D1082362

Windows 10 Inside Out

3rd Edition

Ed Bott
Craig Stinson

Windows 10 Inside Out, 3rd Edition
Published with the authorization of Microsoft Corporation by:
Pearson Education, Inc.

ISBN-13: 978-1-5093-0766-1
ISBN-10: 1-5093-0766-4

Library of Congress Control Number: 2018966103

1 18

Trademarks
Microsoft and the trademarks listed at http://www.microsoft.com on the "Trademarks" webpage are trademarks of the Microsoft group of companies. All other marks are property of their respective owners.

Warning and Disclaimer
Every effort has been made to make this book as complete and as accurate as possible, but no warranty or fitness is implied. The information provided is on an "as is" basis. The author, the publisher, and Microsoft Corporation shall have neither liability nor responsibility to any person or entity with respect to any loss or damages arising from the information contained in this book.

Special Sales
For information about buying this title in bulk quantities, or for special sales opportunities (which may include electronic versions; custom cover designs; and content particular to your business, training goals, marketing focus, or branding interests), please contact our corporate sales department at corpsales@pearsoned.com or (800) 382-3419. For government sales inquiries, please contact governmentsales@pearsoned.com. For questions about sales outside the U.S., please contact intlcs@pearson.com.

Editor-in-Chief: Brett Bartow
Executive Editor: Loretta Yates
Technical Editor: Carl Siechert
Sponsoring Editor: Charvi Arora
Development Editor: Rick Kughen
Managing Editor: Sandra Schroeder
Senior Project Editor: Tracey Croom
Project Editor: Charlotte Kughen
Copy Editor: Rick Kughen
Indexer: Cheryl Lenser
Proofreader: Karen Davis, Gill Editorial Services
Editorial Assistant: Cindy Teeters
Cover Designer: Twist Creative, Seattle
Compositor: Bronkella Publishing LLC
Graphics: TJ Graham Art

To Mackie. He was a good dog.

Contents at a Glance

Table of Contents

About the authors

Ed Bott is an award-winning author and technology journalist who has been researching and writing about Windows and PC technology, in print and on the internet, for more than two decades. He has written more than 30 books, all on Windows and Microsoft Office, which in turn have been translated into dozens of languages and been read worldwide. You can catch up with Ed's latest opinions and get hands-on advice at *The Ed Bott Report* on ZDNet (*zdnet.com/blog/bott*). You can also follow his lively and occasionally irreverent Twitter feed (@edbott). Ed and his wife, Judy, live in northern New Mexico with an adorable English Springer spaniel, Lucy, who was adopted with the help of English Springer Rescue America (*springerrescue.org*). She makes several cameo appearances in this book.

Craig Stinson, an industry journalist since 1981, was editor of *Softalk for the IBM Personal Computer*, one of the earliest IBM-PC magazines. He is the author or coauthor of numerous books about Windows and Microsoft Excel. Craig is an amateur musician and reformed music critic, having reviewed classical music for various newspapers and trade publications, including *Billboard*, the *Boston Globe*, the *Christian Science Monitor*, and *Musical America*. He lives in Bloomington, Indiana.

Introduction

Microsoft Windows has been around for more than three decades. During that time, it has grown to become a mainstay of business and personal computing, running on some 1.5 billion devices worldwide.

The authors of this book began working together in 2001 with the very first title in the Inside Out series, covering Windows XP. Like many of you, we took a break a few years ago, watching from the sidelines as Microsoft released Windows 8 and Windows 8.1. We returned for Windows 10 because, quite frankly, we were excited by the possibilities of "Windows as a service." As we predicted in the first edition of this book, published shortly after the initial release of Windows 10 in 2015, Windows 10 is evolving rapidly.

That evolution has been a key part of our experience over the past three years, as we researched and wrote what turned out to be a very significant revision to the original edition and then did a series of ebook-only updates. This third edition incorporates all that learning and covers the two editions of Windows 10 released in 2018.

One bedrock fact we've discovered over the past three years is that the core features of Windows 10 are familiar and change very slowly. The fundamentals of NTFS security and the registry, for example, have remained reassuringly consistent throughout many generations of Windows. But there's also plenty that's new in Windows 10, some of it obvious (the new Start experience) and some not so obvious (Windows Hello).

The challenge of writing a book like this one is that Microsoft keeps updating Windows 10, releasing new features twice each year instead of every few years, as in the past. To our great relief, we've found that most of the changes in these semi-annual Windows 10 feature updates are evolutionary, not revolutionary. You might notice small changes in a dialog box or in the appearance of a feature, but its fundamental workings remain the same as before. Our goal in this edition is to help you accomplish those familiar tasks using a new set of tools.

Who this book is for

This book offers a well-rounded look at the features most people use in Windows. It serves as an excellent starting point for anyone who wants a better understanding of how the central features in Windows 10 work. If you're a Windows expert-in-training, or if your day job involves IT responsibilities, or if you're the designated computer specialist managing computers and networks in a home or small business, you'll discover many sections we wrote just for you. And if you consider yourself a Windows enthusiast—well, we hope you'll find enough fun and interesting tidbits to hold your attention because, after all, we're unabashed enthusiasts ourselves.

Assumptions about you

This book was written for people who have some experience with Windows and are comfortable with and even curious about the technical details of what makes Windows work. It touches only briefly on some of the basic topics that you'll find covered in more detail elsewhere. (For people who require a more basic introduction, we recommend other Microsoft Press titles, such as *Windows 10 Step by Step* or *Windows 10 Plain & Simple*.)

Whether you've been working with Windows for a few years or a quarter-century, we expect that you're comfortable finding your way around the desktop, launching programs, using copy and paste operations, and finding information in a web browser. We don't assume that you're a hardware tinkerer, hacker, hardcore gamer, or developer.

How this book is organized

Part I, "Windows 10 essentials," offers an overview of what's new in this version, along with details on installing, configuring, and personalizing Windows 10. For this edition, we've added a brand-new chapter covering the tools and techniques for managing Windows security and feature updates.

Part II, "Productivity," covers the essentials of using and managing Universal Windows Platform (UWP) apps and desktop programs, with details on built-in productivity tools (including Mail) and entertainment apps. This section also introduces Microsoft Edge, the new default web browser. In this section, we explain how to organize your personal data using local drives and the built-in OneDrive cloud storage service. Finally, we explain how to find those files as well as answers from the internet, when you need them, using Cortana and Windows 10's powerful search tools.

Part III, "Managing Windows 10," starts with a detailed guide to keeping your user accounts and devices secure. Additional chapters cover routine maintenance tasks and explore tools and techniques for measuring and improving your computer's performance, keeping your network connections fast and secure, and configuring hardware. The section closes with advice on how to back up your important files, how to recover quickly from problems, and how to trouble-shoot issues when they arise.

Part IV, "For IT professionals and Windows experts," leads off with a chapter about Hyper-V, a powerful virtualization platform built into Windows 10 Pro and Enterprise editions. Additional chapters cover advanced tools for managing business networks and the Windows 10 devices connected to those networks. Windows 10 security gets its own in-depth chapter, and we close with a look at the unique features available for mobile computing.,

Finally, we provide three appendixes of reference information: a concise look at the differences between Windows 10 editions, a hands-on guide to the Windows Insider Program, and an overview of help and support resources.

Acknowledgments

For this edition we're once again fortunate to have an expert production team led by Loretta Yates. Proofreader Karen Davis, compositor Tricia Bronkella, and indexer Cheryl Lenser were invaluable additions to our team, asking the right questions and offering excellent suggestions to help smooth away our rough edges. And, as usual, they made it all happen quickly and efficiently, despite all the curveballs that the crazy fast "Windows as a service" development pace threw our way.

They were joined by a very special team member, Carl Siechert, who was our co-author on every previous edition but put on the technical editor's hat for this revision. It was a perfect fit.

And we've saved a special tip of the hat to our longtime colleagues Rick and Charlotte Kughen. This book would never have gotten into your hands without their production magic.

Errata, updates, & book support

We've made every effort to ensure the accuracy of this book and its companion content. You can access updates to this book—in the form of a list of submitted errata and their related corrections—at:

MicrosoftPressStore.com/ Win10InsideOut/errata

If you discover an error that is not already listed, please submit it to us at the same page.

If you need additional support, email Microsoft Press Book Support at:

microsoftpresscs@pearson.com.

Please note that product support for Microsoft software and hardware is not offered through the previous addresses. For help with Microsoft software or hardware, go to *https://support.microsoft.com.*

What you need to know about Windows 10

What kind of people use Windows 10? The list is long and surprisingly diverse.

If you work in a modern office, you probably spend the better part of every workday staring at a display—creating, communicating, researching, analyzing, sharing, and collaborating with co-workers. Yes, you can do some of those tasks on a mobile phone, but when you need to see the big picture, there's nothing that works as well as a PC.

At home, you (and a few hundred million people just like you) use Windows 10 PCs for checking the news, making travel plans, shopping, and staying in touch over social media networks. You probably also play a few games and occasionally edit family photos and videos using that PC.

You might be a developer, in which case you spend a lot of time writing, testing, and debugging code. In the process, you use advanced features (like the Windows Subsystem for Linux) that mere mortals will never touch.

Or perhaps you actually manage PCs in business settings, in which case, you have probably forgotten more about Windows deployment tools and techniques than most people will learn in a lifetime.

The one thing all of you have in common is that you're probably not a newcomer to Microsoft Windows. Regardless of your productivity needs and your level of technical expertise, you've undoubtedly mastered little shortcuts that make you more productive in everyday computing activities.

For decades, one of the defining characteristics of Microsoft Windows—indeed, one of its greatest strengths—has been its respect for backward compatibility. That means most of those old tricks still work, and we don't need to spend a lot of time dwelling on the familiar.

Instead, our goal in this book is to help you become more productive by helping you discover and master some of the big changes in Windows 10. For this, the third edition of *Windows 10 Inside Out*, we've substantially reorganized both the structure and the content based on more than three years of hands-on experience with Windows 10 and lots of feedback from readers like you.

In this introductory chapter, we introduce the most important improvements in Windows 10 and supply some reasons to dig deeper into this powerful operating system.

Windows core features

As we finished writing and editing this edition in late 2018, Microsoft's official tally of devices running Windows 10 had crossed 700 million. That's an enormous number, but it represents only about half of the worldwide population of PCs. The other half are still running older Windows versions, primarily Windows 7.

If you're among the substantial population that has stuck with Windows 7 for the past few years, avoiding Windows 8 and waiting for Windows 10 to mature, you missed some interesting and deep-seated changes to core features in Windows. This section introduces some of those essential changes in the most important parts of the operating system.

The image-based setup process makes upgrading to Windows 10 faster and more reliable. It also powers the recovery tools, shown in Figure 1-1; the Reset This PC option allows you to reinstall Windows without having to search for installation media or product keys, with the option to keep your personal files or wipe the system clean. For more details, see Chapter 15, "Troubleshooting, backup, and recovery."

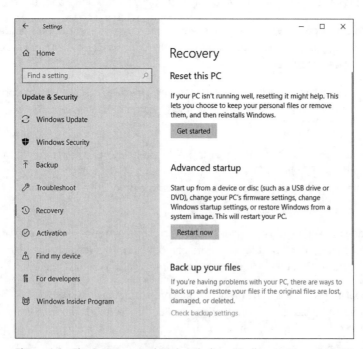

Figure 1-1   The Recovery options in Windows 10 allow you to reset a PC without requiring separate installation media or wiping out your personal files.

NTFS is still the default file system for Windows 10, but the primary file management tool has changed significantly from its Windows 7 predecessor. It's no longer called Windows Explorer; beginning with Windows 8, the name officially changed to File Explorer. The addition of a Microsoft Office–style ribbon, shown in Figure 1-2, makes a number of formerly obscure operations more discoverable and dramatically improves search capabilities by adding a Search Tools tab when you click in the search box. Windows 10 adds a Quick Access region in the navigation pane. We cover File Explorer in exhaustive detail in Chapter 9, "Storage and file management."

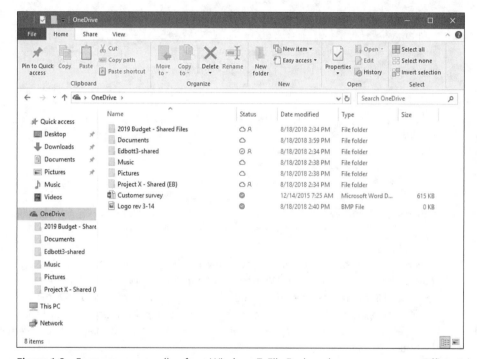

Figure 1-2   For anyone upgrading from Windows 7, File Explorer has a new name, an Office-style ribbon, and a OneDrive node in the navigation pane.

Some of the most important architectural changes in Windows 10 aren't visible, but you can certainly see their impact on performance. Microsoft's engineers have made steady and significant improvements in memory management, for example, which results in faster startups and more efficient management of running processes.

You can monitor system performance in Task Manager, another familiar Windows 7 utility that has received a major makeover in Windows 10. Press Ctrl+Shift+Esc to open Task Manager, and then click the Performance tab to see detailed information about the most important aspects of how the operating system is using available resources, as shown in Figure 1-3.

➤ **For an in-depth look at the new Task Manager, see Chapter 12, "Performance and power management."**

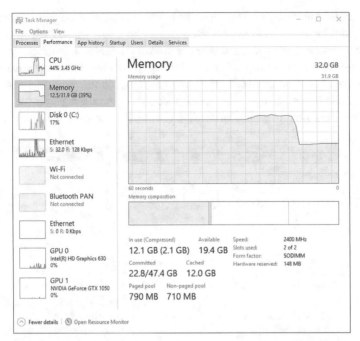

Figure 1-3   The Task Manager Performance tab in Windows 10 offers far more information and is more clearly organized than its Windows 7 predecessor.

Several other major architectural changes in Windows 10 are also on display in the previous figure. The networking stack in Windows 10 continues to improve with each feature update, for example. On modern devices that include multiple graphics processing units (GPUs), you can now assign a specific GPU on a per-app basis to improve performance. Other display-related changes include significant improvements when using multiple displays with different scaling factors.

Not every core feature has survived the relentless parade of semi-annual updates that make up Windows 10, however. HomeGroup, a signature networking feature that debuted in Windows 7 with the goal of making file and printer sharing easier, has been officially removed from Windows 10 beginning with version 1803. We have details of this change in Chapter 13, "Windows networking."

Perhaps the most significant change of all in Windows 10 is the deprecation of a core feature that has been part of Windows for more than two decades. The venerable Internet Explorer is still part of Windows 10, but it has been supplanted as the default browser by Microsoft Edge. The newer browser is built for the modern web, with a new rendering engine in which interoperability has a much higher priority than backward compatibility. We explain the differences between the two browsers, as well as how to configure each one to match your preferences, in Chapter 8, "Microsoft Edge and Internet Explorer."

Microsoft Edge is touch-friendly, with a minimal list of controls. Among its unique features is a Reading View button that reformats and rearranges the text of a cluttered webpage to make a less distracting reading experience. You can see this feature in action in Figure 1-4, with side-by-side Microsoft Edge windows displaying the same page in its original view (left) and in reading view (right).

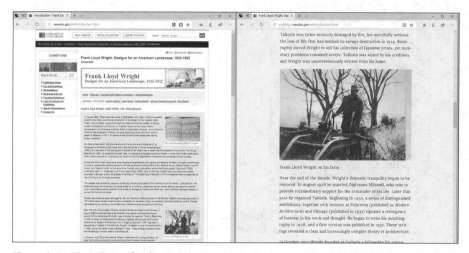

Figure 1-4 The Microsoft Edge web browser has simple controls and a Reading View option that reformats text and removes clutter from webpages.

The version of Microsoft Edge that was included with the initial release of Windows 10 was functional but lacked features that most experienced Windows users expect in a web browser. After more than three years' worth of development, Microsoft Edge has become more polished and powerful. Each Windows 10 feature update has added significant new features to Microsoft Edge, including support for browser extensions, which are delivered through the Microsoft Store app. Figure 1-5 shows some of those extensions in use.

Subsequent feature updates have expanded the capabilities of Microsoft Edge significantly, turning it into a capable viewer of PDF documents and e-books.

CHAPTER 1

Figure 1-5   Microsoft Edge supports browser extensions like those shown here, which add features and connect to other apps and services.

Windows as a service

For decades, the cadence of Windows went something like this: Roughly every three years, a new version of Windows came out. New PCs included the latest Windows version; owners of existing PCs could choose to pay for an upgrade to the new Windows version or choose not to upgrade. The cycle began anew three years later, with the release of yet another new Windows version.

That's all history now.

Before the initial release of Windows 10, Microsoft declared its intention to treat Windows as a service. In the first three years after that release, Windows 10 customers had a chance to see "Windows as a service" in action, with five feature updates that collectively would have qualified as one of the most feature-packed new Windows versions ever.

ABOUT WINDOWS 10 VERSIONS

The most striking difference between Windows 10 and its predecessors is the way Microsoft has chosen to deliver new features. Instead of assembling a long list of features and working on them as part of a new version—Windows 11, let's call it—Microsoft chose to ship those new features in small, bite-size chunks, as part of regular feature updates that are free for every PC running Windows 10.

In November 2015, just a few months after the public debut of Windows 10, Microsoft released the first feature update, version 1511. It contained a slew of changes, many of them aimed at enterprise customers, including changes to Windows Update that allow administrators to delay installation of updates.

On August 2, 2016, almost one year to the day after Windows 10's launch, Microsoft publicly released the Windows 10 Anniversary Update, more prosaically known as version 1607. It included new security features as well as major improvements to some signature features in Windows 10, including Cortana and the Microsoft Edge browser. The Anniversary Update also marked the debut of the Windows Ink platform for pen-equipped devices.

In 2017, Microsoft formally committed to a twice-yearly schedule for feature updates to Windows 10. The Windows 10 Creators Update, version 1703, began rolling out to customers in April 2017; the Fall Creators Update, version 1709, followed six months later; and the April 2018 Update, version 1803, arrived right on schedule six months after that, at the end of April 2018. As we wrapped up this edition, Microsoft released version 1809. You can expect a similar release schedule in 2019 and beyond.

The Windows 10 versioning system starts with a four-digit release date in the format *yymm*, where the first two digits represent the year, and the last two represent the month. Thus, versions 1703 and 1709 were completed in March 2017 and September 2017, respectively. Beginning in 2019, this numbering system will change slightly, with the last two digits representing which half of the year the release belongs to: 19H1, for example.

A separate build number keeps track of update versions. The initial release of Windows 10, for example, was build 10240, version 1607 was build 14393, and version 1809 is build 17763. A version identifier for each monthly cumulative update is appended to that build number.

To see which Windows 10 version is installed on a device, go to Settings > System > About. The example that follows shows a PC running Windows 10 version 1803 with the August 2018 cumulative update (OS Build 17134.228) installed.

CHAPTER 1

Any device running any edition of Windows 10 is eligible for feature updates. Instead of waiting two or three years to be included in a new Windows version or a service pack, new features are delivered automatically, through Windows Update. That's a major change from previous Windows versions, which delivered only security and reliability updates through these Microsoft-managed channels.

> ➤ **The sole exception to the above discussion of feature updates is the Long Term Servicing Channel, available for a specific version of Windows 10 Enterprise. You can read more about this exception in "Servicing channels" in Chapter 5, "Managing updates."**

The new update process also allows Windows users to choose how soon they want to receive those updates.

Previously, Microsoft developed and tested new Windows features privately, occasionally offering the public an advance look in the form of preview versions before releasing them publicly. Beginning with Windows 10, those preview releases are built into the development cycle. As new features make their way into Windows, they're delivered to different "flights," starting with internal testers in Microsoft's engineering group, and then working out to customers who have opted to join the Windows Insider Program and receive preview releases. Each new flight reaches a larger number of people, with fixes for bugs discovered in previous flights incorporated into later ones. Figure 1-6 shows, conceptually, how the process works.

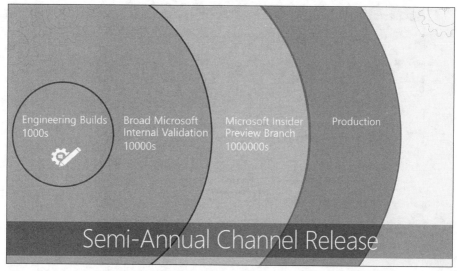

Engineering Builds
1000s

Broad Microsoft
Internal Validation
10000s

Microsoft Insider
Preview Branch
1000000s

Production

Semi-Annual Channel Release

Figure 1-6 For Windows 10, Microsoft delivers new features in "flights" that work their way through a series of test groups before being released to consumers and business customers.

NOTE

In late 2017, Microsoft changed the terminology for the public releases of Windows 10. Instead of Current Branch and Current Branch for Business, these are now called Semi-Annual Channel (Targeted) and Semi-Annual Channel, respectively. Although the name has changed, the philosophy behind each release channel remains the same as before.

After the preview phase concludes, the first public release of a feature update, installed by PC manufacturers and available to the general public through Windows Update, goes to the Semi-Annual Channel (Targeted). That release, previously known as the Current Branch, represents program code that has been tested as part of the preview cycle and corresponds to what have traditionally been General Availability releases of new Windows versions or service packs. The "targeted" designation signals to businesses that they should target test groups within their organizations before deploying feature updates more widely.

IT managers and administrators on enterprise networks can choose a more cautious approach to feature updates by configuring PCs under their management to receive feature updates after they're released to the Semi-Annual Channel (previously known as the Current Branch for Business), typically at least two months after the initial public release.

Microsoft's developers receive unprecedented levels of feedback that shape the development effort in real time. That feedback comes from automated data collection (known formally as diagnostics and informally as *telemetry*) as well as from a Feedback Hub app, shown in Figure 1-7, which is installed with every Windows 10 release.

Figure 1-7   This Windows Feedback app allows anyone using Windows 10 to report bugs and offer suggestions directly to Microsoft.

➤ **For more details on how Windows preview releases work, see Appendix B, "The Windows Insider Program."**

The app landscape

In this book, we pay proper respect to the legacy desktop apps that still account for much of the productivity work we do on PCs. That includes stalwarts like Microsoft Office and a practically endless list of third-party programs. In fact, a few desktop programs are still part of Windows 10, including Windows Media Player, Paint, Notepad, and WordPad. Most of those legacy apps are in maintenance mode at this point, with no new features; they're present largely because third-party apps require them, and some Windows users have long-established workflows that depend on them.

Much more interesting are the Trusted Microsoft Store apps that are designed to work on any device running Windows 10. Some of these apps are provisioned automatically with a new Windows 10 installation; others are downloaded from the Microsoft Store. In either case, because these apps can be updated automatically via the Store, they can incorporate new features and bug fixes without requiring a separate installation, as is usually the case with legacy desktop apps. With the help of a steadily evolving set of application programming interfaces (APIs), these apps can also sync settings and data between Windows 10 devices without having to reconfigure accounts or import data. When you set up a new Windows 10 device and install one of these so-called modern apps, you can literally pick up where you left off on the other device.

Windows 10 includes a lengthy list of productivity, entertainment, and news and information apps as part of a default installation. That list continues to grow, with several apps (Paint 3D and People foremost among them) arriving years after the initial release of Windows 10. Other apps that are part of a default installation of Windows 10 have matured dramatically since their initial release, thanks in part to improvements in the underlying Universal Windows Platform (UWP).

Finally, some relatively recent additions to the Windows 10 platform expand the reach of the Store tremendously. First, those API changes allow developers of traditional desktop programs to deliver and update those programs through the Microsoft Store; the list of programs that have been repackaged in this fashion includes some megahits like Spotify Music and iTunes, as you can see in the Store listings in Figure 1-8.

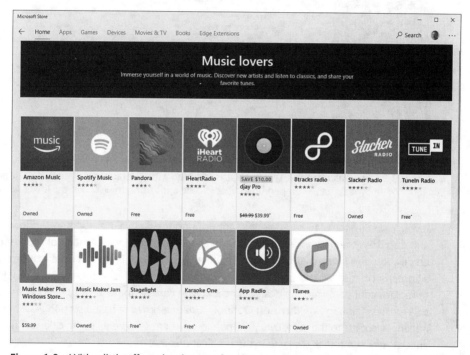

Figure 1-8   With a little effort, developers of traditional desktop programs, like Spotify Music and iTunes, can now deliver and update those apps through the Microsoft Store.

An additional set of APIs supports *progressive web apps*, which are built on the same foundation and open standards as the web but allow features that aren't available in a browser—working offline, for example, or accessing hardware directly. You'll find more details about Trusted Microsoft Store apps and how they differ from legacy desktop programs in Chapter 6, "Installing and configuring apps and desktop programs."

Chief among the productivity apps provisioned with Windows 10 are the three communication apps: Mail, Calendar, and People. These apps work with a broad swath of internet services, including Microsoft's Office 365 and Outlook.com services as well as Google's Gmail and Apple's iCloud. Figure 1-9 shows a month of appointments in the Calendar app.

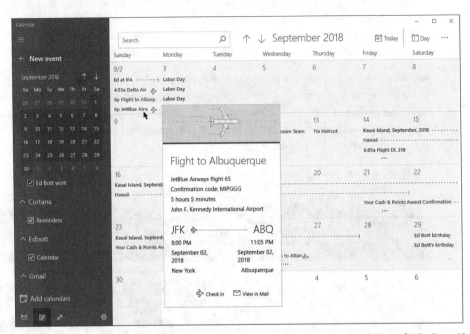

Figure 1-9   The Calendar app, shown here, is included with a default installation of Windows 10. Switch to the companion Mail or People apps using the icons in the lower-left corner.

If you looked at the Mail and Calendar apps during the first year or so after Windows 10's debut and dismissed them as underpowered, it might be worth taking another look. For modern email and calendaring platforms such as Office 365, Outlook.com, and Gmail, these apps offer a light, touch-friendly way to respond to incoming mail or check your calendar. You don't have to replace your preferred mail/calendar client; you can use these apps as needed, in addition to a full desktop app like Microsoft Outlook 2016 or a browser-based session. As a bonus, connecting accounts to the Windows 10 apps allows you to see events in the calendar flyout that appears when you click the date in the notification area.

Windows 10 also includes an assortment of entertainment apps and casual games (the Microsoft Solitaire Collection is included with every edition). The Photos app has become an especially interesting showcase for the Universal Windows Platform, offering tools for editing digital pictures and then organizing them into albums or easy-to-share videos with music, as shown here.

➤ **For more information about apps and utilities included with Windows 10, see Chapter 7, "Using and managing built-in Windows apps."**

These new apps for Windows 10 are delivered and updated through the Microsoft Store, just as their predecessors in Windows 8 were, but that's where the resemblance ends. In Windows 10, Store apps can work in resizable windows alongside conventional Windows desktop applications.

On a tablet, for example, the editing capabilities in the new Photos app work best in full screen. On a large desktop display (or two), the full-screen view is overkill, and the app is perfectly usable in a window, as shown in Figure 1-10.

➤ **For a more thorough look at how Store apps work, see Chapter 6.**

CHAPTER 1

Figure 1-10   The editing controls in the universal Photos app are designed so that they work well in a resizable window on desktop PCs with a large display, a keyboard, and a mouse.

Cloud connections

When you set up a new PC running Windows 10, you can create a local account and sign in, avoiding the cloud completely. If you do that, however, you miss some of the operating system's most compelling features.

Throughout this book, we assume most of our readers are signing in with a Microsoft account (free to individuals) or an Azure Active Directory account associated with their organization. Doing so unlocks access to a variety of cloud services; adding an Office 365 account provides a total of 1 TB of cloud storage for personal files. That's a lot of online storage space.

The OneDrive synchronization client installed with Windows 10 supports connections to cloud storage from both the consumer version of OneDrive and its professional counterpart, One-Drive for Business, with synced files and folders available in File Explorer. And that sync client has been evolving methodically since the original release of Windows 10. It now includes a feature called Files On-Demand, which allows you to see all cloud files in File Explorer, even if they're not synced to the local device. And on consumer accounts, the default settings sync (and back up) key system folders to the cloud, as shown here. That makes recovery easier after a hardware failure or even a successful ransomware attack.

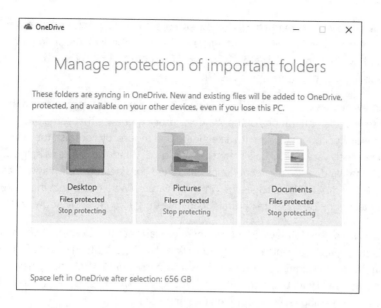

Digital music and photo files stored in OneDrive are also available for playback, viewing, and editing in the Groove Music and Photos apps, respectively.

A second major Windows 10 feature that also depends on the cloud is Cortana. With your permission, this "intelligent personal assistant" handles searches, tracks appointments, and sets reminders. Cortana recognizes your voice, if you choose to enable that option, and can also be, in turn, a calculator, package tracker, translator, and source of real-time sports updates, to list just a few skills from Cortana's résumé.

> ➤ For more information about how OneDrive and Windows 10 work together, see Chapter 9. We cover Cortana's capabilities in Chapter 10, "Cortana and Windows search."

The user experience

How you react to Windows 10 is determined in no small part by how you feel about its predecessor.

With the launch of Windows 8 in October 2012, Microsoft removed the familiar touchstones of the Windows user experience—the Start button and Start menu—and replaced them with a radically redesigned Start screen created for use with touch-enabled devices. It also introduced a new class of touch-friendly apps, delivered through a new Windows Store. (In the Windows 10 era, the store's branding changed. It's now known as the Microsoft Store.)

The innovations in Windows 8 laid an essential foundation for tablets and other touch-oriented devices. But that new design also inspired some passionate and often blunt feedback from

CHAPTER 1

Windows users who weren't pleased with the often-confusing changes to an operating system they had spent years mastering. Microsoft reacted to that feedback by reworking the user experience in Windows 10, bringing back the Start menu from Windows 7 and combining it with live tiles and other features that were introduced in Windows 8.

If you skipped Windows 8 and stuck with Windows 7, as we know many of our readers did, you missed several major iterations of the Windows user experience that some people found difficult to use on conventional PCs with a keyboard and mouse. By contrast, the Windows 10 user experience feels very much like a smooth evolution of Windows 7. After a half-dozen feature updates, the Windows 10 user experience has added considerable polish as well as some impressive all-new capabilities, such as the Timeline feature. (We'll get to that in a minute.) The result should feel significantly more natural for anyone upgrading from Windows 7.

Our lightning tour of the Windows 10 user experience starts at the lock screen, which hints at a few of the security improvements we'll talk about later. Note that instead of entering a password here, we can use a PIN assigned to this device, as shown in Figure 1-11. On some newer devices that support Windows Hello biometric authentication, you can skip that step completely and sign in automatically using facial recognition or a fingerprint.

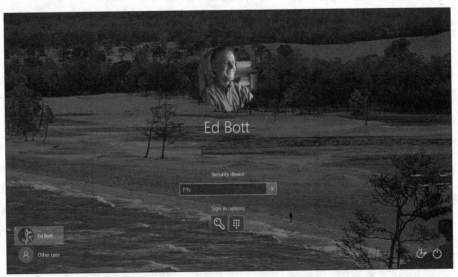

Figure 1-11   The Windows 10 lock screen offers the option to sign in using a PIN (with the option of a hardware security device in this example) instead of a password.

After you successfully sign in, Windows 10 takes you to the Windows desktop. For anyone making the move from Windows 7, this environment should be familiar. The taskbar runs along the bottom, as expected, with a notification area on the right. In the lower-left corner is a stylized Windows logo. Clicking that button opens what Windows designers call the *Start experience*, an example of which is shown in Figure 1-12.

Figure 1-12   The Windows 10 Start experience combines the scrolling list of shortcuts from Windows 7 (left) with live tiles like those from the Windows 8 Start screen (right).

The height and width of the new Start menu are fully adjustable; there's also a full-screen Tablet Mode, which works well on touchscreen devices without a physical keyboard.

Although the basic arrangement of Start in Windows 10 has remained consistent, subsequent updates have introduced some subtle but significant changes. In its current incarnation, the Start experience incorporates a scrolling All Apps list that is permanently available, while the power button and shortcuts to frequently used folders shrink to a slim column of icons on the left. (Click the so-called hamburger button in the upper-left corner to reveal labels for those icons.) Tiles are resizable and can be organized into folders, which expand and collapse to reduce clutter.

Version 1803 introduced the most significant new addition to the Windows 10 experience: a feature called Timeline. Timeline expands the capability of Task View to include not just running apps but also "activities" you've allowed Windows 10 to track on your behalf: websites you've visited using Microsoft Edge, for example, and documents you've opened with apps that support the Timeline APIs. The list of supported apps includes every built-in Windows app (modern apps like Photos as well as legacy programs like Notepad) and all of the Microsoft Office desktop programs. Third-party programs that support the Timeline API, such as the members of the Adobe Creative Cloud family, are also included, and Microsoft plans to release browser extensions that will add content from third-party web browsers to the Timeline.

➤ For a more detailed discussion of Timeline, see "Reviewing, revisiting, resuming with Timeline" in Chapter 3, "Using Windows 10."

The visual design of Windows 10 uses flat icons and a monochromatic color scheme in the notification area and in the Settings app, as shown in Figure 1-13.

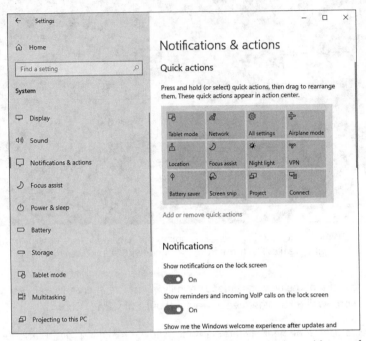

Figure 1-13   The Windows 10 Settings app adds more options with every feature update; its overall design and typography are characteristic of the operating system.

The Settings app debuted in 2012 with Windows 8, and its evolution accelerated under Windows 10. Over that entire period, Microsoft's designers and engineers have been steadily moving user controls from the old Control Panel to their new home. That work has taken major steps forward with each feature update, as new categories appear (Cortana settings, for example, now appear in their own category) and major groups of options migrate permanently to Settings, like the Networking options shown below. The iconography and typography have become more sophisticated over time, and other recent changes include the incorporation of shadows and transparency, part of a major set of visual enhancements Microsoft calls Fluent Design.

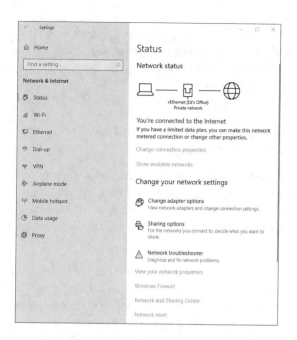

THE PIECES OF WINDOWS 8 THAT DIDN'T SURVIVE

The Windows 8 user interface was radically different from any previous version of Windows. Maybe too radical, based on the clear feedback Microsoft received from customers.

That feedback inspired a thorough rethinking of the Windows user experience, which in turn led to the design you see in Windows 10. In the process, these signature Windows 8 elements were retired:

- **Charms menu.** This vertical row of five buttons, with the Windows logo key at the center, appeared on the right side of Windows 8 PCs in response to a swipe from the right edge or the mouse moving to the upper-right corner of the display. Its five functions have been broken up and moved to the new Start and to Action Center, which now appears where the Charms once did with a swipe from the right or a click of the Notifications icon.

- **Hot corners.** For PCs without a touchscreen, a key navigation principle in Windows 8 involved moving the mouse to a corner and pausing until something happened. Moving the mouse pointer to the upper-left corner and then sliding down, for example, exposed a column of thumbnails for switching between running apps. In Windows 10, moving the mouse to a corner does nothing special, and app switching has been moved to the Task View button and its keyboard shortcuts.

- **Start screen.** The Start screen, filled with colorful live tiles, was the first thing a new Windows 8 user saw. Over time, with Windows 8.1 and a subsequent update, the Start screen was modified to make it less jarring. In Windows 10, the desktop is the default first step, and live tiles appear as part of Start. If you miss the Windows 8–style Start screen, you can restore the experience by configuring Start to run in a full screen or by switching to Tablet Mode.

Recent usage data we've seen suggests that virtually everyone who once used Windows 8 has now moved on to Windows 10. Our experience suggests the learning curve for Windows 10 is not that steep. But it's ironic that one of the biggest challenges for those who made the transition from Windows 8 was unlearning these now-missing elements.

The Windows 10 user experience isn't just an evolution of features you already knew, however; you'll also find plenty of new capabilities to explore.

The search box to the right of the Start button, for example, returns answers directly from the web, without the need to open a browser. These results can be as simple as a link to a Wikipedia article that matches the search terms, but the expanded search results pane can also include weather forecasts, sports scores, biographies, currency conversions, a full-featured calculator, and even a built-in translator.

Another major addition, new in Windows 10 and significantly refined in recent feature updates, is Action Center. This pane appears on the right side when you swipe in from the right on a touchscreen or click the Notifications icon, which appears to the right of the system clock. A badge over that icon shows how many new notifications are available. In addition, you can now tweak notification settings on an app-by-app basis, with more intelligent grouping options. The top of the pane contains notifications from apps (new messages, weather alerts, alarms, reminders), while the bottom contains handy buttons for performing common tasks. Figure 1-14 shows what Action Center looks like in version 1803.

Figure 1-14   The buttons that appear beneath notifications in Action Center allow quick access to system settings.

PC hardware

They don't make PCs like they used to.

We don't mean that as a figure of speech, but rather as a statement of fact that helps to explain why Microsoft Windows 10 exists.

Every year, Microsoft's hardware partners sell hundreds of millions of PCs running the latest version of Windows. Many of those PCs still follow traditional form factors: towers designed to fit under a desk, all-in-one PCs that pack the electronics behind a desktop display, and clamshell-shaped laptops with full keyboards and touchpads.

But the fastest-growing group—and by far the most interesting—have diverged from those familiar designs. The defining characteristic of these next-generation Windows devices is a touchscreen. On touchscreen-equipped laptops, you can choose to perform a task by tapping the screen or by using the keyboard and touchpad. In the case of a tablet running Windows 10, the touchscreen offers the only way to navigate between and within apps.

> ### NOTE
>
> **The core code that makes up Windows 10 runs on a broad assortment of hardware, including the Xbox One game console, HoloLens mixed-reality smart glasses, and the Surface Hub, a large, touch-enabled smart display designed for corporate conference rooms. In this book, we focus on devices designed to perform the functions associated with traditional PCs.**

Then there's the most intriguing category of all: so-called *hybrid devices*, equipped with a touchscreen and a keyboard that can be detached or folded out of the way. The touch-enabled displays in Lenovo's perfectly named Yoga series, for example, can rotate 360 degrees, turning a laptop into a tablet with the keyboard behind the display.

Microsoft's popular Surface devices also help define the category. The Surface Pro and Surface Go device, for example, support Type Covers that magnetically attach to add a keyboard and a precision touchpad. The Surface Book series looks and acts like a traditional laptop until you push the Detach button and remove the screen from the base. When you remove the keyboard from the display and use a Surface Pen, a Surface device becomes a tablet you can use to sketch or take notes.

Windows 10 is the engine that powers all those next-generation devices as well as the large population of traditional PC designs still in use.

On a touchscreen, you swipe and tap to interact with objects on the screen and use an on-screen keyboard to enter and edit text. For devices with detachable keyboards, Windows 10 includes features designed to ease the transition between the traditional PC way of working and the new Tablet Mode. In the case of PCs that aren't touch-enabled, Windows 10 offers the familiar keyboard-and-mouse experience, with no compromises.

> ➤ We offer details on how to be productive with the Windows 10 user experience on traditional PCs and touchscreen-equipped devices in Chapter 3. Our coverage of customization options is in Chapter 4, "Personalizing Windows 10."

Security and privacy

Windows 10 has a broad set of security features, many of them built into the core of the operating system and thus essentially invisible. For example, modern hardware designed for Windows 10 starts up from a Unified Extensible Firmware Interface (UEFI) rather than an old-fashioned BIOS. That hardware design, in turn, enables a Windows 10 security feature called Secure Boot, which protects your PC from an insidious form of malware called *rootkits*.

Other core security features of the operating system are enabled by default, including the Windows Defender Antivirus software included with every installation of Windows 10. (If you or your organization prefer an alternative security software solution, Windows Defender steps aside gracefully.) You can monitor and configure the full set of user-facing security features from a consolidated dashboard called Windows Security. (In versions 1803 and earlier, this app was called Windows Defender Security Center.)

Figure 1-15   The green check marks, red X, and yellow triangle denote the status of each feature. Clicking any option here opens a configuration dialog box for that feature.

Each of the categories listed here can be configured with minimal technical knowledge, making this the primary window into security on Windows 10 PCs running in homes and small offices where a full-time IT department isn't available.

More advanced security options include multi-factor authentication options for PCs as well as BitLocker Disk Encryption, which is available on PCs running Windows 10 Pro or Enterprise editions.

Privacy options in Windows 10 are extensive, with the most confusing choices revolving around the diagnostic data (sometimes referred to as telemetry) that Microsoft collects as part of its product improvement efforts. Recent feature updates include a new tool called the Diagnostic Data Viewer, which allows you to inspect the diagnostic data being sent to Microsoft under your current privacy settings. We discuss this topic in detail in Chapter 18, "Windows security and privacy."

Installing, configuring, and deploying Windows 10

Mechanically, Windows Setup has evolved a bit since Windows 10 debuted in 2015. Those step-by-step details are a big part of this chapter. The more important change, though, is the way in which you're likely to encounter Windows Setup.

In the first year after its release, when Microsoft was offering Windows 10 as a free upgrade, the installed base for the new operating system went from zero to well over 300 million. Most of those early adopters got to Windows 10 by upgrading a PC running an earlier version of Windows. With that free upgrade offer long since ended, we expect that most of the readers of this book who encounter Windows 10 for the first time will do so on a new PC, where the Windows Setup experience is abbreviated. When you first power up a new PC with Windows 10 already installed, you go through the brief Out Of Box Experience (OOBE) setup; then you sign in and get to work.

But sooner or later you'll almost certainly have to deal with one of the other, more complicated Setup options. If you're sitting in front of a PC that has no operating system installed, for example, your only choice is to boot from installation media and perform a clean install. And even though upgrades are less common than they were in that frenetic first year, hundreds of millions of PCs worldwide are still running Windows 7 and should be migrated to Windows 10 (or retired) before support for that old operating system runs out on January 14, 2020.

> ### NOTE
>
> Microsoft's well-publicized free upgrade offer for Windows 10 ended on July 29, 2016, one year after the initial release of Windows 10. On that date, the GWX (Get Windows 10) app, which had offered those updates to PCs running eligible versions of Windows, stopped displaying upgrade notifications; a subsequent update removed the app and its associated software permanently.
>
> Although those persistent offers stopped, the free upgrade offer remained valid through December 31, 2017, for anyone using "assistive technologies," with no restrictions on what those technologies are. That offer, too, has now expired. For full details, see *https://www.microsoft.com/accessibility/windows10upgrade*.

> **Regardless of what the rules might say, the Windows Installer program—Setup.exe—still allows upgrades to Windows 10 on PCs running Windows 7 and Windows 8.1; in our tests in mid-2018, after the release of Windows 10 version 1803, downloading the Windows 10 installation package and running Setup as an upgrade results in a system with an apparently valid digital license. No product key or proof of purchase is required.**

Beyond the mechanics of installation, this chapter also covers the sometimes-confusing details of Windows licensing and activation. Adding an extra complication to that topic is Microsoft's introduction of *digital licenses* (known as *digital entitlements* in the early days of Windows 10).

In this chapter, we cover the nuts and bolts of setup and activation. But first, some suggestions on how to make the process as smooth as possible.

Before you start

Whether you're planning to upgrade an old PC or perform a clean install on a newly built device, you can increase the odds that setup will succeed by taking some common-sense precautions. At the top of this list is checking the hardware on which you plan to install Windows 10 to confirm that it meets the minimum requirements (note that this list is unchanged from the system requirements for Windows 7):

- Processor: 1 gigahertz (GHz) or faster

- RAM: 1 gigabyte (GB) (32-bit) or 2 GB (64-bit)

- Free disk space (system drive): 16 GB

- Graphics card: Microsoft DirectX 9 graphics device with WDDM driver

  ## NOTE

  The free disk space requirement varies, and Microsoft continues to work on improving upgrade scenarios for low disk space. On devices with small amounts of built-in storage, you might be able to upgrade with as little as 10 free gigabytes. If less storage is available, you might be able to add a removable storage device, such as a USB flash drive, to continue. When available storage is severely constrained, you might find that setup fails in unpredictable ways. If you're stuck, check the Microsoft Community forums (*https:// answers.microsoft.com*) to see whether there's a workaround for your situation.

Those are fairly modest requirements, and virtually every PC sold in the past 10 years with Windows 7 or a later version preinstalled should qualify. Note that some older devices that are at or near the minimum for one or more of these hardware components might not perform acceptably.

To download the Windows 10 installation files, you also need internet access. (In fact, reliable internet access is a prerequisite for most tasks we describe in this book.) A Microsoft account is recommended but is not required.

Inside OUT

RIP, Windows Media Center

One of the signature features of Windows for many years has been Windows Media Center. This feature, which debuted with headline billing in a special edition of Windows XP in 2002, enabled a so-called 10-foot interface for using Windows PCs as an entertainment hub in a living room. Media Center grew steadily from its original design, adding support for high-definition TV and digital cable tuners and becoming the centerpiece of the Windows 7 Home Premium, Professional, and Ultimate editions.

After Windows 7 launched, the Windows Media Center team was disbanded, and development of the feature ceased. In Windows 8 and 8.1, the Media Center functionality was available as an extra-cost add-on, but it was a simple port of the Windows 7 version, with no new features.

With Windows 10, Windows Media Center is officially retired. When you run the Windows 10 Setup program to upgrade a PC that has Windows Media Center enabled, the feature will be completely unavailable after the upgrade is complete. There's no registry magic or secret to enable Windows Media Center on Windows 10 either. If this is a make-or-break feature for you, avoid the Windows 10 upgrade on that PC.

Check for potential compatibility problems

In broad terms, any device that was designed for Windows 8.1 should be compatible with Windows 10, as should any apps or device drivers installed on that device. There are, however, exceptions to this rule—some of them minor, others more serious. Your likelihood of encountering compatibility issues goes up when upgrading a PC running Windows 7.

NOTE

Throughout this book, we refer to Windows 8.1 and not to Windows 8. That's deliberate. Windows 8 is no longer a supported operating system, and we assume most of our readers long ago upgraded their Windows 8 PCs to Windows 8.1. If you find yourself in front of a PC running Windows 8, you can upgrade directly to Windows 10—there's no need to upgrade to Windows 8.1 first.

The Windows 10 Setup program includes a compatibility checker that alerts you to any potential compatibility issues before performing the actual installation. We describe its workings in "Upgrading from an earlier Windows version," later in this chapter.

Before you run Setup, though, it's worth taking inventory of your critical apps and devices and checking with the developer or manufacturer to confirm that those products are supported under Windows 10. Pay special attention to any app or device originally designed and developed before the release of Windows 7 in 2009.

Inside OUT

Use dynamic updates

When you use Windows Update to install a feature update for Windows 10, the Setup program automatically checks for and downloads dynamic updates. When you use Windows 10 installation media to perform an in-place upgrade, you're asked whether you want to get the latest updates. If you have an active internet connection, be sure to take advantage of this option.

Dynamic updates can include any or all of the following: critical updates to the Setup program itself; improved or new versions of boot-critical drivers for storage, display, and network hardware detected on your system; and compatibility updates (also known as *shims*) for programs you're currently running. Rolling these updates in at the beginning of the process increases the likelihood that your Windows 10 installation will be successful. After completing the installation, you'll still need to connect to Windows Update to check for the latest updates for Windows and the most recent drivers for detected hardware.

Back up your data and settings

Having an up-to-date backup of important files is, of course, good advice for any time. But it's especially important when you're upgrading an operating system.

The simplest way to back up files is to sync them to the cloud. OneDrive sync capabilities are built in to Windows 10 and Windows 8.1; a sync utility for Windows 7 is available for download from *https://onedrive.com/download*. Move or copy your files into the OneDrive folder and wait for them to be fully synchronized before proceeding.

With large file collections or slow internet connections—or if you just prefer not putting your files in cloud storage—a sufficiently large USB flash drive or an external hard drive makes a perfectly good target for a local backup. If you're upgrading from Windows 7, you can use its built-in backup program; individual files and folders from those backups can be restored in Windows

10 by using the helpfully labeled Backup And Restore (Windows 7) option in Control Panel. (For a complete look at your options, see Chapter 15, "Troubleshooting, backup, and recovery.")

If you're upgrading from Windows 8.1 and you signed in with a Microsoft account, your personalized settings are already being synced to OneDrive. From Windows 7, there's no easy way to back up those settings. Although you can find third-party utilities that promise to accomplish this task, it's probably faster (and less risky) to re-create that handful of settings than it is to mess with transfer utilities. A far more important task is to ensure that you have product keys or other license details for any third-party software that might require reinstallation.

Download or create installation media

For every Windows 10 installation scenario that we cover in the next section, you need access to installation media. To do a clean install on modern hardware, the most common choice is a bootable USB flash drive or, on older hardware, a bootable DVD. For upgrades and reinstallations, you can use the same type of physical media or download an ISO file, which you can then mount directly or use to create your own installation media.

NOTE

The ISO name is ancient, by modern computing standards, dating back to the mid-1980s. And, strictly speaking, it's also meaningless. The name is shorthand for the file system originally used with CD-ROM media, which was designated ISO 9660 by the standards-setting body that published it. These days, an ISO image file is just as likely to use the UDF file system (ISO/IEC 13346), which is commonly found on larger-capacity optical media such as DVDs and Blu-ray discs.

You can still buy a physical copy of Windows 10 in a package that includes installation files on a bootable USB flash drive or a DVD. Be aware, however, that the version on that physical device is likely to be out of date on the day you cut through the shrink wrap. After you finish your installation, you will almost certainly have to download a large feature update immediately.

If you have access to an internet-connected PC running any supported version of Windows, we recommend using Microsoft's Media Creation Tool, which downloads the most recent installation files and then allows you to create a bootable USB flash drive or save the download file in ISO format.

NOTE

IT pros, developers, and service providers with access to a Visual Studio subscription (formerly MSDN) or a Microsoft Partner Program membership can download ISO files in a variety of configurations after signing in to the online portal for the respective service. Volume License customers will find ISO files for Pro and Enterprise editions at the Volume Licensing Service Center.

If the PC you want to upgrade is already running a supported version of Windows, your best starting point is the Download Windows 10 page (*https://aka.ms/downloadwindows10*), which supports a variety of installation scenarios and offers options dynamically, based on the version of Windows you're already running. When you visit this page using a PC that's already running Windows 10, for example, you'll see an offer to run an Update Assistant; this simple tool downloads and installs the most recent feature update (if you don't already have it), so you don't have to wait for it to arrive via Windows Update.

The real star of the Download Windows 10 page, however, is the Media Creation Tool, which is a bootstrap version of the Windows 10 Setup program and shares that program's look and feel. It's a small file (less than 20 MB in size) that takes only seconds to download. (Recent versions of the tool incorporate the Windows version number into the executable filename— MediaCreationTool1803.exe, for example.) After running the tool and accepting a license agreement, you should see a screen that offers the option to upgrade the current PC or create installation media for another PC. Select that second option to reach the step shown in Figure 2-1.

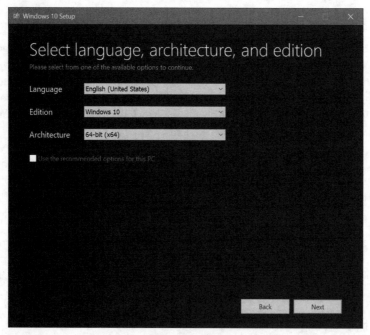

Figure 2-1   These default Media Creation Tool options will create the correct installation media for almost all modern PCs in the United States.

By default, the choices for Language, Edition, and Architecture match the current configuration. If you want to change any of those choices, do so before you click Next.

Choosing the correct installer involves finding the specific combination of three factors that match your needs:

- **Language.** Windows 10 is available in a large number of languages—more than 100—covering nearly 200 countries and regions. Choose the base language that's appropriate for your installation. You can add language interface packs to translate text that's displayed in commonly used wizards, dialog boxes, menus, and other items in the user interface; however, you can't change the parent language except by reinstalling Windows using an edition built for that language.

- **Edition.** In early releases of the Media Creation Tool, this field gave you the option to download either Windows 10 Home or Windows 10 Pro. As of late 2017, only one choice is available in the United States; the download consists of a combined installer that can be used to install any retail edition. Large organizations with volume license contracts can install Windows 10 Enterprise or Education on a system that already has a license to run an edition of Windows that qualifies for the upgrade. We describe the differences between the editions in Appendix A, "Windows 10 editions and licensing options."

- **Architecture.** Windows 10 is available in 32-bit and 64-bit distributions. Choosing Both from this drop-down list causes the Media Creation Tool to download a larger ISO file capable of installing either architecture. Most modern CPUs support either version, and your preference should be for the 64-bit version. In general, 32-bit versions of Windows are appropriate for systems with 2 GB (or less) of RAM, with no option to add memory. Choose a 64-bit version if your system includes 4 GB or more of memory or if you rely on one or more programs that are available only in 64-bit editions. (And note that all your 32-bit programs, including new and old versions of Microsoft Office, will work fine on a 64-bit installation of Windows, so you needn't have any fears in that regard.)

> ➤ Note that the installation files you download are independent of your Windows license. For more details about the intricacies of Windows licensing, see "Activating Windows," later in this chapter.

If you already have an ISO file and a PC running Windows 10, you can create your own installation media with ease.

You can't simply copy installation files to a USB flash drive and use it to perform a clean install. First, you have to make the disk bootable. When creating a bootable drive, you need to consider two factors:

- **Partitioning scheme: MBR or GPT?** You can use a flash drive formatted using either scheme with a Unified Extensible Firmware Interface (UEFI) system; older BIOS-based systems are typically able to recognize only MBR partitions. (For an explanation of the difference and a discussion of the new MBR2GPT tool, see "Managing hard disks and other storage devices," in Chapter 14, "Hardware and devices.")

CHAPTER 2

- **Disk format: NTFS or FAT32?** If you plan to install Windows on a modern UEFI-based system (such as the Microsoft Surface Pro and Surface Book families), the boot files *must* reside on a FAT32 partition on the flash drive. If the drive is formatted using another file system, the PC will not recognize the device as bootable.

One of the simplest ways to create a bootable install drive is to use the built-in Recovery Media Creator tool, RecoveryDrive.exe. Just as in previous Windows versions, this tool can be used to create a bootable drive that includes the recovery partition provided by the OEM. If you perform a clean install or remove that recovery partition to reclaim disk space, the recovery drive can be used only for simple repair operations.

TROUBLESHOOTING

You are unable to create installation media because the Windows image file is too large.

Installation files you download using the Media Creation Tool are specifically designed for use with USB flash drives. If, however, you are trying to use custom installation images, including those downloaded as ISO files from Microsoft's official Visual Studio subscription site, you might encounter a frustrating problem. If any of the Windows Image (.wim) files contained in those ISO files are larger than 4GB, they won't fit on a USB flash drive that's formatted using FAT32. But that disk format is required to perform a clean install on a device that uses UEFI firmware.

There are solutions, although none are particularly appetizing. You can create a multi-partition USB drive, for example, using advanced Windows deployment tools. Or you can store the installation image on a separate removable drive, formatted using NTFS, which might require you to boot from a FAT32-formatted recovery drive, start Setup.exe, remove the recovery drive, and plug in the new drive containing your installation media. Or you can store the installation image on a network location or split the image files.

For the daunting but detailed instructions for all these scenarios, see *https://bit.ly/ deploy-single-usb-drive*.

To run the Recovery Media Creator tool, type **RecoveryDrive** in the search box and then choose the Recovery Drive desktop app from the search results. (Or, if you prefer, search for the Create A Recovery Drive option in Control Panel or Settings.) Figure 2-2 shows this tool in operation.

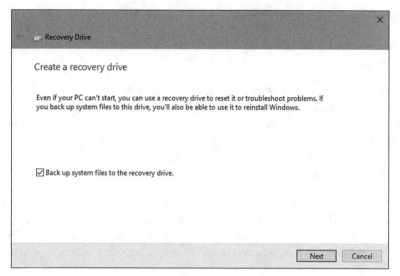

Figure 2-2   Choose the option to back up system files if you want to create a recovery drive using a Windows 10 image preinstalled by an OEM that you can use to reset the current system.

If you used the Media Creation Tool to download an ISO file containing the Windows installation files, you can burn its contents to a DVD (assuming that you have a DVD burner handy and the target system on which you plan to install Windows has an optical drive from which it can start). Or, if you have access to a system running Windows 10, you can make your own bootable media, following these steps:

1.   Create a blank recovery drive using the steps we described earlier, skipping the option to copy system files to the drive.

2.   Double-click the ISO file to mount it as a virtual DVD.

3.   Use File Explorer to drag all files and folders from the virtual DVD to the USB recovery drive.

   NOTE

   Although it's not necessary for most purposes involving Windows 10, some people and organizations want maximum flexibility in creating installable media. If that description fits you, we recommend the free, open source utility Rufus, available at *https://rufus. akeo.ie/*. It allows precise control over partitioning, formatting, and copying installation files to a USB flash drive. If you encounter difficulties using the built-in Windows tools, we strongly recommend this alternative.

Choose your installation method

You have two choices when running Windows Setup: in-place upgrades and custom installations.

Microsoft strongly encourages *in-place upgrades* for anyone moving to Windows 10 on a PC currently running Windows 7 (with Service Pack 1). You can also use this technique to update an older Windows 10 version to a more recent version instead of waiting for a feature update to be installed automatically or to repair an ailing installation by "upgrading" to the currently installed version. To perform an in-place upgrade, start the Windows 10 Setup program from within the current Windows installation.

The default option for an in-place upgrade offers to keep all your data files, installed programs, and settings, at the risk of creating some compatibility issues. But you also have the option to start from scratch, with or without your personal data files; if you choose the latter option, you need to reinstall desktop programs and re-create or sync settings from another system.

You must boot from the Windows 10 media and choose a *custom installation* (sometimes referred to as a clean install) if either of the following conditions is true:

- **You need to adjust the layout of the system disk.** The Windows 10 installer includes disk-management tools you can use to create, delete, format, and extend (but not shrink) partitions on hard disks installed in your computer. Knowing how these tools work can save you a significant amount of time when setting up Windows.

- **You want to install Windows 10 alongside another operating system.** If you want to set up a multi-boot system, you need to understand how different startup files work so that you can manage your startup options effectively. We discuss this option in "Configuring a multi-boot system," later in this chapter.

If the system on which you plan to install Windows 10 is already running a Windows version that supports upgrades (Windows 7, Windows 8.1, or Windows 10), you can start the Setup program from within Windows.

When running Setup from within Windows, you can upgrade from Windows 7 or Windows 8.1 to Windows 10. You can also use the in-place upgrade technique to move from an older version of Windows 10 to a newer one—from version 1803 to version 1809, for example. As we noted earlier, installation files you download using the Media Creation Tool include all retail editions of Windows—Home, Pro, and a few obscure editions most people can safely ignore. In these scenarios, Setup automatically chooses the Windows 10 version that corresponds to the currently installed Windows version. Table 2-1 shows how these upgrade paths work when upgrading an older Windows version.

Table 2-1 Supported upgrade paths by edition

Current version	Supported upgrade
Windows 7 Starter, Home Basic, Home Premium	Windows 10 Home
Windows 7 Professional, Ultimate	Windows 10 Pro
Windows 8.1	Windows 10 Home
Windows 8.1 Pro, Windows 8.1 Pro for Students	Windows 10 Pro

In early versions of the Media Creation Tool, you had the option to choose a specific Windows 10 edition for download. That led to some scenarios that involved an unsupported upgrade path, without the option to transfer programs and settings. If you want to upgrade to a higher Windows edition, your best bet is to perform a supported upgrade first (Windows 8.1 to Windows 10 Home, for example) and then, after Windows 10 is running smoothly, follow the steps we describe later in this chapter to convert the installation to a different edition.

Double-clicking Setup from within Windows does not offer the option to perform a custom install. However, performing an upgrade and choosing Nothing from the list of what you want to keep has essentially the same effect as performing a clean install. After Windows 10 is installed, the Reset This PC option offers an alternative way to accomplish the same task of reinstalling Windows when something isn't working properly.

Note that the installation media must match the architecture of the installed Windows version. You cannot run the 64-bit Setup program on a PC running a 32-bit version of Windows, or vice versa. In addition, you cannot make changes to the layout of a disk when running Setup from within Windows; you must use existing partitions, and Setup will not recognize or use unallocated space on an available hard drive.

If you boot from the Windows 10 installation media, you can delete existing partitions, create new partitions from free space, extend an existing disk partition to unallocated space, or designate a block of unallocated space as the location where you want to install Windows. (We describe these actions later in this chapter.) After booting from the Windows installation media, you cannot upgrade an existing Windows installation. Your only option is a custom installation.

Using either option, you can install Windows 10 on the same volume as an existing Windows version. (You'll find step-by-step instructions in "Performing a clean install" later in this chapter.)

With that background, we're ready to explain the best ways to perform a Windows 10 upgrade or a clean install. We start by breaking down the Windows Installer program.

How Windows 10 Setup works

The Windows Installer (Setup.exe) is used for both in-place upgrades and clean installs. In this chapter, we use the term *Setup* to refer to the operation of this program in either mode. For

CHAPTER 2

upgrades, the installer is streamlined, offering a minimum of options. Booting from Windows 10 installation media offers a much more complete set of options: choosing a specific physical disk for use in dual-boot (or multi-boot) scenarios, creating and formatting partitions, and setting up unattended installations, for example.

In this section, we cover both options. We don't include step-by-step instructions to document every possible upgrade or clean installation scenario. (We do, however, cover some noteworthy changes related to privacy that debuted as part of Windows 10 version 1703.) Given the nearly infinite number of combinations of PC hardware, providing comprehensive instructions would be impossible. And besides, we're confident our readers can make their way through a setup wizard without handholding.

In Windows 10, Setup works in multiple stages, the details of which vary depending on whether you're performing an in-place upgrade or a custom installation. The process is extremely robust and is capable of recovering from a failure at any stage.

Setup first performs a basic system compatibility check to confirm that the system has sufficient free disk space for both the installation and the recovery options, that required CPU features are available, and that both memory and graphics hardware meet minimum requirements. During this phase, Setup also inventories hardware and confirms that critical drivers are available (storage and networking, for example). If any critical drivers are unavailable, Setup stops and rolls back.

In either type of installation, the lengthiest stage occurs with Setup running offline in the Windows Preinstallation Environment (Windows PE), during which it backs up the previous Windows installation (if one exists) into a Windows.old folder and applies the new Windows 10 image.

The remaining stages of installation run after a restart, with the final stage consisting of what's known as the Out of Box Experience (OOBE), with the user signing in and either creating a new profile or migrating an existing one as part of the upgrade. We cover the OOBE process in greater detail in Chapter 11, "Managing user accounts, passwords, and credentials."

Setup does its magic using two folders:

- **C:\$Windows.~BT** is a hidden folder that contains the files used during both the online and the offline phases of installation. When you launch Setup from installation media, such as a mounted ISO file or a bootable DVD or USB flash drive, the initial phase of Setup creates this folder and copies the installation files to it for temporary use, eliminating the possibility of an installation failure caused by prematurely removing or unmounting the installation media.

- **C:\Windows.old** is created only when you perform an upgrade or do a clean install on a volume that already contains a Windows installation. This folder does double duty. During upgrades, it's used as a transfer location to hold files and settings that are moving from the old installation to the new one. After the Setup program completes its work, this folder holds system files from the previous Windows installation as well as any user files that were not migrated during Setup.

NOTE

These temporary installation files are deleted automatically after 10 days. Your previous Windows installation is saved for approximately 30 days in Windows.old, allowing you to roll back to the previous version or recover files if necessary. On systems with limited free disk space, you can remove these files using the Disk Cleanup utility or tools in Settings > Storage. We describe this process in more detail in "Managing disk space" in Chapter 9, "Storage and file management."

If you poke around in the root of the system drive, you might notice additional hidden folders with similar names: $Windows.~WS, for example, is created by the Media Creation Tool when you download Windows 10 installation files, and $GetCurrent is created when you use the Update Assistant.

Upgrading from an earlier Windows version

A streamlined wizard walks you briskly through a Windows 10 upgrade. The process is significantly faster than in earlier versions of Windows, especially on systems with a large number of files. No major upgrade is ever risk free, of course, but the Windows 10 installer is designed to be robust enough to roll back gracefully in the case of a failure.

In Windows 10, you can begin the upgrade process by running the Media Creation Tool and selecting the first option, Upgrade This PC Now. That option downloads the full installation file and then runs the Windows Setup program immediately, downloading additional installation files on the fly. As an alternative, you can use bootable installation media or an ISO file mounted as a virtual drive.

When you kick off a Windows 10 upgrade, Setup performs a series of tasks. First, it runs a compatibility check, which determines whether your PC, peripheral devices, and installed Windows apps will work with Windows 10. (See "Checking compatibility" later in this section for details about warnings that might appear.)

Inside OUT

Upgrade directly from an ISO file

The ISO disc image format was originally devised to make it possible to share DVDs as files, without having to put shiny discs in the mail and wait a few days or weeks. Over time, they've evolved into a virtual alternative that doesn't require discs at all. Both Windows 8.1 and Windows 10 support the capability to mount ISO files directly in File Explorer. Double-click the ISO file to mount it with its own drive letter, after which you

can access files directly or copy those files to a fixed or removable drive for later use. (For Windows 7, you need a third-party utility program to mount an ISO file. We recommend the open source WinCDEmu utility, available at *http://wincdemu.sysprogs.org/*.)

Obviously, this option won't work for a clean install on a freshly formatted drive, but it's ideal for upgrades and feature updates. When you double-click a saved ISO file in Windows 10's File Explorer, its contents appear as a virtual CD/DVD drive in the Devices And Drives area of File Explorer, as in Figure 2-3.

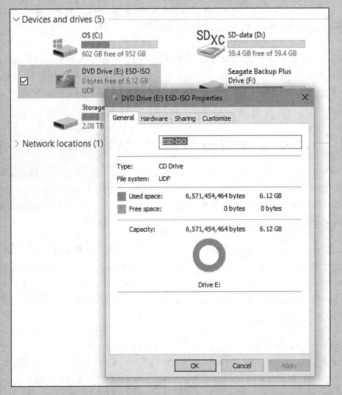

Figure 2-3   In this File Explorer window, drives C and D are physical drives, but drive E is a virtual drive created by double-clicking and mounting an ISO disc image file.

Double-click to open the mounted disk, and then double-click Setup to kick off an upgrade. When you no longer need the virtual drive, right-click its File Explorer icon and click Eject.

When you start an online upgrade from within Windows 8.1, the upgrade keeps all your data files and migrates settings, Windows apps, and desktop programs. Upgrades from Windows 7 preserve data files and desktop programs but do not migrate personalized settings such as your desktop background.

If you have Windows 10 installation media, you can also start the upgrade process from within Windows. Open the DVD or USB flash drive in File Explorer and double-click Setup. The resulting wizard walks you through several steps that aren't part of the streamlined online upgrade. The most important of these is the option to transfer files, apps, and settings, a topic we cover shortly.

Checking compatibility

A compatibility checker is built into the Windows 10 Setup program (replacing the Upgrade Advisor from Windows 7), and it runs as one of the first steps when you kick off an upgrade. A more limited version runs on a clean install, checking for issues such as a BIOS that needs updating or a disk controller or network adapter that has no supported driver.

In most cases, this appraisal turns up nothing, and Setup continues without interruption. If this routine finds any issues, however, it notifies you with a warning dialog box. Setup will refuse to continue if your device doesn't have enough RAM or free disk space. Other causes of hard blocks include a CPU or a BIOS that is not supported, as well as the presence of a hard-disk controller or networking device that lacks a driver. When the compatibility checker turns up any hard blocks, Setup ends immediately, with a message that identifies the problem.

For less severe issues, the Setup program might warn you that specific apps or devices might not work correctly or will have reduced functionality in Windows 10. You might be given the option to fix the issue and try the upgrade again. In these cases, the compatibility checker offers instructions to deal with specific issues:

- You might need to install updates to your current version of Windows before continuing.

- You might need to suspend disk encryption before upgrading.

- Some apps must be uninstalled before the upgrade can continue. (In some cases, they can be reinstalled after the upgrade is complete.)

- Some apps must be updated to a newer version before the upgrade can be completed.

- After the upgrade, you might need to reinstall language packs.

If the upgrade process ends prematurely for any of these reasons, Setup generally cleans up after itself, although you might have to manually remove some leftovers.

Transferring files, apps, and settings

When you upgrade to Windows 10 on a volume that already contains a copy of Windows, you must choose what you want to do with user files, settings, and apps. To choose an alternative option, run Setup from installation media or a mounted ISO file. The default option when upgrading from Windows 7 to Windows 10 is to keep all files and apps. Figure 2-4 shows the additional options available if you click Choose What To Keep.

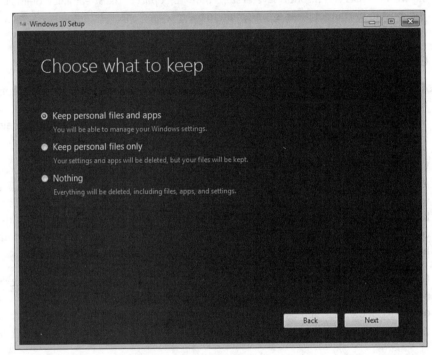

Figure 2-4   When you upgrade from Windows 7 to Windows 10, these three options are available when you first run Setup.

Here's what happens with each option:

- **Keep Personal Files And Apps.** All Windows desktop programs and user accounts are migrated. After the upgrade is complete, you need to sign in with your Microsoft account to install apps from the Windows Store and sync saved settings. When upgrading from Windows 8.1, this option includes the capability to preserve settings.

    ### NOTE

    This option is unavailable if you're installing a Windows edition that is not a supported upgrade path from the current edition.

- **Keep Personal Files Only.** This option is the equivalent of a repair installation. Each user's personal files are available in a new user profile that otherwise contains only default apps and settings.

- **Nothing.** Choose this option if you want to perform a clean install, with your existing installation moved to Windows.old. Note that the descriptive text, "Everything will be deleted," is misleading. Your personal files, as well as those belonging to other user accounts in the current installation, are not deleted. Instead, they are moved to the Windows.old folder, where you can recover them by using File Explorer.

After the initial prep work, Setup restarts in offline mode, displaying a progress screen that is simpler than the one from the initial release of Windows 10.

In this mode, you can't interact with the PC at all. Your PC is effectively offline as the following actions occur.

Windows Setup first moves the following folders from the existing Windows installation on the root of the system drive into Windows.old:

- Windows

- Program Files

- Program Files (x86)

- Users

- ProgramData

During this offline phase, Setup extracts registry values and program data from the Windows.old folder, based on the type of upgrade, and then prepares to add this data to the corresponding locations in the new Windows 10 installation. Third-party hardware drivers are also copied from the old driver store in preparation for the new installation.

Next, Setup lays down a new set of system folders for Windows 10 using the folder structure and files from the compressed Windows image. After that task is complete, Setup moves program files, registry values, and other settings it gathered earlier.

Moving folders minimizes the number of file operations that are required, making upgrade times consistent even when individual user accounts contain large numbers of files. (By contrast, the Windows 7 Setup program moved files individually, which led to some painfully long upgrades.)

To further speed things up, Windows 10 Setup uses hard link operations to move files and folders from the transport location to the new Windows 10 hierarchy. Not having to physically move the file improves performance and allows for easy rollback if something goes wrong during the upgrade.

Setup moves folders associated with individual user accounts as part of a default in-place upgrade. The entire folder is placed within the fresh Windows 10 installation unchanged; every file in the folder and all its subfolders is preserved. (Note that organizations using corporate deployment tools can override some of this behavior, excluding some files or subfolders and merging the contents of default folders with the contents of existing folders from the source operating system.)

This activity is accompanied by several restarts and can take more than an hour, depending on your hardware, although an upgrade on most modern hardware typically goes much faster. At the conclusion of this process, you're confronted with a sign-in screen. That's followed by a single screen that allows you to choose privacy settings for your device.

If you're upgrading from Windows 7 or from a Windows 8.1 PC that was configured to use a local user account, you need to sign in using the credentials for that account. After that, you'll have the option to link your account to a Microsoft account or to continue using a local account.

By signing in with a Microsoft account, you can continue setting up Windows 10 by using your synced settings. The most current version of each preinstalled app is downloaded and installed from the Store before you sign in.

> ➤ For more information about your options when setting up a user account, see Chapter 11, "Managing user accounts, passwords, and credentials."

Performing a clean install

Among some PC traditionalists, it's a badge of honor to wipe a newly purchased PC clean and then set up Windows from scratch. Even if you're not so fastidious, a clean install is sometimes unavoidable: it's the only option for PCs you build yourself and for virtual machines, and it's sometimes the fastest way to get back up and running after a disk failure.

The time-tested road to a clean install involves starting up from a bootable USB flash drive containing the Windows 10 installation files and removing all traces of the currently installed Windows version before proceeding to run Setup.

This is still a perfectly valid installation method, one we'll describe in more detail shortly. But it's no longer the only option, nor is it always the best. For a system that's already running any modern version of Windows, you'll find it much easier to start Setup from within Windows, choose an upgrade install, and choose the option to keep Nothing. After you use Disk Cleanup Manager or the tools in Settings > Storage to remove the old Windows installation, the result is virtually identical to an old-fashioned clean install.

NOTE

For a thorough discussion of how the push-button reset option works, see Chapter 15, "Troubleshooting, backup, and recovery."

Inside OUT

Set up and format your hard disk

In this section, we describe the steps for a clean installation on the simplest of all PC configurations: a single storage device (hard disk or SSD) containing unallocated space ready to be automatically partitioned for use as the system drive. Out in the real world, especially among Windows enthusiasts, we know that disk configurations can be much more complex.

On most desktop PCs and on some notebooks, you can connect multiple physical disk drives. You can choose to install Windows 10 to any fixed volume, including internal IDE and SATA drives as well as eSATA drives, which attach to the system via an external cable but appear to Windows as an ordinary internal drive. You cannot, however, install Windows to an external drive connected via USB or IEEE 1394 (FireWire) or to any form of removable media. (The sole exception is the Windows To Go feature, which requires specially built USB drives and an installed copy of Windows 10 Enterprise edition.)

With a new internal storage device or an existing one, you might have any of several good reasons to tinker with disk partitions. You might prefer to segregate your operating-system files from your data files by placing them on separate volumes, for example, or you might be planning to set up a dual-boot or multi-boot system. In any event, it's always easier to make partitioning decisions before installing Windows than it is to resize and rearrange volumes after they're in use.

For a full inventory of all disk-management tools and techniques available in Windows 10, see Chapter 14. For details about partitioning a drive and managing data storage, see Chapter 9.

That neat option isn't possible if you're starting with a brand-new hard disk, or you want to install a 64-bit Windows 10 edition on a device that's currently running 32-bit Windows, or you want to clean up a messy OEM's partition layout on the system disk, or ... well, you get the idea.

For those scenarios, you need to boot into the Windows 10 Setup program from a USB flash drive (or a DVD drive, if your PC is equipped with one of those increasingly rare peripherals). You might need to read the manual for your device to learn the magic combination of keystrokes and firmware settings that make it possible to start up using a bootable Windows 10 disc or drive.

After the installation process begins, you can follow the instructions as outlined in this section.

When you boot from that media, you pass through a few introductory screens—choosing a language, accepting a license agreement—and eventually reach the Windows Setup dialog box shown in Figure 2-5. You're asked to choose an installation type—Upgrade or Custom. Be aware: "Which type of installation do you want?" is a trick question.

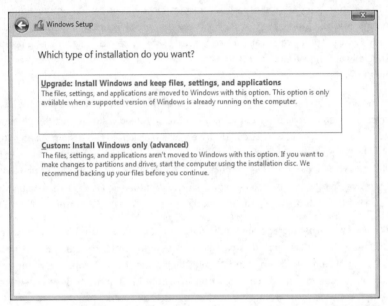

Figure 2-5   When you boot from a USB flash drive or DVD to perform a clean install of Windows, the only option that works from this screen is Custom.

Choosing the Upgrade option raises an error message; you can upgrade Windows only if you start Setup from within Windows.

The Custom option allows you to continue, and you're presented with a list of available disks and volumes. Figure 2-6 shows what you see on a system with a single drive that has not yet been partitioned and contains only unallocated space.

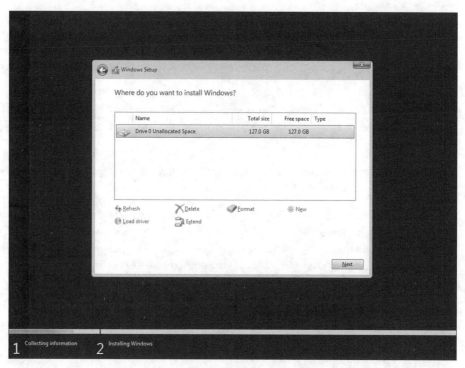

Figure 2-6   In this simple scenario, with a single physical disk that has not been partitioned, click Next to create the necessary partitions and install Windows using the entire physical drive.

Inside OUT

How Windows 10 divides a disk

If you install Windows 10 on a UEFI-based system with a single unformatted disk, Setup creates a default disk layout. Three of its partitions are visible in the Disk Management console, as shown here.

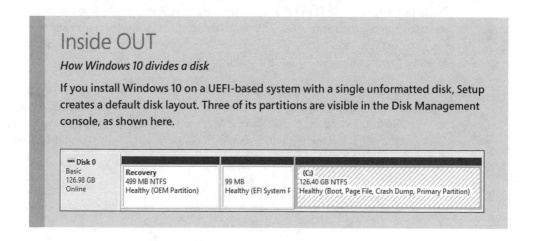

The small (499-MB) recovery partition at the start of the disk in this example contains the Windows Recovery Environment, which allows the system to boot for repair and recovery operations. (This partition might be a different size and in a different location on your PC.)

The EFI system partition is even smaller—on this PC, a mere 99 MB. It contains the files required for the system to start up, including the Windows Hardware Abstraction Layer and the boot loader (NTLDR).

The largest partition is the primary partition, formatted using NTFS, which contains Windows system files, the paging file, and all user profiles.

A fourth partition, required for every GPT disk, is hidden and not visible in Disk Management. This partition, labeled MSR (Reserved), resides between the EFI system partition and the primary partition and is used for post-installation tasks, such as converting a basic disk to a dynamic disk. It's visible when you use DiskPart or the partitioning tools available with a custom installation.

PC makers have the option to add custom OEM partitions to this layout, with those volumes containing files that are part of a custom installation. In addition, some PCs create a second recovery partition at the end of the drive, which contains files you can use to restore the original system configuration.

You can use the tools beneath the list of available drives to manage partitions on a drive that currently contains a Windows installation and user data. For example, if you want a truly fresh start, you can select each partition and click Delete until only unallocated space remains. You can also use these tools to create one or more new partitions, format an existing partition, or extend a partition to include adjacent unallocated space.

To make adjustments to existing disk partitions, boot from Windows 10 installation media (DVD or bootable USB flash drive) and run through Windows Setup until you reach the Where Do You Want To Install Windows page. Figure 2-7 shows a system that contains two physical drives. Drive 0 contains a standard partition layout, with Windows installed on Partition 4. Drive 1 is divided in half, with a data volume and unallocated space.

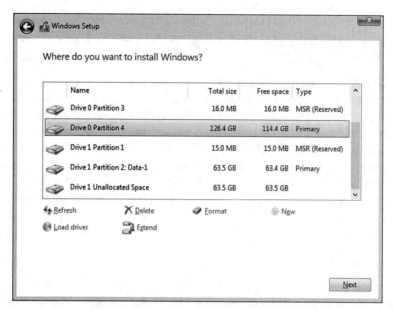

Figure 2-7   Use the disk-management tools in this phase of the Windows 10 installation process to manage disk partitions for more efficient data storage and multi-boot configurations.

You can accomplish any of the following tasks here:

- **Select an existing partition or unallocated space on which to install Windows 10.** Setup is simple if you already created and formatted an empty partition in preparation for setting up Windows, or if you plan to install Windows 10 on an existing partition that currently contains data or programs but no operating system, or if you want to use unallocated space on an existing disk without disturbing the existing partition scheme. Select the partition or unallocated space and click Next.

- **Delete an existing partition.** Select a partition, and then click Delete. This option is useful if you want to perform a clean installation on a drive that currently contains an earlier version of Windows. Because this operation deletes data irretrievably, you must respond to an "Are you sure?" confirmation request. After deleting the partition, you can select the unallocated space as the destination for your Windows 10 installation or create a new partition. Be sure to back up any data files before choosing this option.

- **Create a new partition from unallocated space.** Select a block of unallocated space on a new drive or on an existing drive after deleting partitions, and click New to set up a partition in that space.

  By default, Windows Setup offers to use all unallocated space on the current disk. You can specify a smaller partition size if you want to subdivide the disk into multiple drives. If you have a 4-TB drive, for example, you might choose to create a relatively small partition on which to install Windows and use the remaining space to create a second volume with its own drive letter on which to store data files such as music, pictures, documents, and videos.

- **Extend an existing partition by using unallocated space.** If you're not happy with your existing partition scheme, you can use the Extend option to add unallocated space to any partition, provided that space is immediately to the right of the existing partition in Disk Management, with no intervening partitions. If the manufacturer of your PC initially divided a 128-GB hard disk into two equal volumes, you might decide to rejoin the two partitions when performing a clean install. After backing up your data files to an external drive or to cloud storage, delete the data partition, select the partition to the left of the newly freed space, and click Extend. Choose the total size of the extended partition in the Size box (the default is to use all available unallocated space) and click Apply. You can now continue with Setup.

CAUTION

In both the Disk Management console and the disk-management tools available via Windows Setup, it can be confusing to tell which partition is which. Confusion, in this case, can have drastic consequences if you inadvertently wipe out a drive full of data instead of writing over an unwanted installation of Windows. One good way to reduce the risk of this sort of accident is to label drives well.

Alert observers will no doubt notice that one option is missing from that list. Unfortunately, Setup does not allow you to shrink an existing disk partition to create unallocated space on which to install a fresh copy of Windows 10. The option to shrink a volume is available from the Disk Management console after Windows 10 is installed, but if you want to accomplish this task before running Setup, you need to use third-party disk-management tools.

After you click Next, the installation process switches into a lengthy unattended phase in which it partitions and formats the disk (if necessary), copies the clean Windows 10 image to the system partition, installs device drivers, and starts default services. When those operations are complete, you arrive at a series of screens where you select the default region and keyboard layout.

If you do a clean install using bootable media for Windows 10 Pro, you're faced with one additional choice immediately after Setup completes this. The dialog box shown in Figure 2-8 asks you to choose whether you want to set up the device for personal use or as part of an organization. For an installation of Windows 10 Enterprise, the dialog box asks whether you want to join Azure AD or join a domain. (This portion of Setup has undergone numerous changes since the initial release of Windows 10, all in the interest of reducing confusion when setting up a work PC.)

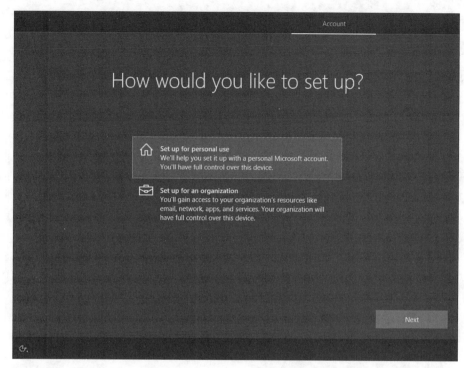

Figure 2-8   This option is available only when you do a clean install of Windows 10 Pro.

If you own the device, or if it is a company PC that will be joined to a Windows domain, choose Set Up For Personal Use and click Next to continue.

If the PC will be managed by your organization using something other than a Windows domain on a local network, choose the second option (Set Up For An Organization). Clicking Next leads you through a series of dialog boxes you use to set up a device for access to online services (from Microsoft and others). The credentials are managed in Azure Active Directory and can be linked to services such as an Office 365 account at a workplace or university.

> ➤ **For more information about setting up user accounts, during Windows installation or afterwards, see Chapter 11.**

Performing an edition upgrade

If you want access to a feature that's not available in your edition of Windows, you can upgrade to a different edition. This scenario is especially common when you purchase a retail PC configured with Windows 10 Home and want to take advantage of features in Windows 10 Pro, but the same technique allows you to upgrade from any edition to any higher edition, including Enterprise and Education editions.

The fastest upgrade path is to enter a product key for the new edition. Open Settings > Update & Security > Activation and look at the two options under the Upgrade Your Edition Of Windows section, as shown here.

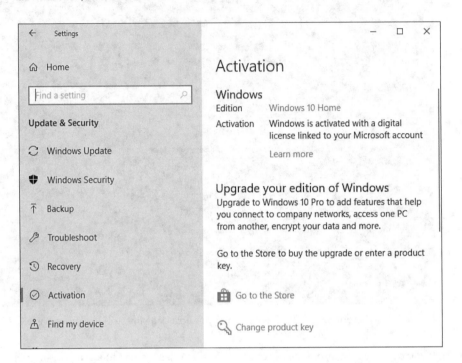

Click Go To The Store and follow the prompts to purchase an upgrade. Or, if you already have a valid product key and associated license for the upgrade, click Change Product Key and enter that 25-character key. In either case, completing the upgrade requires a restart (or two) and typically requires only a few minutes.

Activating Windows

For more than a dozen years, desktop versions of Windows have included a set of anti-piracy and anti-tampering features. In the past, Microsoft has used different names for these capabilities: Windows Activation Technologies and Windows Genuine Advantage, for example. In Windows 10, these features are collectively referred to as the *Software Protection Platform*.

The various checks and challenges in Windows 10, in essence, are enforcement mechanisms for the Windows 10 license agreement, which is displayed during the process of installing or deploying the operating system. (You must provide your consent to complete setup.) We're not lawyers, so we won't attempt to interpret the terms of this legal document. We do recommend you read the license agreement, which is written in relatively plain language compared to many such documents we've read through the years.

CHAPTER 2

NOTE

It's important to understand a potentially confusing concept here: the legal and contractual restrictions imposed by license agreements are completely independent of technical restrictions related to installation.

Licenses are assigned to devices. If you upgrade a system to Windows 10 from Windows 7 and then the system's hard disk fails, you can replace the storage device, perform a clean install of Windows 10, and still be properly licensed. Conversely, it's technically possible to install and activate Windows on a computer that doesn't have an underlying license, but that successful activation doesn't necessarily translate to a valid license. This distinction is especially crucial for businesses (even small ones) that could be the target of a software audit to verify proper licensing.

You can find the license terms for the currently installed Windows edition by going to Settings > System > About. Under the Windows Specifications heading, click Read The Microsoft Software License Terms.

In this section, we explain how the activation and validation mechanisms in Windows 10 affect your use of the operating system.

Product activation happens shortly after you sign in on a PC running a freshly installed copy of Windows 10. Typically, this involves a brief communication between your PC and Microsoft's licensing servers. If everything checks out, your copy of Windows is activated silently, and you never have to deal with product keys or activation prompts.

The activation process is completely anonymous and does not require that you divulge any personal information. If you choose to register your copy of Windows 10, this is a separate (and optional) task.

After you successfully activate your copy of Windows 10, your hardware is still subject to periodic antipiracy checks from Microsoft. This process verifies that your copy of Windows has not been tampered with to bypass activation. It also allows Microsoft to revoke the activation for a computer when it determines after the fact that the original activation was the result of product tampering or that a product key was stolen or used in violation of a volume licensing agreement.

NOTE

A Windows 10 PC that is not activated can still be used. All Windows functions (with the exception of personalization options) work normally, all your data files are accessible, and all your programs work as expected. The nagging reminders are intended to strongly encourage you to resolve the underlying issue. Some forms of malware can damage system files in a way that resembles tampering with activation files. Another common cause of activation problems is a lazy or dishonest repair technician who installs a stolen or "cracked" copy of Windows instead of using your original licensed copy.

Links in the Windows Activation messages lead to online support tools, where you might be able to identify and repair the issue that's affecting your system. Microsoft also offers free support for activation issues via online forums and by telephone.

The activation mechanism is designed to enforce license restrictions by preventing the most common form of software piracy: casual copying. Typically, a Windows 10 license entitles you to install the operating system software on a single computer. If you're trying to activate Windows 10 using a product key that has previously been activated on a second (or third or fourth) device, you might be unable to activate the software automatically.

Windows licensing options

Every copy of Windows is licensed, not sold. Windows 10 supports multiple license types, some of which are new.

- **Full.** A full license is sold directly to retail customers as an electronic distribution or a packaged product. With a full license, Windows can be installed on a computer that was not sold with Windows originally, or it can be used as an upgrade. (Microsoft no longer sells upgrade-only licenses for Windows.) You need a full license to install Windows in a virtual machine, on a Mac or other computer that does not come with Windows preinstalled, or in a dual-boot or multi-boot setup. A full license can be transferred to a different computer; the underlying copy of Windows on the original PC must be removed for the transferred license to be valid.

- **OEM.** An OEM (original equipment manufacturer) license is one that's included with a new computer. This license is locked to the computer on which it's installed and cannot be transferred to a new computer. OEM System Builder packages are intended for use by small PC makers but are often used by consumers and hobbyists in place of a more expensive full license. The system builder is required to provide support for OEM Windows along with the device on which it is installed.

- **Volume.** Volume licenses are sold in bulk to corporate, government, nonprofit, and educational customers and are typically deployed by using enterprise-management tools. A volume license for Windows is available as an upgrade only.

- **Cloud.** If you purchased an upgrade to Windows 10 Enterprise using a subscription option (E3 or E5), your license is associated with your Azure Active Directory account. You can activate that edition of Windows on up to five PCs by signing in with those credentials.

- **Digital license.** PCs that have been upgraded from Windows 7 or Windows 8.1, during or after the free upgrade offer, receive a digital license that is associated with the upgraded hardware on Microsoft's activation servers. The details of a digital license can be linked to a Microsoft account, as we describe later in this section.

Do you need a product key?

The 25-character alphanumeric product key is certainly not dead, although you're increasingly less likely to need such a key to work with Windows 10. On most PCs built by large OEMs and sold through retail channels, Windows can retrieve the embedded license information from the computer's firmware and activate automatically.

Smaller OEMs (in Microsoft's parlance, these are called System Builders) purchase individual copies of Windows that require a product key for activation. The System Builder is required under the terms of the OEM license to include that key as part of the Windows installation and to provide an official copy of that key to the purchaser of the PC.

If you're building your own PC or installing Windows 10 in a new virtual machine, you still need a product key from a retail copy of Windows 10 or an OEM System Builder package. You also need a product key to upgrade a PC that does not already have a valid Windows 10 license.

If you skip the opportunity to enter a product key during a clean install, or if the key you enter fails activation (perhaps because it has been used on another PC), you can go to Settings > Update & Security > Activation and click the Change Product Key button. Enter a valid product key for the currently installed Windows edition using the dialog box shown in Figure 2-9.

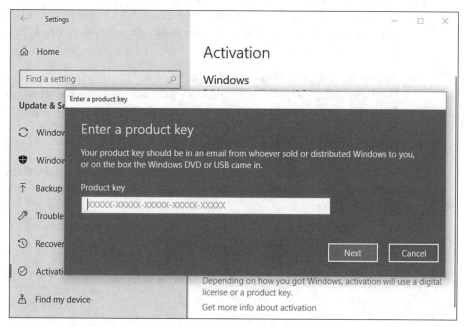

Figure 2-9   When you enter the 25-character alphanumeric product key, Windows automatically checks it and prompts you to complete activation.

CHAPTER 2

Here are some important facts you should know about product keys:

- **A custom product key is stored in firmware on any copy of Windows that is prein-stalled on a new PC by a large computer maker.** This configuration is called System Locked Preinstallation (SLP). Using this configuration, you can reinstall the same edition of Windows and reactivate without having to enter a product key.

- **Your product key matches your edition of Windows.** When you enter a product key as part of a custom install of Windows, the key identifies the edition to be installed. If you purchase a boxed copy of Windows 10 from a retail outlet, the installation media (a DVD or a USB flash drive) contains a configuration file that automatically installs the edition that matches the product key included with that package.

- **Some Windows 10 PCs don't require a product key.** If you upgraded a properly acti-vated copy of Windows 7 or Windows 8.1, you don't need to enter a product key. A record of the edition that device is licensed to use, Home or Pro, is stored with the device's hard-ware ID on Microsoft's activation servers. That digital license can be associated with your Microsoft account for later use. Digital licenses are also associated with upgrades and full licenses of Windows 10 purchased from the Microsoft Store.

- **Product keys are not tied to a specific architecture.** The product key matches a spe-cific Windows 10 edition and will activate a 32-bit or 64-bit copy of that Windows 10 edi-tion on your hardware (assuming the hardware is compatible with the architecture you choose, of course).

- **You are not required to enter a product key when performing a clean install of Windows 10.** You're prompted to enter a valid product key when you perform a clean installation of Windows 10, as shown in Figure 2-10. If you are reinstalling Windows 10 on a PC that has previously been activated and has a digital license, click I Don't Have A Product Key, just to the left of the Next button.

Clicking I Don't Have A Product Key allows Setup to proceed but might require that you select a specific Windows edition to install. Be sure to choose the edition that matches your license.

Figure 2-10   Setup automatically installs the Windows edition that matches the 25-character alpha-numeric product key you enter here and attempts to activate using that key after Setup is complete.

Managing digital licenses

In the first year after the initial release of Windows 10, Microsoft made upgrades from Windows 7 and Windows 8.1 free; as we noted earlier in this chapter, the free upgrade offer was extended until December 31, 2017, for any PCs that use assistive technology. As part of these campaigns, Microsoft also added a new license type. On PCs upgraded using that free offer, the Windows activation server generated a Windows 10 license certificate (Microsoft initially called it a *digital entitlement* but later changed the nomenclature to *digital license*) for the corresponding edition (Home or Pro). That digital license is stored in conjunction with your unique installation ID on Microsoft's activation servers. (You can read more details about this and other license types at *https://support.microsoft.com/help/12440/windows-10-activation*.)

The unique installation ID is essentially a fingerprint of your PC, based on a cryptographic hash derived from your hardware. That hash, reportedly, is not reversible and not tied to any other Microsoft services. So, although it defines your device, it doesn't identify you. But it does make it possible to store activation status for that device online.

Once that online activation status is recorded, you can wipe your drive clean, boot from Windows 10 installation media, and install a clean copy (skipping right past the prompts for a product key); at the end of the process you'll have a properly activated copy of Windows 10.

At any time, you can check the activation status of your device by going to Settings > Update & Security > Activation, as shown in Figure 2-11.

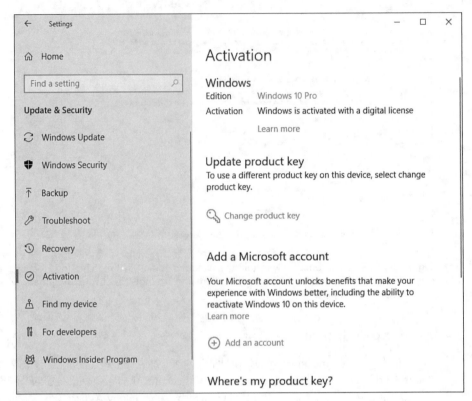

Figure 2-11   Most Windows 10 PCs will be automatically activated, with the successful activation status shown in this dialog box.

One detail worth noting in Figure 2-11 is the suggestion to add a Microsoft account. Doing so creates a record of the digital license that can be retrieved for troubleshooting purposes, as we discuss in the next section.

Troubleshooting activation problems

When you install Windows 10 on a new PC, it attempts to contact Microsoft's licensing servers and activate automatically within three days. Under most circumstances, activation over the internet takes no more than a few seconds. If the process fails, you see several indications that there's a problem. The first is a link at the bottom of every page in Settings: Windows Isn't Activated. Activate Windows Now. If you open any option from the Personalization category in Settings, every option is grayed out and unavailable, with a message in red at the top: "You need to activate Windows before you can personalize your PC." Below that is an Activate Windows Now link.

The most obvious reminder of all appears, naturally, if you click Settings > Update & Security > Activation. Figure 2-12 shows an example of this dire message.

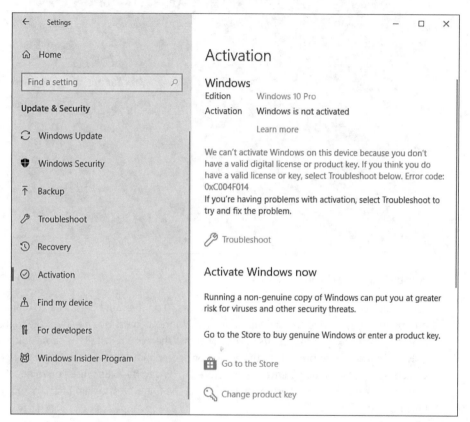

Figure 2-12 In the event of an activation error, you can use options on this Settings page to use a troubleshooting tool, buy a new license from the Microsoft Store, or enter a product key.

If you're confident you have a legitimate Windows 10 license, click Troubleshoot to try to fix the problem. The activation troubleshooter can resolve some simple problems and is especially well suited for activation errors that result from hardware changes or from situations where you inadvertently installed the wrong Windows edition (Home instead of Pro, for example). In fact, if the troubleshooter is unable to resolve your issue, it offers an I Changed Hardware On This Device Recently option, as shown here.

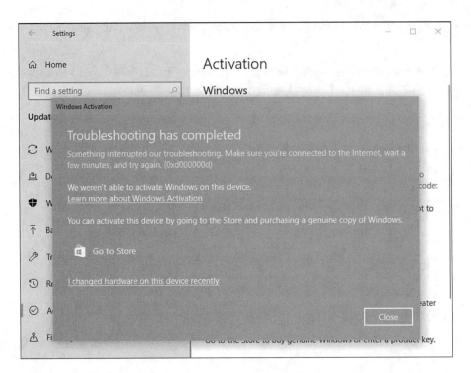

CHAPTER 2

Why are hardware changes an issue?

You're allowed to reinstall and reactivate Windows 10 on the same hardware an unlimited number of times. During the activation process, Windows transmits a hashed file that serves as a "fingerprint" of key components in your system. When you reinstall the same edition of Windows 10 you activated previously, the activation server receives the current hardware fingerprint and compares that value against the one stored in its database. Because you're reinstalling Windows 10 on hardware that is essentially the same, the fingerprints will match, and activation will be automatic.

Just as with earlier Windows versions, this activation process is designed to prevent attempts to tamper with the activation files or to "clone" an activated copy of Windows and install it on another computer. What happens if you upgrade the hardware in your computer? When you activate your copy of Windows 10, a copy of the hardware fingerprint is stored on your hard disk and checked each time you start your computer. If you make substantial changes to your system hardware, you might be required to reactivate your copy of Windows.

You can upgrade almost all components in a system without requiring a new license. Replacing the motherboard on a PC is the most certain way to trigger the activation mechanism, because the activation server assumes you tried to install your copy of Windows on a second computer. If you replaced a defective or failed motherboard with one that is the same model or the manufacturer's equivalent, you do not need to acquire a new operating system license, and you should be able to reactivate your copy of Windows.

To help with this scenario, the activation troubleshooter relies on a feature that was introduced with the Anniversary Update, version 1607: the capability to save a digital license for Windows 10 and link it to your Microsoft account. This step isn't mandatory, but it's handy if you make major changes to a system with a digital license and need to reactivate.

If the PC in question has a valid digital license that has been previously associated with a Microsoft account, you can run the activation troubleshooter to make the match that Microsoft's activation servers can't. Click the Troubleshoot link at the bottom of that Settings page to launch a tool that tries to find the activation record for the PC you're using. If you're not signed in with a Microsoft account, you need to do so, using the account you used previously to activate this PC.

Figure 2-13 shows the activation troubleshooter in action. After signing in with the Microsoft account to which the previous device activation was linked, you'll see a list of linked devices. Select the name associated with the device you're having troubles with and then click Activate.

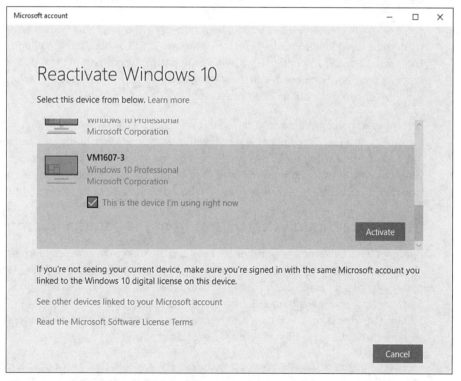

Figure 2-13   Using the activation troubleshooter, you can choose a digital license from a previously activated device to resolve issues that occur if you make significant hardware changes.

If all else fails, your only remaining option is to contact the telephone-based activation support center, explain the circumstances, and—assuming that the support representative accepts your claim—manually enter a new activation code. (If you upgrade your PC with a new motherboard, that is considered a new PC and might require a new license.)

The license agreement for a retail copy of Windows 10 allows you to transfer it to another computer, provided that you completely remove it from the computer on which it was previously installed. An OEM copy, by contrast, is tied to the computer on which it was originally installed. You can reinstall an OEM copy of Windows an unlimited number of times on the same computer. However, you are prohibited by the license agreement from transferring that copy of Windows to another computer after it has been assigned to a device.

Product activation and corporate licensing

Businesses that purchase licenses through a Microsoft Volume Licensing (VL) program receive VL media and product keys that require activation under a different set of rules from those that apply to retail or OEM copies. Under the terms of a volume license agreement, each computer with a copy of Windows 10 must have a valid license and must be activated.

Beginning with the Anniversary Update to Windows 10, Microsoft also made it possible to upgrade to Windows 10 Enterprise from Windows 10 Pro by purchasing a Windows 10 Enterprise E3 or E5 subscription from a Microsoft partner who is part of the Cloud Service Provider program. For more details, see *https://docs.microsoft.com/windows/deployment/ windows-10-enterprise-subscription-activation*.

Enterprise editions of Windows 10 can be installed using Multiple Activation Keys, which allow activations on a specific number of devices within an organization, or they can use Key Management servers to activate computers within an organization. If you encounter activation issues with Windows 10 Pro or Enterprise in a VL deployment, contact the person in your organization who manages your VL agreement—the "Benefits Administrator," as this person is called.

Managing Windows activation from the command prompt

Windows 10 includes a command-line tool you can use to examine the licensing status of a PC, change its product key, and perform other activation-related tasks. Although this feature is primarily intended for automating license administration activities, you can also run the Windows Software Licensing Management Tool interactively. Open a Command Prompt window with administrative privileges, and then run the command slmgr.vbs. If it's run without parameters, this command shows its full syntax in a series of dialog boxes.

One common use of this tool is to display the current licensing status for a device, using the syntax `slmgr.vbs /dli`. Figure 2-14, for example, shows the status of a device running Windows 10 Enterprise that has been properly activated with a Multiple Activation Key.

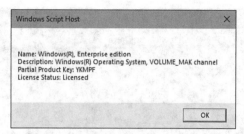

Figure 2-14   This output from the Windows Software Licensing Management Tool shows a system that is properly licensed. If you see an error code here, you need to do some troubleshooting.

For a much more detailed display of information, use the same command with a switch that produces verbose output: **slmgr.vbs /dlv**. Use **slmgr.vbs /ipk <product_key>** to enter the 25-character product key you provide following that switch. The /upk switch uninstalls the current product key, and the /cpky switch removes the product key from the registry to deter attempts to steal and reuse a key. To see all available switches, enter the **slmgr.vbs** command by itself.

Configuring a multi-boot system

If your computer already has any version of Windows installed and you have a second disk partition available (or enough unallocated space to create a second partition), you can install a clean copy of Windows 10 without disturbing your existing Windows installation. At boot time, you choose your Windows version from a startup menu, like the one shown in Figure 2-15. Although this is typically called a *dual-boot system*, it's more accurate to call it a *multi-boot configuration*, because you can install as many copies of Windows or other PC-compatible operating systems as your system resources allow.

Having the capability to choose your operating system at startup is handy if you have a program or device that simply won't work under Windows 10 but can't easily be run in a virtual machine. When you need to use the legacy program or device, you can boot into your earlier Windows version without too much fuss. This capability is also useful for software developers and IT professionals who need to be able to test how programs work under different operating systems using physical (not virtual) hardware.

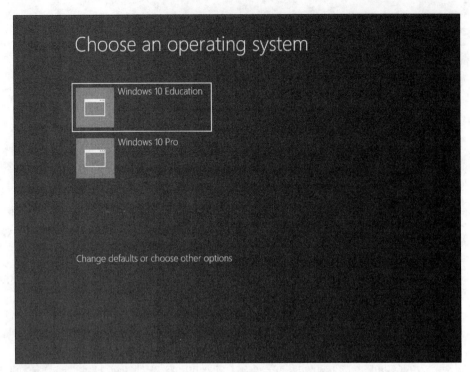

Figure 2-15   This system is configured to allow a choice of operating systems at startup.

TROUBLESHOOTING

After installing Windows 7, you see a text-based boot menu

The preferred way to build a multi-boot system is to install the most recent version last. That option uses the graphical boot menu. If you install Windows 7 as a second operating system on a PC that is currently running Windows 10, you get Windows 7's black-and-white, text-based boot menu. To restore the graphical menu, start Windows 10, open an Administrative Command Prompt, and run the following command: **bcdboot c:\windows**. Restart, and you should see the familiar blue-and-white menu.

For experienced Windows users, installing a second copy of Windows 10 in its own partition can also be helpful as a way to maintain a completely clean environment, separate from confidential work data. It's also useful when you need to experiment with a potentially problematic program or device driver without compromising a working system. After you finish setting up the second, clean version of Windows 10, you'll see an additional entry on the startup menu that corresponds to your new installation. (The newly installed version is the default menu choice; it runs automatically if 30 seconds pass and you haven't made a choice.) Experiment with the program or driver and see how well it works. If, after testing thoroughly, you're satisfied that the program is safe to use, you can add it to the Windows 10 installation you use every day.

To add a separate installation of Windows 10 to a system on which an existing version of Windows is already installed, first make sure you have an available volume (or unformatted disk space) separate from the volume that contains the system files for your current Windows version.

Inside OUT

Use virtual machines whenever possible instead of hassling with multi-boot menus

You can create truly elaborate multi-boot configurations using Windows versions that date back a decade or more. But unless you're running a hardware testing lab, there's no good reason to do that. The much simpler, smoother alternative is to use virtual hardware that faithfully re-creates the operating environment. During the course of researching and writing multiple editions of this book, we installed Windows 10 in virtual machines to capture details of several crucial tasks and processes that can't easily be documented on physical hardware, and we saved many hours compared to how long those tasks would have taken had we set up and restored physical hardware.

We strongly recommend Microsoft's Hyper-V virtualization software, which is a standard feature in Windows 10 Pro (including Windows 10 in S Mode), Enterprise, and Education and on current Windows Server versions. (For more information about Client Hyper-V in Windows 10, see Chapter 16, "Hyper-V.")

To run Windows 10 on a Mac, try Parallels, available at *https://parallels.com*. For other operating systems, check out VMware (*https://vmware.com*), which offers excellent virtualization software for use on desktop Windows machines and servers, and the free VirtualBox package from Oracle (*https://virtualbox.org*).

Using any of these solutions, you can install even the most ancient Windows version. Backing up a machine's configuration and restoring it is as simple as copying a file. You will, of course, need a license for every operating system you install in a virtual machine. If you have a license to use Windows for evaluation purposes, the option to run Windows in a virtual machine can be a tremendous timesaver.

The target volume can be a separate partition on the same physical disk as the current Windows installation, or it can be on a different hard disk. If your system contains a single disk with a single volume used as drive C, you cannot create a multi-boot system unless you add a new disk or use software tools to shrink the existing partition and create a new partition from the free space. (The Disk Management console, Diskmgmt.msc, includes this capability on all supported versions of Windows; you can also use third-party software for this task. For details, see "Shrinking a volume" in Chapter 14.) The new partition does not need to be empty; if it contains system files for another Windows installation, they will be moved to Windows.old. Run Setup, choose the Custom (Advanced) option, and select the disk and partition you want to use for the new installation.

The Setup program automatically handles details of adding the newly installed operating system to the Boot Configuration Data store.

And how do you edit and configure the Boot Configuration Data store? Surprisingly, the only official tool is a command-line utility called Bcdedit. Bcdedit isn't an interactive program; instead, you perform tasks by appending switches and parameters to the Bcdedit command line. To display the complete syntax for this tool, open an elevated Command Prompt window (using the Run As Administrator option) and type the command **bcdedit /?**.

For everyday use, most Bcdedit options are esoteric, unnecessary—and risky. In fact, the only option that we remember using more than once in the past four years is the command to change the text for each entry in the boot menu. By default, the Setup program adds the generic entry "Windows 10" followed by a volume number for each installation. If you set up a dual-boot system using two copies of Windows 10 (one for everyday use, one for testing), you'll find it hard to tell which is which because the menu text will be essentially the same for each. To make the menu more informative, follow these steps:

1. Start your computer and choose either entry from the boot menu. After startup is complete, make a note of which installation is running.

2. Right-click Start, or press Windows key+X, and choose Command Prompt (Admin) from the Quick Link menu. Click Yes in the User Account Control box to open an elevated Command Prompt window. (If you see PowerShell [Admin] on the Quick Link menu, choose that option and then enter **cmd** to drop to a Command Prompt session.)

3. Type the following command: **bcdedit /set {current} description *"Menu description goes here"*** (substituting your own description for the placeholder text and making sure to include the quotation marks). Press Enter.

4. Restart your computer, and note that the menu description you just entered now appears on the menu. Select the other menu option.

5. Repeat steps 2 and 3, again adding a menu description to replace the generic text and distinguish this installation from the other one.

A few startup options are available when you click or tap Change Defaults Or Choose Other Options at the bottom of the boot menu. Doing so leads to the Options menu shown here:

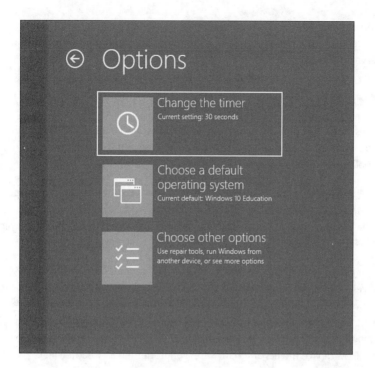

You can choose which installation is the default operating system (this is where descriptive menu choices come in handy) and change the timer that determines how long you want to display the list of operating systems. The default is 30 seconds; you can choose 5 seconds (allowing the default operating system to start automatically unless you immediately interrupt it) or 5 minutes, if you want to ensure you have a choice even if you're distracted while the system is restarting. These options write data directly to the Boot Configuration Data store.

Inside OUT

Installing Windows 10 and Linux in a multi-boot configuration

It's possible to install Windows 10 and Linux in a multi-boot configuration that works much like the Windows multi-boot setup described on the preceding pages. You can set it up to use the Windows 10 boot menu, or you can use a Linux boot loader (most commonly, GRUB) if you prefer. The procedure is a bit more complex than the procedure for installing another version of Windows, and it varies somewhat depending on which Linux distribution you use and which Linux tools (such as partition editors, boot loaders, and the like) you prefer. It's generally easier to set up such a system if the Windows partition is set up first, but it can be done either way: Windows and then Linux, or Linux and then Windows.

An internet search for "dual boot Linux Windows" turns up plenty of detailed instructions, and if you add the name of your Linux distribution to the search input, you're likely to find the specific steps needed to make it work with Windows 10.

CHAPTER 2

For slightly more control over the boot menu timer, use the System Configuration utility, Msconfig.exe. You can use the Boot tab to change the default operating system and set the Timeout interval in any amount between 3 and 999 seconds.

Tweaking and tuning your Windows 10 installation

When Windows Setup completes, you're signed in and ready to begin using Windows 10. For upgrades and clean installs alike, we suggest following this simple checklist to confirm that basic functionality is enabled properly:

- **Check Windows Update.** If you didn't get the latest updates as part of the upgrade process, they should arrive automatically within the next 24 hours. Checking for updates manually lets you install them at your convenience and avoid a scheduled overnight restart.

- **Look for missing device drivers.** Open Device Manager and look for any devices that have a yellow exclamation mark over the icon or any devices that are listed under the Other category. This is also a good time to install any custom drivers supplied by the device maker that might unlock additional features not available with the class drivers provided through Windows Update. For more information on working with device drivers, see "How device drivers and hardware work together" in Chapter 14.

- **Adjust display settings.** You'll want to confirm that the display is set for its native resolution and that any additional tasks, such as color calibration, have been completed.

- **Check your network connection.** If you skipped the option to connect to a network during a clean install, you can complete the task now. On a secure home or small business network, you can open the Network folder in File Explorer to switch from a public network to a private network and allow local file sharing.

- **Verify security settings.** If you use third-party security software, install it now and get the latest updates.

- **Change default programs.** Use this opportunity to set your preferred browser, email client, music playback software, and so on.

- **Adjust power and sleep settings.** The default settings are usually good enough, but they're rarely a perfect match for your preferences. Now is a good time to adjust when your device sleeps and whether it requires a password when it wakes.

Using Windows 10

This chapter covers the basics of the Windows 10 user interface. We'll look at all the things that you tap, click, drag, and drop in order to make Windows do what you want it to do. If you're just arriving in Windows 10 after spending months or years with Windows 7, you'll find both famil-iarity and novelty here. But even if you've been happily and productively working with Windows 10 since the system debuted in July 2015, you might want to give this chapter a quick perusal. Microsoft now provides semiannual updates to Windows, continually introducing new features and enhancing existing ones. The interface has "matured" over these last several years—that is to say, changed in subtle and significant ways for the better. It's worth getting reacquainted to see what's new.

A quick disclaimer: In this chapter and throughout, we write and depict the operating system as it stood in the summer of 2018. Version 1803 is the basis for this book, but by the time you read this, you may be looking at version 1809 (the next feature update after 1803, due in the fall of 2018) or perhaps one of the two versions scheduled for release in 2019. (To see which version you're using, look under Windows Specifications at Settings > System > About.) It's possible that some of the screenshots and step-by-step instructions you find in this book may not match exactly the system you're working with. We hope that our descriptions are clear enough that you'll be able to take small changes in stride.

An overview of the Windows 10 user experience

Before we dive into detailed descriptions of individual features, please join us for a brief tour of Windows 10. Our goal is to introduce the different parts of Windows, new and old, so that we can be sure you're on the same page...or at least looking at the same arrangement of pixels.

Figure 3-1 shows the basic building blocks of Windows 10 and offers a hint of its signature visual style.

Figure 3-1   Start and Action Center are at the core of the Windows 10 experience, with the familiar desktop front and center for conventional PCs.

When you first start up a conventional PC running Windows 10, you see the familiar Windows 7–style desktop and taskbar. Clicking the Start button—the Windows logo in the lower-left–corner—opens Start, which is conceptually similar to its predecessor but differs dramatically in the details.

HOW THE CLOUD CHANGES YOUR EXPERIENCE

One noteworthy difference between the initial Windows 10 experience and the traditional Windows experience that reached its zenith with Windows 7 is the amount of personalization you see when you sign in on a new PC or device. If you use a Microsoft account that you've already used on a different device, the customized settings saved with your account appear automatically on the new device, making it feel familiar right away.

On a clean install or a refresh, you can create a local account, which gives you the standard default layout and themes, as defined by Microsoft. If you sign in to a corporate network, your personalized settings roam according to policies defined by your network administrator. (If your organization allows you to, you can attach a Microsoft account to your domain account, and both your personal and work settings roam together as you switch between devices.)

When you allow your Microsoft account to sync settings between devices, you don't have to go through a tedious process of tweaking the default settings to match those preferences; instead, your visual themes, browser settings, and saved Wi-Fi passwords appear exactly as you expect. If your Microsoft account is connected to OneDrive, your online files, photos, and music collection will be available, too. We discuss these features in more detail in "Syncing your settings between computers" in Chapter 4, "Personalizing Windows 10."

A click on the right side of the taskbar opens Action Center, which is also shown in Figure 3-1. This pane, which uses the full height of your display, contains notifications from apps and services as well as action buttons that allow quick access to settings.

As with previous versions, Windows 10 offers multiple ways to switch between tasks. The Task View button, located at the left end of the taskbar, produces the view shown in Figure 3-2, which also shows a portion of Timeline. We discuss Task View and Timeline in more detail later in this chapter.

Figure 3-2   Use Task View to switch quickly between available windows; the new Timeline feature allows you to switch to activities or sites from the immediate or more distant past.

Navigating Windows 10

Touchscreens might represent the future of computing, but the present is still ruled by more-or-less conventional desktop and laptop PCs, each equipped with a keyboard and a mouse or touchpad. For that type of device, the desktop is where you'll likely spend most of your time, and it's what we concentrate on in this section. We discuss Tablet Mode separately, later in this chapter. (See "Using Windows 10 on a touchscreen device.")

CHAPTER 3

Using and customizing Start

The Windows 7 interface element that you knew as the Start menu is now called Start in Windows 10. Start is divided into three segments. At the very left is a thin column, near the bottom of which appear the current user's name and picture and icons for the Documents and Pictures folders, as well as for Settings and Power. You can display descriptive labels alongside each of those icons by clicking the hamburger menu at the top.

Next to this thin column is a wider column that includes a list of any recently added apps, the apps you use most often, and a scrolling list of all your apps. In the app list, you'll find the names and launch icons for your programs, listed in alphabetical order. You can move through the list by swiping directly on a touchscreen, using two-finger scrolling gestures on a touchpad, or using the scroll wheel with a mouse. Often the quickest way to get from one part of the list to another is by clicking any of the letter headings. That produces an index menu, like this:

You can click or tap any letter or symbol in this menu to jump to the associated part of the all-apps list.

Obviously, you can launch any item in the app list by tapping or clicking it. Alternatively, if you're comfortable typing, you can skip all the scrolling and simply type the beginning characters of an item you want in the search box, directly to the right of the Start button. (See Figure 3-1.) What you're looking for will soon appear at or near the top of the search results. This approach is especially handy when you're not sure exactly where in the app list the item you desire is located. (Where's Notepad, for example? Its default location is within the Windows Accessories folder, several clicks or taps away from the top of the list. You'll get to it more quickly by typing.)

Inside OUT

Change your Start picture

The picture that appears on the left side of Start is the one associated with your user account (the one that also appears on the Welcome screen). If you're not happy with that picture, click it, and then click Change Account Settings. That takes you to the Settings page for your account, where you can choose a different picture or snap one with a webcam.

The remainder of Start consists of tiles. This is the remnant of the Start screen that filled the desktop in Windows 8. As in Windows 8, tiles can be live or not. The live ones update their appearance periodically with relevant content. Windows gives you some tiles to get you going (including some that you might want to get rid of), but, of course, this part of Start is completely customizable, as we discuss shortly.

You can change the size and shape of Start by dragging it up (to a maximum height that is 100 pixels below the top of the display), to the right, or both ways.

Customizing the contents of Start

If you're accustomed to the extensive array of customization options for items on the Start menu in earlier Windows versions, you'll need to make some adjustments. You can remove programs from the Most Used section, but you can't pin program shortcuts to the left side of Start.

You can, however, add or remove certain folder shortcuts from the narrow column of options at the left edge of Start. The Documents and Pictures folders are there by default, but you can put various others there as well. You might want to have File Explorer or Network accessible on the narrow strip, for example. To see the list of possibilities, go to Settings > Personalization > Start, and then click or tap Choose Which Folders Appear On Start.

What if you actually prefer the visual style of Windows 8.1 and would rather work only with tiles instead of program names? To express this preference, visit Settings > Personalization > Start, and turn Show App List In Start Menu to Off. On the same settings page, you might then also want to turn on Use Start Full Screen. Windows 10 will respond by spreading your Start tiles across the full expanse of your screen, much as they might have appeared in Windows 8.1.

If you choose to hide the alphabetical app list, you can easily redisplay it when you need it. With the app list absent, Windows adds two new buttons, called Pinned Tiles and All Apps, near the top of the narrow strip at the left of Start. Clicking All Apps produces a display comparable to the one shown in the following illustration. Clicking Pinned Tiles then restores the visual style of Windows 8.1:

Inside OUT

Master the powerful "other" start menu

Here's some good news for anyone who misses the system shortcuts from earlier iterations of the Start menu. Most of those tools are available as part of a hidden menu,
called the Quick Link menu, that appears when you right-click the Start button or press
Windows key+X, as shown here.

Most of the major system management and troubleshooting tools are on that list, including Disk Management, Event Viewer, and the Computer Management console.

Windows traditionalists will appreciate the fact that the Shut Down Or Sign Out menu item is here, along with links to Settings and Task Manager. The menu also includes the current command-line shell (Windows PowerShell or Command Prompt). The default in Windows 10 version 1803 is PowerShell. If you're not a PowerShell user, you can use an option in Settings > Personalization > Taskbar to replace the two PowerShell options with Command Prompt equivalents.

If you've been using Windows 10 since the Anniversary Update, version 1607, you might notice that the top item in the Quick Link menu has changed from Programs And Features to Apps And Features and the Control Panel item has changed to Settings. These changes reflect the ongoing migration of configuration commands from Control Panel to Settings. Apps is now a top-level entry point in Settings—hence the name change in the Quick Link menu.

Inside OUT

Which programs are included in the Most Used list?

The list of most-used programs—the items that appear at or near the top of the left side of Start—is controlled by Windows. In previous Windows versions, this list included only shortcuts to executable files you open, such as .exe files and .msc files. Windows 10 continues this behavior.

Several types of items are excluded by default, so you won't see things like setup programs, installer and uninstaller packages, Control Panel modules, and MMC consoles. You can find a list of what's excluded in the AddRemoveApps value of the registry key:

`HKLM\Software\Microsoft\Windows\CurrentVersion\Explorer\FileAssociation.`

We do not recommend trying to edit these values manually.

Adding and arranging tiles

Clicking a tile has the same effect as clicking a Start program shortcut or a pinned taskbar button. What makes tiles different is the variety of sizes and their ability to display information or notifications from the app, making a tile *live*.

To pin a program as a tile to the right side of Start, drag it from the app list or the Most Used list on the left side of Start into position. As an alternative, right-click its entry in the app list or the Most Used list on the left side of Start, and then click or tap Pin To Start. The item will take up residence as a medium-sized tile in the first available empty space, and from there you can move and resize it as needed.

To remove a program from the right side of Start, right-click it and then click Unpin From Start.

You can adjust the size of any tile by right-clicking the tile to see the menu shown in Figure 3-3.

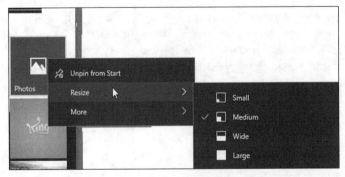

Figure 3-3   These options are available for most modern apps, including those you acquire from the Windows Store. Not all apps support this full list of sizes.

Note that not all tiles support the full range of sizes shown in this figure. Windows desktop pro-grams, for example, offer only the Small and Medium options.

On a touchscreen, you can accomplish the same tile customization tasks with a long press on the tile. That produces two options shown in white circles on the right side of the tile. Tapping the top option unpins the tile, while tapping the ellipsis at the bottom right reveals a menu with Resize and Live Tile items.

NOTE

Options for a specific app might allow additional customization of the live tile. The Pho-tos app, for example, allows you to choose a specific image for its tile.

Right-clicking the tile for a Windows desktop program produces a menu with an extra set of options: Run As Administrator, for example.

Tiles can be arranged into groups, with or without custom group names. Drag tiles, one at a time, into the position you prefer. If the position you choose is sufficiently far from the edge of an existing group, your tile ends up in a new group of its own. You can move it back to an exist-ing group or add other tiles to the new group.

A slim bar sits above every group of tiles. Click (as we have in Figure 3-4) to display a text box where you can type a group name of your choosing. (We created a group named Microsoft Office here.) Click the horizontal lines to the right of the name box to drag the entire group to a new location.

Figure 3-4   Click above any group of tiles to give that group a descriptive label.

CHAPTER 3

Gathering tiles into folders

Another technique for grouping tiles is to create a folder. A folder of tiles looks like an ordinary tile with small icons inside, representing the contents of the folder. The following is a folder of Microsoft Office apps:

When you click or tap a folder, the folder opens to reveal its components, like this:

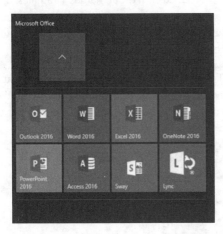

With the folder thus expanded, you can launch a component app in the usual way or return the folder to its former state by clicking the upward arrow.

To create a folder, drag one tile and drop it on top of another. To drop additional apps into the folder, simply drag them to the existing folder.

Using and customizing the taskbar

The taskbar is that strip of real estate along one screen edge (bottom by default) that contains, from left to right, the Start button, the search box, the Task View button, program buttons, notification icons, icons for people, and a clock. The taskbar made its first appearance in Windows 95. In the years since, it has slowly evolved without changing its basic shape.

The Windows 10 taskbar continues to serve the same basic functions as its progenitors—launching programs, switching between programs, and providing notifications—with only subtle changes in functionality.

Every running program with a user interface has a corresponding taskbar button. When you close that program, the button vanishes as well, unless you pinned it to the taskbar. A faint line appears underneath the icon for a running program, and the program with the current focus has a subtle but noticeable transparent shadow to identify it.

The Windows 10 taskbar offers a limited selection of customization options, most of which are available through Settings > Personalization > Taskbar (or right-clicking an empty space on the taskbar or the Task View button and clicking Settings). Figure 3-5 shows the first group of options on that Settings page.

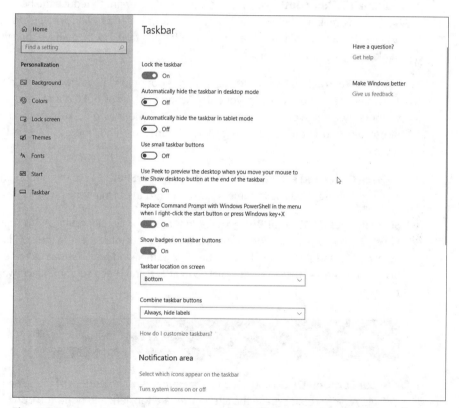

Figure 3-5   For most people, the options set here will be acceptable, especially Lock The Taskbar, which prevents you from accidentally dragging the taskbar to the side of the monitor.

Here is a rundown of the options shown in Figure 3-5:

- **Lock The Taskbar.** On by default, this option prevents you from accidentally dragging the taskbar to the side of the monitor. Note that the shortcut menu that appears when you right-click the taskbar also includes this command. It's there so that you can easily switch in and out of the locked mode when you need to adjust the size or position of the taskbar. Also note that locking the taskbar does not prevent you from rearranging taskbar icons. (If your Windows configuration includes multiple monitors, this command changes to Lock All Taskbars.)

- **Automatically Hide The Taskbar.** By default, the taskbar remains visible at all times. If that's inconvenient for any reason, you can tell it to get out of the way. The Settings page provides separate Hide options for Desktop and Tablet modes. With either option set, the taskbar retreats into the edge of the desktop whenever a window has the focus. To display the hidden taskbar, move the mouse pointer to the edge of the desktop where the taskbar normally resides. On a touchscreen, swipe from that edge toward the center of the screen.

- **Use Small Taskbar Buttons.** Select this option if you want to reduce the height of taskbar buttons, making them similar in size to buttons in earlier Windows versions. In our experience, buttons of this size are too small for practical use. If you have the eyesight of a hawk, your opinion might differ.

- **Use Peek To Preview The Desktop.** With this option on, moving your mouse to the extreme edge of the taskbar (beyond the Action Center button) hides all open windows temporarily, giving you the opportunity to see the underlying desktop. This option is off by default; we don't see a good reason not to turn it on (and Figure 3-5 shows the option set to on).

- **Replace Command Prompt With Windows PowerShell.** Leave this option on if you're a PowerShell user. You'll save some steps getting to the command line.

- **Show Badges On Taskbar Buttons.** Badges are small circular notifications that can appear on the lower-right corner of certain taskbar buttons. In the following illustration, for example, badges on the Alarms & Clock, Weather, and Mail buttons indicate that an alarm has been set, that a weather alert is in effect, and that a stack of mail is waiting to be read.

- **Taskbar Location On Screen.** The taskbar appears at the bottom of the screen by default. As you would expect, the alternatives are top, left, and right. You don't have to visit Settings to change positions, however. Simply unlock the taskbar and drag it.

- **Combine Taskbar Buttons.** The default setting for Combine Taskbar Buttons is Always, Hide Labels. This setting instructs Windows to always group multiple windows from a single application (such as Microsoft Word documents) into a single taskbar button. The Hide Labels setting for this option ensures that each running program has one and only one button, which consists of the program's icon. With either of the other settings (When Taskbar Is Full or Never), Windows gives each window its own separate taskbar button and adds the name of the running program or open document as a label to the right of the program icon, if space permits. It groups windows only when the taskbar becomes too crowded or continues to shrink the size of taskbar buttons as you open more windows. We recommend the default setting here.

> ➤ If you have more than one display attached to a Windows 10 PC, some extra customization options are available for the taskbar. See "Configuring the taskbar with multiple displays," later in this chapter, for details.

Pinning programs to the taskbar

Pinning a taskbar button makes it easy to find and run favorite programs without the need to open Start or use the search box to find the program's shortcut. To pin a program to the taskbar, simply drag its icon or a shortcut (from Start, from the desktop, or from any other folder) to the taskbar. Alternatively, right-click a program icon wherever you find it or the taskbar button for a running program and then click Pin To Taskbar.

To remove a pinned program from the taskbar, right-click the pinned icon and then click Unpin From Taskbar. This command also appears on other shortcuts to the program, including those on the desktop and on Start.

You can use taskbar buttons to launch a program that's not currently running or to switch from one running program to another. You can also click a taskbar button to minimize an open window or to restore a minimized window. If those features sound too obvious, here's a trick you might not know: You can open a new instance of a program that's already running—a new Microsoft Word document, for example, or a fresh File Explorer window—by right-clicking the taskbar button and then clicking the program name; alternatively, hold Shift and click the program name.

Using Jump Lists for quick access to documents and folders

A Jump List is the official name of the menu that appears when you right-click a taskbar button or a tile pinned to Start. Each Jump List includes commands to open the program, to pin the program to the taskbar (or unpin it), and to close all open windows represented by the button.

In addition, for programs developed to take advantage of this feature, Jump Lists can include shortcuts to common tasks that can be performed with that program, such as New Window or New InPrivate Window on a Microsoft Edge Jump List. For Microsoft Office programs, Adobe Acrobat, and other similarly document-centric programs, Jump Lists also typically include links to recently opened files.

Figure 3-6 shows the default Jump List for File Explorer.

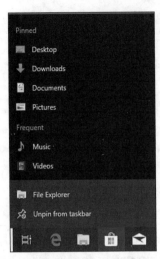

Figure 3-6   Right-click a taskbar button, such as File Explorer, to see a Jump List showing recently opened files and folders with the option to pin items for quick access.

Individual files and folders can't be pinned directly to the taskbar, but you can add them to Jump Lists by using the following techniques:

- To pin a document to the taskbar, drag its icon or a shortcut to any empty space on the taskbar. If the taskbar already has a button for the program associated with the document, Windows adds the document to the Pinned section of the program's Jump List. If the document's program is not on the taskbar, Windows pins the program to the taskbar and adds the document to the program's Jump List.

- To pin a folder to the taskbar, drag its icon or a shortcut to the taskbar. Windows adds the folder to the Pinned section of the Jump List for File Explorer.

- To open a pinned document or folder, right-click the taskbar button and then click the name of the document or folder.

- To remove a pinned document or folder from the Jump List, right-click the taskbar button and point to the name of the document or folder to be removed. Click the pushpin icon that appears.

Changing the order of taskbar buttons

To change the order of buttons on the taskbar, simply drag them into position. Pinned program icons retain their order between sessions, allowing you to quickly find your most used programs in their familiar (to you) location.

Inside OUT

Use shortcut keys for taskbar buttons

The first 10 taskbar buttons are accessible by keyboard as well as by mouse. Press Windows key+1 for the first, Windows key+2 for the second, and so on (using 0 for the tenth). Using one of these shortcuts is equivalent to clicking the corresponding taskbar button: If the button's program isn't running, it starts; if it has a single open window, you switch to that window; if it has multiple open windows, Windows displays previews of all windows and switches to the first window. Hold down the Windows key and tap the number key repeatedly to cycle between all open windows for that program.

Note that when you change the order of a taskbar button, you also change the Windows key+number combination that starts that particular program.

Another useful shortcut key is Windows key+T, which brings focus to the first item on the taskbar. At that point, you can repeatedly press Windows key+T, Shift+Windows key+T, or the arrow keys to select other taskbar buttons. When a taskbar button is selected, you can press Spacebar to "click" the button or press the Menu key to display its Jump List.

CHAPTER 3

Pinning people to the taskbar

To simplify communication with your most important contacts, you can pin them to the area at the right side of your taskbar (in the typical left-to-right taskbar orientation), just to the left of the notification area. Windows displays a thumbnail image for a pinned person if such an image is available or initials if not. The resulting icon can serve as a drop target for a sharing operation (drag a document to a people icon and search options appear), or you can click an icon to review recent communication, see upcoming events for the selected contact, or initiate new communication.

To pin a contact to the taskbar, click the People icon, near the notification area of the taskbar. Then choose Find And Pin Contacts.

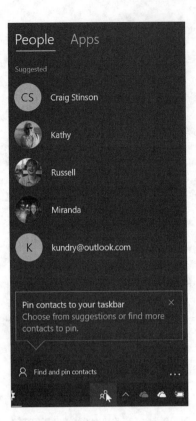

Windows displays a list of suggested contacts. To pin one of those, click it. To locate contacts not on the suggested list, click Find And Pin Contacts.

Pinned contacts appear just to the left of the People icon:

Note that if you use Focus Assist to squelch calls and notifications during particular hours of the day, any contacts you have pinned to the taskbar are automatically "white listed"; that is, their messages break through the Focus Assist screen. (We discuss Focus Assist in Chapter 4; see "Eliminating distractions with Focus Assist.")

By default, you can pin up to three contacts on the taskbar. Windows will accommodate as many as ten, however. To allow for more than three, go to Settings > Personalization > Taskbar and change the number under Choose How Many Contacts To Show. Because adding a lot of contacts to the taskbar might crowd out your application icons, Windows provides an overflow area at the top of the pane that appears when you click the People icon. In this illustration, there are three people in the overflow area:

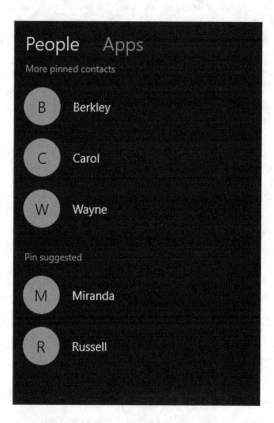

You can put as many people as you want in the overflow area, where they function exactly as they would on the taskbar.

To change the order in which taskbar contacts appear, simply drag and drop. You can also drag and drop to move a contact from the overflow area to the taskbar. Display the overflow area, grab the contact you want, and drag it to the taskbar. Windows moves one of the current taskbar occupants to the overflow area when you do this. To move an existing taskbar resident to the overflow area, drag it laterally. When your mouse reaches the People icon, the People pane appears, and you can deposit the contact in the overflow area. Windows responds by moving someone from the overflow area to the taskbar.

To remove a pinned contact, right-click it and choose Unpin From Taskbar.

Changing the taskbar's size and appearance

The default height of the taskbar is enough to display one button. (If you switch to small buttons, the taskbar automatically shrinks its height to fit.) You can enlarge it—and given the typical size and resolution of computer displays these days, enlarging it is often a great idea. Before you can change the taskbar's dimensions, you need to unlock it. Right-click an unoccupied area of the taskbar; if a check mark appears next to the Lock The Taskbar command, click the command to clear the check mark. Then position the mouse along the border of the taskbar farthest from the edge of the screen. When the mouse pointer becomes a two-headed arrow, drag toward the center of the screen to expand the taskbar. Drag the same border in the opposite direction to restore the original size.

Moving the taskbar

The taskbar docks by default at the bottom of the screen, but you can move it to any other edge. You do this by selecting the Taskbar Location On Screen option in Settings > Personalization > Taskbar.

As an alternative, you can manipulate the taskbar directly. Unlock it, and then drag any unoccupied part of the taskbar in the direction you want to go. (Don't drag the edge of the taskbar closest to the center of the screen; doing that changes the taskbar's size, not its position.)

Adding toolbars to the taskbar

A seldom-used feature of the taskbar is its ability to host other toolbars. Optional toolbars date back to much older versions of Windows, offering shortcuts to folders, documents, and applications. Third parties can also write add-ons that operate entirely within the confines of the taskbar. Built-in toolbars you can choose to install include the following:

- **Address.** The Address toolbar provides a place where you can type an internet address or the name and path of a program, document, or folder. When you press Enter or click the Go button, Windows takes you to the internet address, starts the program, opens the document, or displays the folder in a File Explorer window. The Address toolbar is functionally equivalent to the Run command in Start or the address bar in File Explorer or the Microsoft Edge browser.

- **Links.** The Links toolbar provides shortcuts to internet sites; its contents are drawn from the Favorites Bar in Internet Explorer.

- **Desktop.** The Desktop toolbar provides access to all the icons currently displayed on your desktop. In addition, it includes links to your Libraries, This PC, Network, Control Panel, and other user profile folders. When you click the toolbar's double arrow, a cascading menu of all the folders and files on your system appears.

To install a new toolbar or remove one you're currently using, right-click any unoccupied part of the taskbar or any existing toolbar. Click Toolbars on the menu that appears, and then choose from the ensuing submenu. A check mark beside a toolbar's name means that it's already displayed on the taskbar. Clicking a selected toolbar name removes that toolbar.

In addition, any folder on your system can become a toolbar. To create a new toolbar, right-click an existing toolbar or a spot on the taskbar, click Toolbars, and then click New Toolbar. In the next dialog box, navigate to a folder and click Select Folder.

The folder's name becomes the name of the new toolbar, and each item within the folder becomes a tool.

Configuring the taskbar with multiple displays

If your computer has more than one monitor attached, you have additional options for configuring the taskbar: You can show it on just the main display or on all displays, and you can vary its appearance on each display. To review these options, right-click the taskbar and choose Settings. The following illustration shows the multiple-display options. You'll find them near the bottom of the page at Settings > Personalization > Taskbar.

Selecting the first option shows a taskbar on each monitor. If you set it to Off, the taskbar appears only on the main display. (You specify the "main display" in Settings > System > Display. For details, see "Configuring displays and graphics adapters" in Chapter 4, "Hardware and devices.")

The Show Taskbar Buttons On setting determines where the taskbar button for a particular app appears—on all taskbars or only the one where that app's window resides.

The last setting specifies how taskbar buttons are combined on displays other than the main display.

CHAPTER 3

Customizing the notification area

The notification area extends from the right edge of your taskbar (on a left-to-right arrange-ment) to the People area and application tiles. Typically, this includes the Action Center icon, the clock, and a variety of system and application-specific items.

To customize the system icons, go to Settings > Personalization > Taskbar. Under the Notifica-tion Area heading, click Turn System Icons On Or Off to specify which icons appear. As Figure 3-7 shows, the available items are denoted by icons and switches.

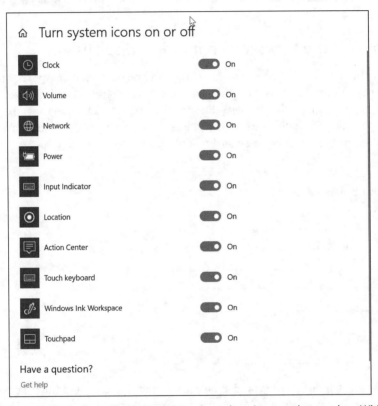

Figure 3-7   Each notification area icon shown here is currently turned on. With a flick of the switch, you can remove any that you don't need or want.

To customize the rest of your notification area, click Select Which Icons Appear On The Taskbar. You'll probably see a longer list, including some items specific to applications or devices on your system. Figure 3-8 shows an example.

You can use the On-Off switches to add or remove items. In case you want them all, Windows provides a master switch at the top of the list.

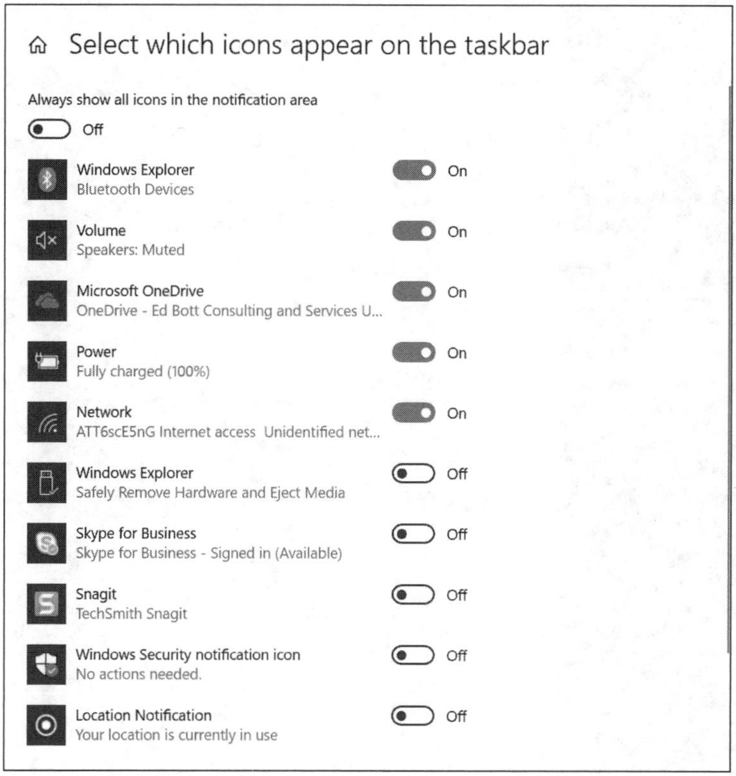

⌂ Select which icons appear on the taskbar

Always show all icons in the notification area
◯ Off

Windows Explorer   On
Bluetooth Devices

Volume   On
Speakers: Muted

Microsoft OneDrive   On
OneDrive - Ed Bott Consulting and Services U...

Power   On
Fully charged (100%)

Network   On
ATT6scE5nG Internet access Unidentified net...

Windows Explorer   Off
Safely Remove Hardware and Eject Media

Skype for Business   Off
Skype for Business - Signed in (Available)

Snagit   Off
TechSmith Snagit

Windows Security notification icon Off
No actions needed.

Location Notification   Off
Your location is currently in use

Figure 3-8   Some icons in this list provide status messages. Others are shortcuts to associated programs.

Using and customizing Action Center

Action Center is the formal name of the pane that appears at the right side of your screen when you swipe in from the right (on a touchscreen), press Windows key+A, or click the small button just to the right of the clock on your taskbar. It serves two important functions. First, it supplies a notification area that can display messages from various apps and system components. These notifications occupy the upper part of Action Center. Second, it provides a panel of Quick Action buttons for such things as switching in and out of Airplane Mode or Tablet Mode, creating a note in OneNote, connecting to a Wi-Fi access point, and so on. The action buttons appear as one or more rows of tiles along the lower edge of Action Center. Figure 3-9 shows an example of Action Center with three notifications and three rows of Quick Action buttons. Notifications are grouped under headings corresponding to the notifying applications. Collapse icons beside each notification to reduce the verbosity of the notification; these are handy if your Action Center is teeming with messages.

CHAPTER 3

Figure 3-9 Action Center consists of two parts: a set of notifications at the top and one or more rows of Quick Action buttons at the bottom.

You can respond to notifications in various ways. If you hover the mouse pointer over a notification, a Close button appears in its upper-right corner, and you can dismiss the notification by clicking there. If you click on the body of the notification, the relevant action occurs. For example, clicking on a news bulletin opens the story in the News app; clicking on a message from Windows Update telling you that a system restart is pending might open a secondary message with more details and a button for effecting an immediate restart.

Some Quick Action buttons are simple commands. Clicking All Settings, for example, opens Settings. Others, such as Tablet Mode and Wi-Fi, are toggle switches. Action Center uses the current accent color to indicate which switches are currently on.

Customizing the Quick Actions panel

To rearrange the contents of the Quick Actions panel, go to Settings > System > Notifications & Actions. The current Quick Actions layout is shown near the top of the page:

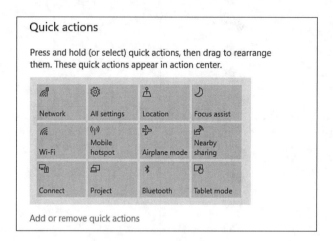

You can change the order in which your Quick Actions are displayed by dragging with the mouse or other pointer. On a touchscreen, press and hold a button to select it, and then drag. Note that you do not have to have an empty space in the panel to do the rearranging; Windows adjusts button positions as you drag.

The arrangement of the Quick Actions panel matters in one way. With the Collapse button that appears directly above the panel in Action Center (shown in Figure 3-9), you can reduce the panel to a single row of four. The row that appears then is the top row shown in Settings > System > Notifications & Actions. You can think of this row as the quickest of your Quick Actions. If you want to get in and out of Airplane Mode effortlessly, for example, you can put that button in the top row, collapse the panel in Action Center, and then swipe in from the right when you board the plane. Your Airplane Mode Quick Action button will be right there, more or less under your thumb.

To change the content of the Quick Actions panel, click Add Or Remove Quick Actions. (See the previous illustration.) The list of choices that appears is appropriate for your hardware. Figure 3-10, for example, shows the Quick Actions available on a Surface Pro 3. Some of these, such as Battery Saver and Rotation Lock, would not appear on a desktop computer.

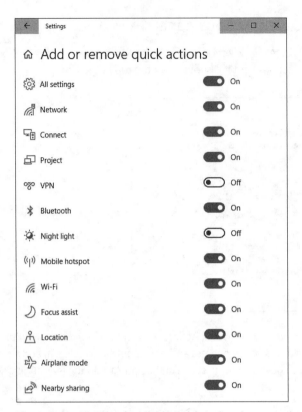

Figure 3-10   The list of available Quick Actions is appropriate for your hardware.

Customizing notifications

The options for controlling which "senders" can deliver messages to the notification area of Action Center are also located at Settings > System > Notifications & Actions, just below those for Quick Actions. Switches here also control whether messages are displayed on your lock screen. The following illustration shows the options governing general notification behavior.

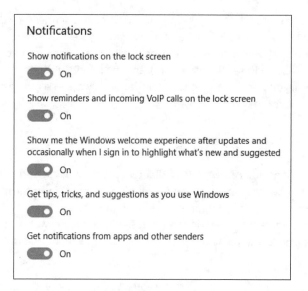

Scroll down from these general switches, and you'll come to switches for individual senders. You can use the switches to squelch or permit notifications from particular senders. Clicking on the sender takes you to a more granular set of controls, such as the ones for the Calendar app, shown next:

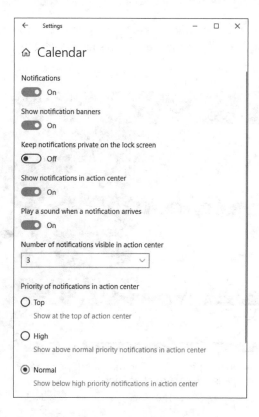

CHAPTER 3

You can use this set of controls for such things as determining whether a sender provides a notification banner (a pop-up that appears briefly when a notification arrives), whether a sound is played, the maximum number of notifications that will be displayed at one time in Action Center (you can use an Expand button to see the remainder), and the priority given to the sender's notifications. For example, if you want your Calendar notifications always to show up at the top of Action Center, you can select Top.

Switching tasks

As in previous Windows versions, you can switch to a different program by clicking its taskbar button. And if you're not sure which icon your document is hidden under, hover the mouse pointer over a taskbar button to display a thumbnail image of the window above the button. If a taskbar button combines more than one window (representing multiple Microsoft Excel spreadsheets, for example), hovering the mouse pointer over the taskbar button displays a preview of each window.

If the live thumbnail isn't enough to help you select the correct window, hover the mouse pointer over one of the preview images. Windows brings that window to the forefront, temporarily masking out the contents of all other open windows.

The alternative to this manual hunt-and-click technique is Task View, which displays large, live thumbnails of running programs on the screen so that you can switch with confidence.

To begin, click the Task View button or use the Windows key+Tab shortcut. On a touchscreen-equipped device, you can swipe in from the left edge. Figure 3-11 shows the results on a system with seven running programs.

Figure 3-11   Opening Task View shows running programs using their windowed dimensions. Clicking or tapping any thumbnail opens it in its current position.

Those thumbnails remain open until you do something, usually by clicking or tapping a thumb-nail to switch to that window or by pressing Esc to return to the current window.

If there are too many open windows to fit as thumbnails on the display, use the up and down arrows at the bottom of the screen to scroll through the full list.

The old-fashioned Alt+Tab task switcher, familiar to every Windows user of a certain age, is still available as well. The concept is similar, but the thumbnails appear only as long as you continue to hold down the Alt key. Hold down Alt and tap the Tab key to cycle (left to right, top to bot-tom) through all open windows. When you've highlighted the window you want to bring to the fore, release the Alt and Tab keys.

When using Task View, you also have the option of closing a window by clicking the red X in the upper-right corner of the preview or, if your mouse scroll wheel supports clicking, by middle-clicking anywhere in the preview image. Other basic window tasks are available on the shortcut menu that appears when you right-click the preview image.

Reviewing, revisiting, resuming with Timeline

Timeline, introduced in version 1803, extends Task View into the past, showing thumbnails for the places you have been and the things you have done within the most recent 30 days. If you forget where you found that important article on the Internet, or if you saved your notes *some-where* (but who knows where?), relax; Windows knows. Press Windows key+Tab or click the Task View button. Then scroll down below the thumbnails for your current apps to get to your time-line. Figure 3-12 shows the beginning two days of a user's timeline.

Figure 3-12   Each tile in Timeline represents an activity or site to which you can return. Initially, two rows of tiles appear for each day heading; you can click links beside the headings to see more.

Each tile represents the combination of an app, a piece of content, and a specific time. Clicking a tile takes you back to the activity in question.

Timeline initially displays two rows of tiles per day, and it selects the activities that it considers to be most "relevant." If you don't find what you're looking for, click the link beside the head to display all activities for the selected day. When you do this, Timeline divides the full day's activities into hourly subgroups. If you're still not finding what you need, press Ctrl+F to get to the search box in the upper-right corner of the display.

The scrollbar at the right side of the display is annotated by date. If you want to rediscover what you were up to on a particular day, drag the annotated scrollbar until that date appears.

What if you don't want to be reminded of certain activities or don't want others to see what you've been doing? You can remove any tile by right-clicking it and choosing Remove. Or you can suppress an entire day's (or hour's if you have expanded a day) history by right-clicking a tile and choosing the command at the bottom of the context menu (Clear All From Earlier Today, for example). Timeline also ignores any Microsoft Edge browsing you do in an InPrivate session.

Timeline is a good example of a feature that is evolving as this book goes to press and one that can be expected to undergo more changes in the future. In its debut with Windows 10 version 1803 in the summer of 2018, Timeline supported Microsoft Edge, the document-oriented components of Microsoft Office (Word and Excel, for example, but not Outlook), Photos, News, Notepad, and Maps. Adobe Acrobat DC and VLC Media Player were among third-party programs supporting Timeline, and you can certainly expect to see others arrive as time passes. Stay tuned.

Inside OUT

Add timeline support to your app

Developers looking to build Timeline support into their applications can find a good introduction to the topic in the blogpost "Application Engagement in Windows Timeline with User Activities," located at *https://bit.ly/Timeline-Win10*.

One of the most useful things about Timeline is its ability to track activities across all systems that share a common Microsoft account. If you leave the office *in medias res*, you can pick up where you left off on another device in another location.

On first use, when you scroll to the bottom of Timeline's array of tiles, you might encounter the message shown in the next illustration:

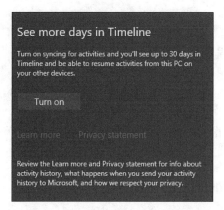

Clicking Turn On in this dialog box enables the syncing of Timeline data across devices and, at the same time, extends Timeline's reach from four days to thirty.

Settings for Timeline are located at Settings > Privacy > Activity History:

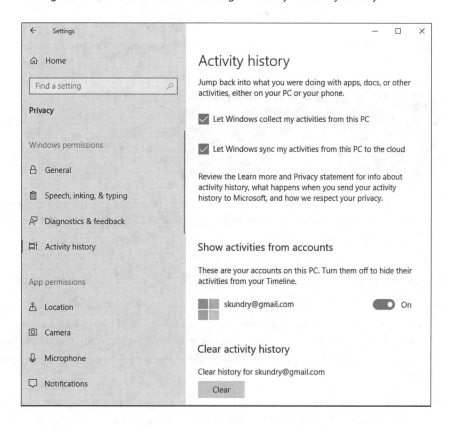

With the first and second check boxes selected, Timeline is enabled, and your sites and activities can be revisited on any device sharing a common Microsoft account. If you open an activity requiring a modern app on a device where that app is not installed, Windows will assist you to install it.

In the Show Activities From Accounts section of the page, you can enable or disable tracking for particular Microsoft accounts, in the event that you have multiple—a work account and a school account, for example. Finally, the Clear button at the bottom of the page provides a way to erase your current history and start fresh.

Switching between virtual desktops

The idea of virtual desktops is straightforward: Instead of just a single desktop, you create a second, third, fourth, and so on. On each desktop, you arrange individual programs or combinations of apps you want to use for a specific task. Then, when it's time to tackle one of those tasks, you switch to the virtual desktop and get right to work.

To create a desktop, click New Desktop at the top of the Task View window.

Virtual desktops show up as a row of thumbnails along the top of the Task View window, like this:

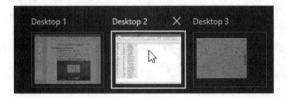

The system depicted here has three virtual desktops, of which the second is currently active. You can switch from one virtual desktop to another by clicking its thumbnail. You'll notice that your taskbar changes to reflect the makeup of the current desktop.

Managing and arranging windows

Windows 10 includes a host of keyboard shortcuts and mouse gestures that greatly simplify the everyday tasks of resizing, moving, minimizing, arranging, and otherwise managing windows. The most useful trick is a collection of "snap" techniques. These have been around for several Windows versions, but Windows 10 adds some extremely useful new tricks to the old familiar methods.

The simplest window-snapping scenario is a PC with a single display, where you want to arrange two windows side by side. You might want to compare two Word documents, move files between the Documents folder and an archive, or do financial research in a web browser and plug the numbers into an Excel spreadsheet.

Drag a window title bar to the left or right edge of the screen, and it snaps to fill that half of the display. As soon as you let go of the title bar, the window snaps into its position and Windows helpfully offers thumbnails for all other open windows to help you choose what to run alongside your first snapped window.

In Figure 3-13, for example, we've just snapped a Microsoft Edge browser window to the left side of the screen and now have a choice of two other running windows to snap opposite it. (If you don't feel like snapping a second window, just press Esc or click anywhere except on one of those thumbnails. They vanish immediately and retain their previous size and position.)

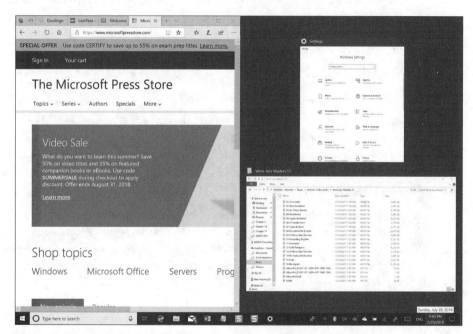

Figure 3-13   When you snap a window to one edge of the display, Windows shows other open windows in thumbnails alongside the snapped window for easy side-by-side arrangement.

Note that the window resizes when the mouse pointer hits the edge of the screen. To use this feature with minimal mouse movement, start your drag action by pointing at the title bar near the edge you're going to snap to.

As soon as you begin dragging a snapped window away from the edge of the screen, it returns to its previous size and position.

Here are a few ways you can snap windows in Windows 10 by using a mouse or by dragging directly on a touchscreen:

- Drag the title bar to the top of the screen to maximize the window, or drag the title bar away from the top edge to restore it to its previous window size.

- Drag a window title bar to any corner of the screen, and it snaps to fill that quadrant of the display. This capability is new in Windows 10 and is most useful on large, high-resolution desktop displays.

- Drag the top window border (not the title bar) to the top edge of the screen, or drag the bottom border to the bottom edge of the screen. With either action, when you reach the edge, the window snaps to full height without changing its width. When you drag the border away from the window edge, the opposite border snaps to its previous position.

Inside OUT

Snap side-by-side Windows at different widths

Although Windows automatically arranges side-by-side windows at equal widths, you don't have to settle for symmetry. On a large desktop monitor, for example, you might want to arrange a news feed or Twitter stream along the right side of your display, using a third or less of the total display width and leaving room for Word or Excel to have a much larger share of the screen real estate.

The secret is to snap the first window and immediately drag its inside edge to adjust the window to your preferred width. Now grab the title bar of the window you want to see alongside it and snap it to the opposite edge of the display. The newly snapped window expands to fill the space remaining after you adjusted the width of the first window.

The rules work the same with multimonitor setups. With two side-by-side monitors, for example, you can drag the mouse to the inside edge of a display and snap a window there, allowing for two pairs of equal-size windows lined up from left to right. By dragging the title bar, you also can move a maximized window from one screen to another on a multimonitor system.

Inside OUT

Shake to minimize distractions

An ancient Windows feature called Aero Shake, introduced with Windows Vista, survives in Windows 10. Grab the window's title bar with the mouse or a finger and quickly move it back and forth a few times. Suddenly, all windows retreat to the taskbar except the one whose title bar you just shook. This move takes a bit of practice, but it's worth mastering. It requires only three smooth "shakes"—a left, right, left motion is best—not maniacal shaking.

Windows 10 includes keyboard shortcuts that correspond with the preceding mouse gestures. These (and a few extras) are shown in Table 3-1.

Table 3-1   Keyboard shortcuts and gestures for resizing and moving windows

Task	Keyboard shortcut	Gesture
Maximize window	Windows key+ Up Arrow	Drag title bar to top of screen
Resize window to full screen height without changing its width	Shift+Windows key+ Up Arrow	Drag top or bottom border to edge of screen
Restore a maximized or full-height window	Windows key+ Down Arrow	Drag title bar or border away from screen edge
Minimize a restored window	Windows key+ Down Arrow	Click the Minimize button
Snap to the left half of the screen	Windows key+ Left Arrow*	Drag title bar to left edge
Snap to the right half of the screen	Windows key+ Right Arrow*	Drag title bar to right edge
Move to the next virtual desktop	Ctrl+Windows key+ Left/Right Arrow	Three-finger swipe on precision touchpad; none for mouse
Move to the next monitor	Shift+Windows Key+ Left/Right Arrow	Drag title bar
Minimize all windows except the active window (press again to restore windows previously minimized with this shortcut)	Windows key+ Home	"Shake" the title bar
Minimize all windows	Windows key+M	
Restore windows after minimizing	Shift+Windows key+M	

* Pressing this key repeatedly cycles through the left, right, and restored positions. If you have more than one monitor, it cycles these positions on each monitor in turn.

The Windows 10 taskbar also exposes some traditional window-management menus. The secret? Hold the Shift key as you right-click a taskbar button. For a button that represents a single window, the menu includes commands to Restore, Move, Size, Minimize, Maximize, and Close the window. For a grouped taskbar button, Shift+right-click displays commands to arrange, restore, minimize, or close all windows in the group.

If you find it disconcerting to have windows snap to a certain size and position when you drag their title bars, you can disable Snap. The options controlling Snap are at Settings > System > Multitasking.

Using a keyboard and mouse in Windows 10

As of version 1803, the options for customizing a keyboard had not yet made the transition from Control Panel to Settings. To find these options, type **keyboard** in the Search box. The options are few, but they might affect your typing comfort level:

The repeat delay—the amount of time Windows waits as you hold down a key before repeating that key—is set, by default, a bit long for the tastes of some proficient typists. You can make it shorter by dragging the slider to the right. On the other hand, if you sometimes find that Windows gives you an unwanted string of repeated characters, you can drag the slider leftward. You might also then want to reduce the repeat rate.

Inside OUT

Reconfigure the Caps Lock key to avoid shouting

If you occasionally find yourself accidentally stuck in Caps Lock mode so that your emails are shouting, or your text documents look like a demand letter from a creditor, consider the following tweak.

On a standard 101-key desktop keyboard, you can disable the Caps Lock key so that it does nothing whatsoever: Open Registry Editor and navigate to HKLM\System\ CurrentControlSet\Control\Keyboard Layout. Add a Binary value called Scancode Map. Set the data for this key to

```
00000000 00000000 02000000 00003A00 00000000
```

Close Registry Editor, restart, and you'll never be stuck in Caps Lock again.

Alternatively, you can use SharpKeys (a free download from *https://github.com/ randyrants/sharpkeys*) to remap the Caps Lock key to anything you might find more useful—a second Windows key, for example.

Mastering keyboard shortcuts

Windows 10 offers so many keyboard shortcuts that mastering them all would be a remarkable feat, a bit like memorizing 80 digits of pi. Learning a handful or several handfuls, on the other hand, can definitely improve your productivity.

Table 3-1, earlier in this chapter, offered a list of keyboard shortcuts having to do with window management. Table 3-2 presents an idiosyncratic selection of everyday shortcuts—the ones that we use most often and would have trouble living without. Because your own needs probably differ from ours, however, you might want to peruse the exhaustive list that appears at *https://aka.ms/keyboard-shortcuts*.

A shortcut for emojis

A recent addition to the repertoire of keyboard shortcuts, one that was introduced in Version 1709, simplifies access to the Windows 10 emoji library. Press Windows key+. or Windows key+; in any window that accepts text input, and the emoji panel appears. Within the panel, you can use the Tab key to navigate between categories of emojis and the left and right arrow keys to move within a category. Mouse and fingers work as well, of course. To change from one category of emoji to another (smiley faces to people, for example), click or tap along the bottom row of the pop-up display. To change the skin tone of an emoji in the people category, click the Skin Tone button, next to the Close button in the upper-right corner of the window. You may choose from six color gradations. The emoji panel remains visible until you press Esc or click the Close button.

The emoji library is also accessible via the Touch Keyboard, and we discuss its use there later in this chapter (see "Using the Touch Keyboard").

Table 3-2 A short list of general-purpose keyboard shortcuts

Shortcut	Effect
Ctrl+C	Copy selection
Ctrl+X	Cut selection
Ctrl+V	Paste Clipboard contents

CHAPTER 3

Ctrl+Z	Undo
Ctrl+Y	Redo
Ctrl+N	Open new window (in many apps)
Ctrl+S	Save
Ctrl+W	Close current window (in many apps)
Ctrl+P	Print (in many apps)
Ctrl+A	Select all
Ctrl+Shift+Esc	Open Task Manager
F2	Rename (in File Explorer)
F3	Search (File Explorer and many browsers)
F5	Refresh (File Explorer and many browsers)
Alt+F4	Close current window
Alt+Enter	Display properties dialog box
Windows key	Display Start
Windows key+E	Open new File Explorer window
Windows key+I	Open Settings
Windows key+R	Open the Run command
Windows key+X	Open the Quick Link menu

Using alternative keyboard layouts

Windows 10 offers keyboard support for more than 300 languages. Most of these languages are available as full language packs, and installing a language pack changes the entire Windows user interface—menus, dialog boxes, and all—to the selected language. But you can also simply install a keyboard layout for another language, without changing the user interface. This might prove handy if you work in an international environment and occasionally need to dash off an email to, say, a Russian-speaking colleague or customer.

To install another keyboard, go to Settings > Time & Language > Region & Language. When you click Add A Language, the entire set of available languages appears, and you can make your choice. When the keyboard is installed, it becomes available through the Input Indicator system icon, which typically lives on the taskbar, adjacent to the clock. Clicking there pops up a menu of available keyboards, along with a Language Preferences command.

CHAPTER 3

Clicking Language Preferences takes you back to Settings > Time & Language > Region & Language.

To remove a language, make it the default, or set options relating to the language, return to Settings > Time & Language > Region & Language, and then click on the language.

CHAPTER 3

Inside OUT

For emojis, accented characters, and language assistance, use the Touch Keyboard

The primary purpose of the Touch Keyboard, as its name suggests, is to facilitate input on a touch-enabled device. We discuss and illustrate it, therefore, later in this chapter. (See "Using Windows 10 on a touchscreen device.") But it's invaluable for certain kinds of input on any computer—which is why it's available on nontouch machines as well as tablets.

To enter an emoji—one of the whimsical characters available on all mobile platforms and on Windows 10—click on the smiley-face icon on the bottom row of the keyboard. To enter a character with a diacritical mark, click and hold the unadorned character; your choices will appear in a pop-up window. Hold the *n*, for example, and the option to type ñ will appear. Hold the *o,* and you'll have the opportunity to enter variants like ò, ö, ô, and even œ. If you've ever labored to memorize ANSI codes or wandered through Character Map in search of the accent you need, you'll certainly appreciate this feature.

As for language assistance, suppose you're a whiz touch typist in English but you hunt and peck in Russian. When you select Russian as your input source, the Touch Keyboard will turn to Cyrillic. You can use it as a visual layout guide while you type with your standard keyboard. Or you can use the Touch Keyboard to do the pecking as well as the hunting.

Taming your mouse or other pointing device

To teach your mouse new tricks, go to Settings > Devices > Mouse. With settings here, you can swap the functions of your left and right mouse buttons (great for left-handed folks) and control how much to scroll each time you roll the mouse wheel. The remainder of the mouse configuration options are still in Control Panel; to get there, click Additional Mouse Options. The Mouse Properties dialog box in Control Panel looks like this:

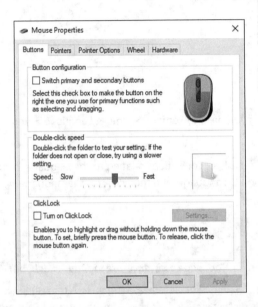

Mouse Properties has settings that define a double-click (that is, how quickly you must twice press the mouse button for it to be detected as a double-click instead of two clicks), change pointer shapes, configure other pointer options, and more. Depending on the mouse you have, you might find additional options in Mouse Properties or in a separate app.

If your computer has a precision touchpad, the Touchpad page in Settings > Devices has a lot to offer, as shown in Figure 3-14.

You can use options here to turn off the touchpad when you have a mouse attached or disable it altogether. Those who've been annoyed when the pointer suddenly hops to a new location while they type (usually because a thumb lightly grazed the touchpad) will shout hosannas about the sensitivity drop-down. Setting this to Low Sensitivity should eliminate most grazing accidents. Other settings determine what various gestures (tapping, double-tapping, tapping with two or three fingers, dragging with two or three fingers, and so on) will do.

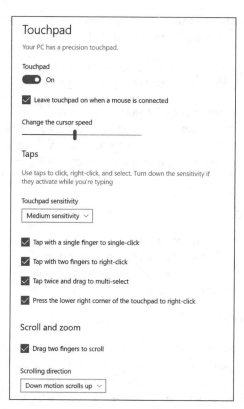

Figure 3-14   Touchpad users are richly rewarded by visiting Settings > Devices > Touchpad.

Using Windows 10 on a touchscreen device

Tablet Mode was specifically designed for sustained use with a touchscreen-equipped device such as a tablet or hybrid PC. We already discussed the Windows user experience with a conventional PC. Tablet Mode introduces a series of significant changes—automatically if it detects you're using a touchscreen device without a keyboard attached, or manually if you want to treat a touchscreen-equipped laptop as if it were a tablet.

Turning on Tablet Mode makes the following changes in the Windows 10 user experience:

- It reconfigures the taskbar, bumping up button sizes, adding a back button, replacing the search box with a search button, and hiding all taskbar buttons. The following comparison shows the normal taskbar on top and the same area in Tablet Mode below it:

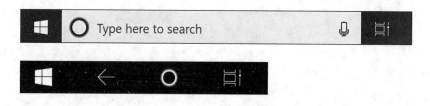

- All apps run in full screen. It's possible to snap two apps side by side, but they have a thick sizing bar between them, similar to the one introduced in Windows 8.

- Start opens in full screen, with the app list hidden by default and accessible only by tapping the hamburger menu icon in the upper-left corner of the display.

Windows 10 makes some assumptions about your preferences based on your hardware. On conventional PCs with a keyboard and mouse, Tablet Mode is off. On dedicated tablets, this mode is on by default. You can adjust these preferences at Settings > System > Tablet Mode. On a hybrid device with a relatively small touchscreen, you might prefer to have Tablet Mode on full time, for example.

Using the Touch Keyboard

The other essential feature of a touchscreen-equipped device, especially one without a keyboard, is the presence of the extremely versatile Windows 10 Touch Keyboard. It allows text entry into dialog boxes, web forms, your browser's address bar, documents, the search box—anywhere you would normally need a physical keyboard to provide input.

Figure 3-15 shows the standard Touch Keyboard.

The Touch Keyboard should appear automatically when you tap to position the insertion point in a place that accepts text entry. On touchscreen-equipped devices, you can make the Touch Keyboard appear by tapping its button, which appears in the notification area on the right of the taskbar. (If this button is hidden, right-click or do a long press on the taskbar and then select the Show Touch Keyboard Button option.)

Figure 3-15   This is the default layout of the Touch Keyboard; use the control in the upper-left corner to change the keyboard display mode, dock or float the keyboard, or jump to language or typing settings.

The limited screen space available for the Touch Keyboard means you have to switch layouts to enter symbols and numbers. Tap the &123 key in the lower-left corner to switch between the standard QWERTY layout and the first of two symbol layouts, as shown in Figure 3-16. Note that the layout includes a dedicated number pad, which is extremely handy for working with spreadsheets and performing other data-entry tasks.

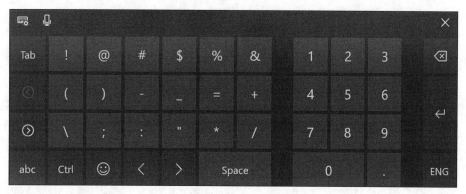

Figure 3-16   Tap the &123 key in the lower-left corner to switch between the standard QWERTY keys and this alternate view of symbols and numbers.

In some respects, the Touch Keyboard is more versatile than its physical counterparts. Entering a typographic symbol like the interrobang or an emoji doesn't require the use of ANSI codes. Instead, you can enter characters directly. To see the vast array of available emojis, click the "happy face" button on the bottom row.

With the emoji keyboard layout visible, the bottom row displays keys you can use to switch between different categories. All the categories offer more symbols than can be displayed at one time in the Touch Keyboard. To explore a category fully, swipe left and right. If you don't have a touch display, you can scroll by clicking the minuscule arrows in the lower-right and -left corners of the emoji layout. Figure 3-17 shows an example of the people category. Note that by clicking and holding the people category icon, you can change the skin tone of the people emojis.

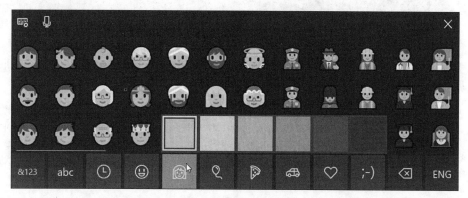

Figure 3-17   Windows 10 supports hundreds of emoji characters. Pick a category from the bottom row and use the arrow keys to scroll through different character sets, 30 at a time.

CHAPTER 3

NOTE

For a full list of officially supported Windows-compatible emoji characters, see *https:// emojipedia.org/microsoft-emoji-list/.*

Dictating text with the Touch Keyboard

By clicking the microphone button near the upper-left corner of the Touch Keyboard, you can dictate text instead of typing. In addition to words, you can dictate punctuation symbols and such editing instructions as "delete last ten words."

Typing with shapes

If you find hunting and pecking is onerous and slow, draw your words instead. Using either the compact or the wide (default) layout of the Touch Keyboard, you can create words by drawing a line from one letter to the next. Windows does an excellent job of recognizing your intentions, and where it cannot it proposes alternative possibilities (just as it would if you misspelled using conventional typing methods). Mobile phones have had this capability for some time, and if you've texted this way on a hand-held platform you'll find it much the same on your Windows tablet.

Changing keyboard styles and docking

Tapping the button in the upper-left corner of the Touch Keyboard reveals a unified settings menu for the keyboard:

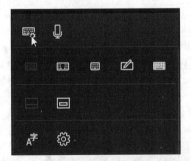

The two options in the middle row of this menu control whether the keyboard floats or is docked against the lower edge of your screen. The bottom row includes buttons to display language settings, typing settings, and tips.

The buttons on the top row of the menu change the layout of the keyboard itself. With the button on the left, you get the default layout shown earlier. The button on the right displays the "full" layout, which, like a typical laptop keyboard, includes Alt and Ctrl keys, a Tab key, and an Fn key. If you're handy with thumbs, you'll like the third button from the left, which compresses the keyboard into a one-handed miniature that takes up a minimum of screen space and functions just like your cell phone. The second layout from the left splits the keyboard into left and right sections, each of which you can operate with one-handed dexterity.

With all these layouts, you can take advantage of Microsoft's superb text-prediction engine. As soon as you finish a word (and sometimes before), likely continuations appear in a row at the top of the keyboard. So, for example, to write "Give me a few minutes to get the money," all you need to type is the first two letters. You can click your way through the rest of the sentence. If you're sending input to a modern (UWP) app, the engine will suggest appropriate emojis as well as text continuations.

Typing suggestions are an opt-in feature. To enable them, go to Settings > Devices > Typing. Under the Typing heading on the Typing page, turn on Show Text Suggestions As I Type On The Software Keyboard.

Inside OUT

Get typing suggestions on the hardware keyboard

The inherent slowness of typing on the Touch Keyboard makes the purpose of typing suggestions self-evident. But you can also take advantage of suggestions and corrections while using your computer's ordinary hardware keyboard. The prediction engine is slightly less versatile in this context as on the Touch Keyboard, because it shows only three suggestions at a time. Even so, suggestions may prove useful, particularly for novice typists or language learners. To turn this feature on, go to Settings > Devices > Typing. Under the heading Hardware Keyboard, turn on Show Text Suggestions As I Type.

Meanwhile, the fourth button from the left in the menu's middle row replaces the keyboard with a handwriting input panel, shown in Figure 3-18. Text that you enter in the input box is automatically translated into characters for entry at the current insertion point.

Figure 3-18   The handwriting panel does a remarkable job at translating even sloppy penmanship into readable results.

Even if your handwriting is so bad that no one but you (and perhaps not even you) can read it, you might be in for a surprise. In the unlikely event that the panel misreads your intent, you can still select from a row of alternatives that appears at the top of the window.

Although the handwriting panel is most useful with devices that support pen input, if you find yourself without a stylus, you can still use it with your fingertip. To do this, visit Settings > Devices > Pen & Windows Ink and turn on Write In The Handwriting Panel With Your Fingertip. On this page, you can also choose which font you want your handwriting efforts to appear in.

Using the Windows Ink workspace

The Windows Ink workspace, shown in Figure 3-19, gathers pen-enabled apps into a pane that appears on the right side of your screen when you tap (or click) the Windows Ink Workspace taskbar button. (If you don't see that button, right-click the taskbar and click or tap the Show Windows Ink Workspace button.)

The three apps shown in the figure are Sticky Notes, Sketchpad, and Screen Sketch. Sticky Notes has been around for many iterations of Windows. Sketchpad is a blank canvas for freehand drawing, and Screen Sketch offers an image of the desktop for drawing. Much as you use the Web Note feature in Microsoft Edge to annotate the current webpage, Screen Sketch gives you a way to mark up whatever is on your desktop. An editing toolbar atop both Screen Sketch and Sketchpad provides basic drawing tools, a ruler for drawing straight lines, and commands to copy, save, share, and delete your work.

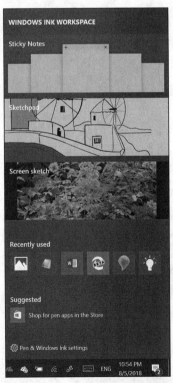

Figure 3-19   The Windows Ink workspace offers a menu of pen-enabled applications, along with links to recently used apps of any kind and links to items you might want to pick up at the Windows Store.

The apps in the Windows Ink workspace, of course, are intended to give you a taste of what you can do with the pen. Much more elaborate pen-friendly programs exist, and you can use them to perform some remarkable feats. Using Microsoft Word, for instance, you can insert handwritten comments and annotations into a document. Another member of the Office family, One-Note, goes even further, indexing your handwritten notes and allowing you to search through an entire notebook for a word or phrase.

Setting pen options

Options relating to your pen are located at Settings > Devices > Pen & Windows Ink. In the lower portion of that settings page, you'll find a set of options for configuring pen shortcuts. (See Figure 3-20.) These options, which require a pen with a shortcut button, govern what happens when you press that button once, press it twice in quick succession, and press and hold.

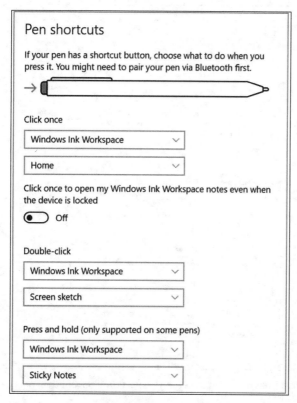

Figure 3-20   With the single-click, double-click, and hold settings, you can train your pen to launch a program, perform a screen capture, summon Cortana, or simply open the Windows Ink workspace.

Within the three sets of drop-downs, you'll find options to launch programs, capture screens, and more.

Working with fonts

Introduced in Windows 10 version 1803 is a Fonts page in Settings (Settings > Personalization > Fonts). If you miss the ancestral font home in Control Panel, you can still visit, but the new Settings page, shown in Figure 3-21, is perhaps easier on the eyes. In the new venue, fonts that include color information are displayed in color, and the page that appears when you click a font presents more information about licensing, trademark, version, manufacturer, and assorted other details. A link at the top of the Fonts page in Settings transports you to the Microsoft Store, where additional fonts are available.

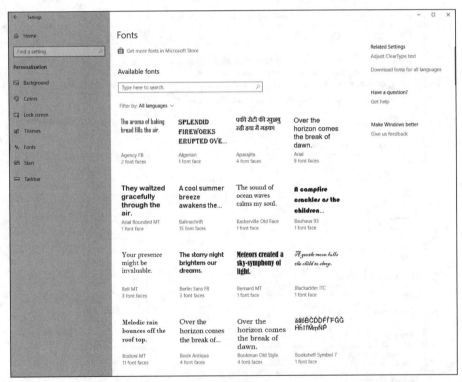

Figure 3-21   Font management has migrated to Settings in version 1803, but the Fonts page in Control Panel remains.

The primary font format used by Windows is TrueType. Windows also supports OpenType and PostScript Type 1 fonts. To install a new font, you can drag its file from a folder or compressed .zip archive to Fonts in Control Panel. But you don't need to open Fonts; the simplest way to install a font is to right-click its file in File Explorer and choose Install. Because font file names are often somewhat cryptic, you might want to double-click the file, which opens the font pre-view window, to see what you're getting. If it's a font you want, click the Install button.

> **NOTE**
>
> **PostScript Type 1 fonts normally consist of two or three files. The one you use to install the font—regardless of which method you use—is the .pfm file, whose file type is shown in File Explorer as Type 1 Font File.**

Making text easier to read

If you like to work at high screen resolutions but find yourself straining to read the text, you can try the following:

- Look for scaling ("zoom") commands in the text-centric programs you use. Many pro-grams, including most modern word processors, include these scaling features. Scaling text up to a readable size is a good solution for particular programs, but it doesn't change the size of icon text, system menus (such as Start), or system dialog boxes.

- To enlarge part of the screen, use the Magnifier tool. (For more information, see "Over-coming challenges" in Chapter 4.)

- Use the scaling options in Display settings. Adjusting the scaling to a higher level enables you to have readable text at higher screen resolutions.

Beginning with version 1809, you can change the size of text everywhere, without changing the overall scaling of your system. Go to Settings > Ease Of Access > Display. Then use the slider under the heading Make Text Bigger. A sample text window will show you how large your text becomes as you drag the slider (see Figure 3-22). You can choose any size from 100 to 225 percent.

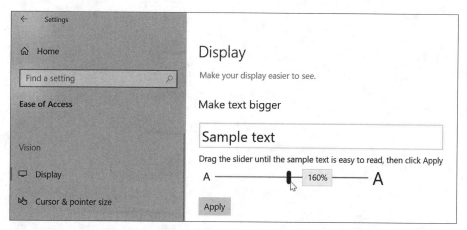

Figure 3-22   By moving this slider, you can magnify the size of text throughout Windows.

CHAPTER 3

Using font smoothing to make text easier on the eyes

ClearType is a font-smoothing technology that reduces jagged edges of characters, thus easing eye strain.

To check or change your font-smoothing settings, type **cleartype** in the search box and then click Adjust ClearType Text. Doing so opens the ClearType Text Tuner, which, in its first screen, has a check box that turns ClearType on when it's selected. The ensuing screens that appear each time you click Next offer optometrist-style choices ("Which Is Better, Number 1 or Number 2?") to help you reach ClearType perfection. If you have more than one monitor attached, the ClearType Text Tuner goes through this exercise for each one.

Windows includes seven fonts that are optimized for ClearType. The names of six of these—Constantia, Cambria, Corbel, Calibri, Candara, and Consolas—begin with the letter c—just to help cement the connection with ClearType. If you're particularly prone to eye fatigue, you might want to consider favoring these fonts in documents you create. (Constantia and Cambria are serif fonts, considered particularly suitable for longer documents and reports. The other four are sans serif fonts, good for headlines and advertising.) The seventh ClearType-optimized font, Segoe UI, is the typeface used for text elements throughout the Windows user interface. (Windows also includes a ClearType-optimized font called Meiryo that's designed to improve the readability of horizontally arrayed Asian languages.)

➤ **For information about how ClearType works, visit Microsoft's ClearType site at** *https://bit.ly/ ClearTypeInfo*.

Personalizing Windows 10

Like every previous version of Windows, Windows 10 offers you innumerable options for personalizing your workspace. These are the choices that make your computing device feel like it's truly your own, embodying your own design preferences as well as choices that make your interaction with Windows work for you. These customizations might not affect your productivity directly, the way that, say, pinning shortcuts to the taskbar does. But creating a visually satisfying workspace makes you more comfortable with your PC, and when you're more comfortable, you're more productive.

With that goal in mind, we introduce the extensive lineup of personalization features in Microsoft Windows 10. Many of the features we discuss in this chapter will be familiar from earlier Windows versions, but a few are genuinely new, including the capability to use the same image on both the sign-in screen and the lock screen.

One important thing to note is that if you use multiple computing devices, all signing into Windows through the same Microsoft account or Azure Active Directory (Azure AD) account, you can choose to have some or all of your customization preferences apply to all such devices. On various personalization screens you can click a Sync Your Settings link (under Related Settings). This action takes you to Settings > Accounts > Sync Your Settings, where you can specify exactly what choices you want to carry over from machine to machine. We discuss the Sync Your Settings page later in this chapter.

Settings vs. Control Panel

We begin with an overview of what you will find at Settings > Personalization. Nearly all your personalization can be accomplished there; that is, the migration of customization choices from Control Panel to Settings that has characterized all recent versions of Windows is nearly complete.

Although you'll find personalization options in both Settings and Control Panel, the latter now contains mostly legacy settings. The far more complete selection is in Settings, where Personalization is one of more than a dozen top-level categories. In this chapter and throughout this book, we guide you to the most effective way to make a specific setting, whether it be through Settings or Control Panel. But you'll find that most of the time we're directing you to Settings. Usually you can find whatever configuration option you need by opening Settings and using its search box.

Inside OUT

Let Microsoft know what you think

On the right side (or the bottom, depending on screen width) of all pages in Settings, you'll find a Give Us Feedback link. Clicking this link takes you to Feedback Hub, a forum in which you can register your thoughts, wishes, and frustrations regarding any aspect of Windows 10. (You can also run Feedback Hub directly. Type the first few characters of **feedback** in the search box or navigate to Feedback Hub in Start.) Feedback Hub is more than a suggestion or complaint box. You can use it to search for and read comments from other users. Microsoft gathers similar comments into "collections," so you can easily learn whether others have been providing feedback similar to your own. If you find an entry that addresses one of your concerns, you can upvote it. A number in bold beside a feedback entry tallies the upvotes and shows you (and Microsoft) which issues are particularly resonant.

Feedback Hub was introduced as part of the Windows Insider Program, and feedback from insiders—testers of upcoming releases—has played an important role in the development of all feature updates since the original release of Windows 10. For some time, however, the hub has been available to all users. You don't have to be part of the Insiders program to be part of the conversation.

Customizing the visual appearance

The most obvious way to personalize your Windows experience is to customize its visual appearance—the desktop background, lock screen picture, accent colors, and so on. These options are neatly arranged under the Personalization heading in Settings.

Selecting the desktop background

You can perk up any desktop with a background image. Your background can be supplied by a graphics file in any of several common formats: BMP, GIF (static only, not animated), JPEG, PNG, and TIFF. If you can't settle on a single image, set up a slide show of images instead. And if you find pictures too distracting, just pick a background color. (That last option might prove especially useful if you like to populate your desktop with files and shortcuts to programs; these icons might be easier to recognize without the distraction of a background image.)

To select any of these options, go to Settings > Personalization > Background. The Background drop-down menu offers the three options shown in Figure 4-1.

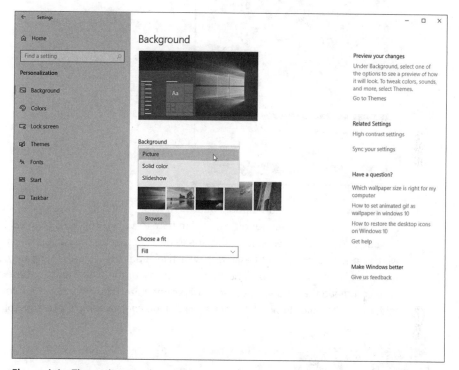

Figure 4-1   The options on the Background page change, depending on which of these three options you select.

Here's what you can do with each of the options in this list:

- **Picture** displays a single image of your choice, scaled to fit the resolution of your display. Windows 10 includes a default selection of images, and PC makers often include additional selections. Click Browse to choose one of your own pictures.

- **Solid Color** covers the background with a color you select from a palette of two dozen shades. You can also create a custom color, and that color then becomes the twenty-fifth item in your palette. Click Custom Color, and then click or tap the color picker that appears, to specify the color you want:

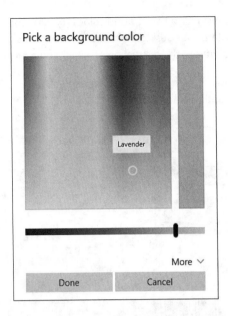

- **Slideshow** is like the Picture option, but with a twist: At an interval you select (at one of six preconfigured intervals ranging from 1 minute to 1 day), Windows changes the desktop background to a new picture from the folder you specify. Unless you specify otherwise, Windows uses the Pictures library (which includes the Pictures folder in your user profile and its counterpart on OneDrive) as sources for the slide show. For best results, we recommend that you select a group of properly sized images, copy them to their own folder, and then click Browse to replace the default choice with your custom folder.

Inside OUT

Restore the photographs furnished with Windows

When you click Browse and select a new picture, your selection replaces the rightmost of the five existing picture choices. But what if you decide you'd rather go back to one of those terrific photos provided with Windows? Getting any one of them back is simple, but not obvious.

Click Browse and navigate to %Windir%\Web\Wallpaper. (On most systems, %Windir% is C:\Windows.) You'll find a handful of nice pictures in subfolders of that folder—including the ones you displaced. If you downloaded any themes from online sources, including those offered by Microsoft, you'll find pictures for those themes in that location as well.

After you choose an image or set up a slide show, select one of the six Choose A Fit options to let Windows know how you want to handle images that are not exactly the same size as your screen resolution:

- **Fill** stretches or shrinks the image so that it occupies the full screen, cropping the image in one or both dimensions so that no blank space remains on the sides or the top and bottom.

- **Fit** reduces or enlarges the image to exactly the width or height of the display, without changing its aspect ratio or cropping the image; this option might result in letterbox bars (using the current background color) on either side or above and below the image.

Inside OUT

Assign separate images to multiple monitors

Of the six fit options we describe here, only Span is specifically intended for use with systems that have additional monitors attached. For the remaining five options, the image you select and the fit options are repeated on each display, and there's no obvious way in Settings to assign a different image to each monitor.

Even though it's not obvious, there's a secret menu that allows you to specify that you want to use an image with a specific monitor. The images you want to use must be available in the list of five thumbnails on the Background page in Settings. Right-click each thumbnail in turn to display a message like the one shown here, with options for each available monitor:

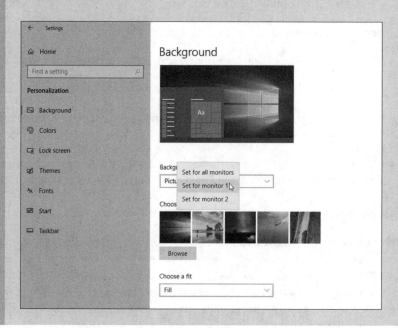

Alas, these settings aren't saved when you switch between single and multiple monitors, as you might with a laptop that occasionally connects to a docking station. If that feature means a lot to you, try the third-party utility DisplayFusion (*https://displayfusion.com*). The software is available in a free version that supports per-monitor background images; a paid Pro version is also available.

- **Stretch** reduces or enlarges the image so that it fits both dimensions, distorting the image if necessary. If there's a significant mismatch between the aspect ratios of the image and the display, the effect can be unpleasant.

- **Tile** repeats the image at its original size to fill all monitors. This option is most effective for abstract backgrounds or for simple, small images where the repeated design looks like a pattern.

- **Center** displays the image at its original size in the center of the screen, without stretching. If the image is smaller than the display resolution, this can leave blank space on the sides or at the top and bottom; if the image is larger than the display, some parts of the image might be cropped away to fit.

- **Span** works like Fill to display a single image across multiple monitors. On a single-monitor PC, this option is the same as Fill.

Here are some other ways to change the desktop background:

- Right-click an image file in File Explorer and choose Set As Desktop Background.

- Right-click an image in Internet Explorer and choose Set As Background.

- Open any image file in Paint, open the File menu, and choose Set As Desktop Background. A submenu lets you choose the Fill, Tile, or Center picture position.

- Use the Photos app to open an image file, click or tap the ellipsis at the right side of the menu bar, tap or click Set As, and then click or tap Set As Background.

Selecting colors

With a beautiful desktop background in place, your next personalization step might be to select a complementary accent color and specify where and how to use it. If you're coming to Windows 10 directly from Windows 7, this group of settings represents a major change. In Windows 7, you can assign separate colors to dozens of different pieces of the Windows interface. In Windows 10, you choose one systemwide accent color from a palette of 48 solid colors (plus an additional color of your own making if you click Custom Color), or you can allow Windows to choose a color that matches your desktop background, as shown in Figure 4-2.

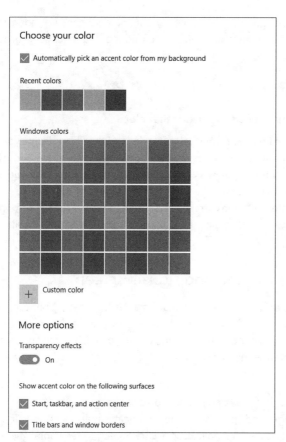

Figure 4-2   Use the first check box to specify that you want Windows to match the accent color to your background automatically.

The Automatically Pick An Accent Color From My Background option is the best choice if you configured a slide show for the desktop background. With this setting on, the accent color changes each time the background picture changes, minimizing the chances that a particular image will represent a poor contrast with a background color you choose manually. On the other hand, be prepared to see shades of purple, pink, and yellow, depending on the image.

The accent color you choose appears in some places automatically—the background of tiles that don't assign a custom color, text links in modern apps, and on the desktop when a background image doesn't fill the display fully.

Turning on the Start, Taskbar, And Action Center option applies the accent color as a background to the taskbar and to Start and Action Center, when they're visible. With this option turned off, those areas have a dark background. A separate Title Bars option turns color on or off for the title bars in desktop programs and modern apps that don't specify a custom color.

Choose Your Default App Mode gives you a choice of light and dark backgrounds for modern apps, including Settings. On some portable devices, you might prefer a dark background as a power-saving measure.

> ### TROUBLESHOOTING
>
> **The Automatic Color option doesn't change the color**
>
> Suppose you turn off the first option and select a color and then later decide you'd rather go back to the automatic color. So, you turn on the option to automatically select an accent color and...nothing happens. When you turn it on, the automatic option doesn't take effect until the *next time* the background changes. If you want to use the automatic color associated with the current background, return to the background page and select the same background again; that triggers Windows to "automatically" select an accent color.

Customizing the lock screen and sign-in screen

The lock screen is a security precaution that prevents someone from seeing or accessing your account when you step away from the computer while you're signed in. To display the lock screen, click Start, and then click your account picture, where you'll find Lock on the menu of available options. Of course, the much faster way to lock the screen is with a keyboard shortcut—Windows key+L.

Just as you can customize the desktop background, you can change the lock screen to your liking by adding custom images and specifying which notifications appear on the lock screen when you're away. Go to Settings > Personalization > Lock Screen to see your options, as shown in Figure 4-3.

These settings closely resemble those for the desktop background. In fact, under the Background menu, you'll find Picture and Slideshow options that work exactly like those under the Background headings, so we won't repeat the detailed instructions here.

The Windows Spotlight option supplies a continually changing assortment of background images along with occasional helpful tips and the option to indicate whether you like or dislike a particular image—that feedback goes into the algorithm that serves future images to you.

The Show Lock Screen Background Picture On The Sign-In Screen option was introduced with the Anniversary Update. After you slide this switch to On, you can clear the lock screen—by clicking, swiping, or tapping any key—and see the box to enter your credentials with the same image behind it.

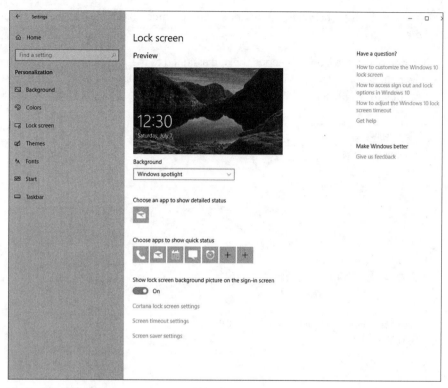

Figure 4-3   The Windows Spotlight option changes the lock screen background at regular intervals, using visually compelling images from Microsoft's vast collection.

NOTE

Windows uses the custom lock screen image for the user who last signed in. On a PC with multiple user accounts and different lock-screen settings, this might result in your seeing a lock screen image configured by another user. If you sign out completely and then restart, Windows might display the default sign-in screen instead.

You can allow one or more apps to display their current status—such as the number of new email messages, upcoming appointments, and so on—on the lock screen. You can also see alarms and reminders here. Depending on your personal preferences, these notifications are either a convenience or a potential privacy issue; if you don't want anyone who passes by your desk to see notifications, go to Settings > System > Notifications & Actions. Under Notifications, turn off Show Notifications On The Lock Screen and Show Reminders And Incoming VOIP Calls On The Lock Screen.

If you choose to use lock-screen notifications, you can configure a single app to display detailed status (the time, title, and location of your next appointment, for example) and up to seven additional apps to show quick status information. Status icons appear in the order you specify here.

Tap one of the app icons to change the app assigned to that position; tap a plus sign to add a new notification to that position. In either case, you'll see a list of apps that support status notifications, as shown here.

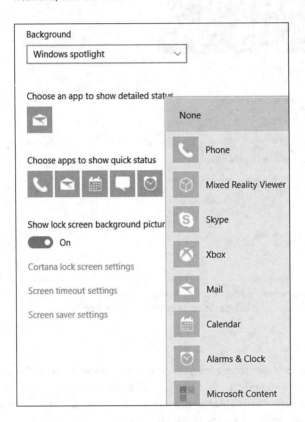

Fine-tuning visual options

Windows 10 contains a handful of legacy customization options that give you fine-grained control over small aspects of the user experience. Most of the options we discuss in this section are in the classic Control Panel, and there's a possibility that some will not survive the transition to the newer Settings app in a future upgrade. So, enjoy the following features while they last.

Customizing mouse pointers

As we noted at the beginning of this chapter, personalization options have been moving from the classic Control Panel to the new Settings app over time. Options to change the appearance of the mouse pointer offer a particularly good example of where this transition is not yet complete.

For example, you might want to change the size and color of the mouse pointer to make it easier to see, especially on a large, high-resolution display where the default white pointer is so small you might find it hard to make it out against light backgrounds.

To quickly change the pointer size and color, go to Settings > Ease Of Access > Cursor & Pointer Size, where you'll see the options shown in Figure 4-4.

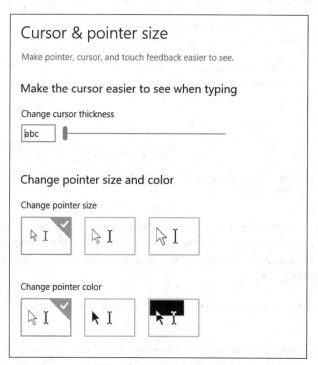

Figure 4-4   A larger pointer, especially one that shifts between dark and light depending on the background, can be easier to pick out on a large display.

Meanwhile, you can find a completely separate entry point to a closely related group of options by going to Control Panel > Ease Of Access > Ease Of Access Center > Make The Mouse Easier To Use. Figure 4-5 shows the resulting options.

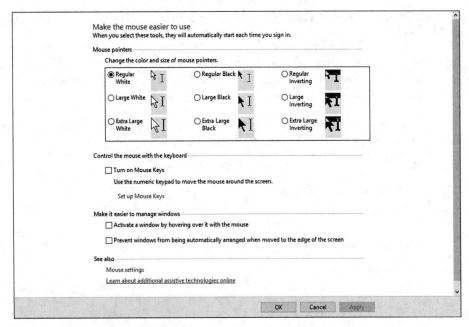

Figure 4-5   The options at the top of this dialog box are an alternative entry point to the same options in the Settings app.

The one unique option here, which isn't in the modern Settings app, is the check box next to Activate A Window By Hovering Over It With The Mouse. This behavior, sometimes known as "focus follows mouse," will be familiar to those who've used Linux-based operating systems. It definitely takes some getting used to.

Elsewhere in Control Panel, some old-style mouse pointer options are still available—at least for now.

If you think an hourglass depicts the passage of time more unambiguously than a rolling doughnut, you can easily bring back the Windows XP–era shape. You can customize the entire array of pointer shapes your system uses by going to Settings > Personalization > Themes > Mouse Cursor, which opens a dialog box like the one shown in Figure 4-6.

On the Pointers tab of the Mouse Properties dialog box, you can select a scheme from the list at the top. For those who are keeping score, this is a third way to set the size and color of the pointer.

What makes this entry point different is the list of options at the bottom, where you can change the pointer associated with specific actions, such as resizing and selecting. Windows wraps up a gamut of pointer shapes as a mouse-pointer scheme. The system comes with an assortment of predefined schemes, making it easy for you to switch from one set of pointers to another as needs or whims suggest.

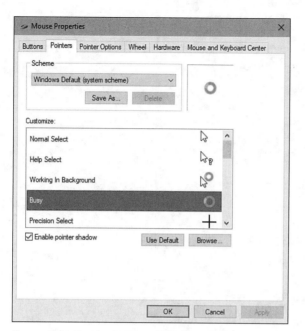

Figure 4-6   Use the options at the bottom of this dialog box to customize the predefined mouse pointer schemes.

Pick a pointer from the Customize box and then click Browse to select an alternative pointer shape. (The Browse button takes you to %Windir%\Cursors and displays files with the extensions .cur and .ani. The latter are animated cursors.)

The pointers included with Windows won't win any cutting-edge design awards; some of them date back to an era when an hourglass actually *was* used for keeping time. If you're inclined to roll your own mouse scheme (by using the Browse button to assign cursor files to pointer types), be sure to use the Save As command and give your work a name. That way you'll be able to switch away from it and back to it again at will.

A few additional settings of interest are available on the Pointer Options tab, shown in Figure 4-7.

If you sometimes struggle to find the mouse even after you've moved it slightly, consider turning on the Display Pointer Trails option. The last option on the page, Show Location Of Pointer When I Press The CTRL Key, provides a clever shortcut when you find yourself involuntarily playing "Where's the pointer?" Tap Ctrl to see a series of concentric circles where the mouse pointer is currently hiding.

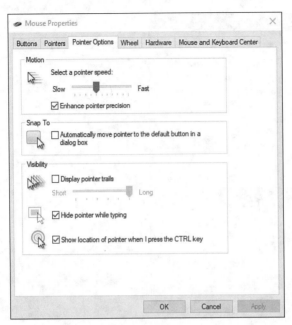

Figure 4-7   Use these pointer options to ease eyestrain by making the mouse pointer easier to spot as it moves.

Making other small visual tweaks

Windows is alive with little animations, such as when you open or close a window. Along with other effects, these can help to direct your focus to the current window or activity. But some folks find them annoying, and an argument can be made that they do take a small bite out of your computer's performance. So, if you don't like them, turn them off!

In the search box of Settings or Control Panel, type **performance** and then choose Adjust The Appearance And Performance Of Windows. The Performance Options dialog box looks like the one shown next, and you can use it to control animations and other effects on a granular level.

On modern hardware with even a moderate graphics processor, these options make little or no difference in actual performance. The loss of animation can be disconcerting, in fact, as you wonder where a particular item went when you minimized it. These options offer the most pay-off on older devices with underpowered graphics hardware.

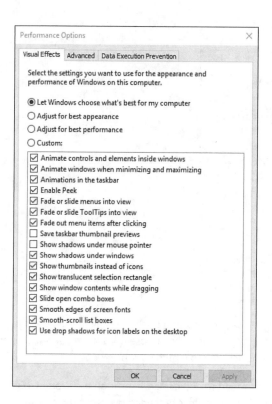

Selecting sounds for events

To specify the sounds that Windows plays as it goes through its paces, go to Settings > Personalization >Themes > Sounds. Custom sound schemes were extremely popular in the early days of Windows, with collections of beeps, gurgles, and chirps that Windows and various apps played in response to various system and application events. Whimsical sounds were typically included in packaged themes that also set up desktop backgrounds and animated cursors. Those sound schemes have gone the way of Pet Rocks, Beanie Babies, and other once-popular fads, but they live on in the Sound dialog box shown here:

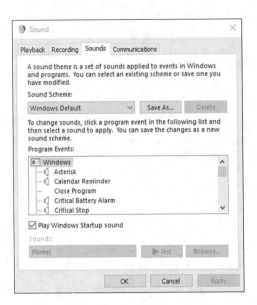

A new installation of Windows comes with only a single scheme, called Windows Default. If you can find and install a custom sound scheme, you can choose it from the Sound Scheme list, or you can customize the current sound scheme to match your preferences.

To see which sounds are currently mapped to events, scroll through the Program Events list. If an event has a sound associated with it, its name is preceded by a speaker icon, and you can click Test to hear it. To switch to a different sound, scroll through the Sounds list or click Browse. The list displays .wav files in %Windir%\Media, but any .wav file is eligible. To silence an event, select None, the item at the top of the Sounds list.

If you rearrange the mapping of sounds to events, consider saving the new arrangement as a sound scheme. (Click Save As and supply a name.) That way, you can experiment further and still return to the saved configuration.

Inside OUT

Mute your computer

If you like event sounds in general but occasionally need complete silence from your computer, choose No Sounds in the Sound Scheme list when you want the machine to shut up. (Be sure to clear the Play Windows Startup Sound check box as well.) When sound is welcome again, you can return to the Windows Default scheme—or to any other scheme you have set up. Switching to the No Sounds scheme won't render your system mute (you'll still be able to play music when you want to hear it), but it will turn off the announcement of incoming mail and other events.

If you want to control sound levels on a more granular level—perhaps muting some applications altogether and adjusting volume levels on others—right-click the volume icon in the notification area and choose Open Volume Mixer. Volume Mixer provides a volume slider (and a mute button) for each output device and each desktop program that emits sounds. You can also mute individual browser tabs in Microsoft Edge.

Personalizing with themes

A theme is a named collection of personalization settings, encompassing background, color, sounds, and mouse cursor. Any time you arrive at a configuration of settings that pleases you and that you might want to return to later (while you continue experimenting, for example), you can make it a theme by simply naming it. To do this, go to Settings > Personalization > Themes. Near the top of the page, you'll see a summary of your current settings and a Save Theme button.

Themes are saved as a .theme file in your %LocalAppData%\Microsoft\Windows\Themes folder. (A .theme file is a standard text file that describes all the theme settings. For complete details about .theme files, see "Theme File Format" at *https://docs.microsoft.com/en-us/windows/ desktop/Controls/themesfileformat-overview*.)

Perhaps more important than the ability to name your own customizations, Settings > Personalization >Themes gives you free access to hundreds of beautiful themes created by professional and amateur photographers all over the world. Most of these are slideshows; a few include sounds as well. If you apply a theme as a slideshow, you can configure the change interval at Settings > Personalization > Background, just as you would for a slideshow of your own photos. The page at Settings >Personalization >Themes shows thumbnails of all the themes that are currently installed and available; to apply one, simply click it. Hundreds more can be found in the Microsoft Store. (Click Get More Themes In Microsoft Store to see what's there.) Click a theme in the store to install it, and then apply it by selecting it at Settings > Personalization > Themes.

Configuring desktop icons

A fresh, cleanly installed Windows 10 desktop (as opposed to one generated by an upgrade installation) includes a single lonely icon—Recycle Bin. If you want to display other system icons, go to Settings > Personalization > Themes > Desktop Icon Settings. The resulting dialog box, shown next, provides check boxes for five system folders—Computer, User's Files (the root folder of your own profile), Network, Recycle Bin, and Control Panel.

If you're really into customization, you can change any of the five icons that appear in the large box in the center. Note that the Control Panel icon does not appear in this center box even if you select its check box; Windows doesn't provide a way to change it.

To change an icon, select it in the center box and click Change Icon. By default, the Browse button displays the selection of alternative icons from the file %Windir%\System32\Imageres.dll. (Be sure to use the horizontal scroll bar to see them all.) If none of these suits you, try browsing to %Windir%\System32\Shell32.dll.

After you populate your desktop with icons, you might want to control their arrangement. If you right-click the desktop, you'll find two commands at the top of the shortcut menu that can help in this endeavor. To make your icons rearrange themselves when you delete one of their brethren, click View > Auto Arrange Icons. To ensure that each icon keeps a respectable distance from each of its neighbors (and that the whole gang stays together at the left side of your screen), click View > Align Icons To Grid. And if you don't want desktop icons to get in the way of your gorgeous desktop background image, click View and then clear the check mark to the left of Show Desktop Icons. (Return to this option if you decide you miss those desktop icons.)

To change the sort order of desktop icons, right-click the desktop and click Sort By. You can sort on any of four attributes: Name, Size, Item Type, or Date Modified. Sorting a second time on any attribute changes the sort order from ascending to descending (or vice versa).

Eliminating distractions with Focus Assist

Focus Assist, formerly known as Quiet Hours, is a feature designed to minimize aural and visual interruptions from your computer at crucial times—for example, when a task requires maximum concentration, or when you're playing a full-screen game or giving a presentation. The feature has been around, under its former name, in previous versions of Windows 10, but beginning with version 1803 it offers greater configurability. To see and configure Focus Assist, visit Settings > System > Focus Assist, shown in Figure 4-8.

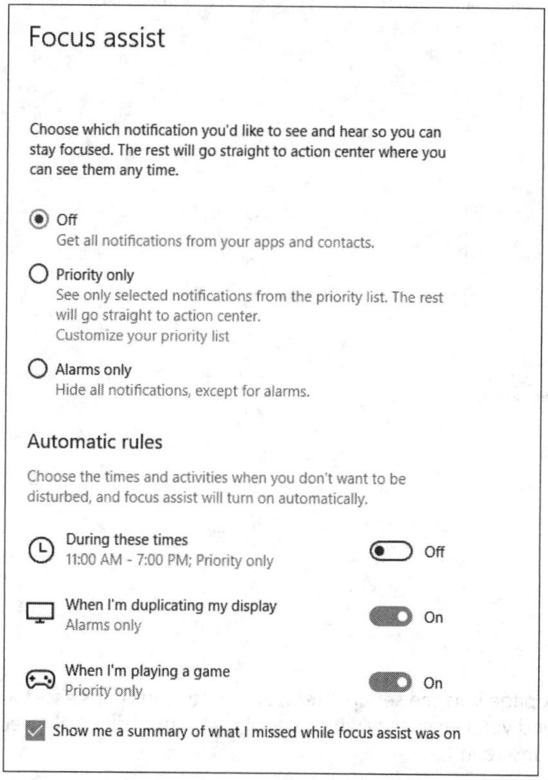

Figure 4-8   You can use the three option buttons at the top of this page to turn Focus Assist on and off, although it might be quicker to do this in Action Center. The Automatic Rules section of the page give you considerable control over when the feature will be activated.

As the option buttons at the top of the settings page suggest, Focus Assist can be in three states—Off, Priority Only, and Alarms Only. Choosing Alarms Only blocks all interruptions except those generated by an alarm clock.

To allow some but not all notifications to sound or appear, choose Priority Only, and then click Customize Your Priority List. The Priority List page, shown in Figure 4-9, gives you considerable control over what interruptions you will accept—and from whom.

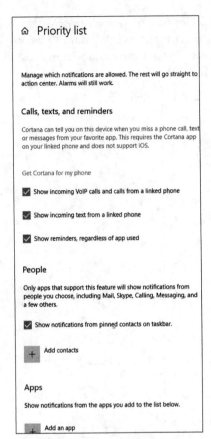

Figure 4-9 On the Priority List page you can set up interactions between Focus Assist and Cortana (on your phone), and you can specify which people and apps will be allowed to send notifications to your screen.

The first three check boxes on this page provide a way for Focus Assist to pass suppressed notifications to your phone. Cortana must be installed on the phone, and if it's not already there, you can click Get Cortana For My Phone.

Options under People permit particular contacts to interrupt you. On the assumption that those contacts you have pinned to your taskbar are particularly important, Windows provides a check box to give them all a blanket pass. Below that check box you can click Add Contacts to make additional allowances.

The bottom of the settings page lists apps that are allowed to interrupt. Click Add An App to expand the list.

The Automatic Rules options shown at the bottom of Figure 4-8 provide additional control over Focus Assist. By default, the feature swings into action whenever you are projecting your screen or playing a game. You can also set a range of hours during which you want your focus to be assisted. Clicking During These Hours takes you to a page where you can specify starting and ending times, a repeat pattern (Daily, Weekends Only, or Weekdays Only), and a focus level (Priority Only or Alarms Only).

To use Focus Assist on an ad hoc basis, you can return to Settings > System > Focus Assist and turn it on or off. A quicker and easier approach is to display Focus Assist in the Quick Actions section of Action Center. (If you don't find it there, visit Settings > System > Notifications & Actions, and then click Add Or Remove Quick Actions.) Clicking Focus Assist in the Quick Actions panel cycles the feature from Off through Priority Only and Alarms Only.

Choosing a screen saver

Screen savers don't save screens, and they certainly don't save energy compared to simply blanking the display.

In the distant past, when screens were invariably CRTs and many offices displayed the same application at all hours of the working day, having an image move about during idle times probably did extend the service life of some displays. Today, this legacy feature is strictly for nostalgia buffs who want to compute like it's 1999.

By default, Windows 10 does not configure a screen saver, although it includes a handful of old favorites. To see what's available, go to Settings > Personalization > Lock Screen, scroll to the bottom of the Lock Screen page, and then click Screen Saver Settings.

In the Screen Saver Settings dialog box (shown next), select an option under Screen Saver. Some screen savers have additional configuration options; click Settings to review your choices.

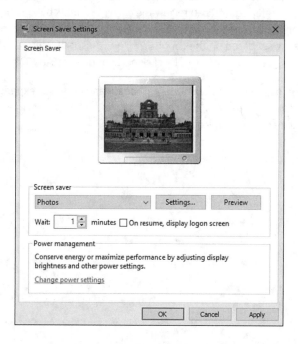

Setting date and time, currency, and other regional options

A personalized experience requires Windows to know some things about you. Not just how to read your handwriting, or your dining preferences, but some basic information about how other people in your part of the world display the date and time, currency symbols, and preferred number formats, such as whether to use a comma or a period as a separator.

In Windows 10, some language options are determined by the base Windows version. Windows configures additional regional settings using your location (with your permission) as well as settings you specify for Cortana.

In most cases, Windows 10 picks the right regional settings. You might need to customize some of these options if you prefer settings from one region (your home, typically) but Windows insists on applying settings for a different region, such as one you're visiting. Your first stop is the Time & Language section in Settings, where you can change time zones and make other time-related settings, as shown in Figure 4-10.

If you have an always-on internet connection, we recommend leaving the top two options enabled. Windows 10 periodically synchronizes your computer's clock to an internet-based time server, fixing any "drift" if your PC's clock isn't working correctly. You can also manually set the PC's time zone here if it's not detected properly. (On a domain-based network, this setting is controlled by the domain server.)

Windows uses your country/region and language settings to provide some personalized content and for regional formats such as the way dates, times, and numbers are displayed and which measurement system is preferred. You can review the current formats by looking at the samples under Formats. Windows uses the formats you set here for displaying dates and times in the taskbar. Initially, these are set based on the country/region you specify during Windows setup, but you can easily change any or all of them by clicking Change Date And Time Formats.

On the Region & Language page, you can set a country or region and add local experience packs (commonly known as language packs) if your edition of Windows supports them. (You can also find local experience packs in the Microsoft Store.)

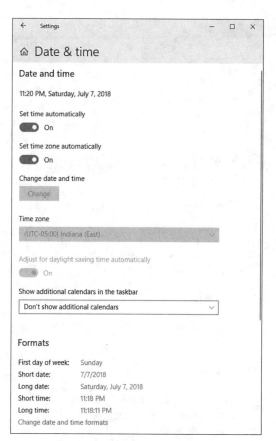

Figure 4-10   The two automatic options at the top of this Settings page usually get the time and date right. Slide either option to Off if you need to make adjustments.

For even more fine-grained control over the full range of settings, you need to go deep into legacy Control Panel options. Click Additional Date, Time, & Regional Settings under the Related Settings heading on the Date & Time page in Settings. That opens the Clock And Region page in Control Panel. Click Change Date, Time, Or Number Formats to open the Region dialog box, with its handful of settings; to display the full collection, click Additional Settings.

After all that clicking, you should see the options shown in Figure 4-11.

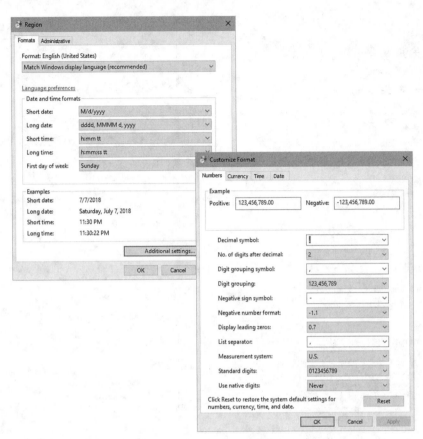

Figure 4-11   For fine-grained control over number formats, you need to dive deep into Control Panel.

If you frequently communicate with people in other time zones, you might want to click Add Clocks For Different Time Zones, under the Related Settings heading at Settings > Date & Time. This opens a dialog box in which you can add one or two clocks to the top of the calendar that appears when you click or tap the clock in the notification area, as shown next.

The agenda section at the bottom of that calendar displays appointments from any account you connected to the Windows Calendar app as well as reminders you set using Cortana.

Beginning with the Creators Update (version 1703), Windows 10 now supports the Traditional Chinese and Simplified Chinese lunar calendars. To install either, go to Settings > Time & Language > Date & Time, and then choose which lunar calendar you want from the list below Show Additional Calendars In The Taskbar. Your calendar will then display the lunar dates below the corresponding Gregorian dates, like this:

CHAPTER 4

Overcoming challenges

Microsoft has a longstanding commitment to making computing accessible and easier to use for persons with vision, hearing, or mobility impairments. Windows 10 groups these options into the Ease Of Access section of Settings. (Alternatively, you can press Windows key+U to open this page directly.) Additional options are available in the Ease Of Access Center in Control Panel.

The options at Settings > Ease Of Access are organized in three groups: Vision, Hearing, and Interaction. Any of the settings can be used alone or in conjunction with others.

Vision options include the following:

- **Magnifier.** This tool enlarges part of the screen, making it easier for people using apps that support closed captioning. To turn Magnifier on from anywhere in Windows, press Windows key+Plus. To turn it off, press Windows key+Esc. For a complete list of Magnifier keyboard shortcuts, scroll to the bottom of Settings > Ease Of Access > Magnifier, and click Show All Keyboard Shortcuts.

- **Color Filters.** These are designed to help users with color-blindness. Available filters include Grayscale, Inverted, Grayscale Inverted, Red-Green (Green Weak, Deuteranopia), Red-Green (Red Weak, Protanopia), and Blue-Yellow (Tritanopia).

- **High Contrast.** This tool configures Windows to use a high-contrast color scheme (by default, white text on a black background) that makes it easier for visually impaired users to read the screen.

- **Narrator.** This tool converts on-screen text to speech and sends it to your computer's speakers. This option allows people who are blind or have severe vision impairments to use Windows.

  The Vision section also includes a Display page, where you can adjust the size of text and other visual elements, increase or decrease the brightness of your display, and configure several other visual aspects of the Windows user interface. For example, if you find the normal animations of windows a distraction, you can turn them off here.

Hearing options include an Audio page, where you can turn on monaural audio, or configure visual behavior to accompany audio alerts. For example, you can choose to make the title bar of the active window, the entire active window, or the entire screen flash in response to an audio alert. Also, in the Hearing section, is Closed Captions, which lets you configure the appearance of closed captioning in videos.

The Navigation section includes the following:

- **Speech.** On the Speech page, you can enable speech recognition by setting the switch under Turn On Speech Recognition to on. With speech recognition enabled, you can dictate text, system commands, and editing commands by speaking instead of typing. When you first enable this feature, a wizard will guide you through some simple setup steps and will lead you to a Microsoft support page where, among other things, you can view and print a table of recognized editing commands.

- **Keyboard.** This collection of tools provides alternate means for Windows users with impaired mobility to enter text using a pointing device. Options that appear when you click Options in On-Screen Keyboard let you control how it works—you can choose whether to select a letter by clicking, for example, or by allowing the pointer to pause over a key for a specific amount of time. Other tools on the Keyboard page allow users with impaired mobility to more easily deal with key combinations and repeated keystrokes.

- **Mouse.** This page includes tools that make the mouse pointer easier to see for visually impaired users. Another tool enables the numeric keypad to move the mouse pointer instead of by using a mouse.

- **Eye Control.** Version 1709 introduced support for eye control, allowing users to manipulate the mouse and keyboard, and to turn narration on or off, by means of the eyes. (Support is currently provided for the Tobii Eye Tracker 4C and the EN-US keyboard layout. Support for additional keyboard layouts and hardware devices is promised for the future.) Version 1803 extended the eye-control feature set with better support for scrolling; improved mouse control; quick access to Start, Timeline, and Settings; and the ability to hide the launchpad as needed to avoid accidental clicking.

The easiest way to configure your computer for adaptive needs in one fell swoop is to open Ease Of Access Center in Control Panel and then click Get Recommendations To Make Your Computer Easier To Use, a link near the center of the page. The link launches a wizard, shown here, that walks you through the process of configuring accessibility options:

CHAPTER 4

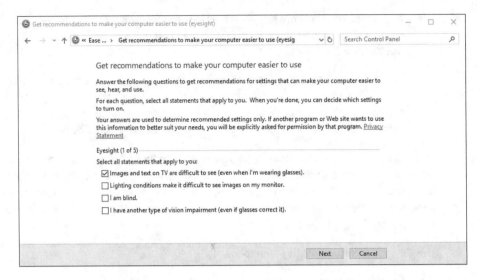

If you want accessibility options to be available at all times, even before signing in to the computer, click the Change Sign-In Settings link in the left pane of Ease Of Access Center in Control Panel. This option (shown next) applies any changes you make to the sign-in desktop. If you choose not to enable this option, you can still turn accessibility features on or off at the sign-in screen; click the small Ease Of Access icon in the lower-right corner of the sign-in screen to display a list of available settings, as shown next. Press the Spacebar to enable each one.

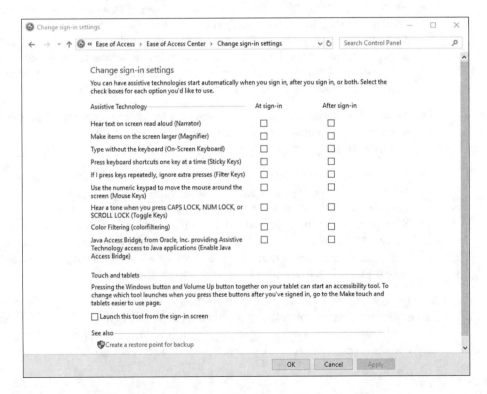

Syncing your settings between computers

When you sign in using a Microsoft account or an Azure Active Directory account, Windows 10 offers the capability to synchronize settings between computers you use. When you sign in on a new PC using that account, Windows retrieves those personalized options from Microsoft OneDrive and applies them to the new device.

To manage synchronization options, go to Settings > Accounts > Sync Your Settings. Figure 4-12 shows the window that appears.

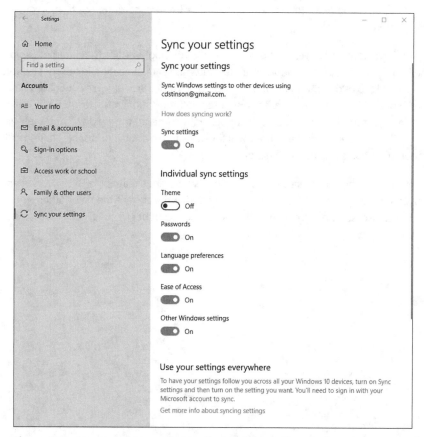

Figure 4-12   You can enable or disable all sync settings with a single setting, or control settings individually. By not syncing themes, for example, you can maintain a unique visual identity for each of your PCs.

The settings available for synchronization include the following:

- **Theme.** This group of settings includes the desktop background, accent color, sound scheme, screen saver, desktop icons, and mouse pointers.

- **Passwords.** This group includes passwords you saved for access to secure websites and other network computers.

- **Language Preferences.** These settings are from the Time & Language page in the Settings app.

- **Ease Of Access.** Any accessibility options you set using Ease Of Access in Settings are in this group.

- **Other Windows Settings.** This group includes settings that don't fit into other categories, including printers, mouse options, File Explorer settings, notification preferences, and more.

If you have used earlier versions of Windows 10, you might notice that Internet Explorer Settings no longer appears on this list. To configure settings synchronization in Internet Explorer, visit the Advanced tab of the Internet Options dialog box. Under Browsing, select Enable Syncing Internet Explorer Settings And Data. To configure synchronization in Microsoft Edge, click the More Settings button (the three dots at the upper-right corner of the window), and then click Settings. Below the Account heading, you'll find a switch to enable or disable sharing of favorites, reading list, top sites, and other settings.

Note that settings are synced on a per-user basis. Settings that apply to all users at your computer, such as screen resolution, are not included in the current theme or other synchronized settings. Also, settings associated with a local user account are not synchronized with other computers.

In Windows 10, the Windows Update service delivers security fixes, performance and reliability improvements, and updated device drivers, just as its predecessors have done for two decades. But this release also assigns a crucial new role to this core Windows feature. In the "Windows as a Service" model, Windows Update delivers regular upgrades to Windows 10, with new and improved features alongside the bug fixes.

If you're accustomed to using Windows Update in earlier versions of Windows, you might be startled by one major change in Windows 10. Whereas Windows 7 and Windows 8.1 users were offered a menu of updates periodically and could pick and choose which updates they wanted to install, Windows 10 bundles all its available updates into cumulative updates. A cumulative update includes all fixes that Microsoft has previously released. When you install the update, the system downloads and applies only those updates you have not previously installed. This major change in the servicing model for Windows is likely to dismay traditionalists who want to retain the option to sort through updates at their leisure, accepting some, delaying others, and rejecting still others.

The second major change in the "Windows as a Service" model is that updates are installed automatically. Most newly discovered vulnerabilities in Windows are patched quickly—usually before they become widespread problems. In fact, many of the worst security incidents in recent years have attacked vulnerabilities that had been patched months or years earlier. The victims tended to be those who failed to keep their Windows PCs properly updated. With Windows 10, Microsoft has taken additional steps to ensure that more systems are updated automatically.

In this chapter, we discuss how Windows Update works, with a special emphasis on how administrators can manage updates effectively on PCs running Windows 10 Pro and Enterprise editions.

An overview of how Windows 10 update works

Windows Update runs as a service that is set to run as needed; its associated services, including the Background Intelligent Transfer Service (BITS), also run automatically, with little or no attention required from you other than an occasional restart. We strongly suggest checking in at regular intervals to confirm that updates are being delivered as expected and that the various Windows Update services are working properly. To do this, go to Settings > Update & Security > Windows Update. Figure 5-1 shows what you'll see if Windows has pending updates available.

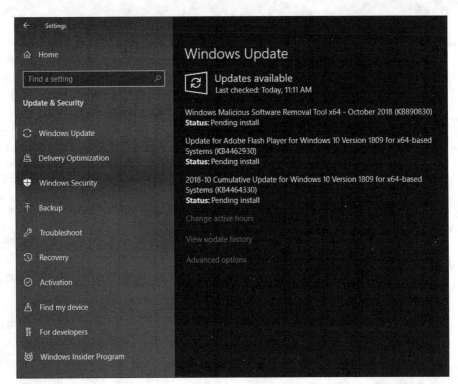

Figure 5-1 When updates are available, you can view their installation status on this page. If a restart is required, you'll see an option to restart immediately or schedule a more convenient time.

The text below the Windows Update heading tells you whether your system was up to date as of the most recent check. If updates are ready to install, you can do so immediately. For updates that require a restart, you can take advantage of the scheduling options we describe later in this chapter. (See "Choosing when updates are installed.")

Windows Update checks daily to see whether new updates are available, so you don't ordinarily need to use the Check For Updates button. If you're preparing for travel, you might want to make a manual check before your departure to avoid having to deal with pending updates while on the road.

Inside OUT

Don't fear automatic updates—manage them

As the global internet has become more pervasive, Microsoft and other software companies, large and small, have ratcheted up the speed at which they deliver updates. Occasionally, those updates end up causing new problems of their own. Among conservative IT pros, it has become practically dogma to stand out of the line of fire when updates are first released. Historically, problematic updates are usually identified within the first week or two and either pulled or fixed, making it safe to deploy them after a suitable delay.

So, are things different this time around? Are monthly cumulative updates in Windows 10 more trustworthy than their predecessors? Is it safe to dive into a new feature update on the day it's released?

There's no right or wrong answer to those questions. But two crucial differences in the modern Windows development process are worth noting. One is Microsoft's use of telemetry, the diagnostic feedback loop that allows it to identify problems in real time, before customers begin lighting up support lines. The other is the maturation of the Windows Insider Program, which allows a large group of early adopters to test feature updates before they are released to the general population.

Yes, seemingly innocuous updates can and do cause problems for some users. But after more than three years' experience with Windows 10, we can testify that those problems are resolved far more quickly than before. On devices running business editions of Windows 10—Pro, Enterprise, and Education—administrators can avoid the occasional flawed update that sneaks into circulation by delaying quality updates, deferring feature updates, and instituting pilot programs in their organizations to evaluate updates first-hand. (We discuss all these options at length in this chapter.) For truly mission-critical systems, where any downtime could be disastrous, and a conservative approach is imperative, the Windows Enterprise Long Term Servicing Channel is an essential option.

CHAPTER 5

What you get from Windows Update

In earlier versions of Windows, security updates and reliability fixes were offered as an ever-growing collection of individual updates, with feature improvements reserved for major version upgrades that typically required payment. This approach meant you could pick and choose which updates to install. But it also meant you were sometimes faced with installing scores of updates (and performing multiple reboots), especially when updating a device that hadn't been used for a few months. That pick-and-choose-your-updates approach changes dramatically with Windows 10.

When you check for new updates in Windows 10, even on a device that hasn't been updated in many months, you are likely to see, at most, only a handful of updates. These updates fall into the following categories.

Quality updates

Windows 10 receives so-called *quality updates*, which fix security and reliability issues, in cumulative packages targeted at each Windows 10 version. (This category includes the fixes delivered like clockwork on the second Tuesday of each month, also known colloquially as Patch Tuesday or, more formally, Update Tuesday.) They are version specific, with separate updates available depending on the currently installed Windows version—1709 or 1803, for example. Each newly released cumulative update supersedes all previous updates for that version. When you install the latest cumulative update, it applies the most recent revision of all quality updates that apply to your Windows 10 version.

Separate quality updates, which are not part of the cumulative packages, address security issues in the Adobe Flash code that is part of Microsoft Edge and Internet Explorer.

Beginning in February 2019, Microsoft plans to change the format of cumulative quality update packages to make them smaller, redistributable, and easier to manage. Details are in this post on the Windows IT Pro blog: *https://bit.ly/update-changes-2019*.

Feature updates

Feature updates are the equivalent of major version upgrades. They are released twice yearly, with code typically finalized in March and September and the actual updates delivered within a month. Because these updates are much larger than quality updates and take significantly longer to install, they have their own set of management options, which we describe later in this chapter.

Inside OUT

Be patient with feature updates

Hundreds of millions of PCs worldwide run Windows 10. When Microsoft releases one of its twice-yearly feature updates, the new version doesn't go to that massive global population overnight. Instead, Microsoft uses its device telemetry to prioritize the timing of update delivery. The feature update goes first to devices that are known to be compatible with it, while devices that have compatibility issues (such as a problematic hardware driver or a third-party antivirus program that needs an update) are blocked. As those compatibility issues are resolved, the update rolls out gradually, but the upshot is that it might be several months before all Windows 10 PCs are running the new version.

It's possible to jump to the head of the line and override those compatibility blocks by installing a feature update manually. Doing so comes with risks, however, including the chance that you'll run into a serious performance or reliability issue.

Servicing stack updates

The *servicing stack* is the code that installs operating system updates to Windows. It also includes the *component-based servicing stack (CBS)*, which powers several Windows-based deployment features, including the Deployment Image Servicing and Management command-line tool (DISM.exe); the System Integrity Check and Repair tool (Sfc.exe), a direct descendant of the Windows XP-era System File Checker tool; and the Windows Features tool (OptionalFeatures.exe).

Servicing stack updates are delivered on an as-needed basis (typically not every month) and include reliability and security fixes. They are version specific, with separate servicing stack updates available depending on the currently installed Windows version. They are typically delivered along with, but separate from, the cumulative quality updates in a given month.

If you are manually installing updates from the Microsoft Update Catalog as part of setting up a new Windows 10 installation, Microsoft recommends installing the most recent servicing stack update before downloading the latest cumulative update. Manually installing the most recent servicing stack update is also a recommended step for troubleshooting Windows Update problems.

Driver updates

Microsoft delivers some device drivers and firmware updates through Windows Update. All Microsoft Surface devices, for example, receive hardware-related updates through this channel. Windows Update provides some third-party drivers to complete setup for devices that are not available in the Windows installation package as well as occasional replacements for installed device drivers that have been deemed to be the source of significant reliability issues.

Windows Defender Antivirus definitions

Windows Defender Antivirus has its own update mechanism that periodically downloads definition updates (sometimes called *signature files*). If you manually check Windows Update, it will download and install any available definition updates that have been released since the most recent Windows Defender check.

Microsoft Malicious Software Removal Tool

The Malicious Software Removal Tool (MSRT) is typically delivered monthly, on Update Tuesday. Its purpose is to detect and remove prevalent malware from Windows computers; it is not a substitute for the comprehensive antimalware code included as part of Windows Defender. MSRT runs automatically in the background; if it detects and removes any threats, it generates a log file and saves it as %windir%\debug\mrt.log.

For additional details about MSRT, including download links and deployment instructions for IT administrators, see *https://bit.ly/msrt-details*.

Servicing channels

With Windows 10 Pro, Enterprise, and Education editions, you have the ability to manage when updates are delivered using Windows Update for Business, which we discuss later in this chapter. Before we get to those details, however, we need to discuss the servicing options for feature updates. Note that this terminology has changed significantly since the original release of Windows 10. For example, in Windows 10 version 1703 and earlier, update settings included what Microsoft called *branch readiness levels*; beginning with version 1709, these are called *servicing channels*. Although the labels have changed, the underlying concept has not. Administrators can choose when to deploy new features by assigning Windows 10 devices to one of the following channels:

- **Semi-Annual Channel (Targeted).** Machines in this channel receive feature updates automatically, shortly after Microsoft releases them via Windows Update. This is the default setting for all retail and OEM Windows editions. (This channel was previously designated as the Current Branch.)

- **Semi-Annual Channel.** Feature updates are not offered to clients in this channel until at least two months after they've been released to the Semi-Annual Channel (Targeted) and Microsoft has declared the update ready for deployment in enterprises. Even then, administrators can delay installation of feature updates by up to 365 days. (Note that this setting changed in Windows 10 beginning with version 1703; the deferral period for previous versions was a maximum of eight months.) Because the Semi-Annual Channel allows for controlled rollout of feature updates over a longer period of time, it's often the best option for the majority of users in an organization. The option to choose this channel is available only on Pro, Enterprise, and Education editions of Windows 10. (This channel was previously designated as the Current Branch for Business.)

- **Long Term Servicing Channel (LTSC).** This channel includes the usual monthly security and reliability updates, but no new features are added for the supported life of that release (up to 10 years).

    LTSC is the only channel that is specific to a single edition, Windows 10 Enterprise LTSC. (Note that pre-2018 releases of this edition are called LTSB, which is short for Long Term Servicing Branch.) This edition is not intended for general-purpose workstations running Office and other productivity applications; rather, it's targeted at specialized devices (such as manufacturing control systems or point-of-sale systems) that run mission-critical applications and where high reliability is the primary goal. For more details, see "Windows 10 editions at a glance" in Appendix A, "Windows 10 editions and licensing options."

NOTE

A fourth servicing option is available for those who want to be ahead of the curve. The Windows Insider Program delivers feature updates *before* they're distributed to the masses. Insider Preview builds allow you to get an early look at new features, test them, and provide feedback to Microsoft—but it also means you install software that hasn't been as widely tested and might cause severe problems. If you want to be a guinea pig, go to Settings > Update & Security > Windows Insider Program. For more details about how the program works and how you can sign up for it, see Appendix B, "The Windows Insider Program."

➤ For additional details about Windows servicing options, visit *https://bit.ly/servicing-options.* To learn the version number and build number of the current release in each servicing channel, go to *https://bit.ly/windows-release.*

Finding technical information about updates

The information that appears in the list of available updates and in your update history is brief and often less than informative. Why, exactly, are you being offered a particular update? Which reliability and security issues, exactly, are addressed in the latest quality update?

For the answers, prepare to do some clicking. Start with Settings > Update & Security > Windows Update > View Update History. That opens a categorized list of all updates installed since the most recent feature update, similar to the one shown in Figure 5-2.

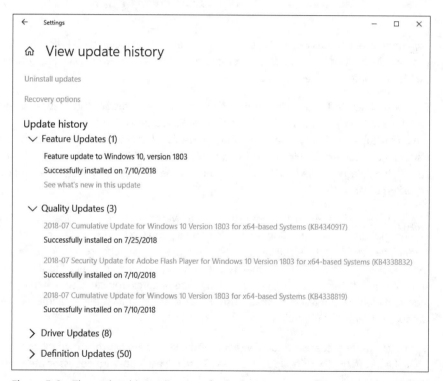

Figure 5-2   The update history list starts fresh after you successfully install a new feature update. Click any hyperlink to see additional details about a quality update.

Each cumulative update listed under the Quality Updates heading includes a descriptive title and the number associated with a related Knowledge Base (KB) article. That KB article, in turn, typically contains a list of key changes—security updates and quality improvements that are new in that cumulative update, along with a listing of any known issues for the update. It also includes a link to the Microsoft Update Catalog, where you can download a standalone package that allows you to install the updates manually. A File Information section provides a link to a list of files and version information associated with the update (in CSV format).

Inside Out

Open any KB article directly

If you're reading about a Knowledge Base article and don't have access to a hyperlink, you can open that KB article directly by using the following URL format: https://support.microsoft.com/help/*nnnnnnn/* and replacing *nnnnnnn* with the seven-digit number following "KB."

For cumulative updates that include security content, the associated KB article typically does not include detailed information about those fixes. That's a noteworthy change from Microsoft's previous update documentation policy.

Previously, Microsoft issued a monthly security summary on the second Tuesday of each month, with links to individual security bulletins that contained details about a security issue, including an executive summary, a severity rating, and a list of affected software. Microsoft stopped issuing those bulletins in March 2017, and as of April 2017 this information is available in a searchable database called the Security Update Guide: *https://portal.msrc.microsoft.com/en-us/security-guidance*.

The Security Update Guide includes listings for all Microsoft products. To see only the most recent updates, use the filters on the guide's home page to specify a date, and then use additional filters to refine the results further. For example, you can choose a specific version (such as Windows 10 version 1803) and specify a security rating (such as Critical) to show only Critical updates for that version during the specified range of dates. You can also search by the industry standard identifier for a security issue, using the Common Vulnerabilities and Exposures (CVE) database, or enter a KB number.

Security updates that are included with a cumulative update get their own release notes, which are linked from the Security Update Guide. These release notes are not associated with a KB number.

Every cumulative update, complete with KB number and minor build number, is also listed on the Windows 10 Update History page. That index is categorized by version; updates for version 1803, for example, are at *https://support.microsoft.com/help/4099479*.

Every update listing also links to the associated page in the Microsoft Update Catalog. There, you can find download links for standalone update packages as well as further details about the updates.

Security updates include a rating of the threat's severity. These are the four ratings that are used, listed in order of severity (with the most severe first):

- **Critical.** A critical vulnerability can lead to code execution with no user interaction.

- **Important.** An important vulnerability is one that can be exploited to compromise the confidentiality or integrity of your data or to cause a denial-of-service attack.

- **Moderate.** A moderate vulnerability is one that's usually mitigated by default settings and authentication requirements. In other words, you'd have to go a bit out of your way for one of these to damage your system or your data.

- **Low.** A vulnerability identified as low usually requires extensive interaction or an unusual configuration to cause damage.

For vulnerabilities with a rating of Critical or Important, Microsoft provides an Exploitability Index that estimates the likelihood that a vulnerability addressed in a security update will be exploited. This information is intended to help Windows administrators prioritize their deployment of updates.

The Exploitability Index includes four values:

- **0 – Exploitation Detected.** The vulnerability is actively being exploited.

- **1 – Exploitation More Likely.** There is a strong likelihood that attackers could consistently exploit this vulnerability, making it an attractive target.

- **2 – Exploitation Less Likely.** Attackers would have difficulty creating exploit code, making it a less attractive target.

- **3 – Exploitation Unlikely.** Successfully functioning exploit code is unlikely to be utilized in real attacks, and the full impact of exploitation is likely to be limited.

For more information about the Microsoft Exploitability Index, see *https://www.microsoft.com/ msrc/exploitability-index.*

Managing Windows Update

Almost all the tools for managing updates have migrated from the old-style Control Panel to the modern Settings app. In this section, we discuss options that are available in every edition, including Windows 10 Home.

Choosing when updates are installed

If Windows needs to restart your system to complete the installation of an update, you have the option to restart immediately or specify a time when you want the system to restart. If you do neither of these things, Windows Update will restart at a time outside your designated active hours. You can set your normal working hours by clicking Change Active Hours on the main Windows Update page and filling out this dialog box:

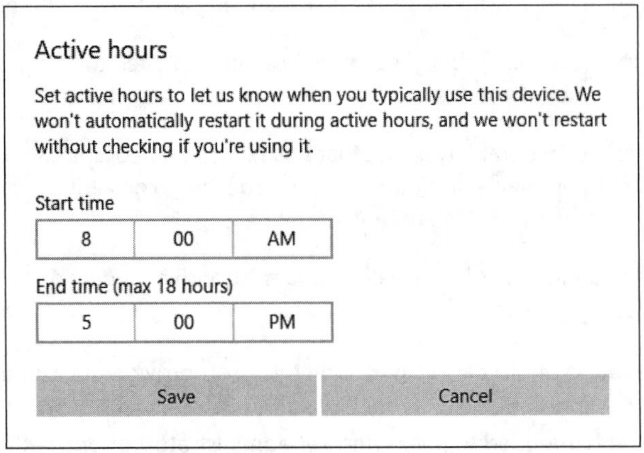

Active hours

Set active hours to let us know when you typically use this device. We won't automatically restart it during active hours, and we won't restart without checking if you're using it.

Start time

8	00	AM

End time (max 18 hours)

5	00	PM

Save	Cancel

The allowable range for prohibiting automatic restarts was increased in version 1703 from 12 to 18 hours. This change should be welcome news to those who work long or variable hours. But even if you're working outside your designated active hours, Windows will not restart your system without notification.

If Windows requires a restart to install one or more updates, you receive a notification in Action Center as well as a similar notification on the main Windows Update page, shown earlier in Figure 5-1.

Restarting immediately, by clicking Restart Now, may be the ideal option if you know you're going to be away from the PC for a meeting or lunch break that will last longer than the few minutes it takes to install a batch of updates. (But watch out for feature updates, which are equivalent to full upgrades and might take as much as an hour or even longer, depending on your hardware.) Save your existing work, close any open files, and then click Restart Now. Be sure to wait for all open apps to close before you head out the door. It's annoying (and a big drag on productivity) to come back from a meeting and discover that the restart hasn't taken place because a dialog box was open, waiting for your approval.

If instead you want to specify a restart time, click Schedule The Restart. You'll see a dialog box like the one shown in Figure 5-3. Slide the switch to the On position and then pick the exact time when you want your PC to restart and begin the installation.

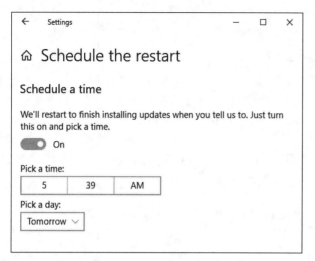

Figure 5-3 If you'd prefer not to have your work interrupted with a restart, even outside your Active Hours settings, enable this option and set a restart time up to one week in the future.

You cannot, of course, postpone this installation indefinitely. Your options on the Pick A Day list include Today, Tomorrow, or any date up to one week from the current day.

Choosing how updates are installed

All editions of Windows 10 include three settings that give you further control over how Windows Update works. Click Advanced Options to see these settings, as shown in Figure 5-4.

If you select Give Me Updates For Other Microsoft Products When I Update Windows, Windows Update expands its scope to include other Microsoft products, such as perpetual-license versions of Microsoft Office. (Office 365 installations use a separate update mechanism.)

The second option, Automatically Download Updates, Even Over Metered Data Connections, applies only if you have configured a metered data network connection, such as an embedded LTE modem or a wireless phone configured as a Wi-Fi hotspot. In those circumstances, Windows normally refrains from downloading updates, out of respect for what is often a pay-as-you-go data plan. Turn this switch to On if you're comfortable that updates won't overrun your data budget.

The final option adds an extra layer of notifications, including pop-up "toast"-style warnings when updates are ready to install.

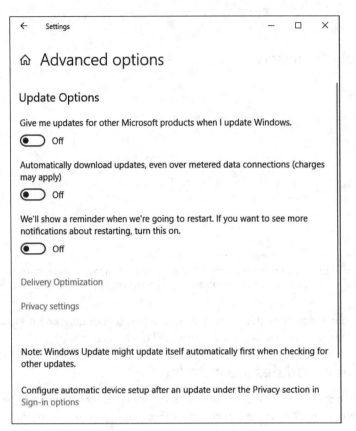

Figure 5-4   The options shown here are available in all Windows 10 editions; on devices running Pro or Enterprise editions, several additional settings are available.

When installing an update entails a restart of your system, Windows normally requires you to sign in before the installation finishes. If you're away from your PC while an upgrade is in progress, you might find the system waiting at the sign-in screen when you return, with additional setup tasks (and additional wait time) after you sign in. You can streamline the process by clicking Sign-in Options, which takes you to the Privacy settings page.

Fine-tuning network bandwidth usage

By definition, Windows Update uses your network connection to download updates for Windows and for Store apps. You can monitor and control network usage by adjusting Delivery Optimization settings. In version 1803 and earlier, you'll find a link to these settings near the bottom of the Advanced Options page. In version 1809, Delivery Optimization gets its own category on the Update & Security page.

These options, which have expanded significantly since the initial release of Windows 10, apply to all Windows 10 editions and allow fine-grained control over the source of updates and the amount of network bandwidth that the update service is allowed to use. You can also check your network bandwidth usage if you're concerned that those updates are slowing down other activities.

The Delivery Optimization page, shown in Figure 5-5, allows you to share updates with other PCs. This peer-to-peer feature, new in Windows 10, is particularly useful if multiple computers in your home or workgroup are likely to be downloading updates over shared bandwidth. By setting Allow Downloads From Other PCs on and choosing PCs On My Local Network, you can share updates with devices on your local network rather than requiring a connection to Microsoft's update servers. The net effect is to reduce usage on your internet connection, which is particularly important if your service provider imposes monthly download quotas.

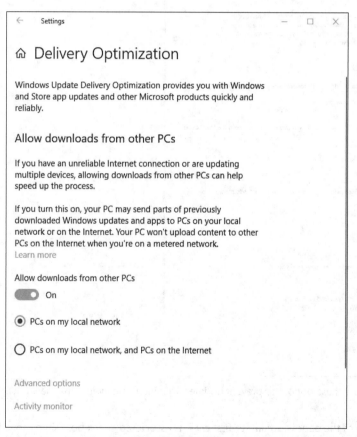

Figure 5-5   Enabling this peer-to-peer option can speed up installation of large updates on a small network, reducing the demands on your internet connection.

The second option expands the range of peer updates to include PCs outside your local network. For a discussion of privacy issues and more information about the delivery optimization process, see *https://bit.ly/wu-delivery-optimization*.

True to its name, the Background Intelligent Transfer Service (BITS) dynamically optimizes bandwidth usage for updates that occur in the background, with the goal of doing so in a way that minimizes the impact of these transfers on other activities. If you prefer more fine-grained control of bandwidth usage, click Advanced Options, near the bottom of the Delivery Optimization page. That opens the Settings page shown in Figure 5-6, which offers control over upload and download speeds as well as allowing you to define upload limits.

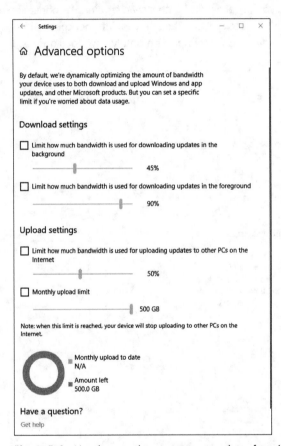

Figure 5-6   Use these options to prevent updates from interfering with other network activity.

To adjust one of the bandwidth limits, first click its associated check box. Then move the slider control left or right. The three bandwidth options can be set to a minimum of 5% and a maximum of 100%. If you prefer to download updates manually and install them as soon as they're available, you might set the second option, Limit How Much Bandwidth Is Used For

Downloading Updates In The Foreground, to its maximum. Conversely, if you have multiple PCs on a small network with a relatively slow shared internet connection, consider setting all PCs to relatively low percentages for uploads and downloads.

The Monthly Upload Limit setting goes from a minimum of 5 GB to a maximum of 500 GB.

If you're curious about the amount of bandwidth that all updates in total have used in the current month, click Activity Monitor (below Advanced Options on the Delivery Optimization page) to display a pair of charts like the ones shown here. The average download speeds are useful for determining whether you need to throttle speeds to avoid affecting other network traffic.

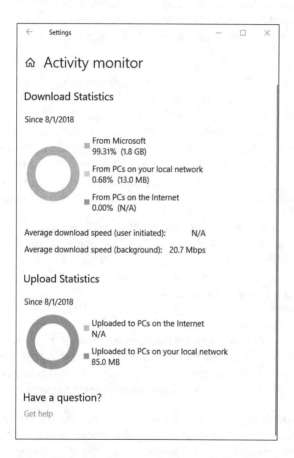

Network administrators can apply even more granular Delivery Optimization settings using Group Policy. These policies, which are available under Administrative Templates > Windows Components > Delivery Optimization, allow you to throttle bandwidth at selected times of day (for both foreground and background traffic), restrict peer selection to the same subnet, automatically join devices into peer groups by using a DHCP server's User option (or the connection's DNS suffix), and prioritize update sharing between peers by delaying the use of the HTTP source.

Deferring and delaying updates

The level of control that administrators have over how and when updates are installed on a device depends on which edition of Windows is installed on that device.

- Devices running Windows 10 Home are assigned to the Semi-Annual Channel (Targeted), and all updates are delivered automatically on a schedule defined by Microsoft's update servers. No options to defer, delay, or pause updates are available on this edition. You don't need to take any additional action aside from observing the occasional reminders to restart your computer and, if you choose, to schedule a restart.

- On devices running Windows 10 Pro, Enterprise, and Education, the default settings are the same as those in Windows 10 Home. As an administrator, however, you can take advantage of additional options collectively known as Windows Update for Business. These controls, available in the Settings app and as part of Group Policy, allow you to shift delivery of feature updates to the Semi-Annual Channel (formerly known as the Current Branch for Business.) That option defers those upgrades until they have been declared ready for deployment by business customers. Additional options allow you to delay installation of quality updates by up to 30 days after they are initially available from Microsoft and to defer installation of feature updates by up to 365 additional days.

- Organizations with a Volume License agreement for Windows have one additional option: They can choose to install Windows 10 Enterprise LTSC/LTSB, which is a part of the Long Term Servicing Channel (formerly the Long Term Servicing Branch). This edition offers 10 years of support and receives no feature updates. For more details about this edition, see "Windows 10 editions at a glance" in Appendix A.

All these Windows Update for Business settings can be found on the Advanced Options page, under the Choose When Updates Are Installed heading, as shown in Figure 5-7. By means of settings here, users of the Pro and Enterprise editions of Windows 10 can change the servicing branch and defer installation of feature and quality updates. These options are also available via Group Policy settings for enterprise administrators, as we explain later in this section.

The first option allows you to change your servicing branch. (The explanatory text in this dialog box still uses the older "branch readiness level" terminology.) Under the default servicing branch, Semi-Annual Channel (Targeted), feature updates are installed when they become available. If you change the servicing branch to Semi-Annual Channel, updates will be deferred until Microsoft has declared them ready for widespread use in organizations.

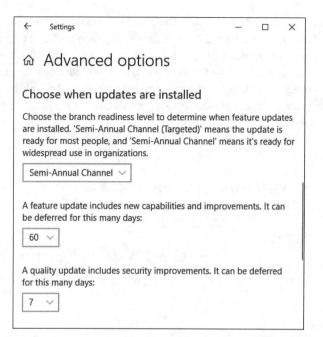

Figure 5-7   These Windows Update settings, available only on Pro, Enterprise, and Education editions, allow administrators to defer quality and feature updates.

The second option allows you to defer feature updates by an additional period of up to 365 days from the time they are made available to the servicing branch you selected above. In Figure 5-7 above, we've set a deferral of 60 days in addition to assigning this device to the Semi-Annual Channel. This has the practical effect of delaying a feature update for roughly four months, and perhaps longer, depending on how long it takes Microsoft to declare the update ready for the Semi-Annual Channel.

The third option allows deferral of quality updates—the cumulative updates that include security and reliability enhancements—by up to 30 days. Selecting a deferral of 7 days, as we've done in Figure 5-7 above, effectively gives you a week to monitor feedback from Microsoft support channels after the regular release of updates on the second Tuesday of each month. If you discover a problem that might affect your PC, you can use the Pause Updates option to delay installation further while you either find a workaround or wait for Microsoft to resolve the issue.

Both deferral settings are persistent.

If you need to pause updates for only a period of time—for example, if you plan to be traveling and don't want to be bothered with the update process—use the Pause Updates switch. Windows Update will refrain from updating your system for 35 days or until you set the Pause Updates switch back to Off.

As we noted earlier, you can also apply Windows Update for Business settings using Group Policy, either as part of a Windows domain using Active Directory or using the Local Group Policy Editor, Gpedit.msc. In releases of Windows 10 up to and including version 1703, the only way to configure Windows Update for Business was through Group Policy. In Windows 10 version 1709 and later, these policy settings are available in Computer Configuration > Administrative Templates > Windows Components > Windows Update > Windows Update For Business. Figure 5-8 shows an example of these policies.

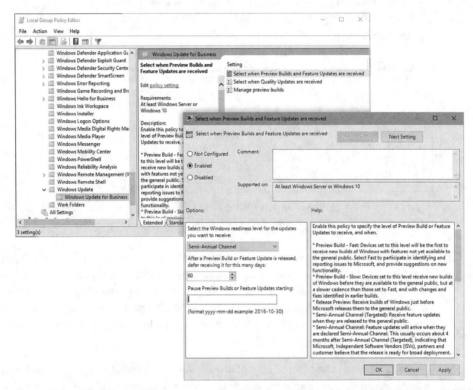

Figure 5-8   Using Group Policy, you can adjust Windows Update for Business settings to defer feature updates. The options shown here defer a feature update until 60 days after Microsoft declares it ready for widespread deployment.

The three policies available for configuration are as follows:

- **Select When Preview Builds And Feature Updates Are Received.** Configure this policy to defer feature updates. After you enable this policy, you can select the "Windows readiness level" that corresponds to the servicing channel. In addition to the Semi-Annual Channel (Targeted) and Semi-Annual Channel options that are available in Settings, this policy also allows you to choose one of three Insider Preview channels. You can then specify an amount of time to defer the update after release. This value is entered in days, with possible values ranging from 0 to 365.

- **Select When Quality Updates Are Received.** With this policy, you can defer the regular cumulative updates (which include security, reliability, and driver updates) for up to 30 days. Deferring quality updates requires a balancing act: Configuring this policy gives you an opportunity to test the latest update on a subset of PCs in your organization before deploying the update widely; that delay can also put your other machines at risk because they haven't received potentially important security fixes.

- **Manage Preview Builds.** This policy, new in Windows 10 version 1709, includes the options to enable or disable preview builds, as you might expect. A third option, Disable Preview Builds Once Next Release Is Public, prevents preview builds from installing after a preview cycle ends and the corresponding feature update is released to the public.

Inside Out

The Windows Update calendar includes more than one Tuesday

Microsoft delivers most scheduled updates on the second Tuesday of each month. Update Tuesday (more commonly known as Patch Tuesday) is the primary day for delivering monthly updates, and it is the only regular release that includes new security fixes.

Additional nonsecurity updates are released on the third and fourth weeks of the month, respectively. (Microsoft refers to these as the "C" and "D" releases, in contrast to the "B" releases on Update Tuesday. Scheduled updates are never released on the first Tuesday of the month, the "A" week.) These are preview releases that are not delivered automatically; they are intended to allow administrators to test the nonsecurity fixes that will be shipped as part of the following month's "B" release.

On rare occasions, an *out-of-band release* appears on Windows Update to fix an urgent security vulnerability (typically one that is being actively exploited) or to resolve a quality issue that has widespread impact. Because out-of-band updates are both urgent and rare, they are issued without respect to the calendar.

Troubleshooting update problems

In our experience, Windows Update is generally reliable, but problems can and do occur. These problems fall into a handful of categories: updates that cause stability problems; updates that fail to install properly; and general problems with Windows Update.

For updates that cause problems, the first step is to remove the offending update. (For particularly nettlesome problems, this might require booting into Safe Mode.) Go to Settings > Update & Security > Windows Update. Click View Update History to display the list of installed updates (as described earlier in this chapter) and then click the unobtrusive Uninstall Updates link at the top of that page.

Doing so takes you back to the old-style Control Panel, where you'll find an inventory of everything that Windows Update has installed for Windows itself and for other Microsoft products, as well as a smattering of updates for third-party products that register those updates with Windows. From this page, as shown in Figure 5-9, you can confirm that a particular update has been installed by referring to its KB number in the list of installed items. Some items may include a support link at the bottom of the page—this leads you to details about the selected update. The Uninstall option appears above the list when you select an update. Click that option to remove the update, but do so only as a last resort, and only when your troubleshooting leads you to suspect that a recently installed update is causing serious performance or reliability issues.

> ➤ **For information about uninstalling a problematic device driver, see "Uninstalling a driver," in Chapter 14, "Hardware and devices."**

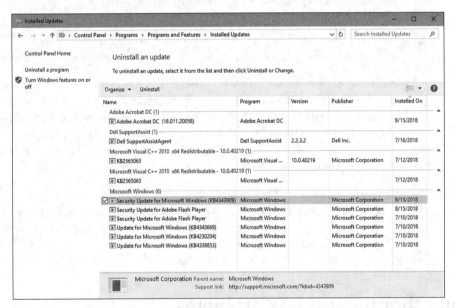

Figure 5-9   If an update is causing problems, you can select it from this list and use the Uninstall option to remove it for troubleshooting purposes.

That action (after a restart) removes the immediate problem. But because of the way Windows Update works, the unwanted item will reappear the next time Windows checks for updates. You can interrupt this cycle by "hiding" the offending update.

To do this, you need to run the Show Or Hide Updates troubleshooter package, which you can download from *https://support.microsoft.com/kb/3073930*. The troubleshooter presents a list of updates that can be hidden. Select the item that you don't want to reinstall. The ruse is temporary, but it should give you respite until a revised update becomes available. For more details about how to use this troubleshooter with problematic hardware drivers, see "Uninstalling a driver," in Chapter 14.

TROUBLESHOOTING

Windows Update is stuck in a reboot loop

In some cases, Windows Update can get stuck in a loop, failing to complete the installation of one or more updates and continually repeating the unsuccessful update process each time you restart.

The solution? Reset Windows Update completely, removing content from the update cache and starting with fresh downloads. In most cases, that's enough to get things unstuck.

Microsoft created a help resource for diagnosing and fixing Windows Update problems, which is available at *https://support.microsoft.com/kb/971058*. The process involves stopping several services, removing the folder containing updates in progress, and reregistering a list of system files. You can download a troubleshooter that performs these steps automatically from *https://aka.ms/wudiag*.

CHAPTER 5

CHAPTER 6

Installing and configuring modern apps and desktop apps

As the title of this chapter suggests, the programs you can run on Microsoft Windows 10 fall into two broad categories. One category consists of so-called *desktop applications*. These are the programs you might have and could have run under Windows 7 and earlier versions. Windows 10 continues to support such programs. (You might also see these programs described as *Win32 applications*.) These traditional applications are designed, for the most part, for use with a keyboard and a mouse, and many of them first came into being during the era when desktop machines dominated the computing landscape.

The other category consists of programs delivered through the Microsoft Store. These programs, optimized for touch, ink, and mobile use (although equally usable on desktop systems with traditional input devices), are variously called *modern apps, trusted Microsoft Store apps,* or *UWP apps*. Windows favors the term *Trusted Microsoft Store app*. If you enter the name of one of these programs in the search box on your taskbar, you see something like the following:

Alarms & Clock
Trusted Microsoft Store app

In this book, for the sake of simplicity, we favor the designation *modern app*, but Windows opts for the wordier handle for good reason. These apps, available only through Microsoft Store—or "sideloaded" with an administrator's permission in managed enterprise environments—have passed a stringent vetting process and can be trusted to be free of malware. They are also "sandboxed," which means they run in secure isolation, free from potentially hazardous interactions with other running processes.

The current name for the development platform is *Universal Windows Platform*, or *UWP*. The keyword here is *universal*. The platform offers a core application programming interface (API) that developers can use to create a single app package, which in turn can be installed on devices with a wide range of sizes and modalities. UWP apps use adaptive controls that tailor the app's behavior to the size and feature set of the target machine. In short, a program you download from Microsoft Store to your tablet can also work on your traditional desktop or notebook PC, an all-in-one device, an Xbox console, or even the HoloLens wearable computer.

In 2016, Microsoft introduced a hybrid app type that combines the capabilities of older desktop apps in a modern package that can be distributed through Microsoft Store. Developers can use the Desktop Bridge tools to convert apps that meet proper standards, including the ability to run as a standard interactive user, with no reliance on kernel-mode drivers or Windows services. The resulting package can be distributed using Microsoft Store to control licensing and enforce security. Optionally, the developer can choose to add UWP features, such as the ability to display live tiles, to the app.

> ➤ For more details on this technology, see the developer-focused documentation for the Desktop to Universal Windows Platform (UWP) Bridge, at *https://bit.ly/DesktopUWPBridge*. The Desktop App Converter is available in Microsoft Store at *https://aka.ms/converter*.

EVOLUTION OF MODERN APPS

UWP apps are the latest step in a years-long progression toward creating a development platform that simplifies work for software developers, makes finding and purchasing apps easier for consumers, and provides a consistent user experience across a range of devices. The efforts started with the release of Windows 8 and the Windows Runtime (WinRT), a common application architecture. With the move to Windows 8.1 and Windows Phone 8.1, developers could create *universal Windows 8 apps*. Although developers could then use a common codebase for Windows and Windows Phone, they still had to create a separate app package for each of the two operating systems, with each offered in a separate Microsoft Store.

Windows 10 advanced the marker with the further development of the Windows Runtime model, now dubbed Universal Windows Platform. UWP provides a common app platform that is available on every device that runs Windows 10—IoT (Internet of Things) devices, mobile devices, PCs, Xbox, HoloLens, and so on. In addition to using the WinRT application programming interfaces (APIs) that are common to all devices, programmers can call on APIs that are specific to a particular device family. They can then create a single app package that can be installed on any Windows 10 device and offered in a single, unified Microsoft Store.

In a direct reflection of this blurring of app categories, Windows 10 gives the Apps category its own top-level heading in Settings. The resulting Apps & Features list (which we discuss in more detail later in this chapter) includes both modern apps and desktop programs. Above this list, you'll find the option, introduced in version 1703, to specify whether apps can be installed from locations other than the Store.

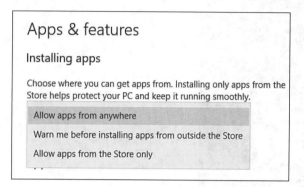

What's in a modern app

Here are some important characteristics of modern apps:

- **Tiles.** Each app gets a tile, which can be displayed on Start or not, as you choose. To add an app to Start, press the Windows key, scroll through the list of apps until you find the one you want, right-click the name of the app, and choose Pin To Start. (You can use similar steps to pin an app to the taskbar or to unpin an app from either location; when you right-click the app, click More to see these options.)

- **Live tiles.** Tiles can be programmed to update dynamically when they're displayed on Start—that is, they can become *live tiles*. Live tiles, for example, can display news headlines, cycle through a set of photos, show calendar information, and so on. If you find a tile to be livelier than you would like, you can render it inanimate by right-clicking it. Then click More, and click Turn Live Tile Off.

- **Notifications and alerts.** Apps can trigger notifications and alerts. To take one example, your calendar app can display appointment information on your lock screen and issue reminders at the appropriate times.

- **Easy sharing between apps.** The capability to pass data between modern apps has been part of the Windows platform since its dawn. The available options vary depending on the current selection and the list of installed modern apps. The redesigned Share panel shown here, for example, offers options for sharing a single image from the OneDrive Pictures folder and is available with a tap on the Share icon in the Photos app.

- **Cortana.** Apps can be integrated with Cortana, allowing you to do such things as issue a voice command to send an email.

- **Security and safety.** Modern apps are prevented from accessing system resources. They also don't store their own configuration information in publicly accessible places, such as .ini files.

- **The ability to run without administrative consent.** Because modern apps are designed to work in a sandbox and can't interact with the operating system except through approved methods, you don't need an administrative token to install or run them. You won't find Run As Administrator on the shortcut menu of a modern app; there's no need for it.

- **Power conservation.** By default, a modern app is suspended within a few seconds if you move away from it. This behavior is particularly valuable on battery-driven systems. Apps can be written to run in the background (allowing you, for example, to play music while you work), but this is an exceptional case.

- **Automatic updates.** Modern apps are updated automatically. Microsoft Store efficiently manages this process for you when an app's publisher makes changes to a program.

- **Per-user installation.** When you install an app, that app is installed only for your user account. Other account holders who want to use the app have to install it as well. Depending on licensing provisions and the number of devices on which you have installed the app in question, other accounts on a system where an app has already been bought and installed might find, on visiting Microsoft Store, that the app is identified as "owned." In that case, these users can install the app without going through a payment process. The same is true for other systems you sign in to with the Microsoft account under which you bought the app.

- **Application-specific volume control.** Beginning with Version 1709, you can set individual volume controls for modern apps that generate sound. If you want to turn down your music player, for example, while maintaining full sound output from Microsoft Edge, you can right-click the speaker icon on your taskbar, click Open Volume Mixer, and then make the desired adjustments. Note that applications appear in Volume Mixer only after they have started to play.

Inside OUT

Develop modern apps

If you're a software developer who's interested in creating UWP apps, Microsoft offers plenty of resources for more information. You'll find a comprehensive collection of information about UWP app development, including links to how-to articles, in the Windows Dev Center at *https://bit.ly/develop-uwp-apps.*

Browsing Microsoft Store

Microsoft Store (shown in Figure 6-1), much improved and expanded since its debut with Windows 8, is your emporium for games, movies, and TV shows, as well as modern Windows apps. (And, since the introduction of Windows 10 version 1703, it has also included the option to buy ebooks that can be read in Microsoft Edge.) Using the menu across the top of the Microsoft Store page, you can switch between these various kinds of offerings. Below the display ad, you'll find some items that Microsoft Store thinks you might be interested in, based on what you downloaded earlier. Further down is a sort of categorized bestseller list—top free games, games that have received stellar ratings from other users, "new and rising" items, and so on.

If you know more or less what you're looking for, you can use the search box to find it. You can search by name or publisher, and the search results will include entertainment offerings as well as apps.

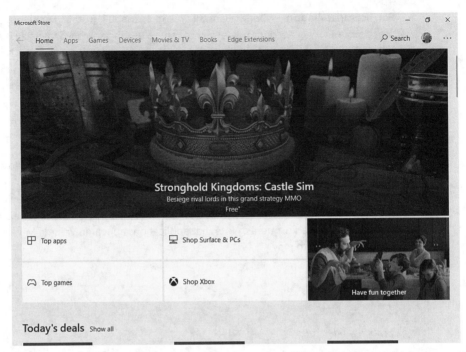

Figure 6-1 Microsoft Store offers a categorized selection of items it thinks you might want to download. Use Search to find what you actually want.

The offerings in Microsoft Store are not organized by price, but if you type **free** in the Search box, you will get a filtered list showing only free items. When you consider the cost of an item, however, you should check to see if the price is adorned with an asterisk and the notation that the app comes with "in-app purchases." This is a delicate way of alerting you that the app, once installed, will give you the opportunity to buy extra goodies. Some apps are quite low-key about this; others have been known to be nearly useless without at least some of the extra items. When you click on an item, the details page that appears might enumerate the extra offerings.

Scrolling to the bottom of an app's details page usually reveals additional useful details, such as the approximate size of the app, the system resources the app is permitted to use, and the number of devices on which the app can be installed.

Buying an app

To begin the process of installing a new app, simply click its price. If money is required, the payment process is managed through your Microsoft account. If your Windows 10 user account signs in locally, rather than through a Microsoft account, you'll be prompted at this point for

Microsoft account credentials, and you'll be guided to create such an account and configure a payment mechanism if you haven't already done so.

While the app is being downloaded and installed, you can follow its progress. A status message—along with Pause and Cancel buttons—appears on the details page in place of the purchase button. Or, if you click the download indicator in the menu bar, you can view the progress of this installation as well as others you queued for download and apps that have been recently installed, as shown in Figure 6-2. (Effective with Windows 10 version 1703, this information is also visible in Action Center, allowing you to track the progress of a download without having to continually return to the Store app.)

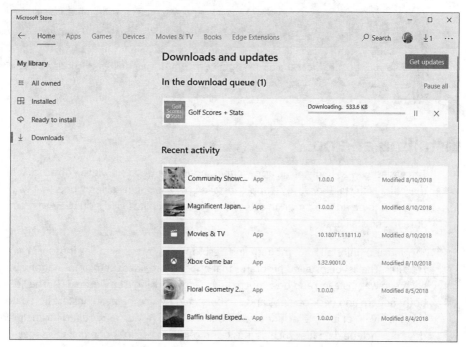

Figure 6-2   While one or more downloads are in progress, an indicator appears in the menu bar. Clicking that indicator displays this list of current and recent downloads.

Next to the progress indicator—either on the details page or the Downloads And Updates page—you can also pause or cancel a download. You might want to pause if you have several lengthy downloads going at once and want to prioritize them.

CHAPTER 6

Inside OUT

Get updates and more information about Microsoft Store apps

On the Downloads And Updates page (shown in Figure 6-2), clicking or tapping the name of any app takes you directly to the details page for that app in Microsoft Store. A button in the upper-right corner lets you check for and retrieve updates to Microsoft Store apps at any time. (In theory, checking for updates shouldn't be necessary because Microsoft Store apps periodically check for and install updates automatically. But if your computer has been offline for an extended time, you might want to oversee the updating process.)

You can display the Downloads And Updates page at any time—even when the download indicator shown in Figure 6-2 is not displayed. Simply click or tap the ellipsis next to your picture (near the upper-right corner of the window) and choose Downloads And Updates.

Uninstalling an app

The easiest way to uninstall an app—either modern or desktop—is to right-click it on Start and then click Uninstall. Because an app is installed per user, uninstalling works that way as well; if you want to be rid of a program everywhere it has been installed, you need to repeat the procedure to uninstall it.

You can also uninstall both modern and desktop apps by opening Settings > Apps > Apps & Features. The list of installed programs that appears provides useful information about when each app was installed and how much disk space it is using (see Figure 6-3). The list includes both modern and desktop apps and can be sorted by size, name, or installation date. Note that the size given for an app includes executable files and resources required for the program. It does not include data files such as music and photo collections or email messages.

If your computer has more than one drive, the Move button for some apps allows you to move the app to a different drive. The entry for a desktop app might display a Modify button, which you can use to add or remove optional features.

To uninstall an app from the Apps & Features list, click its name and then click the Uninstall button.

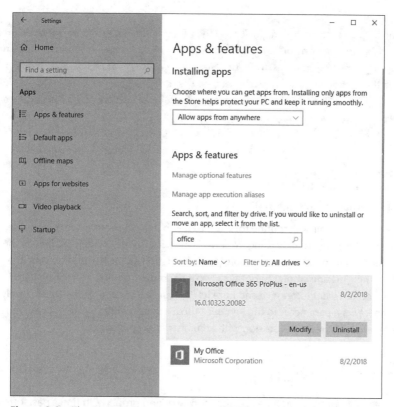

Figure 6-3 The Apps & Features section provides a way to uninstall both modern and desktop apps.

CHAPTER 6

Inside OUT

Find the version number of an app

You'll sometimes need to know the version number of an installed app. Having that number might help, for example, when you're troubleshooting a problem and a support article says something like "this problem has been fixed in version 8.0.20623.2."

Different methods for modern apps and desktop programs reveal the version number.

For a modern app, open Microsoft Store, click the ellipsis next to your picture, and click Downloads And Updates to display a screen similar to the one shown earlier in Figure 6-2. The version number is displayed next to the name of each app.

For desktop programs, you have two places to look. On the Apps & Features page in Settings, use the search box or scroll through the list to find its entry, and then click to see full details for the program, including the version number. Alternatively, open Programs And Features in Control Panel. (In addition to the usual search methods, you'll find a link to Programs And Features at the bottom of the Apps & Features page in Settings.) You'll see the version number for each installed desktop program in a column at the right side of the window. The version number for each program also appears at the bottom of the window when you select that program in the list.

TROUBLESHOOTING

Modern apps won't uninstall

If the normal uninstall routine for a modern app doesn't seem to work, you can remove the troublesome item by using Windows PowerShell. (See Chapter 19, "PowerShell and other advanced management tools," for information about PowerShell.) Use the Get-AppxPackage cmdlet to obtain a list of packages installed on your system. Find the one you want to remove and note its *PackageFullName* property. Then supply this property as a parameter to the Remove-AppxPackage cmdlet. Note that you must be working in a PowerShell session with administrative privileges.

Resetting a modern app

For a variety of reasons, sometimes an app stops working properly. In times past, often the suggested solution was to uninstall and reinstall an app in the hope that would produce a clean installation with default settings. Unfortunately, this approach didn't always work because some settings and data weren't deleted as part of the uninstall process.

Effective with Windows 10 version 1607, there's a better way to repair a modern app that's misbehaving: reset it. Follow these steps:

1. Open Settings > Apps > Apps & Features.

2. Select the app you want to reset, and then click Advanced Options.

3. Click Reset, and then (after reading the warning) click Reset again.

As an alternative to steps 1 and 2 in this sequence, you can right-click an app in Start, click More on the menu that appears, and then click App Settings. The App Settings command, introduced in Windows 10 version 1803, takes you directly to the app's Advanced Options page.

Note that resetting an app permanently deletes all currently saved data and settings for that app. After resetting an app, you need to sign in again (if the app requires it) and re-create your preferences.

Managing permissions and other settings

The Advanced Options page for an app, in addition to offering the potentially handy Reset button just described, also provides access to a variety of other useful and interesting settings. In the following illustration, for example, we see that the Weather app has been granted two permissions—to know our current location and to run as a background process when another app has the focus:

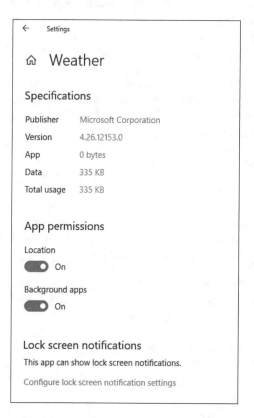

If you've ever granted location permission to an app, you have likely seen a message telling you that you can rescind that permission in Settings. Here is where you would withdraw permission, should you choose to do so.

This illustration also indicates that the Weather app has been permitted to display notifications on the Lock Screen. Clicking the Configure link below this statement would take you to Settings > Personalization > Lock Screen, where you could make any desired adjustments.

Managing line-of-business apps

Enterprises can develop line-of-business (LOB) apps for use within their organizations. Such apps can be deployed either through a private Business Store—managed and deployed by Microsoft Store—or through a process called *sideloading*.

The process of distributing a Windows 10 app through a private Business Store requires that an enterprise have Azure Active Directory accounts for each user in the organization. (These accounts are used instead of Microsoft accounts.) Installation files are managed and deployed by Microsoft Store, which also tracks license usage. Updates are delivered via normal update channels—Windows Update or Windows Server Update Services (WSUS).

LOB apps distributed within an organization without using Microsoft Store don't need to be signed by Microsoft and don't require Azure Active Directory accounts. They do need to be signed with a certificate that's trusted by one of the trusted root authorities on the system. Using a sideloaded app requires three steps:

1. **Turn on sideloading.** In a domain environment, this can be done with Group Policy. For an unmanaged computer, go to Settings > Update & Security > For Developers. Then select Sideload Apps.

2. **Trust the app.** Open the security certificate provided for the app package and choose Install Certificate. In the Certificate Import wizard, select Local Machine and import the certificate to the Trusted Root Certification Authorities folder.

3. **Install the app.** Open PowerShell in the folder with the app package, and then run the Add-AppxPackage cmdlet. Organizations that use mobile device management software can also use that mechanism to deploy packages over the network.

In addition to creating and deploying apps, administrators can use Group Policy to control the use of all apps, including those that are supplied by Windows itself. For example, an organization might choose to remove the Movies & TV app or prohibit it from running.

Apps included with Windows 10

In Windows 10 version 1809, the list of provisioned programs includes the following:

- **Alarms & Clock** shows world time and acts as an alarm, stopwatch, and timer.

- **Calculator** includes a programmer mode (specialized for bitwise operations on binary, octal, and hexadecimal values) along with the more common standard and scientific modes, and it can serve as a handy converter for measurements of volume, length, angles, time, and so on. Beginning with Version 1709, Calculator also performs currency conversions.

- **Calendar** keeps track of appointments and other events. (For details, see Chapter 7.)

- **Camera** captures still images and video.

- **Connect** allows you to use your computer as an extended screen from your phone or other device; when using Windows 10 mobile, this feature is sometimes referred to as *Continuum*.

- **Cortana** is a digital personal assistant; for details, see Chapter 10, "Cortana and Windows Search."

- **Feedback Hub** allows anyone to share bug reports and suggestions with the Windows development team. (Before filing a bug report, use the search box to see if someone else has already reported your issue; if so, you can click Upvote to add your "me too" to that report.)

- **Get Help** puts you in touch with Microsoft's Virtual Agent. You can tell your troubles to the agent, and if that doesn't solve your problem, you can ask to speak to a live human.

- **Groove Music** is a music player. (For details, see Chapter 7.)

- **Mail** creates, sends, receives, and manages email. (For details, see Chapter 7.)

- **Maps** displays maps and aerial photos along with directions between points. (For details, see Chapter 7.)

- **Messaging** shows messages you've sent and received using apps such as Skype. It can't send SMS texts directly, and it only displays SMS texts from mobile operators about data usage on devices with built-in wireless data connectivity.

- **Microsoft Edge** is the modern web browser in Windows 10; for details, see Chapter 8, "Microsoft Edge and Internet Explorer."

- **OneDrive** manages synchronization with your OneDrive cloud storage; for details, see Chapter 9, "Storage and file management."

- **My Office**, an updated version of the Get Office app that was included with Version 1703, provides details about your Office 365 subscription and lists Office files that you have recently worked with.

- **Microsoft Solitaire Collection** includes an updated version of the classic Klondike time-waster, along with four other solo card games and online challenges and tournaments.

- **Microsoft Store**, formerly known as Windows Store, is the place to obtain modern apps of all kinds; see "Browsing Microsoft Store" earlier in this chapter.

- **Movies & TV** plays videos that you create, purchase, or rent. (For details, see Chapter 7.)

CHAPTER 6

- **Microsoft News** provides headlines and links for current news on subjects (and from sources) of your choosing.

- **OneNote** is a place for creating, storing, and managing notes of all kinds.

- **Paint 3D** was introduced in Windows 10 version 1703; for details about how it differs from the classic Paint app, see "Paint 3D," in Chapter 7.

- **People** keeps track of contact information. (For details, see Chapter 7.)

- **Photos** stores, organizes, and displays your collection of pictures, (For details, see Chapter 7.)

- **Skype** is an app for communicating with others via text message or video conferencing.

- **Snip & Sketch** is a tool for capturing and editing screen images. Snip & Sketch, introduced in version 1809, is a more versatile program than Snipping Tool, which is still included but will eventually be phased out.

- **Sticky Notes** provides a place to jot notes—notes that can be enhanced with information from Cortana, turned into a pop-up reminder, and more.

- **Tips** offers videos and other instructional material about Windows 10.

- **Voice Recorder** captures notes in audible form.

- **Weather** displays current conditions and detailed forecasts for locations around the world.

- **Xbox** connects you to the world of computer gaming in genres ranging from card games to shoot-em-ups.

- **Your Phone** connects your Windows 10 device to your Android device, allowing you to send and receive text messages and view the most recent 25 photos taken on your phone.

Previous versions of Windows 10 also included informative apps called Money and Sports. These are now available for free in Microsoft Store, under the names MSN Money and MSN Sports.

Windows 10 also includes the full complement of small programs that have been part of Windows for decades: Notepad, Paint, Character Map, WordPad, and the like. You can find these programs under Windows Accessories in the list of apps on Start.

Installing, running, and managing desktop applications

With only a few rare exceptions, Windows 10 supports virtually all desktop applications that are compatible with Windows 7. If you upgraded from Windows 7 (or from a Windows 8.1 system that itself was upgraded from Windows 7), all your desktop applications from the earlier environment should be happy and ready to go. Desktop programs can be installed anew in the usual ways, from installation media or by download from the internet.

Desktop programs appear in the apps list on Start (or on Start tiles if you put them there) alongside modern apps. Indeed, since the not-so-glorious days of Windows 8 in which switching between modern and desktop apps was a jarring change that made it appear that you were using two completely different operating systems, it's increasingly difficult to differentiate between the two types of apps. They both run in resizable windows on the desktop, and they share many similar features.

You might notice a few differences on Start: desktop applications installed using traditional installer programs do not have a live tile (but then, not all modern apps do either). And as shown in Figure 6-4, the shortcut menu that appears if you right-click is a bit different.

Figure 6-4   When you right-click an app on Start, the menu that appears is slightly different for a modern app (top) than for a desktop application (bottom).

The Run As Administrator and Open File Location commands do not appear on this menu for modern apps. Running modern apps with administrative privileges is never required because such apps don't have the ability to mess with system files. Open File Location is absent from modern app shortcut menus because modern apps are defined by *package* data structures (in %LocalAppData%\Packages), and Windows assumes (correctly) that you have no need to inspect these structures.

Knowing where to find executable files for desktop apps is useful if you like to create shortcuts to your programs. For example, if you were accustomed to having shortcuts on your desktop to the programs you most frequently use, there's no reason not to populate your Windows 10 desktop the same way. Use Start's shortcut menu to go to a program's file location. (That actually takes you to the shortcut's location in the Start Menu folder; if you do want to go to the folder where the program's files are stored, right-click that shortcut in File Explorer and choose

Open File Location.) Then right-click the item in the Start Menu folder and click Create Shortcut. Windows informs you that you can't create a shortcut in that location, but it offers to create a shortcut on the desktop—which is just what you set out to do.

> ## Inside OUT
>
> *Another difference for modern apps: file location*
>
> The executable file (along with supporting files) for a desktop application is normally stored in a subfolder of %ProgramFiles% or %ProgramFiles(x86)%. By contrast, modern apps are stored in a hidden folder called %ProgramFiles%\WindowsApps. This folder is locked so that only Microsoft Store or the Windows System account can view, run, or modify its contents. Although that might frustrate folks who like to crawl through every hidden nook and cranny of their hard drive, there's a good reason for the high security: unlike for most desktop applications, the entire app package is signed, making it possible to validate the contents of any or all files in the package. Instead of running an executable file and calling other resources, Windows runs the entire package in a protected app container environment. Because users (including you) and other apps are prevented from making changes, the app files are safe.
>
> If you're intent on seeing what's in the WindowsApps folder, there is a back door. (Don't worry: although you can view the folder directories, you can't make any changes.) The following steps will get you there:
>
> 1. Open Task Manager. (For details, see "Managing programs and processes with Task Manager," later in this chapter.)
>
> 2. On the Processes tab, right-click the name of a modern app of interest.
>
> 3. In the menu that appears, click Go To Details, which highlights the app's executable on the Details tab of Task Manager.
>
> 4. Right-click, choose Open File Location, and you're in.
>
> 5. Note that system apps, including Microsoft Edge and Cortana, are stored in a different location: C:\Windows\SystemApps.

Running desktop applications as an administrator or another user

As in Windows 7, some desktop applications must be run with an administrative token. If you want to edit the registry, for example, you need to run Registry Editor (regedit.exe) as an administrator. You can run a program as an administrator by right-clicking the executable file or any shortcut for the program (on Start or elsewhere), choosing Run As Administrator, and satisfying the User Account Control (UAC) prompt with either consent or credentials. Here are two additional ways to do it:

- Start a Command Prompt session as Administrator: press Windows key+X and then choose Command Prompt (Admin). If you see two PowerShell options on the Quick Link menu, click PowerShell (Admin) and then type **cmd** from the PowerShell prompt to open a Command Prompt window. There, you can type the name of the executable file for whichever program you want to run as an administrator.

  To run Registry Editor, for example, type **regedit**. Because you already passed UAC inspection for the Command Prompt session, and because whatever you run from Command Prompt is a child process of Command Prompt, you don't have to deal with any further UAC prompts. This method is excellent for situations where you need to run a sequence of programs as an administrator. Keep one administrative-level Command Prompt window open, and run your programs from the command line.

- Type the name of the program you want to run in the taskbar search box, and then press Ctrl+Shift+Enter.

To run a program under a different user account, you can use the Runas command. You can do this from Command Prompt. The syntax is

```
Runas /user:username programname
```

Inside OUT

Use Steps Recorder to troubleshoot misbehaving software

When you need to report details about a software problem to a tech support person, the Steps Recorder tool can prove valuable. Run this program by typing **steps** in the taskbar search box and then clicking the Steps Recorder item that appears. Click Start Record, retrace your steps through the problematic program, and then click Stop Record.

Steps Recorder takes a screenshot and time stamp at each crucial juncture (each mouse click or command) and then appends a verbal description of each step. You can add your own comments along the way. After you stop and save your recording, you can share it with tech support. (Steps Recorder is also an excellent tool for creating documentation to be used by others in your organization.)

After you issue the command, you're prompted to enter the password for the specified user account. Note that the Runas command does not work with File Explorer or with Microsoft Management Console (MMC) snap-ins.

Dealing with compatibility issues

As mentioned, programs that run without problems on Windows 7 should run equally well on Windows 10. Certain older desktop applications might create problems, however. Windows attempts to flag potential compatibility problems when you first run such a program. The Program Compatibility Assistant that appears offers you the alternatives of checking online for solutions (such as downloading a more recent version) or going ahead and running the program.

If you install a program and subsequently run into compatibility issues, a program compatibility troubleshooter might appear. Alternatively, you can run the troubleshooter yourself from Control Panel. You can find it by typing **compatibility** in the Control Panel search box. Under the heading Programs And Features, you'll find the link Run Programs Made For Previous Versions Of Windows. Click this link to launch the troubleshooter, and then click past the opening screen.

The troubleshooter begins by scanning for problems it can detect automatically. If it finds none, it presents a list of applications installed on your system from which you can select the one that's giving you difficulty. Select the offending program and follow the prompts to try to resolve your problem.

Managing programs and processes with Task Manager

Task Manager is a tool that serves two essential purposes. You can use it to track aspects of your system's performance and to see what programs and processes are running, and you can use it to terminate items when the normal shutdown methods aren't working.

> ➤ For information about using Task Manager to monitor system performance, see Chapter 12, "Performance and power management."

The easiest way to run Task Manager is by means of its keyboard shortcut, Ctrl+Shift+Esc. Without a keyboard, right-click or long-tap the taskbar or search box and choose Task Manager. Figure 6-5 shows the Processes tab of Task Manager. If you don't see a tabular layout similar to that shown in Figure 6-5, click More Details at the bottom of the window.

By default, the items listed on the Processes tab are grouped by type—apps at the top, followed by background processes, Windows processes, and so on. Grouping is optional; clear Group By Type on the View menu if you want a single list.

Note that some items in the Apps list have outline controls. You can expand these to see what files or documents are open. In Figure 6-5, for example, the Microsoft Management Console entry has been expanded to reveal the name of the snap-in (Hyper-V Manager) that's currently open. The lists are initially sorted in ascending alphabetical order. Click a heading to reverse the sort. You can also click one of the performance headings to see which processes are using resources on your system. Clicking CPU, for example, gives you a constantly updating readout of how your apps and background processes are taxing the CPU.

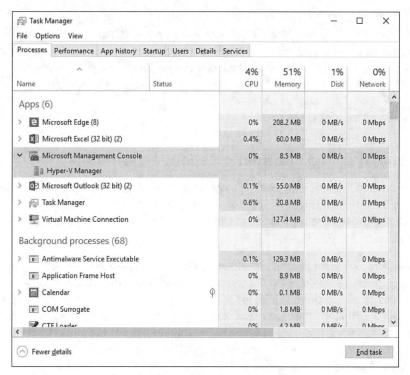

Figure 6-5   Task Manager is useful for terminating recalcitrant applications and processes, as well as for monitoring system performance.

Terminating a program with Task Manager

The Processes tab also includes a Status column. (If it's not visible, right-click a column heading and choose Status.) Most of the time, the entries in this column will be blank, indicating that everything is humming along. If an app hangs for any reason, you'll see the words *Not Responding* in this column. In that case, you can attempt to shut down the miscreant by right-clicking its name and clicking End Task. Don't be too quick on the trigger, however; Not Responding doesn't necessarily mean permanently out to lunch. If the program is using every bit of resources to handle a different task, it might simply be too busy to communicate with Task Manager.

Before you decide to end the program, give it a chance to finish whatever it's doing. How long should you wait? That depends on the task. If the operation involves a large data set (performing a global search-and-replace in a large Microsoft Access database, for instance), it's appropriate to wait several minutes, especially if you see signs of disk activity. But if the task in question normally completes in a few seconds, you needn't wait that long.

Inside OUT

Be smart about shutdowns

When you shut down an app by clicking End Task, Task Manager zaps the item immediately and irrevocably, closing any open files without giving you a chance to save them. (This is equivalent to choosing End Process on the Processes tab of the Windows 7 Task Manager.) Whenever possible, you should try to close the program by the normal methods before resorting to End Task.

Finding detailed information about a program

To see detailed information about the process that's running an app, right-click the app and choose Go To Details. This takes you to a related item on the Details tab. Right-clicking Microsoft Outlook, for example, takes you to Outlook.exe, the name of Outlook's executable file (see Figure 6-6).

For each process, Task Manager includes the following information by default: image name (the name of the process), process ID (PID), status (running or suspended, for example), user name (the name of the account that initiated the process), CPU (the percentage of the CPU's capacity the process is currently using), memory (the amount of memory the process requires to perform its regular functions, also known as the private working set), and description (a text field identifying the process). To display additional information for each process, right-click one of the headings and choose Select Columns.

Inside OUT

Go online to read about programs and processes

Task Manager makes it easy to learn more about items on the Processes or Details tab. Simply right-click an item and choose Search Online. Task Manager opens a browser window and funnels the name of the app and the name of its process to your default search engine. There you'll typically find numerous links to official and unofficial information. If you're suspicious about the legitimacy of anything that shows up in Task Manager, by all means, use this tool as a starting point to find out what others are saying.

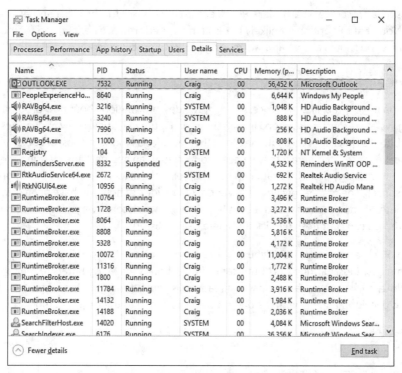

Figure 6-6 Right-clicking an item on the Processes tab takes you straight to the related item on the Details tab.

Assigning a program to a specific processor

If you have a multicore or multiprocessor system (virtually all modern CPUs on desktop and laptop PCs are multicore), you can assign a process to a specific processor—but only after the process is already running. To do this, right-click the process on the Details tab and choose Set Affinity. The following dialog box appears:

To assign a process to a particular CPU, clear the check boxes for the other entries in this dialog box. Note that this option is unlikely to result in any performance benefit, and for most program activities you should allow Windows to assign tasks to processor cores.

Reviewing history

The App History tab, like the Processes tab, provides information about how programs are using system resources. But App History, shown in Figure 6-7, knows only about apps that are distributed as packages through the Store; that includes all modern apps, of course, but desktop applications are listed here if they've been converted to an app package by using the Desktop Bridge technology described earlier in this chapter. App History accumulates its information over some range of time, giving you an approximate idea of how you have been using your computer. If you never clear and restart the history, it will record everything going back one month. You can start fresh by clicking Delete Usage History.

As on other Task Manager tabs, you can sort information on the App History tab by clicking column headings. Clicking CPU Time, for example, brings the heavy hitters to the top of the list. Note, however, that Task Manager already calls your attention to the biggest consumers by means of color mapping, with the darkest colors assigned to the largest numbers.

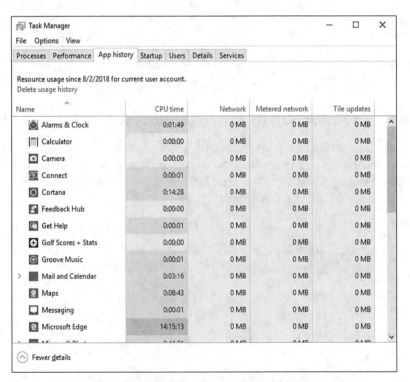

Figure 6-7   The App History tab tells you how much CPU time and other resources an app has used over a period of time.

History is interesting, but you might also find the App History tab useful as a program launcher. Right-click any item in any column, and you'll find a Switch To command. If the program is running, this command brings it front and center. If it's not running, Task Manager launches it.

Managing startup programs

Setting up a desktop application to run automatically when you start Windows is easy. If the program's installer doesn't offer to do this for you (many do) and you want the program to run every time you begin a Windows session, create a shortcut for the program in the Startup folder. Here's one way to do it:

1. On Start, right-click the program you want to run at startup and choose Open File Location. You'll find a shortcut for the program in the File Explorer window that appears.

2. Open a second File Explorer window, and type **shell:startup** in the address bar to navigate to %AppData%\Microsoft\Windows\Start Menu\Programs\Startup.

3. Copy the program's shortcut from the first File Explorer window to the second.

Inside OUT

Run a modern app at startup

You'll find it challenging to launch a modern app from your Startup folder. If you locate the app's executable by starting the program, running Task Manager, right-clicking the program on the Processes tab, clicking Go To Details, right-clicking the process name on the Details tab, clicking Open File Location, and then attempting to create a shortcut in your Startup folder—you'll be stymied by Windows SmartScreen the next time you start Windows. Even if you ignore the SmartScreen warning, Windows still won't run the program, instead throwing out an error message.

The problem is that modern apps, unlike desktop programs, must be run within the context of elaborate data structures called *packages*. (You can see a list of the packages installed on your system and drill down to their component folders by visiting %LocalAppData%\Packages in File Explorer.) A workaround is to create your Startup folder shortcut not to the app but to a data file associated with the app. If .jpg files are associated with the modern Photos app, for example, create a startup shortcut to one of your .jpg files. At startup, Windows will execute the shortcut, which will launch the app.

Suspending or removing startup items

The problem many users have with startup programs is not with creating them (that's easy, and in many cases, it happens without your explicit consent when the program is installed) but getting rid of them. Having too many startup programs not only makes your system take longer to start, it also has the potential to waste memory. If you don't require a program at startup, you should get it out of your list of auto-starting programs.

If you created the startup item in the first place by the method described in the previous section, you can remove it by revisiting the Startup folder and pressing the Delete key. Often, the situation is not so simple, however, because—as you'll see next—there are many other ways by which a program can be made to run at startup.

You can see a list of startup processes on the Startup tab of Task Manager. As Figure 6-8 shows, the Startup tab identifies each item by its estimated impact on the time required to start your Windows environment.

You can't remove a startup item from this list, but you can disable it so that the item will not run automatically at your next startup. To do this, right-click the item and then click Disable.

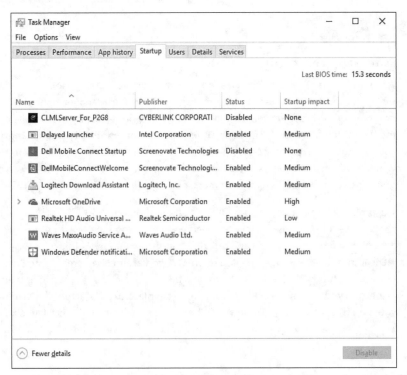

Figure 6-8   The Startup tab in Task Manager shows you which startup programs are enabled and how much impact each is estimated to have on your startup time.

If you're not sure whether an item on the Startup tab is justifying its existence there, try disabling it and restarting. Alternatively, or additionally, you can right-click the item and use the handy Search Online command to learn more about it. (For an alternative way to manage this set of startup programs, go to Settings > Apps > Startup.)

Other ways a program can be made to run at startup

As mentioned, a shortcut in the Startup folder is only one of many ways in which a program can be made to run at startup. Programs that set themselves up to run automatically and administrators who configure systems for others to use have a great many other methods at their disposal, including the following:

- **Run key (machine).** Programs listed in the registry's HKLM\Software\Microsoft\Windows\CurrentVersion\Run key are available at startup to all users.

- **Run key (user).** Programs listed in the HKCU\Software\Microsoft\Windows\CurrentVersion\Run key run when the current user signs in. A similar subkey, HKCU\Software\Microsoft\Windows NT\CurrentVersion\Windows\Run, can also be used.

- **Load value.** Programs listed in the Load value of the registry key HKCU\Software\Microsoft\Windows NT\CurrentVersion\Windows run when any user signs in.

- **Scheduled tasks.** The Windows Task Scheduler can specify tasks that run at startup. (See Chapter 19.) In addition, an administrator can set up tasks for your computer to run at startup that are not available for you to change or delete.

- **Win.ini.** Programs written for 16-bit Windows versions can add commands to the Load= and Run= lines in the [Windows] section of this startup file, which is located in %SystemRoot%. The Win.ini file is a legacy of the Windows 3.1 era and is available only on 32-bit Windows 10 installations.

- **RunOnce and RunOnceEx keys.** This group of registry keys identifies programs that run only once, at startup. These keys can be assigned to a specific user account or to the machine:

    - HKLM\Software\Microsoft\Windows\CurrentVersion\RunOnce

    - HKLM\Software\Microsoft\Windows\CurrentVersion\RunOnceEx

    - HKCU\Software\Microsoft\Windows\CurrentVersion\RunOnce

    - HKCU\Software\Microsoft\Windows\CurrentVersion\RunOnceEx

- **RunServices and RunServicesOnce keys.** As their names suggest, these rarely used keys can control the automatic startup of services. They can be assigned to a specific user account or to a computer.

CHAPTER 6

- **Winlogon key.** The Winlogon key controls actions that occur when you sign in to a computer running Windows. Most of these actions are under the control of the operating system, but you can also add custom actions here. The HKLM\Software\Microsoft\ Windows NT\CurrentVersion\Winlogon\Userinit and HKLM\Software\Microsoft\Windows NT\CurrentVersion\Winlogon\Shell subkeys can automatically launch programs.

- **Group Policy.** The Group Policy console includes two policies (one in Computer Configuration > Administrative Templates > System > Logon and one in the comparable User Configuration folder) called Run These Programs At User Logon that specify a list of programs to be run whenever any user signs in.

- **Policies\Explorer\Run keys.** Using policy settings to specify startup programs, as described in the previous paragraph, creates corresponding values in either of two registry keys: HKLM\Software\Microsoft\Windows\CurrentVersion\Policies\Explorer\Run or HKCU\Software\Microsoft\Windows\CurrentVersion\Policies\Explorer\Run.

- **Logon scripts.** Logon scripts, which run automatically at startup, can open other programs. Logon scripts are specified in Group Policy in Computer Configuration > Windows Settings > Scripts (Startup/Shutdown) and User Configuration > Windows Settings > Scripts (Logon/Logoff).

The Startup tab in Task Manager is a fine way to disable startup behavior established by registry keys. Note, however, that Task Manager might not list every startup item; in particular, the list does not include items established by Group Policy or Task Scheduler. For a somewhat more complete list, run System Information. (Type `system information` in the taskbar search box; the utility should appear at or near the top of the search results.)

In System Information, expand Software Environment and select Startup Programs. Unlike Task Manager, System Information includes items in the All Users startup folder (%ProgramData%\ Microsoft\Windows\Start Menu\Programs\Startup) as well as those in the startup folder for your own account. It also tells you *which* registry keys are responsible for a program's startup status, instead of simply indicating "Registry." Unfortunately, System Information, like Task Manager, also omits Group Policy and Task Scheduler items.

To get the most comprehensive listing of items that run at startup, as well as a handy tool to prevent certain programs from starting, we recommend using Autoruns, a free utility from Microsoft's Windows Sysinternals collection. Autoruns, which you can download from *https:// bit.ly/autoruns*, shows all the registry keys and startup locations listed earlier. It also shows Explorer shell extensions, services, browser helper objects, and more. Autoruns is particularly useful for finding processes that don't belong (such as a Trojan horse or other malware) or that you suspect of causing problems. You can then disable these items without removing them while you test your theory, or you can delete their autorun command altogether.

Select an item, and its details appear at the bottom of the screen, as shown next. Disable an item by clearing the check box next to its name; you can later reenable it by selecting the check box. To clear an item from the autorun list, select it and click Entry, Delete. (Note that deleting removes only the entry in the registry or other location that causes the item to run; it does not delete the program.)

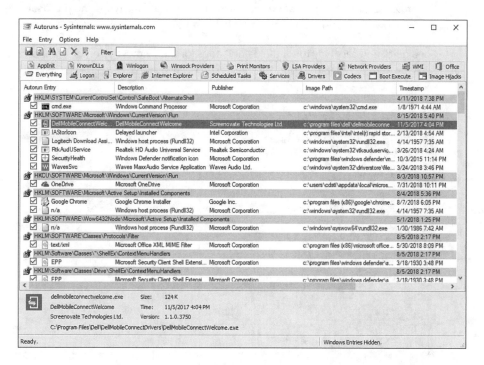

Although the tabs at the top of the Autoruns window filter the list of autorun items into various categories, the number of items can still be daunting. One nice feature of Autoruns is its ability to filter out components that are part of Windows or are digitally signed by Microsoft, because these are presumably safe to run. Commands on the Options menu control the appearance of these items.

You can also use the Compare feature in Autoruns to compare before and after snapshots of the data the program finds. Run Autoruns before you install a new program, save the data, run Autoruns again after you install the program, and compare the results to see what changes to autorun behavior were made by the program's installation.

Setting default programs and file-type associations

Most programs you use in Windows are associated with particular file types and protocols. These associations are what enable you, for example, to open an MP3 file in File Explorer and have your favorite audio program play the file, or click a hyperlink in a document or an email message and have your preferred browser take you to the appropriate website. Some of these associations were probably established by the operating system when you performed a clean install or an upgrade from an earlier version of Windows. (The Windows setup program gives you choices in this matter during the installation process, allowing you, for example, to accept the associations that Windows proposes or keep the ones you established before upgrading.) Regardless of how the associations between programs and file types and protocols are currently set, Windows allows you to see and modify the settings.

For a quick and easy way to set the default apps for the six most common computer tasks, go to Settings > Apps > Default Apps. Figure 6-9 shows an example of what you're likely to see.

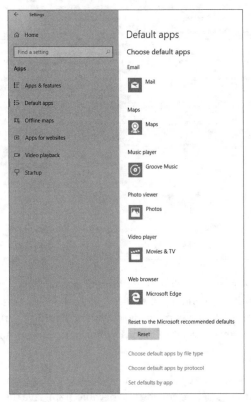

Figure 6-9   The Default Apps page in Settings provides a quick way to change the program associated with certain types of documents.

In the figure, you can see that, for example, Microsoft Edge is the default web browser. To change that, click the Microsoft Edge icon:

Here, two other web browsers are installed on the system: as an alternative to Microsoft Edge (which is given special treatment with the Recommended For Windows 10 label), you can choose Google Chrome or Internet Explorer. If neither of these is satisfying, you can visit the Store to look for something else.

But just because a program is identified in Settings as the default for a file type does not mean that program is assigned to open *every* file type it can open. To see all the file types that a program is capable of opening, click Set Defaults By App at the bottom of the Default Apps list in Settings. Then click the name of an app and click Manage. In the following illustration, for example, we see that Microsoft Edge has been set as the default app for eight of the twelve file types that it can open. But Three types—.pdf, .svg, and .xml—are currently assigned to other programs.

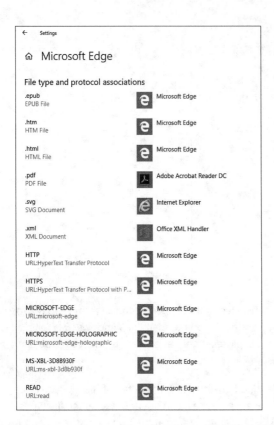

To change the association for a particular file type—for example, to change .xml from Office XML Handler to Microsoft Edge—click the program name in the righthand column next to the file type. Then make your selection in the Choose An App list that appears.

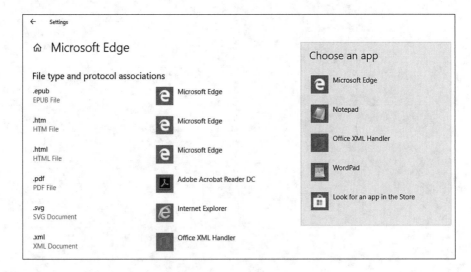

What if, for some reason, you want to assign a file type to a program that does not appear in the Choose An App list? To do this, return to the Default Apps page in Settings and click Choose Default Apps By File Type. As Figure 6-10 shows, Windows responds with a long alphabetized list of all the file types known to your system.

Figure 6-10   By clicking Choose Default Apps By File Type in Settings, you can control the associations for every file type recognized by your system.

Scrolling through the list to the file type in question and clicking the name of the program currently associated with this type allows you to choose a different installed program or visit the Store.

Using a nondefault program on a case-by-case basis

If you just want to open a file occasionally in an application that's not the default for that file type, there's no need to go through all the business of changing the default application. Right-click the file in File Explorer and choose Open With. Windows displays a menu offering the various applications that can open the selected file type. If you don't find the one you want, click Choose Another App. This time a menu similar to the one shown in Figure 6-11 appears.

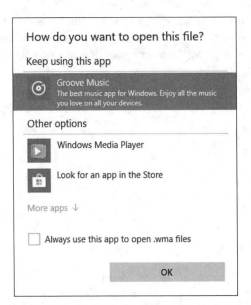

Figure 6-11   Right-clicking a file in File Explorer and choosing Open With > Choose Another App leads to a menu like this.

You can do two things in this menu. You can change the default for the selected file type (by selecting one of the listed apps and then clicking Always Use This App), or you can go for something altogether different by clicking More Apps. Doing this brings up a list of programs, many if not most of which will be completely unsuitable for the selected file type. Select one of these if you're curious to see what will happen. But don't click Always Use This App unless you're quite sure. If the program isn't what you want, it will simply make a nuisance of itself, and you'll have to go to the trouble of making something else the default.

Turning Windows features on or off

If you want to disable or enable certain default Windows features, open Settings and type **turn windows features on or off** in the search box. Run the top search result to display the dialog box shown in Figure 6-12.

Here you can enable Hyper-V Management Tools (if they're not already enabled), disable Internet Explorer 11 if you have no further need for it, and so on. Note that some items in the list have subentries. Those marked by a filled check box (rather than a check mark) have some components enabled and some not.

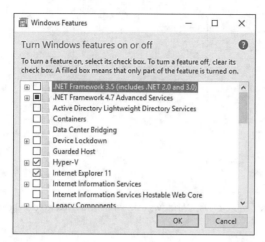

Figure 6-12   The Windows Features dialog box provides a simple way to disable or enable selected programs.

As with so many features in Windows 10, you can find an alternative to some of these options; visit Settings > Apps > Apps & Features > Manage Optional Features to see a much shorter list of features that includes options for uninstalling Internet Explorer 11 and Windows Media Player.

Setting AutoPlay options

AutoPlay is the feature that enables Windows to take appropriate action when you insert removable storage media such as a CD, DVD, or memory card into a drive. The operating system detects the kind of disc or media you inserted and takes the action you requested for that type of media. If you have not already made a decision about what the operating system should do, a window similar to this one appears:

> ⊐   (E:)
> Select to choose what happens with
> removable drives.

If you don't want Windows to take any action, you can simply ignore the message; it disappears after a few seconds. Otherwise, clicking or tapping the message brings you to the screen shown in Figure 6-13.

Notice that your choices here are limited to ones that are appropriate for the device type and Take No Action. (For example, if you insert an audio CD, your only choices are the default app for playing audio CDs and Take No Action.) If you don't want to commit to any of the options on this menu, press Esc.

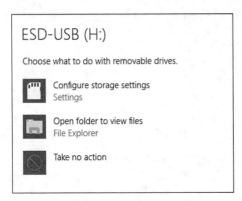

Figure 6-13   When you insert a removable drive, Windows asks what you'd like to do with similar actions in the future.

In any case, if you set a default action for a particular media type and subsequently change your mind and want a different default, open Settings > Devices > AutoPlay. Shown in Figure 6-14, AutoPlay in Settings gives you options for configuring some types of media but not others. You might need to search for AutoPlay in Control Panel to see the rest.

Figure 6-14   The AutoPlay page in Settings lets you configure AutoPlay behavior for some types of media. You might need to visit Control Panel to configure other types.

In the Control Panel counterpart for this corner of Settings, you'll see a dialog box comparable to the one shown in Figure 6-15.

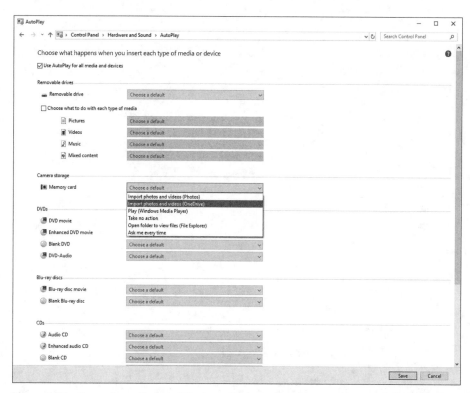

Figure 6-15   For each media type, Windows displays a list of appropriate possibilities you can choose from.

Inside OUT

You don't want a default action?

To have no default action for a given media type, choose Ask Me Every Time as the option for that media type. To suppress the AutoPlay dialog box completely, choose Take No Action.

Using and managing built-in Windows apps

In this chapter we discuss many of the programs that are included with a default installation of Microsoft Windows 10. Our goal is to cover the major productivity apps, as well as the apps you can use to manage and edit media files. We omit detailed coverage of such long-in-the-tooth legacy items as Notepad and Paint (worthy programs though they may be), as well as programs that are essentially self-explanatory, such as Alarms & Clock. And we reserve the bigger topics of Microsoft Edge and Microsoft Internet Explorer for a separate chapter, the one that follows this one.

The list of tools included with Windows grows longer with each iteration, largely because every new version, in addition to introducing new items, must continue to support the work habits developed by users of its predecessors. If you have routinely covered your Windows 7 desktop with color-coded sticky notes, for example, you'll be glad to know that Sticky Notes—now a modern app—is still extant.

In addition to the many legacy applications, Windows 10 offers a whole set of modern productivity and communication apps, all designed for touch and pen as well as more traditional input methods. In addition, not installed by default but available without charge from the Microsoft Store, are mobile versions of three Microsoft Office applications: Word, Excel, and PowerPoint.

NOTE

Because Microsoft regularly delivers feature-enhancing cumulative updates to Windows 10, several apps described in this chapter might have undergone changes—some minor, others significant—by the time you read this. We describe the programs as they appeared as of late 2018, and we'll revisit them with each update to this book.

We begin our survey with a look at the modern communication and productivity apps.

Mail, Calendar, and People

Although they are tightly linked, Mail, Calendar, and People have separate entries in Start. You can switch between them by tapping or clicking icons in the lower-left corner of the window. The People app, populated by the accounts you set up in Mail or Calendar (as well as other sources), provides a directory of potential addressees when you create Mail messages or invite associates to a meeting. Type the beginning of a contact's name or email address on the To line of a message, and if that name or address is among your contacts in People, the To line will be completed for you.

Setting up and using Mail

The first time you open the Mail app, you'll be asked to set up accounts, as shown next. If you sign on to Windows using a Microsoft account, the email address associated with that account appears at the top of this setup page. If that's the only email account you use, you can move on by clicking Ready To Go. If you log on locally or if you have other accounts, click Add Account. Mail supports Exchange, Outlook.com, Google accounts (Gmail and G Suite), Yahoo! Mail, and iCloud, as well as generic accounts based on the POP and IMAP standards. The setup process is straightforward, prompting you for your email address and password:

If your account requires you to enter additional settings, such as the names of your incoming and outgoing servers, scroll to the bottom of the Add An Account list and then click Advanced Setup.

Adding and deleting accounts

To add email accounts subsequently, open Settings by clicking the gear icon in the lower-left corner of the Mail window. Click Manage Accounts > Add Account. To delete an existing account, select it in Settings. Note that you cannot delete the address associated with your Microsoft account.

Linking inboxes

If you have two or more email accounts, Mail will create a separate inbox for each. Thus, you'll see all your messages from the first account, followed by all your messages from the second, and so on. You might find it more convenient to link the accounts, thereby creating a unified inbox. To do this, open Settings > Manage Accounts > Link Inboxes. Mail presents a dialog box listing accounts available to be linked:

Supply a name for the combined inbox if you don't like the one that Mail proposes. Then select each account you want to be part of the combine. If you change your mind, you can unlink the accounts by returning to this dialog box and removing check marks.

Setting sync options

To configure sync options for an account, go to Settings > Manage Accounts, select the account you want to configure, and then click Change Mailbox Sync Settings. Note that with a combined inbox, you still configure the component accounts individually. For example, if you have one email account for personal messages and another for business, you can opt to have the one synced every 15 minutes and the other only once every two hours. If you have an account you use primarily as a repository for commercial messages, you might want to set that account up so that only the most recent week's worth of messages appear in Mail.

The default sync settings, shown in Figure 7-1, reflect Mail's intended use as a mail client for users on the go. To save battery and disk space, Mail, by default, bases its sync frequency on your usage patterns. If you use the app with any significant frequency, it will fetch messages at shorter time intervals. In any case, you can override the program's decision making and configure a predetermined sync interval by opening the drop-down menu at the top of the dialog box. Note that sync settings for an Outlook.com or Office 365 account do not include the option to base downloads on usage patterns.

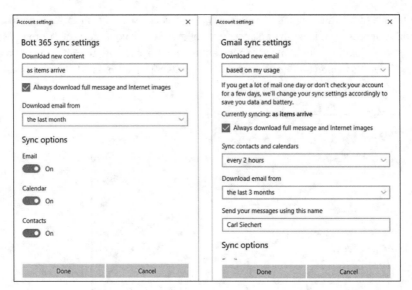

Figure 7-1   Sync settings for a Microsoft mail account (such as Outlook.com or Office 365), left, do not include the option to download content based on your usage patterns, as shown in the Gmail account settings, right.

Because sync settings apply to the device on which they're configured and do not transfer to other devices, you can easily set up different devices for different usage scenarios. Let's say, for example, that you have a desktop computer for use in the office and a tablet for use on the go. You might configure the office PC to download all mail from your server (by opening the Download Email From drop-down menu and clicking Any Time) but have the traveling machine collect only messages from the last two weeks.

Setting notification options

By default, Mail announces the arrival of new mail by posting a notification to Action Center. You have the option of adding banner and audible notifications. Or you can dispense with notifications altogether. To make your wishes known, in Mail go to Settings > Notifications.

Inside OUT

Use Mail for notifications even if you prefer a different mail client

You might already be using a mail client other than Mail and have no need to use Mail for sending and reading messages. If your preferred client does not feed notifications to Action Center, you might still want to set up Mail for that purpose. You can then continue sending and receiving email with the tools you're accustomed to using but rely on Mail to provide Action Center notifications.

Reducing mailbox clutter with Focused Inbox

Focused Inbox is a feature, introduced in version 1703, that makes it easier to focus on messages you care about. With Focused Inbox, two tabs appear above the list of messages in the message header pane—Focused and Other—as shown in Figure 7-2. Incoming messages that Mail deems important appear on the Focused tab, whereas all others fall under Other.

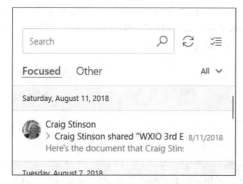

Figure 7-2   Focused Inbox divides messages into two sets, called Focused and Other.

Mail makes the determination based on the message content and on whom you exchange mail with most frequently. You can train the Focused Inbox feature to work more accurately by right-clicking the header for a misfiled message. The menu that appears includes a Move To Focused or Move To Other command (depending on what category of message is selected) that moves a single message or all messages from a particular sender from one category to the other, as shown in the next figure.

To turn the Focused Inbox feature on or off, in Mail go to Settings > Focused Inbox. Note that Focused Inbox might not be available for all types of mail accounts.

Creating a new message

To create a new message, click the New Mail icon. Above the To and Subject lines, you'll find a ribbon that provides an elaborate set of editing tools, derived from Microsoft Word. For example, a wealth of styling options is available via the Format tab on the ribbon. Use the arrows on the ribbon to see the full set of options at your disposal:

To attach a file to your message, click the Insert tab. You can use that part of the ribbon to insert tables, pictures, and hyperlinks as well. Alternatively, you can create an attachment by dragging a file into your new message document. Mail also provides a proofreader; click Options and then click Spelling to check the spelling of your messages.

To add ink to your message, click Draw. A set of drawing tools will appear.

Beginning with version 1703, you can insert *@mentions* into an email message. An @mention of somebody's name highlights their name in the message and adds it to the To line of the message header, helping to ensure that they see your message.

To use this feature, in the body of your message type an @ sign. A list of contacts opens, and you can click the name you want. If you begin typing a name, the list is refined to include only contacts in which the first name, last name, or email address begins with the letters you type.

After you select a contact, the name is highlighted in the message body and the name is added to the To line if it's not already there. You can then edit the name in the message body if you like; for example, you might want to keep things informal by trimming off the last name.

When people receive a message with an @mention, it remains highlighted for good visibility. In addition, the highlighted name is a mailto: link, so when recipients click the name, it opens a new message window with the name already in the To box.

You can filter your inbox to show only messages that include an @mention with your name. Click the arrow at the top of the message header pane and choose Mentions.

Using folders

The pane to the left of the message headers provides a list of system folders—Inbox, Drafts, Sent Items, and Archive—plus any folders you designated as favorites. (If the Mail window is too narrow, you'll need to click the hamburger icon to see the folder list.) Other folders you have created on your mail server or within Mail are listed in an additional pane that appears if you click More. To create a folder in Mail, click More, and then click Create New Folder (the plus icon), to the right of All Folders or, in a combined inbox, to the right of the account name.

You can add any of your own folders to the Favorites list by right-clicking the folder and then clicking Add To Favorites. Once ensconced in the Favorites list, a folder name makes a convenient drag-and-drop target for received messages. You can also move a message from the headers pane to any folder by right-clicking the header and then clicking Move.

Setting up and using Calendar

In Mail, Calendar, and People, you can use the icons at the lower-left corner to switch from one app to another. If you're already running Mail or People, a quick tap takes you straight to Calendar. Alternatively, you can launch Calendar from Start.

Accounts set up in Mail are used in Calendar and vice versa. You can add or modify accounts in Calendar as you would in Mail; click Settings > Manage Accounts. If you're using multiple accounts, your Calendar events will be distinguished by color; you can also set the color by right-clicking an event in the calendar, choosing Categorize, and selecting a color. If the display gets noisy, you can use the check boxes in the left pane, below the thumbnail calendar, to filter particular components of your composite calendar.

If you don't see this pane at the left of your screen, click or tap the hamburger icon in the upper-left corner. Doing this removes or redisplays the left pane. (You'll find it useful particularly on a small display.)

Here you can specify which color is used to display each calendar: Point at a calendar, click the arrow that appears to its right, and then select a color.

You can also add specialty calendars that show schedules for sports teams, your favorite television shows, and so on. To do that, click Add Calendars. (If you have multiple accounts set up in Calendar, you specify which one displays the calendars you add by going to Settings > Calendar Settings > Interesting Calendars.)

Adding an event

To add an event to your calendar, either click or tap New Event, or click the calendar itself. If you click New Event, you get the full Details window for the event. If you click a day or an hour on the calendar, you get a smaller version of this window, and you can move to the full view by clicking More Details. In either case, if you have Calendar configured to use more than one account, you'll want to specify which account the new event should belong to.

In the Details view, you can use the Reminder list to specify your preferences regarding alerts. Calendar defaults to a 15-minute heads-up, but you have lots of alternatives, including None. Note that Calendar's live tile (if you have the app pinned to Start) will also alert you to upcoming events. Set the size to wide if you want to see multiple events on the live tile. Depending on your settings, Cortana can offer reminders as well.

Figure 7-3 shows the details of a recurring event. To create such an item, click the circular Repeat icon and specify your parameters. Calendar offers daily, weekly, monthly, and yearly options.

Figure 7-3 Clicking Repeat opens a new set of options, where you can specify yearly, monthly, weekly, or daily parameters for a recurring event.

Inviting others to a meeting

To create a meeting event and invite others to join, add the email addresses of your invitees to the People section of your Details view. Then click Send. Each of the invitees will get an email message allowing him or her to send back a yes-no-maybe response. The Accept, Tentative, and Decline links, with associated drop-down options, make it easy for the invitee to respond to the invitation.

Setting options

To specify the days of your work week and the hours of your work day, click Settings > Calendar Settings. You can do a few other things as well on the Settings page, such as opting for week numbers and switching to alternative languages and calendars. If you stick with English, the calendar choices include Hijiri, Umm al-Qura, Hebrew Lunar, and Saka Era, in addition to the default Gregorian. Many other options are available for languages other than English.

Printing from Calendar

To print, click Show (the ellipsis icon in the upper-right corner of the Calendar window) and then click Print. There you can specify the starting date for your output as well as whether to print the day, week, work week, or month. A preview button gives you the opportunity to check before you commit.

Adding or editing contacts with People

People acts as a repository for contacts derived from the accounts you set up in Mail or Calendar. You can launch People from the icon at the bottom-left corner of those apps as well as from Start. People lists your contacts, summarizing recent communications and calendar entries for the selected contact in a Timeline pane. In the Timeline pane, you can click an entry to open a message in Mail or Calendar.

When you first run People, the app prompts you to add accounts. Contacts will then be imported from the accounts you name. You can select a variety of accounts, including Outlook, Gmail, Exchange, and iCloud. If you use the People tab in the Photos app (see Photos and Video, later in this chapter) to identify people in your pictures, those people also become available as contacts to the People app.

You can also add contacts directly in People. Click the Plus button along the top of the People window to open an editing form.

People contacts can be pinned either to Start or to the taskbar for easy access and use. Click the Pin Menu button near the upper-right corner of People to pin the current contact to either location. (For more about pinning contacts to the taskbar, see "Pinning people to the taskbar" in Chapter 3, "Using Windows 10.")

Using Skype

Skype, Microsoft's internet video telephony and messaging tool, is the latest member of the Windows 10 family to make the transition from legacy desktop application to universal app and has been installed as part of Windows 10 since version 1703. You can also run Skype in a web browser by going to *https://web.skype.com*.

The modern Skype app, the desktop program, and the web version are functionally similar and use the same accounts and contact lists. You can log in and use whichever seems most convenient and comfortable on the device you're using.

Microsoft continues to invest significant development effort in Skype. At *https://bit.ly/skype-windows10-new*, you can peruse a log of feature changes dating from the present back to September 2016.

Microsoft also offers a more richly featured product called Skype for Business (formerly known as Lync), as part of Office 365 Business and Enterprise subscriptions. For information about features and pricing of Skype for Business, see *https://skype.com/business*.

Getting started

When you first run Skype, the program prompts you to create an account or sign in to an existing one. You can use your Microsoft account if you don't already have a Skype account.

Before you start making calls, you might want to check your video, microphone, and speaker settings. Click the ellipsis icon near the upper-left corner, click Settings, and run the tests under Audio & Video.

To find a contact, in the Search box type your contact's Skype account name, if you know it, or an email address. You can also type the contact's name, but this approach might produce a long list of Skype users with identical first and last names. When you find the person you want to add, click the name to see relevant options, which depend on whether the person has a Skype account, whether you've chatted before, and other factors. You can right-click a name and choose Add To Favorites so that it appears prominently in your list of contacts.

Note that if you receive an unwanted contact solicitation and choose to decline, the Decline button provides additional options to block the request or report it as spam.

With your equipment checked out and your contacts list populated, you might then want to flesh out your own profile—the information your contacts will see about you. The profile screen appears when you click your own picture or name in the upper-left corner of the window, and here you can add phone information and other details. If you shot your profile photo with the rear-facing camera by mistake or simply want to transmit a different image, click Change Picture.

Placing or answering an audio or video call

To initiate an internet call, click your contact's name and then choose one of the options that appear on the right side of the screen:

Click Create Group (the rightmost icon) to add one or more people to the call. The phone icon in the center makes the call audio only. Choose the camera icon on the left to send video as well. You can also switch in and out of video during the call if the need arises—for example, if your internet connection is not strong enough to support video transmission.

Similar buttons appear if someone places a call to you. Before you answer, you'll also get an audio signal to alert you to the call.

Calling people who don't have Skype or aren't online

With Skype, you can also place Voice-over-Internet-Protocol (VoIP) calls to people who don't have Skype accounts or are not online. The calls are charged at per-minute rates that vary by country or region. Before placing a call, you can buy credit by clicking your profile icon and choosing Skype To Phone.

When you're ready to call, press Ctrl+D. On the dialer that appears, type or click the numbers to dial, and then click the phone icon. Note that you can also enter letters, which is handy for phone numbers—usually for a business—that are presented as letters or a word.

While you're on a call, notice that when you switch to another app, Skype switches to mini view—a small window that includes the video (if it's a video call) and controls for muting your microphone and hanging up the call. The window stays in front of other windows, leaving you a small, but unobstructed, view of the action.

Sending text or video messages, pictures, or files

To send a text message, select a contact name and then type in the text box that appears at the bottom of the window. (You can also send text while you're in an audio or video call.) To send a video message to someone, click the video-camera icon to the right of the text box. Your camera will come to life, your shining visage will appear on the screen, and you can click the red Record button when you're ready to start. Click the Send button when you're satisfied and ready to transmit.

To send a photo or a file, click the nearby Add Files icon.

Using OneNote

OneNote is Microsoft's extraordinarily versatile note-taking machine. You can use it as a personal organizer, recording outlined and free-formed notes, drawings, embedded video and audio, attached files, and so on. You can also use it as a collaborative tool, sharing notebooks with other members of a project team.

Like Skype, OneNote comes in desktop and universal-app variants. The universal app is included in all Windows 10 installations; the desktop version, OneNote 2016, is part of the Microsoft Office family, including all Office 365 subscriptions. Versions for your Android device or iPhone are also available through their app stores. The version included with Windows 10 stores its notebooks in OneDrive, which means you can open them from any device in any location with an internet connection. All OneNote users with Office 365 subscriptions can store notebooks locally or in OneDrive. Those with Business or Enterprise subscriptions have access to OneDrive for Business.

With both OneNote 2016 and the universal OneNote app, which should you use? You can use both, and unless you have turned off the option to sync notebooks automatically, your notebooks will be accessible from either version. The universal app might be ideal when you're on the go or when you're concerned with reading your notes (and those that others have shared with you) and making simple annotations. For more extensive editing and note taking, and for such things as inserting recorded audio or video notes, you'll probably want the much larger feature set provided by OneNote 2016.

If you're new to OneNote, these core principles will get you started:

- Notes are stored in notebooks, which are subdivided into sections. Each section consists of one or more pages. OneNote gives you a notebook to start with, and that notebook contains a single section (called Quick Notes) with no pages. Sections are identified by tabs arrayed vertically to the right of the notebook name, and pages are listed vertically, further to the right. Click the plus signs to add notebooks, sections, or pages.

- OneNote saves everything you enter immediately and instantly. If your notebook is stored on OneDrive, you have access to it from anywhere.

- OneNote is a free-form editor. You can type or jot anywhere on the page. With drawing tools, you can create sketches or annotate your notes.

With either version of OneNote, you can share notebooks for collaborative projects. To share an existing notebook, select it in the left column and then click Share. (The notebook must have at least one page and be stored on OneDrive or OneDrive for Business for this link to be available.)

Inside OUT

Don't overlook the My Office app

For several years, Windows included an app called Get Office. In its earliest iterations, it was a somewhat pushy program that served the sole purpose of facilitating the purchase and installation of Office. In Version 1709, the Get Office app was transformed into something much more useful called My Office. It still provides an easy path to purchasing (if necessary), downloading, and installing Office, including its ancillary programs (such as Sway, Microsoft To-Do, and Office Lens) and versions for different platforms. But it's now a convenient hub for all things Office: launching programs, opening recent documents, getting help, and managing your Office account, as shown here.

CHAPTER 7

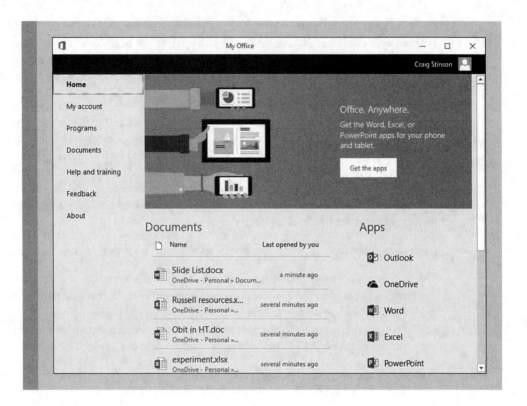

Using Maps

Mapping applications have long been one of the indispensable tools of modern life. Microsoft's modern Maps app should serve you well, whether you want to explore a new city, plot a road trip, find a restaurant or a bank, print a set of turn-by-turn directions to take with you on the road, or just enjoy aerial views of the world or your neighborhood.

On first run, Maps asks for permission to track your location information. If you consent, Maps will plant a marker at your current location. Tapping Show My Location (the target-shaped button in the toolbar on the right side of the screen) at any time or pressing Ctrl+Home displays your current location, assuming the program knows what that is.

Searching for places and services

To find a location, click the Search tool on the left or press Ctrl+F. You can type an address, the name of a person or business in your contacts list, or the name of a place known to Maps—an institution or a restaurant, for example. As shown in Figure 7-4, Maps displays the location on the map, one or more street-side pictures, and other interesting information. If you search for a restaurant known to Maps, you'll also be rewarded with reviews, hours, and website information. The panel of icons in the What's Nearby section of this information pane offers single-click searches for nearby restaurants, attractions, malls, hotels, banks, hospitals, and parking facilities.

Figure 7-4   In addition to displaying your search item on the map, Maps displays a street-side picture and a considerable amount of related information. Clicking Tilt Up displays a 3-D map so you can better visualize the topography.

Getting directions

To get directions, click the Directions icon (to the right of the Search icon) and then type your starting and ending points. (One of them might already be in place if you just searched for it.) Maps responds with a set of route alternatives.

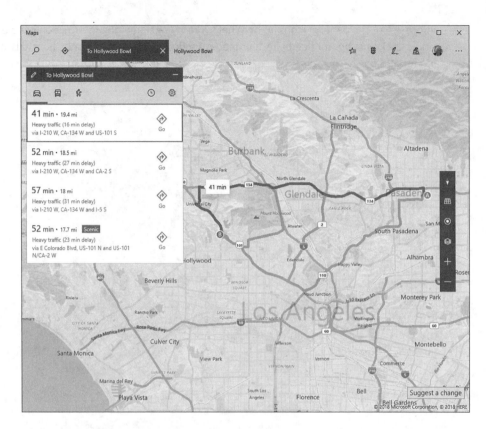

Click or tap the left side of one of these alternatives to see particular steps in the route. Click or tap Go to see and hear turn-by-turn instructions. If you want a more detailed look at traffic conditions than the "Heavy traffic" indication with the directions, tap Map Views (the fourth icon in the bar along the right side) and turn on Traffic. Optionally, Maps can display the location of traffic-jamming incidents and traffic cameras. Click one of those to get a preview of your upcoming drive.

Inside OUT

View traffic conditions on your commute

Click the Traffic icon in the upper-right toolbar to get an idea of the time it'll take you to drive to your home and work locations from your current location.

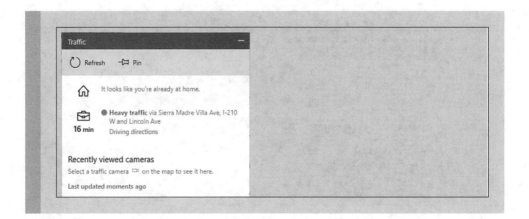

Maps defaults to showing driving directions. To see public transportation information instead, click the bus icon near the upper-left corner of the directions pane. Maps shows you the best route and includes helpful information about how to watch for your stop on the transit system. For a trip from Columbia University to Carnegie Hall, for example, the resulting instructions include this tip about getting off the train: "Previous stop is 66 St – Lincoln Center. If you reach 50 St., you've gone too far." You can also tap on a bus stop on the map to see when the next bus will arrive at that stop.

If you'd rather walk than ride, click the humanoid icon next to the bus icon. Maps calculates its walking time at a rate of about 2.3 miles per hour. If you usually walk or ride public transit, you can change the default by clicking See More (the ellipsis icon in the upper-right corner of the screen), clicking Settings, and opening the Preferred Directions list.

On the right side of a map's display, Maps offers a panel of additional options, allowing you to change the compass heading, switch between plane and elevation views, display your current location, switch between aerial and street views, and zoom in and out.

Sharing maps and creating reminders

To send someone a map, display the map and then click Share. Maps opens a panel of sharing options.

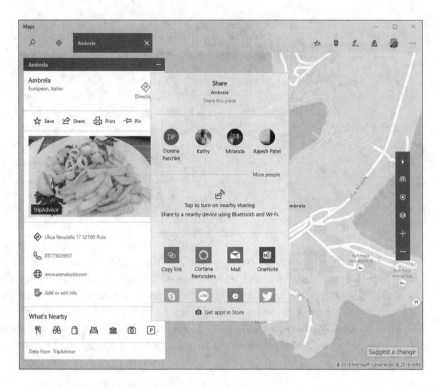

You can create a reminder to yourself associated with a particular place by clicking Share, and then clicking Cortana Reminders. The following appears:

Type what you want to be reminded to do in the box labeled Remember To. Then click Place. On the ensuing screen, you can specify whether you want to be reminded at the time you arrive or the time you depart.

Downloading maps for offline use

If you're out and about without a data connection for your portable device, you can still use maps that you previously downloaded. To take advantage of this feature, go to Settings > Apps > Offline Maps. To download a map, click the plus sign. On subsequent screens, you can choose the particular map you want.

Maps are updated frequently. To ensure that you have the most recent data, set the Map Updates switch at Settings > Apps > Offline Maps to On.

Performing screen captures with Snipping Tool and shortcut keys

Pictures speak louder than words, and sometimes an image capture of the current window or screen can be the ideal way to enhance a PowerPoint presentation, explain a procedure, or remind yourself at some future time of what you were doing and how. All Windows versions, from the very first to the present, have offered two keyboard shortcuts for capturing screens:

- PrtScn captures an image of the entire screen. If you have multiple monitors, the image includes all screens.

- Alt+PrtScn captures an image of the current window.

Both capture methods post bitmaps to the Clipboard, and you can paste the results into any program that accepts graphics.

NOTE

These two screen-capture methods can also save an image file (in PNG format) to OneDrive automatically. To turn this feature on or off, right-click the OneDrive icon in the notification area and choose Settings. You'll find the setting on the Auto Save tab under Screenshots.

Inside OUT

Capture a screen on a tablet PC

If your computer doesn't have a PrtScn key—or it doesn't have any keyboard at all—you can still capture a screen. Hold down the Windows button and press the Volume Down button.

Recent Windows versions offer a third built-in shortcut:

- Windows key + PrtScn captures an image of all current screens (including secondary screens) and saves that image as a PNG file in the Screenshots subfolder of your Pictures folder.

The newest screen capture trick made its debut in version 1703:

- Windows key + Shift + S captures an image of part of the screen. When you press that key combination, the screen dims; then, using the mouse, drag over the area you want to capture. When you release the mouse button, the selected area is copied to the Clipboard. Alternatively, after pressing Windows key + Shift + S, use the arrow keys to move to one corner of the area you want to capture and press Spacebar or Enter. Then use the arrow keys to move to the opposite corner and press Spacebar or Enter again. (This feature used to be part of OneNote, but with version 1703 it moved into Windows itself.) Beginning with version 1809, pressing this hotkey combination adds a toolbar to the top of the screen where you can select the type of screen you want to capture: a rectangle, a freeform snip, or the full screen.

Of course, there are many situations in which what you want is not a full window or screen capture, but a rectangular or freeform capture of a portion of a window. Many third parties offer richly featured tools for these purposes; we're particularly fond of Techsmith's Snagit and have used it for all recent iterations of our books. Windows, however, includes a lightweight utility called Snip & Sketch that serves most basic screen-capture needs. To run it, type **snip** in the Search box; the program should appear at the top of your search results.

Note that Snip & Sketch made its formal debut with version 1809. Earlier versions included a similar but slightly less versatile app called Snipping Tool.

Music, photos, movies, and games

Not that long ago, your PC was the indispensable hub of digital media. Music and movies were delivered on shiny discs, and you needed a desktop or laptop PC to rip CDs, watch a movie while traveling, transfer photos from your digital camera, and share your photos on social media.

Today, the explosion of mobile devices and cloud-based entertainment services means the PC is no longer a hub, and shiny discs are now an endangered species. The PC is still uniquely qualified for tasks that involve editing and managing a media collection and syncing it with cloud services, but for playing those files you're more likely to use a smaller mobile device.

The three core media apps included with Microsoft Windows 10—Groove Music, Photos, and Movies & TV—are tightly connected to the cloud, although the demise of the Groove Music Pass at the end of 2017 removes at least one of our favorite cloud connections. Like other apps built on the Universal Windows Platform, they're touch-friendly but also work well in a window on a conventional PC. And because it's possible to update these apps through the Store, they have evolved significantly since Windows 10's debut in 2015. In the following sections, we cover the most recent releases of these apps.

If you're worried that the digital media landscape in Windows 10 will be completely alien, we can reassure you that a couple of familiar touchstones remain: Windows Media Player is still available for playing music and movies on a desktop or portable PC and, yes, Paint is still around for basic photo-editing tasks. Both programs are essentially unchanged from their Windows 7 incarnations.

In the living room, it's still possible to connect a PC to a home entertainment system directly, although the experience is less enjoyable than it used to be now that Windows Media Center is no longer available with any edition of Windows 10. (In fact, Media Center is removed from your system when you upgrade from a prior edition.) More modern alternatives include streaming content from a Windows tablet or PC to a large display (like your big-screen TV) by using built-in support for the Miracast standard. And if your living room or rec room includes an Xbox One game console, it's easy to connect to a Windows 10 PC.

Music

No, you're not seeing double. Windows 10 includes two programs whose primary purpose is to play digital music files:

- Groove Music is a Universal Windows app and the default app for playing music files in Windows 10. It's the direct successor to the Xbox Music app from Windows 8.1, and it traces its ancestry (at least indirectly) to the late, lamented Zune Music app. Using Groove Music, you can play music files in various formats and stream or download your music collection from OneDrive.

NOTE

On January 1, 2018, Microsoft shuttered the Groove Music Pass subscription service and also ended sales of albums and tracks in the Microsoft Store. The Music tab is no longer available in the Microsoft Store app, and tracks that were added to a music collection as part of a Groove Music Pass subscription no longer play.

- Windows Media Player in Windows 10 is virtually identical to the version shipped with Windows 7. (The single, very large, exception is support for files saved using formats based on lossless compression.) The most distinctive feature of Windows Media Player compared with Groove Music is its ability to play CDs and rip their contents to digital formats. It can also sync content with some older models of portable music players.

Both programs create indexed libraries from the contents of folders in your Music library. The indexes are stored separately.

Both programs support the same selection of audio formats, most of them compressed. For practical purposes, audio files must be compressed; using the uncompressed WAV format, a typical 60-minute CD will consume more than half a gigabyte of disk space. Compressing the files means you can store more music on your hard disk, and it makes the process of backing up and streaming music files easier and more efficient.

When it comes to compression, Windows 10 supports both lossy and lossless formats. Most popular algorithms used to compress audio (and video) files are lossy, which means that they achieve compression by eliminating data. In the case of audio files in the popular MP3 and AAC formats, the data that's tossed out during the compression process consists mostly of frequencies that are outside the normal range of human hearing. The level of compression is determined by the *bit rate*. Higher bit rates preserve more of the original sound quality of audio tracks but result in larger files on your hard disk or portable player. Lower bit rates pack more music into limited space at a cost in fidelity.

The more compressed a music file is (that is, the lower its bit rate), the more likely you are to notice degradations in audio quality.

Windows 10 supports three different lossless compressed formats: Windows Media Audio Lossless, Apple Lossless Audio Codec (ALAC), and Free Lossless Audio Codec (FLAC). When you have a choice of formats, we recommend FLAC, which is widely supported and stores music files efficiently without sacrificing any information. In theory, at least, a track saved in any of these lossless formats should be indistinguishable from the original.

NOTE

Although you can play files saved in lossless formats from a local disk, you cannot use the Windows 10 Groove Music app to stream files saved in those formats from OneDrive.

Using Groove Music

Every installation of Windows 10 sets Groove Music as the default music player, unless you choose a different app when you first set up a user profile. If you used this app in its previous incarnations, the basic look and feel should be familiar. One area that has changed repeatedly over the short life of Windows 10 is the primary navigation list at the top of the pane on the left. With the demise of the Groove Music Pass service, this section now contains only three links: My Music, which displays the contents of albums and songs in your music library (including those stored in OneDrive's Music folder); Recent Plays, which shows the names of tracks and albums you've been listening to lately; and Now Playing, which shows the currently selected album or playlist.

Below those core navigation links is the Playlists option, which opens a pane where you can create custom playlists from tracks in your library and manage previously created playlists.

The navigation pane—that thin column of icons on the left—follows the same interface conventions as other universal apps. If the app's window is wide enough, the labels for the navigation pane appear automatically; to make those labels visible, or to hide them if you want more room for the current view, click the Maximize/Minimize Navigation Pane (aka "hamburger") button at the top of the pane. Figure 7-5 offers an overview of the Groove interface with the navigation pane expanded to show all its labels.

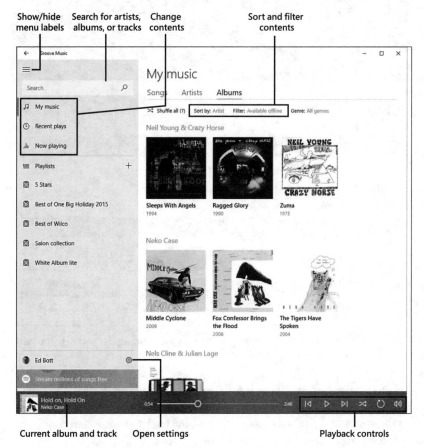

Show/hide menu labels Search for artists, albums, or tracks Change contents Sort and filter contents

Current album and track   Open settings   Playback controls

Figure 7-5   The Groove Music app's contents pane offers multiple views of your collection, available via icons in the navigation pane on the left. Sort or filter the current view using controls at the top.

The design of the Groove Music app isn't difficult to figure out. A menu pane on the left provides a way for you to choose what you want to play, from your local music collection or from content stored in the Music folder in OneDrive. To change the way your collection is displayed, click the My Music tab and then choose Albums, Artists, or Songs. To display the current album or playlist, click Now Playing. Your custom playlists appear at the bottom of the left pane.

Figure 7-6 shows the options that appear when you click to display the contents of an individual album. (A menu of additional options for the album appears when you click the ellipsis to the right of the Add To command.)

Figure 7-6   The options at the bottom apply only to the current selection. Use the Add To option to send tracks or an entire album to a custom playlist.

The option to select individual songs from an album or playlist (or from the Songs view) isn't immediately obvious. When you select an album, for example, track numbers appear to the left of each song. Move the mouse pointer over the track to reveal a check box where the track number had been, along with Play and Add To buttons. (With songs in a playlist or in the Songs view, the check box appears to the left of the track name.) After you click to select one song, check boxes appear to the left of all other tracks in the current album or playlist.

As we noted earlier, Groove Music integrates neatly with OneDrive. Any compatible files you save to the Music folder in OneDrive are available for playback when you sign in using that account on any Windows 10 device. The resulting collection can be displayed along with locally stored files or maintained separately. Use the Filter menu, as shown in Figure 7-7, to specify your preferences.

As Figure 7-8 shows, search terms you enter in the box at the top of the navigation pane return results showing artists, albums, songs, and playlists from your collection.

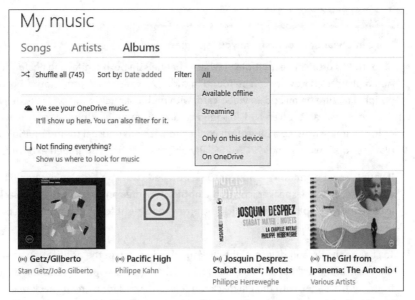

Figure 7-7   Use the Filter menu to show only a subset of your music collection: albums saved in the OneDrive Music folder, for example, or those available offline.

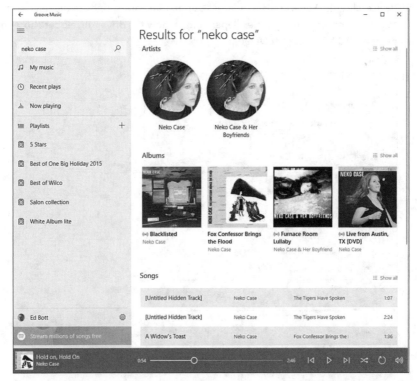

Figure 7-8   Use the search box in the upper-left to display results that match artists, albums, and songs from your collection.

CHAPTER 7

TROUBLESHOOTING

You can't hear any sound from your speakers

Modern PCs often have multiple playback channels, in both digital and analog formats. Audio playback hardware can be found in various locations: on your motherboard; as an optional feature on an add-in video card, with multichannel sound typically delivered over an HDMI cable; on an add-in sound card; or through headphones connected physically or wirelessly using a Bluetooth connection. It's not unusual to find multiple audio playback options in a single PC, especially one that has been upgraded extensively.

If your hardware and drivers appear to be installed correctly, but you're unable to hear any sound, click the speaker icon in the notification area and look at the playback device listed above the volume slider. Click the arrow to its right to choose from a list of alternate playback devices.

To change the default device, right-click the speaker icon in the notification area at the right side of the taskbar and choose Playback Devices. This opens the Sound dialog box from Control Panel, with the Playback tab selected. Look for a green check mark next to the device currently designated as the default playback device. In the following example, the built-in speakers are disabled, and headphones connected via Bluetooth are used for communications programs and for playback. To change the default playback device, click the Speakers/Headphones option that corresponds to the device you want to use (the exact wording varies depending on how the driver developer chose to implement it) and then click Set Default:

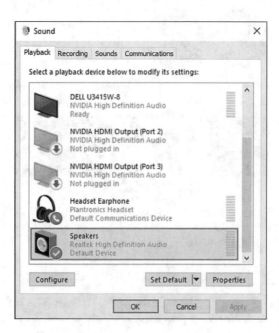

➤ For details on how to configure hardware and install drivers to unlock the functionality of those devices, see Chapter 14, "Hardware and devices."

One new and noteworthy feature that arrived in Groove Music after the release of Windows 10 version 1803 is the playback equalizer. From the Settings page, click Equalizer to open the control shown in Figure 7-9, and then drag the sliders for each of the five frequency ranges up or down. You can choose from eight preset arrangements or create a single Custom setting. Choose the Flat option to play back with no adjustments.

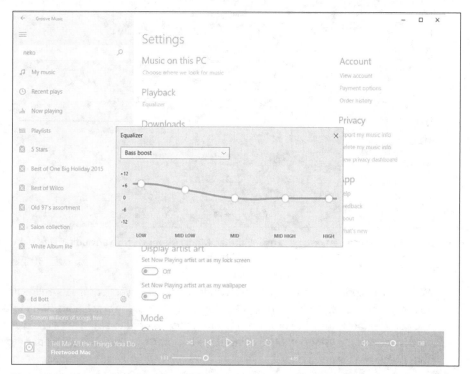

Figure 7-9 The Playback equalizer feature, introduced in mid-2018, allows you to emphasize or soften audio frequencies to compensate for room acoustics or playback equipment.

Using Windows Media Player to rip CDs

If you prefer the familiar Windows Media Player interface to the more modern Groove Music app, relief is a search away. We don't recommend Windows Media Player for new Windows 10 users, but if you're already comfortable with its quirks and you don't want or need to access your music collection from the cloud, it's a thoroughly appropriate choice.

We don't include exhaustive instructions for Windows Media Player in this edition. (If you're interested in that, pick up a copy of *Windows 7 Inside Out* from Microsoft Press, 2011). The single most important task Windows Media Player can perform that Groove Music can't is to convert ("rip") tracks from an audio CD and save them in digital formats on your local hard drive.

Figure 7-10   The best reason to use Windows Media Player is to rip an audio CD to digital format, a task that Groove Music can't perform.

When you're connected to the internet, Windows Media Player consults its online data sources to determine the name of your disc, as well as the names of the artist or artists and tracks and the genre of music the disc contains. This information is used to automatically tag and name tracks. You can use Windows Media Player, File Explorer, or a third-party tag editor to change those tags if necessary.

Windows Media Player copies each CD track to a separate file and stores it, by default, in the Music folder in the user profile of the currently signed-in user (%UserProfile%\Music). Using the album metadata, Windows Media Player creates a folder for each artist and a subfolder for each album by that artist.

The digital files you create by ripping a CD are completely free of technical restrictions on your ability to play them back or make identical copies: you can listen to the saved tracks on your PC or on a mobile device, burn a collection of tracks to a custom CD, or copy those tracks to another PC or to OneDrive. Before you use Windows Media Player to rip a CD, however, it's wise to check the program's settings.

For compatibility with the maximum number of devices, the widely used MP3 format is best.

To set your preferences after inserting a CD, click the Rip Settings button on the Player toolbar. (You can also reach this dialog box by clicking Organize and then Options, and then clicking the Rip Music tab.) Click Format, and then choose one of the eight available formats, as shown in Figure 7-11. If you choose a format that allows lossy compression, use the slider at the bottom of the dialog box to choose a quality level.

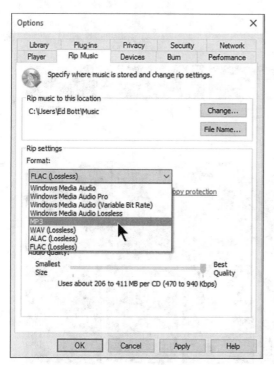

Figure 7-11   Before ripping a CD, be sure to choose a format and quality level here.

As long as you have that dialog box open, use the options at the top to specify the location where you want your ripped files saved and to define the default naming convention for individual tracks.

Photos and videos

Windows 10 includes two built-in apps suitable for viewing, managing, and editing photos in digital image formats. In this section, we concentrate on the Photos app, with a nod to the grizzled elder of image editors, Paint, which remains primarily for compatibility's sake. Another legacy tool from bygone days, Windows Photo Viewer, isn't included with a clean Windows 10 installation, but it might still be available if you upgraded from Windows 7 or Windows 8.1. We can't think of a good reason to use this outdated program.

The Photos app has undergone significant changes since the original edition of this book. These updates, which occur much more frequently than the twice-a-year Windows 10 feature updates, have smoothed the rough edges in its interface and added some notable features. Figure 7-12 shows the user interface of the Photos app as of September 2018, with the entire collection available for browsing and editing.

Figure 7-12   In Collection view, the Photos app displays your collection of digital pictures by date, with newest photos first. Use the timeline on the right to jump to a different date.

As with its music and movie counterparts, the Photos app displays the contents of all files it finds in your Pictures library. It also includes the option to show photos and videos from OneDrive, even if those files are not synchronized with your PC or tablet.

The navigation links above the contents pane include two alternative views you can use to organize photos into albums or browse the contents of your collection by folder rather than by date. A People tab uses facial recognition and manual tagging to help you find pictures containing friends and family members. We discuss Albums and Video Projects later in this chapter.

Several options in the Photos app's Settings page are worth checking before you invest a lot of time and energy learning its inner workings. Figure 7-13 shows some of these options.

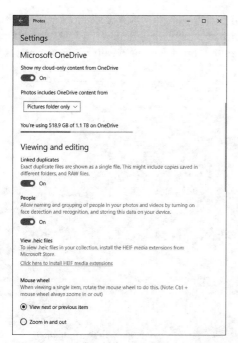

Figure 7-13   To view settings for the Photo app, click the See More menu on the opening page (identified by three dots in the upper-right corner) and then click Settings.

At the top of the page, not shown here, is a Sources list, which allows you to specify which local folders include photos you want to see in your collection. Beneath that entry, shown at the top of the page here, is a switch you can use to include photos and videos from OneDrive. Beneath that switch is an option to select which photos and videos to include from your cloud collection. If you don't want album art from the Music folder and random images from your Documents folder visible in the Photos app, select Pictures Folder Only. If you prefer to see only files in selected folders that are synced to your local PC or device, turn this option off and add the local synced OneDrive folders to your Pictures library.

The Linked Duplicates setting under the Viewing And Editing menu is intended to eliminate the frustration of seeing multiple copies of the same image. This can occur if your camera captures images in RAW format but also saves a lower-resolution copy for easier downloading on space-sensitive mobile devices. You can see the full selection of image files by using File Explorer.

Two options beneath that offer control of people tagging and control of how your mouse wheel behaves when you're viewing a single photo.

Clicking an individual photo from your collection or from a folder or an album opens it for viewing, sharing, and editing, with an array of tools appearing in a bar above the image, as shown in Figure 7-14. (If the menu bar is hidden, click the image to make it reappear.) Note that we clicked the Edit & Create command to display a menu of additional choices; clicking the ellipsis at the end of the menu bar shows a separate drop-down menu with still more options.

Figure 7-14   Double-clicking a photo from the collection displays options for sharing and editing this photo on the menu bar at the top.

If you opened this picture from a folder or album, allow the mouse pointer to hover over either side of the picture to display an arrow you can use to quickly shuffle back and forth through the pictures in a folder. The buttons on the menu bar above the picture allow you to add a photo to an album or other creation, zoom in or out, delete the photo, or rotate it, with options to edit, share, or print the selection on the far right.

Click the ellipsis at the right of the menu bar and then click File Info to see selected details about the image, as shown here. Note that the metadata displayed in the File Info pane is read-only and can't be edited in the Photos app. In the case of photos stored in a local or network folder, you can work with the file and its metadata directly; click Open Folder under the Folder Path heading to open the folder containing the image in File Explorer.

Using the Photos app to crop and edit pictures

The greatest strength of the Photos app is its collection of lightweight editing tools. After opening an image, click or tap Edit & Create > Edit on the menu bar to reveal the lean and efficient layout shown in Figure 7-15. This user experience has evolved substantially over the past few years, from a frankly clunky set of categorized editing tools to the simple but powerful assortment shown here.

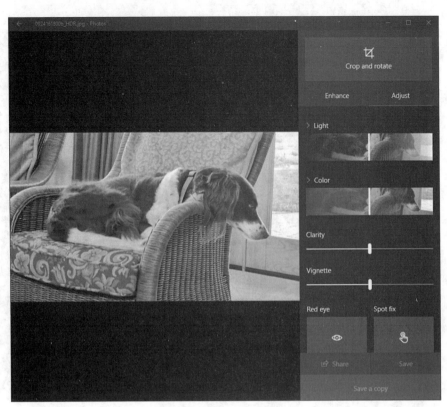

Figure 7-15   The clean layout of editing tools shown here puts you one click away from most useful functions.

To quickly turn a casual shot into something worth keeping and sharing, start by clicking the Crop And Rotate button, at the top of the pane. That reveals the cropping, flipping, rotating, and straightening tools shown in Figure 7-16.

Figure 7-16 The Crop And Rotate tools are the ones you're likely to use most often. The vertical slider just to the right of the photo allows you to straighten a crooked image.

To select the portion of the image you want to keep, cutting out extraneous parts of the picture, grab any of the four corners and drag. Use the controls on the right for more focused tasks:

- **Aspect Ratio.** Click this button to lock a specific aspect ratio into place. The Custom option allows free-form cropping, whereas all other options adjust width and height simultaneously to preserve the ratio you choose:

- **Flip.** Use this option to change a picture to its mirror image, flipping the left-right orientation. This can be useful to make a picture fit a layout. It's generally not a good idea to use this tool with images that contain text.

- **Rotate.** Click or tap this control to shift the angle of the picture 90 degrees at a time, to fix images that are sideways or upside down.

The vertical slider to the right of the image allows you to straighten a picture by moving the horizon of the image in either direction, one degree at a time, for those occasions when you were holding the camera at a slight angle when the picture was snapped.

Click Reset to undo any changes and start over; click Done to close the cropping pane.

All other editing controls are arranged into two groups along the right side of the selected photo. Click Enhance to see the editing options, including 15 predefined filters, shown in Figure 7-17.

Figure 7-17   Select one of the filters on the right to apply that set of effects to the current image. Drag the slider beneath the photo to control the intensity of the filter.

The slider at the top of the editing pane applies algorithmic fixes to lighting, contrast, color, and the like. Move the slider to the left for a darker image, or to the right for more light.

Each of the 15 filters beneath the Enhance slider applies a set of effects that collectively give the image a distinctive look and feel. Use the slider beneath the photo to adjust the intensity of the filter's effects. There's no penalty in trying different filters to see whether you like the result; you can always choose Original (the first item in the list of filters) to remove all effects.

Click Adjust to switch to a different set of editing tools, as shown in Figure 7-18.

Figure 7-18   It's possible to improve a photo with judicious application of these light and color editing tools, which can compensate for poor lighting or exposure.

The two sliders at the top of this pane work in straightforward fashion. Slide the Light bar to the left to make an overexposed photo darker, or to the right to brighten an image that seems a little too dark.

Use the Color slider to change the temperature, tint, or saturation of the image—for example, to compensate for a blue tint from indoor lighting. Move the bar all the way to the left to remove all color, converting the image to monochrome, and to the right to punch up the saturation of the image. Either effect is best used in moderation.

Click the arrow to the left of either slider to expose more fine-grained controls, as shown earlier in Figure 7-18.

If you don't like the results after tinkering with these effects, click the Reset option just above either slider to return it to the neutral setting and start over.

The remaining editing controls in this pane have the following effects:

- **Clarity.** Use this slider to emphasize or deemphasize highlights and shadows, making the image sharper by sliding the bar to the right, or softening its focus by moving that slider to the left.

- **Vignette.** Blurs and defocuses the outside edges of the image, leaving the center portion in focus. This effect, reminiscent of an old-time cameo, is useful when you want to deemphasize a potentially distracting background.

- **Red Eye.** Removes the red-eye effect caused by using a flash when snapping photos of people. (Note that this tool has no effect on pictures of dogs and cats and other nonhuman species.)

- **Spot Fix.** Click this option to change the mouse pointer to a tool that blurs anything you click with it. Use it to remove distractions and clutter from an image, such as blemishes from a close-up portrait.

The options at the bottom of the editing pane remain fixed regardless of which set of tools is in use. Click Undo All to revert the image to its last saved state. Click Save to apply all edits, using the same file name and replacing the current image. Click Save A Copy to leave the original image undisturbed and save the edited image in the same location, with a numeric suffix appended to the file name.

Creating albums and video projects

Previously, we discussed tools for managing an entire collection, which can be organized by date or by folder. Using the second option in the Photos app navigation bar, you can create albums made up of photos and videos you select, which in turn can be viewed as a slide show, uploaded to the cloud, or shared using any app that supports the Windows 10 Share pane. Using the third option, you can turn a selection of photos and videos into a moving picture, complete with narration, music, and transitional effects. Every album and video project has a title and a selection of pictures and videos.

The albums and video project views show creations in OneDrive as well as those stored locally. The Photos app creates some of these projects for you, based on dates, locations, and its own pattern recognition skills. The app can pick out photos containing smiling people, for example, and find pictures that contain animals or bodies of water. You can also create albums and video projects manually, adding photos from any folder as well as from OneDrive.

Switching to Albums view in the Photos app produces a scrolling list of all albums, as shown in Figure 7-19. Those you have created yourself appear at the top; albums created by Photos are shown below. Items stored in OneDrive are denoted by a cloud in the upper-left corner.

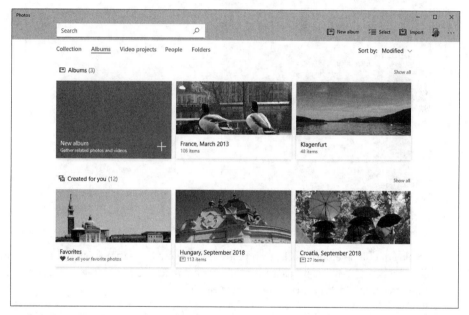

Figure 7-19   The Albums view includes albums you create manually as well as those created for you by the Photos app.

To begin creating a new album, click the big New Album rectangle. That takes you back to Collection view, where you can select items to populate your new album. Alternatively, you can start your creation in Collection view. Right-clicking a photo or video there produces a menu comparable to the following figure.

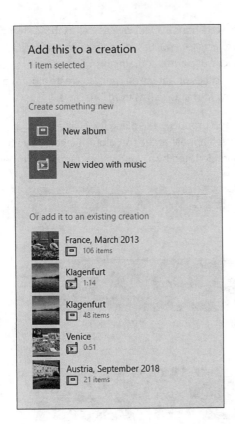

To play or edit an album, click its entry in Albums view. Note that, in addition to expanding an album, you can remove items from it. Albums are made up of pointers to files only, so deletions from an album do not remove the photos within it.

Creating a new video project is similar to creating an album. You can start by clicking the Video Projects item on the main menu bar. Photos responds with tiles for the projects you have already started or finished, along with a selection of items it creates for you. A New Video Project tile, similar to the New Album tile shown in Figure 7-20, gets you started with your new project. Alternatively, you can right-click an item in Collection view and choose New Video With Music from the menu shown in the previous illustration.

After you do either of the foregoing, a tile for your new creation appears in Video Projects view. When you click that tile, Photos responds by creating a video from your selection, as shown in Figure 7-20.

Note that this initial presentation represents the app's choices about sequence, durations, and everything else. You can select individual items on the storyboard and click the headings above the storyboard to edit what Photos has given you. Alternatively, you can start over from scratch by clicking Remove All and then dragging items from the project library to the storyboard.

Figure 7-20 Photos begins the process of creating a new video project by putting all items on the storyboard and making its own decisions about duration, sequence, transitional effects, on so on. You can overrule those decisions.

Editing photos with Paint

Paint (Mspaint.exe) has been a part of Windows since version 1.0. Despite its age, Paint still has a few tricks up its sleeve. Its most useful feature is the capability to save an image in an alternative format. If you saved an image in the space-hogging Windows Bitmap format, for example, you can quickly convert it to a much more efficient, compressed format, such as PNG or JPEG, by using the Save As option on the File menu, as shown in Figure 7-21.

(Paint 3D, which debuted in version 1703, is designed for a completely different set of tasks. Although it has the capability to crop two-dimensional images and export them to alternative formats, the older Paint program is much more suited for the tasks we describe in this section.)

You also can use Paint to resize an image, a capability that's useful if your original image was captured at a high resolution (with a correspondingly large file size) and you plan to post it on a webpage or share it via email, where the large file size might be unwelcome.

Figure 7-21 Use Paint's File menu to convert an image to a different format.

To shrink an image using Paint, click Resize on the Home tab. That opens the dialog box shown in Figure 7-22, which you use to specify a percentage or an actual height or width, measured in pixels. The decrease in file size can be substantial.

Figure 7-22 Use Paint to change the size of an image file; this option is useful when you plan to post an image online and file size is a concern.

Watching movies, recorded TV shows, and video clips

The Movies & TV app is similar in design to Groove Music and Photos. Of the three, it's probably the simplest to use, doing its handful of required tasks very well.

The design of the Movies & TV app follows the same principles as the Photos app, with the navigation bar along the top. The Purchased tab allows you to see content you purchased from the Microsoft Store. (Previous purchases from the Xbox store are also included and can be played back.) Figure 7-23 shows a typical TV library.

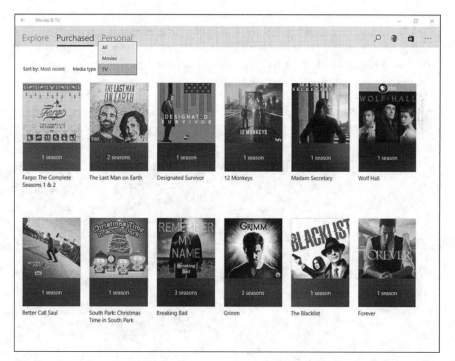

Figure 7-23   Movies and TV programs you purchased through an Xbox or from the Microsoft Store are available for playback here.

Inside OUT

What about DVDs?

In a significant break from the past, Windows 10 doesn't include the capability to play DVDs (or MPEG-2 files ripped from DVDs). That decision is a reflection of two market realities: Most new PCs don't include optical disc drives at all, and the cost of royalties for DVD playback software is significant. On the small percentage of PCs that do ship with optical media drives, the manufacturer typically includes playback software.

Microsoft offers a DVD Player app that is available for purchase in the Store. It should be installed automatically (at no charge) when you upgrade a Windows 7, Windows 8, or Windows 8.1 PC that includes Windows Media Center. If your upgrade doesn't qualify for that offer, we recommend the free VLC software, which contains the necessary codecs and is available in a desktop version from *https://videolan.org*. Although a modern version of the VLC app is available in the Microsoft Store, a prominent warning on this app notes that it does not support DVD playback.

Click Personal on the menu bar to see your collection of personal video files captured in compatible formats, such as those in MP4 formats recorded on a modern smartphone. The player window, shown in Figure 7-24, includes the typical controls for playback, with a slider bar you can use to move to a specific point in the file.

Figure 7-24   Click the double-headed diagonal arrow to zoom a video to full screen, hiding elements such as the title bar and playback controls.

The See More button (indicated by an ellipsis in the lower-right corner of the app) reveals menu options you can use to cast the video to a device such as a large-screen TV—a topic we cover next.

Projecting to another screen

You have a high-definition video on your Windows 10 laptop or tablet. That's fine for watching a rented movie or TV show as you fly cross-country, but that laptop screen isn't big enough for the entire family to share. For that, you need the large, high-definition TV connected to a surround-sound system in your living room.

If you have a long enough HDMI cable, you can connect your laptop's video output to a spare HDMI input on the big-screen TV. That option works, but it's an awkward solution at best. So how do you bring that video to the big screen without tripping over a 15-foot cord?

One answer, if you have the right hardware, is to stream your laptop display (with multichannel surround sound) to the larger, louder living-room system. For this task, you can choose from a variety of wireless standards, each one backed by a large hardware or software company. Windows 10 natively supports a standard called Miracast, which is designed for wirelessly mirroring a mobile display and streaming high-quality sound between mobile devices and large displays, with (in theory) perfect fidelity.

In homes, Miracast is mostly an entertainment option, good for projecting YouTube videos and the occasional webcast to a larger screen. This setup is also effective for a conference room or a classroom, where the Miracast adapter can be permanently attached to a large-screen display and available for connection from any Windows 10 device. The Anniversary Update added the capability for any Windows 10 PC to become a Miracast receiver, allowing you to cast a video from a smaller screen to a larger one.

To project your laptop or tablet display to a TV using Miracast, you need a compatible receiver, such as a TV or Blu-ray player that also supports the standard, or an external adapter that connects to your TV's HDMI port. Although the Miracast standard is relatively new, the technology behind it is well tested, and there are an increasing number of compatible devices on the market. The most versatile option is a thumb drive–sized adapter like the Microsoft Wireless Display adapter shown in Figure 7-25, which plugs into an HDMI input on a TV or monitor and draws power from a USB port on the TV.

A Miracast receiver uses Wi-Fi Direct to turn itself into a special-purpose wireless hotspot. Connecting a Miracast-compatible device to that invisible hotspot allows the device to mirror or extend its display to the larger screen.

CHAPTER 7

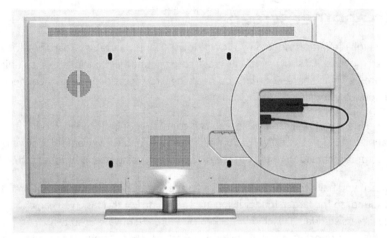

Figure 7-25   The Microsoft Wireless Display adapter plugs into an HDMI port and draws power via a USB connection, turning a TV into a Miracast receiver.

After preparing the Miracast receiver to accept incoming connections (usually a simple matter of turning it on and selecting the matching input on the TV), open Windows 10's Action Center and click or tap the Connect button. That opens up a panel that lists available devices, where you can click or tap the entry for your Miracast receiver, with the goal of making a connection like the one shown in Figure 7-26.

Figure 7-26   Clicking or tapping Connect at the bottom of the Windows 10 Action Center displays this dialog box, from which you can connect to a Miracast device and mirror your laptop or tablet display to a larger device such as a TV.

After successfully connecting to the Miracast receiver, you can duplicate the display on your laptop or tablet to the larger screen, allowing you to wirelessly project a Microsoft PowerPoint presentation to a conference room TV, watch a livestream in your living room, or cue up a music playlist for a party.

All three built-in Windows 10 media apps include a Cast option you can use to send the current video and audio output to a previously configured device.

After you make a Miracast connection, you can change the projection mode just as you would with a second display connected directly to your PC. You use the options in the Connect pane to extend the display so that you can watch a webcast or a video conference call on the large screen while you work on your laptop; use the second screen only; or use the PC screen only, severing the Miracast connection.

Xbox and other forms of online entertainment

Microsoft's Xbox One game console doesn't just connect with Windows 10 devices. It actually is one. The November 2015 update for the Xbox One was the first to be built on the Windows 10 foundation, and subsequent updates have added more features, including support for universal apps that target the console.

Windows 10 includes several features designed to enhance your experience when you play games on desktop PCs, laptops, and tablets powered by Windows 10. These features are conveniently grouped under a Gaming heading in Settings, which debuted in version 1703 and has been steadily evolving ever since.

The Game bar is a pop-up toolbar that appears when you press the default keyboard shortcut, Windows key+G, while playing a game. (You can redefine this shortcut using the Game Bar page in Settings.) As Figure 7-27 illustrates, this compact toolbar offers access to features you can use to share game-playing experiences with other people.

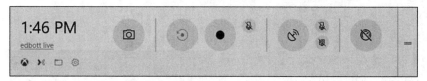

Figure 7-27   The Game bar appears during game play with a tap of its keyboard shortcut, Windows key+G, and allows you to record or broadcast your play session.

If you're especially proud of a gaming achievement, you can capture a single frame or a video clip for posterity by using the tools on the Game bar. From left to right, these tools are:

- **Take Screenshot (Windows key+Alt+PrtScr).** Captures the current frame from your game

- **Record That (Windows key+Alt+G).** Creates a video clip using the most recent few moments from your gameplay. (The exact interval is configurable in Settings.)

- **Record From Now (Windows key+Alt+R).** Use the Game DVR feature to record game play. Tapping this button or using the keyboard shortcut starts and stops recording. The Microphone icon to the right controls whether your recording includes your commentary.

- **Start Broadcasting (Windows key+Alt+B).** Broadcast your game session using the Xbox network.

- **Turn Game Mode On.** With this setting on (some games do this automatically), the system maximizes resources available to the game, improving graphics quality and performance.

Buttons in the lower-left corner include options to open the Xbox app and to adjust Game Bar settings. Tap the gear icon to open the dialog box shown in Figure 7-28, where you can configure game options, including the ability to record game play as a background task.

Figure 7-28 Use this dialog box to adjust settings for the Game Bar itself or click the large blue button to see all Gaming preferences in Windows Settings.

If you own an Xbox One console, we recommend that you check out two apps available for your Windows 10 PC: Xbox One SmartGlass and Xbox app for Windows 10. Xbox One SmartGlass turns a Windows 10 touchscreen device into a capable remote control for your console. You can tap, slide, and type to control games, navigate the Xbox home screen, and pause or play back media files. The Xbox app for Windows 10 allows more direct connections to an Xbox One, including the capability to stream games directly from the console to a Windows 10 device for immediate play even if someone else is using the TV that the Xbox One is connected to.

Microsoft Edge and Internet Explorer

Windows 10 includes not one but two web browsers: Microsoft Edge and Internet Explorer. The former is (relatively speaking) the brash new but rapidly growing kid on the block; the latter is the neighborhood elder. Why two? Because they serve increasingly divergent purposes. Microsoft Edge is a modern browser built to support modern standards and to work well with the web as it exists today; Internet Explorer, by the standards of the World Wide Web, is downright ancient but maintains compatibility with older web-design practices and hence with applications that require such compatibility.

The history of Internet Explorer, from its inception in 1995 to the present, can be viewed as a struggle to maintain compatibility with the past while trying to adapt to an ever-faster pace of change in web development standards. Worthy competing browsers, such as Mozilla Firefox and Google Chrome, didn't have those compatibility burdens, allowing them to progress much more quickly and outperform Internet Explorer.

With Microsoft Edge, Microsoft set out to create a clean-slate, modern browser, free of compatibility freight and engineered to avoid common security hazards. The focus is on support for current and forthcoming web standards and interoperability so that sites developed for other modern browsers will run with minimal or no modifications on Microsoft Edge.

After 20 years of service, the Trident rendering engine of Internet Explorer, Mshtml.dll, has been replaced with the new Microsoft Edge rendering engine, Edgehtml.dll. (The *rendering engine* is what translates HTML and other web code into intelligible, navigable content in a browser or an app using browsing features.) Although the newer engine started with the Trident code as its base, the developers ruthlessly tossed out older features that aren't relevant to the modern web. Among the technologies not included in the new rendering engine are the following:

- ActiveX

- Browser helper objects

- Compatibility view

- Document modes

- Vector Markup Language (VML)

- VBScript

Inside OUT

Microsoft Edge or Internet Explorer?

Internet Explorer 11 is provided with Windows 10 for compatibility reasons, primarily for enterprise environments that require its unique features, such as support for ActiveX controls. Microsoft has pledged to continue to provide technical support and security updates for Internet Explorer, but this legacy browser will not receive new features. That new development work is reserved exclusively for Microsoft Edge.

Large organizations and other users who rely on older web technologies such as ActiveX for their intranets or line-of-business web applications might have reason to make Internet Explorer the default browser. Most others will prefer a more modern browser, with Microsoft Edge earning a place on the short list of candidates for this role thanks to its uncluttered design, touch friendliness, new features, speed, and, above all, enhanced security. By dropping support for technologies like ActiveX and browser helper objects, Microsoft Edge eliminates many of the security hazards that have plagued Internet Explorer over the years.

We know that many of our readers prefer Internet Explorer precisely because of its extensibility options and their longtime familiarity with it. But given its legacy status, we strongly recommend that you have a plan to switch to Microsoft Edge or another modern browser. If you set Microsoft Edge as your default browser, you can still keep Internet Explorer on hand for the occasional website that requires it. Click More > More Tools > Open With Internet Explorer in Microsoft Edge to reopen the current page using your backup browser.

On managed networks, you can deploy Microsoft Edge as the default browser for all users and then turn on a feature called Enterprise Mode, which uses a custom site list to specify particular sites that must use Internet Explorer. Windows 10 version 1607 introduced a new Internet Explorer group policy that restricts Internet Explorer 11 usage to sites on the Enterprise Mode Site List. We cover Enterprise Mode in more detail in "Managing the browsing experience," in Chapter 17, "Managing business PCs."

This chapter assumes that if you're using Internet Explorer, you've been using it a while and you know your way around. We'll have a bit to say here and there about the older browser, but for the most part, we'll focus our attention on Microsoft Edge.

Specifying your default browser

Microsoft Edge is Microsoft's recommended default browser. To make a different browser your default, go to Settings > Apps > Default Apps. Under the Web Browser heading, you should see the name of your current default browser. Click that entry to display a menu that lists Microsoft Edge, Internet Explorer, and any third-party browsers you have installed, along with an invitation to visit the Microsoft Store.

> ➤ **For information about fine-tuning your default settings—for example, assigning particular browsers to particular web protocols—see "Setting default programs and file-type associations" in Chapter 6, "Installing and configuring apps and desktop programs."**

Essential customizations

Before we get to the business of browsing, let's look at some of the ways you can tailor your working environment to suit your needs and tastes. Most of the procedures described in this section begin with a trip to the Settings pane, which is one step removed from the main toolbar in Microsoft Edge. (To keep the user interface touch-friendly and hospitable to small-form-factor devices, the browser, employs relatively few top-level controls.) Figure 8-1 shows some of the choices at More > Settings.

Beginning with Windows 10 version 1809, the many Settings offerings are separated into four tabs. If you've developed habits with earlier versions of Microsoft Edge, this reorganization might take a moment to get used to, but it results in a cleaner and more logical design. You can click the arrow in the upper-left corner of the dialog box to switch between a full-width view of the tab headings and a narrow, icon-only view.

CHAPTER 8

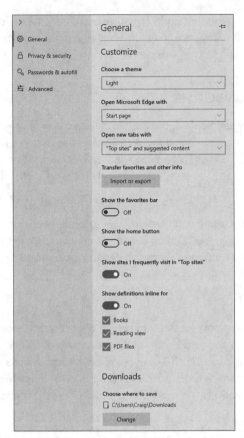

Figure 8-1   Settings in Microsoft Edge are now organized into four tabs. Many basic customization options are located here, on the General tab.

Choosing the light theme or the dark

With the Choose A Theme box, at the top of the General tab, you can flip the user interface in Microsoft Edge from dark text on a light background (the light theme) to light text on a dark background. Note that this reversal does not affect the contents of web pages; it only changes menus and toolbars. Applying the dark theme to these elements might, however, create a pleasing contrast between web pages and the browser itself. Note also that applying the dark theme in Microsoft Edge is different from choosing Dark at Settings > Personalization > Colors > Choose Your Default App Mode. The latter action reverses colors in File Explorer and common dialog boxes but does not affect Microsoft Edge.

Customizing your start and home pages

Microsoft Edge distinguishes between a home page and startup pages. Startup pages, of which you can have one or more, appear at the beginning of each new session. The home page, of which you can have but one, opens only when you click the Home button—which is not displayed by default but can easily be added to your toolbar.

To configure startup pages, click More > Settings and expand the Open Microsoft Edge With menu. Your options are to open with the default Start page (about:start), the new tab page, all pages that were open when you last closed the browser, or one or more pages of your own choosing.

If you select A Specific Page Or Pages, we recommend that you first open the page and then click in the address bar and press Ctrl+C to copy its URL. Paste that address in the box and save it. After you enter a specific startup page in this manner, an Add New Page command appears, as shown in the following illustration. You can use that to specify additional startup pages:

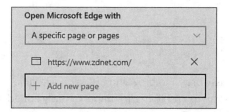

To use a home page in Microsoft Edge, click More > Settings. Then turn the Show The Home Button switch to On. With that option turned on, you can choose where you go when you click the Home button: the Start page, the New Tab page, or a specific page of your choosing.

Displaying the Favorites bar

The Favorites Bar is a special folder whose contents can be displayed below the address bar in Microsoft Edge. By default, it's hidden. To make it visible, click More > Settings and turn on Show The Favorites Bar.

Importing favorites

If you have recently switched your browser default to Microsoft Edge, you might have favorites or bookmarks from another browser that you'll want to import. To do that, go to More > Settings and click Import Or Export. Microsoft Edge then lists your installed browsers, and you can choose which one to import from.

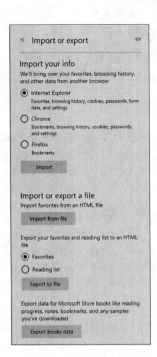

The import feature also migrates saved passwords and browsing history, if available. Select the browser from which you want to import settings and then click Import. Newly added favorites appear in Microsoft Edge in a folder called Imported From *<browser>*, where *<browser>* is the name of the app from which you imported favorites. This is a one-time process. Any subsequent changes you make to the imported favorites are not reflected in the original location, and any new favorites you add in the other browser are exclusive to that browser and not incorporated into Microsoft Edge.

Windows 10 also includes the capability to export Microsoft Edge favorites to a file. Use this option if you want to transfer a curated set of favorites from one Windows 10 PC to another when the two machines aren't using a shared Microsoft account.

Syncing favorites and other settings

If you use Microsoft Edge on multiple systems that log into a common Windows account, you can—and almost certainly should—synchronize your favorites. That way you'll have the same familiar navigational items wherever you work. To do this, visit the General tab at More > Settings. Near the bottom of the screen, under the Account heading, you'll find a switch to turn synchronization on (or off).

With sync on, Microsoft Edge also synchronizes items in your reading list and the list of top sites that it can use to populate a new tab page.

For more about using favorites, see "Browsing with favorites," later in this chapter.

Changing the default search provider

On a clean installation of Windows 10, Microsoft's Bing is, unsurprisingly, the default search provider for both of Microsoft's browsers. With a few simple steps, you can change the default in either browser. The one gotcha is that to change the search provider in Microsoft Edge, you must first have visited the search provider's website. You don't have to do anything there; if the site you have visited supports the OpenSearch standard, you just have to browse to that page once for the provider to show up on the list of available search engines.

With that excursion completed, open Microsoft Edge and go to More > Settings > Advanced. Click Change Search Provider (the very last button, at the bottom of the Advanced tab). To make a change, select an entry from the list that appears:

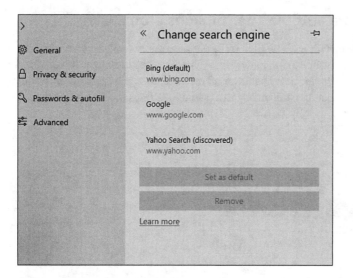

After making a selection, click Set As Default to make that site your new default for searches from the address bar, or click Remove to clear that site from the list of available search providers.

Making text easier to read

Microsoft Edge and Internet Explorer both provide easy ways to make text and graphics on a webpage larger or smaller. If you're working on a touchscreen or on a device with a precision touchpad, you can zoom in and out with the standard touch gestures. Spread two fingers on a page to make the content larger; bring two fingers together to make it smaller.

With a wheel mouse, you can zoom in or out by holding down the Ctrl key as you roll the wheel forward or back. Unlike the Zoom command on the menu (More > Zoom), which magnifies or reduces in increments of 25 percent, each roll of the mouse wheel changes the display magnification by a more granular 5 percent. Zooming with the mouse wheel has the advantage of maintaining the position of whatever object you're pointing to when you begin zooming. Suppose, for example, that you're zooming in to get a better look at a graphical element lying near the right edge of the screen. If you use other zooming methods, the element you care about will eventually drift out of the window. However, if you zoom in by pointing to it and rolling the wheel, the element retains its position relative to your mouse pointer as it gets larger.

If a mouse is not at hand, hold down Ctrl and press the + (the plus sign) to increase magnification; hold down Ctrl and press - (the minus sign) to zoom back out. To return to normal (100%) magnification, press Ctrl+0.

Changes to display magnification are persistent, so if you nearly always require a certain zoom level, you can set it once and not have to worry about it again.

Setting media autoplay permissions globally

Sites that begin playing media on their own, without your explicit approval, can be a serious distraction and annoyance. A welcome improvement in the current version of Microsoft Edge is the ability to turn this autoplay behavior off on a site-by-site basis. You can also turn media autoplay off globally on the Advanced tab at More > Settings:

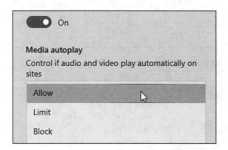

As this illustration shows, you can choose either to limit or to block global autoplay behavior. To limit means to permit silent media but squelch the rest. To block is to suppress the silent players along with the noisy ones.

Because some sites might not function well with suppressed autoplay, you might prefer to control this behavior on a site-by-site basis. We discuss the procedure for doing that later in this chapter. (See "Controlling media autoplay and permissions for particular sites.")

Getting around in Microsoft Edge

Microsoft Edge continues the trend toward visual simplicity (the minimization of "chrome") that has been characteristic of all modern browsers. Unlike Internet Explorer, Microsoft Edge has no menu bar. Figure 8-2 shows the layout of the toolbar (the second line of the display, under the browser tabs) as it stood in Version 1809. Notice that the toolbar controls are well spaced to accommodate fingers and a stylus.

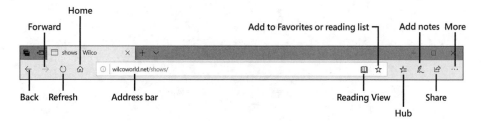

Figure 8-2   The user-interface controls in Microsoft Edge are spaced to accommodate fingers or a stylus.

The Hub button, fourth from the right on the toolbar shown in Figure 8-2, is actually a gateway to five separate items: Favorites, Reading List, Books, History, and Downloads. Clicking Hub opens a tabbed pane comparable to the one shown in Figure 8-3.

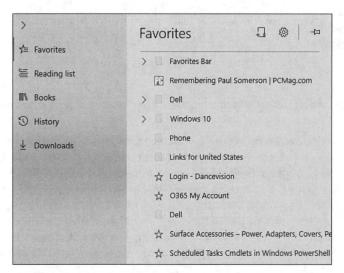

Figure 8-3   The Hub dialog box provides access to five separate items: Favorites, Reading List, Books, History, and Downloads.

By gathering so much functionality into a single location, the Hub serves the interest of finger-navigability. Beginning with version 1809, however, you also have the option of breaking out Hub tabs into separate toolbar controls. You might want to do this if conserving space on the toolbar is not a priority for you and if, for example, you want to get directly to an item such as History without having to click the Hub control first. To add or remove toolbar controls for Hub items, go to More > Show In Toolbar. You will see a list of checked and unchecked items comparable to Figure 8-4.

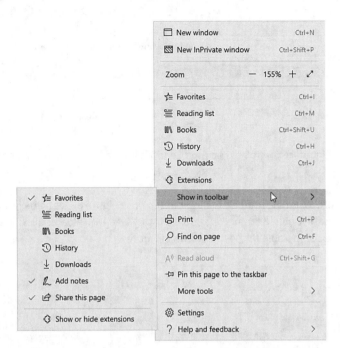

Figure 8-4 You can choose to display or suppress toolbar controls for the items in the list at the left.

Note that by deselecting everything in this list, you could totally disencumber the right side of your toolbar, removing everything there except the More button. You can still get to any Hub item by clicking More or by using the keyboard shortcut shown on the More menu. You can, of course, revisit More > Show In Toolbar to restore oft-used items to the toolbar.

Note also that the Favorites button is the gateway to all five of the elements in the Hub, even though the favorites list is only one component of what appears there. (Hub is the term that earlier versions of Microsoft Edge employed, and it still seems like a useful name for this multi-purpose apparatus.)

Navigating with the Start page and address bar

Unless you configured it to do otherwise, a new instance of Microsoft Edge opens on the Start page, with a large box near the top of the page:

After you enter text in this box you can press Enter or click the magnifier icon (in version 1803 it's a Web Search button). Either action passes the text you entered to your default search provider.

If the Start page is not present (as is the case if you've used about:blank to open a blank page, or if you're already viewing a page), simply type in the address bar and then press Enter. If Microsoft Edge can parse your input as a web address, it takes you there directly. Otherwise, it sends your input to the default search provider. When you use the address bar, Microsoft Edge does its best to simplify your typing task. As you type, the browser offers a proposed completion of your entry, along with a list of matching sites from your browsing history and other possible destinations:

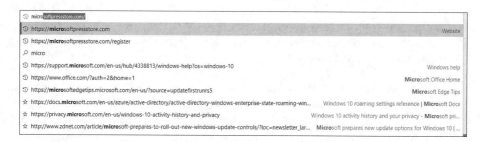

The retrograde clock icons in this list represent items from history. The star icons denote items in your favorites. If you have opted in, information gathered by Cortana about your interests and locations might also appear in the list.

Using tabs

Like all modern browsers, both Microsoft Edge and Internet Explorer allow you to keep multiple pages open on separate tabs in the same application window and switch between them quickly. This feature is a tremendous timesaver for anyone doing research or trying to juggle multiple tasks.

In either Microsoft Edge or Internet Explorer, you can open a new tab in any of several ways:

- To open a new tab, press Ctrl+T, or click the New Tab button, just to the right of the current tabs. The content of the new tab in Microsoft Edge is determined by your choice under Open New Tabs With, at More > Settings.

- To open a link in a new tab without shifting focus from the current tab, right-click the link and choose Open In New Tab, or hold down Ctrl while you click the link.

- To open a link in a new tab and shift focus to the newly opened tab, hold down Ctrl+Shift and click.

- To duplicate a tab, press Ctrl+K, or right-click the tab and choose Duplicate from the shortcut menu. Note that the duplicated tab also includes the history associated with the original tab.

- To close any open tab, point to its tab heading and click the X at the right side. To close the current tab, press Ctrl+W.

- To pin a tab to the browser window so that it appears in a place of honor to the left of all open tabs, right-click its tab heading and choose Pin from the shortcut menu. Pinned tabs occupy a tiny amount of space (on the theory that you know what each pinned tab is and therefore you don't need to see its heading). Pinned tabs reopen every time you open a new Microsoft Edge window.

To reposition a tab within an array of tabs, drag the tab you want to move laterally. To peel a tab off from the current browser window and make it appear in a new window, drag the tab away from the tab bar and release it.

If more tabs are open than will fit in the browser window, a scrolling arrow appears to the left of the first tab or to the right of the last (or both). Click the arrow to scroll in the indicated direction. You can also use keyboard shortcuts to cycle between tabs: press Ctrl+Tab to move from left to right or Ctrl+Shift+Tab to go from right to left.

You can view thumbnails to see which pages are open when the visible text and web site icon (favicon) on the tab itself isn't useful. Point to any inactive tab heading to display an up-to-date thumbnail of that page. For Internet Explorer, you can also point to the program's taskbar icon to display thumbnails for all open tabs, move the mouse pointer over a tab to preview that page, and click to make that the current tab. Note that the thumbnail that appears when you point to the taskbar icon for Microsoft Edge displays only the current tab.

It's easy to open so many tabs that navigation is difficult or impossible; that's especially true when you're working with multiple tabs from the same site, with similar titles and icons for each. Microsoft Edge includes a tab preview bar to help you overcome too-many-tabs syndrome.

Click the down arrow just to the right of the New Tab button to open the tab preview bar, as shown in Figure 8-5. Use the left and right arrows at either side of the tab preview bar to scroll through all open tabs, or point to any open tab and use the mouse wheel to scroll horizontally.

Figure 8-5   For easier navigation, click the arrow to the right of the New Tab button to show thumbnails of every open tab.

To collapse the tab preview bar, click the upward-pointing arrow to the right of the New Tab button.

Silencing a noisy tab

When browsing the web, there is perhaps no feeling more frustrating than to suddenly hear sound bursting out of your PC speakers because a video began automatically playing on a web page. Beginning with Windows 10 version 1803, you no longer have to open each tab to find the offender; instead, scan the tab headings and look for a speaker icon, which indicates that sound is playing from that tab. Click the icon to immediately mute the sound without having to open the tab itself. Click again to unmute the tab's audio stream.

Controlling media autoplay and permissions for particular sites

Clicking the speaker icon on a website's tab shuts the site up immediately. But the next time you open that site, you might find it singing to you once again. To squelch media autoplay on that site in a persistent manner, click the Show Site Information button. For secure sites–that is, those that use the https protocol–the button you're looking for is the lock image directly to the left of the address bar. For sites that are not secure, you'll see an information symbol (the letter i) instead of a lock. In the case of a secure site, clicking opens a Website Identification dialog box that resembles this:

CHAPTER 8

If the site is not secure, you will be admonished with something like this:

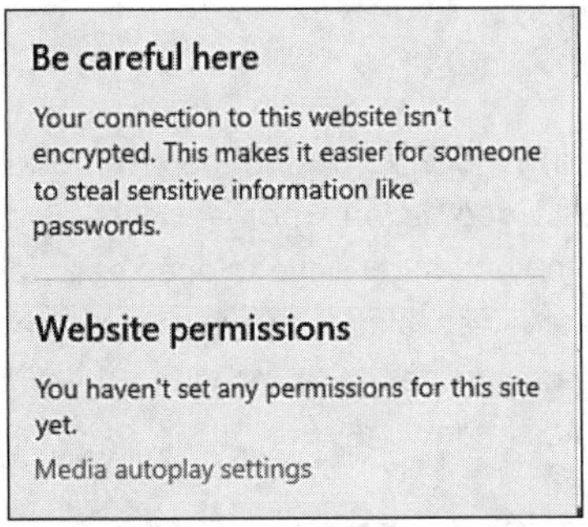

Be careful here

Your connection to this website isn't encrypted. This makes it easier for someone to steal sensitive information like passwords.

Website permissions

You haven't set any permissions for this site yet.

Media autoplay settings

To change media autoplay behavior, click Media Autoplay Settings. The drop-down menu that appears will offer three choices: Allow, Limit, and Block. These are the same options you have when setting autoplay permissions globally, as discussed earlier in this chapter.

For both secure and insecure sites, the link to apply media autoplay settings appears under the heading Website Permissions. If you have granted or refused a permission requested by a site—such as to allow notifications or use your location information—your choice will appear here and you can change your mind if you want. For example, in the secure-site illustration above, the user has been asked to accept notifications and has declined. Clicking the on-off switch reverses that decision. The Clear Permissions button returns the site to the state it was in before it requested permission—in which case it would almost certainly ask again. Clicking Manage Permissions, the link at the bottom of the dialog box, takes you to Manage Permissions, on the Advanced tab of More > Settings. We discuss that option later in this chapter.

Setting tabs aside for easy reuse

Microsoft Edge allows you to set aside all tabs that are open in the current window so that those tabs no longer clutter your display but can be recalled easily when you want them back. Saved tabs appear in a pane similar to Figure 8-6.

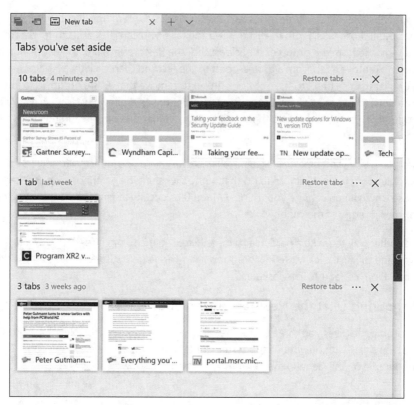

Figure 8-6 Tabs that you have set aside appear in a pane like this one, grouped by the date on which they were set aside.

The controls for setting tabs aside and restoring them appear in the very left corner of the Microsoft Edge window, before the first website tab:

Open set-aside pane

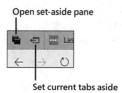

Set current tabs aside

Click the second of these controls to park your current tabs. Click the leftmost control to open the pane of tabs you have already set aside.

Setting tabs aside not only clears away clutter, it also frees up memory and other resources in use by all those tabs. From the list of set-aside tabs, you can click any tab to restore it and remove its tile from the group of set-asides; click the Restore Tabs link to restore all tabs in that group. To remove a tab from a group, point to the tab and then click the X that appears as you hover over it. Click the X to the right of a group to remove that entire group. Click the ellipsis (three dots) to the right of any group to expose options that allow you to save all the tabs in that group as Favorites or share them to any supported target app, including OneNote and email.

Note that if you want a particular tab available every time you launch Microsoft Edge, the simplest solution is to pin that tab. To do that, right-click the tab and choose Pin. Right-click and choose Unpin if you change your mind. Pinned tabs occupy a minuscule amount of visual space near the left edge of the window.

Yet another way to make a particular tab easily reusable is to pin it to Start or the taskbar. To pin a page to Start, click More > More Tools >Pin This Page To Start. To pin to the taskbar, click More > Pin This Page To The Taskbar.

Configuring what the New Tab button does

Microsoft Edge gives you three options regarding the behavior of the New Tab button. You can have "top sites," with or without suggested content, or you can have a blank page. The options, configurable on the General tab at More > Settings, are shown here:

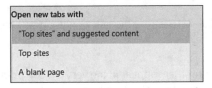

If you choose either of the first two options, new tabs will open with one or two rows (depending on screen width) of "top sites." On a clean install, this list contains up to eight suggested sites, chosen based on your regional settings. After you have used your system for a while, the array of sites will adjust to your browsing habits. You will then see something more akin to the following.

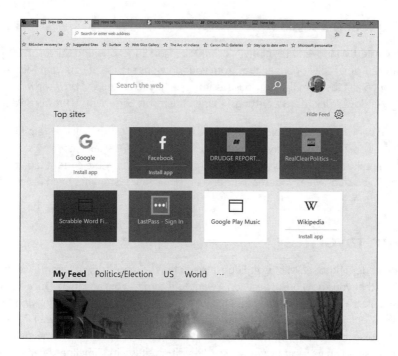

If you find the selection of sites arbitrary or irrelevant, you can eliminate any that you don't want to see by pointing to the thumbnail and clicking the X. After you've used Microsoft Edge for a while, the Top Sites section of the new tab page should reflect your browsing history more and more accurately and become a useful navigational tool. You can drag the tile for any site to a different position. Allow the mouse pointer to hover over any thumbnail and then click the pen icon to edit the link for that tile. If you've removed enough tabs to leave a blank space, click the plus sign at the right of the row to add a new thumbnail.

The suggested content consists of a feed of news stories and advertising provided by Microsoft News. The provider is not configurable, but you can add a few categories to the default array by clicking the ellipsis button at the right.

Reopening closed tabs

Did you accidentally close a tab before you were quite finished with it? No problem. Right-click any tab that's currently open and choose Reopen Closed Tab (or use the keyboard shortcut Ctrl+Shift+T). The page you most recently closed reappears in its previous location. You can repeat this procedure for other tabs you might have closed.

Internet Explorer, but not Microsoft Edge, includes a command you can use to reopen a par-ticular closed tab without having to reopen others that were closed later. Right-click a tab and choose Recently Closed Tabs to display a menu from which you can choose the page you want to revisit.

Restoring your last session

When you restart Windows without first closing Microsoft Edge, opening Microsoft Edge in the new session automatically opens all tabs from your previous session. If you want Microsoft Edge to always open all tabs from the previous session, even if you closed the browser window before restarting Windows, click More > Settings > Open Microsoft Edge With > Previous Pages.

The new tab page in Internet Explorer includes a Reopen Last Session link that reloads every page that was open the last time you closed Internet Explorer. This can spare you some anguish if you accidentally close the browser when you meant to close only the current tab. It can really rescue you if you sit down at your machine and find that your system has been restarted in your absence.

Browsing with favorites

Like every modern browser, Microsoft Edge lets you build a repository of favorite webpages—destinations that you know or suspect you'll want to return to now and then. Once a page has been designated a favorite, you can reopen it with only a few clicks instead of having to search for it again or pull it up from your browsing history. Your browsing history is available for reuse as well, of course (see "Browsing through history" later in this chapter), and Timeline can help you return to sites you've recently visited (see "Revisiting sites with Timeline," later in this chapter), but for pages you visit regularly, a well-placed favorite can be more convenient.

Although Internet Explorer and Microsoft Edge both allow you to save favorites, the two lists are saved in different places and are not shared.

➤ **For information about displaying the favorites bar, importing favorites from another browser, and synchronizing favorites across devices, see "Essential customizations," earlier in this chapter.**

NOTE

The quickest way to add the current page to your favorites in Microsoft Edge is by pressing Ctrl+D. This shortcut works in Internet Explorer (and most third-party browsers) as well.

To add a shortcut for the current page to Favorites or to the Favorites Bar, click the star at the right side of the address bar in Microsoft Edge. As Figure 8-7 shows, that action opens the Add To Favorites Or Reading List dialog box, where you can choose to add the link to your favorites or your reading list. Click Favorites if that's not already selected (as indicated by the underscore and the accent color), edit the name of the saved shortcut if you'd like, choose a location, and click Add.

Figure 8-7 As part of its effort to keep the user interface controls well spaced for touch friendliness, Microsoft Edge combines Add To Favorites and Add To Reading List in a single dialog box, accessed by clicking the star-shaped icon on the right side of the address bar.

To use your favorites, once you have created them, click the Favorites, just to the right of the separator line next to the Add To Favorites button in the address bar (on a default toolbar). You can also get to the favorites list by pressing Ctrl+I.

And no, it's not your imagination. You can scroll through your saved favorites, rename them, and organize them into folders, but there's no way to search directly in the Favorites pane. Entering a search term in the address bar should turn up a saved favorite that contains your term, but in our experience this workaround is inconsistent at best.

Inside OUT

Always rename favorites

Get in the habit of assigning a descriptive name when you save a favorite. Make sure the name you choose contains the words your future self is likely to use as search terms. Steer clear of extra-long file names. Web designers often create outrageously long page titles, packing descriptions and keywords together with the goal of ranking higher on search engines. Shorter, more meaningful names are easier to spot when you're scrolling through a folder full of favorites. And speaking of folders, by all means use them to categorize your favorites. The more favorites you accumulate, the happier you'll be that you have them organized.

Click a favorite to launch it in the current tab. Hold down Ctrl as you click to open the link in a new tab (or right-click the link and then click Open In New Tab). Hold down Shift and click to open the link in a new window. The menu that appears when you right-click also gives you the means to rename or remove a shortcut as well as an option to edit the URL associated with each

CHAPTER 8

saved favorite. Right-click any empty space in the Favorites list to create a new folder on the fly or sort the list by name.

TROUBLESHOOTING

You can't find your Microsoft Edge favorites

Internet Explorer saves its favorites in a subfolder of your user profile, %UserProfile%\Favorites; Microsoft Edge, by contrast, keeps its favorites tucked away in a folder deeply nested under %LocalAppData%\Packages\Microsoft.MicrosoftEdge_8wekyb3d8bbwe. We don't recommend that you go poking around in search of those favorites; you can't do anything useful with the File Explorer entries there anyway. If you try to add a favorite by manually creating a file alongside the others, Microsoft Edge simply ignores it. Use the Favorites list in Microsoft Edge to delete a favorite or rename it.

Inside OUT

Share or save a page

Given its name, you might expect the Share button on the Microsoft Edge toolbar to be exclusively for sharing a webpage with other people. But clicking the Share button also makes it possible to save a page for your own reference, using any installed app that can act as a share target, as shown here:

The system from which you're sharing might offer a different set of targets, depending on which apps are installed and registered as eligible to share content. The format of the shared content depends on the target, but typically it consists of a hyperlink, a thumbnail, and a summary of the page.

Using the reading list to save links for later

Favorites are a great way to preserve and categorize websites to which you expect to return periodically. When you just want to save a link to a page so that you can read it later, when you have more time, the reading list in Microsoft Edge is a better alternative.

To save the current page to the reading list, click the star at the end of the address bar, just as if you were saving a favorite, but click Reading List instead. Give the page a name, and click Add.

Microsoft Edge proposes the name of the page as the name of your reading list item, but you can (and often should) replace that with something easier to recognize. Above the name field, Microsoft Edge displays an image taken from the page you're saving, assuming that it finds one near the beginning of the page.

When you finally have some spare time to read your saved items, click Favorites and then click the Reading List icon or use the keyboard shortcut Ctrl+M. Pages you added to the list are ordered chronologically, with the most recent on top. Click and read.

When you've finished with an item, right-click it and choose Delete.

Browsing through history

Microsoft Edge and Internet Explorer each maintain separate histories of the sites you visit. If you need to return to a site and you neglected to make it a favorite (or save it to your reading list in Microsoft Edge), you should be able to find it by looking through the history listings. (If you have recently been to a site in Microsoft Edge, you might also be able to use Timeline to get back to it. We discuss Timeline next.)

To inspect your history in Microsoft Edge, click Hub, and then click the History tab. Microsoft Edge presents sites in descending chronological order, using relative dates and times: Last Hour, Earlier Today, Yesterday, Last Week, and so on.

Use the outline controls at the left to expand date categories. As you move the mouse pointer over each item, an X appears to its right, allowing you to quickly clean up pages you don't want or need in your history. As Figure 8-8 shows, each item has its own date and time stamp.

For a more thorough pruning of your history, right-click any entry in the history list and choose the last option on the shortcut menu to delete all visits to that domain. To erase the entire history in Microsoft Edge, click Clear History at the top of the list.

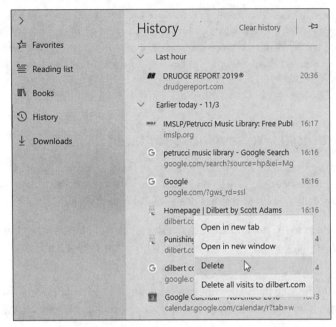

Figure 8-8   Microsoft Edge organizes your browsing history in reverse chronological order. Right-click to erase a single entry or remove all visits to a particular domain.

Revisiting sites with Timeline

Timeline, which we discussed in Chapter 3, "Using Windows 10" (see "Reviewing, revisiting, resuming with Timeline"), provides a chronologically ordered set of tiles that link to recent activities you've undertaken, including sites that you have opened in Microsoft Edge. You can use Timeline as an alternative way to retrace your steps. To open Timeline, press Windows key+Tab or click the Task View button near the left side of your taskbar.

Should you use Timeline instead of History? You might want to experiment to see which you prefer. History is deeper. Timeline stores only 30 days of activity data, so if you're looking for something older, you'll need History. But you might find Timeline more visually appealing, and its tiles often provide a graphic snippet of the site you're looking for. It also supports the capability to search for page titles, which isn't an option in History. On the other hand, it's also more visually distracting. Along with your browsing history, you'll find tiles for all sorts of other activities.

Using Reading View in Microsoft Edge

Zooming in is an excellent way to make small text easier on the eyes. But for more improvement in reading comfort, try Reading View in Microsoft Edge. Introduced in Windows 8 with the modern app version of Internet Explorer, Reading View removes distracting elements from a webpage and reformats the text so that you can focus on what you're trying to read. Reading View is especially useful on pages that are cluttered with ads and where the designer has used type that's too small or has contrast problems with the background.

To display a page in Reading View, click the Reading View icon, which resembles an open book; it's located near the right end of the address bar. If Reading View is not available (because the page is not suitable for that kind of display), the icon will be dim. (The icon might also be dim for a few seconds while Microsoft Edge analyzes your page to see whether it can be displayed in Reading View.) To switch back to normal view, click the Reading View icon again or click Back.

Figures 8-9 and 8-10 show the same page in normal display and in Reading View.

Figure 8-9   In its normal display, the text you want to read might be surrounded by navigational elements, ads, and other distractions.

In converting a page to Reading View, Microsoft Edge removes such distractions as ads and navigational display elements, while retaining hyperlinks, source information, and graphics that the Reading View algorithm determines are integral to the article. Reading View also makes some intelligent layout decisions—for example, offering multicolumn layouts when the width of the browser window allows it. Generous amounts of white space, a soft sepia background, and a specially designed font further augment readability. (The background and font size can be customized.)

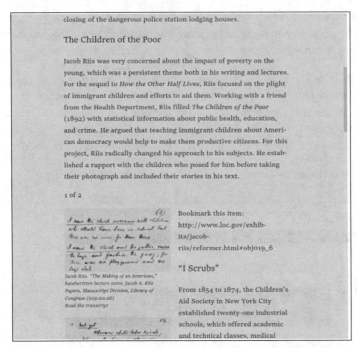

Figure 8-10   In Reading View, the navigational elements have been removed (although hyperlinks are retained), and a generous amount of white space has been added to enhance readability.

A toolbar appears in the upper-right corner of the window in Reading View. (Press Shift+Control+O if you don't see it. Use the same keyboard shortcut or click on empty page space to get rid of the toolbar.) With the first item in the toolbar, Text Size selected, the toolbar looks like this:

You can use the Text Size buttons to increase or decrease the font size. Under Page Themes you'll find four options controlling the background and foreground colors. The same four foreground/background combinations are selectable under the toolbar's Learning Tools heading, along with eighteen additional theme choices. If you like your background pink, yellow, or green, for example, Learning Tools is the place to go. Other options at Learning Tools let you change the inter-word spacing, download a set of grammar tools to support readers for whom English is not native, and more.

If reading is still a challenge, you can ask Reading View to read to you. Turn on your speakers or plug in your headset and click the Read Aloud button on the toolbar. (The Read Aloud option is also available in PDF files and e-books.)

Inside OUT

Get definitions for words without a trip to the dictionary

In Version 1809, if you come upon an unfamiliar word in Reading View, a PDF file, or an e-book, simply select the word and Microsoft Edge will provide its definition:

Percutaneous Coronary Interve

percutaneous

[pərkyooˈtānēəs] ◀))

(adjective) made, done, or effected through the skin.

"percutaneous needle biopsy"

...

www.nhlbi.nih.gov
2 mins read

more

P CI requ   ch is the
  insertion of a catheter tube and injection of
  contrast dye, usually iodine-based, into your

To hear the word pronounced, click the speaker button. To read a more elaborate definition, with etymology and dictionary source, click More. (If you don't see the definition display, visit the General tab at More > Settings and change the settings under Show Definitions Inline For.)

Beginning with version 1803, you can right-click a word or phrase and then click Ask Cortana. As we explain in Chapter 10 , "Cortana and Windows Search" (see "Using Cortana in Microsoft Edge"), that action opens a pane with a definition or other useful information.

Annotating Microsoft Edge pages and PDF files

The Add Notes feature in Microsoft Edge lets you draw on, highlight, add text annotations to, and clip sections of webpages you want to call attention to. You can also annotate PDF document files that you open in Microsoft Edge. You can draw with your fingers or a pen (on a touchscreen) or use the mouse and keyboard on a conventional display that lacks touch capabilities. After you mark up a page, you can email it, send it to OneNote (or another sharing

CHAPTER 8

target). Also, you could simply save it to your own favorites or reading list. In the case of a PDF document, you can save it as a file. Figure 8-11 shows an example of a page with a red circle and some yellow highlighting.

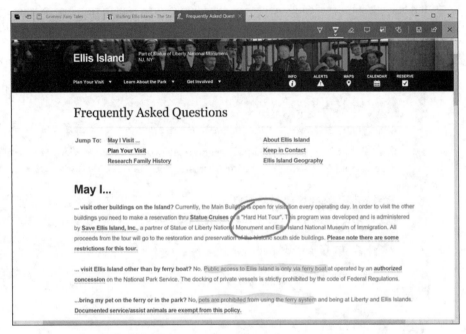

Figure 8-11   The pen and highlighter are two of the tools you can use to create web notes.

To begin creating a web note, click Add Notes, the icon to the left of Share on the toolbar (or press Ctrl+Shift+M). Microsoft Edge opens a set of drawing tools for your use, shown next:

Click the drop-down arrows on the Pen and Highlighter tools to change size and color options. If you inadvertently leave a stray mark or change your mind about an annotation, use the Eraser tool and try again. To get rid of all the marks you've made, click the Eraser tool and then choose Clear All Ink from the menu. (Alternatively, you can exit drawing mode without saving and then come back for another go.)

No pen? Tap the Touch Writing button and use your finger to draw.

To add a text box to the page, use the mouse to click Add A Note, and then click to indicate where you want the text to go. To copy a snippet to the Clipboard, click the Clip tool, and then select the area you want to copy.

The Save Web Note tool, on the right side of the toolbar, offers OneNote, Favorites, and Reading List as destinations. If you save to your favorites or the reading list, you'll be able to pull the page back up at any time and review your annotations. The Share icon presents a full assortment of sharing options using installed apps that support this functionality.

Inside OUT

Use a web note to freeze a webpage

Website content tends to be ephemeral. If you need to capture the current state of a rapidly changing webpage, grab it with a web note and save it to your reading list, favorites, or OneNote. If you don't care to annotate it, you can simply click Make A Web Note and then click Share. There are many other ways to take screenshots, but this one is right at hand as you browse, and it captures the entire page, not just what you see in the confines of your screen. When you reopen your web note from wherever you put it, you can quickly switch back to the "live" version of the site by means of the Go To Original Page link that appears atop the web note.

CHAPTER 8

Extending Microsoft Edge

When Microsoft Edge first arrived in the original release of Windows 10, its single greatest weakness for many was a lack of support for browser extensions. Modern competitors, especially Google Chrome, had built a thriving ecosystem of add-ins that used JavaScript and HTML to extend the capabilities of the browser.

That shortcoming was resolved with Windows 10 version 1607, and the absence of extension support is no longer a valid objection to adopting Microsoft Edge. You can now peruse the Microsoft Store and find a great many useful extensions. Not surprisingly, some of the most useful extensions in the first wave came from Microsoft, including the OneNote Web Clipper and Office Online extensions. The selection of third-party extensions grew slowly but now covers multiple entries in crucial categories, such as password managers and ad blockers.

To see all installed extensions, click More > Extensions, which displays a list like the one shown in Figure 8-12. Click Explore More Extensions to search for additional extensions.

Let the mouse pointer rest over any extension to reveal a gear icon, which is your hint that clicking opens additional options for the extension, including allowing its use for InPrivate browsing or uninstalling it if it turns out not to meet your needs, as shown in the figure at the bottom of the next page.

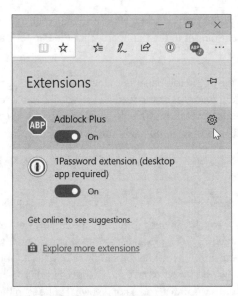

Figure 8-12 Installed extensions show up on this list. Click any extension to see settings, including the option to show the extension's button or uninstall it.

To browse for new extensions, open the Microsoft Store and click the Edge Extensions category.

Reading ebooks in Microsoft Edge

Browsers aren't just for webpages. For example, Windows 10 sets Microsoft Edge as the default program for opening PDF files, and beginning with Windows 10 version 1703, it's also capable of opening ebooks in the standard EPUB format.

You can find a large selection of compatible books for purchase in the Store, in a new Books category. You can also open a locally saved EPUB file by double-clicking it in File Explorer. (Note that books you open this way must be unprotected by digital rights management features.)

The ebook reading experience in Microsoft Edge has evolved dramatically since its initial appearance. Figure 8-13 shows what you might see when reading an ebook in a current release of Windows 10.

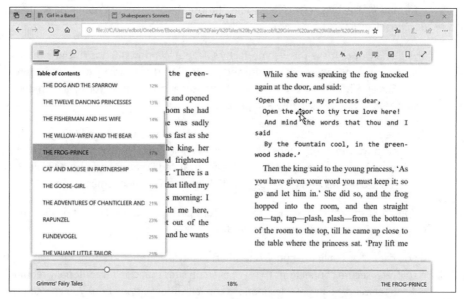

Figure 8-13   The floating toolbar above the book-reading window in Microsoft Edge allows you, among other things, to view a table of contents and make text larger or smaller.

Microsoft Edge can narrate your book if you want it to. Click the Read Aloud button (the second icon in the group on the right) to get started. When narration is in progress or paused, you can click the Previous Paragraph or Next Paragraph button to skip back or forward. Tap the Voice Settings button, shown at the top of the next page, to choose a different voice and to speed up or slow down the narration.

Privacy and security issues

The beauty of the web is that you can use it to connect instantly to an almost unlimited world of information. The bad news is that some of those destinations are potentially dangerous to your PC's health and to your privacy.

There's no way to make the web perfectly safe, but Windows 10 does include features that help you minimize concerns over security and privacy. We discuss many of those features, including SmartScreen Filter, in Chapter 11, "Managing user accounts, passwords, and credentials," and Chapter 18, "Windows security and privacy."

To make sure that SmartScreen Filter is on in Microsoft Edge version 1809, go to the Privacy & Security tab at More > Settings. The switch you're looking for is at the bottom of the pane. (In version 1803, go to More > Settings > View Advanced Settings and turn on Help Protect Me From Malicious Sites And Downloads With Windows Defender SmartScreen.)

In Internet Explorer, click Tools > Safety > Turn On SmartScreen Filter. If the link says "Turn Off . . . ," that means the feature is already enabled.

If you care about online security, one smart practice you should adopt for everyday browsing is to prefer secure connections (HTTPS) even on sites that don't traditionally require it. Insecure links to seemingly harmless destinations can leak information about you and can also be used to spoof sites, potentially compromising a machine using a man-in-the-middle attack. Recent releases of Microsoft Edge flag the addresses of sites that are insecure as well as those that contain a mix of secure and insecure content. In that spirit, we have gone out of our way in this book to use HTTPS links. In this section, we focus primarily on features that are unique to web browsing.

Protecting your privacy

Unless you go to extraordinary lengths, such as using a virtual private network for every browser session, simply connecting to a webpage reveals information about your PC, your internet service provider, and your general location. When combined with other details, even a single, seemingly harmless visit to a webpage can become part of your permanent online profile, used by companies and organizations you've never heard of.

You can't completely disappear online, but you can take some common-sense precautions to cover your tracks and avoid disclosing too much about yourself.

Clearing your browser history and other personal information

Your browser keeps a copy of webpages, images, and media you've viewed recently. This cached information is saved to generally inaccessible locations, but even so, it might give other people who have access to your computer more information than you might want them to have—especially when combined with cookies, saved form data, saved passwords, and other details.

To wipe away most of your online trail in Microsoft Edge, click More > Settings > Privacy & Security. Then, under the Clear Browsing Data heading, click Choose What To Clear. These steps take you to the set of check boxes shown in Figure 8-14. (To get to the comparable location in Internet Explorer, click Tools > Safety > Delete Browsing History.)

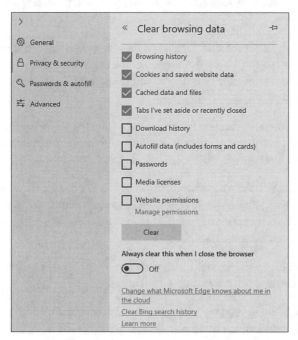

Figure 8-14   Use the options under Clear Browsing Data to specify which elements of your browsing history you want Microsoft Edge to erase.

In Windows 10 version 1809, these choices are as follows:

- **Browsing History.** This is simply a list of sites you've been to since you last cleared your history, whether you went to them directly or followed another site's hyperlinks. You can also view this list from the History tab of the Hub and right-click any entry to delete that item or all saved addresses from that domain.

- **Cookies And Saved Website Data.** A *cookie* is a small text file that enables a website to store persistent information on your hard disk. Cookies, particularly first-party cookies, are generally benign and useful. Note that removing cookies via this option does not block their arrival in the future. (To do that, see "Blocking cookies and sending Do Not Track requests" later in this chapter.)

- **Cached Data And Files.** These are local copies of pages and media content from sites you visit. The browser saves local copies of this data to speed up its display on subsequent visits.

- **Tabs I've Set Aside Or Recently Closed.** This option allows you to quickly clear traces of tabs you've set aside.

- **Download History.** This is the list that appears on the Downloads tab of the Hub. Deleting this history here (or clicking Clear All at the top of the Downloads list—the actions are equivalent) does not remove the downloads themselves, which remain where you put them.

- **Autofill Data.** Your browser allows you to store some information—for example, your shipping or email address—that you use to fill out forms, simplifying reuse. This option erases all such saved entries.

- **Passwords.** As we discuss later in this chapter (in "Allowing or not allowing your browser to save sign-in credentials"), there are pros and cons associated with saving sign-in credentials for websites. If you change your mind after you've allowed the browser to store these credentials, you can erase the data here.

- **Media Licenses.** This category includes the digital rights management information that allows you to play audio and video files on the current device.

- **Website Permissions.** When you visit a webpage, it can request permission to perform specific actions, such as delivering notifications, switching to full screen, or using your location for personalization. Click this check box to remove all saved permissions, or click Manage Permissions to review and modify these settings on a per-site basis.

After making your selections, click Clear. To automatically clear the selected data every time you shut down the browser or sign out, turn on the Always Clear This When I Close The Browser setting.

Squelching history temporarily with InPrivate browsing

If you want to cover your local tracks only for a particular browsing session, don't bother fussing with history settings or clearing items after the fact. Instead, open an InPrivate window. In Microsoft Edge, click More > New InPrivate Window. In Internet Explorer, click Tools > Safety > InPrivate Browsing. In either browser, you can use the keyboard shortcut Ctrl+Shift+P to open an InPrivate window. When you subsequently close the InPrivate session, the browser deletes any data it stored (session cookies and other temporary files, for example), and no record of the visit is saved in history.

Be aware that browsing privately is not the same as browsing anonymously. Sites you visit can record your IP address, and your network administrator or internet service provider (which includes anyone in control of a public Wi-Fi hotspot) can see which sites you connect to and can capture any unencrypted information you transmit or receive.

During an Internet Explorer InPrivate session, toolbars and extensions are disabled by default. If you want them enabled, click Tools > Internet Options. On the Privacy tab, clear Disable Toolbars And Extensions When InPrivate Browsing Starts. For Microsoft Edge, you can allow or prohibit the use of extensions in InPrivate mode on a per-extension basis, as we describe in "Extending Microsoft Edge," earlier in this chapter.

Blocking cookies and sending Do Not Track requests

Cookies—small bits of information that websites store on your hard disk—come in two flavors. First-party cookies are used by the site you're currently visiting, generally for such purposes as personalizing your experience with the site, storing shopping-cart information, and so on. Third-party cookies are used by a site other than the one you're visiting—such as an advertising network or social media service that has placed an ad or a sharing button on the site you're currently visiting.

Cookies do not carry executable code (they're text files), and they can't be used to spread viruses or malware. A cookie can provide a website only with information you supply while visiting the site; a cookie has no access to the Windows file system and can't read your address book or financial records, for example. The information a cookie gathers can be read only by pages in the same domain as the one that created the cookie.

Nevertheless, privacy concerns arise when advertisers and web-analytics companies begin to correlate the information from third-party cookies to build a profile of your activities. Because it's not always obvious who's sending you a cookie and what purposes that cookie serves, some people are understandably wary about allowing cookies on their systems.

The most effective way to block this form of tracking is with the use of ad-blocking extensions for Microsoft Edge. A cruder solution, available in both of the Microsoft browsers included with Windows 10, allows you to block either all cookies or third-party cookies. In Microsoft Edge, visit the Privacy & Security tab at More > Settings. Then open the drop-down list below the Cookies heading. You'll see the following simple set of choices:

In Internet Explorer, click Tools > Internet Options. On the Privacy tab, click Advanced to open the Advanced Privacy Settings dialog box. There, you can express your preferences separately for first-party and third-party cookies. In addition to accepting or blocking cookies, you can ask to be prompted each time a first or third party wants to deliver or update a cookie. You're likely to find this choice more trouble than it's worth. In addition, you can also choose to allow all session cookies—cookies that are deleted at the end of your browsing session. In a separate group of settings (which you can access by clicking Sites on the Privacy tab of the Internet Options dialog box), you can block or allow cookies on a per-domain basis.

Sending Do Not Track requests

Some websites use *tracking* capabilities to gather information about your browsing history, information you enter in your browser, and other details of your online life to build a profile that companies can use for targeted advertising and other purposes. If that bothers you, you can ask them to stop.

The Do Not Track (DNT) standard, which is nearing final approval after years of development by a committee of the World Wide Web Consortium (W3C), is now supported by all modern browsers. If DNT is enabled, when you visit a site, the browser sends a DNT=1 header with every request for a new page. Alas, this seemingly straightforward option is not widely accepted, nor is it backed by any technical or legal enforcement mechanisms.

In Windows 8, the option to send Do Not Track requests was turned on by default (included with Internet Explorer's "express settings"). This provoked controversy and resistance from both competing browsers and the advertising industry because the standard, as codified by the W3C, stipulates that DNT requests must result from an active decision by end users. Microsoft reversed its position on the matter, and in both Microsoft Edge and Internet Explorer, DNT is initially turned off. To turn it on in Microsoft Edge, click More > Settings . On the Privacy & Security tab, turn on Send Do Not Track Requests. In Internet Explorer, click Tools > Safety > Turn On Do Not Track Requests.

A far more effective solution for the problem of excessive tracking is ad-blocking software, which has the salutary side effects of speeding page loading times and blocking the most common vectors for serving malware via web exploits. At the time we wrote this chapter, at least six offerings in this category were available in the Store as extensions for Microsoft Edge.

Controlling Flash content

Historically, one of the most problematic parts of any browser, from the standpoint of security and reliability, is a reliance on third-party add-ins. Microsoft Edge includes Adobe's Flash Player, but effective with Windows 10 version 1703, this feature is set to work in "click to run" mode.

As a result, Microsoft Edge now blocks Flash content on untrusted pages by default until you explicitly choose to play that content. When Microsoft Edge blocks Flash content, it displays a puzzle icon in the address bar; the first time it does so, it includes a pop-up tip to alert you to this otherwise subtle change in the user interface, as shown in Figure 8-15. Click the puzzle icon to allow the content to play once or every time you return to the same site.

Figure 8-15   This explanatory message appears the first time you encounter a blocked piece of Flash content in Microsoft Edge.

Managing and securing your web credentials

When you sign in to a password-protected website using Microsoft Edge or Internet Explorer, you have the option to save your user name and password so that it can enter those credentials for you automatically when you revisit that site. In Microsoft Edge, the prompt looks like this:

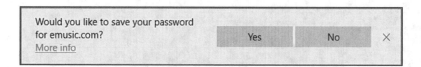

If you click Yes, the user name and password are saved for you. If you click No, the user name is saved but not the password, and you won't be asked to save that password again. Internet Explorer has a similar process for requesting to save credentials.

When you revisit the website, your browser automatically fills in your credentials for you, with the password field masked. (Saved credentials are not filled in automatically when you use InPrivate mode, but the password is filled in when you manually enter the user name.)

If you have multiple credentials saved for a specific site (for example, if you sign in to Microsoft services using more than one Microsoft account), you can position the insertion point in the user name field and press the Down Arrow key to choose from a list of saved credentials.

CHAPTER 8

TROUBLESHOOTING

Windows 10 won't save your user name and password

If your browser doesn't offer to save a specific set of credentials for you, first confirm that the option to save passwords is turned on. Next, check the list of saved credentials (in Microsoft Edge or using Control Panel's Credential Manager) as described in the following sections. If you see an entry for the uncooperative site, delete it and try again. If that fails, you might be facing a website whose designers have blocked the browser from saving credentials. A third-party password manager or an alternative browser might work; otherwise, your only option is entering the password manually.

Windows 10 is responsible for managing web credentials, which are stored in a secure, encrypted vault. Saved credentials can be accessed by either browser after you're properly authenticated.

Allowing or not allowing your browser to save sign-in credentials

Saving web credentials is an optional feature. It can save you time and trouble when you're revisiting sites—shopping sites, for example—that require you to sign in to an account. It also means anyone who sits down at your unlocked computer can sign in to those same sites without your permission. If you're comfortable typing in your own passwords, or if you use a third-party password manager, you can turn off credential saving in Microsoft Edge. Click More > Settings. On the Passwords & Autofill tab, slide the Save Passwords switch to the Off position. In Windows 10 version 1803, similar options appear under Autofill Settings when you click More > Settings > Advanced Settings:

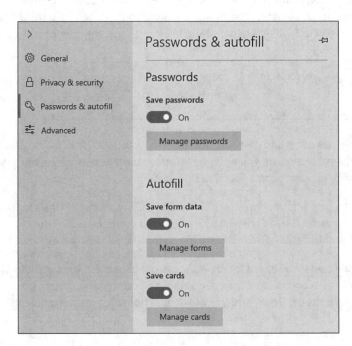

CHAPTER 8

This group of settings also includes options for saving form entries and cards that (with your permission) automatically fill information such as addresses and credit card numbers in web forms. The latter feature was introduced in Windows 10 version 1803.

Note that disabling the offer to save passwords does not affect any previously saved credentials. To view and manage those credentials, click Manage Passwords (just below that switch). Rest the mouse pointer over any individual entry in the list of all saved credentials, and click the X to remove that item. Right-click to see the option to open that site in a new tab.

If you click a saved password in this list, Microsoft Edge displays the URL, user name, and encrypted password, like this:

You can modify the user name or password in this dialog box and then save your changes, but for your security, Microsoft Edge will not show you (or anyone else using your computer) the current password. (You can, however, inspect passwords using Credential Manager, which we discuss next.)

To reach the comparable setting in Internet Explorer, click Tools (or press Alt+X) and open the Internet Options dialog box. On the Content tab, under the AutoComplete heading, click Settings. The option to save passwords (and to be prompted for approval each time Internet Explorer finds new credentials to save) appears in the AutoComplete Settings dialog box, along with numerous similar options.

Viewing and deleting credentials with Credential Manager

The Manage Passwords button in Internet Explorer's AutoComplete Settings dialog box takes you to Credential Manager, a destination you can also reach by typing Credential Manager in the search box. The Web Credentials section of Credential Manager displays a list of user names and passwords saved by either Microsoft Edge or Internet Explorer. Clicking an item reveals details, as shown in Figure 8-16.

The list of credentials here is identical to the one you can see in Microsoft Edge. The Remove option provides a way to clean out credentials you no longer need. Clicking Show allows you to see the saved password for a site, but a casual snoop won't be able to steal that information. For your security, you must first reenter the password you use to sign in to Windows or provide acceptable biometric proof, such as on a device that uses Windows Hello facial recognition.

Figure 8-16   Credential Manager, a part of Control Panel, lists all web credentials saved by either browser.

Configuring security zones in Internet Explorer

Internet Explorer uses a system of "security zones" that apply security settings differently for different categories of websites. The zones are called Internet, Local Intranet, Trusted Sites, and Restricted Sites, and you can configure them by going to the Security tab of the Internet Options dialog box, shown in Figure 8-17. In its quest for a simpler browsing experience, Micro-soft Edge does not include an equivalent system.

The four zones are intended to be used as follows. The Restricted Sites zone, designed for sites that you trust the least (or explicitly distrust), has the highest security settings—that is, the maximum in safeguards. The Trusted Sites zone has, by default, a medium level of protection, blocking the download of unsigned ActiveX controls and prompting for permission before downloading other material considered potentially unsafe. The Internet Zone—with medium-high settings—is reserved for all nonintranet sites you have not assigned to the Trusted Sites or Restricted Sites zone. The Intranet Zone, with low security settings, is populated with intranet sites you have not explicitly moved to Trusted Sites or Restricted Sites, sites that bypass your proxy server, and all network servers accessed via a UNC path (\\server_name).

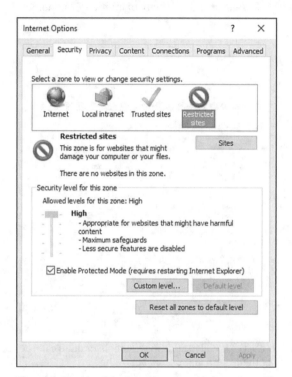

Figure 8-17 Use this dialog box to add sites to specific zones in Internet Explorer or to modify the security settings associated with a zone.

To add sites to a zone, select the zone and click Sites. To change the security settings for a zone, adjust the slider or click Custom Level.

Managing and troubleshooting add-ons in Internet Explorer

One reason Internet Explorer has been relegated to the legacy category is that its add-on model is fundamentally flawed. Through the years, Microsoft's engineers have knocked down some of the most troubling vulnerabilities, but add-ons still remain the weakest link in Internet Explorer. To view information about add-ons, click Tools > Manage Add-Ons.

The Toolbars And Extensions section of the Manage Add-Ons dialog box, shown in Figure 8-18, provides information about whatever ActiveX controls, browser helper objects, and other add-ons you have installed in Internet Explorer. You can inspect version numbers, see how many times an add-on has been used or blocked, and view details of the performance impact of any add-on. More importantly, you can disable an add-on completely, either as a troubleshooting step or as a way to improve the performance and reliability of Internet Explorer.

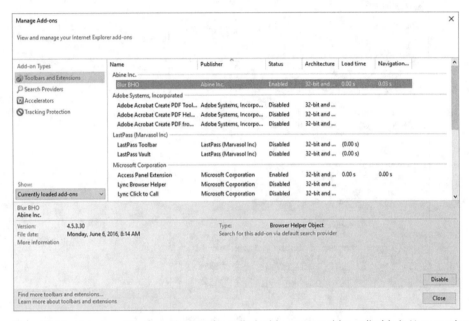

Figure 8-18   Select an item from the list of installed add-ons to enable or disable it. You can view a summary of details about the item in the pane below the list.

When you select an item from the list of add-ons, you can see more details about it in the pane below, including the publisher's name, the version number and file date (if available), and the add-on type. Buttons in the lower-right corner let you disable or enable the add-on.

If you're ready to be completely overloaded with information, double-click an add-on's name in the list. If the selected add-on is an ActiveX control, you see an information-rich dialog box like the one shown next.

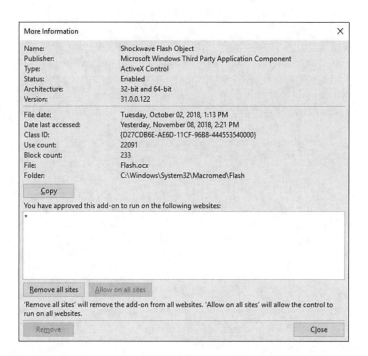

In the large box here, the asterisk—the wildcard character for "all"—indicates you have approved the add-on to run on all sites. If you're particularly cautious, you might want the option to approve websites on a site-by-site basis. In that case, click the Remove All Sites button. From that point forward, whenever you visit a site that uses that ActiveX control, Internet Explorer will request your permission to run it. If you grant your OK, the domain is added to the list of approved sites.

Storage and file management

Unless you use your computer exclusively as a game machine, learning to manage your "stuff"—your documents, programs, and communications—is probably the single most critical computing skill you need to acquire. The addition of cloud services adds extra flexibility as well as new organizational challenges, especially as you juggle multiple devices with different storage capacities.

In this chapter, we cover the best way to manage files on local volumes and in the cloud.

Microsoft's cloud storage service, OneDrive, offers 5 GB of free storage with every free Microsoft account. Its sync engine, built into Windows 10, is now shared by OneDrive and OneDrive for Business. A relatively new OneDrive feature, Files On-Demand, allows you to browse through your cloud storage without having to fill up all of your local storage. In this chapter, we explain how to configure OneDrive so that your most important files are available when you need them, even if you're not connected to the internet.

The primary tool for managing files in Microsoft Windows 10, regardless of where they are located, is File Explorer (the direct descendant of what was known as Windows Explorer in Windows 7 and earlier versions). File Explorer is an amazingly powerful tool, filled with features that can streamline your work processes and make it easier to find digital music files and photos. Most Windows users barely scratch the surface of File Explorer, which is why we devote a significant section of this chapter to a master class in its rich feature set.

Finally, this chapter also covers the tools and techniques for working with existing local drives—internal, external, and removable—including managing volumes and monitoring disk usage.

> ➤ File Explorer also includes a search box, which we cover in Chapter 10, "Cortana and Windows search," along with additional details about Windows 10's powerful indexing and search tools.

CHAPTER 9

Organizing personal data with user profile folders and libraries

Windows uses a logical organizational structure that helps keep data together in known system folders. As we explain in this section, you can change the location of some of these folders to make best use of your available storage. You can also create virtual storage locations called *libraries* to make searching easier.

What's what (and where) in your user profile

Your personal files and settings are stored by default in your *user profile*, which is created by copying the contents of the Default profile to a new folder when you sign in to a user account for the first time on a device. In addition to predefined folders for personal documents and digital media files, this new profile also includes the details that define the desktop environment: the user's own registry settings (HKEY_CURRENT_USER) as well as user data and settings for installed apps and desktop programs.

> **NOTE**
>
> **Although you can customize the Default profile, doing so requires the use of enterprise deployment tools and is impractical for home and small business installations.**

In addition to individual user profiles, the operating system creates a Public profile containing a group of folders for common document types that mirror those in your user profile. You can see the Public Documents, Public Music, Public Pictures, and Public Videos folders in their matching libraries. The advantage of these folders is that other users can save files to these locations from different user accounts on the same computer or from across the network.

Local user profiles are stored in %SystemDrive%\Users. Each user's profile is stored in a subfolder whose name is based on the user account name (for example, C:\Users\Katy). The entire path for the current user's profile is accessible via another commonly used environment variable, %UserProfile%. If you have File Explorer's navigation pane set to show all folders, you can see the subfolders of your profile by clicking your user name in the navigation pane.

> **TROUBLESHOOTING**
>
> **Your user account name and user profile folder name don't match**
>
> As we mentioned earlier, Windows creates the user profile folder when you first sign in to a device. If you do so with a local or domain account, the name of the profile folder matches the user name (unless there's already a folder with that name from a previous installation, in which case Windows appends a dot and the name of the PC to the folder name). Signing in with an Azure AD account creates a profile name consisting of your username with the extension .AzureAD.

This naming convention breaks down if you sign in for the first time using a Microsoft account. In that case, Windows creates a folder name using the first five characters of the user name associated with the Microsoft account. If your user name is six characters or longer, the folder name (which is also shown in File Explorer as the profile name) is truncated. So the profile folder for edbott@example.com becomes C:\Users\edbot.

If that folder name bothers you, we have some bad news: There's no supported way to change the user profile folder name after that first sign-in. But you can make sure it doesn't happen again. The trick is to create a local user account with the same name as what you want to use for your user profile folder. (Follow the instructions in "Creating and managing user accounts," in Chapter 11, "Managing user accounts, passwords, and credentials.") Then, after signing in for the first time using that local account, you can connect your Microsoft account.

To see the folders included in your user profile, open its folder directly from C:\Users or from the drop-down menu at the left of the address bar. As you can see from Figure 9-1, the list includes some familiar destinations. (Because third-party apps can add their own data folders to the user profile, your system might include some additional folders.) In that same figure, you might also notice the dark theme support for File Explorer, newly added in version 1809.

Figure 9-1   Your user profile contains folders intended for specific types of data as well as a hidden AppData folder for data that should be accessed only from within an app.

CHAPTER 9

Inside OUT

What's in the AppData folder?

The hidden AppData folder, introduced in Windows Vista, is used extensively by programs as a way to store user data and settings in a place where they'll be protected from accidental change or deletion. This folder contains application-specific data—customized dictionaries and templates for a word processor, synchronized copies of messages stored on an email server, custom toolbar settings, and so on.

It's organized into three subfolders, named Local, LocalLow, and Roaming. The Roaming folder (which is also accessible via the environment variable %AppData%) is for data that's made available to a roaming profile (a profile stored on a network server; the server makes the profile available to any network computer where the user signs in). The Local folder (which is also accessible via the system variable %LocalAppData%) is for data that should not roam. This location includes the Temp folder (accessible with the environment variable %Temp%), where Windows and apps create files that are strictly for temporary use. The LocalLow folder is used by applications that run at a lower integrity level, such as Internet Explorer in Protected Mode or Mozilla's Firefox browser in Private Mode.

The personal data folders (Documents, Downloads, Music, Pictures, and Videos) serve as the default location for applications that use those file types. You'll also find folders containing the contents of synced OneDrive and SharePoint data stores. Here's everything you need to know about the remaining folders:

- **3D Objects.** Apps like Paint 3D and Mixed Reality Viewer store their data files here by default. This system folder made its first appearance in Windows 10 version 1709.

- **Contacts.** This folder first appeared in Windows Vista and was designed to store contact information used by Windows Mail. It is not used by any programs included in Windows 10 and is maintained for compatibility purposes with third-party personal information management programs.

- **Desktop.** This folder contains items that appear on the user's desktop, including files and shortcuts. (A Public counterpart also contributes items to the desktop.) A link to this location appears in the Quick Access section of the navigation pane.

- **Favorites**. Internet Explorer saves shortcuts to websites here. (Microsoft Edge, as we note in Chapter 8, "Microsoft Edge and Internet Explorer," handles its favorites collection differently.) To manage Internet Explorer favorites in File Explorer, type the shortcut **shell:favorites** in the address bar.

- **Links.** In Windows 7, this folder contains shortcuts that appear in the Favorites list at the top of the navigation pane. Its contents are not used in Windows 10.

- **Saved Games.** This folder is the default storage location for apps that can save a game in progress.

- **Searches.** This folder stores saved search specifications, allowing you to reuse previous searches. (We explain how to use this feature later in this chapter.)

Inside OUT

Customize the Send To menu

The SendTo folder, in %AppData%\Microsoft\Windows, contains shortcuts to some folders and applications that appear on the Send To submenu when you right-click a file or folder in File Explorer (or on the desktop). The SendTo folder is not hidden. You can add your own items to the Send To menu by creating shortcuts here. Type **shell:sendto** in the File Explorer address bar or in the Run dialog box (Windows key+R) to open this folder and add or delete shortcuts.

Relocating personal data folders

The organizational scheme that Windows uses for personal data folders—keeping documents, music, pictures, and so on in visible subfolders of %UserProfile%—is perfectly appropriate for most configurations. In fact, for portable devices and all-in-one PCs that have only a single storage device, it's the only option.

On desktop PCs that include options for multiple storage devices, some users prefer to store documents and other personal data on a volume other than the system drive. With this configuration, it's easier to organize large collections of data, in particular, digital media files, which have a way of overwhelming available space on system volumes. (It's a good idea to keep a portion of your system drive free for maintenance, such as updates, and for performance, which reduces available data storage even further.)

This option is especially attractive on desktop PCs where Windows is installed on a solid-state drive (SSD) to maximize performance. Adding a second, much larger conventional hard disk—at a cost per gigabyte that's typically a fraction of an SSD—makes it possible to store large amounts of data without compromising system performance.

The easiest, safest way to accomplish this goal is to store personal data in folders on a separate drive, and then include those folders in your libraries and set them as the default save location, a topic we cover in the next section. This approach leaves you with a default set of profile folders, which you can still use when it's convenient to do so, but it keeps the bulk of your data files on a separate drive.

CHAPTER 9

Not everyone loves libraries, however, and there's no requirement to love them. You can still move some or all of your profile subfolders in Windows 10, just as you could in earlier versions. To relocate a user profile folder by editing its properties, follow these steps:

1. Open your user profile folder by starting at This PC, navigating to C:\Users, and then double-clicking your profile name. Alternatively, enter **%UserProfile%** in the address bar.

2. Right-click a folder you want to relocate and choose Properties. (Or select the folder, and then click Properties on the Home tab.)

3. On the Location tab of the properties dialog box, enter the address you want to relocate the folder to. For example, to move the Downloads folder from C:\Users\Edbott\ Downloads to X:\Downloads, type or paste the path as shown here:

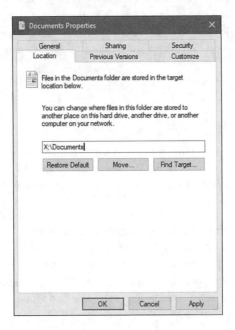

4. Click OK. Windows asks permission to create the target folder if it doesn't already exist. Click Yes. A Move Folder dialog box similar to this one appears:

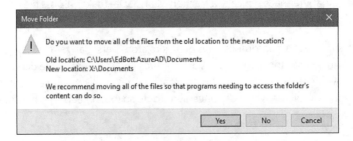

5. Unless you have some good reason not to move the existing files from the original location to the new one, click Yes.

It's really not a good idea to click No in this dialog box. First, it's difficult to imagine why you would want to divide your personal documents into two identically named folders on different volumes. (If you want to keep your existing files separate from those you save in the future, move the old files to a subfolder in the new location instead of leaving them in the old location.) Second, because %UserProfile% is a system-generated folder, not an ordinary data folder that corresponds to a fixed disk location, leaving some files behind will give you two subfolders with the same name in %UserProfile%.

A relatively new option in Windows 10 allows you to relocate specific folders from your personal profile to OneDrive. We cover this option in more detail later in this chapter.

Using libraries

A *library* is a virtual folder that aggregates the contents of multiple folders stored on your computer, on your network, or in the cloud. You can sort, filter, group, search, arrange, and share the data in a library as if it were in a single location. Windows 10 gives you several by default: Documents, Music, Pictures, Saved Pictures, and Videos. You can create additional libraries to suit your storage needs, and you can customize any library by changing or adding to the physical folders that make up that library.

The important things to understand about libraries are the following:

- A library can encompass multiple folders on multiple disks on multiple networked devices.

- All folders in a library must be capable of being indexed, which in turn means you can perform fast searches covering the full contents of a library by entering a search term in the search box while viewing the contents of a library in File Explorer. That action quickly pulls up all matching documents, even if they're located on a networked PC or server or on an external drive. (It also means that you cannot add a shared folder to a library if it's located on a network-attached storage device that doesn't support Windows indexing.)

- Library files are automatically backed up by the Windows 10 File History feature.

Libraries are useful for large collections of digital media files, where archived files are stored in a shared network folder or on an external drive, with current projects on a local drive. They're also invaluable for keeping team projects organized—create a library that includes your local project folder and the shared folders where your coworkers store graphics and final submissions.

Figure 9-2 illustrates a library search. Here we created a custom library called Research, made up of a synced OneDrive folder, a local folder containing scanned documents, and a shared network folder. Searching for the term *population* returns a single results list containing eight matching items—four Word documents, three Excel worksheets, and a PDF file—stored in three different locations.

CHAPTER 9

To create a new library, right-click the Libraries heading in the navigation pane, and then click New > Library. Give the new library a descriptive name and then press Enter. Your newly created library appears in the navigation pane. Open it and then click the Include A Folder button to populate the library.

Using the Include Folder In dialog box, select the folder you want to use as the default location for saving files in this library, and then click Include Folder. That opens the library and lists the contents of the folder you just selected.

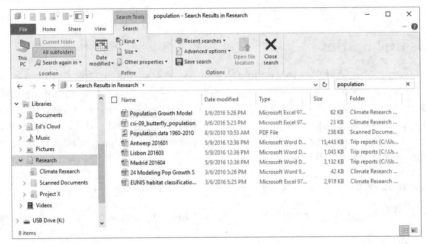

Figure 9-2   The custom library shown here includes folders on two separate local drives and one on a network server. Search results cover all three locations.

To add more folders to the library, click the Manage tab under the Library Tools heading. Then click Manage Library to get to the Library Locations dialog box, shown in Figure 9-3.

In this dialog box, you can delete folders as well as add them, of course, and you can change the library's default save folder. The default save folder is important for applications that expect to save their documents in particular places—a music service, for example, that expects to save downloaded songs in a certain folder within the Music library. It's also the folder that File Explorer will use if you drag a file to the library's heading in the navigation pane.

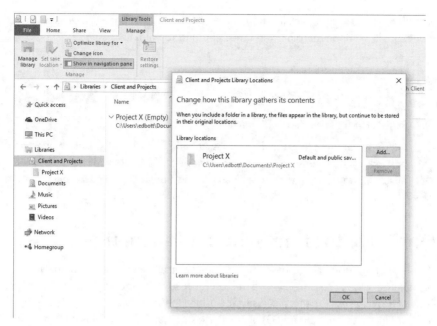

Figure 9-3 The first folder you add to a library becomes the default location for saving files within that library. Use the Manage Library button to add more folders and change settings.

What locations can you add to a library? The most important consideration is that the folder must be indexed so that it can be included in searches. Folders and network shares in any of the following locations are eligible for inclusion:

- The system drive.

- An additional volume on an internal local drive formatted using NTFS or FAT32.

- An external USB or IEEE 1394 (FireWire) hard drive, formatted using NTFS or FAT32.

- A USB flash drive, if the device appears in the navigation pane, under the This PC heading. (Most removable drives do not satisfy this condition.)

- A shared network folder that's indexed using Windows Search; this includes any shared folder from another computer in your workgroup as well as shared folders on Windows-based servers.

- A shared network folder that has been made available offline and is therefore available in your local index.

➤ For more details on how to manage the search index, see "Configuring the Windows Search Index" in Chapter 10.

To delete a library, right-click its entry in the navigation pane and click Delete. The library is gone, but its component folders and their contents remain.

> ## Inside OUT
>
> *Open a file or folder location from a library*
>
> Because libraries are virtual folders, it's sometimes difficult to perform operations directly on their contents. If you want to see a file or folder in its actual location in File Explorer, right-click and choose Open File Location or Open Folder Location.

Using OneDrive to store, sync, and share files

OneDrive, Microsoft's cloud-based file-storage service, is a crucial part of the Windows 10 experience. When you sign in with a Microsoft account, Windows 10 synchronizes settings and stores recovery keys for encrypted storage using OneDrive. Every newly created free Microsoft account includes 5 gigabytes (GB) of OneDrive storage. (Some older accounts include larger allotments that are grandfathered in.) You can expand that storage capacity with paid upgrades to OneDrive or get a massively increased cloud storage allotment (1024 GB per user) with an Office 365 Home or Personal subscription.

OneDrive for Business, which shares a sync client with the consumer OneDrive service, offers enterprise-class management capabilities and 1024 GB of file storage for each Office 365 Business and Enterprise subscription. We explore the differences between the two OneDrive services more fully later in this section.

OneDrive offers a sync client for every major desktop and mobile operating system. In Windows 10, this sync client is built in and is updated automatically. Before we get to that sync client, though, let's start with an overview of OneDrive and OneDrive for Business.

How OneDrive and OneDrive for Business work

Despite the shared brand name, Microsoft's two cloud-based file-storage services have different origins. A common sync client, introduced in 2017, has helped bring the management tools together, but there are some big differences in how the two services work.

Because these are web-based services, Microsoft regularly updates the back-end services and can change the web-based interface independently of the local sync client. As a result of this steady evolution, some screenshots in this section might appear different from those you see when you sign in to your online account.

OneDrive, the consumer service, is designed for personal use, with special views that showcase photo libraries and albums, as well as the ability to store a music collection that can be streamed through the Groove Music app in Windows 10. OneDrive is the default storage option for Office 365 Home and Personal editions.

Files stored in OneDrive are organized into folders and subfolders just as they would be on a local drive. Figure 9-4 shows the top-level folders in a OneDrive account, as viewed in a web browser. Note the range of options available in the command bar for the selected folder, as well as the additional menu choices available from the More (ellipsis) menu.

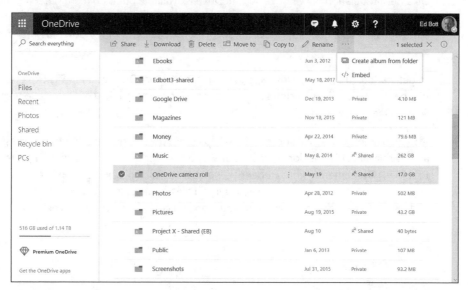

Figure 9-4   When using OneDrive in a web browser, you can perform most file-management tasks and have the ability to create, edit, and collaborate on Office documents.

Clicking the usage graph in the lower-left corner opens a page with details about storage for that subscription.

OneDrive for Business offers a similar web-based view, with one crucial difference: Subscription settings aren't accessible from the navigation pane on the left. That's because a OneDrive for Business subscription is managed by a company administrator, with additional security and collaboration options appropriate for use in an organization.

Both services allow subscribers to share files and folders with other people. The consumer edition of OneDrive allows complete control of sharing: You can choose to make a file, a photo, or an entire folder public. You can also share access by using a link that doesn't require signing in with a Microsoft account.

Sharing options for OneDrive for Business are managed by a company administrator, who might apply restrictions on sharing files with other people, especially in folders that contain confidential company information.

Both OneDrive and OneDrive for Business include built-in versioning, so you can see the history of a document and download an earlier version if you want to recover a portion of an earlier draft. The Recycle Bin for both services makes it possible to retrieve deleted documents for up to 30 days.

Setting up and using OneDrive

On a new installation of Windows 10, OneDrive is available but is *not* configured by default. Setting up OneDrive is simple, but you're under no obligation to use it. (For information about removing all visible traces of OneDrive, see "Disable OneDrive in Windows 10" later in this section.)

To get started, run the OneDrive app in Start, click the OneDrive entry in File Explorer's navigation pane, or click the gray cloud icon in your notification area. Any of these actions opens the Set Up OneDrive wizard.

After you enter your email address, the setup wizard determines whether that address is associated with a OneDrive personal account or a OneDrive for Business account and prompts you to sign in. After entering your credentials, you see the dialog box shown in Figure 9-5, which recommends a local folder to hold your synced files. Your inclination might be to just click Next and move on quickly; we recommend you stop and consider your options here.

Figure 9-5   The default location for storing your synced files is a folder in your user profile. Click Change Location to specify that you want the folder on a separate data drive.

Inside OUT

Disable OneDrive in Windows 10

Maybe you're philosophically opposed to storing files in the cloud. Maybe you prefer a cloud service from another provider. Or maybe you just don't see the need for OneDrive. Regardless of the reason, if you don't want to use OneDrive, you're free to ignore it. If you're asked to sign in to the sync client, click Cancel, and all your files will remain on your local drive or your network. From OneDrive Settings, you can tell Windows not to load the sync client at startup, making it even easier to steer clear of the cloud.

That option does, however, leave the OneDrive icon in the navigation pane of File Explorer. To make it disappear, you need to make a simple registry edit.

In Windows 10 Pro or Enterprise, you can use Group Policy to make this change. Open Local Group Policy Editor (Gpedit.msc) and go to Computer Configuration > Administrative Templates > Windows Components > OneDrive. Double-click the policy Prevent The Usage Of OneDrive For File Storage and set it to Enabled. After you restart your PC, you'll find that the OneDrive icon is no longer in the navigation pane and the sync client no longer runs.

On devices running Windows 10 Home, where Group Policy isn't available, you must edit the registry manually. Using Registry Editor, navigate to HKLM\Software\Policies\Microsoft\Windows\OneDrive. (If that key doesn't exist, you need to create it.) Add a new DWORD value, **DisableFileSyncNGSC**, and set it to **1**. Restart the PC to make the policy setting effective.

Note that this change applies to every user of the selected device. Any previously synced files stored in the local OneDrive folder are still available but are no longer linked to their cloud counterparts.

The default location is a folder in your user profile, with the name OneDrive followed by a hyphen and either the word "Personal" or, in the case of OneDrive for Business accounts, the name of your organization. (Allow the mouse pointer to hover over the file name if it's truncated.) You can't change the folder name, but we can think of two good reasons to click Change Location and select a different drive. First, if your business name is long, consider choosing a folder with a shorter path to avoid running into problems with lengthy path names. Second, if your system drive is a relatively small SSD and you have a separate data drive with multiple terabytes of storage, you definitely want to choose that data drive for synced files.

Beginning with Windows 10 version 1709, the space-saving Files On-Demand feature is automatically enabled when you connect a new account. A full listing of files and folders in your

OneDrive account appears in File Explorer, and you can open any file by double-clicking it; if the file is currently available only online, the OneDrive sync client downloads it automatically and keeps the local copy in sync with the cloud.

You can disable the Files On-Demand feature if you prefer; in that configuration, only files and folders you choose to sync from the cloud to the local device are visible in File Explorer. To find this setting, right-click the OneDrive or OneDrive for Business shortcut in File Explorer or in the notification area, and then click Settings; on the Settings tab, clear the Save Space And Download Files As You Use Them box under the Files On-Demand heading.

With Files On-Demand enabled, you can selectively show or hide files and folders in File Explorer. Open the OneDrive Settings dialog box for the account you want to adjust, click the Account tab, and then click Choose Folders. By default, all folders and all files are selected. From the list of folders, as shown in Figure 9-6, clear the check box for any you want to keep online without displaying in File Explorer.

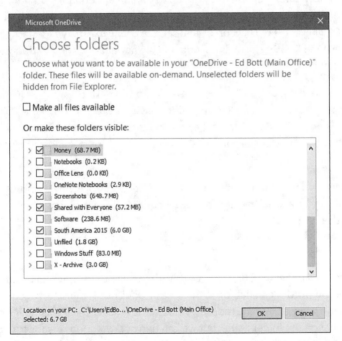

Figure 9-6   Clear the Make All Files Available check box if you prefer not to see the contents of some OneDrive folders in File Explorer.

Inside OUT

Move your local storage folder after setup is complete

Unlike many other data folders in your user profile, the OneDrive sync folders don't include a Location tab as part of the properties dialog box. That's why we recommend that you make this configuration decision wisely when you first link your OneDrive account to your PC.

But if you realize after the fact (and after syncing lots of files) that you want to move the OneDrive folder, there's a relatively simple workaround.

Right-click the OneDrive icon in the notification area and then click Settings. On the Account tab of the resulting dialog box, click Unlink This PC—don't worry, your local files and those in the cloud are unaffected. After OneDrive confirms that your account is unlinked, move the (now unsynced) local folder, and then go through OneDrive setup again, specifying the folder that contains your relocated date folder as the sync location. (You'll be asked to confirm that you want to merge the local files into your cloud storage.)

When setup is complete, OneDrive confirms that the files in the cloud match those in the new location. The process should go swiftly, with no loss of data.

On a device with sufficient storage, you can sync your entire cloud file collection; just make sure there's enough disk space to handle all the photos, music files, video clips, and documents stored there. On devices that have limited local storage, you can selectively sync folders in the cloud to the local device so that those files are available even when you're offline. To designate any file or folder for offline access, right-click its icon in File Explorer and choose Always Keep On This Device.

Repeat this process if you want to set up one or more OneDrive for Business accounts. (You can link only a single OneDrive personal account.) Note that the Microsoft account you link in OneDrive does not have to be the same one you use to sign in to Windows 10, although that's the most common (and logical) configuration.

At any time, you can change your OneDrive configuration: right-click the OneDrive icon associated with that account in File Explorer's navigation pane or in the taskbar (the OneDrive account icon is white; OneDrive for Business icons are blue) and then click Settings. From the resulting dialog box, you can add a new account, unlink an existing account, change the selection of folders that are visible, and limit the amount of bandwidth your system uses when syncing files.

Inside OUT

Use the OneDrive sync client to sync your SharePoint folders

The OneDrive sync client can now be used to sync SharePoint Online team sites, including Microsoft Teams and Office 365 Groups, as well as OneDrive folders. An Office 365 administrator has to explicitly enable the syncing of SharePoint assets. The easiest way to accomplish this task is to navigate to the shared folder in a web browser and then click Sync. For more information, see *https://bit.ly/sync-sharepoint*.

Syncing files and folders

Any file or folder you save in your local OneDrive or OneDrive for Business folder is automatically copied to a corresponding location in the cloud. If you have multiple devices (including PCs, Macs, tablets, and mobile phones) using the same OneDrive or OneDrive for Business account, changes, additions, and deletions you make to files and subfolders on one device are synchronized with all those other devices. So, for example, if you routinely work on the same documents on separate computers at the office and at home, saving to the OneDrive folder on each system ensures that you can retrieve the latest version from anywhere.

If for any reason you need to interrupt this normal syncing activity, right-click the OneDrive or OneDrive for Business icon in your notification area and choose Pause Syncing. You can pause for two hours, eight hours, or a complete day:

When Files On-Demand is enabled, items in your local OneDrive folder that are available only online are marked in File Explorer with a cloud icon; those that have been downloaded manually are tagged with a green check mark in a white circle; files and folders that have been set to be always available on the current device are marked with a white check mark on a solid green background. Items that are currently being synced are denoted by rotating arrows. You can get detailed information about a sync operation in progress by clicking the OneDrive icon in your notification area, as shown in Figure 9-7.

The three icons in the navigation bar along the bottom of this status display are live. Click Open Folder to open the corresponding OneDrive or OneDrive for Business folder in File Explorer. Click View Online to open the OneDrive account in a browser window. Click More to open a menu that leads to OneDrive Settings and other options.

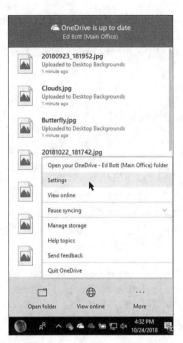

Figure 9-7   Click the cloud icon in the notification area (white for personal, blue for a OneDrive for Business account) to display this sync status window.

Sharing OneDrive files and folders

To share a file or folder in your personal OneDrive, you can right-click the item in File Explorer and then click Share A OneDrive Link. This creates a link to the shared file or folder and copies that link to the Clipboard so that you can paste it into an email message or a chat window.

This type of sharing link is convenient but not secure. Anyone who has the link can access the files, so this option is not appropriate for sharing files that contain confidential information. For situations where you need more security, click the More OneDrive Sharing Options menu item. That opens OneDrive in your web browser, where you will find a full range of sharing options, including the ability to allow or disallow editing and to set an expiration date for the share.

Sharing options and procedures are a bit different in OneDrive for Business. Right-click a One-Drive for Business item in File Explorer and click Share. This opens a dialog box where you can specify a name or email address; note that options to share outside your organization might be restricted by your administrator. You can also assign read-only or edit permissions, and choose various other options.

To share a resource from your Office 365 groups or other SharePoint repositories, select the resource in the OneDrive for Business website and click Share on the command bar. Depending on how your site is set up, you might see a message restricting the share to members of your organization.

Inside OUT

Share and sync files between accounts

One of OneDrive's best-kept secrets is the capability for friends and coworkers to work together using shared folders. (The authors and editors of this book and its predecessors have made extensive use of shared folders for their collaborative work.) The technique is simple: You mark a folder as shared, giving your colleagues access to it when they sign in with an account that has permission to read and write to that folder.

On the other end, your colleague opens OneDrive on the web and clicks Shared in the navigation pane on the left. She then opens the shared folder and clicks Add To My One-Drive. The folder is now available in her list of folders that are eligible to be synced. Both of you now have full access to the contents of the shared folder.

For this technique to be most effective, you should name the shared folder carefully, using a descriptive name such as "Shared Files for Budget Committee," so that everyone who sees it knows immediately that it's a shared folder.

Mastering File Explorer

You can't become a Windows expert without learning how to move quickly and confidently through File Explorer. This general-purpose tool is used throughout Windows for all sorts of file-management tasks, for opening and saving files in Windows programs, and even in parts of the Windows shell. The more you understand about how File Explorer works, the more effective you'll be at speeding through tasks without unnecessary delays. Because it's vital to know your way around, we begin this section with a short tour.

Figure 9-8 shows the default File Explorer layout.

Ribbon

Quick Access Toolbar   Address bar   Search box   Click to minimize/expand ribbon

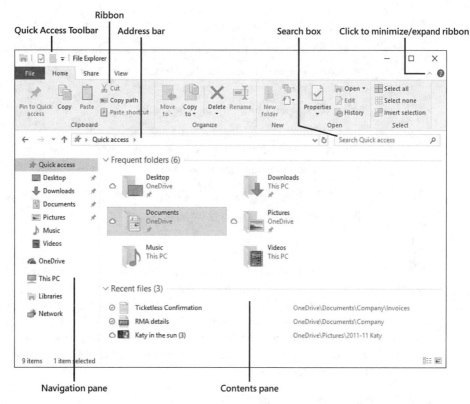

Navigation pane   Contents pane

Figure 9-8   File Explorer includes the navigation and display elements shown here, some of which can be customized.

Inside OUT

Zip through File Explorer with keyboard shortcuts

You can find File Explorer in various places in Windows 10, but if you're handy with the keyboard, don't bother hunting for it. Press Windows key+E to open a new instance of File Explorer directly. If you want to jump to an open instance of File Explorer, use the taskbar keyboard shortcut, Windows key + *number*, where *number* marks the position of the File Explorer icon on the taskbar. By default, the File Explorer icon is in the second position on the taskbar, right after the icon for Microsoft Edge, so unless you've changed the layout, Windows key + 2 should switch between open File Explorer windows.

After File Explorer is open, you have a wide assortment of keyboard shortcuts to choose from. Pressing Ctrl+N opens a new window on the same folder. Ctrl+W closes the current window. The following additional keyboard shortcuts work in File Explorer:

- **Alt+Up Arrow.** Go up one level.
- **Alt+Left Arrow.** Go to previous folder in history.

CHAPTER 9

- **Alt+Right Arrow.** Go to next folder in history.

- **Alt+D.** Move the focus to the address bar and select the current path.

- **F4.** Move the insertion point to the address bar and display the contents of the drop-down menu of previous addresses.

- **Alt+Enter.** Show properties of the selected file.

- **Tab.** Cycle through the following elements: navigation pane, file list, column headings, address bar, search box.

- **F11.** Switch in and out of full-screen mode.

- **Ctrl+Shift+N.** Create a new subfolder in the current folder.

- **Ctrl+Shift+E.** Expand the navigation pane to the current folder.

If you've used any of the recent versions of Microsoft Office, or if you're coming to Windows 10 by way of Windows 8, you won't be startled to see the ribbon atop File Explorer. If, by any chance, this aspect of the user interface is new to you, the only thing you need to know is that it replaces the old system of drop-down and cascading menus with a set of top-level tabs—Home, Share, and View in the example shown in Figure 9-8. Click a tab heading to display available commands for that tab, which are organized into groups—Clipboard, Organize, New, Open, and Select on the Home tab, for example.

More important points to note are the following:

- The command bar from Windows 7 days is gone. The ribbon itself provides the context-specific commands that used to appear on the command bar.

- Unlike its Office counterpart, the commands and groups on the File Explorer ribbon cannot be customized. What you see is what you get.

- The ribbon can be minimized or not, according to your preference. If the ribbon is minimized, it looks very much like a menu, with the commands for a tab appearing only when you click the tab heading. To switch between the full ribbon and this minimized version, use the Expand/Minimize arrow to the right of the tab headings, or just double-click any tab heading.

- When you select one or more files that File Explorer recognizes as pictures, music, or videos, an additional tab appears at the right side of the ribbon, under a color-coded heading. Likewise, selecting a library from the navigation pane or clicking in the search box displays additional tabs with commands relevant to those contexts. These extra tabs can appear side by side. If you display the contents of the Pictures folder, for example, and then click in the search box, new tabs appear under the Search Tools and Picture Tools headings, as shown in the next figure.

- Most of what's on the ribbon is also available on the menus that appear when you right-click files or folders. If you ever become impatient when trying to find a command on the ribbon, right-click in the contents pane and look there. Microsoft adopted the ribbon to reduce the number of cascading submenus that we all used to have to traverse. But sometimes the old ways seem simpler; it's your choice.

To the left of the ribbon tabs, displayed in blue, is the File menu. There you'll find commands for opening a new File Explorer window and for adjusting folder and search options, as well as a list of recently used folders for quick navigation. If you're proficient with managing files at the command line, the most interesting options on this menu are the ones that allow you to open a Windows PowerShell session, using the current folder as the path, with or without administrative privileges. (You can replace the PowerShell commands with their Command Prompt equivalents by going to Settings > Personalization > Taskbar and turning off the switch Replace Command Prompt With Windows PowerShell In The Menu When I Right-click The Start Button Or Press Windows Key + X.)

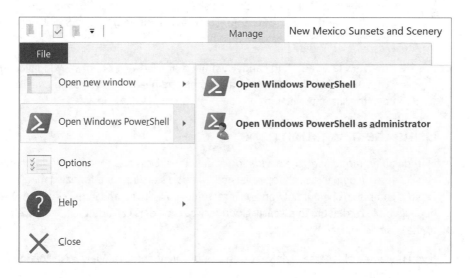

Inside OUT

Use the keyboard with the ribbon (if you prefer)

Devoted keyboard users will appreciate that any command on the ribbon can be accessed and applied without the mouse. Within File Explorer, tap Alt and notice the letters and numbers that appear under the ribbon tabs and the Quick Access Toolbar. Tap one of those letters—V for View, for example—and the appropriate tab itself appears, adorned with its own set of shortcut letters. Follow the shortcuts to your destination.

The design goal of the ribbon is to put the commands you use most often front and center, easy to find. A secondary benefit is that it makes less frequently used commands easier to discover. Here are a few gems that merit your attention:

- The Copy Path command, on the Home tab, puts the path of the current folder or file on the Clipboard. This is handy for sending someone a link to a network share via email. (As an alternative, you can click in the address bar and press Ctrl+C, or you can press Shift as you right-click a file or folder, and then click Copy As Path on the shortcut menu.)

- The Move To and Copy To commands, also on the Home tab, drop down a list of likely targets (recently used folders) for your move and copy operations. If none of those recent folders are appropriate, click Choose Location.

- The Zip command, on the Share tab, instantly creates a Zip (compressed) file from the current selection, thereby providing an alternative to the time-honored approach of right-clicking and choosing Send To, Compressed (Zipped) Folder. (See "Using compressed (zipped) folders" later in this chapter.)

- On the View tab, you'll find handy commands for showing or not showing files and folders with the Hidden attribute. Another command nearby lets you assign the Hidden attribute to the current selection.

Using the navigation pane

In its default arrangement, the navigation pane on the left is arranged into nodes that expand and collapse on demand. Each top-level node offers a starting point for navigating through files on your computer, on your network, on local removable drives, and in the cloud. (A OneDrive node is visible by default; third-party cloud service providers can add their own top-level nodes to the navigation pane.)

If you prefer the older, tree-style view with a single hierarchy, click View > Navigation Pane > Show All Folders.

With the Show All Folders option selected, the navigation pane looks like the example shown in Figure 9-9. (Note that the Quick Access menu shown here is collapsed, making the listing even more compact.) The top level of the folder hierarchy, under the Desktop heading, includes your profile folders (which you can expand by clicking your user name in the navigation pane), removable drives (which also appear directly under This PC), OneDrive accounts, SharePoint sites, Control Panel, Recycle Bin, and any folders you've created directly on the desktop.

Figure 9-9   Selecting the Show All Folders option changes the navigation pane to one that more closely resembles the file-management tool in older Windows versions.

From the Navigation Pane menu on the View tab, you can clear the Navigation Pane entry to make this element completely disappear. Unless you're working on a tiny tablet with extreme space constraints, we can't imagine why you would want to choose this option. This same menu does, however, contain two additional selections you might find useful:

- **Expand To Open Folder.** By default, opening any folder in the contents pane displays its contents there and doesn't affect the navigation pane. If you select Expand To Open Folder, File Explorer expands the navigation pane to show the parent folder of the folder you select in the contents pane, making it easier to see where the selected item fits in the File Explorer hierarchy and move or copy files between folders in that hierarchy.

- **Show Libraries.** If you choose to directly manage files stored in libraries (as discussed in "Using libraries" earlier in this chapter), you might want to include them in your navigation pane. When the Show Libraries option is selected, all your libraries—those that Windows provides and any you create yourself—appear in a node in the navigation pane. If you want to see only particular libraries, click the Libraries node heading, and then right-click each library you want to remove and click Don't Show In Navigation Pane. To restore a library to this node, use the Show In Navigation Pane command. Both commands are also in the Manage group on the Libraries Tools tab.

Navigating faster with Quick Access shortcuts

The Quick Access node, which appears at the top of the navigation pane in all configurations, is new in Windows 10. When it's selected, the contents pane displays two groups of shortcuts: frequently used folders at the top, recently used files beneath it. Windows makes some intelligent choices about what to display under Quick Access, but you can customize this to suit your needs.

In the Frequent Folders section, you'll find some folders marked with pins and others without one. The pinned folders always appear under Quick Access (unless you unpin them). The unpinned folders are ones you recently worked with, and these folders are replaced by others if you begin to use them less frequently. You can unpin a pinned folder by right-clicking it and then clicking Unpin From Quick Access. And you can make any folder anywhere a permanent resident of Quick Access by right-clicking it and then clicking Pin To Quick Access.

The Recent Files section of Quick Access contains files you recently worked with, sorted with the most recently used one at the top. By right-clicking a file name and clicking Open File Location, you can go directly to the folder in which the file resides. If you find that you don't need to see a particular file (and want to make room for another), you can right-click that file and then click Remove From Quick Access.

Quick Access is an extremely handy navigational tool because it gathers together the stuff you're most likely to be concerned with, regardless of where that stuff is actually stored. But if you don't need it, or you're not keen on having passersby see what you've been working on, you can suppress the Frequent Folders section or the Recent Files section, or both. To do this, click View > Options. On the General tab of the Folder Options dialog box, you'll find the check boxes you need in the Privacy section, as shown in Figure 9-10.

(If you just want to cover your immediate tracks without changing the overall behavior of File Explorer, it's probably simpler to click Clear in the Privacy section.)

Figure 9-10   Use these settings to control whether files and folders you've recently opened or edited are visible in the Quick Access pane.

Inside OUT

Customize the Quick Access Toolbar

As its name implies, the Quick Access Toolbar—that set of icons in the upper-left corner of File Explorer, above the ribbon—puts commonly used functions close at hand (or close to your mouse pointer). If you'd like those items a few centimeters closer, you can move the Quick Access Toolbar by clicking the arrow at the end and then clicking Show Below The Ribbon.

This menu also includes a short list of six commonly used items you can add to the Quick Access Toolbar, including Undo, Redo, and New Folder. But don't be fooled by that paltry selection. You can add any command or even entire groups of commands to the Quick Access Toolbar. To add a command, right-click it and then click Add To Quick Access Toolbar.

To add an entire group of commands to the Quick Access Toolbar, right-click the name at the bottom of the group and then click Add To Quick Access Toolbar. In this example, we added the Panes group from the View tab, making it easier to add the Preview or Details pane even if the View tab isn't visible:

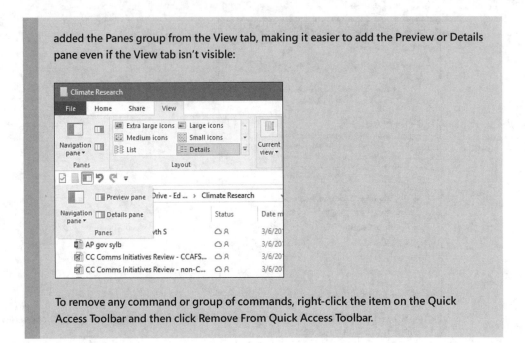

To remove any command or group of commands, right-click the item on the Quick Access Toolbar and then click Remove From Quick Access Toolbar.

Layouts, previews, and other ways to arrange files

You can adjust the display of any individual folder's contents in File Explorer by means of options in the Layout group on the View tab. As Figure 9-11 shows, your choices are numerous: icons in your choice of four sizes, List, Details, Tiles, and Content. Display options are folder-specific and persistent.

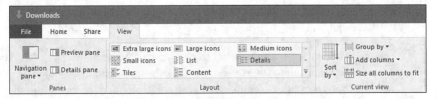

Figure 9-11   The View tab provides a large set of options for displaying content in File Explorer.

You can get a look at each display option by hovering the mouse pointer over it on the View tab. File Explorer gives you a preview of each choice, making it easier for you to decide.

The range of options for the various icon views is larger than it looks. Although there are four discrete choices available on the View tab—small, medium, large, and extra-large—the actual number of sizes is 76. You can cycle smoothly through all 76 sizes by choosing one of them, holding down the Ctrl key, and turning the wheel on your mouse. With each step, you'll see the icons grow or shrink (although at some of the smaller sizes the change is barely perceptible).

Content view arranges listings in multiline bands that take up the full width of the window, while List view displays file names only, arranged in columns.

Details view is one of the most important alternatives, offering a multicolumn tabulation of your files that unlocks a wide range of sorting, filtering, and grouping options, as we discuss later in this chapter, "Sorting, filtering, and grouping in File Explorer."

The default arrangement of column headings is determined by the folder type, but you can tailor this arrangement in any folder. To add or remove a column heading while in Details view, right-click anywhere in the row of column headings. (Alternatively, click the View tab and then click Add Columns in the Current View group.) If the list of column headings that appears doesn't include the one you want, click the option at the bottom of the list. As Figure 9-12 shows, the Choose Details dialog box that appears next provides you with a wealth of choices. In fact, Figure 9-12 shows only the first 15 choices in a vast array of possibilities.

In the Choose Details dialog box, you can use the Move Up and Move Down buttons to change the order in which column headings appear. (You can also change the column order in File Explorer by dragging headings with the mouse.)

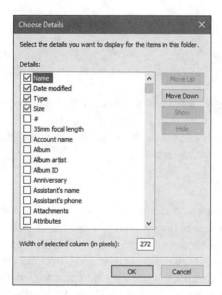

Figure 9-12   Use this dialog box to select which headings are displayed in Details view.

CHAPTER 9

Inside OUT

Change display settings in Open and Save dialog boxes

In many programs, you can change display settings in common file-management dialog boxes (Save As and Open), although the lack of a ribbon means you can't use the View tab to do so. To switch between views in one of these File Explorer–based dialog boxes, use the keyboard shortcuts: Ctrl+Shift+6 for Details view, Ctrl+Shift+2 for Large Icons, and so on. You can also use the unlabeled Change Your View button, with its drop-down list of standard views, which is available in the command bar above the contents pane. As an alternative, right-click an open space in the dialog box (you might have to enlarge the dialog box first) and then click View.

Initially, all folders intended for the storage of user data (including those you create) are assigned one of five folder templates that define the default headings File Explorer considers appropriate for the content type. The logic is straightforward: You'll probably want to sort a folder full of MP3 tracks by track number, and the Date Taken column is extremely useful for filtering digital photos, but neither column would be particularly useful in a folder full of Microsoft Word documents.

Inside OUT

Customize folder templates

Not sure what folder "type" you're in? Right-click a blank space in the folder and then click Customize This Folder. On the Customize tab of the properties dialog box for the selected folder, look at the selection in the Optimize This Folder For drop-down list, which shows the folder type that's currently in effect.

The View tab also contains commands to show an optional pane on the right side of the contents pane. This pane can either show a preview of the currently selected file—supported file formats include most image files, Microsoft Office documents, and PDF files—or details about the current file (a topic we discuss in the next section). Either command is a toggle. Click once to make the pane visible; click again to hide the pane. If you use either capability regularly, it's worth memorizing the keyboard shortcuts: Alt+P for Preview, Alt+Shift+P for Details.

Using compressed (zipped) folders

Depending on the file type, you can dramatically reduce the amount of disk space used by one or more files by compressing those files into a zipped folder. You can also combine multiple files into a single Zip file while preserving the folder hierarchy of that group of files.

Don't be fooled by the name: A zipped folder (also known as a Zip file or archive) is actually a single file, compressed using the industry-standard Zip format and saved with the .zip file name extension. Any version of Windows can open a file saved in this format, as can other modern operating systems. The format is also accessible with the help of many third-party utilities.

To create a new archive using zipped folders, follow these steps:

1. In File Explorer, display the folder in which you want the new archive to reside.

2. Right-click any empty space in the folder, and then click New > Compressed (Zipped) Folder.

3. Name the folder.

To add files and folders to your archive, drag and drop them onto the zipped folder icon in File Explorer (or double-click to open the zipped folder in its own window and then drag items into it). You can also use the Clipboard to copy and paste items. To remove an item from the zipped folder, double-click the folder to display its contents, right-click the item, and then click Delete.

You can also create a compressed folder from the current selection by clicking Zip on the Share tab in File Explorer. Windows creates an archive file with the same name as the selected object. Use the Rename command (or press F2) to replace the default name with a more descriptive one.

To extract individual files or folders from a zipped folder, open it in File Explorer and then drag the items you want to extract to a new location, or use the Clipboard to copy and paste. To extract all items from a zipped folder to a specific location, right-click the zipped folder icon and then click Extract All, or open the zipped folder in File Explorer and click Extract All on the Extract tab on the ribbon.

Sorting, filtering, and grouping in File Explorer

Regardless of the view settings you've chosen for a folder, you can adjust the way its contents are displayed at any time by changing the sort order, filtering the contents by one or more properties to include only selected items, and grouping and arranging the contents by a particular heading. In any view, the sort and group options are available by right-clicking anywhere in the contents pane and choosing a Sort By or Group By option. In most cases, however, these actions are easier to accomplish by switching to Details view and using the column headings, which is also the preferred way to filter.

Note that all these techniques also work with virtual folders, such as search results and libraries.

Sorting a folder's contents

To sort a folder in Details view, click the heading you want to use as a sort key. For example, to sort by Date Modified, click the Date Modified heading. Click again on the same heading to reverse the sort order. An up arrow or down arrow above the heading indicates whether the folder is sorted in ascending or descending order by the current field.

In all other views, right-click any empty space in the contents pane and select a value from the Sort By menu. A bullet next to Ascending or Descending indicates the current sort order; choose the other option to reverse the sort order.

Filtering folder contents

In Details view only, you can use headings to filter the contents of a folder. If you rest your pointer on a heading, a drop-down arrow appears at the right. Clicking the arrow reveals a set of filter check boxes appropriate for that heading. In most cases, the filter list is built on the fly from the contents of the current file list. If you're looking for a particular type of file—a Word or PDF document, for example, or an executable file—you can filter by type to show only those files. Figure 9-13 shows the filter list for the Type field in the Downloads folder, with the contents filtered to show only files whose type matches Application.

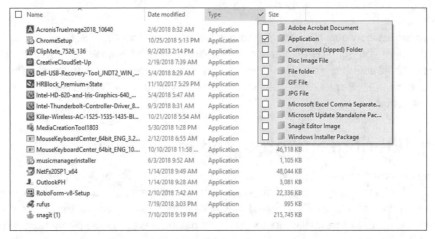

Figure 9-13 When you click the drop-down arrow to the right of a column heading, a set of filtering options appropriate for that heading appears.

Select the check box next to any item to add it to the filter list; clear the check box to remove a previously selected item from the filter. After you filter the list in Details view, you can switch to any other view and the filter will persist. Look in the address bar to see the specific filter applied, and then click the folder name to the left of the search term in the address bar (also known as a *breadcrumb*) to remove all filtering without switching back to Details view.

If you filter by Size or Name, you get a much more limited set of choices that includes ranges rather than discrete values.

A single filter can include multiple items from each heading's filter list, which are treated as a logical OR—in other words, File Explorer displays items that match any of the selected check boxes. A filter can also include multiple headings, which together function as a logical AND, with File Explorer displaying only items that satisfy the criteria applied to each heading. So, for example, you can filter a picture folder to show only photos where the value in the Rating column is four or five stars and the value in the Date Taken field is in this year, resulting in a list of your favorite photos of the year, suitable for a year-end newsletter or family photo album.

When a folder is filtered, check marks appear to the right of headings used for filtering. The values on which you have filtered appear in the address bar. You can perform most common file-management tasks on the items in the results list, including renaming individual files or using the Clipboard to copy or move files from their current location to a new folder.

Inside OUT

Use the date navigator to zoom through time

If you click a date heading, the filter options display a date navigator like the one shown next, with common date groupings available at the bottom of the list. You can also click Select A Date Or Date Range and use the calendar to filter the file list that way.

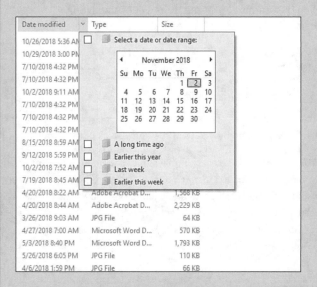

The date navigator is much more powerful than it looks at first glance. Use the calendar to zoom in or out and narrow or expand your view of the contents of a folder or a search. Initially, the calendar shows the current month, with today's date highlighted. Click the month heading to zoom out to a display showing the current year as a heading with the current month highlighted. You can then drag or hold down Ctrl and click to select multiple months.

Click the year to zoom out again to show the current decade. Click once more to show the current century. In any calendar view, you can use the arrows to the left and right of the column heading to move through the calendar a month, year, decade, or century at a time. To zoom back in, click any month, year, decade, or century on the calendar control. This technique is especially valuable with folders or search results containing hundreds or thousands of files and folders.

Grouping folder contents

If sorting and filtering don't give you enough ways to organize or locate files, try grouping. When you group items, File Explorer collects all the items that have some common property, displaying each group under a heading that can be expanded or collapsed in most views.

List view offers a particularly interesting perspective, with each group of results appearing under a column heading. The grouped arrangement is saved as part of the custom view settings for that folder; the next time you open the folder, it will still be grouped.

To group items in a File Explorer window, open the View tab, click Group By, and then click the property you want to use. File Explorer displays a bullet before the selected property. You can remove the grouping by returning to Group By and choosing None.

Inside OUT

Use check boxes to simplify file selection

File Explorer offers two modes of file and folder selection—with and without check boxes. You can switch between them by means of the Item Check Boxes command on the View tab.

With check boxes on, you can select multiple items that are not adjacent to one another by clicking or tapping the check box for each one in turn; to remove an item from the selection, clear its check box. In either case, there's no need to hold down the Ctrl key. (This option is especially useful when you're trying to select files using a touchscreen.) In any case, though, Ctrl-selecting and Shift-selecting work as they always have, with or without check boxes.

Managing disk space

At the dawn of the Windows 10 era, several long-term trends converged to make data storage more of a performance issue than it has been in years.

For many years, the trend with conventional hard disks was simple: more storage space at a lower cost per gigabyte. Each new Windows version required more space than its predecessor, but the accompanying new generation of hardware meant there was plenty of room for system files and data.

The advent of solid-state drives (SSDs) and flash memory changed all that. SSDs are dramatically faster than conventional hard disks. They're also more reliable than hard disks because they have no moving parts. However, although the gap is narrowing, SSDs are still far more expensive per gigabyte than conventional hard disks, causing PC makers to choose smaller default disks for new PCs.

On a desktop PC, you have the option to expand storage by replacing the primary drive with one that's faster, larger, or both; on most full-size desktop PCs, you can also install additional drives to make room for extra data files. Many portable devices, on the other hand, provide built-in primary storage that is soldered to the system board and can't be replaced. For some portable devices, the option to expand storage using inexpensive removable media is available. Microsoft's Surface Pro PCs, for example, include a slot that accepts removable storage in the form of a MicroSD card, which can be treated as dedicated storage and used for File History.

➤ **For a full discussion of the ins and outs of setting up new hard drives and SSDs in Windows 10, see "Managing hard disks and other storage devices," in Chapter 14, "Hardware and devices." For a discussion of how to use removable storage for backup, see "Using File History to protect files and folders" in Chapter 15, "Troubleshooting, backup, and recovery."**

Managing storage on a Windows 10 device involves two separate challenges:

- Setting default file locations to make the best use of available storage

- Performing occasional maintenance to ensure useful space (especially on the system drive) isn't being wasted with unnecessary files

For an overview of how much total storage is available and what's in use on a Windows 10 device, open Settings > System > Storage to see a page like the one shown in Figure 9-14. This example shows a desktop PC with an internal system drive (C) and an external drive, both approximately 1 TB in size.

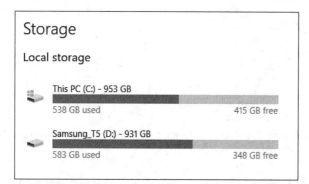

Figure 9-14   The Storage page in Settings shows all available volumes, with an indication of how much space is currently in use on each.

Inside OUT

Why is actual storage capacity lower than advertised disk sizes?

When you use Microsoft's built-in disk utilities to view the storage capacity of a disk, the capacity is reported by using the binary system (base 2) of measurement: 1 KB is 1,024 bytes, 1 MB is 1,024 KB, 1 GB is 1,024 MB, and so on. Thus, measured in binary terms, 1 GB is calculated as 1,073,741,824 bytes. But the makers of storage devices and the PC makers who build SSDs and hard disks into their products typically advertise storage using the convenient metric that 1 GB is equal to 1 billion bytes. That difference is why a system advertised with 32 GB of storage displays only about 28 GB when detailed in Disk Management and other Windows tools. Fortunately, those same tools also report the number of bytes of storage, which allows more accurate comparisons with the advertised space.

Regardless of how many drives are available, you can see which types of files are using that space, color-coded by file type. Open Storage in Settings and click any drive to show a breakdown of storage space in use, as in Figure 9-15.

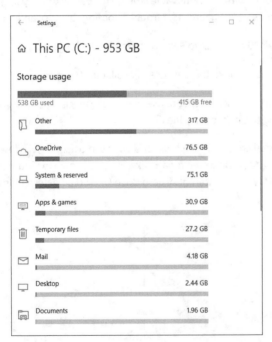

Figure 9-15   This screenshot shows just the start of a long list that displays a detailed breakdown of how much space is in use, grouped by type of file.

Click or tap any category to see more details about what's in it. Here are some examples of what you'll find in each category:

- **System And Reserved.** This category is typically large and includes files that are essential to the operation of the system. The actual amounts of storage in use depend on the type of device and how much memory it contains. Figure 9-16, for example, shows the breakdown for this category on a Windows 10 desktop PC with 16 GB of RAM.

- **Apps And Games.** This category includes default apps as well as those you downloaded from the Microsoft Store.

- **Documents, Pictures, Music, Videos.** These separate categories show how much space is in use in the default save locations for the respective file types. Note that this value is not the total found in the libraries of the same names.

- **Mail.** This value measures the space used by local copies of messages saved using the default mail app. Clicking or tapping the Manage Mail button takes you to the default email app: Mail or Microsoft Outlook, for example.

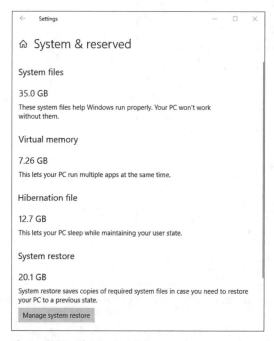

Figure 9-16 The System & Reserved category shows how much space is in use by Windows, space reserved for virtual memory, and hibernation files.

- **OneDrive.** The total amount of space used by local copies of files synced from OneDrive.

- **Desktop.** This total should be small unless you use the desktop as a dumping ground for downloads and other potentially large files.

- **Maps.** If you have a large collection of offline maps, this category can get fairly large.

- **Other Users.** This category displays the total amount of space in use for data files from other user accounts, not broken down by file types.

- **Temporary Files.** This category includes files that are managed by Windows but are not typically necessary for the operation of a Windows 10 device. On the system shown in Figure 9-17, with just a few clicks, you can recover almost 20 GB of storage space from the Recycle Bin.

- **Other.** If you have large collections of files that don't slot into the standard categories, you might see a very large Other category. The types of large files that might show up in this category include Hyper-V virtual machines and associated VHD files as well as ISO files.

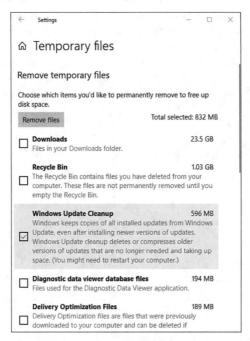

Figure 9-17 With several options in this category, you can free up large amounts of disk space.

As you click to navigate deeper into the categories in the Storage section of Settings, you'll find buttons and links for managing files contained in that category by using File Explorer.

Changing default save locations

On systems with multiple drives (including removable media), you can change the default location for specific file types. If you have a large music collection, for example, you might prefer to store MP3 files on a disk you dedicate for that purpose. To make that possible, open the Storage page in Settings and click Change Where New Content Is Saved, as shown in Figure 9-18.

NOTE

Changing the default location for a file type affects the storage of new items. It does not move current items.

When you set the default save location for these categories to a secondary drive, Windows 10 creates folders on the secondary drive, with subfolders that correspond to the category name for each file type within a folder named after your user account name.

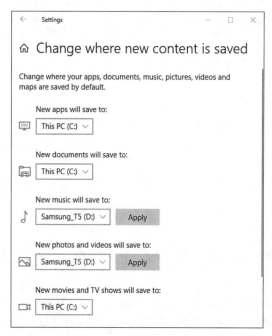

Figure 9-18   You can change the default location for new files you save in default categories. Existing files remain in their current locations.

Note that if you are redirecting an item type that is currently stored in a library, Windows expands the library definition to include the new location.

➤ For information about libraries, see "Using libraries" earlier in this chapter.

Cleaning up unneeded files

A feature called Storage Sense is designed to free up disk space automatically by deleting files you don't need. Because this feature has the potential to guess wrong and remove files you really do need, it is turned off by default. To turn Storage Sense on and fine-tune its capabilities, go to Settings > System > Storage and click Change How We Free Up Space Automatically. That opens a page like the one shown in Figure 9-19.

In addition to the option to automatically purge unused temporary files, Storage Sense includes the option to automatically clear the contents of the Recycle Bin, the Downloads folder, and locally available copies of files from OneDrive, OneDrive for Business, and SharePoint accounts. For each such category, you can specify an age for files: from 1 day to 60 days, or Never.

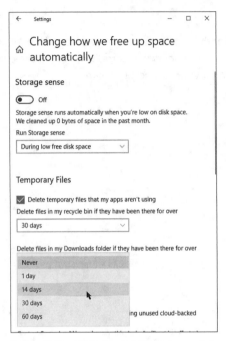

Figure 9-19   With the Storage Sense switch set to On, options to delete unnecessary files become available.

These settings take effect only when you flip the Storage Sense switch to the On position. To run Storage Sense manually, scroll to the bottom of that Settings page and click Clean Now.

Additional options for tidying up are available via the legacy Disk Cleanup utility (Cleanmgr.exe). You can use the search box to locate this tool; as an alternative, open File Explorer, right-click the disk you want to tidy up, choose Properties, and then click Disk Cleanup. Note that this utility initially opens in standard user mode, allowing you to manage files available to your user account but blocking access to system files. To enable the full range of Disk Cleanup options, click Clean Up System Files, entering the credentials for an administrator account if necessary. That restarts the utility and unlocks access to the full range of cleanup options, as shown in Figure 9-20.

CAUTION

You might be tempted to obsess over disk space usage and use every trick to create as much free space as possible. That strategy might come back to haunt you, however. If you remove previous Windows installations, for example, you lose the ability to roll back to a previous version to recover from compatibility problems. As a general rule, you should keep at least 20 percent of total disk capacity free. That allows enough room to process temporary files properly without affecting performance dramatically. Beyond that baseline, think long and hard before deleting what might be important files.

Figure 9-20   When you start Disk Cleanup using administrative credentials, you have the option to remove Windows installation files and previous Windows versions.

Recovering lost, damaged, and deleted files and folders

It takes only a fraction of a second to wipe out a week's worth of work. You might accidentally delete a folder full of files or, worse, overwrite an entire group of files with changes that can't be undone. Whatever the cause of your misfortune, Windows includes tools that offer hope for recovery. If a file is simply lost, try searching for it. (See "Using Windows Search" in Chapter 10.) For accidental deletions, your first stop should be the Recycle Bin, a Windows institution since 1995.

> ➤ Windows 10 includes a considerably more powerful recovery tool called File History—but it's available only if you set it up in advance. See "Using File History to protect files and folders" in Chapter 15, "Troubleshooting, backup, and recovery."

The Recycle Bin provides protection against accidental erasure of files. In most cases, when you delete one or more files or folders, the deleted items go to the Recycle Bin, not into the ether. If you change your mind, you can go to the bin and recover the thrown-out items. Eventually, when the bin fills up, Windows begins emptying it, permanently deleting the files that have been there the longest.

The following kinds of deletions do not go to the Recycle Bin:

- Files stored on removable disks such as USB flash drives

- Files stored on network drives, even when that volume is on a computer that has its own Recycle Bin

- Files deleted from a command prompt

- Files deleted from compressed (zipped) folders

You can bypass the Recycle Bin yourself, permanently deleting an item, by holding down the Shift key while you delete the item. You might choose to do this if you're trying to reclaim disk space by permanently getting rid of large files and folder subtrees.

To see and adjust the amount of space currently used by the Recycle Bin for each drive that it protects, right-click the Recycle Bin icon on your desktop and then click Properties. In the Recycle Bin Properties dialog box (shown in Figure 9-21), you can select a drive and enter a different value in the Custom Size box. Windows ordinarily allocates up to 10 percent of a disk's space for recycling. (When the bin is full, the oldest items give way to the newest.) If you think that amount of space is excessive, enter a lower value. If you're certain you don't need to recover files from a particular drive, select the Don't Move Files To The Recycle Bin setting for that drive.

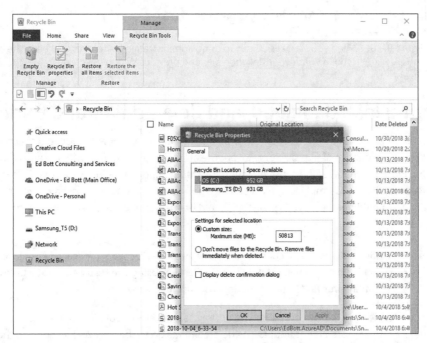

Figure 9-21   You can use the Recycle Bin Properties dialog box to alter the amount of space devoted to the bin—or to turn the feature off for selected drives.

Note that the Recycle Bin for OneDrive folders shows only deleted copies of locally synced files. A separate OneDrive Recycle Bin is available from the browser-based interface and includes all deleted files.

Whether the Recycle Bin is enabled or disabled, Windows normally displays a confirmation prompt when you delete something. If that prompt annoys you, clear the Display Delete Confirmation Dialog check box.

Restoring files and folders

When you open the Recycle Bin, Windows displays the names of recently deleted items in an ordinary File Explorer window. In Details view, you can see when each item was deleted and which folder it was deleted from. Use the column headings to sort the folder—for example, to display items that have been deleted most recently at the top, with earlier deletions below. Alternatively, you can organize the bin by disk and folder by clicking the Original Location heading. If these methods don't help you find what you're hoping to restore, use the search box.

Note that deleted folders are shown only as folders; you don't see the names of items contained within the folders. If you restore a deleted folder, however, Windows re-creates the folder and its contents.

The Restore commands on the Manage tab (Restore All Items and Restore The Selected Items) put items back in the folders from which they were deleted. If a folder doesn't currently exist, Windows asks your permission to re-create it. Note that if your Recycle Bin contains hundreds or thousands of deleted files dating back weeks or months, Restore All Items can create chaos. That command is most useful if you recently emptied the Recycle Bin and all of its current contents are visible.

If you want, you can restore a file or folder to a different location. Select the item, click the Home tab, click Move To, and then choose a new location. Or, simplest of all, you can drag the item out of the Recycle Bin and drop it in the folder where you want to save it.

Purging the Recycle Bin

A deleted file sitting in your Recycle Bin takes up as much space as it did before it was deleted. If you're deleting files to free up space for new programs and documents, transferring them to the Recycle Bin won't help. You need to remove them permanently. The safest way to do this is to move the items to another storage medium—a different hard disk or a removable disk, for example.

If you're sure you'll never need a particular file again, however, you can delete it in the normal way, and then purge it from the Recycle Bin. Display the Recycle Bin, select the item, and then press Delete.

To empty the Recycle Bin entirely, click Empty Recycle Bin on the Manage tab.

Managing existing disks and volumes

No matter how well you plan, your approach to deploying storage resources is likely to change over time. The Disk Management tool (Diskmgmt.msc) can help you adjust to changing requirements. You can expand volumes (assuming space is available), shrink volumes, reformat, relabel, assign new drive letters, and more. We'll consider these options next.

> ➤ This section assumes you are working with physical disks that have already been prepared for use with Windows and volumes that already contain data. For details on how to use Disk Management with new physical disks, see "Managing hard disks and other storage devices" in Chapter 14.

Extending a volume

What do you do when a disk begins to fill up? The most common solution is to prune away unneeded files to recover disk space, as we discussed earlier in this chapter. But Disk Management will be happy to make an NTFS volume larger for you, provided unallocated space is available on the same hard disk. This configuration is unusual and only likely to occur when the disk you're working with was originally partitioned into multiple volumes and you have deleted the second volume. To accomplish the expansion, right-click the volume you want to expand and then click Extend Volume. Click Next to move past the Extend Volume Wizard's welcome page. The Select Disks page, shown in Figure 9-22, appears.

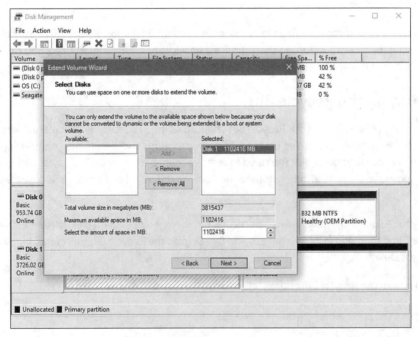

Figure 9-22   Use the Extend Volume Wizard to extend a volume into unallocated space on the same disk or another hard disk with free space.

The Selected list, on the right side of this dialog box, initially shows the disk whose volume you intend to extend. The Maximum Available Space In MB box shows you how much larger you can make the volume, assuming you want to confine your expansion to the current disk. The Select The Amount Of Space In MB box, initially set to equal the maximum available space, is where you declare the number of megabytes you want to add to the volume, and the Total Volume Size In Megabytes (MB) box shows you how big your volume is about to become.

When you're ready to continue, click Next, review your orders on the ensuing page, and then click Finish. If your volume resided on a basic disk to begin with, it remains basic after the expansion—provided that the space into which you expanded was contiguous with the original volume. Note that no separate formatting step is required; the new territory acquires the same formatting as the original.

Volume extension is subject to the following limitations:

- Only NTFS-formatted volumes can be extended.

- A logical drive can be extended only within the extended partition that contains it.

- The system and boot partitions can be extended only into contiguous unallocated space.

Inside OUT

Increase storage space with NTFS compression

If you're thinking of expanding a partition because you're short of space, consider compressing your files and folders instead. You can compress individual files, particular folders, or entire volumes. Items compressed in this manner are decompressed on the fly when you open them and compressed again when they are closed. You won't achieve huge savings in storage space this way—less than you would get by using compressed (zipped) folders—but the convenience of NTFS is high and the cost, in terms of performance, is virtually unnoticeable.

To compress a volume, open This PC in File Explorer, right-click the volume, click Properties, and then, on the General tab of the properties dialog box, select Compress This Drive To Save Disk Space. To compress a particular folder or file, right-click it in File Explorer, click Properties, and then click Advanced on the General tab of the properties dialog box. In the Advanced Attributes dialog box, select Compress Contents To Save Disk Space. Note that this form of compression is available only on NTFS volumes and that NTFS compression is incompatible with encryption that uses the Encrypting File System. You can have one or the other, but not both.

CHAPTER 9

Shrinking a volume

Provided space is available, you can shrink an NTFS-formatted volume to make more space available for other volumes. (This option is most common on very large physical disks where you want to segregate different types of data.) To do this, right-click the volume in either the volume list or graphical view pane and then click Shrink Volume. Disk Management responds by analyzing the disk, and then it reports the amount of shrinkage possible, as shown here:

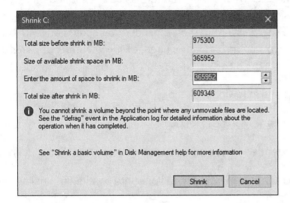

Enter the number of megabytes by which you want to reduce your volume, and then click Shrink. Disk Management defragments the disk, moving all its data to a contiguous block, and then performs the shrink.

Be aware that two types of system-managed files—paging files and volume shadow copy files—cannot be moved during the defragmentation process. This means you might not have as much room to shrink as you would like. Microsoft also advises that the amount by which you can shrink a volume is "transient" and depends on what is happening on the volume at the time. In other words, if you're trying to eliminate, say, 10 GB from the volume and Disk Management can manage only 7, take the 7 and then try for more later.

Deleting a volume

Deleting a volume is easy—and irreversible. All data is lost in the process, so be sure you have backed up or no longer need whatever the volume currently contains. Then right-click the volume and click Delete Volume. The volume reverts to unallocated space, and if it happens to have been the last volume on a dynamic disk, the disk itself is converted to basic.

Converting a FAT32 disk to NTFS

To convert a FAT or FAT32 disk to NTFS, use the command-line Convert utility. The essential syntax is

```
convert d: /fs:ntfs
```

where *d* is the drive letter you want to convert. For information about optional parameters, type **convert /?** at the command prompt.

The Convert utility can do its work within Windows if the drive to be converted is not in use. However, if you want to convert the system volume or a volume that holds a paging file, you might see an error message when you run Convert. In that case, you must schedule the conversion to occur the next time you start Windows. After you restart the computer, you see a prompt that warns you that the conversion is about to begin. You have 10 seconds to cancel the conversion. If you allow it to proceed, Windows runs the Chkdsk utility and performs the conversion automatically. During this process, your computer will restart twice.

Assigning or changing a volume label

In Windows 10, as in previous versions of Windows, you can assign a descriptive text label to any volume. Assigning a label is purely optional, but it's a good practice, especially if you have a multi-boot system or if you set up separate volumes to keep your data organized. You can use Data as the label for your data drive, Music for the drive that holds your collection of digital tunes, and so on.

You can enter a volume label when you format a new volume, or you can do it at any time afterward by right-clicking a volume (in Disk Management or in File Explorer), clicking Properties, and entering text in the edit field near the top of the General tab.

Assigning and changing drive letters

You can assign one and only one letter to a volume. For all but the following volumes, you can change or remove the drive letter at any time:

- The boot volume

- The system volume

- Any volume on which the paging (swap) file is stored

To change a drive-letter assignment, right-click the volume in Disk Management and then click Change Drive Letter And Paths. (You can do this in either the upper or lower pane.) To replace an existing drive letter, select it and click Change. To assign a drive letter to a volume that currently has none, click Add. Select an available drive letter from the Assign The Following Drive Letter list, and then click OK twice.

> ### TROUBLESHOOTING
>
> **The drive letter for your card reader has disappeared**
>
> Windows 10 does not display empty drives by default. If your computer has a set of drives for memory cards, you might be accustomed to seeing those drives listed in File Explorer whether the drives are empty or not. If you want to make the empty drives visible, open File Explorer, click the View tab, and then select Hidden Items.

Mapping a volume to an NTFS folder

In addition to (or in place of) a drive letter, you can assign one or more paths to NTFS folders to a volume. Assigning a drive path creates a mounted volume (also known as a mounted drive, mounted folder, or volume mount point). A mounted volume appears as a folder within an NTFS-formatted volume that has a drive letter assigned to it. Besides allowing you to sidestep the limitation of 26 drive letters, mounted volumes offer these advantages:

- You can extend storage space on an existing volume that's running low on free space. For instance, if your digital music collection has outgrown your drive C, you can create a sub-folder of your Music folder and call it, say, More Music. Then you can assign a drive path from a new volume to the More Music folder—in effect increasing the size of your origi-nal Music folder. The More Music folder in this example appears to be part of the original Music folder but actually resides on the new volume.

- You can make commonly used files available in multiple locations. Say you have an enor-mous collection of clip art that you store on drive X, and each user has a subfolder in his or her Documents folder where desktop publishing files are stored. In each of those per-sonal folders, you can create a subfolder called Clip Art and assign that folder's path to volume X. That way, the entire clip art collection is always available from any user's desk-top publishing folder, and no one has to worry about creating shortcuts to X or changing drive letters while they work.

To create a mounted volume, follow these steps:

1. In Disk Management, right-click the volume you want to change (in either the graphical view pane or the volume list pane), and then click Change Drive Letter And Paths.

2. Click Add to open the Add Drive Letter Or Path dialog box.

3. Select Mount In The Following Empty NTFS Folder. (This is the only option available if the volume already has a drive letter assigned.)

4. Click Browse. The Browse For Drive Path dialog box that appears shows only NTFS volumes, and the OK button is enabled only if you select an empty folder or click New Folder to create one.

5. Click OK to add the selected location in the Add Drive Letter Or Path dialog box, and then click OK to create the drive path.

You can manage files and subfolders within a mounted volume just as though they were stored in a regular folder. In File Explorer, the mounted volume appears within the list of folders, iden-tified by a drive icon with a shortcut arrow. And as Figure 9-23 shows, when you right-click the folder icon and then click Properties, the General tab reveals that the folder is actually a mounted volume and provides more details about the drive to which the folder is mapped.

Figure 9-23   The properties dialog box for a mounted drive identifies the volume that actually holds its files.

Click the Properties button on the General tab to see more details about the drive to which the folder is mapped.

If you use the Dir command in a Command Prompt window to display a folder directory, a mounted volume is identified as <JUNCTION> (for junction point, yet another name for a mounted volume), whereas ordinary folders are identified as <DIR> (for directory, the MS-DOS term for a folder).

CAUTION

When creating mounted volumes, avoid establishing loops in the structure of a drive— for example, by creating a drive path from drive X that points to a folder on drive D and then creating a drive path on drive D that points to a folder on drive X. Windows allows you to do this, but it's invariably a bad idea because an application that opens subfolders (such as a search) can go into an endless loop.

To see a list of all the mounted drives on your system, click View > Drive Paths in Disk Management. A dialog box like the one shown in Figure 9-24 appears. Note that you can remove a drive path from this dialog box; if you do so, the folder remains in the same spot it was previously located, but it reverts to being a regular, empty folder. The files and folders remain in that volume, accessible if you assign a drive letter or a different empty folder to it.

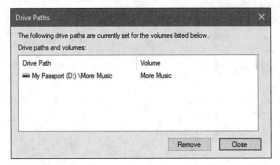

Figure 9-24   This dialog box lists all the mounted drives on a system and shows the volume label, if any, of each mounted drive.

Permanently wiping all data from a disk

Formatting a volume results in a root folder that appears to be empty. Because of the way formatting works, however, someone with data-recovery tools might be able to restore deleted files even after you format the volume. If you're discarding or recycling an old computer or hard disk, you don't want to risk the possibility of it landing in the hands of someone who might search it for recoverable data that can be used for identity theft or other nefarious purposes.

If your old disk is headed for the dumpster, you can ensure that the data can't be recovered by removing the disk drive from the computer and physically destroying the disk. Using tools as varied as a power saw, drill, torch, or sledgehammer, you can render the disk inoperable. (Be sure you're wearing safety goggles.) Although this method is effective, it has several disadvantages: it takes time and considerable physical effort, and it has all the usual risks associated with tools. In the case of an otherwise functional piece of hardware, you're left with a disk that can't be sold or donated to someone who can use it.

As we discuss in Chapter 14, the Format command (with the /P switch) and the Cipher command (with the /W switch) can be used to overwrite everything on a disk, but these tools are impractical for cleaning the system partition.

> ## Inside OUT
>
> ### *Use BitLocker drive encryption to wipe a drive clean*
>
> One highly effective method using built-in tools is to reinstall Windows 10 Pro or Enterprise using a local account with a long, completely random password you create by simply mashing the keyboard. Don't write that password down. Use the built-in BitLocker management tools to encrypt the entire drive, including empty space. Then restart the computer using a Windows recovery drive and use the disk management tools to remove all partitions from the system drive. Even if a would-be data thief can reconstruct the partitions, they'll be unable to gain anything useful from the encrypted system drive.

Another simple solution is to use a third-party disk-wiping tool. A free one that we like is Darik's Boot And Nuke (DBAN), which you can download from *https://dban.org*. DBAN is a bootable disk that securely wipes a computer's hard disks. If you're worried that DBAN or another purported disk-wiping utility might surreptitiously steal your data before destroying it, remove your concerns by disconnecting your computer from your network before using the program.

If your disk contains highly sensitive material and you want to be absolutely sure its data can't be recovered, search for a utility that conforms to the United States Department of Defense DoD 5220.22-M standard for clearing and sanitizing media. This standard requires each sector to be overwritten with different characters several times, thus defeating even the most sensitive data-recovery tools. Programs that meet the standard include Active@ KillDisk (*http://www.killdisk.com*) and BCWipe (*https://www.jetico.com*).

Working with virtual hard disks

Using Disk Management, you can create a virtual hard disk (VHD) in the same formats used by the Windows 10 Hyper-V Manager program. A VHD file encapsulates all the characteristics of a simple disk volume in a single file. Once you've created, initialized, and formatted a VHD file, you can mount the file so that it appears as a disk drive in File Explorer and Disk Management; unlike a physical disk, however, you can back up or move the entire disk by copying the VHD file. This type of file can be a useful alternative to Zip files for archiving and sharing large amounts of information with a detailed folder hierarchy.

> ➤ For more information about Hyper-V Manager, see Chapter 16, "Hyper-V."

To create a virtual hard disk, open Disk Management and click Action, Create VHD. Disk Management responds with the Create And Attach Virtual Hard Disk dialog box, as shown in Figure 9-25.

CHAPTER 9

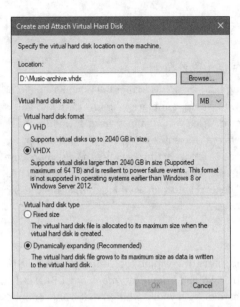

Figure 9-25   You can create a virtual hard disk using either of two formats. The Dynamically Expanding option makes the best use of existing disk space.

Specify a file name with a fully qualified path. It's easiest to do this with the help of the Browse
button, but note that the file cannot be stored in your %SystemRoot% (usually C:\Windows)
folder.

New in Windows 10 is the option to create a virtual hard disk in either of two formats. The VHD
format supports disks up to 2 TB; these can be used on systems running Windows 7, Windows 8
or 8.1, or Windows 10. The VHDX format supports much larger disks, up to 64 TB, but it's not
supported by earlier versions of Windows. The VHDX format was introduced with Windows
Server 2012, and the option to create gigantic virtual disks is perhaps primarily of interest to
server administrators. VHD is still the default format in Windows 10. However, because metadata
in VHDX disks continuously tracks changes (a service not provided in VHD), they are, as the dialog box indicates, more resilient to power failures. For that reason, you might prefer the newer
format even if your size requirements are well under 2 TB. Provided that you don't require
interoperability with Windows 7 or Windows 8.1, we don't know of a good reason not to prefer
VHDX.

If you want the disk to expand in size as you add files to it, select Dynamically Expanding. Otherwise, select Fixed Size. (The Recommended option changes depending on which VHD format
you chose.) Either way, you must also specify a size (that's a maximum size if you select Dynamically Expanding). The minimum size is 3 MB; the maximum is the amount of free space available
on your (real) disk. After you finish with the Create And Attach Virtual Hard Disk dialog box, Disk
Management adds the new virtual disk to its graphical view pane as an unknown, uninitialized
disk with unallocated space.

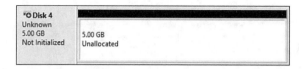

Right-click the area at the left side of this display (with the disk number), and then click Initialize Disk. The Initialize Disk dialog box that appears gives you the option of setting up a disk with a Master Boot Record or a GUID Partition Table:

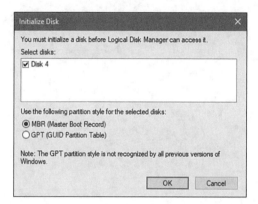

Select MBR (Master Boot Record) if you want the VHD to be usable in older versions of Windows; choose GPT (GUID Partition Table) if you're working with a disk larger than 2 TB. After completing these steps, you can follow the procedures described earlier in this chapter to create one or more volumes on the new disk. After you have created a volume, formatted it, and assigned it a drive letter, the disk appears like any other in Disk Management and File Explorer.

To remove a virtual hard disk, right-click the disk-number box at the left side of Disk Management's graphical view pane, and then click Detach VHD. Disk Management informs you that deleting the disk will make it unavailable until you reattach it. The dialog box also reminds you of the location of the file that encapsulated your virtual hard disk.

To reattach a virtual disk, click Action, Attach VHD in Disk Management. Then type or browse to the location of the VHD or VHDX file. (It will be identified in File Explorer as Hard Disk Image File.)

CHAPTER 9

CHAPTER 10

Cortana and Windows search

Microsoft founder Bill Gates first articulated his vision of "information at your fingertips" back in 1994, at the dawn of the internet era. A quarter-century later, we're almost there.

In Windows 10, the search box to the right of Start neatly ties together all the ways you might want to search for answers. You can quickly open apps and jump to a system setting, find local files and folders, search through your music collection, and track down a picture.

You can also extend your search to the web without having to open a browser. Type your request into the search box and get an instant answer right in the Start menu. Or you could skip the typing and just say "Hey Cortana" to perform that search with the help of Microsoft's web-connected intelligent assistant. If you connect Cortana to cloud services like Office 365, you can get personalized answers to questions like "What's on my calendar next week?"

Perhaps more than any other feature in Windows, the search tools have the potential to change the way you work. If your filing philosophy involves the digital equivalent of throwing everything into a giant shoebox, you'll be startled at how easy it is to find what you're looking for. Even if you consider yourself an extremely well-organized Windows user, we predict you'll find ways to integrate File Explorer's search tools into your everyday routine.

But we begin with the unified search capability that sets Windows 10 apart from its predecessors.

Using Windows search

Search, as a Windows 10 feature and as an online service, is evolving at breathtaking speed. The results that show up when you enter text in the search box are powered in large part by online services that are constantly improving, as are the Windows features you use to make those requests.

In the initial release of Windows 10, Cortana was a feature layered over traditional Windows search capabilities. If you didn't want the help of an occasionally sassy assistant, you could turn off Cortana with a simple switch.

In all currently supported releases of Windows 10, that on-off switch is gone (although, as we explain later in this section, you can accomplish the same goal with Group Policy). Cortana's "personality" has also been toned down, and the personalized features are now neatly integrated with other search capabilities in Windows 10, as well as with external devices such as mobile phones (there's a Cortana app for iPhone and in the Google Play Store for Android devices).

Beginning with version 1709, Settings now includes a top-level Cortana section, and you can sync your search history between devices. You still have full control over what personal information is available to Cortana, and you have extensive customization capabilities as well.

Search is built into Windows 10 as an integral feature that gets prime real estate, just to the right of the Start button. By default, on desktop and laptop PCs, you'll find a search box here. In Tablet Mode (or if you change the default setting), a search button appears, which expands to reveal a box when you tap or click it. And if even that icon is too much, you can hide it completely.

Beginning with the Windows 10 October 2018 Update, version 1809, clicking in the search box opens a wide panel designed to help you focus your search efforts. As Figure 10-1 shows, you can narrow the scope of your search before you begin typing, using any of the five options at the top of the panel.

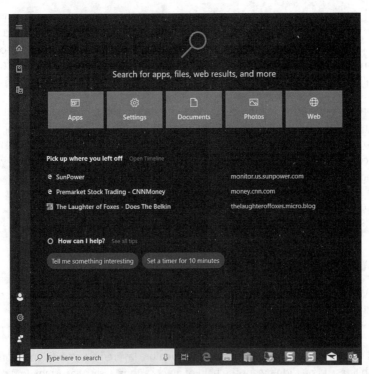

Figure 10-1 Clicking in the search box displays these filtering options. Pick one of the five tiles along the top, and then type a search term to display a filtered results list.

For most simple tasks, such as searching for an app or a setting, the fastest route to success is to tap the Windows key and begin typing. The results, as shown in Figure 10-2, are businesslike and efficient, with no personality. This example shows the new, wider search results experience that debuted in version 1809; in earlier releases of Windows 10, the default results list occupies a single column.

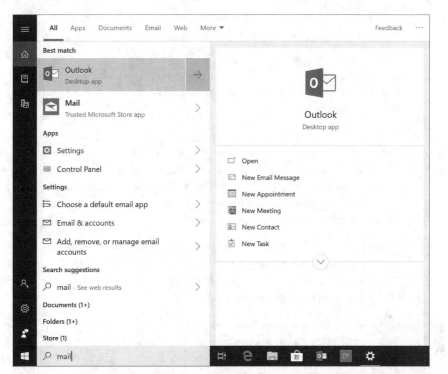

Figure 10-2 Type a word or phrase in the search box, and you get a categorized list of results that match the search term, including apps and settings. Use the options at the top to change the search scope.

Windows highlights the top item on the results list, but you can use the arrow keys to scroll up and down through the list. You can also use the mouse to select the arrow to the right of any entry and make its properties or Jump List options visible on the right side of the wide results pane.

If the first pass doesn't find the exact item you were hoping for, you can narrow the scope of the search by choosing a category from the list above the results pane. The Apps, Documents, Email, and Web categories are visible by default; click More to expand the list of available categories to include Folders, Music, People, Photos, Settings, and Videos. Choosing one of those categories immediately changes the search results list to show only the category you selected.

Choosing a category has a simple but powerful action: It inserts a prefix in the search box, before the search term. If you're more comfortable with the keyboard, you can accomplish the same result by typing the category prefix manually: **folder:** or **photos:**, for example.

Inside OUT

Turn off Cortana using Group Policy or a registry edit

As with most things Windows, you can remove the search button or box completely if you're really convinced you won't use it. Right-click the taskbar and then click Cortana > Hidden. With that option set, you can still access Cortana's full feature set by tapping the Windows key and typing.

To turn off all of Cortana's features, leaving only the ability to search for local apps, files, and settings, you need to make a simple registry edit. On a system running Windows 10 Pro or Enterprise edition, you can use Group Policy to apply this setting across multiple machines; on a single PC, use the local Group Policy Editor, gpedit.msc, to open the policy Computer Configuration > Administrative Templates > Windows Components > Search > Allow Cortana and set it to Disabled.

On a system running Windows 10 Home, you must manually edit the registry to make this configuration change. Find the key HKLM\Software\Policies\Microsoft\Windows\Windows Search (which you might need to create if it doesn't exist), and then create the DWORD value AllowCortana and set it to 0.

In either case, this change applies to all user accounts. Restart the PC, and you'll notice that the text in the search box has changed from "Type here to search" to "Search Windows." Clicking in the search box displays only a simple prompt. In addition, Cortana's Notebook is unavailable, and only a few settings are available when you click the Cortana heading in Settings.

When you enter a word or phrase in the search box, results from the web can appear directly in the results list, in a panel that pops out to the right of the initial display of search results in Start. This feature, which was added in version 1709, allows you to get instant answers to questions in a wide array of categories. If your question is clear and unambiguous and you have a working internet connection, your answer appears immediately, as is the case here.

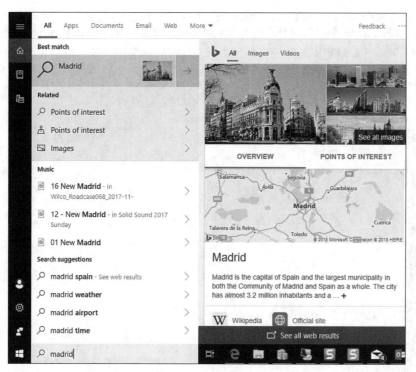

Figure 10-3 When the best match for a search term is on the web, a pop-out like this appears to the right of the results list.

You can use this same technique for the following types of queries:

- **Dates and times.** Use the search box to check the dates of upcoming holidays and events. ("When is Thanksgiving this year?" and "What time does the Super Bowl start?")

- **Biographical details.** If someone is famous enough or holds a public office, you can ask for more information. ("How old is Bill Gates?" "Who is governor of New Mexico?").

- **Definitions.** Not sure of the meaning of an unfamiliar word? You can view a definition in the results pane, with an option to hear the word's pronunciation or jump to an online dictionary. ("What does *phlegmatic* mean?")

- **Sports scores.** You can see scores and standings for any team or league, even for games that are in progress.

- **Stock prices.** To get the current price and a chart for any stock or index on a major exchange, enter a dollar sign followed by the ticker symbol: $MSFT, $DJIA

- **Weather.** Type **weather** followed by a city name to see a five-day forecast that can help you decide whether to pack an umbrella or sunscreen for an upcoming trip.

CHAPTER 10

The expanded results pane can also display interactive controls. Enter an arithmetic problem, and Windows search shows the result in a calculator where you can continue your number-crunching. If you ask how to convert units of measurement, the resulting display allows you to choose from an enormous number of conversions, including length, volume, and even fuel efficiency. Figure 10-4 shows a conversion that might not be as practical as gallons to liters but could help settle a bet over your favorite space opera.

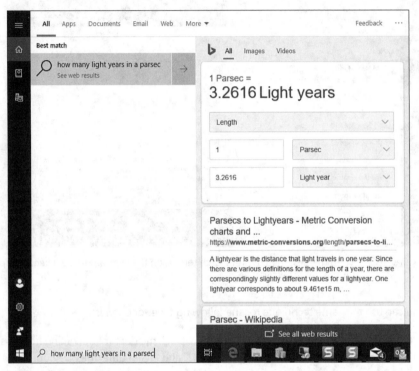

Figure 10-4 These live widgets appear in the search results when you ask a question that involves calculation or conversion.

Besides conversions, you can also do basic math by entering an appropriate query in the taskbar search box. Enter any valid mathematical format—addition, subtraction, multiplication, division, exponentiation, and more, with support for using parentheses to group operations—and see the answer directly in the results pane.

The search box is also able to look up current exchange rates and convert any amount in one currency to its equivalent in another. Feel free to be brief: For users in the United States, entering any amount with a dollar sign in front opens a conversion window with Euro selected as the target currency. You can keep typing to specify a different target currency ("$1850 in GBP") or use controls in the widget, as shown here, to change the amount, choose a different currency, and even reverse the conversion.

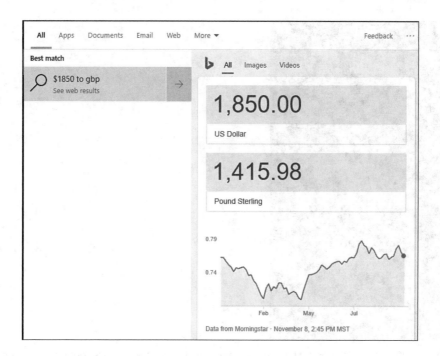

So far, none of what we've done using the search box involves Cortana. In the next section, we discuss what Cortana adds to this basic search experience.

What you can do with Cortana

Cortana, the intelligent search assistant built into Windows 10, adds an adult's voice and a (programmed) sense of humor to the core search experience. With your permission, Cortana also has the capability to anticipate actions and to perform additional tasks, such as adding items to a to-do list and delivering regular updates that match your interests and your schedule, as defined in a notebook full of settings.

In many ways, Cortana today is still like a child prodigy. Despite the pleasant female voice (no additional voice options are available) and the mostly natural intonations, "she" is really a web service, which is constantly learning and adding capabilities.

To get started with Cortana, you have to sign in with a Microsoft account or an Azure Active Directory account and agree to some terms, as shown in Figure 10-5. (You can change these and other settings later.) Doing so gives Cortana permission to search your information on your behalf.

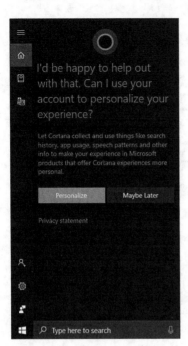

Figure 10-5 Cortana doesn't have access to personal information unless you provide your consent first.

The other feature you might want to configure now is how Cortana responds to your verbal commands. You can, of course, always click the microphone icon at the right side of the search box and begin speaking. To foster a more conversational approach, go to Settings > Cortana > Talk To Cortana and tell Cortana you want a response when you say "Hey Cortana" followed by a spoken request. You can also specify that you want to use the keyboard shortcut Windows key + C to tell Cortana to start listening. (That latter option is especially useful if you have two or more Cortana-aware devices and you don't want them trying to answer the same query simultaneously.)

For a lengthy (but still not exhaustive) list of things Cortana can do for you, just ask: "What can you do?" (If your system doesn't support input via a microphone, click in the search box and type the question.) The categorized list includes all the Windows search tricks we mentioned earlier as well as a variety of personalized tasks. Results appear in the Start window, using Cortana's voice or a pop-out results pane.

Cortana can also control music playback on a multitude of music apps, including Spotify, iHeartRadio, and TuneIn Radio, even when the display is locked. (For maximum flexibility, open the Music section in Cortana's notebook and connect the Microsoft account you use with one or more of those services.) You can ask Cortana to play music by a specific artist; a track, title, genre, or playlist; or the call sign or frequency for a radio station, optionally specifying the app to use.

In addition to taking over search duties for files, folders, settings, music, and so on, Cortana can return results based on information you've given permission to search. For example, you can enter a list of symbols for stocks and mutual funds to your watch list, and then ask, "How did my stocks do today?" If you connect an Office 365 account, Cortana can also check for email from specific people and offer reminders on when you need to leave to arrive on time for an appointment.

Other tasks Cortana can complete on your behalf include adding appointments and reminders, creating notes and to-do lists, and checking your calendar for upcoming events. Figure 10-6, for example, shows the response when you ask Cortana to set a reminder. Reminders don't have to be triggered by a time. They can also be attached to a location or to a person. (This type of reminder is most effective when you also have the Cortana app running on your mobile device; the Cortana app is available on iOS and Android.)

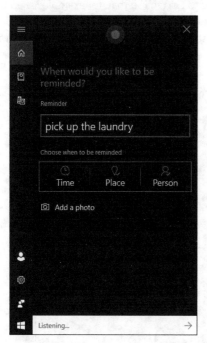

Figure 10-6   If you ask Cortana to set a reminder or create an appointment, you get this crisply efficient form.

You can also set recurring reminders in Cortana, including "Every Month" (useful for paying bills or remembering household maintenance tasks) and "Every Year" (so you don't forget a birthday or an anniversary). Cortana can also monitor the status of flights and track packages on your behalf.

CHAPTER 10

Your timers and alarms appear as notifications, and you can ask Cortana to show you your reminders any time.

Configuring Cortana and search options

Cortana is most helpful when you fill in the notebook, shown in Figure 10-7, to indicate the topics that are most relevant to you. Click the icon below Home on the left to open Cortana's notebook. (Those three icons are properly labeled if you click the button at the top of the navigation pane.) The appearance of this notebook changed dramatically in Windows 10 version 1803, transforming from a single long list to one that is organized into two tabs. Despite the change in appearance, the underlying contents of the Notebook, as shown in Figure 10-7, are essentially the same. Your name and email address are at the top. The Organizer tab contains lists, reminders, and tasks, while the Manage Skills tab allows you to define your interests in fine-grained detail. You can connect accounts and services to Cortana so that, for example, calendar items and commitments from email messages make it into your daily agenda. Next, the notebook provides dozens of sections where you can list your preferences—favorite sports teams, preferred cuisines and restaurant budgets, and news topics you want to follow.

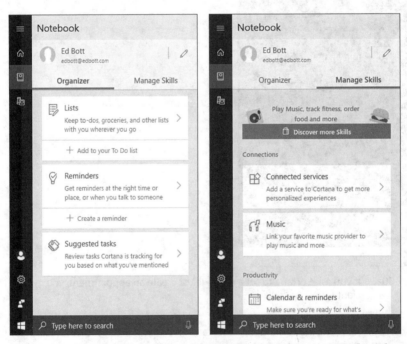

Figure 10-7   Click the notebook icon, just below the home icon in the upper-left corner to open Cortana's notebook, where you can add items to track and customize your interests on these two tabs.

Click any category to fill in information that can help make for more tailored recommendations and reminders later. If this seems like a tedious process, remember two things: First, you can do this over time. Just pop in every so often and check out a category or two. Second, all your settings are saved with your Microsoft account and available for you when you use other devices. That includes mobile devices running the Cortana app on Android and iOS.

You have every right to be concerned about privacy when using a service that knows so much about your daily routine. That's why Cortana has options to eliminate your device history and your local search history. To delete personal information saved on Microsoft's servers, open Settings > Cortana > Permissions & History, click or tap Change What Cortana Knows About Me In The Cloud, and follow the instructions. Two additional options allow you to manage what Cortana can access from the current device (location, email, calendar, communication history, and browsing history) and from other connected services.

You can adjust other Windows search–related privacy settings using options on the Cortana Settings page, shown in Figure 10-8. (Note that these options moved to the Windows 10 Settings app beginning with version 1709.) These settings affect whether Windows search returns results based on content you've stored in OneDrive and other cloud services as well as your activity history, as recorded in Timeline.

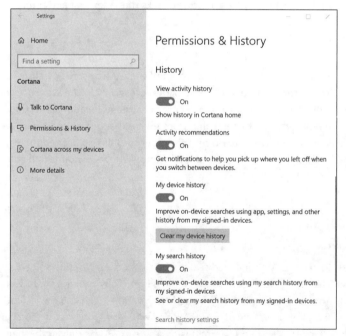

Figure 10-8   The Cortana Settings pane provides options to control how much of your information from the cloud is available for search.

Using Cortana in Microsoft Edge

Cortana has a special relationship with Microsoft Edge, the default browser in Windows 10, which we discuss at length in Chapter 8, "Microsoft Edge and Internet Explorer." A search result might pop up in your browser immediately if you type something about which Cortana is particularly knowledgeable. Enter a flight number or the name of a foreign currency, for example, and you'll get status or rate information, exactly as it would appear in the search results pane from Start. Cortana also has a fairly broad knowledge of restaurants.

If Cortana doesn't volunteer the information you need, take matters into your own hands. If you run across an interesting term while viewing a webpage in Microsoft Edge, right-click the word, name, or phrase and then click Ask Cortana. That opens a sidebar with additional information drawn from online sources.

Configuring the Windows search index

At its heart, the Windows Search service relies on a speedy, powerful, and well-behaved indexing service that does a fine job of keeping track of files and folders by name, by properties, and (in supported formats) by contents. All those details are kept in the search index, a database that keeps track of indexed file names, properties, and the contents of files. As a rule, when you do most common types of searches, Windows checks the index first and returns whatever results it finds there.

> ### NOTE
>
> The search index is stored by default in %ProgramData%\Microsoft\Search\Data. Default permissions for this folder are set to allow access only to the System account and to members of the Administrators group. You can change its location using the Indexing Options dialog box (available by searching from the taskbar or Control Panel). We can't, however, think of a good reason to do so. This folder contains no user-editable files, and we recommend that you leave it in its default location with its contents undisturbed.

Inside OUT

When do searches skip the index?

Although we focus mostly on indexed searches in this section, Windows 10 actually includes two search engines. The second engine is informally known as *grep* search. (The name comes from an old UNIX command derived from the full name *global | regular expression | print*.) Windows Search uses the index whenever you use the search box on the taskbar, and in libraries. In those circumstances, search looks only in the index and ignores any subfolders that are excluded from the index.

Windows uses the grep search engine if you begin your search from the This PC folder, from the root of any local drive (including the system drive), or from a local file folder. Grep searches include the contents of all subfolders within the search scope regardless of whether they're included in the search index. For a more detailed examination of non-indexed searches, see "Advanced search tools and techniques" later in this chapter.

To build the index that makes its magic possible, Windows Search uses several separate processes. The index is constructed dynamically by the Windows Search service, SearchIndexer.exe. It includes metadata for all files in all locations that are prescribed to be indexed; for documents in formats that support indexing of file contents, the indexer extracts the text of the files and stores it alongside the file properties for quick retrieval.

The Windows Search service begins running shortly after you start a new Windows session. From that point on, it runs in the background at all times, creating the initial index and updating it as new files are added and existing ones are changed or deleted. Protocol handlers do the work of cracking open different data stores to add items to the index. Property handlers allow Windows Search to extract the values of properties from items and store them properly in the index. Filters extract the contents of supported file types so that you can do full-text searches for those items.

Which files and folders are in the index?

Indexing every 0 and 1 on your hard disk would be a time-consuming and space-consuming task—and ultimately pointless. When you search for a snippet of text, you're almost always looking for something you wrote, copied, or saved, and you don't want the results to include random program files that happen to have the same snippet embedded in the midst of a blob of code. (Yes, we know some developers might disagree, but they're the exception.) So the default settings for the indexer make some reasonable inclusions and exclusions.

Certain locations are specifically included. These include all user profiles (but not the AppData folder), the contents of the Start menu, and your Internet Explorer history. Locally synced files from OneDrive as well as offline files stored in the client-side cache (CSC) are automatically included in your local index. You can explicitly add other folders to the index, but Windows 10 eliminates the need to do that. Instead, just right-click the folder, click Include In Library, and select an existing library or create a new one; when you do so, Windows automatically adds that folder to the list of indexed locations and begins indexing its contents without requiring additional steps on your part.

To see which folders are currently being indexed, open the Indexing Options dialog box. You can get there in various ways, including by entering **Indexing Options** in the search box on the taskbar. In Figure 10-9, the Indexing Options dialog box shows four default folders that are included in the index as well as two we've added to libraries.

To get more information about what's being indexed, click Modify, which opens the Indexed Locations dialog box.

CAUTION

We strongly recommend that you not try to manage locations manually using the Indexed Locations dialog box. If you add a folder to a library and then remove it from the list of indexed locations, the folder remains in the navigation pane under the associated library, but none of its contents will be visible in the library itself.

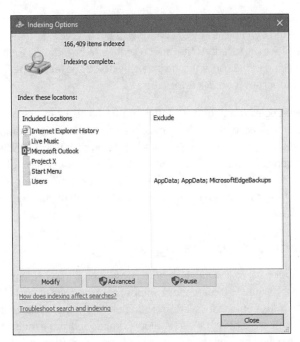

Figure 10-9   The Indexing Options dialog box shows the top level of locations that are included in the index. Subfolders (for example, all the profile subfolders of Users) are not shown here.

In its default view, the list of folders and other data stores in the Indexed Locations dialog box shows only locations that are accessible to your user account. To see (and manage) locations from other user profiles, click Show All Locations. As the User Account Control (UAC) shield icon makes clear, you need to be signed in as an administrator (or provide an administrator's credentials) to continue.

Within that list of indexed locations, the Windows Search service records the file name and properties (size, date modified, and so on) of any file or folder. Files marked as System and Hidden are indexed but are displayed in search results only when you change File Explorer settings to show those file types. Metadata for common music, image, and video file formats is included in the index by default. The indexer also includes the contents of a file and its custom properties if the file format has an associated property handler and filter, as is the case with most popular document formats.

To see whether a particular file format supports content indexing, open the Indexing Options dialog box, click Advanced, and then click the File Types tab. Find the extension associated with the file type and then look in the Filter Description column for the name of the filter that handles that extension. If you see File Properties Filter, the file type does not support content indexing. File types that are supported have a named filter, such as Microsoft Office Filter, Open Document Format ODT Filter, HTML Filter, or Reader Search Handler.

The list of formats on the File Types tab on your computer might include more file types if you installed Windows programs that include custom property handlers and filters, such as the Office Open XML Format Word Filter installed with Microsoft Office 365.

Windows Search does not index the content of files that are saved without a file name extension, nor does it index the contents of files that are protected by Information Rights Management (IRM) or digital rights management (DRM).

A handful of locations are specifically excluded from indexing. Even if you manually specify that you want your system drive (normally C) to be included in the index, the following files and folders will be excluded:

- The entire contents of the \Windows folder and all its subfolders. (The Windows.old folder that's created by an upgrade installation of Windows 10 is also excluded.)

- \$Recycle.Bin (the hidden folder that contains deleted files for all user accounts).

- \Users\Default and all of its subfolders. (This is the user profile template used to create a profile for a new user.)

- The entire contents of the \Program Files and \Program Files (x86) folders and all their subfolders.

- The \ProgramData folder (except the subfolder that contains shortcuts for the shared Start menu).

Monitoring the index and tuning indexer performance

The status message at the top of the Indexing Options dialog box offers real-time updates on what the indexer is doing at the moment. "Indexing complete" means there are no pending tasks. The status message lists the number of items (files, folders, and so on) that are currently in the index.

"Indexing paused" means the service has temporarily stopped all indexing tasks; you'll see this message if you check the indexer status shortly after you start the computer because the default setting for the Windows Search service is Automatic (Delayed Start).

If indexing tasks are currently underway, the status message displays an increase or decrease in the number of items indexed as new, changed, and deleted files are processed. The indexer is designed to throttle itself whenever it detects that the system is working on other, presumably more important tasks. As a result, you'll most likely be told that "Indexing speed is reduced due to user activity" when you first check.

That message indicates the indexing service has backed off in response to your activity and is operating at a fraction of its normal speed. If the number of files to be indexed is big enough (if you copied a folder with several thousand documents, for instance), you'll see the indexing speed pick up dramatically after you keep your hands off the keyboard and mouse for a minute or so.

The exact speed of indexing depends on various factors, including the speed of your CPU and storage subsystem as well as the number, size, and complexity of documents and whether their full contents are being indexed. Unfortunately, the status message in the Indexing Options dialog box doesn't include a progress bar and doesn't indicate how many files are yet to be indexed, so there's no easy way to tell whether the current task is barely underway or nearly complete. If you haven't recently added any new folders to the index but have simply been changing a few files in the course of normal work, the index should stay close to complete (assuming you've ever had a complete index).

In the past, some websites for performance-obsessed Windows users complained about the performance hit that Windows Search causes; some even recommended disabling the Windows Search service to improve overall system performance. We recommend you leave it running. In our experience, the Windows Search service uses only a small percentage of available CPU resources even at its busiest. The indexing service is specifically designed to back off when you use your computer for other activities, switching to low-priority input/output (I/O) and allowing foreground I/O tasks, such as opening Start, to execute first. When Windows 10 first builds its index, or if you copy a large number of files to the system at once, indexing can take a long time and cause some spikes in CPU and disk activity, but you shouldn't notice a significant impact on performance.

File Explorer accesses the index directly, so even if the indexer is busy processing new and changed files, it shouldn't affect the speed of a search operation. In normal operation, retrieving search results from even a very large index should take no more than a few seconds. You might notice a delay in opening a folder that contains a large number of compressed folders, including Zip files and ISO disk images.

TROUBLESHOOTING

You encounter problems finding files that should be in the search index

If you're certain that the files you're looking for are in an indexed location but they don't turn up in search results, the index might have become corrupted. As with so many Windows features, there's a troubleshooter for that.

Open Settings and begin typing **Find And Fix Problems With Windows Search** in the search box. The resulting troubleshooter automatically finds and fixes any problems it can detect. If it finds none, it leads you through a series of steps to identify and resolve your problem.

Alternatively, you can manually rebuild the search index. From the Indexing Options dialog box, click Advanced, and then click Rebuild, under the Troubleshooting heading, as shown here:

We recommend you restart your system before trying to rebuild the index, to ensure that no open files are interfering with the indexing process. Rebuilding the index might take a considerable amount of time, especially if you have a large number of files to index. To maximize the efficiency of the reindexing process, start the operation when you know you don't need to use your PC and you can leave it powered on—before lunch or at the end of your workday, for example.

Managing file properties and metadata

Every file you view in File Explorer has a handful of properties that describe the file itself: the file name and file name extension (which is associated with the program that opens that type of file), the file's size, the date and time it was created and last modified, and any file system attributes. These properties are stored in the file system and are central to displaying the contents of a folder or other location and performing simple searches.

In addition to these basic file properties, many data-file formats can store custom metadata. These additional properties can be added by a device or by software; in some cases, they can be modified by the user. When you take a digital picture, your camera or smartphone might add the device make and model, exposure time, ISO speed, and other details to the file when it's saved. When you buy a digital music track or album, the individual audio files include custom properties (often referred to as *tags,* from the IDv3 tag format used in MP3 files) that identify the artist, album, track number, and other details. You can also add free-form tags to digital images saved in formats that support that additional metadata. Microsoft Word and other Microsoft Office programs automatically add your name to the Author field in documents you create; you can fill in additional properties such as keywords and comments and save them with the file.

The simplest way to view metadata for a folder is to click Details Pane on the View tab in File Explorer. Doing so opens a pane on the right that displays a thumbnail of the selected file (if a thumbnail is available), plus metadata saved as file properties. You can click through a group of files in rapid succession, with the contents of the details pane changing with each new selection. Figure 10-10 shows these details for a photo saved in JPEG format; you can see the date the photo was taken, the make of the camera, the dimensions of the picture, the exposure settings, and quite a bit more.

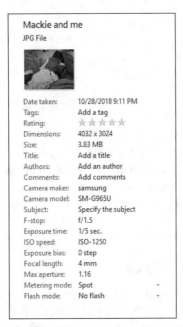

Figure 10-10   The Details Pane in File Explorer shows a selection of properties from the currently selected file. Some are directly editable; others are fixed and can't be changed.

Saving custom information as metadata can make it easier to find that file (and others like it) using the search tools we describe later in this chapter.

The properties displayed in the details pane are an excellent starting point, but they might not represent every detail available for the selected file. To see the complete list, right-click the item and click Properties (or select the item and press Alt+Enter). Then click the Details tab in the properties dialog box.

Inside OUT

Rate your favorite digital media files

For digital photos, music, and other media files, you'll notice that the Rating field is available in the details pane. Instead of providing a box to enter free-form text or a number, this field shows five stars, all displayed in gray if this value is empty. You can rate any file on a scale of one to five stars by clicking or tapping the appropriate star in the details pane. Adding ratings is a useful way to filter large media collections so that they show only the entries you previously rated highly. Ratings are also useful for assembling playlists and slide shows.

Figure 10-11 shows a side-by-side comparison of the properties dialog box and the details pane for a music track. A casual listener might not care that scrolling down through the properties dialog box reveals such exotica as Period, Mood, Beats-Per-Minute, and Initial Key, but a professional DJ can certainly find uses for those extra details.

Figure 10-11   The Details tab in a file's properties dialog box (left) offers a more exhaustive set of editable properties than the simpler details pane (right).

In either place, the details pane or the properties dialog box, you can edit many (but not all) of the item's properties. Some properties, such as file size, photo dimensions, and MP3 bitrate, are calculated by the file system or are otherwise fixed and cannot be directly modified. But you can edit custom metadata if the format of the underlying file allows you to do so.

To enter or change a property's value, simply click and type. If you add two or more words or phrases to a field that accepts multiple entries (such as Tags or Authors), use semicolons to separate them. Press Enter or click Save to add the new or changed properties to the file.

You can edit properties for multiple files at one time. This is especially useful when you're correcting an error in an album or artist name; just select all the songs in the album's folder. When more than one file is selected, you'll note that some properties in the details pane (such as track numbers and song titles) change to indicate that the specified field contains multiple values. A change you make to any field is written to all the files in your selection.

Metadata is saved within the file itself, using industry-standard data storage formats. Software developers who need to create a custom file format can make its metadata available to Windows by using an add-in called a property handler, which opens the file format to read and write its properties. Because metadata is saved within the file itself, the properties you edit in File Explorer or a Windows program are fully portable. This opens some useful possibilities:

- You can move files to other computers, even those running other operating systems, without losing the files' tags and other metadata.

- You can edit a file in an application other than the one in which it was created without losing any of the file's properties (assuming the other application properly adheres to the file format's standard for reading and writing metadata).

- A file's properties are visible to anyone who has read access to the file.

Inside OUT

Remove personal metadata for privacy's sake

Metadata within a file can tell a lot about you. Cameras record data about when (and, with some cameras, precisely where) a picture was taken and what camera or smartphone was used. Microsoft Office automatically adds author and company information to documents and spreadsheets. With user-created tags, you can add personal and business details that might be useful on a local copy but are unwise to disclose to the wider world.

To scrub a file of unwanted metadata, select one or more files in File Explorer, click Home > Properties > Remove Properties. This opens the Remove Properties dialog box, an example of which is shown here:

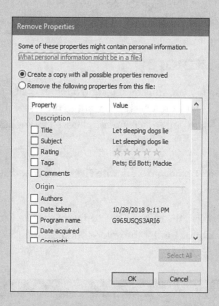

At this point, you have two choices. The default option creates a copy of your file (using the original file name with the word "Copy" appended to it) and removes all properties that can be changed, based on the file type. With the second option, Remove The Following Properties From This File, you select the check boxes next to individual properties and permanently remove those properties from the file when you click OK. (If no check box is visible, that property is not editable.)

Of course, common sense should prevail when it comes to issues of privacy. This option zeroes out metadata, but it does nothing with the contents of the file itself. You'll need to be vigilant to ensure that a digital photo doesn't contain potentially revealing information in the image itself or that sensitive personal or business details aren't saved within a document's contents.

You can edit custom properties only in files saved using a format that accommodates embedded metadata. For digital image files, Windows supports the JPEG, GIF, and TIFF formats, but you cannot save metadata in bitmap images and graphics files saved in PNG format because these formats were not developed with metadata in mind. Among music file formats, MP3, WMA, and FLAC fully support a wide range of properties designed to make it easy to manage a music collection; files saved in the uncompressed WAV (.wav) format do not support any custom tags. Plain text and Rich Text Format (.rtf) files do not support custom metadata; files saved in Word formats expose a rich set of additional properties, as do all other native file formats from Microsoft Office programs.

In some cases, you'll find that you're unable to view or edit metadata in a file even though the underlying format supports metadata. In that case, the culprit is a missing property handler.

Searching from File Explorer

To use File Explorer's search tools, start by selecting a folder or library. That defines the *scope* of your search—the set of files from which you want to draw search results. (If you're not sure which folder contains the files you're looking for, choose Libraries or Quick Access from the navigation pane.)

➤ **For a refresher course on how to work with File Explorer and libraries, see Chapter 9, "Storage and file management."**

Next, click in the search box in the upper-right corner of the File Explorer window. That action adds a Search tab to the ribbon, under the color-coded Search Tools heading, as shown in Figure 10-12.

Figure 10-12   Clicking in the search box to the right of the address bar reveals the Search Tools tab on the ribbon.

We'll get to those tools in a moment, but for now, just start typing a word or phrase in the search box. As you type, File Explorer will display a list of all files and folders whose name, properties, or contents match that search term.

The following rules govern how searches work:

- Whatever text you type as a search term must appear at the beginning of a word, not in the middle. Thus, entering **des** returns items containing the words *des*ire, *des*tination, and *des*troy but not un*des*irable or sad*des*t. (You can override this behavior by using wildcard characters, as we explain in "Advanced search tools and techniques" later in this chapter.)

- Search terms are not case sensitive. Thus, entering **Bott** returns items with *Ed Bott* as a tag or property, but the results also include files containing the words *bott*om and *bott*le.

- By default, searches ignore accents, umlauts, and other diacritical marks. If you routinely need to be able to distinguish, say, Händel from Handel, open the Indexing Options dialog box, click Advanced (for which you'll need administrative credentials), and then select Treat Similar Words With Diacritics As Different Words.

- To search for an exact phrase, enclose the phrase within quotation marks. If you enter two or more words without using quotes, the search results list includes items that contain all of the words individually.

Search results for indexed folders appear so quickly that you might have a substantial number of results before you type the second or third character in the search string. A complicating factor: If your search term is part of a subfolder name, your results list includes the entire contents of that subfolder.

Inside OUT

See all files in a folder and its subfolders

If you open File Explorer to a particular folder and you want to avoid the tedium of opening subfolders to view their contents, try using the wildcard character that's been around as long as Microsoft has been making operating systems. Entering an asterisk (*) in the search box immediately returns all files and subfolders in the current folder and all its subfolders. Assuming the list is of manageable size, you can then group, filter, sort, or otherwise rearrange the items within the folder to find exactly what you're looking for.

If simply entering a search term doesn't return the needed results, you have two options. The easiest is to build a new search (or refine the current one) using the point-and-click commands on the ribbon's Search tab. The other is to use the powerful but cryptic search syntax to build a search manually.

We start with the Search tab (under the Search Tools heading), which offers a wealth of options to create and refine a search. The choices you make here return results from the current search scope. To change the scope, use the options in the Location group.

In Figure 10-13, for example, OneDrive – Personal is selected in the navigation pane, and All Subfolders (the default) is selected in the Location group on the ribbon. Clicking Date Modified and selecting Today from the drop-down list returns all files that were added or changed in all locally synced OneDrive folders today.

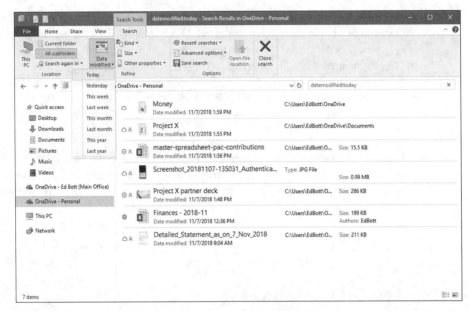

Figure 10-13   To make the Search tab visible, click in the search box, and then use its options to build a search from scratch or refine an existing search.

If you're looking for an invoice you're certain was created last month, you can click Last Month from the Date Modified list. If the set of results is still too large to scan, you can use additional options on the Search tab to refine the search, or click in the search box and enter a word or phrase that you know was in the file's name or its contents.

Three filters get top billing in the Refine group on the Search tab:

- **Date Modified.** This property represents the most recent date a file or folder was saved. For a downloaded program file, it shows the date you saved the file locally, not the date the developer created it.

- **Kind.** This field shows predefined groups of file types, including those for some items that aren't stored in File Explorer. The most common choice to make here is Document, which includes text files, any file saved in a Microsoft Office format, and PDF files. Try Music, Movie, or Picture if you're looking for digital media files.

- **Size.** This list shows a range of sizes. If you're trying to clear space on your system drive, choosing Huge (16 – 128 MB) or Gigantic (>128 MB) is a good way to locate large files that can safely be deleted or archived on an external drive.

Using any of the previous three filters adds a search operator, followed by a colon and a parameter, in the search box. Clicking Other Properties on the Search tab offers additional, context-specific options to refine the search results. What makes these options different is that they fill in the name of the operator, followed by a colon, and then position the insertion point so that you can complete the definition. For a folder optimized for General Items, this list contains the following four options:

- **Type.** Enter a file extension (pdf, xls, or docx, for example) or any part of the description in the Type field in Details view; enter **Excel**, for example, to return Excel workbooks in any format.

- **Name.** Enter a string of text here. The results list will show any file or folder that contains that exact string at the beginning of any word in its name.

- **Folder Path.** Enter a string of text here. The results list will show any file or folder that contains that exact string anywhere in its full path. If you enter **doc**, the results will include all files and folders in your Documents folder and any of its subfolders (because Documents is part of the path for those subfolders), as well as the contents of any other folder whose name contains a word beginning with those three letters.

- **Tags.** Almost every data file contains this field, which is stored as metadata in the file itself. You can add one or more tags to any file using the Details pane or the Details tab in its properties dialog box.

The list of available options changes slightly for other folder types. Documents folders include Authors and Title operators, and Photos folders include Date Taken and Rating, for example.

To run the same search from a different location, click Search Again In and choose an available scope. Or just switch to a different node in the navigation pane and start again.

Advanced search tools and techniques

The search capabilities in Windows 10 are direct descendants of standalone tools and Windows features that date back to the turn of the 21st century. Those original search tools relied on something called Advanced Query Syntax (AQS), which survives, only slightly modified, in a mostly undocumented form today.

You can see some vestiges of AQS when you build a search using the Search tab. Each entry you make from the ribbon adds a corresponding query to the search box. When you learn the query syntax, you can create your own advanced searches and even save them for reuse, as we explain in this section.

NOTE

The advanced search syntax we describe here works in the File Explorer search box but not in searches from the taskbar.

CHAPTER 10

The most basic query typically begins with a keyword (or a portion of a word) typed in the search box. Assuming you begin typing in a location that supports indexed searches (the task-bar search box or your locally synced OneDrive folder, for example), the list of search results will include any item in that location containing any indexed word (in its name or properties or content) that begins with the letters you type. You can then narrow the results list by using additional search parameters.

Advanced queries support the following types of search parameters, which can be combined using search operators:

- **File contents.** Keywords, phrases, numbers, and text strings

- **Kinds of items.** Folders, documents, pictures, music, and so on

- **Data stores.** Specific locations in the Windows file system containing indexed items

- **File properties.** Size, date, tags, and so on

In every case, these parameters consist of a word that the search query recognizes as a property or other index operator, followed by a colon and the value to search for or exclude. (When Windows Search recognizes a word followed by a colon as a valid property, it turns that operator blue.) You can combine search terms using Boolean operators and parentheses.

The value that immediately follows the colon can take several forms. If you want a loose (partial) match, just type a word or the beginning of a word. Thus, **type:Word** turns up files of the type Microsoft Word Document, Microsoft Word 97 – 2003 Document, Microsoft Word 97 – 2003 Template, Microsoft Word Macro-Enabled Document, and so on. To specify a strict (exact) match, use an equal sign and, if necessary, quotation marks, as in this example:

```
type:="Microsoft Word Document"
```

You can also use Boolean operators (AND, OR, and NOT) and parentheses to combine criteria. If you have fond memories of MS-DOS, you'll welcome using ***** and **?** as wildcards, and you can dramatically change the behavior of a search by means of the innocuous-looking tilde (~) character (which forces Windows to perform a strict character search in indexed locations, as discussed later in this section).

Of course, all these techniques become much more useful when you're able to reuse your carefully crafted search criteria, as we explain in "Saving searches and clearing search history" at the end of this chapter.

Searching by item type or kind

To search for files with a particular file name extension, you can simply enter the extension in the search box, like this:

```
*.ext
```

(Note that this method of searching does not work for .exe or .msc files.) The results include files that incorporate the extension in their contents as well as in their file names—which might or might not be what you want. You'll get a more focused search by using the ext: operator, including an asterisk wildcard and a period like this:

```
ext:*.txt
```

NOTE

As with many properties, you have more than one way to specify an exact file name extension. In addition to ext:, you can use fileext:, extension:, or fileextension:.

File name extensions are useful for some searches, but you'll get even better results using two different search properties: Type and Kind. The Type property limits your search based on the value found in the Type field for a given object. Thus, to look for files saved in any Microsoft Excel format, type this term in the search box:

```
type:excel
```

To find any music file saved in MP3 format, type this text in the search box:

```
type:mp3
```

To constrain your search to groups of related file types, use the Kind property, in the syntax kind:=*value*. Enter **kind:=doc**, for example, to return text files, Microsoft Office documents, Adobe Acrobat documents, HTML and XML files, and other document formats. This search term also accepts **folder**, **pic**, **picture**, **music**, **song**, **program**, and **video** as values to search for.

Changing the scope of a search

You can specify a folder or library location by using **folder:**, **under:**, **in:**, or **path:**. Thus, **folder:documents** restricts the scope of the search to your Documents library, and **in:videos mackie** finds all files in the Videos library that contain *Mackie* in the file name or any property.

Searching for item properties

You can search on the basis of any property recognized by the file system. (The list of available properties for files is identical to the ones we discuss in "Layouts, previews, and other ways to arrange files" in Chapter 9.) To see the whole list of available properties, switch to Detail view in File Explorer, right-click any column heading, and then click More. The Choose Details dialog box that appears enumerates the available properties.

When you enter text in the search box, Windows searches file names, all properties, and indexed content, returning items where it finds a match with that value. That often generates more search results than you want. To find all documents of which Jean is the author, omitting documents that include the word Jean in their file names or content, you type **author:jean** in the search box. (To eliminate documents authored by Jeanne, Jeannette, or Jeanelle, add an equal sign and enclose jean in quotation marks: **author:="jean".**)

When searching on the basis of dates, you can use long or short forms, as you please. For example, the search values

`modified:9/29/16`

and

`modified:09/29/2016`

are equivalent. (If you don't mind typing the extra four letters, use **datemodified:** instead.)

To search for dates before or after a particular date, use the less-than (<) and greater-than (>) operators. For example,

`modified:>09/30/2015`

searches for dates later than September 30, 2015. Use the same two operators to specify file sizes below and above some value.

Use two periods to search for items within a range of dates. To find files modified in September or October 2016, type this search term in the Start menu search box:

`modified:9/1/2016..10/31/2016`

You can also use ranges to search by file size. The search filters suggest some common ranges and even group them into neat little buckets, so you can type **size:** and then click Medium to find files in the range 100 KB to 1 MB.

Again, don't be fooled into thinking that this list represents the full selection of available sizes. You can specify an exact size range—using operators such as >, >=, <, and <=. (Also, you can use the "**..**" operator.) For example, **size:0 MB..1 MB** is the same as **size:<=1 MB**. You can specify values using bytes, KB, MB, or GB.

Inside OUT

Make your searches flexible

You don't need to enter a precise date as part of a search term. Instead, Windows Search recognizes "fuzzy" date qualifiers like *today*, *yesterday*, *this week*, and *last month*. This technique lets you create saved searches you can use to quickly open a window showing only the files you've worked on this week or last week. A search that uses dates picked from the calendar wouldn't be nearly as useful next month for identifying current projects, but one built using these relative dates will continue to be useful indefinitely.

Using multiple criteria for complex searches

You can use the Boolean operators **AND**, **OR**, and **NOT** to combine or negate criteria in the search box. These operators need to be spelled in capital letters (or they will be treated as ordinary text). In place of the **AND** operator, you can use a plus sign (**+**), and in place of the **NOT** operator, you can use a minus sign (**–**). You can also use parentheses to group criteria; items in parentheses separated by a space use an implicit **AND** operator. Table 10-1 provides some examples of combined criteria.

Table 10-1   Some examples of complex search values

This search value	Returns
Siechert AND Bott	Items in which at least one indexed element (property, file name, or an entire word within its contents) begins with or equals *Siechert* and another element in the same item begins with or equals *Bott*
title:("report" NOT draft)	Items in which the Title property contains the word *report* and does not contain a word that begins with *draft*
tag:tax AND author:Doug	Items authored by Doug that include *Tax* in the Tags field
tag:tax AND author:(Doug OR Craig) AND modified:<1/1/18	Items authored by Doug or Craig, last modified before January 1, 2018, with *Tax* in the Tags field

> ### NOTE
>
> When you use multiple criteria based on different properties, an AND conjunction is assumed unless you specify otherwise. The search value **tag:Ed Author:Carl** is equivalent to the search value **tag:Ed AND Author:Carl**.

Using wildcards and character-mode searches

File-search wildcards can be traced back to the dawn of Microsoft operating systems, well before the Windows era. In Windows 10, two of these venerable operators are alive and well:

- The asterisk (*), also known as a star operator, can be placed anywhere in the search string and will match zero, one, or any other number of characters. In indexed searches, which treat your keyword as a prefix, this operator is always implied at the end; thus, a search for **voice** turns up *voice*, *voices*, and *voice-over*. Add an asterisk at the beginning of the search term (***voice**), and your search also turns up any item containing *invoice* or *invoices*. You can put an asterisk in the middle of a search term as well, which is useful for searching through folders full of data files that use a standard naming convention. If all your invoices start with **INV**, followed by an invoice number, followed by the date (**INV-0038-20180227**, for example), you can produce a quick list of all 2018 invoices by searching for **INV*2018***.

- The question mark (?) is a more focused wildcard. In index searches, it matches exactly one character in the exact position where it's placed. Using the naming scheme defined in the previous item, you can use the search term **filename:INV-????-2018*** to locate any file in the current location that has a 2018 date stamp and an invoice number (between hyphens) that is exactly four characters long.

To force Windows Search to use strict character matches in an indexed location, type a tilde (~) as the first character in the search box, followed immediately by your term. If you open your Documents library and type **~??v** in the search box, you'll find any document whose file name contains any word that has a *v* in the third position, such as *saved, level*, and, of course, *invoice*. This technique does not match on file contents.

Searching nonindexed locations

In both the previous examples, we described the behavior of searches in indexed locations, such as a library or a folder within a library. In other locations, the grep search engine kicks in. By default, anything you enter in one of these locations is treated as a character search that can match all or any part of a word. Thus, if you open a data folder that is not in a library and enter the search term **voice**, you get back *voices* and *voice-over* and *invoice*. The behavior of wildcards varies slightly as well. In a grep search, **??voice** matches *invoice* but not *voice*. In an indexed search, the wildcards at the beginning of the term are ignored in favor of loose matches. (Extra question marks at the end of a search term are ignored completely.)

When Windows does a grep search of the folder's contents, a green progress bar traversing your address bar warns you that the search is likely to be slow. While the search is still underway, you can click the Search tab and refine the search.

By default, when searching nonindexed locations, Windows looks at file names and basic properties (date modified and size) only. You can change this behavior so that Windows searches the contents of files that include a property handler and filter. To do this, click the Search tab, click Advanced Options, and then click File Contents, as shown in Figure 10-14.

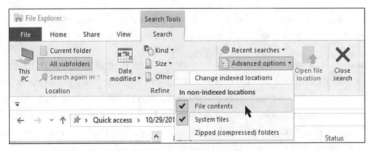

Figure 10-14   When searching in locations that aren't part of the index, Windows looks only at file names and properties. Select this box to include the contents of files in those locations.

Be aware that choosing this option can add significantly to your search times.

Inside OUT

Search shared remote folders

When you connect to a shared folder on a networked computer, the search engine can detect whether the Windows Search service is running and whether the location you've accessed is already part of the remote index. If it is, great! Your query gets handed off to the remote search engine, which runs it on the other machine and returns its results to your computer. Note that for an indexed search of a shared folder, that folder must be included in the list of indexed locations on the remote computer, and the remote computer must be running version 4.0 or later of Windows Search. All versions of Windows released since 2008 are supported.

Saving searches and clearing search history

After you have completed a search and displayed its results in File Explorer, you can save the search parameters for later reuse. Click Save Search on the Search tab. The saved search is stored, by default, in %UserProfile%\Searches. You can run the search again at any time, using the then-current contents of the index, by clicking that saved search in the navigation pane or Searches folder.

When you save a search, you're saving its specification (technically, a persistedQuery), not its current results. If you're interested in the XML data that defines the search, right-click the saved search in your Searches folder, choose Open With, and choose a text editor like Notepad or WordPad.

Recent searches are also included in a history list. To see what you have searched for, click in the search box in File Explorer and then, in the Options group on the Search tab, click Recent Searches. If the list of recent searches gets unwieldy or you want to eliminate older searches that are no longer relevant, click Clear Search History at the bottom of this list.

CHAPTER 10

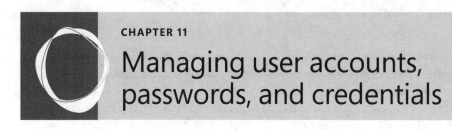

Managing user accounts, passwords, and credentials

Before you can begin working with a device running Microsoft Windows 10, you must sign in with the credentials for a user account that is authorized to use that device. User accounts are an essential cornerstone of Windows security and are key to providing a personalized user experience. As an administrator, you determine which user accounts are allowed to sign in to a specific device. In addition, you can configure user accounts on a Windows 10 device to accomplish the following goals:

- Control access to files and other resources.

- Audit system events, such as sign-ins and the use of files and other resources.

- Sync files and settings between different computers when signing in with the same account.

- Sign in automatically to email and other online services.

- Require each user to provide additional proof of their identity (also known as multi-factor authentication) when signing in for the first time on a new device.

The credentials associated with a user account consist of a user name and password that serve as identification and, in theory, ensure that no one can use the computer or view files, email messages, and other personal data associated with a user account unless they're authorized to do so.

If your computer is in a seemingly secure location where only people you trust have physical access to it, you might be tempted to allow family members or coworkers to share your user account. We strongly caution against using that configuration and instead recommend that you create a user account for each person who uses the computer. Doing so allows each account to access its own user profile and store personal files and user preferences within that profile. With fast user switching, a feature described in this chapter, you can switch between user accounts with only a few clicks.

With the right hardware and some initial setup, you can sign in and sign out without having to enter your full credentials. The Windows Hello feature allows you to sign in using biometric information, such as facial recognition or a fingerprint reader. A relatively new feature called Dynamic Lock allows you to configure Windows to lock the screen when you step away from your PC while carrying a Bluetooth-paired phone, as we explain later in this chapter.

Creating and managing user accounts

When you configure Windows 10 for the first time on a new computer (or on a PC with a clean installation of Windows), the setup program creates a profile for one user account, which is an administrator account. (An *administrator account* is one that has full control over the computer. For details, see "User accounts and security groups" at the end of this chapter.) Depending on what type of account you select during setup, that initial account can be a Microsoft account, an Azure Active Directory (Azure AD) account, or a local user account. A fourth user account type—an account on a local Active Directory domain—is available only on a managed network after this initial local account is created and you join the machine to the domain. (For information about the differences between these account types, see the next section, "Choosing an account type.")

If you upgrade to Windows 10 from Windows 7 or Windows 8.1 and you had local accounts set up in your previous operating system, Windows migrates those accounts to your Windows 10 installation. These migrated accounts maintain their group memberships and passwords.

After signing in for the first time, you can go to Settings > Accounts to create new user accounts and make routine changes to existing accounts. The Your Info page provides an overview of your account, similar to the one shown in Figure 11-1.

Inside OUT

Quickly change your user account picture

Using a feature that was introduced in the Windows 10 Anniversary Update, version 1607, the Your Info page keeps track of the three account pictures you've used most recently. Under the Create Your Picture heading, click Camera to snap a selfie using a webcam or other connected camera, or click Browse For One to select a picture you saved previously. After you select a picture, the one you were using previously moves to one of the two smaller circles on the right. Click any of the three saved pictures to make it the primary one that appears on the sign-in page and as a thumbnail on the left side of Start.

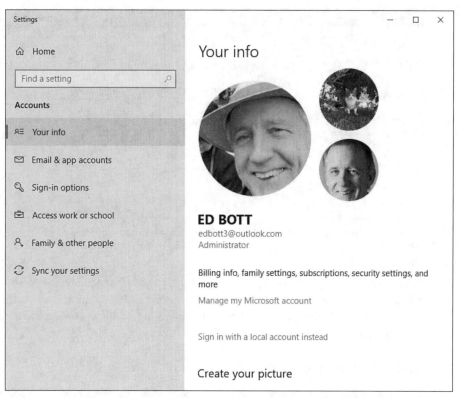

Figure 11-1 The Your Info page offers an overview of your user account along with tools administrators can use to manage all accounts associated with the current device.

You'll find different options and settings in Accounts depending on the type of account you use
(Microsoft account, Azure AD account, or local account), whether your account is a member
of the Administrators group, and—if your computer is joined to a domain—group policies in
effect. On a computer joined to an Active Directory domain, all management of user accounts
beyond basic tasks such as selecting a picture is normally handled at the domain level.

You'll find some account-related settings under the User Accounts heading in the old-school
Control Panel, which is shown in Figure 11-2. Several of these settings duplicate functions that
are available in Settings > Accounts.

CHAPTER 11

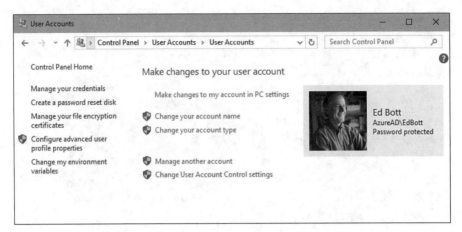

Figure 11-2   Visiting this old-school Control Panel page is rarely necessary, as most options for creating and managing accounts are available in the modern Settings app.

You can add a new account only from the Accounts page in Settings. You can remove an account or change its type from that location or its Control Panel counterpart. All the esoteric options along the left side of the User Accounts page, as well as the Change User Account Control Settings option, are available only in Control Panel.

Choosing an account type

As we mentioned earlier, Windows 10 supports four different account types.

Microsoft account

When you set up a new account on a device running Windows 10, the default options strongly encourage you to sign in using a Microsoft account. You've probably used Microsoft accounts for years, perhaps without even knowing it. If you've signed up for a Microsoft service, including Outlook.com (or its predecessor, Hotmail), Office 365 Home or Personal, Skype, or Xbox Live, you already have a Microsoft account. Every email address that ends with msn.com, hotmail.com, live.com, or outlook.com is, by definition, a Microsoft account.

During setup, you can enter the email address associated with an existing Microsoft account, or you can create a new email address in the outlook.com domain. However, you do not need a Microsoft address to create a Microsoft account; you can set up a Microsoft account using an existing personal email address from any email provider, including Gmail and other non-Microsoft services.

Inside OUT

Avoid using a business email address as a Microsoft account

As we noted earlier in this section, you can use any personal email address as a Microsoft account. That includes free Gmail and Yahoo Mail accounts as well as accounts supplied by an internet service provider.

If you have an email address on a custom domain as part of a work or school account, however, Microsoft will no longer allow you to use that address as a Microsoft account. The new account creation process detects commercial accounts with custom domains that are hosted on Office 365 Exchange Online or Gmail servers and rejects attempts to use them for a Microsoft account.

That is, frankly, a welcome change. Previously, if you used a work email address for a Microsoft account, you were inconvenienced every time you tried to sign in to either service because Windows 10 would ask whether you meant to use your Microsoft account or your work or school account. If you're saddled with this unfortunate configuration, you can set things right by assigning a new email alias to your Microsoft account, making it the primary address, and then deleting the unwanted work address. We provide detailed instructions for accomplishing this task later in this section.

Signing in with a Microsoft account allows you to synchronize PC settings between multiple computers. If you use more than one PC—say, a desktop PC at work, a different desktop at home, a laptop for travel, and a tablet around the house—signing in with a Microsoft account lets you effortlessly use the same desktop background, stored passwords, browser favorites and history, account picture, accessibility configuration, and so on. The synchronization happens automatically and nearly instantly.

➤ For more details on how to configure synchronization options, see "Syncing your settings between computers," in Chapter 4, "Personalizing Windows 10."

Some features in Windows 10, including Cortana and OneDrive, require the use of a Microsoft account or an Azure AD account. It's possible to use OneDrive and other universal apps that depend on a Microsoft account even if you sign in to Windows with a local account. However, in this configuration you must sign in to each app individually, and some features might be unavailable or less convenient to use.

Under normal circumstances, you'll associate a single personal email address with your Microsoft account and use that address to sign in to Windows. But because every Microsoft account supports up to 10 email aliases, you can use any alias associated with your primary address to sign in using your Microsoft account.

To manage Microsoft account aliases, go to *https://account.live.com/names/Manage* and sign in with your Microsoft account. Under the Account Alias heading, click Add Email to create a new alias or use an existing personal email address as an alias. After verifying the added email address, you can make it the primary address and, if you wish, remove the old address. (Every alias uses the same password as the original account.)

Under the Sign-In Preferences heading, you can also change the settings for email aliases so that a specific alias can't be used to sign in to your Microsoft account. That precaution allows you to use aliases to send and receive email but prevents them from being used to access your Microsoft account.

Local account

A *local account* is one that stores its sign-in credentials and other account data on your PC. A local account works only on a single computer. It doesn't require an email address as the user name, nor does it communicate with an external server to verify credentials.

This type of account was the standard in Windows for decades. In Windows 10, Microsoft recommends the use of a Microsoft account rather than a local user account for PCs that aren't part of a managed business network. But using a Microsoft account is not a requirement; local accounts are still fully supported.

You might prefer a local account if your home or small business network includes computers running Windows 7 or earlier (that is, versions that do not explicitly support the use of Microsoft accounts). For details, see "Sharing files, printers, and other resources over a local network" in Chapter 13, "Windows networking."

In addition, some folks have privacy and data security concerns about storing personal information on the servers of a large corporation, whether that infrastructure is managed by Microsoft, Google, Apple, Amazon, or another cloud provider. Signing in with a local account minimizes the amount of information your PC exchanges with Microsoft's servers.

Inside OUT

How should you handle the password reset questions for a local account?

When you set up a new local account using Windows 10 version 1803 or later, you're required to choose three security questions (from a list of six) and provide answers to those questions. The intent of this feature is to help you reset your password if you forget it. (You can choose different questions and change your answers any time by going to Settings > Accounts > Sign-In Options and clicking the Update Your Security Questions link.)

The questions on offer aren't particularly robust. Some of these details, like your first pet's name or the name of the first school you attended, might be easy pickings for an attacker who knows you. A thief who steals your laptop probably won't have easy access to that information, but someone in your immediate circle might.

On a home PC in a secure location, this option might be useful, especially if you're setting up a PC for a forgetful relative. But if you find the idea of answering those questions to be too risky, here's an alternative approach: *Don't tell the truth.* Windows doesn't make even the slightest effort to check whether your answers are true or even sensible. Instead of answering the questions you're asked, think of a three-word challenge phrase and use those words in place of the actual answers. If you'd prefer to render the question-based password reset feature completely unusable, by yourself or a would-be attacker, just mash the keys randomly and enter a long stream of gibberish as the "answer" to each question.

As an alternative, consider creating a password reset disk, which you can lock away in a secure location separate from your PC. You need removable media, such as a USB flash drive, external hard drive, or memory card. After signing in to your account, open Control Panel > User Accounts and click Create A Password Reset Disk. Follow the Forgotten Password Wizard's instructions. You can have only one password reset disk for each local user account. If you make a new one, the old one is no longer usable. We explain how to reset your password using this disk later in this chapter.

CHAPTER 11

You can switch between using a Microsoft account and a local account by going to Settings > Accounts > Your Info. On this page (shown earlier in Figure 11-1), click Sign In With A Local Account Instead. Windows leads you through a few simple steps to create a local account, which you'll then use for signing in.

If you're currently signed in using a local account, the link on that page reads Sign In With A Microsoft Account Instead. Click that link to replace your local account with a Microsoft account. As part of making the switch, you need to enter your local password one more time. A few screens later, you're connected to an existing Microsoft account or a new one you create. From that time forward, you sign in using your Microsoft account.

Azure Active Directory account

The third type of account, available during the initial setup of Windows 10 Pro, Enterprise, or Education, is a work or school account using Azure Active Directory. Azure AD offers some of the advantages of a Microsoft account, including support for two-factor authentication and single sign-on to online services, balanced by the capability of network administrators to impose restrictions using management software. These accounts are most common in medium-size and large businesses and schools.

Organizations that subscribe to Microsoft's business-focused online services—including Business or Enterprise editions of Office 365, Microsoft Intune, and Microsoft Dynamics CRM Online—automatically have Azure AD services as part of their subscription. Every user account in that service automatically has a corresponding Azure AD directory entry.

You can connect an Azure AD account to a new Windows 10 installation during the initial setup of Windows 10, as we explain in "Performing a clean install," in Chapter 2, "Installing, configuring, and deploying Windows 10." You can also associate a Windows 10 device with Azure AD after it has been set up using a local account or a Microsoft account. To accomplish this task, go to Settings > Accounts > Access Work Or School, and then click Connect. The resulting dialog box, shown here, gives you two options:

The default option allows you to continue using your Microsoft account or your local account to sign in to Windows and simply connects your Azure AD account for easier access to Office 365 services, including email and OneDrive for Business. If that's your goal, click Next and follow the prompts.

If you want to reconfigure the PC so that you sign in to Windows using your Azure AD account, don't enter an email address in the Set Up A Work Or School Account dialog box; instead, click the Join This Device To Azure Active Directory link at the bottom of that dialog box. That option opens the dialog box shown in Figure 11-3. After you sign in using your Azure AD credentials, you have one final chance to confirm that you want to sign in with your organization's credentials and allow administrators to apply policies to your device.

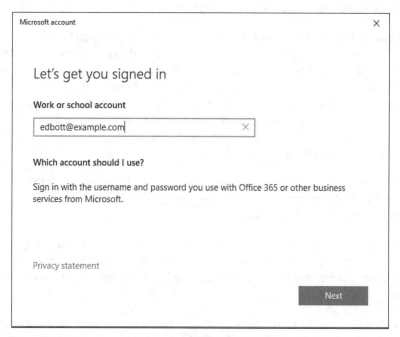

Figure 11-3   Enter credentials from an Azure Active Directory account, such as an Office 365 Enterprise subscription, to join the device to that directory.

After connecting a Windows 10 PC to Azure AD, you can view and edit your user profile by going to Settings > Accounts > Your Info and clicking Manage My Account. You can use the options on the Profile page to request a password reset and manage multi-factor authentication settings. The Applications tab includes any apps that have been set up by your administrator for single sign-on.

Active Directory domain account

In organizations with Windows domains running Active Directory services, administrators can join a PC to the domain, creating a domain machine account. (This option is available only with Windows 10 Pro, Enterprise, or Education editions.) After this step is complete, any user with a domain user account can sign in to the PC and access local and domain-based resources. We cover this account type more fully in Chapter 17, "Managing business PCs."

Changing account settings

With options in Settings and Control Panel, you can make changes to your own account or to another user's account.

To change your own account, go to Settings > Accounts > Your Info, shown earlier in Figure 11-1. Even quicker: Open Start, click or tap your account picture at the top of the column of icons on the left, and then choose Change Account Settings.

Here, you can change your account picture, either by browsing for a picture file or by using your webcam to take a picture. If you sign in with a Microsoft account, the Manage My Microsoft Account link opens your default web browser and loads your account page at *https://account.microsoft.com*. On that page, you can change your password or edit the name associated with your Microsoft account. Click other links along the top of the page to review your subscriptions and Store purchases, change your payment options, and get information about other devices associated with your Microsoft account. You can also set security and privacy options, which we discuss in more detail later in this chapter.

If you have added one or more users to your computer, you (as a computer administrator) can make changes to the account of each of those users. (For information about adding users, see "Adding a user to your computer" later in this chapter.)

To change a user's account type, go to Settings > Accounts > Family & Other People. Click the name of the account you want to change, and click Change Account Type. (Your choices are Standard User or Administrator. For details, see "User accounts and security groups" later in this chapter.)

If the person signs in with a Microsoft account, there are no other changes you can make. (You can't make changes to someone else's Microsoft account at *https://account.microsoft.com*.) For users who sign in with a local user account, you can make a few additional changes, but you must start from User Accounts in Control Panel (shown earlier in Figure 11-2). Click Manage Another Account, and then click the name of the account you want to change. You can make the following changes:

- **Account Name.** The name you're changing here is the full name, which is the one that appears on the sign-in screen, on the Start menu, and in User Accounts.

- **Password.** You can create a password and store a hint that provides a reminder for a forgotten password. If the account is already password protected, you can use User Accounts to change the password or remove the password. For more information about passwords, see "Setting or changing a password" later in this chapter.

- **Account Type.** Your choices here are the same as in Settings > Accounts: Administrator (which adds the account to the Administrators group) or Standard User (which adds the account to the Users group).

If you sign in with a local user account, you can make the following additional changes to your own account (that is, the one with which you're currently signed in) by clicking links in the left pane:

- **Manage Your Credentials.** This link opens Credential Manager, where you can manage stored credentials that you use to access network resources and websites.

- **Create A Password Reset Disk.** This link, available only when you are signed in with a local account, launches the Forgotten Password Wizard, from which you can create a password reset tool on removable media. As an alternative, recent updates to Windows 10 allow you to recover from a lost password using answers to reset questions.

- **Manage Your File Encryption Certificates.** This link opens a wizard you can use to create and manage certificates that enable the use of Encrypting File System (EFS). EFS, which is available only in Pro and Enterprise editions of Windows 10, is a method of encrypting folders and files so that they can be used only by someone who has the appropriate credentials. For more information, see "Encrypting information" in Chapter 18, "Windows security and privacy."

- **Configure Advanced User Profile Properties.** This link is used to switch your profile between a local profile (one that is stored on the local computer) and a roaming profile (one that is stored on a network server in a domain environment). With a local profile, you end up with a different profile on each computer you use, whereas a roaming profile is the same regardless of which computer you use to sign in to the network. Roaming profiles require a domain network running Windows Server Active Directory services.

- **Change My Environment Variables.** Of interest primarily to programmers, this link opens a dialog box in which you can create and edit environment variables that are available only to your user account; in addition, you can view system environment variables, which are available to all accounts.

Deleting an account

As a local administrator, you can delete any local account or Microsoft account set up on a Windows 10 PC, unless that account is currently signed in. To delete an account, go to Settings > Accounts > Family & Other People (the Family option is unavailable, and this category is called simply Other People, if you're signed in using an Azure AD account), and click the name of the account you want to delete. Then click Remove. Windows then warns about the consequences of deleting an account, as shown in Figure 11-4.

CHAPTER 11

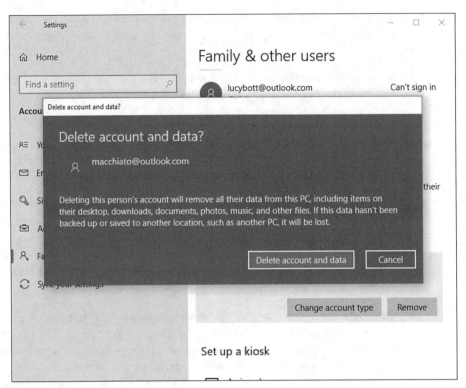

Figure 11-4   Before you click Delete Account And Data, be sure you have saved any local data you don't want to lose.

NOTE

Windows won't let you delete the last local account on the computer, even if you signed in using the built-in account named Administrator. This limitation helps to enforce the sound security practice of using an account other than Administrator for your everyday computing.

After you delete an account, of course, that user can no longer sign in. Deleting an account also has another effect you should be aware of: You cannot restore access to resources that are currently shared with the user simply by re-creating the account. This includes files shared with the user and the user's encrypted files, personal certificates, and stored passwords for websites and network resources. That's because those permissions are linked to the user's original security identifier (SID)—not the user name. Even if you create a new account with the same name, password, and so on, it will have a new SID, which will not gain access to anything that was restricted to the original user account. (For more information about security identifiers, see "Introducing access control in Windows" later in this chapter.)

Inside OUT

Delete an account without deleting its data

Earlier versions of Windows included an option for preserving an account's data files—documents, photos, music, downloads, and so on stored in the user's profile—when you delete the user account. Windows 10 offers that option too, but you won't find it in Settings. Instead, open User Accounts in Control Panel. Click Manage Another Account, select the account you want to remove, and then click Delete The Account.

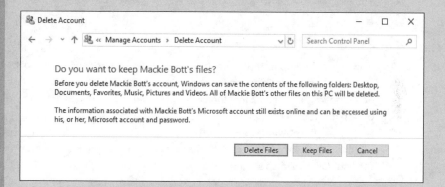

This option gives you a choice about what to do with the account's files:

- **Delete Files.** After you select Delete Files and confirm your intention in the next window, Windows deletes the account, its user profile, and all files in that account's user profile.

- **Keep Files.** Windows copies certain parts of the user's profile—specifically, files and folders stored on the desktop and in the Documents, Favorites, Music, Pictures, and Videos folders—to a folder on your desktop, where they become part of your profile and remain under your control. All other folders in the user profile are deleted after you confirm your intention in the next window that appears; email messages and other data stored in the AppData folder are also deleted, as are settings stored in the registry.

Managing the sign-in process

Users of Windows (as well as most other operating systems) are familiar with the time-honored sign-in method: At the sign-in screen, select your name (if it's not already selected) and then enter a password. This continues to be a valid technique in Windows 10.

CHAPTER 11

NOTE

When you first turn on your computer or return to it after signing out, the *lock screen* is displayed. The lock screen normally shows a snazzy picture, the current time and date, and alerts from selected apps. (You can select your own lock screen picture and specify what information you want displayed on the lock screen. For details, see "Customizing the lock screen and sign-in screen" in Chapter 4.) To get from the lock screen to the sign-in screen, click anywhere, press any key, or (if you have a touchscreen) swipe up.

Inside OUT

Press Ctrl+Alt+Delete without a keyboard

Some network administrators enable a policy that requires you to press Ctrl+Alt+Delete to switch from the lock screen to the sign-in screen. That's tough to do on a tablet with no keyboard—until you know the trick: On an older device with a dedicated Windows button (usually on the bezel along the right or bottom edge of the screen), press that button and the power button simultaneously. If you're using a tablet that has no dedicated Windows button, such as the Surface Pro 4 or Surface Book, press the power button and Volume Down simultaneously.

Windows 10 has other sign-in options that add security as well as convenience:

● You can enter a numeric PIN.

● You can trace a pattern of gestures on a picture.

● With appropriate hardware, you can use Windows Hello—a biometric sign-in method that authenticates you by reading your fingerprint, your face, or your iris.

These three methods each provide a form of *two-factor authentication*, a means of identifying yourself with multiple proofs. In the case of Windows sign-ins, the components include two of the following: something you know (such as a PIN or the gesture pattern), something you have (the device itself, which is registered with Microsoft's servers), and something that's inseparable from you (your fingerprint, face, or iris).

The device you sign in on acts as an authentication component because your information (the PIN or your biometric data) is stored, in encrypted form, on the device—not on a remote server. So, for example, if someone learns your PIN, that person can use it only on that device; he can't use it to sign in to your account on any other device. If someone steals your computer, that person can't sign in unless she knows your PIN.

In the following sections, we explain how to set up each of these sign-in methods: password, PIN, picture password, and biometric. You configure each of these variations on the Sign-In Options page in Settings, Accounts, as shown in Figure 11-5.

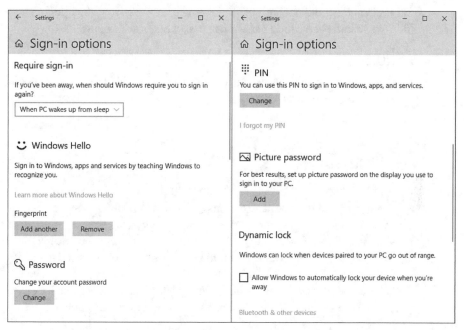

Figure 11-5   Choices on the Sign-In Options page in Settings depend on your computer's hardware. For example, Windows Hello options are available only if you have a compatible fingerprint reader or camera.

If you set up more than one option for signing in, you can choose a method other than the default by clicking Sign-In Options on the sign-in screen. This ability might come in handy, for example, if Windows Hello fails to recognize your face or fingerprint. Icons for each of the options you set up then appear as shown next; click or tap one to switch methods.

Note that these alternative sign-in options also work for some applications, including the Store.

Setting or changing a password

When you set up a Microsoft account, you're required to create a password. Similarly, if you add a local user account to your computer, Windows 10 requires you to specify a password. Earlier versions of Windows did not have this requirement, however, so if you upgrade from an earlier version, you might need to add passwords for existing local accounts.

NOTE

If you sign in with a local account, you must add a password before you can use a PIN, picture password, or Windows Hello.

Inside OUT

For extra security, turn on two-factor authentication

The single greatest advantage of signing in with a Microsoft account or an Azure AD account, as far as we're concerned, is support for two-factor authentication, which provides security for your PC and its data. This feature requires that you prove your identity when signing in on a new device for the first time by supplying a code from a previously verified device, such as your smartphone. If an attacker manages to steal your Microsoft account password, he won't be able to do any damage because he doesn't have access to your device and thus can't provide the additional verification required.

To turn on this feature, go to *https://account.live.com/proofs* and sign in using your Microsoft account. There, you can add approved contact info for receiving security requests and turn on two-step verification. For devices that are connected to an organization using Azure AD, an administrator must enable multi-factor authentication.

To make identity verification even simpler, we highly recommend installing the Microsoft Authenticator app, which is available on Android and iOS smartphones. This app handles authentication for Azure AD and Microsoft accounts; it also supports most third-party accounts, including those provided by Google, Facebook, and Amazon. The Authenticator app supports fingerprint-based approvals on compatible hardware and works with several types of smart watches.

To set or change your own Microsoft account password, go to Settings > Accounts > Sign-In Options. Click or tap Change under Password. If Windows Hello is set up, you first need to enter your PIN or supply biometric authentication. Next, you must enter your existing password to confirm your identity. Windows then asks you to enter your new password twice.

Changing the password for a local account requires an extra step: You must specify a password hint. The password hint appears after you click your name on the sign-in screen and type your password incorrectly. Be sure your hint is only a subtle reminder because any user can click your name and then view the hint. (Windows will not allow you to create a password hint that contains your password.)

NOTE

If you sign in with a local account, you can use a quicker alternative: Press Ctrl+Alt+Delete, and click Change A Password. This method does not include the option to enter a password hint.

You can also set or change the password for the local account of another user on your computer. To do so, open User Accounts in Control Panel, click Manage Another Account, and click the name of the user whose password you want to change. Then click Change The Password or (if the account doesn't currently have a password) Create A Password.

CAUTION

If another user has files encrypted with EFS, do not create or change a password for that user; instead, show the user how to accomplish the task from his or her own account. Similarly, do not remove or change another user's password unless the user has forgotten the password and has absolutely no other way to access the account. (For more information, see the sidebar "Recovering from a lost password.") If you create, change, or remove another user's password, that user loses all personal certificates and stored passwords for websites and network resources. Without the personal certificates, the user loses access to all encrypted files and all email messages encrypted with the user's private key. Windows deletes the certificates and passwords to prevent the administrator who makes a password change from gaining access to them—but this security comes at a cost!

CHAPTER 11

RECOVERING FROM A LOST PASSWORD

It's bound to happen: Someday when you try to sign in to your computer and are faced with the password prompt, you will draw a blank.

For a Microsoft account or an Azure Active Directory account, clicking a link on the sign-in screen (either I Forgot My Password or I Forgot My PIN) connects to Microsoft's servers and leads you through the steps to verify your identity and reset your password or PIN. During this process, an alternative method is offered: use Microsoft Authenticator—an app you install on your mobile device—to verify your identity and sign in.

Another alternative for a Microsoft account is to use another computer or a mobile device to go to *https://account.live.com/password/reset*. Answer a series of questions there, and you'll be able to send a code to one of the alternative verification methods on your account—a text message to your mobile device or an email message to an account you control. Enter the code to prove your identity, and you can reset your password.

For a local account, if the password hint doesn't jog your memory, you have two supported options. The first asks you to correctly answer the three password reset questions you chose when you set up the local account initially. The second option is to use a password reset disk, which you presumably created before you needed it and then stashed in a safe place.

When password amnesia sets in, take your best guess at a password. If you're wrong, Windows informs you that the password is incorrect and offers both a hint and a Reset Password link. For Windows 10 version 1803 or later, that option offers blanks to fill in answers to the three password reset questions; if you have a password reset disk, scroll down and click Use A Password Reset Disk Instead. That opens the Password Reset Wizard, which in turn asks for the location of the password reset disk, reads the encrypted key, and then asks you to set a new password. After you sign in using the new credentials, your password reset disk remains usable in case you forget the new password; you don't need to make a new one.

If you can't remember the password and neither of the above options works, you're out of luck. A local administrator can sign in and change or remove your password for you, but you'll lose access to your encrypted files and email messages and your stored credentials. If that prospect gives you chills, perhaps you should consider switching to a Microsoft account.

Using a PIN

To set up a PIN for signing in to your computer, go to the Sign-In Options page and click Add under the PIN heading. After entering your password to confirm your identity, you enter numbers in a dialog box like the one shown in Figure 11-6. The minimum length is four digits (0–9 only), but your PIN can be as long as you want. If you prefer something more complex and harder to guess, select the Include Letters And Symbols option.

Figure 11-6   A PIN serves as a convenient alternative for signing in to Windows and verifying your identity in apps and services. You can choose a PIN that's longer than the minimum of four characters.

To sign in using a PIN, type the numbers on your keyboard. Beginning with version 1703, key-presses in the numeric keypad area of the keyboard register as numbers while you type in the PIN box on the sign-in screen, regardless of whether Num Lock is set; in earlier versions, those keys acted as arrow keys if Num Lock was off. If your computer doesn't have a keyboard, a numeric pad appears on the screen so that you can tap your PIN. (If the numeric pad does not appear, tap in the PIN-entry box.)

Inside OUT

Make your PIN even stronger

You might be worried that a four-digit numeric PIN is too easy to guess. You'll probably rest a little easier knowing that Windows 10 offers only five incorrect tries before lock-ing you out. After four incorrect attempts, you're required to enter a challenge phrase (which incidentally confirms that your keyboard is working correctly). After the fifth incorrect attempt, a would-be intruder is locked out. At that point, Windows requires you to either enter the password or restart the device and try signing in again. After a handful of failed tries, Windows stops accepting new guesses and requires you to enter your password.

And imagine intruders' surprise when they learn that a PIN can be more than four digits long. When you set up your PIN, make it six digits instead of four, allowing up to 1 mil-lion possible numeric combinations and trying the patience of even the most persistent attacker. Even an eight-digit PIN (100 million numeric combinations) is still easier to enter than a complex password.

If you sign in to an Active Directory domain or Azure AD, a network administrator can use Group Policy on Windows 10 Pro or Enterprise to mandate a minimum PIN length and to force the use of letters and numbers, making the PIN practically unguessable. These settings are in the Group Policy Editor under Computer Configuration > Adminis-trative Templates > Windows Components > Windows Hello For Business.

Using a picture password

With a picture password, you can sign in on a touchscreen using a combination of gestures (specifically, circles, straight lines, and taps) that you make on a picture displayed on the sign-in screen. The easiest way to get comfortable with a picture password is to go ahead and create one.

To get started, go to Settings > Accounts > Sign-In Options. Under Picture Password, click Add. Verify your identity by entering your password to display an introductory screen where you can choose a picture. You then get to select one of your own pictures to appear on the sign-in screen. When you're satisfied with your selection, click Use This Picture.

On the next screen that appears, you specify the three gestures you'll use to sign in. These gestures can consist of circles, straight lines, and taps. After repeating the series of gestures to confirm your new "password," click Finish.

To sign in with a picture password, on the sign-in screen you must perform the same three gestures, in the same order, using the same locations, and in the same direction. You don't need to be *that* precise; Windows allows minor variations in location.

Using Windows Hello for biometric sign-ins

With the proper hardware, you can sign in simply by swiping your fingerprint or, even easier, showing your face in front of your computer's camera. (Some Windows 10 Mobile devices also support iris recognition.) You might also be asked to verify your identity when making a purchase or accessing a secure service. When Windows Hello recognizes a fingerprint or face, it greets you by briefly displaying your name and a smiley face on the sign-in screen before going to your desktop.

To use Windows Hello for biometric sign-ins on a PC, you need one of the following:

- A fingerprint reader that supports the Windows Biometric Framework; if this hardware isn't built in, you can add a USB-based fingerprint reader.

- An illuminated 3-D infrared camera such as those found on the Surface Pro, Surface Book, and other advanced devices; note that a standard webcam will not work.

NOTE
You must add a PIN as described earlier in this chapter before you can use Windows Hello.

To set up Windows Hello, go to Settings > Accounts > Sign-In Options. Under Windows Hello, click Set Up for the biometric device you want to use. Windows asks you to enter your PIN to verify your identity. After that, you need to enter your biometric data. With face recognition, that involves staring into the camera; to set up a fingerprint reader, follow the prompts (as shown in Figure 11-7) to swipe your fingerprint several times, until Windows Hello has recorded the data it needs.

If you're setting up fingerprint scanning, you can enroll additional fingers (so that you don't have to be particular about using the same finger all the time) by clicking Add Another after you complete registration for a fingerprint. (To add another fingerprint later, return to Settings > Accounts > Sign-In Options and click Add Another.) You can also associate an additional fingerprint with a different user account on the same device. Sign in to the alternate account, and set up the second fingerprint there. When you restart, you can choose your account by choosing the fingerprint associated with that account.

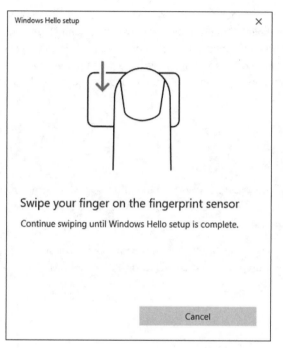

Figure 11-7   Setup for Windows Hello guides you through the brief process of scanning and storing your biometric data.

Signing out, switching accounts, or locking your computer

When you're finished using your computer, you want to be sure you don't leave it in a state in which others can use your credentials to access your files or read and reply to email messages. For security's sake, you need to sign out, switch accounts, or lock your computer:

- **Sign Out.** With this option, all your programs close, and the lock screen appears.

- **Switch Account.** With this option, also known as fast user switching, your programs continue to run. The sign-in screen appears, ready for the sign-in credentials of the person you select. Your account is still signed in, but only you can return to your own session, which you can do when the user who is currently signed in chooses to sign out, switch accounts, or lock the computer.

- **Lock.** With this option, your programs continue to run, but the lock screen appears so that no one can see your desktop or use the computer. Only you can unlock the computer to return to your session; however, other users can sign in to their own sessions without disturbing yours.

To sign out, switch accounts, or lock your computer, open Start and click or tap your picture above the column of icons on the left. That displays a menu with Lock and Sign Out options; on a device with more than one user account set up, it also includes a profile picture and username for other available accounts. On a computer that's joined to a domain, Switch Account appears instead of individual account names. You can then enter an account name on the sign-in screen.

Inside OUT

Use keyboard shortcuts

To lock your computer, press Windows key+L. (You might also find it more convenient to use this shortcut for switching accounts; the only difference is that it takes you to the lock screen instead of to the sign-in screen.)

For any of these actions—sign out, switch accounts, or lock—you can start by pressing Ctrl+Alt+Delete, which displays a menu that includes all three options.

Using Dynamic Lock

Windows 10 version 1703 introduces a new way to lock a computer, called Dynamic Lock. With Dynamic Lock, your computer automatically locks when it becomes separated from your phone, such as when you step away from your desk with your phone in your pocket or purse. To use Dynamic Lock, follow these steps:

1. If you haven't already done so, pair your Bluetooth-enabled phone to your computer. For more information, see "Setting up Bluetooth devices" in Chapter 14, "Hardware and devices."

2. Open Settings > Accounts > Sign-In Options.

3. Select the Dynamic Lock check box.

After following these steps, Windows polls your phone several times each minute. (This does place a small hit on your phone's battery life.) When it discovers that the phone is no longer in range, the computer locks. Be aware, however, that locking doesn't occur instantly; Windows polls your phone only periodically, and it takes some time for you to get far enough away so that your phone is out of range.

How far is "out of range"? That sensitivity depends on several factors, including the signal strength of your two devices and the number of walls and other obstructions between the devices. A registry value sets the threshold, but calibrating it takes some experimentation. Rafael Rivera has created a tool for working with Dynamic Lock threshold values; you can read about it at *https://bit.ly/DynLock*.

Unfortunately, there is no corresponding dynamic unlock feature. When you return to your computer, even with phone in hand, you'll need to sign in using one of the usual methods: Windows Hello, password, PIN, or picture password.

Sharing your PC with other users

Personal computers are usually just that—personal. But there are situations in which it makes sense for a single PC to be shared by multiple users. In those circumstances, it's prudent to configure the shared device securely. Doing so helps to protect each user's data from inadvertent deletions and changes as well as malicious damage and theft.

NOTE

In this section, we offer advice for configuring a PC with Microsoft accounts and local accounts. Azure AD and domain accounts are administered centrally.

When you set up your computer, consider these suggestions:

- **Control who can sign in.** Create accounts only for users who need to use your computer's resources, either by signing in locally or over a network. If an account you created is no longer needed, delete or disable it.

- **Use standard accounts for additional users.** During setup, Windows sets up one local administrative account for installing programs, creating and managing accounts, and so on. All other accounts can and should run with standard privileges.

- **Be sure that all accounts are protected by a strong password.** This is especially important for administrator accounts and for other accounts whose profiles contain important or sensitive documents. Windows 10 requires a password on all local accounts. If you have local accounts that were migrated from Windows 7, make sure they're all password-protected.

- **Restrict sign-in times.** You might want to limit the computing hours for some users, especially children. The easiest way for home users to do this is by setting up family accounts; for details, see "Controlling your family's computer access," later in this chapter.

- **Restrict access to certain files.** You'll want to be sure that some files are available to all users, whereas other files are available only to the person who created them. The Public folder and a user's personal folders provide a general framework for this protection. You can further refine your file-protection scheme by selectively applying permissions to varying combinations of files, folders, and users.

Adding a user to your computer

To allow another user to sign in on your computer, you as administrator must add that user's account. Go to Settings > Accounts > Family & Other Users, shown in Figure 11-8. (In Windows 10 version 1803 and earlier, this setting is called Family & Other People.) There, you'll find controls for adding and managing two separate sets of accounts. Those you add as family members are subject to restrictions that an adult member of the family can manage using a web-based interface. (For details, see the next section, "Controlling your family's computer access.") Accounts you create under the Other Users heading have all the rights and privileges associated with their account type: administrator or standard.

NOTE

The Family & Other Users page is available only when you sign in with an administrator account. On a PC that's joined to a Windows domain or connected to Azure AD, the family options are not available, and this tab appears as Other Users.

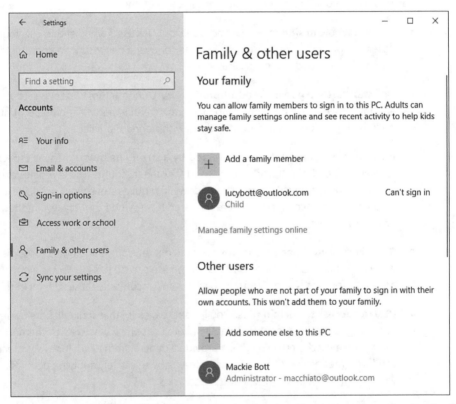

Figure 11-8   Under Other Users, you can add a local account or a Microsoft account. Family members must have a Microsoft account.

To add a user who's not a family member, under Other Users click Add Someone Else To This PC. Windows then asks for the email address of the new user. If the email address is already associated with a Microsoft account, all you need to do is click Next, and the new user is ready to go. (The first time the new user signs in, the computer must be connected to the internet.) If the email address you provide is not associated with a Microsoft account, Windows provides a link to sign up for a new Microsoft account.

What if you want to add a local account? At the first screen—when Windows asks for an email address—instead click the link near the bottom: I Don't Have This Person's Sign-In Information. In the next dialog box, shown in Figure 11-9, ignore the offer to set up a new Microsoft account and instead click Add A User Without A Microsoft Account.

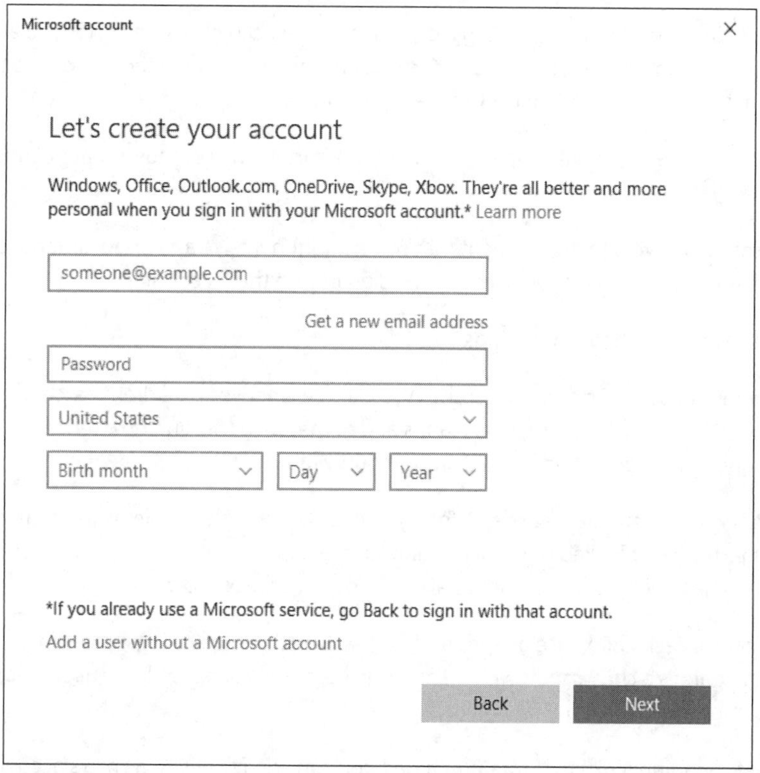

Figure 11-9   Microsoft really, really wants you to set up a Microsoft account. To refuse the offer and set up a local account instead, click the Add A User Without A Microsoft Account option at the bottom of this dialog box.

That option opens a different dialog box where you can specify a user name and password for the new user. You're also required to choose and answer three security questions for the local account. (If your computer has only local accounts set up, you go directly to this final dialog box, skipping the two that guide you toward a Microsoft account.) Click Next, and your work is done.

Controlling your family's computer access

Previous versions of Windows had a feature called Parental Controls (Windows Vista and Windows 7) or Family Safety (Windows 8), which allowed parents to restrict and monitor their children's computer use. Windows 10 offers similar capabilities, but the implementation is completely different. Those earlier versions stored their settings on your PC, but in Windows 10 family settings are now stored and managed as part of your Microsoft account.

This architectural change has some obvious benefits:

- You don't need to make settings for each child on each computer. After you add a family member on one PC, you manage the settings for each child in the cloud, and those settings apply to all the family PCs where they sign in.

- You can manage your children's computer use from any computer that's connected to the internet.

Family settings have one requirement that some might perceive as a disadvantage: Each family member must have a Microsoft account and sign in with that account.

What can you do with family settings?

- Monitor each child's computer use. You can see what your children search for on the web and which sites they visit, which apps and games they use, and how much time they're signed in to each Windows 10 computer they use.

- Block inappropriate websites. When you enable this feature, Microsoft-curated lists of sites that are blocked or explicitly allowed are used by default, but you can supplement these lists with sites you want to always block or always allow.

- Control each child's use of apps and games. Based on age ratings, you can limit the apps and games a child can download and purchase. You can also block specific apps and games from running.

- Set spending limits for Store purchases. You can add money to a child's account and remove other purchase options.

- Restrict when your children can use the computer, and for how long.

You can add a family member using the online management interface or from within Windows 10; go to Settings > Accounts > Family & Other Users, and click Add A Family Member. Windows asks whether you want to add an account for an adult or a child; the difference is that an adult can manage family settings, whereas a child's activity is governed by family settings.

You then enter the family member's email address; if a Microsoft account is not associated with that address, Windows gathers the needed information to set one up. Because all family settings are managed online using Microsoft accounts, there is no option to use a local account.

NOTE

If you don't see the Family & Other Users page, confirm that you're signed in with a Microsoft account and that your account type is administrator.

All other management tasks occur online. Click the Manage Family Settings Online link under the Your Family heading or visit *https://account.microsoft.com/family* to get started. Figure 11-10 shows a portion of the interface for setting up both daily limits and the times during which a child can use a Windows 10 PC and an Xbox One console.

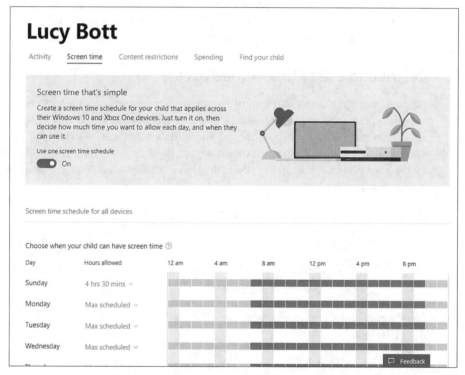

Figure 11-10 With Screen Time settings, you specify an allowable range of times for a child's daily use of a PC and Xbox One console, plus an optional overall daily limit.

After you select a Microsoft account for the new family member, Microsoft Family sends an email invitation to that person. (If you use the web-based interface to add a child's account, you can sign in on the child's behalf using their credentials.) A new family member can sign in to your computer right away, but family settings take effect only after that family member opens the email message and clicks the Accept Invitation button. (Until that happens, the word *Pending* appears next to the family member's name on the Family & Other Users page.)

> ### TROUBLESHOOTING
>
> **The email invitation never arrives**
>
> Despite repeated attempts on your part to set up a new family member, sometimes the invitation isn't sent. To get around this, click Manage Family Settings Online. (Alternatively, browse to *https://account.microsoft.com/family*.) On the webpage that appears, click the Add button for a child or an adult.
>
> Note that when you sign in to one of your other computers, your family's accounts are already in place; you don't need to add family members on each device. However, by default, the other family members cannot sign in to these other devices. To enable access, click the name of the family member and then click Allow. To disable access for a family member on a specific device, click Block.

Restricting use with assigned access

Assigned access is a rather odd feature you use to configure your computer so that a single designated user (one you've already added to your computer) can run only a single modern app. When that user signs in, the specified app starts automatically and runs full-screen. The user can't close the app or start any others. In fact, the only way out is to press Ctrl+Alt+Delete (or press the Windows button and power button simultaneously), which signs out the user and returns to the sign-in screen.

The use cases for this feature are limited, but here are a few examples:

- A kiosk app for public use (see "Setting up a kiosk device" in Chapter 17 for more information)

- A point-of-sale app for your business

- A game for a very young child

If you can think of a use for this feature, click Set Up Assigned Access at the bottom of the Family & Other Users page.

Introducing access control in Windows

We've saved this fairly technical section for last. Most Windows users never need to deal with the nuts and bolts of the Windows security model. But developers, network administrators, and anyone who aspires to the label "power user" should have at least a basic understanding of what happens when you create accounts, share files, install software drivers, and perform other tasks that have security implications.

The Windows approach to security is discretionary: Each securable system resource—each file or printer, for example—has an owner. That owner, in turn, has discretion over who can and cannot access the resource. Usually, a resource is owned by the user who creates it. If you create a file, for example, you are the file's owner under ordinary circumstances. (Computer administrators, however, can take ownership of resources they didn't create.)

NOTE

To exercise full discretionary control over individual files, you must store those files on an NTFS volume. For the sake of compatibility, Windows 10 supports the FAT and FAT32 file systems used by early Windows versions and many USB flash drives, as well as the exFAT file system used on some removable drives. However, none of the FAT-based file systems support file permissions. To enjoy the full benefits of Windows security, you must use NTFS. For more information about file systems, see "Choosing a file system" in Chapter 14.

WHAT ARE SECURITY IDENTIFIERS?

Windows security relies on the use of a security identifier (SID) to identify a user. When you create a user account on your computer, Windows assigns a unique SID to that account. The SID remains uniquely associated with that user account until the account is deleted, whereupon the SID is never used again—for that user or any other user. Even if you re-create an account with identical information, a new SID is created.

A SID is a variable-length value that contains a revision level, a 48-bit identifier authority value, and a number of 32-bit subauthority values. The SID takes the form S-1-x-y1-y2- . . . . S-1 identifies it as a revision 1 SID; x is the value for the identifier authority; and y1, y2, and so on are values for subauthorities.

You'll sometimes see a SID in a security dialog box (for example, on the Security tab of a file's properties dialog box) before Windows has had time to look up the user account name. You'll also spot SIDs in the hidden and protected $RECYCLE.BIN folder (each SID you see in this folder represents the Recycle Bin for a particular user) and in the registry (the HKEY_USERS hive contains a key, identified by SID, for each user account on the computer), among other places. The easiest way to determine your own SID is with the Whoami command-line utility. For details, see the following Inside Out sidebar.

Not all SIDs are unique (although the SID assigned to your user account is always unique). A number of commonly used SIDs are constant among all Windows installations. For example, S-1-5-18 is the SID for the built-in Local System account, a hidden member of the Administrators group that is used by the operating system and by services that sign in using the Local System account. You can find a complete list of such SIDs in the Microsoft Knowledge Base article "Well-known security identifiers in Windows operating systems" (*https://support.microsoft.com/kb/243330*).

To control which users have access to a resource, Windows uses the SID assigned to each user account. Your SID (a gigantic number guaranteed to be unique) follows you around wherever you go in Windows. When you sign in, the operating system first validates your user name and password. Then it creates a security access token. You can think of this as the electronic equivalent of an ID badge. It includes your user name and SID, plus information about any security groups to which your account belongs. (Security groups are described later in this chapter.) Any program you start gets a copy of your security access token.

Inside OUT

Learn about your own account with Whoami

Windows includes a command-line utility called Whoami (Who Am I?). You can use Whoami to find out the name of the account that's currently signed in, its SID, the names of the security groups of which it's a member, and its privileges. To use Whoami, start by opening a Command Prompt window. (You don't need elevated privileges.)

Then, to learn the name of the signed-in user, type **whoami**. (This is particularly useful if you're signed in as a standard user but running an elevated Command Prompt window—when it might not be obvious which account is currently "you.") If you're curious about your SID, type **whoami /user**. For a complete list of Whoami parameters, type **whoami /?**.

With User Account Control (UAC) turned on, administrators who sign in get two security access tokens—one that has the privileges of a standard user and one that has the full privileges of an administrator.

Whenever you attempt to walk through a controlled "door" in Windows (for example, when you connect to a shared printer), or any time a program attempts to do so on your behalf, the operating system examines your security access token and decides whether to let you pass. If access is permitted, you notice nothing. If access is denied, you get to hear a beep and read a refusal message.

In determining whom to let pass and whom to block, Windows consults the resource's access control list (ACL). This is simply a list of SIDs and the access privileges associated with each one. Every resource subject to access control has an ACL. This manner of allowing and blocking access to resources such as files and printers has remained essentially unchanged since Windows NT.

WHAT ARE ACLS?

Each folder and each file on an NTFS-formatted volume has an ACL (also known as DACL, for discretionary access control list, and commonly called NTFS permissions). An ACL comprises an access control entry (ACE) for each user who is allowed access to the folder or file. With NTFS permissions, you can control access to any file or folder, allowing different types of access for different users or groups of users.

To view and edit NTFS permissions for a file or folder, right-click its icon and choose Properties. The Security tab lists all the groups and users with permissions set for the selected object, as shown here. Different permissions can be set for each user, as you can see by selecting each one.

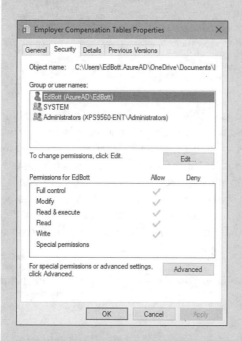

To make changes to the settings for any user or group in the list, or to add or remove a user or group in the list, click Edit. (Use caution. Setting NTFS permissions without understanding the full consequences can lead to unexpected and unwelcome results, including a complete loss of access to files and folders. Above all, avoid delving into the inner workings of NTFS permissions when your goal is to manage network sharing, which is governed by a separate set of options. For details, see Chapter 13, "Windows networking."

The access granted by each permission type is as follows:

- **Full Control.** Users with Full Control can list contents of a folder, read and open files, create new files, delete files and subfolders, change permissions on files and subfolders, and take ownership of files.
- **Modify.** Allows the user to read, change, create, and delete files but not to change permissions or take ownership of files.
- **Read & Execute.** Allows the user to view files and execute programs.
- **List Folder Contents.** Provides the same permissions as Read & Execute, but can be applied only to folders.
- **Read.** Allows the user to list the contents of a folder, read file attributes, read permissions, and synchronize files.
- **Write.** Allows the user to create files, write data, read attributes and permissions, and synchronize files.
- **Special Permissions.** The assigned permissions don't match any of the preceding permission descriptions. To see precisely which permissions are granted, click Advanced.

UAC, which was introduced in Windows Vista, adds another layer of restrictions based on user accounts. With UAC turned on, applications are normally launched using an administrator's standard user token. (Standard users, of course, have only a standard user token.) If an application requires administrator privileges, UAC asks for your consent (if you're signed in as an administrator) or the credentials of an administrator (if you're signed in as a standard user) before letting the application run. With UAC turned off, Windows works in the same (rather dangerous) manner as pre–Windows Vista versions: Administrator accounts can do just about anything (sometimes getting those users in trouble), and standard accounts don't have the privileges needed to run many older programs.

➤ For more information about UAC, see "Windows security and privacy" in Chapter 13.

Permissions and rights

Windows distinguishes two types of access privileges: permissions and rights. A permission is the ability to access a particular object in some defined manner—for example, to write to an NTFS file or to modify a printer queue. A right is the ability to perform a particular system action, such as signing in or resetting the clock.

The owner of a resource (or an administrator) assigns permissions to the resource either programmatically (through management software) or interactively using its properties dialog box. For example, if you're the printer owner or have administrative privileges, you can restrict someone from using a particular printer by visiting the properties dialog box for that printer. Administrators set rights via the Local Security Policy console. For example, an administrator could grant someone the right to install a device driver. (The Local Security Policy console is available only in the Pro, Enterprise, and Education editions of Windows 10. In the Home edition, rights for various security groups are predefined and unchangeable.)

NOTE

In this book, as in many of the Windows messages and dialog boxes, *privileges* serves as an informal term encompassing both permissions and rights.

User accounts and security groups

The backbone of Windows security is the ability to uniquely identify each user. While setting up a computer—or at any later time—an administrator creates a user account for each user. The user account is identified by a user name and is normally secured by a password, which the user provides when signing in to the system. Windows then controls, monitors, and restricts access to system resources on the basis of the permissions and rights associated with each user account by the resource owners and the system administrator.

Account type is a simplified way of describing membership in a security group, which is a collection of user accounts. Windows classifies each user account as one of two account types:

- **Administrator.** Members of the Administrators group are classified as administrator accounts. By default, the Administrators group includes the first account you create when you set up the computer and an account named Administrator that is disabled and hidden by default. Unlike other account types, administrators have full control over the system. Among the tasks that only administrators can perform are the following:

  - Create, change, and delete user accounts and groups

  - Install and uninstall desktop programs

  - Configure automatic updating with Windows Update

  - Install an ActiveX control

  - Install or remove hardware device drivers

  - Share folders

  - Set permissions

- Access all files, including those in another user's folder

- Take ownership of files

- Copy or move files into the %ProgramFiles% or %SystemRoot% folders

- Restore backed-up system files

- Grant rights to other user accounts and to themselves

- Configure Windows Firewall

- **Standard user.** Members of the Users group are classified as standard user accounts. A partial list of tasks available to standard user accounts includes the following:

  - Change the password and picture for their own user account

  - Use desktop programs that have been installed on the computer

  - Install system and driver updates using Windows Update

  - Install and run apps from the Microsoft Store

  - Install approved ActiveX controls in Internet Explorer

  - Configure a secure Wi-Fi connection

  - Refresh a network adapter and the system's IP address

  - View permissions

  - Create, change, and delete files in their document folders and in shared document folders

  - Restore their own backed-up files

  - View the system clock and calendar, and change the time zone

  - Set personalization options, such as themes, desktop background, and so on

  - Select a display dots-per-inch (DPI) setting to adjust text size

  - Configure power options

  - Sign in in Safe Mode

  - View Windows Firewall settings

Assigning an appropriate account type to the people who use your computer is straightforward. At least one user must be an administrator; naturally, that should be the person who manages the computer's use and maintenance. All other regular users should each have a standard user account.

WHAT HAPPENED TO THE ADMINISTRATOR ACCOUNT?

Every computer running Windows has a special account named Administrator. In versions of Windows before Windows 7, Administrator was the primary account for managing the computer. Like other administrator accounts, the Administrator account has full rights over the entire computer. But in Windows 10, the Administrator account is disabled by default.

In Windows 10, there's seldom a need to use the Administrator account instead of another administrator account. With default settings in Windows, the Administrator account does have one unique capability: It's not subject to UAC, even when UAC is turned on for all other users. All other administrator accounts (which are sometimes called Protected Administrator accounts) run with standard-user privileges unless the user consents to elevation. The Administrator account runs with full administrative privileges at all times and never needs your consent for elevation. (For this reason, of course, it's rather risky. Any application that runs as Administrator has full control of the computer—which means applications written by malicious or incompetent programmers can do significant damage to your system.)

Inside OUT

And the Guest account?

Historically, the built-in Guest account provided a way to offer limited access to occasional users. Not so in Windows 10. Although this account still exists, it's disabled by default, and the supported tools for enabling it (the Local Users And Groups console, for example) do not work as expected. In our experience, trying to trick Windows 10 into enabling this capability is almost certain to end in frustration. In the cloud-centric world of Windows 10, the Guest account no longer works as it used to, and enabling it can cause a variety of problems. A better solution (if your guests don't have their own device that can connect to your wireless network) is to set up a standard account for guest use.

Security groups allow a system administrator to create classes of users who share common privileges. For example, if everyone in the accounting department needs access to the Payables folder, the administrator can create a group called Accounting and grant the entire group access to that folder. If the administrator then adds all user accounts belonging to employees in the accounting department to the Accounting group, these users will automatically have access to the Payables folder. A user account can belong to one group, more than one group, or no group at all.

In large networks based on Active Directory domains, groups can be a valuable administrative tool. They simplify the job of ensuring that all members with common access needs have an identical set of privileges. We don't recommend creating or using groups other than the built-in Administrators and Users groups on standalone and workgroup-based computers, however.

Permissions and rights for group members are cumulative. That means that if a user account belongs to more than one group, the user enjoys all the privileges accorded to all groups of which the user account is a member.

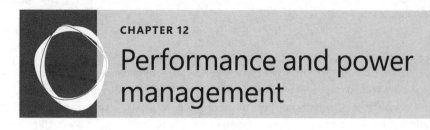

Performance and power management

Viewing details about your system....................420

Managing services....................................426

Monitoring performance with Task Manager 433

Using Resource Monitor to pinpoint performance problems 437

Power management on desktop systems 439

Is there such a thing as a Windows 10 computer that meets every performance desire and expectation of its user(s)? Perhaps. After all, the system is designed to perform well straight out of the box. And yet, for many (ourselves included), performance adequacy is always a receding target. Whether you're mainly a gamer, a video editor, a number cruncher, or a humble writer, speed thrills. More is never less; it's always more.

Still, the out-of-the-box performance of a Windows 10 PC should be acceptable, assuming that the device you're using is capable of the work you're asking it to perform. A small tablet with a low-power mobile processor will almost certainly struggle at a processor-intensive task like video processing, for example.

But even a workstation-class PC can perform poorly if you have a problem with a major subsystem or if Windows is configured incorrectly. In our experience, the most common causes of poor performance (in no particular order) are these:

- **Defective hardware.** Memory and disk errors are most obvious when they cause system crashes, but hardware-related problems can also cause performance to drag. Check with your hardware manufacturer to see what diagnostic tools are available.

- **Outdated or flawed device drivers.** PC and device makers are responsible for supplying drivers for the individual hardware components that go into their hardware. If you do a clean install, Windows might install a generic driver instead of one written specifically for that device. We have seen performance problems vanish immediately after a simple driver upgrade. Always be certain you're using the best possible drivers for all system devices. (Don't assume that a newer driver is automatically better than an older one, however; any driver update has the potential to cause new problems.)

- **Inadequate hardware resources.** Windows 10 should perform basic tasks well on even low-end hardware that was designed and built five or more years ago. But more demanding tasks, such as digital media encoding, can push some systems to the breaking point. The performance-monitoring tools we identify later in this chapter should help you identify areas where hardware resources are being pushed to the limit.

- **Out-of-control processes or services.** Sometimes, a program or background task that normally runs just fine will spin out of control, consuming up to 100 percent of CPU time or grabbing increasing amounts of memory or other system resources. In the process, of course, performance of all other tasks slows down or grinds to a halt. Knowing how to identify and kill this sort of process or service and prevent it from recurring is a valuable troubleshooting skill.

- **Malware.** Viruses, Trojan-horse programs, spyware, and other forms of unwanted software can wreak havoc on system performance. Be sure to check for the possibility that malware is present on a system that exhibits otherwise unexplained performance problems.

In general, our approach to optimizing performance is prosaic. Given that there's no magic registry setting that will suddenly send a system into warp speed, we recommend using quality parts, making sure all devices have correct and up-to-date drivers, having plenty of memory on board, maintaining enough free disk space to allow for a large paging (swap) file, having a speedy Internet connection, and keeping your system abreast of enhancements and security fixes delivered via Windows Update.

Several of these measures are discussed elsewhere in this book. See, for example, Chapter 14, "Hardware and devices"; Chapter 9, "Storage and file management"; and Chapter 5, "Managing updates." In this chapter we focus on diagnosis, discussing tools that you can use to gather information about your system and identify any performance bottlenecks that might be present. We'll conclude with the subject of power management. (Note, however, that power-management topics relating specifically to battery-driven portable systems are discussed separately in Chapter 20, "Maximizing productivity on a portable PC.")

Windows 10 offers two valuable tools for monitoring the performance of your system in real time: Task Manager and Resource Monitor. Task Manager has been a mainstay of Windows through many versions. In Chapter 6, "Installing and configuring apps and desktop programs." we described its use for terminating recalcitrant processes and disabling unwanted startup programs. Task Manager also includes valuable performance-monitoring tools, which we describe later in this chapter. For zeroing in on performance issues with even more detail, you can use an advanced tool called Resource Monitor. In combination, these tools help you to keep an eye on CPU, memory, disk activity, and network usage.

Viewing details about your system

For answers to basic questions about your operating system and computer, there's no better place to start than System, which displays the current Windows edition and whether it is a 32-bit or 64-bit version; basic system details, including processor type and installed memory; details about the computer name and network membership (domain or workgroup); and the current activation status.

Windows 10 offers two versions of this information. On a tablet or touchscreen-enabled system, you'll probably use the Settings app. Open Settings > System > About to display details like those shown in Figure 12-1. A faster way to get to the About page in Settings is to right-click the Start button (or press Windows key+X) and then click System.

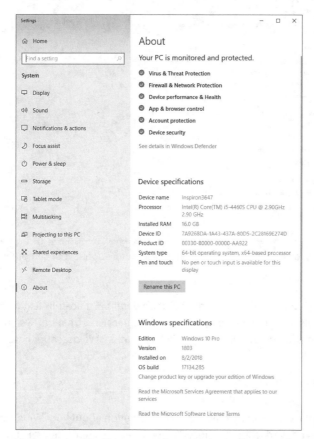

Figure 12-1   This About page, found in the Settings app, includes basic details about the local PC along with the option to change its name.

An alternative display that includes most of the same information is in the old-style Control Panel, shown in Figure 12-2. If File Explorer is open, you can bypass Control Panel to reach the same destination: right-click This PC and click Properties.

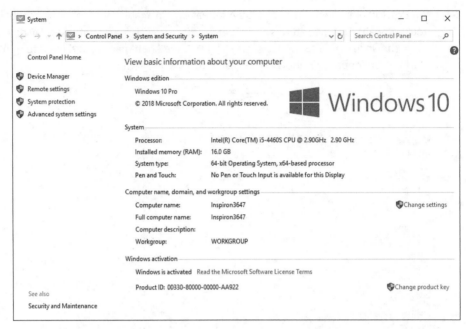

Figure 12-2   The System page in Control Panel provides basic details about your computer's configuration.

For the most exhaustive inventory of system configuration details in a no-frills text format, Windows offers three tools that provide varying levels of technical information: Systeminfo, Windows Management Instrumentation, and System Information. We describe these tools in the following sections.

Systeminfo

Systeminfo.exe is a command-line utility that displays information about your Windows version, BIOS, processor, memory, network configuration, and a few more esoteric items. Figure 12-3 shows sample output.

To run Systeminfo, open a Command Prompt window, type **systeminfo**, and then press Enter. In addition to the list format shown in Figure 12-3, Systeminfo offers two formats that are useful if you want to work with the information in another program: Table (fixed-width columns) and CSV (comma-separated values). To use one of these formats, append the **/fo** switch to the command, along with the Table or Csv parameter. You also need to redirect the output to a file. For example, to store comma-delimited information in a file named Info.csv, enter the following command:

```
systeminfo /fo csv > info.csv
```

```
C:\WINDOWS\system32\cmd.exe                                          —    □    ×

Microsoft Windows [Version 10.0.17134.285]
(c) 2018 Microsoft Corporation. All rights reserved.

C:\Users\Craig>systeminfo

Host Name:                  INSPIRON3647
OS Name:                    Microsoft Windows 10 Pro
OS Version:                 10.0.17134 N/A Build 17134
OS Manufacturer:            Microsoft Corporation
OS Configuration:           Standalone Workstation
OS Build Type:              Multiprocessor Free
Registered Owner:           N/A
Registered Organization:    N/A
Product ID:                 00330-80000-00000-AA922
Original Install Date:      8/2/2018, 03:55:52
System Boot Time:           9/16/2018, 23:54:04
System Manufacturer:        Dell Inc.
System Model:               Inspiron 3647
System Type:                x64-based PC
Processor(s):               1 Processor(s) Installed.
                            [01]: Intel64 Family 6 Model 60 Stepping 3 GenuineIntel ~2901 Mhz
BIOS Version:               Dell Inc. A08, 6/29/2015
Windows Directory:          C:\WINDOWS
System Directory:           C:\WINDOWS\system32
Boot Device:                \Device\HarddiskVolume2
System Locale:              en-us;English (United States)
Input Locale:               en-us;English (United States)
Time Zone:                  (UTC-05:00) Eastern Time (US & Canada)
Total Physical Memory:      16,301 MB
Available Physical Memory:  7,544 MB
Virtual Memory: Max Size:   18,733 MB
Virtual Memory: Available:  7,510 MB
Virtual Memory: In Use:     11,223 MB
Page File Location(s):      C:\pagefile.sys
Domain:                     WORKGROUP
Logon Server:               \\INSPIRON3647
Hotfix(s):                  7 Hotfix(s) Installed.
                            [01]: KB4230204
                            [02]: KB4287903
                            [03]: KB4343669
                            [04]: KB4343902
                            [05]: KB4456655
                            [06]: KB4457146
                            [07]: KB4457128
Network Card(s):            6 NIC(s) Installed.
                            [01]: Realtek PCIe GBE Family Controller
                                  Connection Name: Ethernet
                                  Status:          Media disconnected
                            [02]: Dell Wireless 1705 802.11b/g/n (2.4GHZ)
                                  Connection Name: Wi-Fi
                                  DHCP Enabled:    Yes
```

Figure 12-3   The command-line utility Systeminfo.exe provides an easy way to gather information about all your network computers in a single database.

Using the **/S** switch, you can get system information about another computer on your network. (If your user name and password don't match that of an account on the target computer, you also need to use the **/U** and **/P** switches to provide the user name and password of an authorized account.) When you've gathered information about all the computers on your network, you can import the file you created into a spreadsheet or database program for tracking and analysis. The following command appends information about a computer named Bates to the original file you created:

```
systeminfo /s Bates /fo csv >> info.csv
```

Windows Management Instrumentation command-line utility

This tool with the extra-long name is better known by the name of its executable, Wmic.exe. Wmic provides an overwhelming amount of information about hardware, system configuration details, and user accounts. It can be used in either of two ways.

Enter **wmic** from a command prompt, and the utility runs in console mode, wherein you can enter commands and view output interactively. Alternatively, you can add global switches or aliases, which constrain the type of output you're looking for, and see the output in a Command Prompt window or redirect it to a file. For example, use the following command to produce a neatly formatted HTML file:

```
wmic qfe list brief /format:htable > %temp%\hotfix.html
```

You can then open that file in a web browser to see a list of all installed updates on the current system. To see the full syntax for Wmic, open a Command Prompt window and type **wmic /?**.

System Information

System Information—often called by the name of its executable, Msinfo32.exe—is a techie's paradise. It displays a wealth of configuration information in a simple tree-and-details arrangement, as shown in Figure 12-4. You can search for specific information, save information, view information about other computers, and even view a list of changes to your system.

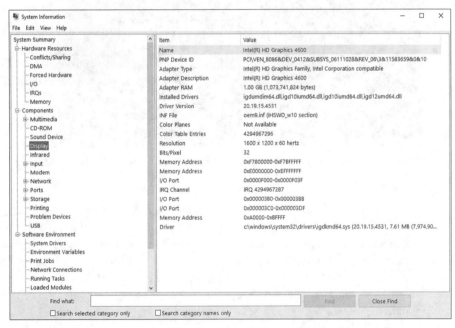

Figure 12-4   System Information is for viewing configuration information only; you can't use it to actually configure settings.

To start System Information, begin typing **system information** in the search box or type **msinfo32** at a command prompt.

You navigate through System Information much as you would through File Explorer: Click a category in the left pane to view its contents in the right pane. To search for specific information, use the Find What box at the bottom of the System Information window. (If the Find bar is not visible, press Ctrl+F, or click Edit and then clear the check box next to Hide Find.)

The Find feature is basic but effective. Here are a couple of things you should know:

- Whenever you type in the Find What box to start a new search, Find begins its search at the top of the search range (which is the entire namespace unless you select Search Selected Category Only)—not at the current highlight.

- Selecting Search Category Names Only causes the Find feature to look only in the left pane. When this check box is cleared, the text in both panes is searched.

Using the System Information tool, you can preserve your configuration information—which is always helpful when reconstructing a system—in several ways:

- **Save the information as an .nfo file.** You can subsequently open the file (on the same computer or on a different computer with System Information) to view your saved information. To save information in this format, click File, Save. Saving this way always saves the entire collection of information.

- **Save all or part of the information as a plain-text file.** To save information as a text file, select the category of interest and click File, Export. To save all the information as a text file, select System Summary before you export it.

- **You can print all or part of the information.** Select the category of interest; click File, Print; and be sure that Selection is selected under Page Range. To print everything, select All under Page Range—and be sure to have lots of paper on hand. Depending on your system configuration and the number of installed applications, your report could top 100 pages. (Even better, consider "printing" to PDF and saving the results.)

Regardless of how you save your information, System Information refreshes (updates) the information immediately before processing the command.

Inside OUT

Save your system information periodically

Saving system configuration information when your computer is working properly can turn out to be useful when you have problems. Comparing your computer's current configuration with a known good baseline configuration can help you spot possible problem areas. You can open multiple instances of System Information to display the current configuration in one window and a baseline configuration in another. Save the configuration in OneDrive, and you'll be able to retrieve the information even after a hard-disk replacement.

Managing services

A *service* is a specialized program that performs a function to support other programs. Many services operate at a low level (by interacting directly with hardware, for example) and need to run even when no user is signed in. For this reason, they're often run by the System account (which has elevated privileges) rather than by ordinary user accounts. In this section, you'll learn how to view installed services; start, stop, and configure them; and install or remove them. We'll also take a closer look at some services used in Windows 10 and show you how to configure them to your advantage.

For the most complete view of services running on your computer, use the Services console. You can also view running services and perform limited management functions by using Task Manager. In this section, we discuss both tools.

Using the Services console

You manage services with the Services snap-in (Services.msc) for Microsoft Management Console, shown in Figure 12-5. To view this snap-in, type **services** in the search box and then click the Services desktop app at the top of the results list. (You must have administrator privileges to gain full functionality in the Services console. Running it as a standard user, you can view service settings, but you can't start or stop most services, change the startup type, or make any other configuration changes.)

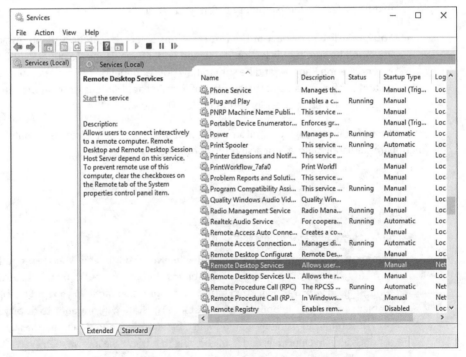

Figure 12-5   Use the Services console to start, stop, and configure services.

The Extended and Standard views in the Services console (selectable by clicking a tab near the bottom of the window) have a single difference: The Extended view provides descriptive information of the selected service in the space at the left edge of the details pane. This space also sometimes includes links for starting, stopping, or pausing the selected service. Unless you need to constrain the console display to a small area of your screen, you'll probably find the Extended view preferable to the Standard view.

The Services console offers plenty of information in its clean display. You can sort the contents of any column by clicking the column title, as you can with similar lists. To sort in reverse order, click the column title again. In addition, you can do the following:

- Start, stop, pause, resume, or restart the selected service, as described in the following section.

- Display the properties dialog box for the selected service, in which you can configure the service and learn more about it.

Most essential services are set to start automatically when your computer starts, and the operating system stops them as part of its shutdown process. A handful of services that aren't typically used at startup are set with the Automatic (Delayed Start) option, which starts the associated service two minutes after the rest of startup completes, making the startup process smoother. The Trigger Start option allows Windows to run or stop a service as needed in response to specific events; the File History service, for example, doesn't run unless you enable the File History feature.

But sometimes you might need to manually start or stop a service. For example, you might want to start a seldom-used service on the rare occasion when you need it. (Because running services requires system resources such as memory, running them only when necessary can improve performance.) On the other hand, you might want to stop a service because you're no longer using it. A more common reason for stopping a service is because it isn't working properly. For example, if print jobs get stuck in the print queue, sometimes the best remedy is to stop and then restart the Print Spooler service.

CHAPTER 12

Inside OUT

Pause instead of stopping

If a service allows pausing, try pausing and then continuing the service as your first step instead of stopping the service. Pausing can solve certain problems without canceling jobs in process or resetting connections.

Starting and stopping services

Not all services allow you to change their status. Some prevent stopping and starting alto-gether, whereas others permit stopping and starting but not pausing and resuming. Some ser-vices allow these permissions to only certain users or groups. For example, most services allow only members of the Administrators group to start or stop them. Which status changes are allowed and who has permission to make them are controlled by each service's discretionary access control list (DACL), which is established when the service is created on a computer.

To change a service's status, select it in the Services console. Then click the appropriate link in the area to the left of the service list (if you're using the Extended view and the link you need appears there). Alternatively, you can use the Play/Pause/Stop controls on the toolbar or right-click and use the corresponding command.

You can also change a service's status by opening its properties dialog box and then clicking one of the buttons on the General tab. Taking the extra step of opening the properties dialog box to set the status has only one advantage: You can specify start parameters when you start a service by using this method. This is a rare requirement.

Configuring services

To review or modify the way a service starts up or what happens when it doesn't start properly, view its properties dialog box. To do that, double-click the service in the Services console. Figure 12-6 shows an example.

Figure 12-6   Specify a service's startup type on the General tab, where you can also find the actual name of the service (in this case, BTAGService) above its display name.

Setting startup options

On the General tab of the properties dialog box (shown in Figure 12-6), you specify the startup type:

- **Automatic (Delayed Start).** The service starts shortly after the computer starts in order to improve startup performance and user experience.

- **Automatic.** The service starts when the computer starts.

- **Manual.** The service doesn't start automatically at startup, but it can be started by a user, program, or dependent service.

- **Disabled.** The service can't be started.

The Trigger Start option cannot be configured manually from the Services console. Instead, you have to use SC (Sc.exe), a command-line program that communicates with the Service Control Manager. If you'd rather not tinker with the arcane syntax of this command, try the free Service Trigger Editor, available from Core Technologies Consulting, at *https://bit.ly/servicetriggereditor.*

You'll find other startup options on the Log On tab of the properties dialog box, as shown in Figure 12-7.

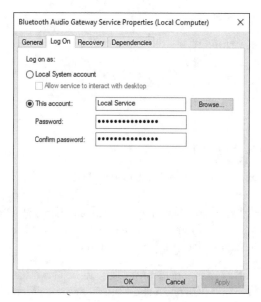

Figure 12-7   On the Log On tab, you specify which user account runs the service.

CHAPTER 12

NOTE

If you specify a sign-in account other than the Local System account, be sure that account has the requisite rights. Go to the Local Security Policy console (at a command prompt, type **secpol.msc**), and then go to Security Settings\Local Policies\User Rights Assignment and assign the **Log On As A Service** right to the account.

Specifying recovery actions

For various reasons—hardware not operating properly or a network connection being down, for example—a service that's running smoothly might suddenly stop. By using settings on the Recovery tab of the properties dialog box, you can specify what happens if a service fails. Figure 12-8, for example, shows the default settings for the Bluetooth Audio Gateway service.

Figure 12-8   Use the Recovery tab to specify what happens if a service fails.

You might want to perform a different action the first time a service fails than on the second or subsequent failures. The Recovery tab enables you to assign a particular response to the first failure, the second failure, and all subsequent failures, from among these options:

- **Take No Action.** The service gives up trying. In most cases, the service places a message in the event log. (Use of the event log depends on how the service was programmed by its developers.)

- **Restart The Service.** The computer waits for the time specified in the Restart Service After box to elapse and then tries to start the service.

- **Run A Program.** The computer runs the program you specify in the Run Program box. For example, you could specify a program that attempts to resolve the problem or one that alerts you to the situation.

- **Restart The Computer.** Drastic but effective, this option restarts the computer after the time specified in the Restart Computer Options dialog box elapses. In that dialog box, you can also specify a message to be broadcast to other users on your network, warning them of the impending shutdown.

Viewing dependencies

Many services rely on the functions of another service. If you attempt to start a service that depends on other services, Windows first starts the others. If you stop a service upon which others are dependent, Windows also stops those services. Before you either start or stop a service, therefore, it's helpful to know what other services your action might affect. To obtain that information, go to the Dependencies tab of a service's properties dialog box, as in the example shown in Figure 12-9.

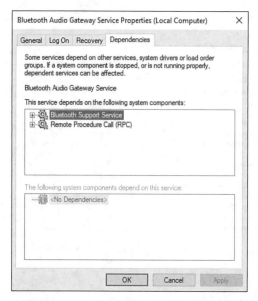

Figure 12-9   The Dependencies tab shows which services depend on other services or drivers.

The outline controls in the Dependencies tab can be expanded to show dependents of the dependents.

Managing services from Task Manager

Using the Services tab in Windows Task Manager, you can start and stop services and view several important aspects of the services, both running and available, on your computer. You can also use this tab as a shortcut to the Services console.

To open Task Manager, use any of the following techniques:

- Right-click Start (or press Windows key+X), and then click Task Manager on the Quick Link menu.

- Right-click the taskbar, and then click Task Manager.

- Press Ctrl+Alt+Delete, and then click Task Manager.

- Press Ctrl+Shift+Esc.

The Services tab is shown in Figure 12-10.

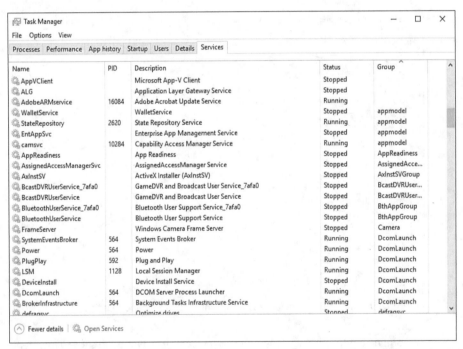

Figure 12-10   By sorting on the Group column, you can see groups of related services together.

NOTE

If Task Manager shows only a list of running apps and does not have a row of tabs across the top, click More Details.

To start, stop, or restart a service, right-click its name on the Services tab and then click Start, Stop, or Restart.

Using the Services tab, you can also associate a running service with its process identifier (PID) and then further associate that PID with other programs and services being run under that PID. For example, Figure 12-10 shows four services running with PID 564. Right-clicking one of the services with PID 564 gives you several choices, including one to stop the service and one called Go To Details. Clicking the latter opens the Details tab in Task Manager with the particular process (typically, Svchost.exe) highlighted.

Determining the name of a service

As you view the properties dialog box for different services, you might notice that the service name (shown at the top of the General tab) is often different from the name that appears in the Services console (the display name) and that neither name matches the name of the service's executable file. (Many services run as part of a service group, under Services.exe or Svchost.exe.) The General tab (shown earlier in Figure 12-6) shows all three names.

So how does this affect you? When you work in the Services console, you don't need to know anything other than a service's display name to find it and work with it. But if you use the Net command to start and stop services from a Command Prompt window, you might find using the actual service name more convenient; it's often much shorter than the display name. You'll also need the service name if you're ever forced to work with a service's registry entries, which can be found in the HKLM\System\CurrentControlSet\Services*service* subkey (where *service* is the service name).

And what about the executable name? You might need it if you have problems running a service; in such a case, you need to find the executable and check its permissions. Knowing the executable name can also be useful, for example, if you're using Windows Task Manager to determine why your computer seems to be running slowly. Although the Processes tab and the Services tab show the display name (under the Description heading), because of the window size it's sometimes easier to find the more succinct executable name.

Monitoring performance with Task Manager

The Performance tab of Task Manager gives you a quick overview of your system's performance as measured in multiple dimensions, including CPU, memory, disk, and network usage. The small thumbnail graphs at the left report current data in real time; clicking any of these thumbnails displays a much larger version, with additional information below the chart. Figure 12-11 shows the performance data for a desktop PC, roughly 50 seconds after opening Task Manager. (If you don't see a tabular layout similar to that shown in Figure 12-11, click More Details.)

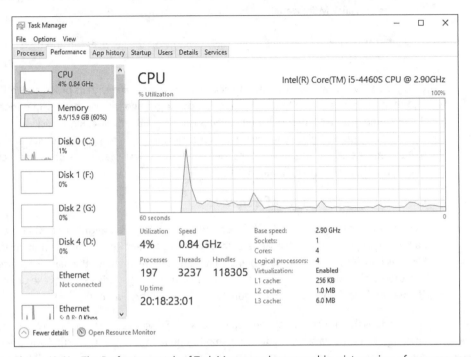

Figure 12-11 The Performance tab of Task Manager gives you a big-picture view of resource usage.

Inside OUT

How long has your PC been running?

Many of the details below the performance graph on the CPU tab in Task Manager are obscure and only of use to developers. You probably don't need to know how many handles are in use by your current workload, for example. But one detail here is interesting as a benchmark of stability. The Up Time measure shows the amount of time that has elapsed—in days, hours, minutes, and seconds—since the machine was last restarted. Thanks to monthly updates that usually include mandatory restarts, it's unlikely you'll ever see this number go beyond 30 days.

The graphs to the right show 60 seconds' worth of data, with updates at one-second intervals. In Figure 12-11, for example, the CPU graph shows a large spike caused by opening Task Manager, followed by several smaller spikes as other activities make demands on the CPU.

By keeping this pane open as you work, you can see what the impact of a given activity is. For example, you might monitor CPU usage when encoding a video file to see whether the operation pins CPU usage at 100 percent; if so, that might be evidence that you need to upgrade your PC to one with a more powerful CPU that's capable of doing the same work faster, generating less heat, and allowing you to do other things while the task completes in the background.

The Memory option offers a snapshot of memory usage, as shown in Figure 12-12. Note that the total amount of memory is visible above the graph, with details about the physical memory itself (number of sticks and slots, for example) below, alongside the amount of RAM in use and the amount available.

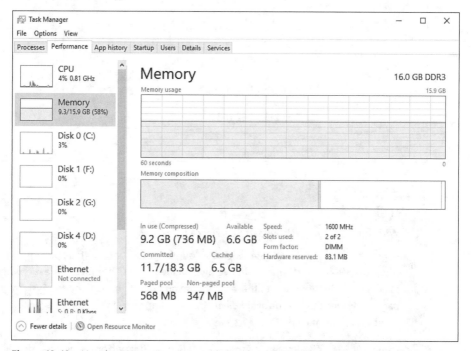

Figure 12-12   Use the Memory option on the Performance tab to see how much of your system's RAM is in use. If the value is at 100 percent, it's time to close some apps to improve performance.

On this page, a detailed Memory Composition bar chart appears below the main graph. At first glance, it appears to be just an alternate view of the main Memory Usage chart, but hover the mouse pointer over any segment to see its real purpose. The ScreenTips that appear over each segment explain what each one represents.

CHAPTER 12

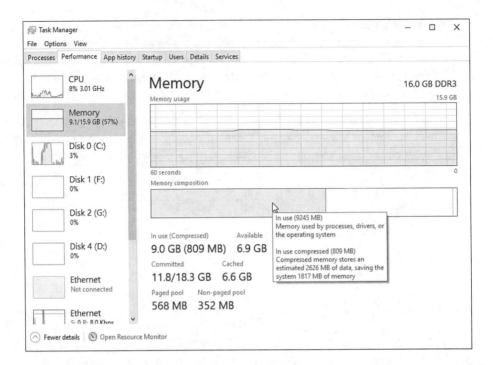

Inside OUT

What happened to the Windows Experience Index?

Beginning with Windows Vista, Microsoft published a set of numbers purporting to quantify your system's performance in five distinct areas. These numbers were merged into an overall score. In Windows 10, these values are no longer reported on the System Properties page. However, they're still available if you're willing to run the Windows System Assessment Tool (Winsat.exe).

Using WinSAT, as it's known for short, you can run a full performance analysis (by typing **winsat formal** at an elevated command prompt) or test individual Windows subsystems (type **winsat –?** for the full syntax). You can also save the output as an XML file or redirect the verbal output of the tests to a text file for subsequent review. To see the most recent set of detailed results, type **winsat query** in a Command Prompt window. This report shows the raw test results instead of the Windows Experience Index scores and provides a more detailed look at your system's performance.

Windows keeps a history of WinSAT performance results you can use for comparisons. You'll find them in %SystemRoot%\Performance\WinSAT\DataStore, each one stamped with the date and time it was run. Minor variations in results between WinSAT runs are normal, and they usually occur because of other processes and services interfering with resource usage. Keeping even an informal record of detailed results over time can help you determine whether a significant change in test scores is normal or a sign of a problem to be found and fixed.

The Disk options, likewise, graph the performance of all nonremovable disks on the current system. Each disk gets its own entry on the left side, with details about the selected disk's performance on the right, as shown in Figure 12-13. The top graph depicts the percentage of time the disk is busy processing read or write requests; the bottom graph shows the disk transfer rate.

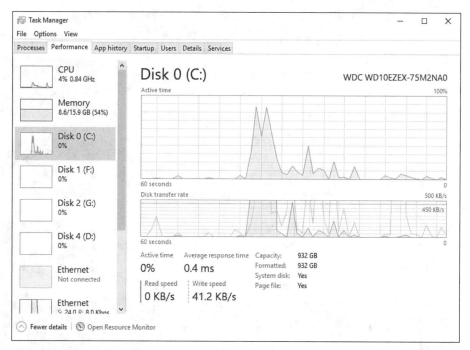

Figure 12-13   The Disk options in Task Manager let you see the throughput of a fixed disk and determine whether a particular activity is causing a bottleneck.

Using Resource Monitor to pinpoint performance problems

Like the Performance tab in Task Manager, Resource Monitor gives you both instantaneous and recent-history readouts of key performance metrics. Also like Task Manager, Resource Monitor can show you, in excruciating detail, what each process is doing.

To open Resource Monitor, you can search for it from the Start menu or use its command line, **perfmon /res**, from a Command Prompt window. But the fastest way is to click the link at the bottom of the Task Manager Performance tab. This is, in our opinion, the preferred way to use this utility. Start with a quick overview from Task Manager, and if you need more information, call on Resource Monitor.

CHAPTER 12

When you first open Resource Monitor, you see the Overview tab shown in Figure 12-14, which provides both detailed tables and charts that summarize performance in four areas.

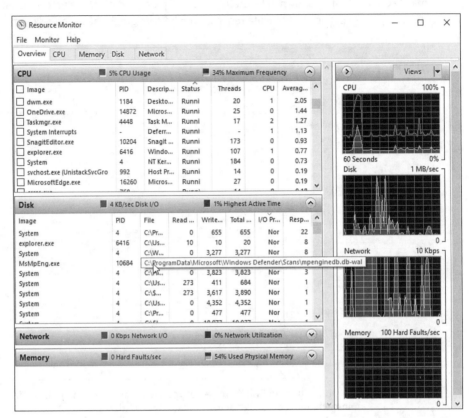

Figure 12-14   Use the check boxes in the top section of Resource Monitor to limit the results to a specific process. ScreenTips show details for files that are truncated in the list below.

Using the tabs along the top of the Resource Monitor window, you can switch to a different context and focus on a specific type of resource usage. The basic layout of each tab is similar and consists of a handful of common elements.

One or more tables contain details about the resource featured on that tab. The first table on each tab is called the key table; it contains a list of all processes currently using the selected resource, with a check box to the left of each process you use to filter the data displayed in additional tables on the tab. The key table at the top of the Overview tab lists all running processes in a display that is similar to the Processes tab of Task Manager.

Resource Monitor is overkill for most performance troubleshooting tasks. But it shines when you want to see exactly which process or file is responsible for an unexplained burst of activity.

Power management on desktop systems

Power-management features in Windows 10 can be broadly divided into two groups. Features in the first group apply universally to all Windows devices, even those that are permanently tethered to AC power. Allowing a PC or tablet to sleep or hibernate cuts the amount of power it consumes, which translates into monetary savings for you and a benefit for society at large.

For portable devices—including notebooks, hybrid devices, and tablets—paying attention to power management has additional productivity benefits. Anything you do to extend the battery life of a portable device helps you avoid having to quit working because your battery gave up the ghost. We discuss power management on portable systems elsewhere in this book.

➤ **For a thorough discussion of power management on portable systems, see Chapter 20, "Maximizing productivity on a portable PC."**

As with several other Windows features, the transition of power-management settings from the traditional Control Panel to the modern Settings app is not yet complete. Figure 12-15 shows the simple Power & Sleep page at Settings > System. Two options here specify the amount of idle time before the screen goes dark and the amount of time before the system goes to a lower-power setting called sleep.

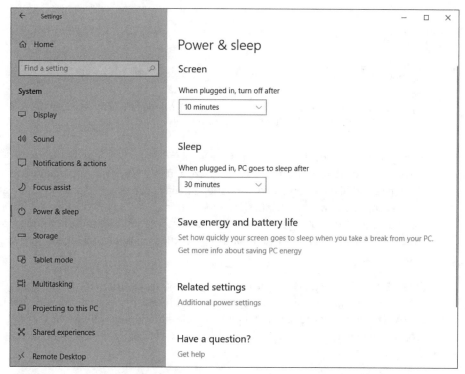

Figure 12-15   On this page, at Settings > System > Power & Sleep, you can set basic power parameters for a desktop computer.

Clicking the Additional Power Settings link on the Power & Sleep page in Settings opens the Power Options page in Control Panel, where you'll find an extensive selection of power settings, some extremely esoteric.

The old-school Power Options page in Control Panel, shown in Figure 12-16, is based on power plans, which represent a collection of saved settings. With older versions of Windows, it was common to find at least three power plans, with a hardware maker sometimes defining its own plan as well. In the Windows 10 era, you're likely to find only one or two. This example includes a Balanced plan and a Power Saver plan.

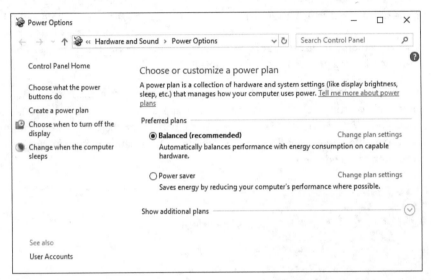

Figure 12-16   Default power options in Windows 10 include one or more power plans. You can create additional plans for special purposes.

Initially, Windows provides one or more power plans: Balanced is the sole option on most modern devices, but you might also see Power Saver and High Performance. (Click Show Additional Plans to see additional plans.) The recommended Balanced plan darkens the screen after ten minutes and sends the system into sleep mode after 30 minutes. (Note that original equipment manufacturers might change the names or parameter settings for these plans.) You can tailor any plan to your liking by clicking Change Plan Settings or by clicking one of the links at the left side of the screen.

For each option, the choices in the drop-down menu range from 1 minute (probably more annoying than most people will accept) to 5 hours (useful if you want the computer to sleep only when you're away for a long time). To disable either option, choose Never from the drop-down menu.

You can create a new plan altogether (while keeping the original plans provided by Windows or your device maker) by clicking Create A Power Plan on the left side of the screen. Doing so takes you to the Create A Power Plan page, shown in Figure 12-17.

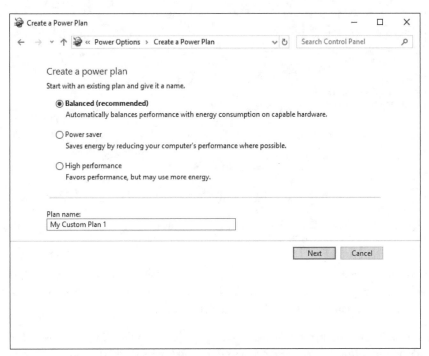

Figure 12-17   On the Create A Power Plan page, you can modify an existing plan or create a new one from scratch.

The Power Saver plan is set to turn off the display after 5 minutes and put the computer to sleep after 15 minutes. The High Performance plan is set by default to go dark at 15 minutes and never go to sleep. This might be the right choice for a system that must always be on alert. (Returning from a screen-darkened state is quick; returning from sleep takes a little longer.)

To create a new power plan, start with one of the existing ones, provide a name or accept the default name My Custom Plan 1, and then click Next. After clicking Next, you will find the usual Display and Sleep controls.

On the page that appears when you click Next, you will also see an option called Change Advanced Power Settings. Click here to arrive at the dialog box shown in Figure 12-18.

Figure 12-18   These advanced options give you granular control over power-management settings in Windows 10.

The options on the Advanced Settings tab, which are tailored to your hardware and software environment, provide a great deal of finely detailed control over power-related events. Click the outline controls to explore the choices available to you.

One of the options on the Advanced Settings page lets you tailor the behavior of your computer's power button. You can also do this by clicking Choose What The Power Buttons Do on the main Power Options page in Control Panel, shown earlier in Figure 12-16. Following this path brings you to the page shown in Figure 12-19.

The drop-down control associated with the power button gives you the following choices:

- Do nothing

- Sleep

- Hibernate

- Shut down

- Turn off the display

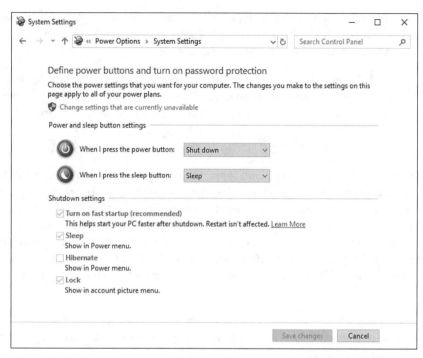

Figure 12-19   Drop-down menu controls on this page govern your system's behavior in response to pressing the power button or sleep button.

The same options, with the exception of Shut Down, are available for your computer's sleep button. Note that in sleep, your computer continues to use a small amount of power; in hibernate, open files and information concerning the state of your system are written to a file on disk, and the computer shuts down almost entirely. (A small amount of power remains available to your keyboard, enabling you to emerge from hibernation by pressing a key, if that option is enabled for the device.) Hibernation reduces power consumption to an absolute minimum, but restarting from this state takes longer than waking from sleep.

The four check boxes at the bottom of the page shown in Figure 12-19 cover a miscellany of settings. Changing any of these requires an administrator's credentials. Click Change Settings That Are Currently Unavailable to make the check boxes selectable. The settings are as follows:

- **Turn On Fast Startup (Recommended).** This option, on by default, results in slightly quicker startups. The system accomplishes this by writing Windows kernel information to disk when you shut down.

- **Sleep.** This one is also enabled by default. If for some reason you'd rather not have the Sleep command appear when you click Power on Start, clear the box.

- **Hibernate.** This option, not set by default, puts Hibernate on Start's Power menu. If you want to hibernate occasionally but don't want to alter the behavior of your sleep or power button, you'll need this menu option.

- **Lock.** The account picture menu is the menu that pops up when you click your account picture in the column at the left edge of Start. Lock, equivalent to pressing Windows key + L, normally is on the menu. Use this check box if you want to remove it.

Configuring power options from the command line

If your work entails managing power settings for multiple systems and users, you'll find the powercfg command-line utility invaluable. With powercfg, you can query and set power schemes and parameters, export power settings to a file, import the file on remote systems, and more. (Many powercfg actions work only in an elevated Command Prompt window.) Even if your concerns are only with your own systems, you might find **powercfg /batteryreport, powercfg /energy,** and **powercfg /sleepstudy** useful. These commands generate reports that are not available via the interactive power-management features described earlier in this section.

To generate a list of commands available with powercfg, open a Command Prompt window and type **powercfg /?**.) For syntax details and usage examples of any powercfg command, type **powercfg /?** *command*.

Modern computing is defined by our ability to communicate and share with one another by using devices of all shapes and sizes. These days, most of that activity happens over the world's largest global network, the internet, using a variety of widely accepted hardware and software standards. The internet is also the driving force behind cloud-based services, which are transforming the way we work and play.

The same network standards that allow connections to the internet can also be used to create a local area network (LAN), which makes it possible to share files, printers, and other resources in a home or an office.

In the not-so-distant past, setting up a network connection was a painful process, one that often required professional help. Today, network hardware is ubiquitous, and setting up a network connection in Microsoft Windows 10 requires little or no technical knowledge. That doesn't mean the process is entirely pain-free; troubleshooting network problems can be maddeningly frustrating, and understanding the basics of networking is tremendously helpful in isolating and fixing problems.

In this chapter, we cover the essentials of connecting a Windows 10 device to wired and wireless networks in a home or small office. We also explain how to share resources securely and how to check the status of your network connection to confirm that it's working properly. And when you want access to an *entire computer* rather than just its resources, a feature called Remote Desktop allows you to do exactly that, and a section of this chapter is devoted to showing you how.

As of Windows 10 version 1803, a feature that facilitated easy resource sharing over a home network has been removed. HomeGroup first appeared in Windows 7, but it's now gone. That doesn't mean the end of easy sharing, of course. Later in this chapter, we discuss alternatives to HomeGroup, including Nearby Sharing, a brand-new feature in version 1803.

Windows 10 networking essentials

Before you can connect to the internet or a local area network, your Windows 10 device needs a network adapter, properly installed with working drivers.

Since the release of Windows 7, Microsoft's hardware certification requirements have mandated that every desktop PC, laptop, all-in-one, and portable device include a certified Ethernet or Wi-Fi adapter. Some portable devices also include modems that connect to mobile broadband networks, and Bluetooth adapters support limited types of direct connections between PCs.

You'll typically find wired Ethernet adapters in desktop PCs and all-in-ones, where a permanent wired network connection is appropriate. These adapters can be integrated into the mother-board or installed in an expansion slot and accept RJ45 plugs at either end of shielded network cables. (Most such devices also include a wireless network adapter.)

Most modern wired adapters support the Gigabit Ethernet standard, which allows data transfers at up to 1 gigabit (1,000 megabits) per second. (Older devices might be limited to the Fast Ethernet standard, which transfers data at 100 megabits per second.) In an office or a home that is wired for Ethernet, you can plug your network adapter into a wall jack that connects to a router, hub, or switch at a central location called a *patch panel*. In a home or an office without structured wiring, you need to plug directly into a network device.

Inside OUT

Connect to a wired network using a USB port

If you crave the consistent connection speed and reliability of a wired network but have a portable PC or mobile device that lacks a built-in Ethernet connection, consider invest-ing in a USB network adapter. A USB 2.0 port will support Fast Ethernet speeds, whereas a modern device with a USB 3.0 or USB Type-C port should be capable of Gigabit Ether-net speeds. Some network docking stations and USB hubs include an Ethernet adapter; this option allows you to use a single USB connection for instant access to a wired net-work and other expansion devices while you're at your desk, and use Wi-Fi when you're on the go.

In recent years, wireless networking technology has enjoyed an explosion in popularity. Wireless access points are a standard feature in most home routers and cable modems, and Wi-Fi connections are practically ubiquitous. You can connect to Wi-Fi, often for free, in hotels, trains, buses, ferries, airplanes, and even public parks in addition to the more traditional hotspot locations such as cafés and libraries.

All laptops and mobile devices designed for Windows 10 include a Wi-Fi adapter, which consists of a transceiver and an antenna capable of communicating with a wireless access point. Wireless adapters are also increasingly common in desktop and all-in-one computer designs, allowing them to be used in homes and offices where it is impractical or physically impossible to run network cables.

Ethernet and Wi-Fi are the dominant networking technologies in homes and offices. Alternatives include phone-line networks, which plug into telephone jacks in older homes, and powerline technology, which communicates using adapters that plug into the same AC receptacles you use for power. The availability of inexpensive wireless network gear has relegated phone-line and power-line technologies to niche status; they're most attractive in older homes and offices, where adding network cable is impractical, and wireless networks are unreliable because of distance, building materials, or interference. (A hybrid approach, useful in some environments, allows you to plug a Wi-Fi extender into an existing power line to increase signal strength in a remote location.)

You don't need to rely exclusively on one type of network. If your cable modem includes a router and a wireless access point, you can plug network cables into it and use its wireless signal for mobile devices or for computers located in areas where a network jack isn't available.

Windows 10 detects and configures network hardware automatically, installing drivers from its built-in collection. A wired internet connection should be detected automatically; you're prompted to enter the access key for a wireless connection during the setup process.

CHAPTER 13

NOTE

In this chapter, we assume you have an always-on broadband connection in your home or office or that you're connecting to the internet through a public or private Wi-Fi connection with internet access. Although Windows 10 supports dial-up connections, we do not cover this option.

Checking the status of your network

As we noted earlier, most network connections in Windows 10 should configure themselves automatically during setup. Tools included with Windows 10 allow you to inspect the status of the current connection and either make changes or troubleshoot problems.

The most easily accessible network tool is the status icon that appears by default in the notification area at the right side of the taskbar. Its icon indicates the current network type (wired or wireless) and the status of the network. Click that icon to display the network flyout, which presents options relevant to your type of network connection.

NOTE

A portable computer with no physical Ethernet adapter sometimes shows the icon for a wired connection rather than wireless. That can occur when you have a virtual network adapter set up for virtual machines as well as when you have a USB Ethernet adapter. (For details about virtual network adapters and virtual switches, see Chapter 16, "Hyper-V.")

Figure 13-1 shows the network flyout for a laptop with a wired Ethernet adapter, connected through a docking station, and a connected Wi-Fi adapter. Both networks appear to be operating properly. (A status of Limited, rather than Connected, would indicate problems with the network's ability to connect to the internet.)

Figure 13-1   The network icon in the notification area shown here indicates that the wired connection is the primary connection. The flyout above shows that the system also has a secured Wi-Fi connection.

Every available network is shown on this list, including wired connections and wireless access points that are broadcasting their names. The icon for each available wireless connection indicates its signal strength, with the list ranked in descending order by signal strength.

The three buttons visible at the bottom of the network flyout in Figure 13-1 are available on any device that has a Wi-Fi adapter. Click or tap Wi-Fi to temporarily disable wireless connections. Doing so changes the network flyout as shown in Figure 13-2. By default, Wi-Fi remains disabled until you manually tap the Wi-Fi button again. If you want your Wi-Fi holiday to be temporary, select an alternative option from the Turn Wi-Fi Back On list; you can choose 1 Hour, 4 Hours, or 1 Day.

Figure 13-2   Click the Wi-Fi button to turn the wireless adapter off or back on. By default, you have to do so manually, or you can set a timer under the Turn Wi-Fi Back On menu.

The option to disable Wi-Fi temporarily comes in handy when you're traveling and have access only to a weak wireless signal (which might drain your PC's battery as it repeatedly tries to make a connection), or a paid Wi-Fi option that you've decided is too expensive. Setting a timer allows you to reconnect without having to remember to turn Wi-Fi back on manually.

Clicking or tapping Airplane Mode shuts down all wireless communications, including Wi-Fi, Bluetooth, cellular, GPS, and near field communication (NFC). (You can selectively enable wireless devices by opening Settings > Network & Internet > Airplane Mode.) The third button, available on any device with a Wi-Fi adapter, activates the system as a mobile hotspot. For information about using your device as a mobile hotspot, see "Mobile hotspots and other metered connections," later in this chapter.

A red X or yellow triangle over the network icon means your connection is not working properly. The yellow triangle is Windows 10's way of warning that something's wrong with the connection; a red X usually indicates a more serious problem with the adapter.

Network management tools

As with so many other parts of Windows 10, the knobs and dials and switches that control networking have steadily migrated from the old Control Panel to a home in the modern Settings app. You can find every network setting you need by going to Settings > Network & Internet, where you'll see the clearly organized Status page shown in Figure 13-3. (If you prefer the old-style interface, click the Network And Sharing Center link near the bottom of that page.)

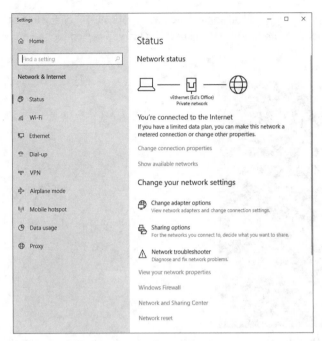

Figure 13-3   You can accomplish just about any network-related task from this starting point in Settings.

NOTE

For slightly faster access to network settings, click the network icon in the notification area, right-click the Network icon, and then click Network & Internet Settings.

The move to the modern Settings app hasn't removed every trace of the old-style Control Panel, however. Clicking Change Adapter Options, for example, leads to the not-so-modern dialog box shown in Figure 13-4. As we explain in the next section, you'll need to visit this page to adjust TCP/IP configuration settings.

We'll get into the details of the other options on this page in the remainder of this chapter.

NOTE

Network adapters that begin with vEthernet are virtual adapters created when you create a virtual switch with Hyper-V. If you've enabled the Application Guard feature in Microsoft Edge (which is also based on Hyper-V virtualization), you'll see an additional virtual adapter named vEthernet (Hvsilcs). Various diagnostic tools will show other virtual adapters used for specialized functions, such as W-Fi Direct connections. In general, we recommend that you avoid trying to manage these adapters manually.

Figure 13-4 This group of settings has not yet shed its old Control Panel look and feel. At some point in the not-too-distant future, expect them to be replaced by equivalent options in the Settings app.

TCP/IP configuration

Transmission Control Protocol/Internet Protocol (TCP/IP) is the default communications protocol of the internet and for modern local area networks; in Windows 10, it's installed and configured automatically and cannot be removed. Most of the time, your TCP/IP connection should just work, without requiring any manual configuration. (We cover some troubleshooting techniques at the end of this chapter.)

Networks that use the TCP/IP protocol rely on *IP addresses* to route packets of data from point to point. On a TCP/IP network, every computer has a unique IP address for each protocol (that is, TCP/IPv4 and TCP/IPv6) in use on each network adapter. An IPv4 address is a 32-bit number that is normally expressed as four 8-bit numbers (each one represented in decimal format by a number from 0 through 255) separated by periods. A 128-bit IPv6 address is usually shown as eight 16-bit numbers (each one represented in hexadecimal format) separated by colons. In addition to the IP address, each computer's TCP/IP configuration has the following additional settings:

- A *subnet mask*, which tells the network how to distinguish between IP addresses that are part of the same network and those that belong to other networks

- A default gateway, which is a computer that routes packets intended for addresses outside the local network

- One or more Domain Name System (DNS) servers, which are computers that translate domain names (such as www.microsoft.com) into IP addresses

CHAPTER 13

Inside OUT

IPv6 and Windows 10

The longer you've worked with Windows, the more likely you are to be familiar with the granddaddy of Windows networking, Internet Protocol version 4, also known as IPv4. A default network connection in Windows 10, wired or wireless, uses IPv4 but also enables the newer IP version 6. IPv6 is on by default and has been the preferred protocol in all desktop and server versions of Windows for over a decade, since the release of Windows Vista.

Without getting into the minutiae of network addressing, suffice it to say that IPv4, with its addresses based on four groups of numbers from 0 to 255, has a big problem. When the internet was young, that address space, consisting of 4.3 billion unique combinations of dotted addresses, like 192.168.1.108 or 10.0.0.242, seemed huge. Unfortunately, nobody anticipated just how big the internet would become, and the authorities who assign IP addresses on the internet have literally run out of IPv4 addresses.

The solution is IPv6, which uses 128-bit addresses and therefore has a maximum address space of 3.4×10^{38} addresses, which we are confident is enough to last for the next few generations of internet users. IPv6 is slowly but surely taking over large swaths of the internet. The giant American internet and cable provider Comcast has fully enabled its network for IPv6, with most of its competition not far behind. Major mobile carriers are also providing the majority of traffic on native IPv6 connections.

Major content providers are enabled for IPv6 as well. You can read about Microsoft's IPv6 efforts at *https://bit.ly/ms-ipv6*. Almost all of Google's services now work over IPv4 and IPv6, as does Yahoo. Facebook's giant data centers now run IPv6 exclusively, and Netflix has supported IPv6 for years.

Windows veterans might be tempted to shy away from IPv6, preferring the more familiar IPv4. In our experience, that's a mistake. IPv6 is here to stay. Learn about it and embrace it.

Windows provides several methods for assigning IP addresses to networked computers:

- **Dynamic Host Configuration Protocol (DHCP).** This is the default configuration for Windows 10. A DHCP server maintains a pool of IP addresses for use by network devices. When you connect to a network, the DHCP server assigns an IP address from this pool and sets subnet masks and other configuration details. Many corporate networks use DHCP to avoid the hassle of managing fixed addresses for constantly changing resources; all versions of Windows Server include this capability. Most routers and residential gateways also incorporate DHCP servers that automatically configure computers connected to those devices.

- **Automatic Private IP Addressing (APIPA).** When no DHCP server is available, Windows automatically assigns an IP address in a specific private IP range. (For an explanation of how private IP addresses work, see the sidebar "Public and private IP addresses" later in the chapter.) If all computers on a subnet are using APIPA addresses, they can communicate with one another without requiring additional configuration. APIPA was introduced with Windows 98 and works the same in all versions of Windows released since that time.

- **Static IP Addressing.** By entering an IP address, subnet mask, and other TCP/IP details in a dialog box, you can manually configure a Windows workstation so that its address is always the same. This method takes more time and can cause some configuration headaches, but it allows a high degree of control over network addresses.

- **Alternate IP Configuration.** Use this feature to specify multiple IPv4 addresses for a single network connection (although only one address can be used at a time). This feature is most useful with portable computers that regularly connect to different networks. You can configure the connection to automatically acquire an IP address from an available DHCP server, and you can then assign a static backup address for use if the first configuration isn't successful.

To see details of your current IP configuration, open Settings > Network & Internet and then, depending on your connection type, click Wi-Fi or Ethernet. Click the name of the current network, at the top of the page, and scroll down to see a compact but information-rich list of network details like those shown here:

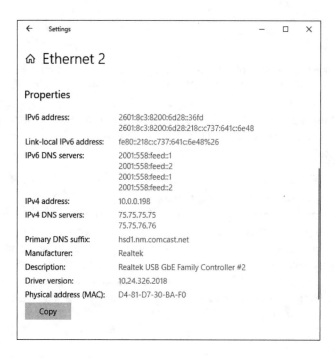

CHAPTER 13

For a more comprehensive view of your network, go to Settings > Network & Internet > Status and click View Your Network Properties. That option shows a far more detailed list of network properties, covering every installed network adapter. Figure 13-5 shows the top of one such list on a Windows 10 PC; you can tell from this display that the IP address was automatically assigned by the DHCP server in a router at IP address 10.0.0.1.

Figure 13-5   This more expansive view of network properties includes details about DHCP servers and link speeds not found in the Properties pages for an individual adapter.

On most home and business networks, IP addresses are assigned automatically by Dynamic DHCP servers; in some cases, you might need (or prefer) to use static IP addresses, which are fixed numeric addresses.

Static IP addresses are useful if you plan to set up a web server, a mail server, a virtual private network (VPN) gateway, or any other computer that needs to be accessible from across the internet. Even inside a local network, behind a router or firewall, static IP addresses can be useful. For instance, you might want to configure the router so that packets entering your network on a specific port get forwarded to a specific computer. If you use DHCP to assign addresses within the local network, you can't be certain that the address of that computer will remain the same over time. But by assigning that computer a static IP address that's within the range of addresses assigned by the DHCP server, you can ensure the computer always has the same address and is thus always reachable.

This procedure works best if you first allow the DHCP server to assign addresses. Open the properties of the connection and make a note of the current settings.

To set a static IP address, follow these steps:

1. Go to Settings > Network & Internet > Status and click Change Adapter Options.

2. In the Network Connections folder, right-click the connection whose settings you want to change and choose Properties.

3. In the list of installed network items, select Internet Protocol Version 4 (TCP/IPv4) or Internet Protocol Version 6 (TCP/IPv6), and then click Properties.

4. In the Internet Protocol (TCP/IP) Properties dialog box, select Use The Following IP Address and fill in the blanks. You must supply an IP address, a subnet mask (for IPv6, the length of the subnet prefix, which is usually 64 bits), and a default gateway.

5. Select Use The Following DNS Server Addresses, and then fill in the numeric IP addresses for one or more DNS servers as well. Figure 13-6 shows the dialog box with all fields filled in.

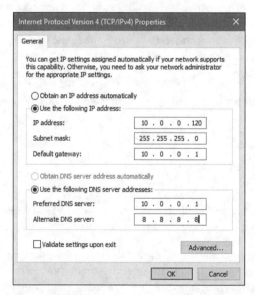

Figure 13-6   When assigning static IP addresses, you must fill in all fields correctly. To avoid making a mistake that could cause you to lose your network connectivity, select Validate Settings Upon Exit.

6. Repeat steps 3-6, if necessary, for an additional protocol, and click OK to save your changes.

CHAPTER 13

PUBLIC AND PRIVATE IP ADDRESSES

Any computer that's directly connected to the internet needs a public IP address—one that can be reached by other computers on the internet—so that information you request (web-pages and email, for instance) can be routed back to your computer properly. When you connect to an internet service provider, you're assigned a public IP address from a block of addresses registered to that ISP. If you use a dial-up connection, your ISP probably assigns a different IP address to your computer (drawn from its pool of available addresses) each time you connect. If you have a persistent connection to your ISP via a DSL or cable modem, your IP address might be permanent—or semipermanent if you turn off your computer when you leave your home or office to travel and your assigned IP address is changed when you reconnect on your return.

On a home or small office network, you don't need to have a public IP address for each computer on the network. In fact, configuring a network with multiple public addresses can increase security risks and often requires an extra fee from your ISP. A safer, less costly solution is to assign a single public IP address to a router or residential gateway (or a computer that performs that function). All other computers on the network connect to the internet through that single address. Each of the computers on the local network has a private IP address that's not directly reachable from the outside world. To communicate with the internet, the router on the edge of the network uses a technology called Network Address Translation (NAT) to pass packets back and forth between the single public IP address and the multiple private IP addresses on the network.

The Internet Assigned Numbers Authority (IANA) has reserved the following three blocks of the IPv4 address space for use on private networks that are not directly connected to the internet:

- 10.0.0.0–10.255.255.255
- 172.16.0.0–172.31.255.255
- 192.168.0.0–192.168.255.255

In addition, the Automatic Private IP Addressing feature in all post-1998 Windows versions uses private IP addresses in the range 169.254.0.0 through 169.254.255.255.

Routers and residential gateways that use NAT almost always assign addresses from these private ranges. Linksys routers, for instance, typically assign addresses starting with 192.168.1.x. If you're setting up a small business or a home network that will not be connected to the internet, or that will be connected through a single proxy server, you can freely use these addresses without concern for conflicts. Just make sure that all the addresses on the network are in the same subnet.

Mobile hotspots and other metered connections

Some devices with data connections on a cellular network allow you to turn the device into a mobile Wi-Fi hotspot—a feature sometimes referred to as *tethering*. This capability is invaluable when you need to get some work done on a portable PC, and an affordable, reliable Wi-Fi connection isn't available. Most modern smartphones, including iPhones and Android devices, can act as a hotspot, although the cellular data provider must allow this capability.

The downside of using a mobile hotspot where you pay by the megabyte or gigabyte is potentially higher costs (especially if you're roaming outside your home network) or the risk that you'll hit your data limit and have your connection throttled or stopped completely. To avoid that possibility, Windows 10 identifies mobile hotspots as metered connections and automatically limits certain types of background activity. By default, the list of restricted activities includes downloads from Windows Update and always-on connections to an Exchange Server connection in Microsoft Outlook.

If Windows 10 doesn't realize that a specific network is on a pay-as-you-go connection, open Settings > Network & Internet > Wi-Fi, and click or tap Manage Known Networks. In the list of networks that appears, tap the one you want to mark as metered, and then tap Properties. Slide the Set As Metered Connection switch to the On position, as shown in Figure 13-7.

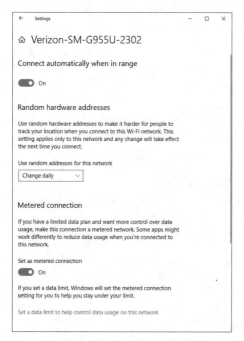

Figure 13-7   On pay-as-you-go networks, you can reduce the amount of data used by telling Windows 10 to treat the connection as metered.

For even more aggressive management of a potentially expensive wireless network, click Set A Data Limit To Help Control Data Usage On This Network. That opens a dialog box where you can set a data limit on a per-connection basis; the limit can apply monthly or on a one-time basis, and you can set the limit to a specific value, expressed in MB or GB.

To see how much data you've used on each connection over the past 30 days, open Settings > Network & Internet > Data Usage. That page shows total data usage over the past 30 days. Click any connection to see that usage broken down on a per-app basis.

Finally, we would be remiss not to note that recent versions of Windows 10 have expanded the Mobile Hotspot feature to support sharing of any network connection on a Windows 10 PC. If you've paid for Wi-Fi on an airplane, for example, you can share that connection securely with up to eight other devices.

You'll find all the options you need by going to Settings > Network & Internet > Mobile Hotspot. There are four settings to pay attention to here.

1. To begin sharing your network connection, flip the Mobile Hotspot switch to the On position.

2. Choose which connection you want to share. In the screenshot shown here, Ethernet is the only option, but you might find yourself in a location where you have multiple connections: wired, Wi-Fi, or even mobile data.

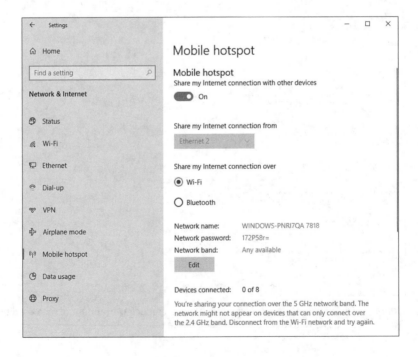

3. Choose how to share your connection: over Wi-Fi or Bluetooth.

4. Click Edit to change the connection name, replace the default random password with one of your own choosing, and customize the type of connection.

With that setup complete, you can turn on your mobile hotspot from the network flyout or from Settings and connect any Wi-Fi- or Bluetooth-capable device (including a mobile phone) to your Windows 10 network connection.

Setting the network location

A desktop PC connected to a wired home or small office network typically remains in a single location. In contrast, mobile devices running Windows 10 can connect to different types of networks—a corporate domain, a wireless hotspot at a coffee shop, or a private home network. Each type of network has its own security requirements. Windows uses network locations to categorize each network and then applies appropriate security settings. When you connect to a new network, Windows applies one of three security settings:

- **Public.** This is the default setting for any new, untrusted network connection. Network discovery is turned off for public networks, and unsolicited incoming connections are blocked, making it more difficult for other people on the same access point to try to connect to your computer. This option is appropriate for networks in public places, such as wireless hotspots in coffee shops, hotels, airports, and libraries. It's also the correct choice if your desktop or laptop PC is directly connected to a cable modem or other broadband connection without the protection of a router and hardware firewall.

- **Private.** This option is appropriate when you're connecting to a trusted network, such as your own network at home—if and only if that network is protected by a router or residential gateway (a consumer device that combines a cable modem, router, and wireless access point in a single box) or comparable internet defense. When you make this choice, Windows enables network discovery for sharing with other users on the network.

- **Domain.** This option is applied automatically when you sign in to Windows using a computer that's joined to a Windows domain, such as your company network. In this scenario, network discovery is enabled, allowing you to see other computers and servers on the network by using accounts and permissions controlled by a network administrator.

➤ If you have a mobile computer that connects to multiple networks, keep in mind that the Windows Defender Firewall maintains separate network security profiles for private (home or work), public, and domain-based networks. For more information about Windows Firewall, see Chapter 18, "Blocking intruders with Windows Defender Firewall."

The location of the current network is shown on the Network Status page, below the name of the network. (See Figure 13-3 earlier in this chapter.)

To change the profile of a wireless network from Public to Private, or vice versa, go to Settings > Network & Internet and click Wi-Fi. Click or tap the icon under the Wi-Fi switch to open the properties page for the active connection, shown in Figure 13-8. If you're using a version earlier than version 1709, your choice here serves the same purpose, but the wording is not as clear: When Make This PC Discoverable is Off, the network is public. Slide the switch to On to make the network private.

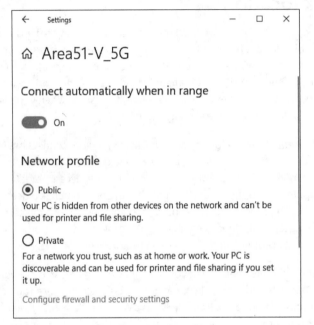

Figure 13-8   A PC on a Private network is "discoverable," and it's safe for other PCs and network devices to connect to this computer. When you set the network location to Public, outside access is blocked.

The procedure on a wired network is the same; click Ethernet to select the connection and toggle the network profile. Note, however, that the option to change a wired network from Private to Public might not be available in some managed configurations. In those cases, you can use the PowerShell commands **Get-NetConnectionProfile** and **Set-NetConnectionProfile**, which are documented at *https://docs.microsoft.com/powershell/module/netconnection*.

Inside OUT

Workgroups vs. domains

Computers on a network can be part of a workgroup or a domain.

In a workgroup, the security database for each computer (including, most significantly, the list of user accounts and the privileges granted to each one) resides on that computer. When you sign in to a computer in a workgroup, Windows checks its local security database to see whether you provided a user name and password that matches one in the database. Similarly, when network users attempt to connect to your computer, Windows again consults the local security database. All computers in a workgroup must be on the same subnet. A workgroup is sometimes called a *peer-to-peer network*.

By contrast, a domain consists of computers that share a security infrastructure, Active Directory, which in turn is managed on one or more domain controllers running Windows Server. Microsoft's cloud-based alternative, Azure Active Directory, provides a subset of this infrastructure without requiring IT departments to manage local servers. Active Directory and Azure Active Directory can be combined to create effective hybrid environments. When you sign in using a domain account, Windows authenticates your credentials against the security database defined by your network administrator.

In this chapter (and throughout this book), we focus primarily on workgroup networks.

CHAPTER 13

Connecting to a wireless network

In this section, we assume you have already configured a wireless access point (often included as a feature in cable modems and DSL adapters supplied by your broadband provider) and confirmed that it is working correctly, or that you are in a location with a public or private wireless access point managed by someone else.

Whenever your computer's wireless network adapter is installed and turned on, Windows scans for available wireless access points. If it finds at least one (and you're not already connected to a wireless network), it alerts you via the wireless network icon, which looks a bit like an antenna. If you see a bright dot at the end of an otherwise gray antenna, connections are available.

Unless you're out in the country, far from civilization, you're likely to see lots of access points available for connection, most of them owned by your neighbors or nearby visitors. Assuming those networks are adequately secured with a network security key you don't know and can't guess, you'd have no luck connecting to them.

Clicking or tapping the entry for a secure wireless access point that doesn't have a saved connection displays a check box asking whether you want to connect automatically to that network in the future. If this is a place you expect to visit again (or in the case of a coffee shop, again and again, and again...), select that box and click Connect to enter and save your credentials. Note that saved Wi-Fi network security keys are synced between devices when you sign in with a Microsoft account, so you might find that a brand-new device, one you've never used before, automatically connects to your home or office Wi-Fi without having to ask you.

Clicking the Connect button for a secure wireless access point reveals a box in which you're expected to enter a passphrase, as in Figure 13-9. If what you enter matches what's stored in the access point's configuration, you're in. Getting in is easy on a network you control, where you set the network security key. For a secured access point controlled by someone else—a doctor's waiting room, a coffee shop, a friend's office—you need to ask someone, typically the network owner, for the passphrase or key.

Figure 13-9   Connecting to a secure network for the first time requires that you correctly enter a passphrase or security key.

To disconnect from a Wi-Fi access point, click or tap its entry in the network flyout and then tap Disconnect. Doing so automatically turns off the option to connect automatically to that network in the future.

Windows 10 saves credentials for every Wi-Fi access point you connect to, giving you the option to connect with a tap when you revisit. If that thought makes you uncomfortable, you can see and manage the full list of networks by opening Settings > Network & Internet > Wi-Fi and clicking Manage Known Networks. That list can be startlingly long, especially if you're a frequent traveler. Tap any name in the list (use the search box if the list is long and you want to find a specific saved network), and you'll see two buttons, as in Figure 13-10. Tap Properties to view information about the network and turn off the option to connect automatically, as shown earlier in Figure 13-7. Tap the Forget button to delete any saved security information and remove the network name from the list. (In Windows 10 version 1709 and later, the Properties and Forget buttons are also available for any nearby Wi-Fi networks: Open the network flyout and click any visible network to see those options.)

Figure 13-10   Wireless networks you connect to are saved in this list. Tap Forget to delete the saved security key and remove the network from the list.

Inside OUT

Decoding Wi-Fi standards

The most popular wireless networks use one of several variants of the IEEE (Institute of Electrical and Electronics Engineers) 802.11 standard, also known as Wi-Fi. On modern Wi-Fi networks, you're likely to encounter one of the following four standards (going from oldest to newest):

- **802.11g.** This standard was current up until 2009, just before the release of Windows 7. It's still in use on some older PCs and wireless access points. It can transfer data at a maximum rate of 54 megabits per second using radio frequencies in the 2.4-GHz range. 802.11g-based networks largely supplanted those based on an earlier standard, 802.11b, which offers a maximum speed of 11 megabits per second.

- **802.11n.** Using this standard, adopted in 2009, you can expect to see dramatic improvements in speed (600 megabits per second) as well as significantly greater range. Unlike the earlier standards, the 802.11n standard allows use of the 5-Ghz frequency range as well as 2.4 GHz. However, not all 802.11n hardware supports both bands.

- **802.11ac.** Also known as Wi-Fi 5, this standard was finalized in 2014 and builds on the 802.11n specification. It allows multiple links at both ends of the wireless connection, advertising throughput rates of 500 megabits per second per link, with a theoretical maximum speed of up to 2,600 megabits per second.

- **802.11ax.** As of late 2018, this standard had not yet been finalized. It promises greater efficiency and theoretical maximum speeds of 11 gigabits per second.

For the maximum throughput, use 5-Ghz 802.11ac devices throughout your network. The 5-Ghz band is subject to less radio interference than 2.4 Ghz and is capable of a higher maximum theoretical data rate. If you must maintain compatibility with older 2.4-Ghz devices, the ideal solution is to use a dual-band wireless access point.

Connecting to a hidden network

Every wireless network has a name, formally known as a *service set identifier* but typically referred to as an *SSID*. In an effort to enforce security through obscurity, some wireless networks are set up so that they don't broadcast their SSID. Connecting to such a hidden network is a bit more challenging because its name doesn't appear in the list of available networks on the network flyout or in Network & Internet Settings. Making such a connection is possible, however, as long as you know the network name and its security settings.

NOTE

Configuring a router so that it doesn't advertise its name has been incorrectly promoted by some as a security measure. Although it does make the network less accessible to casual snoops, lack of a broadcast SSID is no deterrent to a knowledgeable attacker. Furthermore, attackers can learn the SSID even when they're not near your wireless access point because it's periodically broadcast from your computer, wherever it happens to be. We provide these steps to help you connect to a hidden network managed by someone else; we don't recommend that you configure your home or office network in this fashion without a good reason.

If one or more nearby networks aren't broadcasting their SSID, scroll to the bottom of the network flyout and choose Hidden Network from the list of available networks. Click or tap that entry, enter the correct SSID, and click Connect. After passing that test, you can enter the passphrase or security key to complete the connection.

To configure settings for a network that isn't in range so that you can connect to it automatically when you arrive at the location where it's available, open the Manage Known Networks list, shown earlier in Figure 13-10, and click Add. That opens a dialog box like the one shown in Figure 13-11. This example illustrates how to connect to a corporate network using the 802.11x standard, which requires user-level authentication rather than shared keys or passphrases.

Figure 13-11   Click the Add button at the top of the list of known networks to manually add a wireless network, such as this secure corporate network, that is not in range.

Wireless security

On a conventional wired network, especially in a private home or office, physical security is reasonably easy to maintain: If someone plugs a computer into a network jack or a switch, you can trace the physical wire back to the intruder's computer. On wireless networks, however, anyone who comes into range of your wireless access point can tap into your network and intercept signals from it.

If you run a small business, you might want to allow internet access to your customers by using an open internet connection. Some internet service providers create secure guest accounts on their customers' cable modems that allow other customers of that service to connect using their network credentials.

Other than those scenarios, however, you probably want to secure your network so that the only people who can connect to it are those you specifically authorize. Doing that means configuring security settings on your wireless access point or router. When you connect to a network, known or unknown, the level of security is determined by the encryption standard chosen by the network owner and supported by network hardware on both sides of the connection.

Depending on the age of your hardware, you should have a choice of one or more of the following options, listed in order of preference:

- **Wi-Fi Protected Access 2 (WPA2).** Based on the 802.11i standard, WPA2 provides the strongest protection for consumer-grade wireless networks. It uses 802.1x-based authentication and Advanced Encryption Standard (AES) encryption; combined, these technologies ensure that only authorized users can access the network and that any intercepted data cannot be deciphered. WPA2 comes in two flavors: WPA2-Personal and WPA2-Enterprise. *WPA2-Personal* uses a passphrase to create its encryption keys and is currently the best available security for wireless networks in homes and small offices. *WPA2-Enterprise* requires a server to verify network users. All wireless products sold since early 2006 must support WPA2 to bear the Wi-Fi CERTIFIED label.

- **Wi-Fi Protected Access (WPA).** WPA is an earlier version of the encryption scheme that has since been replaced by WPA2. It was specifically designed to overcome weaknesses of WEP. On a small network that uses WPA, clients and access points use a shared network password (called a *preshared key*, or *PSK*) that consists of a 256-bit number or a passphrase that is from 8 to 63 bytes long. (A longer passphrase produces a stronger key.) With a sufficiently strong key based on a truly random sequence, the likelihood of a successful outside attack is slim. Most modern network hardware supports WPA only for backward compatibility.

- **Wired Equivalent Privacy (WEP).** WEP is a first-generation scheme that dates back before the turn of the century. It suffers from serious security flaws that make it inappropriate for use on any network that contains sensitive data. Most modern Wi-Fi equipment supports WEP for backward compatibility with older hardware, but we strongly advise against using it unless no other options are available.

You might see other encryption options, including the 802.11x standard, which allows corporate networks to enforce access through user credentials such as Active Directory. Those configurations are typically designed for use on large enterprise networks and are beyond the scope of this book.

Inside OUT

Beef up security at the access point

If your data is sensitive and your network is in an apartment building or an office complex where you can reasonably expect other people to wander into range with wireless adapters, you should take extra security precautions in addition to enabling WPA. Consider any or all the following measures to protect your wireless access point from intruders:

- Change the network name (SSID) of your access point to one that doesn't match the hardware defaults and doesn't give away any information about you or your business.

- Disable remote administration of the access point; if you need to change settings, you can do so directly, using a wired connection.

- Whether you decide to allow remote administration of the access point or not, set a strong password so that a visitor can't tamper with your network settings.

- Check the firmware and drivers for wireless hardware (access points and adapters) at regular intervals and install the most recent versions, which might incorporate security fixes.

- Consider using a virtual private network (VPN) for wireless connections. A VPN sends all wireless traffic over an encrypted connection, making it impossible for others to snoop on your wireless traffic. Corporate network administrators can help set up a VPN using your company's security infrastructure. For unmanaged Windows 10 devices, VPN software and services are available.

When setting up a wireless access point for a home or small office, choose a strong passphrase. A passphrase for WPA or WPA2 can be up to 63 characters long and can contain letters (case-sensitive), numbers, and spaces (no spaces at the beginning or end, however). Many devices generate a random alphanumeric key, but you might prefer to use a memorable phrase instead of random characters. If you do, choose a phrase that's not easily guessed, and make it long. Also, consider incorporating letter substitution or misspellings to thwart attackers. Because the phrase can be saved and synced between devices, you shouldn't need to enter it often.

CHAPTER 13

You must use the same encryption option on all wireless devices on your network—access points, routers, network adapters, print servers, cameras, and so on—so choose the best option that's supported by all your devices. If you have an older device that supports only WEP (and it can't be upgraded with a firmware update), consider retiring or replacing that device.

Using Hotspot 2.0

Today, wireless hotspots are nearly ubiquitous at airports, hotels, coffee shops, fast-food restaurants, and many other places. In most cases, you use the same procedure to connect to one of these networks as you do to connect to your own Wi-Fi network.

The original version of Windows 10 also included support for easier wireless connections. Using these tools promised internet access in additional locations, at greater convenience, and for lower costs than the public Wi-Fi hotspots you find at airports, hotels, and so on.

Two Windows 10–supported alternative wireless connections that we described in earlier editions of this book—Wi-Fi Sense and Paid Wi-Fi—have been discontinued. A third, Hotspot 2.0, continues to be supported as of late 2018.

Hotspot 2.0 (which also goes by the names *HS2* and *Wi-Fi Certified Passport*) is designed to make Wi-Fi connection effortless *and* secure. Based on the 802.11u Wi-Fi standard, all Hotspot 2.0 networks use WPA2-Enterprise security. Once you enroll in Hotspot 2.0 and download a profile, your computer automatically connects to a secure Wi-Fi hotspot when you're in range.

To use Hotspot 2.0, your device must support it. To confirm that it does, open a command prompt window and type

```
netsh wlan show wirelesscapabilities
```

If ANQP Service Information Discovery is shown as Supported, you're good to go.

Next, you need to set up an account with a Hotspot 2.0 provider and download the profile. Start by going to Settings > Network & Internet > Wi-Fi, and turn on Let Me Use Online Sign-Up To Get Connected (below the Hotspot 2.0 Networks heading). When you're in range of a Hotspot 2.0 network, Windows displays a list of providers for online sign-up. Follow the provider's instructions for creating an account and installing the profile.

Thereafter, whenever you're near a Hotspot 2.0 access point, your device automatically and seamlessly connects to the network. Because Hotspot 2.0 uses a certificate installed as part of the profile as your login credential, you won't need to enter a user name or password to get online securely.

Transferring pictures, links, and other items between nearby devices

Not everything in Windows networking is a holdover from bygone days. An important new feature, Nearby Sharing, allows you to transfer files, pictures, and videos between two devices running Windows 10 version 1803 or later. In addition, you can share links to web pages, from Microsoft Edge or from non-Microsoft browsers that include an extension to add links to the

Windows Timeline. Both devices can be yours, allowing you to quickly move files between a laptop and desktop PC, for example. Or, with your express permission, you can transfer files or share a web link with someone else. The recipient sees a prompt to accept the shared item and has to accept the transfer request. Both computers must have Bluetooth, and both must be running Windows 10 version 1803 or later. Additionally, they must be within Bluetooth range—typically about 30 feet—to allow easy discovery of other devices eligible for sharing.

Nearby Sharing is disabled by default. To enable it, open Settings > System > Shared Experiences and turn on Nearby Sharing. See Figure 13-12.

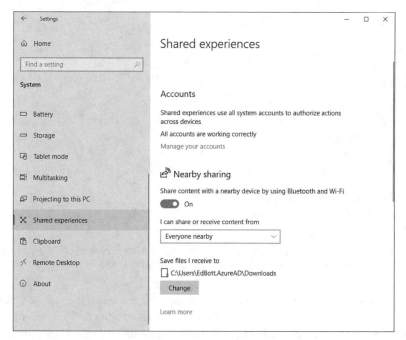

Figure 13-12   Using Nearby Sharing, you can limit transfers to your own devices or enable sharing with everyone nearby—with your permission and theirs, of course.

Under the heading I Can Share Or Receive Content From, you have two choices: Everyone Nearby and My Devices Only. With the second option selected, you can share or receive files only between devices on which you've connected a matching Microsoft account.

By default, files you receive are stored in your profile's Downloads folder. To specify a different destination folder, click Change.

With Nearby Sharing turned on, you can send one or more files, photos, or videos, or a web page link, to another device from any app that supports the Share feature in Windows 10. In File Explorer, right-click a file and choose Share from the shortcut menu, or select multiple items and click Share, on the Share tab. In Microsoft Edge, click Share to send a link to the current page. In the Photos app, open a photo or video or select multiple items from your photo collection and click Share. Devices that are available to receive shared files appear in the center of the Share tab, below your contacts, as shown in Figure 13-13.

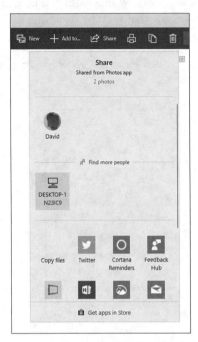

Figure 13-13   Nearby Windows 10 devices that are eligible to receive shared files appear in the center of this pane. Click the computer icon to send a transfer request to that PC.

On the device you've selected to share the items with, a sharing invitation appears above the notification area. (If it disappears too quickly for you to react, open the Action Center to retrieve it.) Figure 13-14 shows a notification for a screenshot, captured with the Snip & Save tool. As the intended recipient, you can decline the request, save the file in the default folder, or save the file and open it as soon as the download is complete.

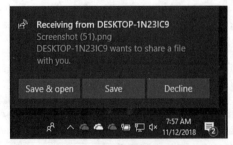

Figure 13-14   When you share files, photos or videos, you have the option to open them as soon as the transfer is complete. For links to web pages, the only options are Open and Decline.

The Nearby Sharing feature assumes that both the sender and the recipient of the shared item are in close physical proximity and ready to act promptly. The pop-out notification remains visible for about five seconds; if you don't respond within 20 seconds or so, the action is canceled on the sharing device.

Connecting to another computer with Remote Desktop

Sharing computer resources over a network, when properly configured, gives you access to all the files you might need, wherever they're stored. But sometimes even that's not enough. You might need to run a program that's installed only on another computer, or you might need to configure and manage another computer's files and settings in ways that can be done only by sitting down in front of that computer. For those occasions, a Remote Desktop session is the perfect solution.

With Remote Desktop, applications run on the remote computer; your computer is effectively used as a dumb terminal. You can use a low-powered computer or even a mobile device to connect to a remote computer directly. Remote Desktop connections are encrypted, so your information is secure.

NOTE

The computer that you want to control—the one at the remote location—is called the *remote computer*. The computer you want to use to control the remote computer is called the *client computer*. By default, Remote Desktop traffic is sent and received using Remote Desktop Protocol (RDP) over TCP port 3389.

In this section, we focus on the most common scenario: configuring a PC running Windows 10 Pro, Enterprise, or Education or any supported version of Windows Server to allow incoming Remote Desktop connections and using a second PC running any edition of Windows 10 as the remote client over a local network. (PCs running Windows Home edition can be used as a Remote Desktop client but do not allow hosting Remote Desktop sessions.)

Inside OUT

Configuring Remote Desktop connections from outside your local network

Remote Desktop connections are relatively easy over a local network, especially when no third-party security software is installed. But trying to connect to Remote Desktop over the internet is far more problematic. To make that long-distance connection through the internet, you must be able to reach the remote computer by using a known public IP address, and you have to get through a router and past any security software between the two computers.

CHAPTER 13

The solutions to these issues depend on your specific hardware configuration. In broad strokes, they require configuring your Remote Desktop client to connect to the external IP address on your router and then configuring your router to pass traffic on port 3389 to the internal IP address of the Remote Desktop server. Then, of course, you have to worry about whether your broadband provider will change your external IP address. If you're a networking expert, those general guidelines should give you all the information you need to set up your remote session over the internet.

If, on the other hand, you're not a networking expert, that probably sounds like more trouble than it's worth. We agree, which is why we suggest instead using any of several third-party programs that can securely provide remote access without the hassles or security risks of allowing direct connections through your network boundary. We recommend Splashtop Business Access (*https://www.splashtop.com/business*), which offers an excellent feature set at a fraction of the cost of some better-known commercial packages.

Installing Remote Desktop client software

Windows 10 includes a desktop program for remote access called Remote Desktop Connection. Although this program's feature set and appearance have remained largely unchanged since its debut nearly 20 years ago, it's still perfectly suitable for remote connections. If you're sitting in front of a PC running Windows 7, you can use this app to connect to a Windows 10 PC configured as a Remote Desktop Server.

A newer alternative, called Microsoft Remote Desktop, is available in the Microsoft Store. (To see its listing, go to *https://aka.ms/urdc*.) This Universal Windows Platform app works on a wide variety of Windows 10 device types, and it includes some capabilities not available in Remote Desktop Connection. In this section, we describe how to use both programs.

And even if you don't have a PC available, you might still be able to connect to a Remote Desktop server using a non-Windows device. Microsoft has Remote Desktop clients for mobile devices running iOS and Android as well as Apple-branded PCs running MacOS. For download links and installation instructions, see *http://bit.ly/remote-desktop-clients*.

Enabling inbound remote desktop connections

For security reasons, incoming Remote Desktop sessions are not allowed without your explicit permission. To grant access on a computer running Windows 10 Pro, Enterprise, or Education, go to Settings > System > Remote Desktop and slide the Enable Remote Desktop switch to the On position. (You must be signed in using an administrator account to make this change, and you must confirm the configuration change in a separate step.)

Enabling Remote Desktop starts a service that listens for incoming connections on port 3389. It also creates an exception in Windows Firewall that allows authenticated traffic on this port. (If you're using third-party security software that includes a firewall, you need to configure it to allow incoming access to TCP port 3389.)

With that step out of the way, the current user account and any user account that's a member of the local Administrators group can connect remotely to the computer. To allow access for other user accounts that are not members of the local Administrators group, click Select Users That Can Remotely Access This PC and add the accounts.

Using the Remote Desktop app

As we noted earlier, Remote Desktop is a UWP app that's not included with Windows; it is, however, available as a free download from the Store. Remote Desktop offers several features not found in Remote Desktop Connection. Its visual approach shows all your remote connections on the home screen, allowing you to open one with a single click or tap. In addition, Remote Desktop includes several performance enhancements that optimize your connection quality. It supports multiple instances, so you can operate two or more Remote Desktop sessions simultaneously, each in its own window. And, of course, as a modern app, it's touch friendly.

The Remote Desktop app window is downright Spartan until you've saved a desktop or two. Adding a desktop takes minimal effort: Click the Add (+) button and then click Desktop. Add A Desktop appears in the right pane, as shown in Figure 13-15. Enter the name or IP address of the PC to which you want to connect, and then click Save to add its tile on the left side of the app window.

> ### NOTE
>
> When you click Add, Remote Desktop also offers the option to connect to "remote resources," which are server-based apps used by some large organizations. Visit *https:// bit.ly/remoteresources* for more information on this feature, which we do not cover here.

All the other fields in the Add A Desktop pane are optional. By default, the User Account field is set to Ask Me Every Time. In this configuration, you're prompted for your user name and password each time you connect to the desktop. If you know you'll always want to use the same account, you can add its credentials here, and Remote Desktop will sign you in every time without prompting. Click the arrow at the right side to select a previously configured user account. If the account you want to use doesn't appear in the list, click the plus sign above the User Account box and add the necessary details.

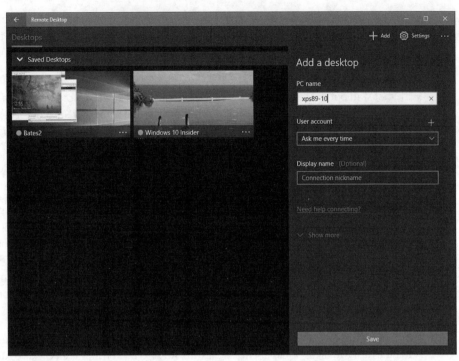

Figure 13-15   In the PC Name box, you can specify the remote computer by name or IP address.

In addition to those two settings, you can save a handful of other parameters, including some that come into view when you click Show More:

- **Display Name.** Provide a friendly descriptive name that appears under the icon for a remote computer in the main Remote Desktop window instead of the PC name or IP address.

- **Group.** If you have multiple saved connections, you can group them by adding a group name and then selecting a group for each connection.

- **Gateway.** To reach a remote desktop through a gateway server on a corporate network, specify its name or IP address, along with the name of a user account with access permission.

- **Connect To Admin Session.** For connecting to a computer running Windows 10, this option has no effect, and you can safely ignore it. It enables administrative access on some older Windows Server configurations.

- **Swap Mouse Buttons.** This option is appropriate for left-handed individuals who have used Settings > Devices > Mouse to set the primary mouse button as Right instead of

Left. Enabling this setting swaps the functionality of the left and right mouse buttons while you work in the remote desktop session to match the local settings.

- **Display Settings.** These settings let you specify a screen resolution and display size for the remote desktop. If you don't specify a resolution here, Remote Desktop uses the resolution of the client computer, displayed full screen, by default. After selecting a custom resolution, you can also choose a custom scaling factor.

- **Update The Remote Session Resolution On Resize.** With this setting on, you can resize a Remote Desktop session in a window and have the display resolution adjust to your changes.

- **Local Resources.** The three settings under this heading allow you to share the client computer's Clipboard contents and microphone with the remote computer and choose whether audio plays on the remote computer, on the client computer, or on neither.

Working in a Remote Desktop session

After you save a connection in the Add A Desktop pane, an icon for that connection appears in Remote Desktop. Click the icon to open a connection to the remote computer. Along the way, you might encounter a couple of obstacles:

- If you specified Ask Me Every Time in the User Account box, Remote Desktop asks for the user name and password of an account authorized on the remote computer to make a connection. Select Remember Me, and you won't need to enter this information in future sessions.

- By default, Remote Desktop sessions you create on your local network use self-hosted digital certificates that aren't recognized as trusted by the client computer. If you're certain that you're connecting to the right computer, select the Don't Ask About This Certificate Again check box (so you won't be bothered in future sessions) and click Connect.

After bounding past those hurdles, Remote Desktop attempts to open a connection. If the account you use for the remote connection is already signed in to the remote computer—or if no one is signed in to the remote computer—the remote computer's desktop then appears on your computer.

If a different user account is signed in to the remote computer, Windows lets you know that you'll be forcing that person to sign out and gives you a chance to cancel the connection. On the other end, the signed-in user sees a similar notification that offers a short time to reject the remote connection before it takes over. Note that only one user at a time can control the desktop of a computer running Windows. Whoever is currently signed in has the final say on whether someone else can sign in.

CHAPTER 13

While you're connected to the remote computer, the local display on that computer (if it's turned on) does not show what you see on the client computer but instead shows the lock screen. A person who has physical access to the remote computer can't see what you're doing (other than the fact that you're signed in remotely).

When you connect to a remote computer using the UWP Remote Desktop app without specifying a custom resolution, the remote computer takes over your entire screen using the resolution of the client computer. At the top of the screen, in the center, a tiny toolbar with two controls appears. Click the magnifying glass icon to zoom the remote display; click the ellipsis (three dots) icon to reveal two buttons in the upper-right corner, as shown here.

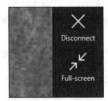

Click Disconnect to end your remote session. The remote computer remains locked, ready for someone to sign in locally. Click Full Screen to toggle between full-screen and windowed views of the remote desktop.

While the display is in full-screen mode, you can move the mouse pointer to the top edge of the screen to display the Remote Desktop title bar. It includes the usual window controls (minimize, resize, and close). Move the mouse pointer to the bottom edge of the screen to display the task-bar for your local computer. Clicking any icon on the local taskbar shifts the focus away from the remote session and back to your local computer. If you're running the Remote Desktop app on a touchscreen-equipped PC, you can reveal either of these controls by swiping in from the top or bottom edge of the screen.

Ending a remote session

When you're through with a Remote Desktop session, you can lock, sign out, or disconnect. If the remote computer is running Windows 10, you'll find these options in the usual places where comparable options appear on your local computer, Lock and Sign Out appear when you click the user avatar on Start on the remote computer, and Disconnect appears when you click Power on Start. For remote machines running earlier Windows versions, these options appear in the lower-right corner of the remote session's Start menu. (You must click the arrow to see all the options.)

Locking the computer keeps the remote session connected and all programs running, but it hides everything behind a sign-in screen that requests a password; this is comparable to pressing Windows key+L to lock your computer.

Signing out closes all your programs, exits your user session, and disconnects.

If you disconnect without signing out, your programs continue to run on the remote computer, but the connection is ended. The sign-in screen is visible on the remote computer, and it's available for another user. If you sign in later—either locally or through a remote connection—you can pick up right where you left off. As an alternative to the Start commands, you can disconnect by clicking the Disconnect button, displaying the Remote Desktop title bar and clicking the Back button, or simply closing the Remote Desktop window.

Adjusting Remote Desktop app settings

At the top of the Remote Desktop app window, to the right of the Add button, is a Settings button that exposes a pane filled with options to customize the app experience. Here, you can edit credentials for saved user accounts, for example; to remove a user account, choose a user name from the list, click the pen icon above the name, and then click the faint Remove This Account link at the bottom of the Edit An Account pane.

Other settings on this list that are potentially useful include a Start Connections In Full Screen switch, which you should turn off if you prefer to run remote sessions in a window, as well as a Prevent The Screen From Timing Out switch that can reduce the annoyance of having to sign back in if you leave an open session to work on other tasks.

Using Remote Desktop Connection

Remote Desktop Connection is a desktop app that should be familiar to longtime Windows users accustomed to remote administration tasks. To start it, in the search box, type **remote** and then click Remote Desktop Connection, or enter its command directly: Mstsc.exe (that name is a holdover from the olden days and is short for Microsoft Terminal Services Connection). A dialog box like the one shown in Figure 13-16 appears. In the Computer box, type the name of the remote computer or its IP address. If you've previously used the app, the last connection will be visible, and a drop-down list will show PCs you previously connected to.

Figure 13-16   You can specify the remote computer by name or IP address.

NOTE

Both the Windows 10 Remote Desktop app and Remote Desktop Connection support the use of Jump Lists. If you pin either icon to Start or the taskbar and save credentials, you can right-click to choose saved PCs from the Jump List to go straight to a remote session.

After entering the PC name, you can click Connect and begin the process of connecting to the remote PC immediately. As with the UWP Remote Desktop app (described in the preceding section), Windows warns if your connection will knock off another user who's signed in to the remote computer and gives that user veto power over your connection request.

Changing screen resolutions and display settings

When you make a default connection, the display from the remote computer fills your entire screen, using the resolution of the client computer. Along the top of the screen, in the center, a small title bar appears. This title bar, dubbed the *connection bar* in Remote Desktop Connection, lets you switch between your own desktop and the remote desktop. The Minimize, Maximize, and Restore buttons work as they do in other programs:

The pushpin button locks the connection bar in place. If you click the pushpin to unlock the connection bar, it disappears completely, retracting into the top of the screen. To make the connection bar reappear, "bump" the mouse pointer to the top edge of the screen. To keep the connection bar visible at all times, click the pushpin again. The Close button disconnects the remote computer (but does not sign you out of the remote computer) and closes Remote Desktop Connection. You can pick up where you left off by reopening Remote Desktop Connection and reconnecting or by signing in locally at the remote computer.

> ## Inside OUT
>
> *Move the connection bar*
>
> If the connection bar covers a part of the screen you need to see, you can slide it left or right to reveal whatever's hidden underneath.

You might prefer to use less than your full screen resolution for the remote desktop. (This option is especially useful if you have a large monitor and the work you want to do with Remote Desktop is just another task among several.) You must set the resolution—along with a number of other options—before you connect to the remote computer. After you start Remote Desktop Connection, click the Show Options button (shown previously in Figure 13-12) to expand the dialog box. Then click the Display tab, which is shown in Figure 13-17. You can set the screen resolution to any size that's supported on the client hardware. Set it to full screen by moving the slider all the way to the right.

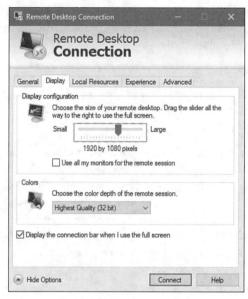

Figure 13-17   Use this slider to adjust the screen resolution when running a Remote Desktop session in a window instead of a full screen.

Remote Desktop Connection allows the use of multiple monitors, as long as the remote computer is running Windows 7 or later. To configure the connection for use with more than one monitor on the client software, select Use All My Monitors For The Remote Session.

Configuring other remote options

The Remote Desktop Connection client software offers a wide range of additional configuration options. We won't go through every tab, but here are a few options that you might find useful:

- **Saved credentials.** On the General tab, you can enter a user name and then select the Allow Me To Save Credentials check box. After you save credentials (in encrypted form, of course), they're entered automatically, allowing you to connect without extra steps. You'll find Edit and Delete buttons to manage saved credentials on the main Remote Desktop dialog box, as shown earlier in Figure 13-15.

- **Local Resources.** On the expanded connection dialog box, click the Local Resources tab to select whether you want to access printers connected to the local computer, whether you want the Clipboard contents to be shared between the local and remote session, and how you want remote audio handled.

- **Performance.** You'll find performance-related options on the Experience tab of the Remote Desktop Connection dialog box. If you're using a slow, bandwidth-challenged, or metered connection, you should disable as many features as possible to reduce the amount of information that must be transmitted across the wire and keep the mouse and windows movements responsive. On the other hand, if you're connecting to another desktop over a fast local area network, you might as well enable all features to enjoy the full experience of working at the remote computer.

Inside OUT

Use your pen in Remote Desktop Connection

In addition to keyboard, mouse, and touch input, if your client computer supports the use of a pen or stylus, you can use it in a Remote Desktop session. You won't see pens mentioned on the Local Resources tab because no configuration is required. You need to have Windows 10 or Windows Server 2016 on the remote computer and the client computer. You can use this feature to add handwriting and other drawings even if the remote computer has no built-in pen capability. You can use the full pen capabilities of the local computer; for example, pens that vary in line width based on the pressure you apply to the screen can use this feature on remote documents.

Saving a Remote Desktop configuration

Changes you make in the expanded Remote Desktop Connection dialog box are automatically saved in a hidden file named Default.rdp (stored in your default save location for documents), and they're used the next time you open Remote Desktop Connection. But you might want to have several different Remote Desktop Connection configurations for connections to different computers. If you have a portable computer, you might want different settings for use with different connections to the same computer (for example, a slow Wi-Fi connection from a hotel versus a fast LAN at your branch office).

To save a configuration, after you make all your settings, click the General tab, and click Save As.

To reuse a stored configuration at a later time, start Remote Desktop Connection, click Show Options, click Open, and then double-click the stored file. More simply, select it from the Jump List for Remote Desktop Connection (on the taskbar or Start menu), or double-click the stored file in File Explorer.

Sharing files, printers, and other resources over a local network

Much of the networking infrastructure of Windows 10 is a refinement of features that were developed decades ago, when the Internet was still an interesting experiment. Today, the simplest way to share files, digital media, and other resources, even between computers in the same home or office, is through a cloud-based service like OneDrive. There are, however, still valid reasons for Windows PCs to connect and share resources across a local area network.

These traditional networking tools and techniques are fully supported in Windows 10, and you can use them alongside OneDrive sharing if you want to. The underlying system of share permissions and NTFS permissions for controlling access to objects remains in Windows 10, working much like it has in previous versions of Windows going all the way back to Windows NT in the early '90s. That's our starting point for this section.

Inside Out

What happened to HomeGroup?

The HomeGroup feature, originally introduced as part of Windows 7 and maintained through Windows 10 version 1709, allowed Windows devices to share resources on a home network. Alas, as of version 1803, HomeGroup is gone.

You need not shed any tears, however. HomeGroup was developed at a time when a major computing challenge, particularly for users of small home networks, was sharing files stored on a network computer. In the years since, cloud storage services such as OneDrive have become a convenient, safe way to store your files in a way that allows you to access them from any device on any platform. But they have also evolved as a collaboration platform and now provide an easy, secure way to share your files, photos, and videos with other users—whether they're in the next room or across the country. (For details, see "Using OneDrive to store, sync, and share files" in Chapter 9, "Storage and file management.")

If you don't want to use OneDrive or a similar service, you can still use the network sharing capabilities built in to Windows to share files. The difference now—and the reason HomeGroup is no longer needed—is that Windows networking supports the use of Microsoft accounts. It's no longer necessary to create identical local user accounts on each computer in order to share.

Another benefit of HomeGroup was the ability to share a printer with other network users. Here, too, time and technological progress have made that feature irrelevant. Today, you have a choice of feature-packed home printers that can connect directly to any PC via Wi-Fi, with no network fussiness required. And even for USB-connected printers, the availability of standard credentials means printing is no longer painful.

CHAPTER 13

NOTE

Beginning with version 1803, Windows 10 adds another way to easily share with another computer in close proximity. We covered the new Nearby Sharing feature earlier in this chapter.

Understanding sharing and security models in Windows

Much like Windows 7, Windows 10 offers two ways to share file resources, whether you're doing so locally or over the network:

- **Public folder sharing.** When you place files and folders in your Public folder or its sub-folders, those files are available to anyone who has a user account on your computer. Each person who signs in has access to his or her own profile folders (Documents, Music, and so on), and *everyone* who signs in has access to the Public folder. (You need to dig a bit to find the Public folder, which—unlike other profiles—doesn't appear under Desktop in the left pane of File Explorer. Navigate to C:\Users\Public. If you use the Public folder often, pin it to the Quick Access list in File Explorer.)

  By default, all users with an account on your computer can sign in and create, view, mod-ify, and delete files in the Public folders. The person who creates a file in a Public folder (or copies an item to a Public folder) is the file's owner and has Full Control access. All others who sign in locally have Modify access.

  Settings in Advanced Sharing Settings (accessible from Settings > Network & Internet, discussed in the next section) determine whether the contents of your Public folder are made available on your network and whether entering a user name and password is required for access. If you turn on password-protected sharing, only network users who have a user account on your computer (or those who know the user name and password for an account on your computer) can access files in the Public folder. Without password-protected sharing, everyone on your network has access to your Public folder files if you enable network sharing of the Public folder.

  You can't select which network users get access, nor can you specify different access levels for different users. Sharing via the Public folder is quick and easy—but it's inflexible.

- **Advanced sharing.** By choosing to share folders or files outside the Public folder, you can specify precisely which user accounts are able to access your shared data, and you can specify the types of privileges those accounts enjoy. You can grant different access privileges to different users. For example, you might enable some users to modify shared files and create new ones, enable other users to read files without changing them, and lock out still other users altogether.

You don't need to decide between sharing the Public folder and sharing specific folders, because you can use both methods simultaneously. You might find that a mix of sharing styles works best for you; each has its benefits:

- Sharing specific folders is best for files you want to share with some users but not with others—or if you want to grant different levels of access to different users.

- Public folder sharing provides a convenient, logical way to segregate your personal documents, pictures, music, and so on from those you want to share with everyone who uses your computer or your network.

Configuring your network for sharing

If you plan to share folders and files with other users on your network, you need to take a few preparatory steps. (If you plan to share only with others who use your computer by signing in locally, you can skip these steps. And if your computer is part of a domain, some of these steps—or their equivalent in the domain world—must be done by an administrator on the domain controller. We don't cover those details in this book.)

1. **Be sure that all computers use the same workgroup name.** With modern versions of Windows, this step isn't absolutely necessary, although it does improve network discovery performance.

2. **Be sure that your network's location is set to Private.** This setting makes it possible for other users to discover shared resources and provides appropriate security for a network in a home or an office. For details, see "Setting the network location," earlier in this chapter.

3. **Be sure that Network Discovery is turned on.** This should happen automatically when you set the network location to Private, but you can confirm the setting—and change it if necessary—in Advanced Sharing Settings, which is shown in Figure 13-18. To open Advanced Sharing Settings, go to Settings > Network & Internet; on the Status page, click Sharing Options.

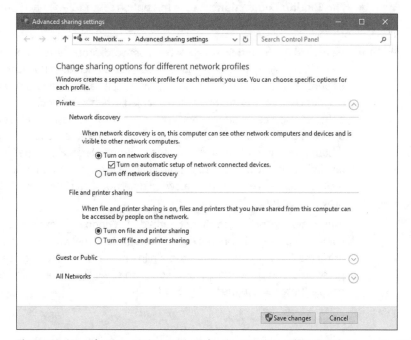

Figure 13-18   After you review settings for the Private profile, click the arrow by All Networks (below Guest Or Public) to see additional options.

4. **Select your sharing options.** In Advanced Sharing Settings, make a selection for each of the following network options. You'll find the first option under the Private profile; to view the remaining settings, expand All Networks.

   - **File And Printer Sharing.** Turn on this option if you want to share specific files or folders, the Public folder, or printers; it must be turned on if you plan to share any files (other than media streaming) over your network.

     The mere act of turning on file and printer sharing does not expose any of your computer's files or printers to other network users; that occurs only after you make additional sharing settings.

   - **Public Folder Sharing.** If you want to share items in your Public folder with all network users (or, if you enable password-protected sharing, all users who have a user account and password on your computer), turn on Public folder sharing. If you do so, network users will have read/write access to Public folders. With Public folder sharing turned off, anyone who signs in to your computer locally has access to Public folders, but network users do not.

   - **Media Streaming.** Turning on media streaming provides access to pictures, music, and video through streaming protocols that can send media to computers or to other media playback devices. In an era where most people stream their music collections from services like Spotify, this option is increasingly esoteric and nearly irrelevant.

   - **File Sharing Connections.** Leave this option set to 128-bit encryption, which has been the standard for most of this century.

   - **Password Protected Sharing.** When password-protected sharing is turned on, network users cannot access your shared folders (including Public folders, if shared) or printers unless they can provide the user name and password of a user account on your computer. With this setting enabled, when another user attempts to access a shared resource, Windows sends the user name and password that the person used to sign in to her own computer. If that matches the credentials for a local user account on your computer, the user gets immediate access to the shared resource (assuming permissions to use the resource have been granted to that user account). If either the user name or the password does not match, Windows asks the user to provide credentials.

     With password-protected sharing turned off, Windows does not require a user name and password from network visitors. Instead, network access is provided by using the Guest account. As we explain in Chapter 11, "Managing user accounts, passwords, and credentials," this account isn't available for interactive use but can handle these tasks in the background.

5. **Configure user accounts.** If you use password-protected sharing, each person who accesses a shared resource on your computer must have a user account on your computer. Use a Microsoft account or, for a local account, use the same user name as that person uses on his or her own computer and the same password as well. If you do that, network users will be able to access shared resources without having to enter their credentials after they've signed in to their own computer.

Sharing files and folders from any folder

Whether you plan to share files and folders with other people who share your computer or those who connect to your computer over the network (or both), the process for setting up shared resources is the same as long as the Sharing Wizard is enabled. We recommend you use the Sharing Wizard even if you normally disdain wizards. It's quick, easy, and certain to make all the correct settings for network shares and NTFS permissions—a sometimes-daunting task if undertaken manually. After you configure shares with the wizard, you can always dive in and make changes manually if you need to. (Although it's possible to use the Advanced Sharing options to configure network sharing independently of NTFS permissions, we don't recommend that technique and do not cover it in this edition.)

To be sure the Sharing Wizard is enabled, open File Explorer Options. (Type **folder** in the search box, and then choose File Explorer Options. Or, in File Explorer, click View > Options.) In the dialog box that appears, shown next, click the View tab. Near the bottom of the Advanced Settings list, see that Use Sharing Wizard (Recommended) is selected:

CHAPTER 13

With the Sharing Wizard at the ready, follow these steps to share a folder or files:

1. In File Explorer, select the folders or files you want to share. (You can select multiple objects.)

2. Right-click and choose Give Access To > Specific People. (In versions before 1709, the command is Share With.) Alternatively, click or tap the Share tab and then click Specific People in the Share With box. You might need to click the arrow in the Share With box to display Specific People. The File Sharing dialog box appears, as shown in Figure 13-19.

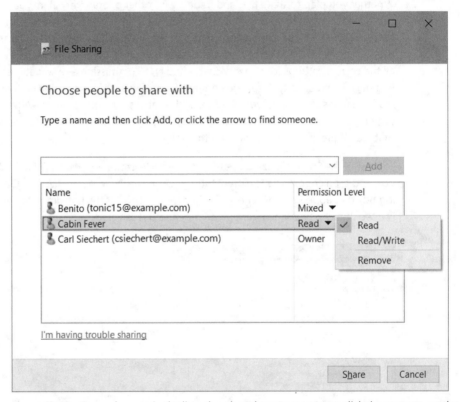

Figure 13-19 For each name in the list other than the owner, you can click the arrow to set the access level—or remove that account from the list.

3. In the entry box, enter the name or Microsoft account for each user with whom you want to share. You can type a name in the box or click the arrow to display a list of available names; then click Add. Repeat this step for each person you want to add.

    The list includes all users who have an account on your computer, plus Everyone. Guest is included if password-protected sharing is turned off. If you want to grant access to someone who doesn't appear in the list, click Create A New User, which takes you to User Accounts in Control Panel.

NOTE

If you select Everyone and you have password-protected sharing enabled, the user must still have a valid account on your computer. However, if you turned off password-protected sharing, network users can gain access *only* if you grant permission to Everyone or to Guest.

4. For each user, select a permission level. Your choices are

   ▪ **Read.** Users with this permission level can view shared files and run shared programs, but they cannot change or delete files. Selecting Read in the Sharing Wizard is equivalent to setting NTFS permissions to Read & Execute.

   ▪ **Read/Write.** Users assigned the Read/Write permission have the same privileges you do as owner: they can view, change, add, and delete files in a shared folder. Selecting Read/Write sets NTFS permissions to Full Control for this user.

NOTE

You might see other permission levels if you return to the Sharing Wizard after you set up sharing. Contribute indicates Modify permission. Custom indicates NTFS permissions other than Read & Execute, Modify, or Full Control. Mixed appears if you select multiple items and they have different sharing settings. Owner, of course, identifies the owner of the item.

5. Click Share. After a few moments, the wizard displays a page like the one shown in Figure 13-20.

6. In the final step of the wizard, you can do any of the following:

   ▪ Send an email message to the people with whom you're sharing. The message includes a link to the shared items.

   ▪ Copy the network path to the Clipboard. This is handy if you want to send a link via another application, such as a messaging app. (To copy the link for a single item in a list, right-click the share name and choose Copy Link.)

   ▪ Double-click a share name to open the shared item.

   ▪ Open File Explorer with your computer selected in the Network folder, showing each network share on your computer.

   When you're finished with these tasks, click Done.

CHAPTER 13

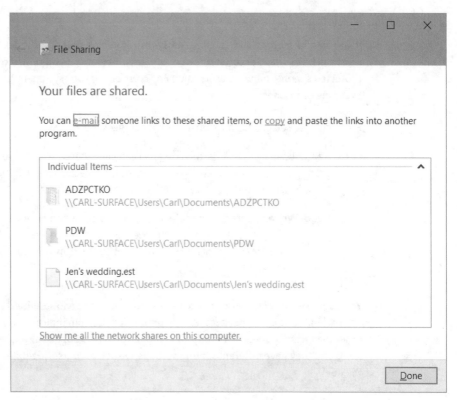

Figure 13-20   The Sharing Wizard displays the network path for each item you shared.

Creating a share requires privilege elevation, but after a folder has been shared, the share is available to network users no matter who is signed in to your computer—or even when nobody is signed in.

Inside OUT

Use advanced sharing to create shorter network paths

Confusingly, when you share one of your profile folders (or any other subfolder of %SystemDrive%\Users), Windows creates a network share for the Users folder—not for the folder you shared. This behavior isn't a security problem; NTFS permissions prevent network users from seeing any folders or files except the ones explicitly shared. But it does lead to some long Universal Naming Convention (UNC) paths to network shares. For example, sharing the PDW subfolder of Documents (as shown in Figure 13-16) creates the network path \\CARL-SURFACE\Users\Carl\Documents\PDW. If this same folder had been anywhere on your computer outside the Users folder, no matter how deeply nested, the network path would instead be \\CARL-SURFACE\PDW. Other people to whom you granted access wouldn't need to click through a series of folders to find the files in the intended target folder.

Network users, of course, can map a network drive or save a shortcut to your target folder to avoid this problem. But you can work around it from the sharing side, too: Use advanced sharing to share the folder directly. (Do this after you've used the Sharing Wizard to set up permissions.) And while you're doing that, be sure the share name you create doesn't have spaces. Eliminating them makes it easier to type a share path that works as a link.

Stopping or changing sharing of a file or folder

If you want to stop sharing a particular shared file or folder, select it in File Explorer and on the Share tab, click Remove Access (Stop Sharing in versions before 1709). Or right-click and choose Give Access To > Remove Access. Doing so removes access control entries that are not inherited. In addition, the network share is removed; the folder will no longer be visible in another user's Network folder.

To change share permissions, right-click and choose Give Access To > Specific People. In the File Sharing dialog box (shown earlier in Figure 13-15), you can add users, change permissions, or remove users. (To stop sharing with a user, click the permission level by the user's name and choose Remove.)

Sharing a printer

Although Windows doesn't have a wizard for sharing a printer over the network, the process is fairly simple. You configure all options for a printer—shared or not—by using the printer's properties dialog box, which you access from Settings > Devices > Printers & Scanners.

To make a printer available to other network users, select a printer, click Manage, and then click Printer Properties. On the Sharing tab, select Share This Printer and provide a share name, as shown in Figure 13-21.

Unlike for shared folders, which maintain separate share permissions and NTFS permissions, a single set of permissions controls access to printers, whether by local users or by network users. (Of course, only printers that have been shared are accessible to network users.)

CHAPTER 13

Figure 13-21   The share name for a printer can include spaces.

When you set up a printer, initially all users in the Everyone group have Print permission for documents they create, which provides users access to the printer and the ability to manage their own documents in the print queue. By default, members of the Administrators group also have Manage Printers permission—which allows them to share a printer, change its properties, remove a printer, and change its permissions—and Manage Documents permission, which lets them pause, restart, move, and remove all queued documents. As an administrator, you can view or modify permissions on the Security tab of the printer properties dialog box.

Setting server properties

In addition to setting properties for individual printers by using their properties dialog boxes, you can set other properties by visiting the Print Server Properties dialog box. To get there, open Settings > Devices > Printers & Scanners. Then, under Related Settings, click Print Server Properties.

The first three tabs control the list of items you see in the properties dialog box for a printer:

- The Forms tab controls the list of forms you can assign to trays using the Device Settings tab in a printer's properties dialog box. You can create new form definitions and delete any you create, but you can't delete any of the predefined forms.

- On the Ports tab, you can configure the ports that appear on the Ports tab in a printer's properties dialog box.

- The Drivers tab offers a list of all the installed printer drivers and provides a centralized location where you can add, remove, or update drivers.

On the Advanced tab, you can specify the location of spool files. (You might want to change to a folder on a different drive if, for example, you frequently run out of space on the current drive when you attempt to print large documents.) You can also set notification options on this tab.

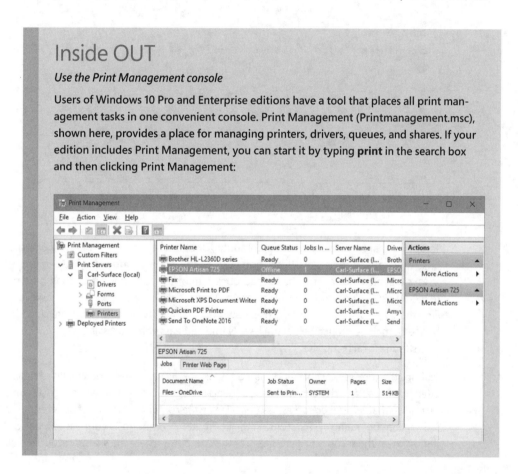

Inside OUT

Use the Print Management console

Users of Windows 10 Pro and Enterprise editions have a tool that places all print management tasks in one convenient console. Print Management (Printmanagement.msc), shown here, provides a place for managing printers, drivers, queues, and shares. If your edition includes Print Management, you can start it by typing **print** in the search box and then clicking Print Management:

Finding and using shared resources on a Windows network

The Network folder is your primary gateway to available network resources, just as This PC is the gateway to resources stored on your own system. The Network folder (shown in Figure 13-22) contains an icon for each computer that Windows discovers on your network; double-click a computer icon to see that computer's shared resources, if any.

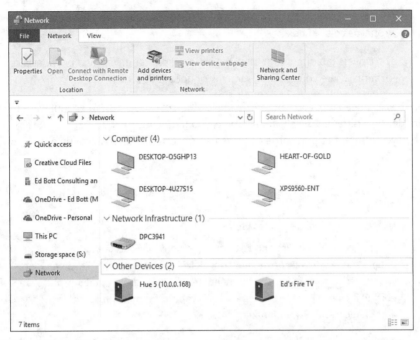

Figure 13-22 The Network folder shows all computers on your network, not just those in your workgroup.

To open a shared folder on another computer, double-click its icon in the Network folder. If you have the proper permissions, this action displays the folder's contents in File Explorer. It's not always that easy, however. If the user account with which you signed in doesn't have permission to view a network computer or resource you select, a dialog box (shown next) asks you to provide the name of an account (and its password, of course) that has permission. Don't be fooled by the Domain reference below the User Name and Password boxes; in a workgroup, that value refers to the local computer.

Perhaps the trickiest part of using shared folders is fully understanding what permissions have been applied to a folder and which credentials are in use by each network user. It's important to recognize that *all network access is controlled by the computer with the shared resources*; regardless of what operating system runs on the computer attempting to connect to a network share, it must meet the security requirements of the computer where the shared resource is actually located.

Working with mapped network folders

Mapping a network folder makes it appear to applications as though the folder is part of your own computer. Windows assigns a drive letter to the mapped folder, making the folder appear like an additional hard drive. You can still access a mapped folder in the conventional manner by navigating to it through the Network folder. But mapping gives the folder an alias—the assigned drive letter—that provides an alternative means of access.

To map a network folder to a drive letter, follow these steps:

1. Open This PC in File Explorer, and on the ribbon's Computer tab, click Map Network Drive. (Alternatively, after you open a computer in the Network folder, right-click a network share and choose Map Network Drive.)

CHAPTER 13

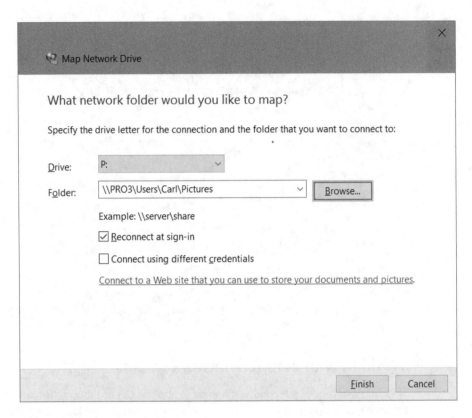

2. Select a drive letter from the Drive list. You can choose any letter that's not already in use.

3. In the Folder box, type the path to the folder you want or, more easily, click Browse and navigate to the folder.

4. Select Reconnect At Sign-In if you want Windows to connect to this shared folder automatically at the start of each session.

5. If your regular sign-in account doesn't have permission to connect to the resource, select Connect Using Different Credentials. (After you click Finish, Windows asks for the user name and password you want to use for this connection.)

6. Click Finish.

In File Explorer, the "drive" appears under This PC.

If you change your mind about mapping a network folder, right-click the folder's icon in your This PC folder. Choose Disconnect on the resulting shortcut menu, and the connection will be severed.

Connecting to a network printer

To use a printer that has been shared, open the Network folder in File Explorer and double-click the name of the server to which the printer is attached. If the shared printers on that server are not visible, return to the Network folder, click to select the server, and then, on the ribbon's Network tab, click View Printers. Right-click the printer and choose Connect. Alternatively, from the Devices And Printers folder, click Add A Printer and use the Add Printer Wizard to add a network printer.

Troubleshooting network problems

Network connectivity problems can be a source of great frustration. Fortunately, Windows 10 includes several tools and wizards that can help you identify and solve problems. Even better, Windows has built-in network diagnostic capabilities, so in many cases, if there is a problem with your network connection, Windows knows about it before you do, displays a message, and often solves the problem.

When a network-dependent activity (for example, browsing to a website) fails, Windows works to address the most common network-related issues, such as problems with file sharing, website access, newly installed network hardware, connecting to a wireless network, and using a third-party firewall.

If you encounter network problems that don't trigger an automatic response from Windows, you should first try to detect and resolve the problem with one of the built-in troubleshooters. Open Settings > Network & Internet; on the Status page, click Network Troubleshooter to fix an issue. If the options shown in that troubleshooter don't address your problem, go to Settings > Update & Security > Troubleshoot to see additional choices.

> ## Inside OUT
>
> ### Skip the troubleshooting menu
>
> For fastest access to the main networking troubleshooter, right-click the network icon in the notification area and choose Troubleshoot Problems; doing so launches the Windows Network Diagnostics troubleshooting wizard immediately.

Each of the troubleshooting wizards performs several diagnostic tests, corrects some conditions, suggests actions you can take, and ultimately displays a report that explains the wizard's findings. Sometimes, the problem is as simple as a loose connection.

If the diagnostic capabilities leave you at a dead end, you'll find that restarting the affected network hardware often resolves the problem, because the hardware is forced to rediscover the network. Here's a good general troubleshooting procedure:

1. Isolate the problem. Does it affect all computers on your network, a subset of your network, or only one computer?

2. If it affects all computers, try restarting the internet device (that is, the cable or DSL modem). If the device doesn't have a power switch, unplug it for a few moments and plug it back in.

3. If the problem affects a group of computers, try restarting the router to which those computers are connected.

4. If the problem affects only a single computer, try repairing the network connection for that computer. Open Settings > Network & Internet and, on the Status page, click Change Adapter Options. Then, in Network Connections, select the connection and click Diagnose This Connection. If the troubleshooter doesn't resolve the problem, select the connection and click Disable This Network Device; then click Enable This Network Device, which causes Windows to reinitialize it.

Inside OUT

As a last resort, use Network Reset

The Status page in Settings > Network & Internet offers much of the same information and links to additional tools, such as Network And Sharing Center. It also includes a Network Reset command. If you're unable to resolve networking problems by using the network troubleshooter, click Network Reset to remove your network adapters, reinstall them, set other networking components to their default settings, and restart your computer.

Network troubleshooting tools

When the built-in troubleshooters don't solve the problem, it might be time to dig deeper into the Windows toolbox. The following list includes some of the command-line utilities you can use to diagnose, monitor, and repair network connections. To learn more about each utility, including its proper syntax, open a Command Prompt window and type the executable name followed by /?.

- **IP Configuration Utility (Ipconfig.exe).** Displays all current Transmission Control Protocol/Internet Protocol (TCP/IP) network configuration values and refreshes Dynamic Host Configuration Protocol (DHCP) and DNS settings.

- **Name Server Lookup (Nslookup.exe).** Displays information about Domain Name System records for specific IP addresses, host names, or both so that you can troubleshoot DNS problems.

- **Net services commands (Net.exe).** Performs a broad range of network tasks. Type **net** with no parameters to see a full list of available command-line options.

- **Network Command Shell (Netsh.exe).** Displays or modifies the network configuration of a local or remote computer that's currently running. This command-line scripting utility has a huge number of options, which are fully detailed in Help.

- **TCP/IP Ping (Ping.exe).** Verifies IP-level connectivity to another internet address by sending Internet Control Message Protocol (ICMP) packets and measuring the response time in milliseconds.

- **TCP/IP Traceroute (Tracert.exe).** Determines the path to an internet address and lists the time required to reach each hop. It's useful for troubleshooting connectivity problems on specific network segments.

As is the case with other command-line utilities, the Windows PowerShell environment includes cmdlets that offer much of the same functionality along with the scripting capability of PowerShell. You can get a list that includes many of the more commonly used network-related cmdlets by entering the following at a PowerShell prompt:

```
get-command -module nettcpip, netadapter
```

➤ For more information about PowerShell, see "An introduction to Windows PowerShell" in Chapter 19, "PowerShell and other advanced management tools." For details about the Net TCP/IP cmdlets, go to *https://bit.ly/NetTCPIP*. On that page, you'll also find (using the navigation pane on the left) details about other network-related cmdlets, including those for Network Adapter, Network Connection, and Network Connectivity Status.

Troubleshooting TCP/IP problems

When you encounter problems with TCP/IP-based networks, such as an inability to connect with other computers on the same network or difficulty connecting to external websites, the problems might be TCP/IP related. You'll need at least a basic understanding of how this protocol works before you can figure out which tool to use to uncover the root of the problem.

Checking for connection problems

Any time your network refuses to send and receive data properly, your first troubleshooting step should be to check for problems with the physical connection between the local computer and the rest of the network. Assuming your network connection uses the TCP/IP protocol, the first tool to reach for is the Ping utility. When you use the Ping command with no parameters,

CHAPTER 13

Windows sends four echo datagrams—small Internet Control Message Protocol (ICMP) packets—to the address you specify. If the machine at the other end of the connection replies, you know that the network connection between the two points is alive.

To use the Ping command, open a Command Prompt window (Cmd.exe) and type the command **ping *target_name*** (where *target_name* is an IP address or the name of another host machine). The return output looks something like this:

```
C:\>ping www.example.com

Pinging www.example.com [93.184.216.34] with 32 bytes of data:
Reply from 93.184.216.34: bytes=32 time=54ms TTL=51
Reply from 93.184.216.34: bytes=32 time=40ms TTL=51
Reply from 93.184.216.34: bytes=32 time=41ms TTL=51
Reply from 93.184.216.34: bytes=32 time=54ms TTL=51

Ping statistics for 93.184.216.34:
    Packets: Sent = 4, Received = 4, Lost = 0 (0% loss),
Approximate round trip times in milli-seconds:
    Minimum = 40ms, Maximum = 54ms, Average = 47ms
```

If all the packets you send come back and the time values are roughly equal, your TCP/IP connection is fine, and you can focus your troubleshooting efforts elsewhere. If some packets time out, a "Request timed out" message appears, indicating your network connection is working, but one or more hops between your computer and the target machine are experiencing problems. In that case, repeat the Ping test using the **–n** switch to send a larger number of packets; `ping –n 30 192.168.1.1`, for example, sends 30 packets to the computer or router at 192.168.1.1.

NOTE

The –n switch is case-sensitive; don't capitalize it.

A high rate of timeouts, also known as *packet loss*, usually means the problems are elsewhere on the network and not on the local machine. (To see the full assortment of switches available for the Ping command, type **ping** with no target specified.)

If every one of your packets returns with the message "Request timed out," the problem might be the TCP/IP connection on your computer or a glitch with another computer on that network. To narrow down the problem, follow these steps, in order, stopping at any point where you encounter an error:

1. Ping your own machine by using any of the following commands:

```
ping ::1
ping 127.0.0.1
ping localhost
```

These are standard addresses. The first line is the IPv6 address for your own computer; the second line is the IPv4 address; the third line shows the standard host name. If your local network components are configured correctly, each of these three commands should allow the PC on which the command is run to talk to itself. If you receive an error, TCP/IP is not configured properly on your system. For fix-it details, see "Repairing your TCP/IP configuration" later in this chapter.

2. Ping your computer's IP address.

3. Ping the IP address of another computer on your network.

4. Ping the IP address of your router or the default gateway on your network.

5. Ping the address of each DNS server on your network. (If you don't know these addresses, see the next section for details on how to discover them.)

6. Ping a known host outside your network. Well-known, high-traffic websites are ideal for this step, assuming that they respond to ICMP packets.

7. Use the PathPing command to contact the same host you specified in step 6. This command combines the functionality of the Ping command with the Traceroute utility to identify intermediate destinations on the internet between your computer and the specified host or server.

CHAPTER 13

Inside OUT

Choose your test site carefully

In some cases, pinging an external website results in a string of "Request timed out" messages, even when you have no trouble reaching those sites. Don't be misled. Some popular sites block all ICMP traffic, including Ping packets, as a routine security measure. Some routers and residential gateways are also configured to block certain types of ICMP traffic. Try pinging several sites before concluding that your internet connection is broken.

If either of the two final steps in this process fails, your problem might be caused by DNS problems, as described later in this chapter. (For details, see "Resolving DNS issues.") To eliminate this possibility, ping the numeric IP address of a computer outside your network instead. (Of course, if you're having DNS problems, you might have a hard time finding an IP address to ping!) If you can reach a website by using its IP address but not by using its name, DNS problems are indicated.

If you suspect that there's a problem on the internet between your computer and a distant host or server, use the Traceroute utility (Tracert.exe) to pinpoint the problem. Like the Ping command, this utility works from a command line. You specify the target (a host name or IP address) by using the syntax **tracert target_name**, and the utility sends out a series of packets, measuring the time it takes to reach each hop along the route. Timeouts or unusually slow performance indicate a connectivity problem. If the response time from your network to the first hop is much higher than the other hops, you might have a problem with the connection to your internet service provider; in that case, a call to your ISP's support line is in order. Problems further along in the traceroute might indicate congestion or hardware problems in distant parts of the internet that are out of your ISP's hands. These symptoms might disappear when you check another URL that follows a different path through the internet.

If your testing produces inconsistent results, rule out the possibility that a firewall program or NAT device (such as a router or residential gateway) is to blame. If you're using Windows Defender Firewall or a third-party firewall program, disable it temporarily. Try bypassing your router and connecting directly to a broadband connection such as a DSL or cable modem. (Use this configuration only for testing and only very briefly because it exposes your computer to various attacks.)

If the Ping test works with the firewall or NAT device out of the picture, you can rule out network problems and conclude that the firewall software or router is misconfigured. After you complete your testing, be sure to enable the firewall and router again.

Diagnosing IP address problems

You can also get useful details of your IP configuration by using the IP Configuration utility, Ipconfig.exe, in a Command Prompt window. Used without parameters, typing **ipconfig** at a command prompt displays the DNS suffix; IPv6 address, IPv4 address, or both; subnet mask; and default gateway for each network connection. To see exhaustive details about every available network connection, type **ipconfig /all**.

The actual IP address you see might help you solve connection problems:

- If the address is in the format 169.254.*x.y*, your computer is using Automatic Private IP Addressing (APIPA). This means your computer's DHCP client was unable to reach a DHCP server to be assigned an IP address. Check the connection to your network.

- If the address is in one of the blocks of IP addresses reserved for use on private networks (for details, see the sidebar "Public and private IP addresses" earlier in this chapter), make sure that a router or residential gateway is routing your internet requests to a properly configured public IP address.

- If the address of your computer appears as 0.0.0.0, the network is either disconnected or the static IP address for the connection duplicates an address that already exists on the network.

- Make sure you're using the correct subnet mask for computers on your local network. Compare IP settings on the machine that's having problems with those on other computers on the network. The default gateway and subnet mask should be identical for all network computers. The first one, two, or three sets of numbers in the IP address for each machine should also be identical, depending on the subnet mask. A subnet mask of 255.255.255.0 means the first three IP address numbers of computers on your network must be identical—192.168.0.83 and 192.168.0.223, for instance, can communicate on a network using this subnet mask, but 192.168.1.101 will not be recognized as belonging to the network. The gateway machine must also be a member of the same subnet. (If you use a router, switch, or residential gateway for internet access, the local address on that device must be part of the same subnet as the machines on your network.)

NOTE

Are you baffled by subnets and other related technical terms? For an excellent overview of these sometimes confusing topics, read Knowledge Base article 164015, "Understanding TCP/IP Addressing and Subnetting Basics" (*https://support.microsoft.com/kb/164015*), which offers information about IPv4. For comparable details about IPv6, see the "Introduction to IPv6" white paper at TechNet (*https://bit.ly/ipv6-intro*).

Repairing your TCP/IP configuration

If you suspect a problem with your TCP/IP configuration, try either of the following repair options:

- **Use the automated repair option.** Right-click the connection icon in Network Connections and click Diagnose.

- **Release and renew your IP address.** Use the **ipconfig /release** command to let go of the DHCP-assigned IPv4 address. Then use **ipconfig /renew** to obtain a new IP address from the DHCP server. To renew an IPv6 address, use **ipconfig /release6** and **ipconfig /renew6**.

NOTE

If these methods don't work, you can use the Netsh utility to restore the TCP/IP stack to its original configuration when Windows was first installed. The utility restores all registry settings relating to the TCP/IP stack to their original settings, which is effectively the same as removing and reinstalling the protocol. The utility records a log of the changes it makes. For details about this drastic, but effective, solution, see Microsoft Knowledge Base article 299357 (*https://support.microsoft.com/kb/299357*). Another option is to reset the network adapter; go to Settings > Network & Internet > Network Reset.

Inside OUT

Translate names to IP addresses and vice versa

The Nslookup command is a buried treasure in Windows. Use this command-line utility to quickly convert a fully qualified domain name to its IP address. You can tack on a host name to the end of the command line to identify a single address; for instance, you can type **nslookup ftp.microsoft.com** to look up the IP address of Microsoft's File Transfer Protocol (FTP) server. Or type **nslookup** to switch into interactive mode. From this prompt, you can enter any domain name to find its IP address.

If you need more sophisticated lookup tools, you can find them with the help of any search engine. A good starting point is DNSstuff (*https://dnsstuff.com/tools*), which offers an impressive collection of online tools for looking up domains, IP addresses, and host names. The site also offers form-based utilities that can translate obfuscated URLs and dotted IP addresses, both of which are widely used by spammers to cover their online tracks.

Resolving DNS issues

The Domain Name System (DNS) is a crucial part of the internet. DNS servers translate host names (*www.microsoft.com*, for instance) into numeric IP addresses so that packets can be routed properly over the internet. If you can use the Ping command to reach a numeric address outside your network but are unable to browse websites by name, the problem is almost certainly related to your DNS configuration.

Here are some questions to ask when you suspect DNS problems:

- **Do your TCP/IP settings point to the right DNS servers?** Inspect the details of your IP configuration, and compare the DNS servers listed there with those recommended by your internet service provider. (You might need to call your ISP to get these details.)

- **Is your ISP experiencing DNS problems?** A misconfigured DNS server (or one that's offline) can wreak havoc with your attempts to use the internet. Try pinging each DNS server to see whether it's available. If your ISP has multiple DNS servers and you encounter problems accessing one server, remove that server from your TCP/IP configuration temporarily and use another one instead.

- **Have you installed any "internet accelerator" utilities?** Many such programs work by editing the Hosts file on your computer to match IP addresses and host (server) names. When Windows finds a host name in the Hosts file, it uses the IP address listed there and doesn't send the request to a DNS server. If the owner of the server changes its DNS records to point to a new IP address, your Hosts file will lead you to the wrong location.

Temporary DNS problems can also be caused by the DNS cache, which Windows maintains for performance reasons. If you suddenly have trouble reaching a specific site on the internet and you're convinced there's nothing wrong with the site, type this command to clear the DNS cache: **ipconfig /flushdns**.

A more thorough solution is offered by **ipconfig /registerdns**, which renews all DHCP leases (as described in the previous section) *and* reregisters all DNS names.

Hardware and devices

It's probably only a slight exaggeration to say that no two computers are alike. Motherboards, storage devices and controllers, video and network adapters, and peripherals of all shapes and sizes combine to create a nearly infinite number of possible computer configurations.

The good news for anyone using Windows 10 is that most of these devices should just work. For most common hardware upgrades, Windows detects the device automatically and installs a driver so that you can use the device and its full array of features. This chapter covers those installations as well as devices that need to be added manually and those that have optional configuration steps.

Over the past few years, feature updates to Windows 10 have added native support for some new types of hardware, including devices built using the USB Audio 2.0 and Bluetooth LE standards as well as High Dynamic Range (HDR) video. For the most part, new devices using these standards should just work if you're using the most recent version of Windows 10. Beginning with Version 1803, Windows 10 adds support for a simplified Bluetooth device setup experience called Swift Pair. This chapter also covers display-related improvements in recent versions, including support for high-DPI hardware configurations typically found in high-end, business-class notebooks, as well as the Night Light feature that makes portable computing easier on the eyes.

In this chapter, we cover the traditional nerve center of hardware, Device Manager, as well as the newer hardware configuration options in Settings. We explain how drivers work (and how to work with drivers). We also offer hints on the best ways to set up specific device configurations, including hard disks, multiple monitors, Bluetooth adapters, and printers.

Adding, configuring, and removing hardware devices

Since its introduction in Windows 95, Plug and Play technology has evolved tremendously. Early incarnations of this technology were notoriously unreliable, leading some users to dismiss the feature as "plug and pray." As this now-mature technology enters its third decade, however, hardware and software standards have converged to make most device configuration tasks completely automatic.

Any computer that was certified as compatible with Windows 7 or later supports the Plug and Play device standard, which handles virtually all the work of configuring computer hardware and attached devices. A Plug and Play device identifies itself to Windows by using unique identifiers in a well-organized hierarchy, listing its required resources (including drivers), and allowing software to configure it.

Plug and Play devices can interact with the operating system, with both sides of the conversation responding to device notification and power management events. A Plug and Play driver can load automatically when Windows detects that a device has been plugged in, and it can suspend its operations when the system sleeps and resume without issue when the system wakes.

> **NOTE**
>
> **Although you still can find older devices that require non–Plug and Play inputs—such as scanners, plotters, and similar peripherals that connect to serial and parallel ports— these legacy devices are becoming increasingly rare. If you own this type of device, we recommend retiring it if possible and replacing it with a supported modern alternative. If you have no choice but to keep it around, look for a community of fellow owners of that device; they're the most likely to be able to help you with configuration issues.**

Installing a new Plug and Play device

When you install a Plug and Play device for the first time, the Plug and Play manager queries the device to determine its hardware ID and any compatible IDs. It then compares the hardware ID with a master list of corresponding tags drawn from all the Setup Information files in the %SystemRoot%\Inf folder. If it finds a signed driver with a matching tag, it installs that driver package and makes other necessary system modifications with no intervention required from you. If everything goes as expected, the only subtle indication you might see is a progress dialog box (typically minimized) that displays a green bar over its taskbar icon and then vanishes when its work is complete.

> **NOTE**
>
> **Any user can plug in a new device and begin using it if a driver for that device is included with Windows 10 or is available via Windows Update. Installing a new driver that is downloaded from a third-party site and is digitally signed by a third party rather than by Microsoft requires an administrator's credentials.**

If Windows detects a Plug and Play device (after you've plugged it into a USB port, for instance) but cannot locate a digitally signed driver that matches the device ID, it looks for generic driver packages that match any compatible IDs reported by the device. If that search still doesn't turn up a suitable driver, the Plug and Play manager installs a stub for the device and awaits the arrival of a proper driver. These partially installed devices appear in Device Manager, under the Other Devices heading, with a yellow exclamation point over the device name, as in Figure 14-1.

Figure 14-1   If Windows 10 can't find drivers for a new Plug and Play device, it adds a yellow exclamation point to the Device Manager listing and files the device under the Other Devices heading.

CHAPTER 14

TROUBLESHOOTING

Drivers for built-in devices are missing

Device Manager might show some devices in the Other Devices category, with a yellow exclamation point indicating that the correct drivers are missing, after a clean installation of Windows 10. This usually occurs on a PC where some low-level devices built into the motherboard aren't recognized during Windows 10 setup. Try checking Windows Update manually to see if the correct drivers turn up; if that search doesn't retrieve the desired drivers, check with the device manufacturer to see whether drivers are available for download. Pay special attention to chipset drivers, which add the necessary entries to the Windows Plug and Play database to allow the correct built-in drivers to be installed.

When Windows Update can't find a signed driver (and, thankfully, those occasions are becoming rarer as the Windows ecosystem matures), you need to manually install a device driver, a topic we cover in more detail later in this chapter.

The built-in Windows drivers are perfectly adequate for many device classes. Some devices, especially complex ones like scanners and all-in-one printers, might require utility software and additional drivers to enable the full range of features for that device.

How device drivers and hardware work together

Before Windows can work with any piece of hardware, it requires a compatible, properly configured device driver. Drivers are compact control programs that hook directly into Windows and handle the essential tasks of communicating your instructions to a hardware device and then relaying data back to you. After you set up a hardware device, its driver loads automatically and runs as part of the operating system, without requiring any further intervention on your part.

Many individual technologies used in Windows 10 devices use minidriver models, where the device driver is made up of two parts. Typically, Microsoft writes a general class driver that handles tasks that are common to devices in that category. The device manufacturer can then write device-specific code to enable custom features.

Windows 10, even more than its recent predecessors, includes a surprisingly comprehensive library of class drivers that allow most devices to function properly without requiring any additional software. There are class drivers for pieces of hardware that are, these days, typically integrated into a larger system: audio devices, network adapters, webcams, and display adapters, for example. Windows 10 also includes drivers for external add-ons (wired and wireless) including printers, monitors, keyboards, scanners, mice and other pointing devices, smartphones, and removable storage devices.

This core library is copied during Windows setup to a protected system folder, %SystemRoot%\System32\DriverStore. (Driver files and associated elements are stored in the FileRepository subfolder.) Anyone who signs in to the computer has Read & Execute permissions for files that are saved in that location, but only an installation program working with authorization from a member of the Administrators group can create or modify files and folders there.

You can add new drivers to the driver store in a variety of ways, including the following:

- Windows Update offers drivers when it detects that you're running a device that's compatible with that driver but is currently using an older version. (You can also search for the most recent driver via Windows Update when installing a new device.)

- A Windows quality or feature update can refresh the driver store with new and updated drivers.

- As an administrator, you can add signed third-party drivers to the driver store by running an installer program. All drivers added to the driver store in this fashion are saved in their own subfolder within the FileRepository folder, along with some supporting files created by Windows 10 that allow the drivers to be reinstalled if necessary.

Any driver that has been added to the store is considered to be trusted and can be installed without prompts or administrator credentials. All drivers, new or updated, that are downloaded from the Windows Update service are certified to be fully compatible with Windows 10 and are digitally signed by Microsoft.

Inside OUT

Copy the FileRepository folder before a clean reinstall

If you're planning a clean reinstall of Windows 10 using bootable installation media rather than the Reset function, consider copying the FileRepository folder from %SystemRoot%\System32\DriverStore to removable media, such as a USB flash drive. After your clean install is complete, you can quickly reinstall any custom drivers by using the Update Driver option from Device Manager and specifying that saved folder as the location for the new driver files.

A Windows hardware driver package must include a Setup Information file (with the extension .inf). This is a text file that contains detailed information about the device to be installed, including the names of its driver files, the locations where they are to be installed, any required registry settings, and version information. All devices with drivers in the DriverStore folder include Setup Information files in the %SystemRoot%\Inf folder.

Although the Setup Information file is a crucial part of the driver installation process, you don't work with it directly. Instead, this file supplies instructions that the operating system uses during Plug and Play detection, when you use a setup program to install a device or when you manually install a driver update.

CAUTION

The syntax of Setup Information files is complex, and the intricacies of .inf files can trip up even experienced software developers. If you find that a driver setup routine isn't working properly, you might be tempted to try editing the Setup Information file to work around the hang-up. Trust us: That approach is almost certain to fail. In fact, by tinkering with .inf files to install a driver that's not certified to be compatible with your hardware, you run the risk of corrupting registry settings and making your system unstable.

When Windows completes the installation of a driver package, it performs all the tasks specified by the Setup Information file and copies the driver files themselves to %SystemRoot%\System32\Drivers.

Inside OUT

For Windows 10, signed drivers only

For all editions of Windows 10, all new kernel-mode drivers must be submitted to Microsoft and digitally signed by the Windows Hardware Developer Center Dashboard portal. (Kernel-mode drivers run at the same level of privilege as Windows itself, as opposed to user-mode drivers, which run in the context of the currently signed-in user and cannot cause the system to crash.) In an additional change that took effect 90 days after the initial release of Windows 10 in 2015, any new drivers submitted to Microsoft must be signed by a valid Extended Validation Code Signing Certificate—a higher-cost option that provides extra assurance about the identity of a software publisher.

The net effect of these changes is to make it extremely difficult for malware to be delivered as part of a driver update. Drivers that were properly signed under the previous rules and were released before those two Windows 10 milestones will continue to work, but Windows 10 will not load new kernel-mode drivers unless they're signed by that Microsoft-controlled portal.

Driver signing establishes an initial threshold of trust, but by itself it's not necessarily an indicator of quality. For that you need to look at the signature a little more closely.

The highest level of quality is found with drivers that have passed compatibility and reliability tests for that category of device, as defined in Microsoft's Hardware Lab Kit. Those devices earn the right to use the Windows logo and can be included on Microsoft's Certified Products List.

Hardware developers who simply want to deliver a signed driver to their customers can submit the driver to Microsoft and "attest" to its quality rather than submitting actual test results. The Attested Signing Service signature is different from the one for a logo-certified device, but Windows 10 treats them the same, allowing either type of signed driver to be installed by any user with no prompts.

In the distant past, users could change default settings to allow installation of unsigned drivers and even completely eliminate warnings about the accompanying security risks. Those options are available by changing advanced startup settings in Windows 10, but they require disabling Secure Boot and fundamentally undermine the device's security. As a result, we strongly recommend against using them except for limited test scenarios.

Getting useful information from Device Manager

The more you know about individual hardware devices and their associated driver software, the more likely you are to make short work of troubleshooting problems or configuring advanced features for a device. In every case, your starting point is Device Manager, a graphical utility that provides detailed information about all installed hardware, along with controls you can use to configure devices, assign resources, and set advanced options.

NOTE

In Windows 10, Device Manager also includes categories that don't represent actual hardware—print queues, for example, or anything under the Software Devices heading. In this section, we focus only on physical hardware devices and their associated drivers.

The easiest way to open Device Manager (Devmgmt.msc) is to right-click the Start button (or press Windows key+X) and then click the Device Manager shortcut on the Quick Link menu. Alternatively, type **device** in the search box and then click the Device Manager entry from the top of the results list. (Device Manager is also available as a snap-in under the System Tools heading in the fully stocked Computer Management console.)

As Figure 14-2 shows, Device Manager is organized as a hierarchical list that inventories every piece of hardware within or connected to your computer. The default view shows devices by type.

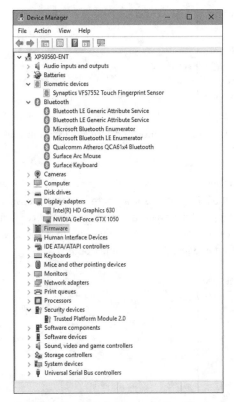

Figure 14-2   Click the arrow to the left of any category in Device Manager to expand or collapse the list of individual devices within that category.

To view information about a specific device, double-click its entry in Device Manager's list of installed devices. Each device has its own multitabbed properties dialog box. Most hardware devices include a selection of tabs, including General and Driver. The General tab lists basic facts about the device, including the device name and type, the name of its manufacturer, and its current status, as in the example in Figure 14-3.

Figure 14-3   The General tab supplies basic information about a device and indicates whether it's currently functioning properly.

The Driver tab, shown in Figure 14-4, lists version information about the currently installed driver for the selected device. Although the information shown here is sparse, it covers the essentials. You can tell at a glance who supplied the driver, and you can see who digitally signed it; you can also determine the date and version number of the driver, which is important when considering whether you should download and install an available update.

Figure 14-4   The Driver tab, which is available for every installed device, offers valuable information and tools for managing installed drivers.

Clicking the Driver Details button on the Driver tab leads to another dialog box that lists the names and locations of all files associated with that device and its drivers. Selecting any file name from this list displays details for that file in the lower portion of the dialog box. (We'll get to the other buttons in the next section.)

Click the Details tab for a potentially overwhelming amount of additional information, arranged in a dialog box in which you can see one property and its associated value at a time. To see the full list of properties available for inspection, click the arrow to the right of the current entry in the Property box; Figure 14-5 shows the typically dense result.

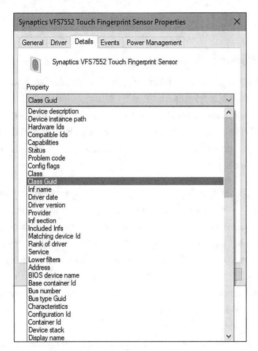

Figure 14-5   Most device properties you can select from this list return obscure details, but a few are useful for troubleshooting purposes.

Choosing a property tucks the list away and displays the value associated with that property, as in the example shown here, which lists the Plug and Play Hardware IDs associated with the selected device.

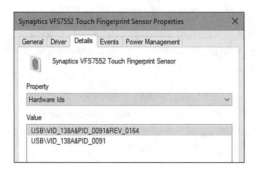

TROUBLESHOOTING

Device Manager shows an unknown device

Most modern hardware built for Windows 7 or later just works with Windows 10. But occasionally you might find mysterious entries under the Other Devices heading in Device Manager, with few or no details, no associated drivers, and no clue about what to do next. This problem is most likely to appear after you perform a clean install of Windows 10 on a device originally designed for another operating system, but the issue can also occur with older external hardware.

You can often get important clues by opening the properties dialog box for the device and looking on the Details tab. The Hardware IDs property, in particular, can be invaluable. The first three characters, followed by a backslash, identify the bus to which the device is connected: USB or PCI, for example. The string VID_ followed by a number is a Vendor ID code; PID_ is a Product ID code; REV_ is the revision code. Use your favorite search engine to look on the web for the first value to identify the vendor that made the device, which might be help to narrow your search; look for a combination of the first two values to identify a specific device.

In addition to this basic information, the properties dialog box for a given device can include any number of custom tabs. The wireless network adapter in the laptop PC shown in Figure 14-6, for example, adds a custom tab (Advanced) that you can use to configure the device at the hardware level—setting allowed wireless modes, for example.

By design, the information displayed in Device Manager is dynamic. When you add, remove, or reconfigure a device, the information stored here changes as well.

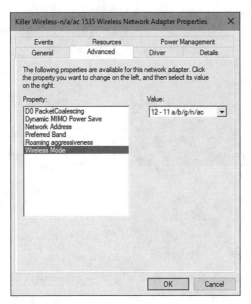

Figure 14-6   You can configure advanced properties for some devices, such as the allowed wireless modes for this network adapter, using Device Manager.

Enabling and disabling devices

Any device listed in Device Manager can be disabled temporarily. You might choose this option if you're certain you won't need an installed device under normal conditions, but you want to keep it available just in case. On a desktop PC with a permanent wired Ethernet connection, for example, you can keep a Wi-Fi adapter installed but disabled. That configuration gives you the option to enable the device and use the wireless adapter to connect to a hotspot on a mobile device if the wired network is temporarily unavailable.

Right-click any active entry in Device Manager to see a shortcut menu with a Disable command. To identify any device that's currently disabled, look for the black, downward-pointing arrow over its icon in Device Manager, as shown here. To turn a disabled device back on, right-click its entry in Device Manager and then click Enable Device.

CHAPTER 14

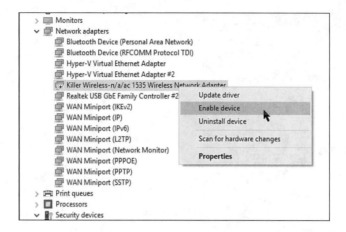

Adjusting advanced device settings

As we mentioned earlier, some devices include specialized tabs in the properties dialog box available from Device Manager. You use the controls on these additional tabs to change advanced settings and properties for devices. For example:

- Network cards, modems, input devices, and USB hubs often include a Power Management tab you can use to control whether the device can force the computer to wake up from Sleep mode. This option is useful if you have fax capabilities (yes, some businesses still use faxes) enabled for a modem or if you use the Remote Desktop feature over the internet on a machine that isn't always running at full power. On both portable and desktop computers, you can also use this option to allow Windows to turn off a device to save power.

- The Volumes tab for a disk drive contains no information when you first display the properties dialog box for that device. Click the Populate button to read the volume information for the selected disk, as shown in Figure 14-7, and click the Properties button to check the disk for errors, run the Defrag utility, or perform other maintenance tasks. Although you can perform these same tasks by right-clicking a drive icon in File Explorer, this option might be useful in situations where you have multiple hard disks installed and you suspect that one of those disks is having mechanical problems. Using this option, you can quickly see which physical disk a given volume is stored on.

CAUTION

DVD drives offer an option to change the DVD region, which controls which discs can be played on that drive. The DVD Region setting actually increments a counter on the physical drive itself, and that counter can be changed only a limited number of times. Be extremely careful with this setting, or you might end up losing the capability to play any regionally encoded DVDs in your collection on that device.

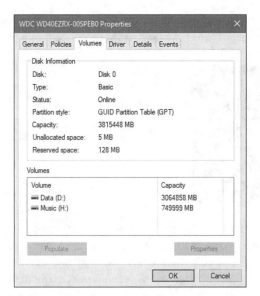

Figure 14-7 After you click the Populate button, the Volumes tab lists volumes on the selected drive. Select any volume and click Properties for full access to troubleshooting and maintenance tools.

- When working with network cards, you can often choose from a plethora of performance-related settings on an Advanced tab. Randomly tinkering with these settings is almost always counterproductive; however, you might be able to solve specific performance or connectivity problems by adjusting settings as directed by the device manufacturer or a Microsoft Support article.

Setting up Bluetooth devices

Bluetooth is one of those rare standards that passes the "it just works" test consistently. These days, virtually every portable device supports Bluetooth for wirelessly connecting headsets and pairing fitness devices. Many desktop PCs include Bluetooth support as well, for connecting keyboards and mice.

Recent feature updates have added a bevy of new features designed to make Windows 10 devices work better with Bluetooth LE devices such as fitness monitors. In Settings, the Bluetooth & Other Devices page combines the previously separate Bluetooth and Connected Devices pages. From this location, you can manage Bluetooth accessories, wireless docks, Xbox wireless controllers, and media devices by using a single interface.

Before you can use one Bluetooth device with another, you have to pair them, a process that generally involves making the external device discoverable (typically, by pressing and holding a pairing button for a few seconds or going into the settings menu on the device) and switching to the Bluetooth & Other Devices page in Settings > Devices. In version 1803, Windows 10 added support for a new feature called Swift Pair for Bluetooth that makes this process nearly effortless. If the device supports Swift Pair, making that device discoverable prompts Windows to display a notification like the one shown here. Click Connect to complete the pairing process:

To pair a device that doesn't support this feature, first make sure Bluetooth is turned on; then click Add Bluetooth Or Other Device and choose Bluetooth from the Add A Device dialog box. Figure 14-8 shows a Surface Pen, successfully discovered in Windows 10. (Making the pen discoverable requires holding down the top button for several seconds until a light flashes.) Tap the device name to complete the connection, and make the device usable with Windows 10, running in this example on a Surface Pro.

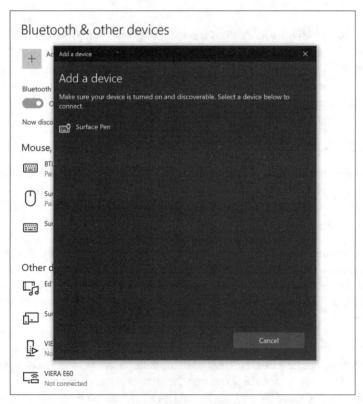

Figure 14-8 Before using a Bluetooth device with a Windows 10 PC, you have to make the device discoverable and then pair it with the PC.

Bluetooth connections represent a security risk—a low one, to be sure, but a risk nonetheless. That's why pairing a keyboard, for example, requires that you use the keyboard to enter a code from the PC's screen. Without that precaution, an attacker might be able to connect a wireless keyboard to your computer without your knowledge and then use it to steal data or run unauthorized and potentially dangerous software.

The Bluetooth & Other Devices page in Settings contains an on-off switch for the Bluetooth adapter. On mobile PCs, this is a power-saving feature. On a desktop PC without a touchscreen, be careful before disabling Bluetooth, because doing so could render your wireless keyboard and mouse—and thus the entire PC—unusable. The only cure, in that case, is to plug in a wired keyboard or mouse and turn the setting back on.

Managing USB devices

Universal serial bus, more commonly known as USB, is one of the oldest and most reliable Plug and Play standards in the world. Through the years, the USB standard has progressed from version 1.1 to 2.0 to 3.2, with the jump to USB 3.1 and beyond making a monumental difference in the speed of data transfer between USB-connected devices (up to 20 Gb/sec for USB 3.2 Gen 2x2 devices).

In an unfortunate bit of timing that has inspired some confusion, a new USB Type-C connector arrived at the same time as USB 3.1 began to appear in high-end computing machinery, including Microsoft's Surface Book 2, Surface Pro (2017), and Surface Go. With the help of so-called alternate modes (and appropriate adapters), you can use a USB Type-C port to connect to devices using HDMI, DisplayPort, Thunderbolt, and Mobile High-Definition Link (MHL) connections. One popular USB Type-C category is the multi-port hub, which accepts HDMI and DisplayPort cables, RJ-45 plugs from wired networks, traditional USB Type-A cables, and even laptop-grade power supplies, transforming a portable PC into a fully connected desktop PC through a single USB Type C input. The USB Type-C connector is reversible (no more flipping the USB plug three times until you find the right orientation). These new connectors are compatible with older USB devices but require an adapter.

> NOTE
> USB Type-C connectors typically support USB 3.1 and can connect to older USB devices using adapters. However, because the USB Type-C specification mandates support only for the older, slower USB 2.0 standard, you have no guarantee of USB 3.1 compatibility. This is most likely to be a problem with off-brand devices that were released as part of the first wave of USB Type-C support.

All USB devices are Plug and Play compatible. Knowing the types of connectors and the highest standard supported on your device can help ensure that you avoid compatibility hassles and carry the right cables.

Updating and uninstalling drivers

If you're having a hardware problem that you suspect is caused by a device driver, your first stop should be Device Manager. Open the properties dialog box for the device, and use the following buttons on the Driver tab to perform maintenance tasks:

- **Update Driver.** This choice opens the Update Driver Software dialog box, which we describe in the next section.

- **Roll Back Driver.** This option uninstalls the most recent manually updated driver and rolls back your system configuration to the previously installed driver. This option is available from Safe Mode if you need to remove a driver that's causing blue-screen (Stop) errors. Unlike System Restore, this option affects only the selected device. If you have never updated the selected driver or if you updated it through Windows Update, this option is unavailable.

- **Uninstall Device.** This button completely removes driver files and registry settings for the selected device. For driver packages you downloaded and installed separately, it also offers the option to completely remove the associated driver files. Use this capability to remove a driver that you suspect was incorrectly installed, and then reinstall the original driver or install an updated driver.

Inside OUT

Create a safety net before tinkering with drivers

When you install a new hardware driver, Windows automatically attempts to create a new System Restore checkpoint. That doesn't mean it will be successful, especially if System Restore is turned off or if a problem with your System Restore settings has caused this utility to suspend operations temporarily. To make certain you can roll back your changes if necessary, set a new System Restore checkpoint manually before making any kind of hardware configuration change. (For more details, see "Rolling back to a previous restore point" in Chapter 15, "Troubleshooting, backup, and recovery.")

Disabling automatic driver updates

Microsoft uses the Windows Update mechanism to deliver drivers for many devices. Using this feature, you can plug in a new device with relative confidence it will work without extra effort on your part. You also can use it to automatically receive updated drivers, which typically fix reliability, stability, and compatibility problems.

The dark side of driver updates is that they can occasionally cause a previously functional device to act up or even shut down. For that reason, some cautious Windows users prefer to disable automatic driver updates. In previous Windows versions and in the initial release of Windows 10, an advanced setting in Control Panel > System allowed you to specify that you never want to automatically install drivers from Windows Update. Effective with version 1607, this option has been replaced by a Group Policy setting.

If you're willing to accept the burden of manually checking for driver updates in exchange for the assurance of not being inconvenienced by a defective driver update, you can turn on this setting by opening the Local Group Policy Editor (Gpedit.msc) and going to Computer Configuration > Administrative Templates > Windows Components > Windows Update. Double-click the Do Not Include Drivers With Windows Updates policy, and set it to Enabled.

If you want to script this change, or if you're working with Windows 10 Home, where Group Policy is not supported, open Registry Editor using an administrator's credentials, and go to the key HKLM\Software\Policies\Microsoft\Windows\WindowsUpdate. Then add a new DWORD value, **ExcludeWUDriversInQualityUpdate**, and set it to **1**.

Updating a device driver manually

Microsoft and third-party device manufacturers frequently issue upgrades to device drivers. In some cases, the updates enable new features; in other cases, the newer version swats a bug that might or might not affect you. New Microsoft-signed drivers are often (but not always) delivered through Windows Update. Other drivers are available only by downloading them from the device manufacturer's website. Kernel-mode drivers must still be digitally signed before they can be installed.

If the new driver includes a setup program, run that program to copy the necessary files to your system's driver repository. Then start the update process by opening Device Manager, selecting the entry for the device you want to upgrade, and clicking the Update Driver button on the toolbar or the Update Driver option on the right-click shortcut menu. (You can also click Update Driver on the Driver tab of the properties dialog box for the device.)

That action opens the dialog box shown in Figure 14-9.

CHAPTER 14

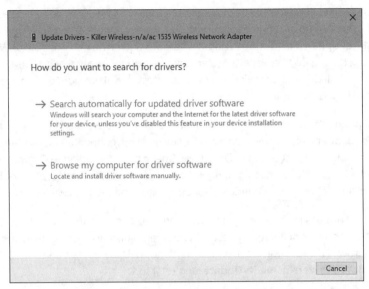

Figure 14-9 When manually updating a driver, try the automatic option first unless you want to select a specific driver you previously downloaded.

Click Search Automatically For Updated Driver Software if you know that the driver file is available on a removable media device or you want to check Windows Update. Click Browse My Computer For Driver Software to enter the location of a downloaded driver package or choose from a list of available drivers in the driver store folder. Clicking the Browse My Computer For Driver Software option opens a dialog box like the one shown in Figure 14-10, with two options for manually selecting a driver.

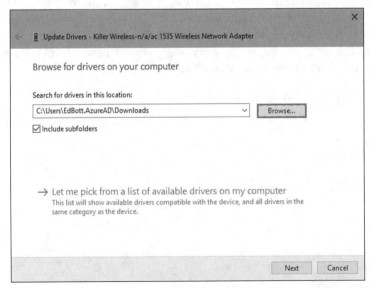

Figure 14-10 If you've downloaded a driver package that doesn't include an installer, select its location here to allow the update to proceed.

If you've downloaded the driver files to a known location or copied them to removable storage, click Browse to select that location, and then click Next to continue. (If you have a copy of the FileRepository folder from a previous Windows installation on the same hardware, you can choose that location.) With the Include Subfolders option selected, as it is by default, the driver update software will do a thorough search of the specified location, looking for a Setup Information file that matches the hardware ID for the selected device; if it finds a match, it installs the specified driver software automatically.

Use the second option, Let Me Pick From A List Of Available Drivers On My Computer, if you know that the driver software you need is already in the local driver store. In general, choosing this option presents a single driver for you to choose. In some cases, as in the example in Figure 14-11, you can see previous versions of a driver, with the option to replace a new driver with an older one for troubleshooting purposes. If you need to install an alternative driver version that isn't listed, clear the Show Compatible Hardware check box and then choose a driver from an expanded list of all matching devices in the device category.

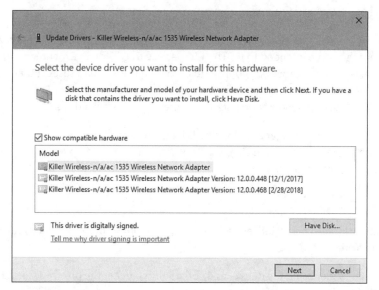

Figure 14-11   Clear the Show Compatible Hardware check box only if you're absolutely certain that Plug and Play has selected the wrong driver and you want to manually install a different driver.

Inside OUT

Make sure that update is really an update

How do you know whether a downloaded version is newer than the currently installed driver on your system? A good set of release notes should provide this information and is the preferred option for determining version information. In the absence of documentation, file dates offer some clues, but they're not always reliable. A better indicator is to inspect the properties of the driver files themselves. After unzipping the downloaded driver files to a folder on a local or network drive, right-click any file with a .dll or .sys extension and choose Properties. On the Version tab, you should be able to find details about the specific driver version, which you can compare with the driver details shown in Device Manager.

Rolling back to a previous driver version

Unfortunately, manually updated drivers can sometimes cause new problems that are worse than the woes they were intended to fix. This is especially true if you're experimenting with prerelease versions of new drivers. If your troubleshooting leads you to suspect that a newly installed driver is the cause of recent crashes or system instability, consider removing that driver and rolling your system configuration back to the previously installed driver.

To do this, open Device Manager and double-click the entry for the device you want to roll back. Then go to the Driver tab and click Roll Back Driver. The procedure that follows is straightforward and self-explanatory.

Uninstalling a driver

There are at least three circumstances under which you might want to completely remove a device driver from your system:

- You're no longer using the device, and you want to prevent the previously installed drivers from loading or using any resources.

- You've determined that the drivers available for the device are not stable enough to use on your system.

- The currently installed driver is not working correctly, and you want to reinstall it from scratch.

Inside OUT

Manage Plug and Play drivers

Removing and reinstalling the driver for a removable Plug and Play device requires a little extra effort. Because these drivers are loaded and unloaded dynamically, you can remove the driver only if the device in question is plugged in. Use the Uninstall button to remove the driver before unplugging the device. To reinstall the device driver without unplugging the device, open Device Manager and choose Action, Scan For Hardware Changes.

To remove a driver permanently, open Device Manager, right-click the entry for the device in question, and click Uninstall. (If the entry for the device in question is already open, click the Driver tab and click Uninstall.) Click OK when prompted to confirm that you want to remove the driver, and Windows removes the files and registry settings completely. You can now unplug the device.

If you installed the driver files from a downloaded file, the Confirm Device Uninstall dialog box includes a check box (shown in Figure 14-12) you can select to remove the files from the driver store as well. This prevents a troublesome driver from being inadvertently reinstalled when you reinsert the device or restart the computer.

Figure 14-12   Be sure to select this check box so that a troublesome driver doesn't reinstall itself automatically.

Note that you can't delete driver software that's included with Windows 10.

If the troublesome device driver was delivered through Windows Update, removing it is only a temporary fix. The next time Windows checks for new updates, it will download and install that same driver, unless you take steps to exclude that driver. To do that, use the troubleshooting package Microsoft created expressly for this problem. You can read more about this tool at *https://bit.ly/show-hide-update*; download it directly from *https://bit.ly/wushowhide*.

After downloading the package, run it and follow the prompts, choosing the Hide Updates option. After checking for available updates, the troubleshooter displays a list of driver and other updates that apply to the current system. Select the check box to the left of the unwanted driver and finish the wizard. If you find that a later update has resolved the problem, rerun the troubleshooter and choose the Show Updates option to make the driver available again via Windows Update.

TROUBLESHOOTING SPORADIC HARDWARE ERRORS

When your computer acts unpredictably, chances are good that defective hardware or a buggy device driver is at fault.

In those circumstances, using a powerful troubleshooting tool called Driver Verifier (Verifier. exe) is a terrific way to identify flawed device drivers. Instead of your computer locking up at a most inopportune time with a misleading Blue Screen of Death (BSOD), Driver Verifier stops your computer predictably at startup with a BSOD that accurately explains the true problem. Although this doesn't sound like a huge improvement (your system still won't work, after all), Driver Verifier performs a critical troubleshooting step: identifying the problem. You can then correct the problem by removing or replacing the offending driver. (If you're satisfied that the driver really is okay despite Driver Verifier Manager's warning, you can turn off Driver Verifier for all drivers or for a specific driver. Any driver that Driver Verifier chokes on should be regarded with suspicion, but some legitimate drivers bend the rules without causing problems.)

Driver Verifier works at startup to thoroughly exercise each driver. It performs many of the same tests that are run as part of the Windows certification and signing process, such as checking for the way the driver accesses memory.

Beware: If Driver Verifier finds a nonconforming driver—even one that doesn't seem to be causing any problems—it will prevent your system from starting. Use Driver Verifier only if you're having problems. In other words, if it ain't broke...

To begin working with Driver Verifier, open an elevated Command Prompt window and type **verifier**. In the Driver Verifier Manager dialog box, shown next, select Create Standard Settings. (If you want to assess current conditions before proceeding, select the last option: Display Information About The Currently Verified Drivers.)

When you click Next, the Driver Verifier Manager displays a list of all currently installed drivers that match the conditions you specified. Note that the list might contain a mix of hardware drivers and some file-system filter drivers, such as those used by antivirus programs, backup utilities, CD- and DVD-burning apps, and other low-level system software.

At this point, you have two choices:

- Go through the list and make a note of all drivers identified, and then click Cancel. No changes are made to your system configuration; all you've done is gather a list of suspicious drivers, which you can then try to remove or disable manually.

- Click Finish to complete the wizard and restart your computer. Don't choose this option unless you're prepared to deal with the consequences, as explained in the remainder of this sidebar.

If your computer stops with a blue screen when you next sign in, you've identified a problem driver. The error message includes the name of the offending driver and an error code.

To resolve the problem, boot into Safe Mode using Windows 10's Recovery Environment and disable or uninstall the problem driver. You'll then want to check with the device vendor to get a working driver that you can install.

To disable Driver Verifier so that it no longer performs verification checks at startup, run Driver Verifier Manager again and select Delete Existing Settings in the initial dialog box. Alternatively, at a command prompt, type **verifier /reset**. (If you haven't yet solved the driver problem, of course, you'll be stopped at a BSOD, unable to disable Driver Verifier. In that case, boot into Safe Mode and then disable Driver Verifier.)

You can configure Driver Verifier so that it checks only certain drivers. To do that, open Driver Verifier Manager, select Create Standard Settings, click Next, and select the last option: Select Driver Names From A List. With this option, you can exempt a particular driver from Driver Verifier's scrutiny—such as one that Driver Verifier flags but you're certain is not the cause of your problem.

NOTE

Driver Verifier has been included with every version of Windows since Windows 2000 and is included with Windows 10. For information about using Driver Verifier, see the Microsoft Support article 244617, "Using Driver Verifier to identify issues with Windows drivers for advanced users," at *https://support.microsoft.com/kb/244617*.

Printers and print queues

To install a modern printer that plugs into a USB port on the PC where you plan to use it, just connect the device. Plug and Play does the rest of the work. (See "Installing a new Plug and Play device" earlier in this chapter.)

NOTE

Although it's nearly certain there are still some non–Plug and Play printers out there, connecting to creaky parallel ports on PCs from the late Cretaceous period, we are happy to bid those devices adieu, and we urge you to do the same. We don't cover manual connection options for legacy devices in this book.

Wireless printers that connect over Wi-Fi or by using Bluetooth also support Plug and Play. Follow the manufacturer's instructions to complete the wireless connection, or skip ahead a few pages to our explanation of the Add A Printer option.

➤ You can share a printer for use by other users on the same local network. On a simple home or small business network, follow the instructions in "Sharing files, printers, and other resources over a local network" in Chapter 13, "Windows networking." On business networks, the procedure is more formal; see "Sharing files, printers, and other resources over a local network," also in Chapter 13.

To configure a printer or work with documents in a print queue, go to Settings > Devices > Printers & Scanners. Click any installed printer to show buttons like those visible in Figure 14-13.

Figure 14-13 This Settings page shows installed printers and scanners. Click any item in the list to reveal the three buttons shown here.

The Open Queue button, naturally, takes you to a list of pages waiting to print. Click Manage to see options that include the familiar printer-queue dialog box as well as links to printer settings and the extremely useful Print A Test Page command. Click Manage > Printer Properties to see status information and other configuration options.

Printers aren't exactly like snowflakes, but there are far too many variations in hardware and software design for us to offer more than the most general advice: Get to know your printer by inspecting these settings, and don't be afraid to read the manual.

To make a wireless or networked printer available locally, go to Settings > Devices > Printers & Scanners and click Add A Printer Or Scanner. If the planets are properly aligned, the autodiscovery software might locate your printer and walk you through setting it up. If you're not so lucky, click The Printer I Want Isn't Listed to open the manual options shown in Figure 14-14. In this example, we chose the Select A Shared Printer By Name option, clicked Browse, and located the shared printer on a network server.

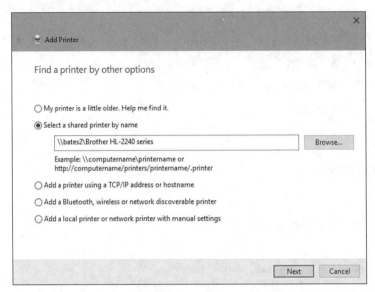

Figure 14-14   The Add Printer Wizard offers numerous paths to connect to a printer, especially those that are available over a network.

Among the "other options" available on this page in the Add Printer Wizard is one that you can use to connect to a network printer using its Universal Naming Convention (UNC) name. The device shown in Figure 14-13 earlier, for example, is connected to a printer on a server named Bates2, making its UNC address \\BATES2\Brother HL-2240 Series. You can also use an IP address for a device that has a permanently assigned address, and you can enlist the help of a wizard to connect a wireless or Bluetooth printer.

Inside OUT

Find a printer's TCP/IP address or host name

Often the easiest way to determine the TCP/IP address or host name for a printer is to use the printer's control panel to print a configuration page, which usually includes this information.

One of the simplest ways to connect to a shared network printer doesn't involve any wizards at all. Just use File Explorer to browse to the network computer (entering and saving credentials for the share, if necessary), where you should see an entry for any shared printer available to you. Double-click that icon to begin the process of connecting to that printer. Because Windows requires a local copy of the network printer's driver, you'll need an administrator's credentials.

> ## Inside OUT
> *Use a compatible driver*
>
> If you can't find a driver that's specifically designed for your printer, you might be able to get away with using another driver. Check the hardware documentation to find out whether the printer emulates a more popular model, such as a Hewlett-Packard LaserJet. If so, choose that printer driver, and then print some test documents after completing setup. You might lose access to some advanced features available with your model of printer, but this strategy should allow you to perform basic printing tasks.

Managing hard disks and other storage devices

When you connect a new storage device to a PC running Windows 10, a new entry, complete with driver, appears in Device Manager. But unlike with most other hardware, that's not where you perform initial setup and configuration tasks. Instead, you'll probably use the Disk Management console (Diskmgmt.msc), which offers a graphical interface for initializing, partitioning, and formatting storage devices.

For those who need to incorporate disk-management tasks in scripts (as well as for those who simply prefer carrying out administrative tasks at the command prompt), Windows also provides a powerful command-line program called DiskPart. Everything you can do with Disk Management you can also do by using DiskPart; you just have to work harder and more carefully.

Knowing when to use which tool is the secret of disk wizardry in Windows 10. Disk Management, for example, is ideal for shrinking and expanding volumes, while the Clean command in DiskPart makes short work of preparing a disk to be formatted for a new role. That command has no counterpart in Disk Management.

> ## NOTE
> Accessing Windows Management Instrumentation (WMI) through Windows PowerShell provides another method for managing disks. This method has the additional advantage of custom programmability, which can be useful for hardware manufacturers and other high-volume operations. Windows also includes a second command-line tool for file-system and disk management, called Fsutil. You can use this utility to find files by security identifier (SID), change the short name of a file, and perform other esoteric tasks. These specialized tools and techniques are beyond the scope of this book.

In this chapter, we cover the tasks required to prepare a new drive for use on a Windows 10 PC. For instructions on the tasks required to maintain and reconfigure an existing disk drive, see Chapter 9, "Storage and file management."

CHAPTER 14

Running Disk Management

To run Disk Management, type `diskmgmt.msc` at a command prompt, or press Windows key+X (or right-click the Start button) and then click Disk Management. You need administrative credentials to run Disk Management. Figure 14-15 illustrates the Disk Management console.

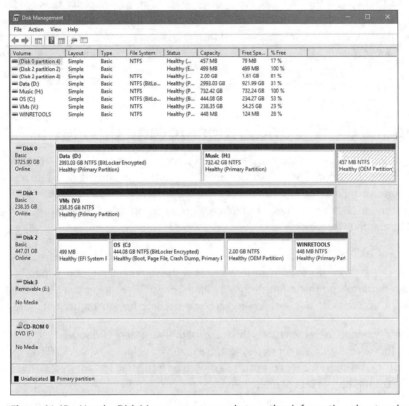

Figure 14-15   Use the Disk Management console to gather information about and manage hard disks and removable disks.

Disk Management provides a wealth of information about physical disks and the volumes, partitions, and logical drives in place on those disks. You can use this utility to perform the following disk-related tasks:

- Check the size, file system, status, and other properties of disks and volumes

- Create, format, and delete partitions, logical drives, and dynamic volumes

- Assign drive letters to hard disk volumes, removable disk drives, and optical drives

- Create mounted drives

- Convert basic disks to dynamic disks and vice versa

- Create spanned and striped volumes

- Extend or shrink partitions

Disk Management displays information in two panes. In its default arrangement, the upper pane lists each volume on your system and provides information about the volume's type, status, capacity, available free space, and so on. You can carry out commands on a volume by right-clicking any entry in the first column of this pane (the column labeled Volume) and choosing a command.

In the lower pane, each row represents one physical device. The heading at the left of each row shows the name by which that device is known to the operating system (Disk 0, Disk 1, and so on), along with its type, size, and status. To the right are areas that display information about the volumes of each device. Note that these areas are not by default drawn to scale. To change the scaling used by Disk Management, click View and then Settings. You'll find various options on the Scaling tab of the Settings dialog box.

Right-clicking a heading at the left in the lower pane displays commands pertinent to an entire storage device. Right-clicking an area representing a volume provides a menu of actions applicable to that volume.

Managing disks from the command prompt

To use DiskPart, start by running Windows PowerShell or Command Prompt (Cmd.exe) with elevated privileges.

➤ **For more information about PowerShell and Cmd, see Chapter 19, "PowerShell and other advanced management tools."**

When you run DiskPart, it switches to a command interpreter, identified by the DISKPART> prompt. If you type **help** and press Enter, you see a screen that lists all available commands.

> ### UNDERSTANDING DISK-MANAGEMENT TERMINOLOGY
>
> The current version of Disk Management has simplified somewhat the arcane language of disk administration. Nevertheless, it's still important to have a bit of the vocabulary under your belt. The following terms and concepts are the most important:
>
> - **Volume.** A volume is a disk or subdivision of a disk that is formatted and available for storage. If a volume is assigned a drive letter, it appears as a separate entity in File Explorer. A hard disk can have one or more volumes.

- **Mounted drive.** A mounted drive is a volume that is mapped to an empty folder on an NTFS-formatted disk. A mounted drive does not get a drive letter and does not appear separately in File Explorer. Instead, it behaves as though it were a subfolder on another volume.

- **Basic disk and dynamic disk.** The two principal types of hard-disk organization in Windows are called basic and dynamic:

  - A basic disk can be subdivided into as many as four partitions. (Disks that have been initialized using a GUID Partition Table can have more than four.) All volumes on a basic disk must be simple volumes. When you use Disk Management to create new simple volumes, the first three partitions it creates are primary partitions. The fourth is created as an extended partition using all remaining unallocated space on the disk. An extended partition can be organized into as many as 2,000 logical disks. In use, a logical disk behaves exactly like a primary partition.

  - A dynamic disk offers organizational options not available on a basic disk. In addition to simple volumes, dynamic disks can contain spanned or striped volumes. These last two volume types combine space from multiple disks. We expect that very few of our readers will ever use dynamic disks.

- **Simple volume.** A simple volume is a volume contained entirely within a single physical device. On a basic disk, a simple volume is also known as a partition.

- **Spanned volume.** A spanned volume is a volume that combines space from physically separate disks, making the combination appear and function as though it were a single storage medium.

- **Striped volume.** A striped volume is a volume in which data is stored in 64-KB strips across physically separate disks to improve performance.

- **Active partition, boot partition, and system partition.** The active partition is the one from which an x86-based computer starts after you power it up. The first physical hard disk attached to the system (Disk 0) must include an active partition. The boot partition is the partition where the Windows system files are located. The system partition is the partition that contains the bootstrap files that Windows uses to start your system and display the boot menu.

Even if you prefer to avoid the command line and don't intend to write disk-management scripts, you should know about DiskPart, because if you ever find yourself needing to manage hard disks from the Windows Recovery Environment (Windows RE), you will have access to DiskPart but you won't have access to the Disk Management console. (Windows RE is a special environment you can use for system-recovery purposes if a major hardware or software problem prevents you from starting Windows.)

CAUTION

DiskPart is not for casual experimentation. Its primary purpose is for scripting rather than for interactive use. The DiskPart command-line interpreter is dense and cryptic, with a complex structure that requires you to list and select objects before you act on them. For more details about DiskPart, see "DiskPart Commands" (*https://bit.ly/diskpart-commands*). Although this article dates from Windows Vista days and some of the comparisons it makes between DiskPart and the Disk Management console are out of date, its tutorial information about the syntax and usage of DiskPart is still accurate.

Setting up a new hard disk

Whether you're installing Windows on a brand-new disk or simply adding a new disk (internal or external) to an existing system, you should consider how you want to use the new storage space before you begin creating volumes. If your goal is to set up a large space for backup or media storage, for example, you might want to devote the entire disk to a single volume. On the other hand, if your plan is to establish two or more separate volumes—perhaps one for each family member on a shared home computer—decide how many gigabytes you want to assign to each partition. You can change your mind later, but it's easiest to adjust the number of volumes on a disk and their relative sizes before you fill a volume with a large amount of data.

Installing Windows on a new disk

When you run the Windows 10 setup program on a computer with a single, raw hard disk (such as a desktop computer you built yourself from new parts or any PC in which you've replaced the system drive with a new physical drive), you're presented with a screen identifying the disk and its size. If you want to create a single volume encompassing the entire disk, you can click Next to proceed, and Setup will take care of initializing the disk, creating a new volume, and formatting it. Otherwise, you can click New, and then in the same screen, you can choose the size of the volume you want to create for your Windows installation.

If you decide not to use the entire disk for Windows, you can create additional volumes from within the Setup program. But there's no particular need to do this. After you install Windows, you can use Disk Management to create one or more additional volumes in the unallocated space remaining on the disk.

> ➤ For more information about setting up Windows, see Chapter 2, "Installing, configuring, and deploying Windows 10."

Adding a new disk to an existing Windows installation

When you open Disk Management for the first time after installing a new hard disk, Windows offers to initialize the disk, as shown in Figure 14-16. This action defines the partition style for the disk and is an essential first step before you can use Disk Management to perform any further actions.

CHAPTER 14

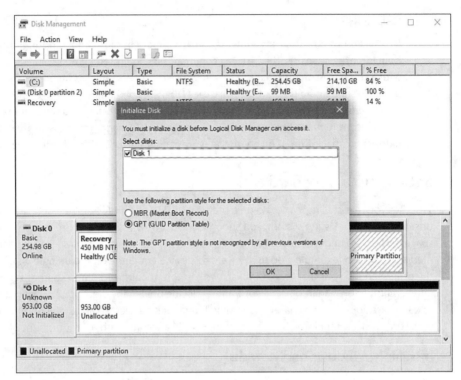

Figure 14-16   You must initialize a disk using one of these two partition styles before you can create a new volume and format it for data storage.

MBR (master boot record) and GPT (GUID Partition Table) are terms describing alternative methods for maintaining that information that defines a disk's subdivisions. Which partition style should you choose? In general, choose MBR only when compatibility with older operating systems is required. GPT disks support larger volumes (up to 18 exabytes) and more partitions (as many as 128 on a basic disk). In earlier versions of Windows, you could convert a disk from MBR to GPT (or vice versa) only before a disk had been partitioned for the first time (or after all partitions have been removed). Beginning with version 1703, Windows 10 includes a utility called MBR2GPT that provides a way past this limitation. GPT is required on drives that contain the Windows partition on UEFI-based systems.

Inside OUT

Convert an MBR disk to GPT

Windows 10 version 1703 introduced a utility called MBR2GPT.exe that does what its name implies—it converts a system disk from the Master Boot Record partition style to GUID partition table. The primary purpose of the tool is to facilitate the conversion of systems running in legacy BIOS mode to UEFI. (You can't use this tool on a non-system disk.) MBR2GPT is designed for administrators to run during deployment, from the

Windows Preinstallation Environment (Windows PE); you can also run it from the Windows 10 command line, using the /AllowFullOS switch. It completes its task without deleting data on the target disk.

Like DiskPart and Fsutil, described earlier in this chapter, MBR2GPT requires a high level of technical competence. Full documentation is provided at *https://technet.microsoft. com/en-us/itpro/windows/deploy/mbr-to-gpt*. Information about converting from BIOS to UEFI can be found at *https://technet.microsoft.com/en-us/windows/mt782786.aspx*.

After this task is complete, you need to create one or more volumes in the unallocated space, assign a drive letter to each volume, label the volumes (if you don't want them to be identified in File Explorer as simply "New Volume"), and format them. You can carry out all these steps with the help of a wizard. To begin, right-click anywhere in the area marked Unallocated and then click New Simple Volume. The New Simple Volume Wizard appears.

1. **Specify Volume Size.** This page displays the maximum and minimum amounts of space you can devote to the new volume. The wizard doesn't give you the option of designating volume space as a percentage of unallocated space, so if your goal is to create two or more volumes of equal size, you need to do a bit of arithmetic before going on.

2. **Assign Drive Letter Or Path.** You can assign any available drive letter to the new volume. Note that the letters A and B, which used to be reserved for floppy disks, are no longer reserved. You also have the option to assign no drive letter.

3. **Format Partition.** You don't have to format the new volume immediately, but there is rarely a good reason to wait. Your choices, as shown in Figure 14-17 are as follows:

    ▪ **File System.** A file system is a method for organizing folders (directories) and files on a storage medium. For hard disk volumes larger than 4 GB (4,096 MB), your only options are NTFS (the default) and exFAT. If you're formatting removable media such as USB flash drives or a writable optical disc, other file systems are available. For more information, see "Choosing a file system" later in this chapter.

    ▪ **Allocation Unit Size.** The allocation unit size (also known as the cluster size) is the smallest space that can be allocated to a file. The Default option, in which Windows selects the appropriate cluster size based on volume size, is the best choice here.

    ▪ **Volume Label.** The volume label identifies the drive in File Explorer. The default label is "New Volume." It's a good idea to give your new volume a name that describes its purpose.

CHAPTER 14

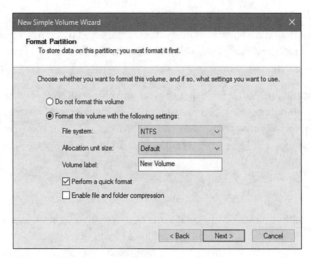

Figure 14-17   You use the Format Partition page to specify your new volume's file system, allocation unit size, and volume label.

4. Select the Perform A Quick Format check box if you want Disk Management to skip the sometimes lengthy process of checking the disk media. Select Enable File And Folder Compression if you want all data on the new volume to use NTFS compression.

The wizard's final page gives you one more chance to review your specifications. You should actually take a moment to read this display before you click Finish.

After Disk Management has done its work and disk formatting is complete, a dark blue bar appears over the new volume in the console's graphical view pane:

If your disk still has unallocated space (as the disk in this example does), you can add another volume by right-clicking that part of the display and then clicking New Simple Volume again.

Choosing a file system

Formatting a disk prepares it for data storage; the first step in formatting is choosing a file system. Windows 10 supports the following file systems: FAT (File Allocation Table), NTFS, exFAT (Extended File Allocation Table); optimized for use with flash drives), CDFS (Compact Disc File System; also sometimes identified as ISO-9660), and UDF (Universal Disk Format). Windows 10 provides read/write ability for the Resilient File System (ReFS), but creation capability is limited to Windows 10 Pro for Workstations.

The formatting choices available for a specific volume depend on the type of media you're formatting. With hard disks, the only options made available by Disk Management are NTFS and exFAT. If you want to format a hard disk in FAT32, you need to use the Format command with the **/FS** switch at the command prompt. (Type **format /?** at the command prompt for details.) The only good reason to do this, however, is for the sake of compatibility with devices running non-Microsoft operating systems that don't natively support NTFS.

If you're formatting a USB flash drive or a MicroSD card, on the other hand, either FAT32 or exFAT is a reasonable choice. Because NTFS is a journaling file system, reading and writing files on NTFS disks involves more disk input/output than similar operations on FAT32 and exFAT disks. Flash drives can perform a finite number of reads and writes before they need to be replaced—hence, they might have a longer life expectancy under FAT32 or exFAT than under NTFS. On UEFI systems, FAT32 is required for bootable installation media. (For more information about exFAT, see the "exFAT vs. FAT32" sidebar later in this chapter.) For a tabular comparison of file systems, see *https://bit.ly/file-systemcomparison*.

In general, for any fixed drive, NTFS is your best choice. It offers a number of important advantages over the earlier FAT and FAT32 file systems:

- **Security.** On an NTFS volume, you can restrict access to files and folders by using permissions. (For information about using NTFS permissions, see "What are ACLs?" in Chapter 11, "Managing user accounts, passwords, and credentials.") You can add an extra layer of protection by encrypting files if your edition of Windows 10 supports it. (Windows 10 Home does not support file encryption using EFS; all other editions do.) On a FAT or FAT32 drive, anyone with physical access to your computer can access any files stored on that drive.

- **Reliability.** Because NTFS is a journaling file system, an NTFS volume can recover from disk errors more readily than a FAT32 volume. NTFS uses log files to keep track of all disk activity. In the event of a system crash, Windows 10 can use this journal to repair file-system errors automatically when the system is restarted. In addition, NTFS can dynamically remap clusters that contain bad sectors and mark those clusters as bad so that the operating system no longer uses them. FAT and FAT32 drives are more vulnerable to disk errors.

- **Expandability.** Using NTFS-formatted volumes, you can expand storage on existing volumes without having to back up, repartition, reformat, and restore.

- **Efficiency.** On partitions greater than 8 GB, NTFS volumes manage space more efficiently than FAT32. The maximum partition size for a FAT32 drive created by Windows 10 is 32 GB; by contrast, you can create a single NTFS volume of up to 16 terabytes (16,384 GB) using default settings, and by tweaking cluster sizes you can ratchet the maximum volume size up to 256 terabytes.

- **Optimized storage of small files.** Files on the order of a hundred bytes or less can be stored entirely within the Master File Table (MFT) record, rather than requiring a minimum allocation unit outside the MFT. This results in greater storage efficiency for small files.

EXFAT VS. FAT32

Microsoft introduced the Extended FAT (exFAT) file system first with Windows Embedded CE 6.0, an operating system designed for industrial controllers and consumer electronics devices. Subsequently, exFAT was made available in Windows Vista Service Pack 1 (SP1). Its principal advantage over FAT32 is scalability. The exFAT file system removes the 32-GB volume and 4-GB file-size limitations of FAT32. It also handles more than 1,000 files per directory. Its principal disadvantage is limited backward compatibility. Some non-PC consumer electronics devices might be able to read earlier FAT systems but not exFAT.

If you're formatting a flash drive and you expect to store large video files on it, exFAT might be a good choice for the file system. On the other hand, if you're planning to use that flash drive to share photos with a local print shop, FAT32 is definitely the way to go.

Inside OUT

Formatting does not remove a volume's data

Whatever formatting options you choose, you're warned that the action of formatting a volume makes that volume's data inaccessible. That's true. Whatever data is there when you format will no longer be available to you by normal means after you format. Unless you use the Format command with the **/P** switch, however, the data remains in some form and might be recoverable by someone who has physical access to the device and the right tools. If you're really concerned about covering your tracks, either use **Format /P**:*x* (where *x* represents the number of passes) or wipe the disk after you format it by using the command-line program Cipher.exe, with the **/W** switch. (Type **cipher /?** at the command prompt for details.) For information about other ways to clean a disk, see "Permanently wiping all data from a disk" in Chapter 9.

Working with solid-state drives

Many newer computers are equipped with a solid-state drive (SSD), which is a chunk of flash memory instead of a spinning magnetic disk coupled with an onboard disk controller and the requisite power and data connectors. Such drives can provide improved performance, increased battery life, better durability, reduced likelihood of damage caused by drops and shocks, faster startup times, and reductions in noise, heat, and vibration. These benefits come at a price: SSDs typically cost more and have less storage capacity than current hard disk drive (HDD) models, although the gap is closing.

Conventional hard disk drives are typically the biggest performance bottleneck in any computing environment. If you can speed up disk activity, especially reads, the effects on system startup and application launch times can be breathtaking. On our test platform, which has a conventional hard disk and an older solid-state drive configured for dual booting, the total boot time when using the SSD is roughly one-fourth the time required to boot from the HDD. On very recent hardware, with the latest generation of SSDs, we routinely see boot times of less than 15 seconds. Close examination of log files created by the Windows System Assessment Tool (WinSAT), which are stored in %SystemRoot%\Performance\WinSAT\DataStore, shows radically higher throughput and faster times in the DiskMetrics section of the SSD-based system.

Although the underlying technology in SSDs and HDDs is completely different, for the most part, the devices are treated identically by Windows, and you don't need to concern yourself with the differences. Behind the scenes, Windows does several things differently on SSDs, including the following:

- SuperFetch, ReadyBoost, ReadyBoot, and ReadyDrive, features designed to overcome hard disk bottlenecks, are unnecessary and are disabled by default on most SSDs. (Windows analyzes disk performance and disables these features only on SSDs that are fast enough to make these features superfluous.)

- When creating a partition on an SSD, Windows properly aligns the partition for best performance.

- Windows 10 supports the TRIM command. SSDs have to erase blocks of data before those blocks can be reused; they can't write directly over deleted data as rotating disks can. The TRIM command makes this process more efficient by reclaiming deleted space in the background. You can find more details in this Wikipedia article: *https://en.wikipedia.org/wiki/Trim_(computing)*.

Using Storage Spaces

Storage Spaces is a technology introduced with the server editions of Windows in 2012 and with Windows 8 and Windows 8.1. With this technology, you can aggregate collections of disks into "storage pools" and then create virtualized disks ("storage spaces") within those pools. For example, you could take two 3-TB disks (Serial-Attached SCSI, Serial ATA, or USB) and use Storage Spaces to combine them into a single 6-TB virtualized disk.

You can also use Storage Spaces to establish resiliency for critical data. For example, using your two 3-TB disks, you could create a mirrored storage space in which each file saved on one of the physical disks is mirrored on the other; if one of the physical disks fails, your data is preserved.

Three types of resiliency are available:

- **Two-way mirror.** The system writes two copies of your data. You can lose one physical disk without data loss. A minimum of two physical disks is required. The amount of storage available is half of the total storage pool or the capacity of the smaller disk, whichever is less.

- **Three-way mirror.** The system writes three copies of your data. You can lose two physical disks without data loss. A minimum of three physical disks is required, and the amount of storage available is approximately one-third of the storage pool.

- **Parity.** The system stripes data across physical disks while also maintaining parity information that allows it to protect and recover your data more efficiently in the event of drive failure. A minimum of three drives is required.

Simple (nonresilient) storage spaces are recommended if you prefer a large virtual disk to separate physical disks. You might make this choice, for example, if you have a large media collection and several older (hence smaller) disks that are not currently in service. Simple storage spaces are also a good choice for space-intensive operations (video editing, for example) that do not require resiliency. Files in a simple storage space are striped across physical disks, resulting in better performance.

Use parity for maximum resiliency, but note that write performance is degraded by the requirement for the system to calculate and store parity information. This choice might be appropriate for archival storage.

Note the following:

- You can create a storage space only on freshly formatted blank disks. If you begin with formatted disks, Storage Spaces will erase all data on the physical components of a pool (with due warning to you, of course) before setting up the storage space, and such erased data cannot be recovered via the Recycle Bin or other data-recovery tools.

- Storage spaces should not be used as a substitute for backups. They do not protect you against theft, fire, or other catastrophic events that affect the entire collection of physical disks.

To set up a storage space, go to Settings > System > Storage and click Manage Storage Spaces, under the More Storage Settings heading. (Or begin typing **storage spaces** in the search box and click the shortcut when it appears in the search results.) Click Create A New Pool And Storage Space, and respond to the UAC prompt. A display comparable to the one shown next appears.

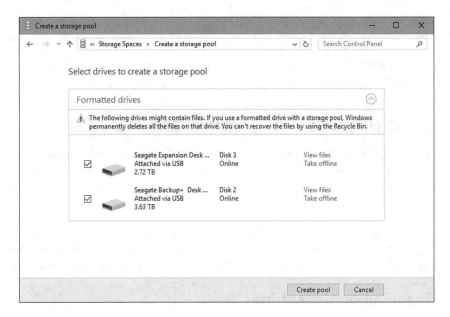

After noting the warning about the erasure of existing data on the available drives, select the drives you want to use, and then click Create Pool. The Create A Storage Space window appears. The example shown below represents a Storage Space configured as a two-way mirror with two disks of identical size:

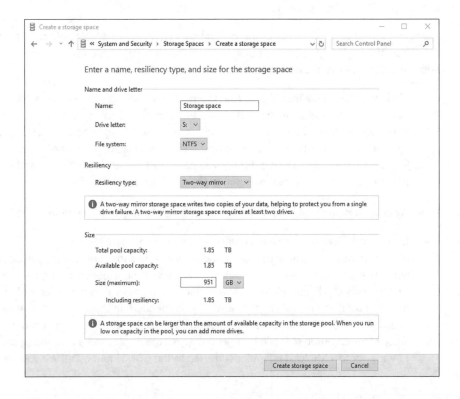

Choose a drive letter, file system, and resiliency type, adjust the capacity if needed, and then click Create Storage Space.

For much more information about Storage Spaces, see *https://bit.ly/storage-spaces and https:// bit.ly/storage-spaces-faq*.

Configuring displays and graphics adapters

On a desktop or portable PC with a single screen (and, when connecting to an external monitor, the proper cable), you shouldn't need to do anything to configure your display. All modern display adapters deliver up-to-date drivers via Windows Update, and the display is capable of configuring itself as soon as it's connected.

In this chapter, we cover a handful of scenarios when you might need to review and adjust these settings manually. We also explain how to use a new feature, introduced in version 1803, that provides per-app control over graphics settings on PCs that contain two graphics processing units (GPUs).

Changing display settings

As we noted earlier, Windows typically does a good job of configuring display settings. To review them, go to Settings > System > Display. This group of settings has been greatly expanded over the course of multiple feature updates, removing all related settings from the old-style Control Panel and making many tasks simpler than in previous releases. Figure 14-18 shows this new Settings page, with display options for a Surface Laptop.

The Brightness settings at the top of this dialog box are typically available only on a laptop PC. We discuss the Night Light settings a bit later in this section. Pay particular attention to the settings under the Scale And Layout heading:

- **Change The Size Of Text, Apps, And Other Items.** On high-resolution monitors, you can increase the apparent size of apps and text, a process known technically as *scaling*. Here, too, Windows recommends a scaling factor based on the size of the display and the resolution. You might choose a larger or smaller scaling factor for your own personal comfort. On a system with a single display, you can adjust the scaling by using a slider below the thumbnail of the current monitor on the Display page in Settings.

   ➤ We cover scaling in "Making text easier to read" in Chapter 3, "Using Windows 10."

- **Resolution.** Every display has a native resolution, one where the number of physical pixels matches the number of pixels Windows wants to show. Configuring the display at a nonnative resolution generally results in a subpar viewing experience, often with a blurry, stretched display. Figure 14-18 shows a Surface Pro running at its native resolution of 2256 by 1504 pixels, as indicated by the word "Recommended" in the label. Click that value to open a full list of other supported resolutions. Why would you choose a non-native resolution? One common scenario is projecting to a large display—in a conference room, for example, or to a Miracast adapter connected to the HDMI input on a TV. If you choose the option to duplicate displays on both monitors, you need to set the resolution to match what your audience is seeing, even if it looks distorted on your built-in display.

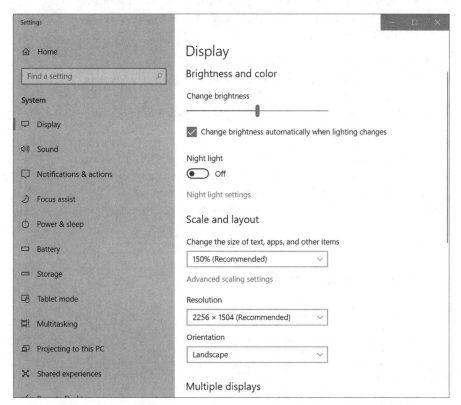

Figure 14-18 If you see "Recommended" after the first two options under the Scale And Layout heading, that means Windows has correctly configured your display resolution and scaling.

TROUBLESHOOTING

Display options stop at 1920 by 1080 even though your monitor supports higher resolutions

The most likely cause of this problem is an HDMI connection that's incapable of handling the desired resolution. If either the display adapter or the monitor supports only the HDMI 1.3 standard, you're limited to Full HD (1920 by 1080) resolution. If both ends of the connection support HDMI 1.4 or later, you need to use a High Speed HDMI cable (a standard HDMI cable is limited to Full HD resolution). In most cases, the best workaround is to switch to a different connection, if one is available. The DisplayPort 1.2a standard, which uses mini and full-sized connectors and also works with USB-C adapters, supports 4K (3840 by 2160 or 4096 by 2160) resolutions, and the HDMI 1.4 standard supports 5K displays (5120 by 2880).

- **Orientation.** This setting is available on portable devices that can be used as tablets and on external displays that can be rotated 90 degrees for use in portrait mode. For a laptop or desktop computer where the orientation of the display is fixed, changing orientation would result in an odd, mostly unreadable display; thus, this setting is typically unavailable.

An increasingly popular configuration for high-powered portable PCs is the inclusion of two GPUs. Some models in Microsoft's Surface Book line, for example, can switch between the power-saving but still capable built-in Intel graphics and a more powerful discrete GPU based on an Nvidia chipset. If you own a PC that includes two GPUs, a feature that first appeared in Windows 10 version 1803 allows you to associate a GPU with a specific app.

To configure custom per-GPU options, go to Settings > System > Display and click Graphics Settings. On a Surface Book, that opens the Graphics Settings page shown in Figure 14-19. As you can see, we've already customized this device to give an extra GPU boost to Microsoft Edge and to the built-in Virtual Machine Connection app.

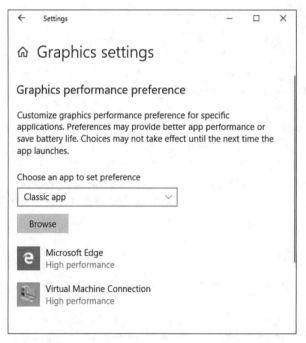

Figure 14-19   On high-end devices with switchable GPUs, you can assign a GPU to specific apps for better performance or to maximize power saving.

The technique to add an app to this list varies. For a Windows desktop program, choose Classic App, and then click Browse and locate the executable file for that program. For a UWP app, choose Universal App and then select the app from the resulting drop-down list. Click Add to create a new entry on the list for your selected program, and then click Options to open the Graphics Specifications dialog box shown in Figure 14-20. The top portion identifies which GPU is for power saving and which is for high performance, and the options below allow you to tell Windows which GPU to use for that app.

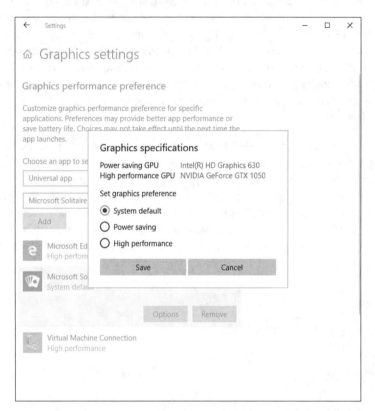

Figure 14-20   With System Default selected, Windows will automatically choose the appropriate GPU. To override that choice, choose Power Saving or High Performance from this dialog box.

At any time, you can see which GPU is in use for a given app by opening Task Manager and looking at the GPU Engine column on the Performance tab. Click the GPU Engine column heading to sort the list so that all apps currently using either GPU appear at the top of the list.

Version 1803 also adds support for High Dynamic Range (HDR) displays. If your system includes hardware compatible with this feature, you can adjust its performance by going to Settings > Apps > Video Playback.

Controlling scaling on high-DPI displays

So-called high-DPI displays are typically found today on high-end portable PCs. Some models in Microsoft's Surface Book series, for example, have a screen size of 13.5 inches (measured diagonally) and a native resolution of 3000 by 2000 pixels. That translates to 267 pixels per inch (a measure sometimes referred to in casual usage as dots per inch, or DPI).

That density is far greater than (typically more than double) the density of a high-resolution desktop display or a budget-priced laptop PC with a similar display size running at a lower native resolution. If you use a high-DPI system at normal (100 percent) scaling, the icons and text will be so small as to be unreadable. That's why, by default, the Surface Book is configured to run Windows 10 at 200 percent scaling. The result is an impressively sharp display. Everything in the Windows interface and in universal Windows apps is magnified at twice its normal size, using multiple physical pixels to create each effective pixel (at 200 percent scaling, each effective pixel is made from four physical pixels). The most popular classic desktop apps look great on primary high-DPI displays, as does any desktop app that was built using Windows Presentation Foundation (WPF).

Beginning with version 1703, Windows 10 includes new display code that improves rendering for some older desktop apps that previously looked a little blurry on high-DPI displays. If you notice that a desktop program isn't scaling properly, you can use another new option that debuted in version 1703 to change its behavior. Find the program's executable file, right-click to open its properties dialog box, click Change High DPI Settings on the Compatibility tab, select the Override High DPI Scaling Behavior setting, and change it to System (Enhanced). This setting overrides the way the selected program handles DPI scaling, eliminating the use of bitmap stretching and forcing the application to be scaled by Windows:

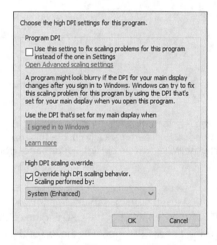

Windows 10 supports scaling factors from 100 percent all the way to 450 percent, with most elements of the user interface looking crystal-clear even at the highest scaling levels. That includes Start, Cortana, File Explorer, and the Windows taskbar.

In general, scaling produces a display that looks perfectly natural. In some scenarios, however, scaling issues can cause problems, including blurry text, desktop programs that appear too large or too small, or interface elements such as menus and toolbars that are clipped or overlap.

These types of scaling problems are most likely to occur when you try to change the display scaling dynamically. This can happen in a variety of scenarios: connecting a portable PC with a high-DPI internal display to a larger external monitor, for example, using a video output or a laptop dock; projecting that high-DPI display to a large TV screen; or making a Remote Desktop connection. Any of those scenarios can result in some unfortunate scaling combinations, especially when using desktop apps that weren't written to handle scaling changes gracefully.

When that happens, the only sure cure is to close all running apps, sign out of Windows, and then sign back in. Ironically, the same problem occurs in reverse when you disconnect from the docking station.

Using multiple displays

When you attach a second (or third or fourth) display to your computer, the Display page in Settings changes. Thumbnails, one for each attached display, appear in a preview pane like the one shown in Figure 14-21. You can drag the displays to either side of one another (or even move one above the other), adjusting the alignment of displays to match their actual physical alignment, with the goal of having your mouse pointer move naturally between displays without a jarring shift when crossing the bezels.

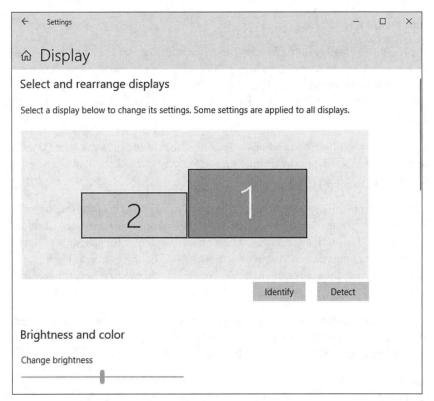

Figure 14-21   With multiple monitors, you can arrange each so that it matches the physical layout. Drag the monitor thumbnail up, down, or to either side of another display's thumbnail.

It's worth noting that the thumbnails have only a casual relationship to the size of the physical displays they represent. In Figure 14-21, for example, display 1 is a Dell laptop with a 15-inch screen, with a display resolution of 3840 × 2160 and scaling set to 250 percent. Display 2 is a 34-inch external display, which is dramatically larger than the laptop's built-in display but actually has a significantly lower resolution of 3440 × 1440 and a scaling factor of 100 percent.

If you're working with two or more displays and you're not sure which is which, click the Identify button, which temporarily positions a large number on each display that corresponds to the number on its thumbnail. Note that you can drag the thumbnail for display 1 to the right of display 2 if that's the way they're physically arranged on your desktop. Doing so allows your mouse to cross borders gracefully when you move the pointer.

To manage how multiple displays work together, use the controls under the Multiple Displays heading near the bottom of Settings > System > Display. You can duplicate the display on multiple desktops, extend the display, or disconnect a particular display so that it's not in use. An even easier shortcut is to press Windows key + P, which opens the Project pane on the right side of the main display. This option is especially useful when connecting a laptop to an external display. Choose Second Screen Only to temporarily stop using the laptop's built-in display and use only the (presumably larger) external monitor.

Night Light

The Night Light feature, introduced in the Windows 10 version 1703 feature update, is based on a relatively recent scientific discovery: Blue light suppresses the secretion of melatonin, disrupting circadian rhythms and disrupting your sleep. To adjust for this effect, you can turn on the Night Light feature, which favors warm colors and reduces the amount of blue light on a display.

To enable this feature, go to Settings > System > Display and slide the Night Light switch to On. To make fine-grained adjustments in how this feature works, click Night Light Settings, which opens the dialog box shown in Figure 14-22.

The Color Temperature At Night slider allows you to fine-tune how the display looks by adjusting the values of red and yellow. Use the Schedule settings to automatically turn on Night Light at sunset and turn it off after sunrise, based on the current location; as an alternative, you can assign specific hours based on your sleep schedule or use the button at the top of the dialog box to turn the feature on or off manually. (You might choose to ignore the schedule if you're on a transcontinental flight in a darkened airplane cabin, for example.)

And one major caveat: obviously, turning on the Night Light feature severely distorts the color of your display; if you're editing photos or videos or doing any other kind of work that depends on accurate color fidelity, don't use this feature.

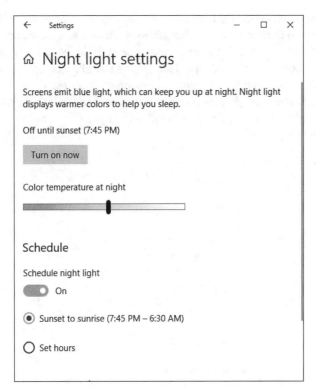

Figure 14-22   If you regularly check your email and perform work-related tasks right before bed-
time, consider scheduling Windows 10 to reduce the amount of blue light in the display at night.

Speakers, microphones, and headsets

Windows 10 supports a broad array of high-quality audio outputs, capable of delivering multichannel surround sound to sophisticated home theater setups or just driving the tiny speakers
on a laptop. As with other hardware subsystems, most of this capability is built into the Windows core drivers and doesn't require custom drivers from hardware manufacturers. (That, of
course, doesn't prevent OEMs from including custom drivers and audio control software with
their Windows 10 PCs.)

As of version 1809, the most common audio settings have migrated to the modern user experience. After you open Settings > System > Sound, you can choose the correct output or input
device, adjust the master volume level, and test your microphone's sensitivity. To make additional adjustments to an output or input device, including renaming or disabling a device, click
Device Properties. Click App Volume And Device Preferences to assign inputs and outputs and
adjust volume on a per-app basis.

A few useful built-in capabilities are buried deep in the configuration dialog boxes of the old audio subsystem, as found in Control Panel. The first allows you to test your surround-sound (or stereo) audio configuration to confirm that every speaker is working properly. From the bottom of the Sound page in Settings, click Sound Control Panel; in the Sound dialog box, select the correct playback device (the default device is identified by a green check mark) on the Playback tab. Click Configure to open the test app. Pick your speaker layout and then click Test to cycle through all the speakers, with a visual display showing which one should be playing. To end the test, click Stop, as shown in Figure 14-23.

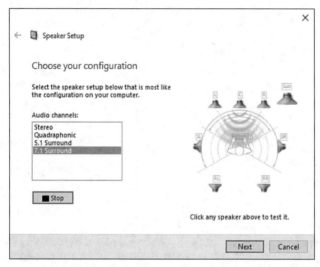

Figure 14-23   You can use this speaker setup test to confirm you haven't accidentally wired the right speakers to left and vice versa.

Windows 10 also allows you to designate a device, typically a headset, for use as the default communications device, as shown in Figure 14-24. (This configuration is designed for ease of use with communication apps such as Skype. For all other applications, such as playing music and videos, you can use a different playback device—external speakers, usually. This device is designated as the *default device*.) After making that designation, you can change playback behavior so that other sounds automatically reduce their volume when your communication device is in use, and the sound of, say, a New Mail Message notification would interfere with your communication.

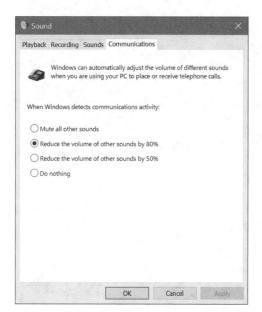

Figure 14-24 Using this well-hidden option, you can reduce other sounds (music and notifications, for example) when Windows detects that you're trying to communicate.

Troubleshooting, backup, and recovery

As they say, stuff happens. That might not be exactly the way you remember that quote, but it's certainly true whenever hardware and software are involved.

Although Microsoft Windows generally has become more stable and reliable over time, your computing experience will never be perfect. Apps stop responding or crash (shut down unexpectedly). Once in a while, a feature of Windows walks off the set without warning. And on rare occasions, the grim BSOD ("Blue Screen of Death," more formally known as a *Stop error* or *bugcheck*) arrives, bringing your whole system to a halt.

In a fully debugged, perfect world, such occurrences would never darken your computer screen. But you don't live there, and neither do we. So the prudent course is to learn to use the many tools Windows provides for diagnosing errors and recovering from problems. We examine these essential tools in this chapter.

And while those troubleshooting tools can help you understand what happened and maybe help you prevent it from happening again, they can't help you recover, which is why this chapter also explains how to use the backup tools included with Windows 10. Our goal is to help you prepare for the inevitable day when you need to restore a lost file (or an entire drive's worth of files). We also explain your options for resetting Windows when the operating system becomes damaged, for whatever reason.

Getting to know your troubleshooting toolkit

As any detective will tell you, solving a mystery requires evidence. If your mystery involves inexplicably slow performance or crashes, you have several places to look for clues.

Built-in troubleshooters

The most obvious first step on the road to resolving performance issues (including features that mysteriously stop working) is the set of troubleshooters at Settings > Update & Security >

Troubleshoot. Here you will find a categorized roster of tools to deal with a wide assortment of common problems.

There's nothing magical about any of these troubleshooters. Their purpose is to ensure that you check the most common causes of problems, including some that might seem obvious. (Is the network cable plugged in? Is the printer turned on?) Running a troubleshooter is an obvious first step when confronting most common problems: The troubleshooter can fix some issues and, more importantly, establishes a baseline for further troubleshooting.

A troubleshooter might lead you through several steps and ask you to check settings or connections. At the end, it displays its results, which include a View Detailed Information link that leads to a troubleshooting report similar to the one shown in Figure 15-1.

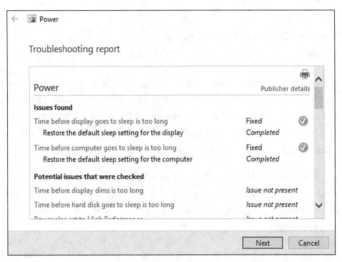

Figure 15-1   The troubleshooting report lists issues and indicates whether they were fixed. For any issues that are detected, you can click a link to see more granular information about that item.

Windows Error Reporting

The Windows Error Reporting service runs continuously in the background, keeping track of software and driver installations (successful and otherwise) as well as crashes, hangs, and other system events that indicate a possible problem with Windows. (In fact, although the service and programs that enable the feature are called Windows Error Reporting, the term you're more likely to see in Windows is *problem reporting*.) If you've authorized Windows 10 to send these reports as part of its diagnostics tracking, Microsoft provides these details to the developers of the program that caused the error (including Microsoft developers when the issue occurs with a feature in Windows, Office, or another Microsoft program). The goal, of course, is to improve quality by identifying problems and delivering fixes through Windows Update and Office Update.

In previous versions, Windows was downright chatty about reporting crashes, successful updates, and minor speed bumps. In Windows 10, most of these problem reports (including diagnostic reports sent after successful upgrades) are completely silent, but each report is logged. You can use the history of problem reports on a system to review events and to see whether any patterns demand additional troubleshooting.

To open the Problem Reports log, type **problem reports** in the search box and then click View All Problem Reports. Figure 15-2 shows a portion of the error history for a computer running Windows 10 version 1809.

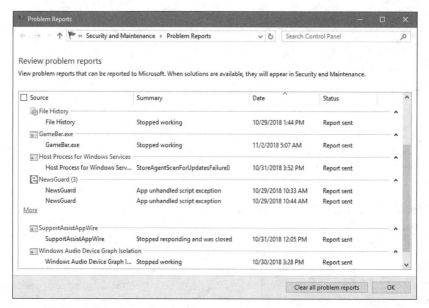

Figure 15-2   The list of saved problem reports displays the two most recent reports in each group.

If the words *Solution Available* appear in the Status column for an item, right-click that item and then click View Solution. That shortcut menu also includes commands to group the entries in the list of problem reports by source, summary, date, or status—or you can choose Ungroup to see the entire, uncategorized list. With the list grouped or not, you can sort by any field by clicking the field's column heading.

You can see a more detailed report about any event in this log by double-clicking the event. (See Figure 15-3.) The Description field usually is written clearly enough to provide potentially useful information. The rest of the details might or might not be meaningful to you, but they could be helpful to a support technician. Some reports include additional details sent in a text file you can inspect for yourself.

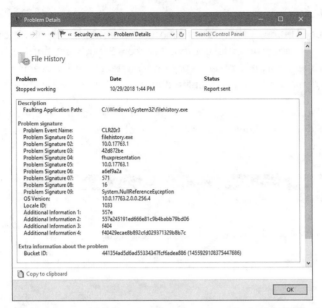

Figure 15-3   Double-clicking an entry in the problem reports list displays details about the problem that might be useful to a support technician.

Feedback and diagnostics

By default, Windows 10 configures your system so that it sends a generous amount of diagnostic and feedback information, including error reports that could inadvertently contain personal information. If you're concerned about data use or privacy, you can dial back the amount of diagnostic information using the settings we describe in "Configuring privacy options," in Chapter 18, "Windows security and privacy."

In addition to this automated feedback, Windows 10 allows you to send problem reports and feature suggestions to Microsoft. In some cases, the operating system will directly ask for your feedback on features. If you prefer not to be asked for feedback, go to Settings > Privacy > Diagnostics & Feedback. The Feedback Frequency setting near the bottom of this page controls how often Microsoft asks you about your use of features. (And yes, "Never" is an option.)

Windows 10 also includes the Feedback Hub app, which you can use to send problem reports and suggestions to Microsoft. (This app was previously available only to registered members of the Windows Insider Program.) We recommend that you search for existing feedback before filling out your own problem report. You can filter and sort the list of search results to see if your specific issue has already been reported; in some cases, Microsoft responds with a note the issue has been fixed (or is on the list for repair in a future update).

If you find an existing feedback entry that describes your issue, you can add a comment and an upvote. If you discover a new issue, feel free to create your own feedback item by clicking Report A Problem or Suggest A Feature. In the spirit of setting expectations, we are compelled to add that items you submit here are not the same as support tickets. You probably won't get personal support from a Microsoft engineer or support tech, although your feedback will be considered, especially if the number of upvotes hits double or triple digits.

Reliability Monitor

Windows 10 keeps track of an enormous range of system events, which you can monitor using Event Viewer, as we describe in the following section. For a day-by-day inventory of specific events (successful and unsuccessful) that affect your system's overall stability, open Reliability Monitor, shown in Figure 15-4. (Type **reliability** in the search box, and then click the top result, View Reliability History.)

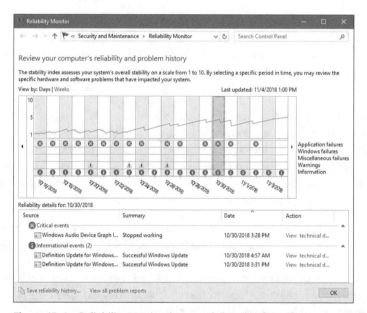

Figure 15-4 Reliability Monitor keeps a daily tally of significant events affecting system stability. Select any day to see details in the pane on the bottom.

Each column in the graphical display represents events of a particular day (or week, if you click that option in the upper-left corner). Each red X along the first three lines below the graph (the various "Failures" lines) indicates a day on which problems occurred. The "Warnings" line describes minor problems unrelated to system reliability, such as a program whose installation process didn't complete properly. The last line below the graph—the line marked Information— identifies days on which an app or an update was installed or removed. You can see the details about the events of any day by clicking on the graph for that day. Reliability Monitor retains its system stability records for up to one year but clears the history with the installation of each new feature update.

This history is most useful when you begin experiencing a new problem and are trying to track down its cause. Examine the critical events for the period when you first began to experience the problem, and see whether they correspond with an informational item, such as a program installation. The alignment of these events could be mere coincidence, but it could also represent the first appearance of a long-term problem. Conjunctions of this sort are worth examining. If you think a new software application has destabilized your system, you can try uninstalling it.

Double-clicking any problem report exposes its contents, which are filled with technical details that are potentially useful, confusing, or both. Note that these reports are identical to those you can find in the listing of problem reports we discussed earlier in this chapter.

Event Viewer

Technically, we probably should have included Event Viewer (Eventvwr.msc) in the previous section. It is, after all, just another troubleshooting tool. But we think that this, the most powerful of all the diagnostic tools in Windows 10, deserves marquee billing in this chapter.

In Windows, an *event* is any occurrence that is potentially noteworthy—to you, to a system or network administrator, to the operating system, or to an application. Events are recorded by the Windows Event Log service, and their history is preserved in one of several log files, including Application, Security, Setup, System, and Forwarded Events. You can use Event Viewer, a Microsoft Management Console (MMC) snap-in supplied with Windows, to review and archive these event logs, as well as other logs created by the installation of certain applications and services.

You can examine the history of errors on your system by creating a filtered view of the Application log in Event Viewer. Why would you want to do this? The most likely reasons are to troubleshoot problems that have occurred, to keep an eye on your system to forestall problems, and to watch out for security breaches. If a device has failed, a disk has filled close to capacity, a program has crashed repeatedly, or some other critical difficulty has arisen, the information recorded in the event logs can help you—or a technical support specialist—figure out what's wrong and what corrective steps are required.

To start Event Viewer, find it by searching for **event** and then click Event Viewer or View Event Logs in the search results. (Alternatively, enter **eventvwr** in the Run box or at a command prompt.)

> NOTE
>
> Event Viewer requires administrator privileges for full functionality. If you start Event Viewer while signed in as a standard user, it starts without requesting elevation. However, the Security log is unavailable, along with some other features. To get access to all logs, right-click and choose Run As Administrator.

Figure 15-5 offers an overview of Event Viewer, which uses the basic three-pane Microsoft Management Console to organize and display a truly massive amount of data from event logs.

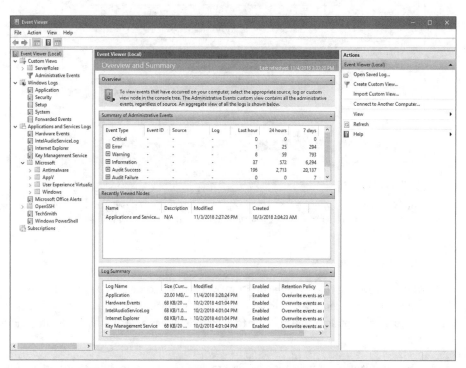

Figure 15-5   Event Viewer's console tree (left) lists available logs and views; the details pane (center) displays information from the selected log or view; the Actions pane (right) provides a menu of tasks relevant to the current selection.

When you select the top-level node in Event Viewer's console tree, the details pane displays summary information, organized into groups, in decreasing order of severity. With this view, you can see at a glance whether any significant events that might require your attention have occurred in the past hour, day, or week. You can expand each category to see the sources of events of that event type. This simple count can flag potential problems easily. If, for example, you see an unusually large number of recent errors from a particular source, you might want to dig deeper into that list to determine whether a particular error is a sign of a reliability or performance problem. To do that, you can right-click an event type or an event source under Summary Of Administrative Events, and then click View All Instances Of This Event, as shown in Figure 15-6.

The resulting filtered list of events is drawn from multiple log files, sparing you from having to search in multiple places. Armed with this information, you can quickly scroll through and examine the details of each one, perhaps identifying a pattern or a common factor that will help you find the cause and, eventually, the cure for whatever is causing the event.

CHAPTER 15

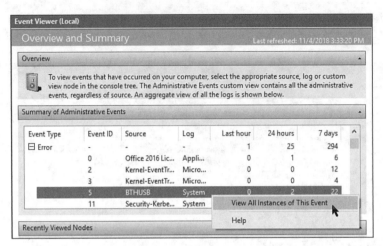

Figure 15-6   The summary view is organized by event type, in order of severity. Expand any category and then right-click a source to view all instances of that event.

Types of events

As a glance at the console tree confirms, events are recorded in one of several logs. Logs are organized in the console tree in folders, and you can expand or collapse the folder tree using the customary outline controls. The following default logs are visible under the Windows Logs heading:

- **Application.** Application events are generated by applications, including programs you install, programs that are preinstalled with Windows, apps from the Microsoft Store, and operating system services. Program developers decide which events to record in the Application log and which to record in a program-specific log under Applications And Services Logs.

- **Security.** Security events include sign-in attempts (successful and failed) and attempts to use secured resources, such as an attempt to create, modify, or delete a file.

- **Setup.** Setup events are generated by application installations.

- **System.** System events are generated by Windows itself and by installed features, such as device drivers. If a driver fails to load when you start a Windows session, for example, that event is recorded in the System log.

- **Forwarded Events.** The Forwarded Events log contains events gathered from other computers.

Under the Applications And Services Logs heading, you'll find logs for individual applications and services. The difference between this heading and the Windows Logs heading is that logs under Applications And Services record events related only to a particular program or feature, whereas the logs that appear under Windows Logs generally record events that are systemwide.

If you expand the Microsoft entry under Applications And Services Logs, you'll find a Windows subfolder, which in turn contains a folder for each of hundreds of features that are part of Windows 10. Each of these folders contains one or more logs.

Viewing logs and events

When you select a log or a custom view from the console tree, the details pane shows a list of associated events, sorted (by default) in reverse chronological order, with each event occupying a single line. A preview pane below the list displays the contents of the saved event record. Figure 15-7 shows one such listing from the System log.

> **NOTE**
>
> The Windows Event Log service records the date and time each event occurred in coordinated universal time (UTC). Event Viewer translates those time values into dates and times appropriate for the currently configured time zone.

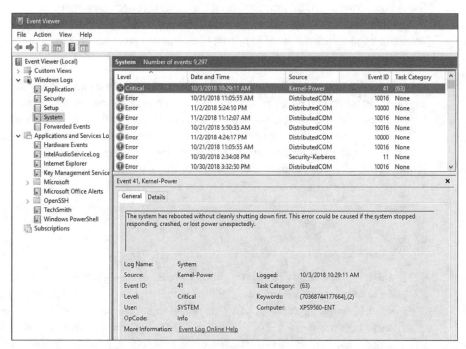

Figure 15-7   All the details you need for an individual event are visible in this preview pane. Double-click an event to see those same details in a separate window.

CHAPTER 15

Events in most log files are classified by severity, with one of four entries in the Level field:

- *Critical* events are the most severe, with this category including Stop errors and other events that have the potential to damage data.

- *Error* events represent a possible loss of data or functionality. Examples of errors include events related to a malfunctioning network adapter and loss of functionality caused by a device or service that doesn't load at startup.

- *Warning* events represent less significant or less immediate problems than error events. Examples of warning events include a nearly full disk, a timeout by the network redirector, and data errors on local storage.

- Other events that Windows logs are identified as *Information* events.

The Security log file uses two different icons to classify events: A key icon identifies Audit Success events, and a lock icon identifies Audit Failure events. Both types of events are classified as Information-level events; "Audit Success" and "Audit Failure" are stored in the Keywords field of the Security log file.

The preview pane shows information about the currently selected event. (Drag the split bar between the list and preview pane up to make the preview pane larger so that you can see more details, or double-click the event to open it in a separate dialog box that includes Next and Previous buttons and an option to copy the event to the Clipboard.)

The information you find in Event Viewer is evidence of things that happened in the past. Like any good detective, you have the task of using those clues to help identify possible issues. One hidden helper, located near the bottom of the Event Properties dialog box, is a link to more information online. Clicking this link opens a webpage that might provide more specific and detailed information about this particular combination of event source and event ID, including further action you might want to take in response to the event.

Inside OUT

Export data from Event Viewer

You can save selected events, all events in the current view, or all events in a particular log to a file for archival purposes, for further analysis in a different program, or to share with a technical support specialist. (To select events for exporting, hold down the Ctrl key and click each event you want to include.) The command to export events is on the Action menu, but the command name varies depending on the current view and selection: Save Selected Events, Save Filtered Log File As, Save Events In Custom View As, or Save Events As.

Saving event data in Event Viewer's native (.evtx) format creates a file you can view only in Event Viewer (or a third-party application capable of reading native event logs). However, Event Viewer can export log data to XML and to tab-delimited or comma-delimited text files, and you can import these easily into database, spreadsheet, or even word-processing programs.

Customizing the presentation of tabular data in Event Viewer

If you have a passing familiarity with Details view in File Explorer, you'll feel right at home with the many tabular reports in Event Viewer. You can change a column's width by dragging its heading left or right. You can sort on any column by clicking its heading; click a second time to reverse the sort order. Right-click a column heading and choose Add/Remove Columns to make more or fewer columns appear.

As with files and folders in File Explorer, you also have the option to group events in Event Viewer. To do that, right-click the column heading by which you want to group and then click Group Events By This Column. Figure 15-8, for example, shows the System log with events grouped by Source and sorted by Date And Time in descending order. Note that you can expand or collapse each grouping using the tiny arrows at the end of each group heading.

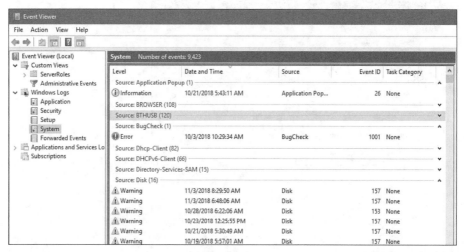

Figure 15-8   In this view, we right-clicked the Source heading and chose the option to group events, and then we clicked the Date And Time heading to bring the most recent events to the top of each group.

Filtering the log display

As you can see from a cursory look at your System log, events can pile up quickly, obscuring those generated by a particular source or those that occurred at a particular date and time. Sorting and grouping can help you find relevant events, but filtering is even more effective, especially when using multiple criteria. With a filter applied, all other events are hidden from view, making it much easier to focus on the items you currently care about.

To filter the currently displayed log or custom view, click Filter Current Log or Filter Current Custom View in the Action pane on the right. A dialog box like the one shown in Figure 15-9 appears. To fully appreciate the flexibility of filtering, click the arrow by each filter. You can, for example, filter events from the past hour, 12 hours, day, week, month, or any custom time period you specify. In the Event Sources, Task Category, and Keywords boxes, you can type text to filter on (separating multiple items with commas), but you'll probably find it easier to click the down arrow and then select each item you want to include in your filtered view. In the Includes/Excludes Event IDs box, you can enter multiple ID numbers and number ranges, separated by commas; to exclude particular event IDs, precede their number with a minus sign.

Click OK to see the filtered list. If you think you'll use the same filter criteria again, click Save Filter To Custom View in the Action pane on the right. To restore the unfiltered list, in the Event Viewer window, click Clear Filter.

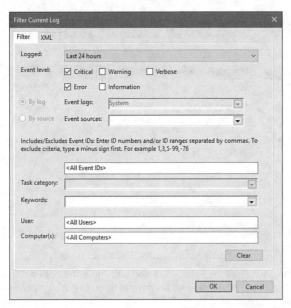

Figure 15-9   If you don't select any Event Level check boxes, Event Viewer includes all levels in the filtered results. Similarly, any other field you leave blank includes all events without regard to the value of that property.

NOTE

Event Viewer also includes an anemic search capability, which you access by clicking Action, Find. You can perform more precise searches by filtering.

Working with event logs on a remote computer

Event Viewer, like many other Microsoft Management Console applications, provides the option of viewing logs on a remote computer as well as your local computer. You might find this useful if you run a help desk and need to troubleshoot a remote user's system. To point Event Viewer to another computer, select the top heading in the outline tree, click Action, and then click Connect To Another Computer. In the Select Computer box, type the IP address or name of the computer you want to connect to.

To manage logs on a remote computer, you need to enable the Remote Event Log Management exception in the Windows Firewall settings on the remote computer. For other details about using Event Viewer remotely, see *https://technet.microsoft.com/library/cc766438.aspx*.

Dealing with Stop errors

If Windows has ever suddenly shut down, you've probably experienced that sinking feeling in the pit of your stomach. When Windows 10 encounters a serious problem that makes it impossible for the operating system to continue running, it does the only thing it can do, just as every one of its predecessors has done in the same circumstances. It shuts down immediately and displays an ominous text message whose technical details begin with the word *STOP*. Because a Stop error typically appears in white letters on a blue background, this type of message is often referred to as a *blue-screen error* or the *Blue Screen of Death (BSOD)*. (If you're running an Insider Preview release of Windows 10, this screen will be green.) When a Stop error appears, it means there is a serious problem that demands your immediate attention.

Windows 10 collects and saves a variety of information in logs and dump files, which a support engineer or developer armed with debugging tools can use to identify the cause of Stop errors. You don't have to be a developer to use these tools, which are available to anyone via download from *https://bit.ly/windows-debugging-tools*. (Don't worry; you can't break anything by simply inspecting a .dmp file.) If you know where to look, however, you can learn a lot from these error messages alone, and in many cases, you can recover completely by using standard troubleshooting techniques.

Customizing how Windows handles Stop errors

When Windows encounters a serious error that forces it to stop running, it displays a Stop message and then writes debugging information to the page file. When the computer restarts, this information is saved as a crash dump file, which can be used to debug the specific cause of the error.

You can customize two crucial aspects of this process by defining the size of the crash dump files and specifying whether you want Windows to restart automatically after a Stop message appears. By default, Windows automatically restarts after a Stop message and creates a crash dump file optimized for automatic analysis. That's the preferred strategy in response to random, isolated Stop errors. But if you're experiencing chronic Stop errors, you might have more troubleshooting success by changing these settings to collect a more detailed dump file and to stop after a crash.

To make this change, type **advanced** in the search box and then click View Advanced System Settings in the results list. (Or, in the Run or search box, type the undocumented command **systempropertiesadvanced** and press Enter.)

On the Advanced tab of the System Properties dialog box, under Startup And Recovery, click Settings. Adjust the settings under the System Failure heading, as shown in Figure 15-10.

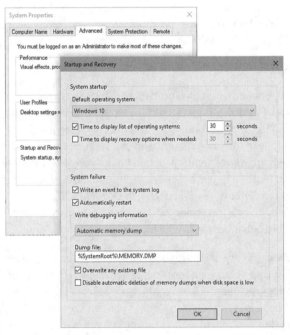

Figure 15-10   By default, Windows manages the size of the memory dump file and restarts automatically after a Stop error. You can pick a larger or smaller dump file here.

If you want Windows to pause at the Stop error message page, clear the Automatically Restart check box and click OK.

From the same dialog box, you can also define the settings for crash dump files. By default, Windows sets this value to Automatic Memory Dump, which contains the same information as a kernel memory dump. Either option includes memory allocated to kernel-mode drivers and programs, which are most likely to cause Stop errors.

TROUBLESHOOTING

Available storage drops dramatically after a stop error

If the paging file size is set to System Managed Size and the Automatic Memory Dump option is selected, Windows can automatically increase the size of the paging file if it needs the space to save a kernel dump file. The increased paging file size is at least equal to the amount of installed RAM. Windows records the time of this event in the registry, at HKLM\SYSTEM\CurrentControlSet\Control\CrashControl\LastCrashTime. It reverts to the normal, smaller paging file size in four weeks.

On a PC with a large amount of RAM and a relatively full system drive, this increase in the size of the paging file can noticeably reduce the amount of available storage. If you've resolved the underlying issue that caused the crash, you can safely delete the LastCrashTime registry entry and immediately revert your paging file to its normal, smaller size.

Because this file does not include unallocated memory or memory allocated to user-mode programs, it usually will be smaller in size than the amount of RAM on your system. The exact size varies, but in general, you can expect the file to be no larger than one-third the size of installed physical RAM, and much less than that on a system with 16 GB of RAM or more. The crash files are stored in %SystemRoot% using the file name Memory.dmp. (If your system crashes multiple times, each new dump file replaces the previous file. If you have sufficient disk space, you can change these default settings so that a new crash dump file does not overwrite any previous dump files.)

If disk space is limited or you're planning to send the crash dump file to a support technician, you might want to consider setting the system to store a small memory dump (commonly called a *mini dump*). A small memory dump contains just a fraction of the information in a kernel memory dump, but it's often enough to determine the cause of a problem. Under Write Debugging Information, select Small Memory Dump (256 KB).

What's in a Stop error

The exact text of a Stop error varies according to what caused the error. But the format is predictable. Don't bother copying down the error code from the blue screen itself. Instead, look through Event Viewer for an event with the source BugCheck, as shown in the example in Figure 15-11.

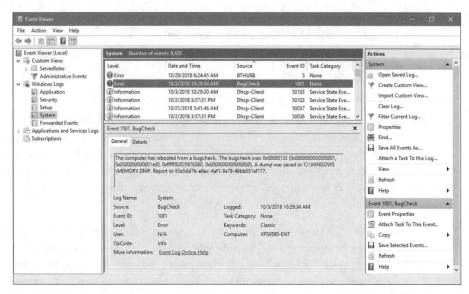

Figure 15-11 Decoding the information in a Stop error can help you find the underlying problem and fix it. Start with the error code—0x00000133, in this example.

You can gather important details from the bugcheck information, which consists of the error number (in hexadecimal notation, as indicated by the *0x* at the beginning of the code) and up to four parameters that are specific to the error type.

Windows 10 also displays the information in Reliability Monitor, under the heading Critical Events. Select the day on which the error occurred, and then double-click the "Shut down unexpectedly" entry for an event with Windows as the source. That displays the bugcheck information in a slightly more readable format than in Event Viewer, even using the term *BlueScreen* as the Problem Event Name.

For a comprehensive and official list of what each error code means, see the Microsoft Hardware Dev Center "Bug Check Code Reference" at *https://bit.ly/bug-check-codes*. A code of 0x00000144, for example, points to problems with a USB 3 controller, whereas 0x0000009F is a driver power state failure. (Our favorite is 0xDEADDEAD, which indicates a manually initiated crash.) In general, you need a debugger or a dedicated analytic tool to get any additional useful information from a memory dump file.

Inside OUT

Create your own Stop error

If for any reason—curiosity, a desire to test debugging procedures, or whatever—you want to generate a Stop error on demand, Windows 10 will accommodate you. As outlined at *https://bit.ly/force-Stop*, the steps involve making a small registry edit and then pressing a multikeystroke sequence on your USB or PS/2 keyboard.

Inside OUT

Troubleshoot Stop errors with more powerful tools

Microsoft Windows Volume Licensing customers who have purchased a Software Assurance subscription have access to a powerful Crash Analyzer tool, which is included with the Microsoft Diagnostics and Recovery Toolset, otherwise known as DaRT. Crash Analyzer can examine the memory dump file created by a Stop error and, usually, pinpoint the cause of the problem. For details about DaRT, see *https://docs.microsoft.com/microsoft-desktop-optimization-pack/dart-v10/*.

If you're troubleshooting a PC with a retail or OEM Windows license, consider using the free NirSoft BlueScreenView utility, which does a good job of reading the memory dump file and identifying the most probable cause of the Stop error. Download the tool from *https://www.nirsoft.net/utils/blue_screen_view.html*.

Isolating the cause of a Stop error

If you experience a Stop error, don't panic. Instead, run through the following troubleshooting checklist to isolate the problem and find a solution:

- **Don't forget to rule out hardware problems.** In many cases, software is the victim and not the cause of blue-screen errors. Common hardware failures such as a damaged hard disk or a corrupted solid state disk (SSD), defective physical RAM, an overheated CPU chip, or even a bad cable or poorly seated memory module can result in Stop errors. If the errors seem to happen at random and the message details vary each time, there's a good chance you're experiencing hardware problems.

- **Check your memory.** Windows 10 includes a memory diagnostic tool you can use if you suspect a faulty or failing memory chip. To run this diagnostic procedure, type **memory** in the search box and click Windows Memory Diagnostic in the search results. This tool requires a restart to run its full suite of tests, which you can perform immediately or defer until your next restart.

- **Look for a driver name in the error details.** If the error message identifies a specific file name and you can trace that file to a driver for a specific hardware device, you might be able to solve the problem by disabling, removing, or rolling back that driver to an earlier version. The most likely offenders are network interface cards, video adapters, and disk controllers. For more details about managing driver files, see "Updating and uninstalling drivers" in Chapter 14, "Hardware and devices."

- **Ask yourself, "What's new?"** Be suspicious of newly installed hardware and software. If you added a device recently, remove it temporarily and see whether the problem goes away. Take an especially close look at software in the categories that install services or file-system filter drivers; these hook into the core operating system files that manage the file system to perform tasks such as scanning for viruses. This category includes backup programs, multimedia applications, networking tools, security software, and DVD-burning utilities. You might need to uninstall the program to resolve the problem; check with the program's developer to see if the issue has been fixed in an updated version that's newer than the one you're running.

- **Search Microsoft Support.** Make a note of the error code and all parameters. Search Microsoft Support using both the full and the short formats. For instance, if you're experiencing a KMODE_EXCEPTION_NOT_HANDLED error, use **0x1E** and **0x0000001E** as your search keywords.

- **Check your system BIOS or firmware.** Is an update available from the manufacturer of the system or motherboard? Check the BIOS or firmware documentation carefully; resetting all BIOS options to their defaults can sometimes resolve an issue caused by overtweaking.

- **Are you low on system resources?** Stop errors are sometimes the result of a critical shortage of RAM or disk space. If you can start in Safe Mode, check the amount of physical RAM installed, and look at the system and boot drives to see how much free disk space is available.

- **Is a crucial system file damaged?** To reinstall a driver, restart your computer in Safe Mode. (See the following section.) If your system starts in Safe Mode but not normally, you very likely have a problem driver. Try running Device Manager in Safe Mode and uninstalling the most likely suspect. Or run System Restore in Safe Mode. If restoring to a particular day cures the problem, use Reliability Monitor to determine what changes occurred on or shortly after that day.

Troubleshooting in Safe Mode

In earlier Windows versions, holding down the F8 key while restarting gave you the opportunity to start your system in Safe Mode, with only core drivers and services activated. On modern hardware, with UEFI firmware, that's no longer possible. Safe Mode is still available, but you have to work a little harder to get there.

If you can start Windows and get to the sign-in screen, you can then click the Power button in the lower-right corner of that screen. Hold down Shift as you click Restart to go to the Windows Recovery Environment, where you can take various actions, including restoring Windows from an image backup, running System Restore to revert to a saved restore point, and resetting your PC. (We discuss all three topics later in this chapter.)

When you first arrive in the Windows Recovery Environment, a menu similar to the one in Figure 15-12 appears. Your menu might look slightly different, with a custom option supplied by the OEM. The Use Another Operating System option appears only on a PC that has been configured to boot into multiple operating systems.

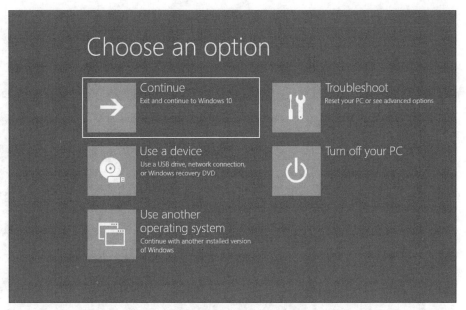

Figure 15-12   The main menu for the Windows Recovery Environment offers a range of trouble-shooting options. The Use Another Operating System choice is available only on multi-boot systems.

To get to Safe Mode, you'll need to navigate through several menus. Click Troubleshoot in this menu, and then click Advanced Options. On the Advanced Options menu, click See More Recovery Options. Click Startup Settings and then (finally!) click Restart. You will then see the Startup Settings menu, as shown in Figure 15-13.

In Safe Mode, you can access certain essential configuration tools, including Device Manager, System Restore, and Registry Editor. If Windows appears to work properly in Safe Mode, you can safely assume there's no problem with the basic services. Use Device Manager, Driver Verifier, and Event Viewer to try to figure out where the trouble lies. If you suspect that a newly installed device or program is the cause of the problem, you can remove the offending software while you're running in Safe Mode. Use Device Manager to uninstall or roll back a hardware driver; use Control Panel to remove a desktop program or utility. Then try restarting the system normally to see whether your changes have resolved the problem.

> ➤ For more information about Device Manager, see "Getting useful information from Device Manager" in Chapter 14. We explain how to use Driver Verifier in "Troubleshooting sporadic hardware errors," also in Chapter 14. You'll find a detailed discussion of Event Viewer earlier in this chapter.

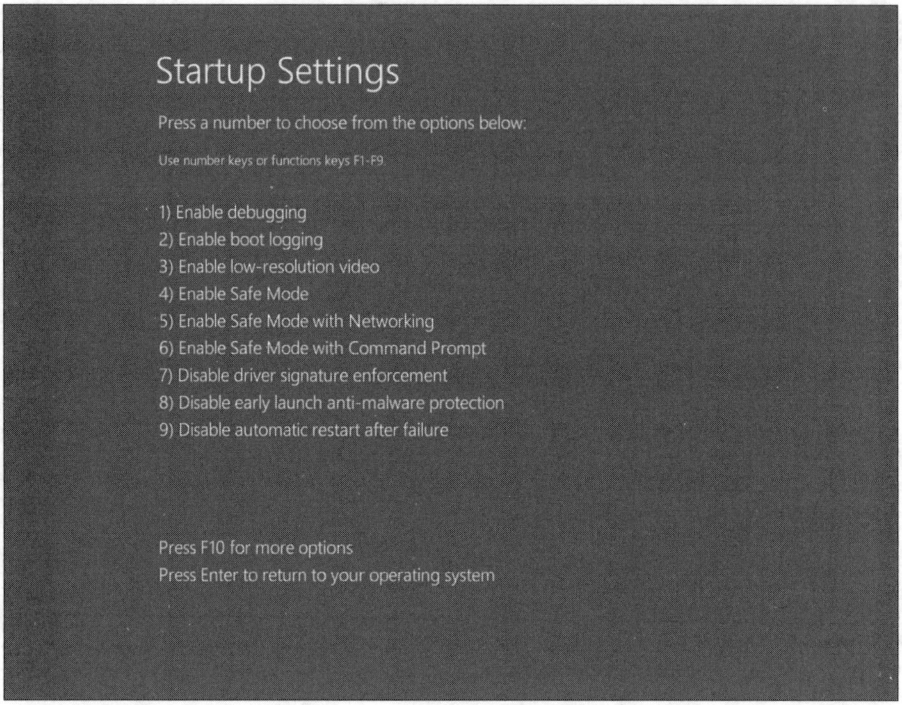

Startup Settings

Press a number to choose from the options below:

Use number keys or functions keys F1-F9.

1) Enable debugging
2) Enable boot logging
3) Enable low-resolution video
4) Enable Safe Mode
5) Enable Safe Mode with Networking
6) Enable Safe Mode with Command Prompt
7) Disable driver signature enforcement
8) Disable early launch anti-malware protection
9) Disable automatic restart after failure

Press F10 for more options
Press Enter to return to your operating system

Figure 15-13   Use the Startup Settings menu to boot into Safe Mode, where you can perform tasks such as removing a troublesome program or driver that prevents you from starting normally.

If you need access to network connections, choose the Safe Mode With Networking option, which loads the base set of Safe Mode files and adds drivers and services required to start Windows networking.

The third Safe Mode option, Safe Mode With Command Prompt, loads the same stripped-down set of services as Safe Mode, but it uses the Windows command interpreter (Cmd.exe) as a shell instead of the graphical Windows Explorer (Explorer.exe, which also serves as the host for File Explorer). This option is unnecessary unless you're having a problem with the Windows graphical interface. The default Safe Mode also provides access to the command line. (Press Windows key+R, and then type **cmd.exe** in the Run dialog box.)

The six additional choices on the Startup Settings menu are of use in specialized circumstances:

- **Enable Debugging.** Use this option if you've installed debugging tools and want to switch into a special mode that is compatible with those tools.

- **Enable Boot Logging.** With this option enabled, Windows creates a log file that lists the names and status of all drivers loaded into memory. To view the contents of this file, look for Ntbtlog.txt in the %SystemRoot% folder. If your system is hanging because of a faulty driver, the last entry in this log file might identify the culprit.

- **Enable Low-Resolution Video.** This option starts the computer in 640-by-480 resolution using the current video driver. Use this option to recover from video problems that are caused not by a faulty driver but by incorrect settings, such as an improper resolution or refresh rate.

- **Disable Driver Signature Enforcement.** Use this option if Windows is refusing to start because you installed an unsigned user-mode driver. Windows will start normally, not in Safe Mode. (Note that you cannot disable the requirement for signed kernel-mode drivers.)

- **Disable Early Launch Antimalware Protection.** This is one of the core security measures of Windows 10 on a UEFI-equipped machine. Unless you're a security researcher or a driver developer, we can't think of any reason to disable this important security check.

- **Disable Automatic Restart After Failure.** Use this option if you're getting Stop errors (blue-screen crashes) and you want the opportunity to see the crash details on the Stop error screen instead of simply pausing there before restarting.

Checking disks for errors

Errors in disk media and in the file system can cause a wide range of problems, from an inability to open or save files to blue-screen errors and widespread data corruption. Windows is capable of recovering automatically from many disk errors, especially on drives formatted with NTFS.

Inside Out

Check the status of a disk or volume

You can check the properties of any drive—including the volume label, file system, and amount of free space available—by right-clicking the drive in File Explorer's This PC folder and then clicking Properties. You can see the same details and more in Disk Management (Diskmgmt.msc). Of particular interest are details about the status of a disk or volume.

Under normal circumstances, the status information displayed here should report that each disk is online and each volume is healthy. A disk status message of Not Initialized means the disk does not contain a valid signature. It might have been prepared on a system running a non-Microsoft operating system, such as Unix or Linux, or the drive might be brand new. If the disk is used by another operating system, do nothing. To prepare a new disk for use with Windows 10, right-click the disk and click Initialize Disk.

A volume status message of Healthy (Unknown Partition) indicates that Windows does not recognize the partition; this occurs with some partitions created by another operating system or by a computer manufacturer that uses a special partition to store system files. You cannot format or access data on an unknown partition using Windows 10's built-in tools. If you're certain the partition is unnecessary, use Disk Management (or a third-party tool) to delete it and create a new partition in the free space created.

To perform a thorough inspection for data errors, run the Windows Check Disk utility (Chkdsk. exe). Two versions of this utility are available—a graphical version that performs basic disk-checking functions, and a command-line version that provides a much more extensive set of customization options.

To check for errors on a local disk, follow these steps:

1. In File Explorer, open This PC, right-click the icon belonging to the drive you want to check, and then click Properties.

2. On the Tools tab, click Check. (If you're using a standard account, you need to supply credentials for an account in the Administrators group to execute this utility.) Unless Windows is already aware of problems with the selected disk, you're likely to see a message that says you don't need to scan the drive.

3. If you want to go ahead and check the disk, click Scan Drive. Windows will perform an exhaustive check of the entire disk. If there are bad sectors, Windows will locate them and recover readable information where it can.

The command-line version of Check Disk gives you considerably more options. You can also use it to set up regular disk-checking operations using Task Scheduler (as described in "Task Scheduler" in Chapter 19, "PowerShell and other advanced management tools.") To run this command in its simplest form, open a Command Prompt window using the Run As Administrator option, and then type **chkdsk** at the prompt. This command runs Chkdsk in read-only mode, displaying the status of the current drive but not making any changes. If you add a drive letter after the command (*chkdsk d:*, for instance), the report applies to that drive.

To see descriptions of the command-line switches available with the Chkdsk command, type **chkdsk /?**. Here is a partial list of the available switches:

- **/F** Instructs Chkdsk to fix any errors it detects. This is the most commonly used switch. The disk must be locked. If Chkdsk cannot lock the drive, it offers to check the drive the next time you restart the computer or to dismount the volume you want to check before proceeding. Dismounting is a drastic step; it invalidates all current file handles on the affected volume and can result in loss of data. You should decline the offer. When you do, Chkdsk makes you a second offer—to check the disk the next time you restart your system. You should accept this option. (If you're trying to check the system drive, the only option you're given is to schedule a check at the next startup.)

- **/V** On FAT32 volumes, /V displays verbose output, listing the name of every file in every directory as the disk check proceeds. On NTFS volumes, this switch displays cleanup messages (if any).

- **/R** Identifies bad sectors and recovers information from those sectors if possible. The disk must be locked. Be aware that this is a time-consuming and uninterruptible process.

The following switches are valid only on NTFS volumes:

- **/I** Performs a simpler check of index entries (stage 2 in the Chkdsk process), reducing the amount of time required.

- **/C** Skips the checking of cycles within the folder structure, reducing the amount of time required.

- **/X** Forces the volume to dismount, if necessary, and invalidates all open file handles. This option is intended for server administrators. Because of the potential for data loss, it should be avoided.

- **/L[:size]** Changes the size of the file that logs NTFS transactions. If you omit the size parameter, this switch displays the current size. This option is intended for server administrators. Because of the potential for data loss, it also should be avoided in normal use.

- **/B** Reevaluates bad clusters and recovers readable information.

Inside Out

Offer remote support with Quick Assist

Quick Assist offers a new name and a streamlined interface to the Windows Remote Assistance tool available in earlier Windows versions. After making a Quick Assist connection as the helper, you can see the other computer's screen on your system, run diagnostic tools such as Task Manager, edit the remote system's registry, and even use a stylus to annotate the remote display.

Two ground rules apply: The computer giving assistance must be able to sign in with a Microsoft account (Quick Assist will prompt for one if the user is signed in using a different account type), and both systems must be running Windows 10, version 1607 or later.

The simplest way to run Quick Assist executable (Quickassist.exe) is to start typing **quick** in the Search box. The program should quickly appear at the top of the search results. After running the program, the party asking for help chooses Get Assistance, and the party offering support chooses Give Assistance.

The helper sees a six-digit security code and has 10 minutes to supply that code to the person asking for assistance, who enters the code to complete the connection. (You can use the Send Email link to do this, but it's probably simpler to use the phone. The two of you are likely to want to be in touch via phone in any case.) After both parties successfully enter the matching code, the Quick Assist connection is complete.

As the helper, you can choose to view the screen or ask for permission to take control, with the explicit permission of the person receiving assistance. From that point forward, the helper can see the remote screen in the Quick Assist window, with a toolbar that offers the ability to open Task Manager, annotate the screen, and send messages via a chat window. At any time, the person receiving assistance can pause screen sharing or end the Quick Assist session.

Windows 10 backup and recovery options

Through the years, the backup and recovery tools in Windows have evolved, but their fundamental purpose has not changed. How well you execute your backup strategy will determine how easily you're able to get back to where you were after something goes wrong—or to start over with an absolutely clean slate. When you reach into the recovery toolkit, you're hoping to perform one of the following three operations:

- **Full reset.** If you're selling or giving away a PC or other device running Windows 10, you can reset it to a clean configuration, wiping personal files in preparation for the new owner. Some Windows users prefer this sort of clean install when they just want to get a fresh start, minus any cruft from previous installations.

- **Recovery.** The "stuff happens" category includes catastrophic hardware failure, malware infection, and system corruption, as well as performance or reliability problems that can't easily be identified with normal troubleshooting. The recovery process involves reinstalling Windows from a backup image or a recovery drive.

- **File restore.** When (not if) you accidentally delete or overwrite an important data file or (ouch) an entire folder, library, or drive, you can call on a built-in Windows 10 tool to bring back the missing data. You can also use this same feature to find and restore earlier versions of a saved file—an original, uncompressed digital photo, for example, or a Microsoft Word document that contains a section you deleted and now want to revisit.

In Windows 10, the primary built-in tool for backing up files is called File History. Its job is to save copies of your local data files—every hour is the default frequency—so that you can find and restore your personal documents, pictures, and other data files when you need them.

Inside OUT

Integrating the cloud into your backup strategy

It's tempting to think of Microsoft OneDrive and other cloud-based storage services as a primary backup. But that strategy is potentially dangerous as well. Cloud services are generally reliable, but it's not out of the question that one might fail or be temporarily unavailable. Moreover, online accounts can be compromised. There are risks associated with using the cloud as your only backup medium. And even when you think you have a backup, it might not be what you expect. On some services, for example, cloud backups of photos might be converted to a lower resolution than the original images, meaning that your only copy of a priceless photo is an inferior compressed version.

Having a complete archive of files backed up to the cloud does offer the reassurance that you can recover any or all those saved files in the event of an accident or natural disaster, such as a fire or flood, that wipes out your primary device and its separate local backup. Given the ubiquity and relatively low cost of online storage services, a truly conscientious approach might be to keep copies of important files in two separate cloud-based services. Just remember that those distant archives are not a replacement for comprehensive local backups on an external storage device or a networked PC.

Windows 10 also includes the old-style Windows 7 Backup And Restore tool. You'll find both backup solutions by opening Settings > Update & Security > Backup, as shown in Figure 15-14.

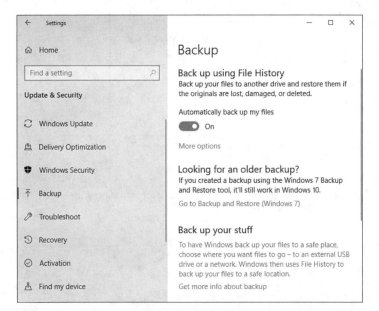

CHAPTER 15

Figure 15-14 The File History feature is the preferred backup solution for Windows 10, but the older Windows 7 Backup and Restore program is still around.

Despite its advanced age, the Windows 7 backup tool can still do one impressive digital magic trick that its newer rivals can't: It can create an image of the system drive that can be restored to an exact copy of the original saved volume, complete with Windows, drivers and utilities, desktop programs, settings, and data files. System image backups were once the gold standard of backup and are still the best way to capture a known good state for quick recovery.

The disadvantage of a full image backup is that it's fixed at a moment in time and doesn't capture files created, changed, or deleted since the image was created. If your primary data files are located in the cloud or on a separate volume from the system drive, that might not be a problem.

The final backup and recovery option in Windows 10 is the "push-button reset" feature, which allows you to reinstall Windows, with the option to keep or discard personal data files. Using this option, you can reset a misbehaving system on the fly, rolling back with relative ease to a clean, fully updated Windows 10 installation. You'll find the Reset This PC option on the Settings > Update & Security > Recovery page. (See Figure 15-15.)

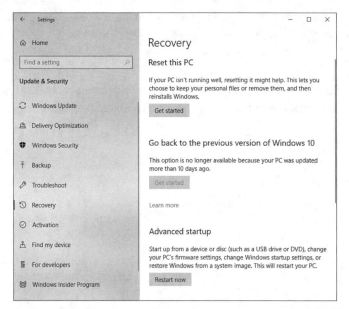

Figure 15-15 The Reset This PC option gives you a fresh start by rolling your system back to a clean Windows 10 installation.

Inside OUT

Do you need the OEM recovery image?

The Windows 10 Reset feature, in a major change from Windows 8.1, is capable of reinstalling Windows without requiring a recovery partition or any external media. Instead, it uses the existing Windows system files to create a new, clean, side-by-side copy. The result, at least in theory, allows you to recover the sometimes significant disk space used by original equipment manufacturer (OEM) recovery images.

The OEM image restores the device to its original, factory-installed configuration, complete with custom drivers and utilities as well as bundled (and potentially unwanted) software. Depending on when the machine left the factory, this option is likely to be significantly out of date. Despite those shortcomings, we recommend keeping this partition on any device that's still under the manufacturer's warranty; delete it only if you're running short of space for storing data.

You can safely remove the OEM recovery image if you're confident you have a reliable way to restore your system to a clean image (to pass it along to a new owner, for example). Creating your own recovery drive or system image, as we explain in this chapter, fills either bill. Removing the OEM partition might require a trip to the Command Prompt window and some judicious use of the DiskPart utility, as we explain in "Managing disks from the command prompt" in Chapter 14.

Windows 10 also includes a built-in option to turn a USB flash drive into a bootable recovery drive. Using this recovery drive, you can restore Windows, even after a complete system drive failure.

In the remainder of this section, we discuss these backup and recovery options in more detail.

Using a recovery drive

Windows 10 includes the capability to turn a USB flash drive into a recovery drive you can use to perform repairs or completely reinstall Windows. The Recovery Media Creator (Recoverydrive.exe) creates a bootable drive that contains the Windows Recovery Environment.

> ➤ For instructions on how to create a recovery drive, with or without Windows installation media, see "Download or create installation media," in Chapter 2, "Installing, configuring, and deploying Windows 10."

To use the recovery drive, configure your PC so that you can boot from the USB flash drive. (That process, which is unique for many machines, might involve tapping a key or pressing a combination of buttons such as Power+Volume Up when restarting.)

If you see the Recover From A Drive option when you restart, congratulations—the system has recognized your recovery drive, and you are (fingers crossed) a few minutes away from being back in business.

Inside OUT

Download a recovery image

If your system won't start, but you can get to the internet on another machine, you might be able to download a recovery image from your hardware vendor and then copy that to a USB flash drive. Microsoft, for example, offers this service for its Surface models. (Go to *https://support.microsoft.com/surfacerecoveryimage*, sign in with your Microsoft account, and select a registered device.) For other vendors, check support offerings to see whether an image is available. If a custom recovery image is not available, you can use Microsoft's Media Creation Tool to download the latest version of Windows 10 and copy it to a USB flash drive or save it as an ISO file. For details, see "Download or create installation media," in Chapter 2.

The menu that appears when you start from a recovery drive allows you to repair a PC that has startup issues. Choose Troubleshoot to get to the Advanced Options menu, where you can choose to perform a startup repair, use System Restore to undo a problematic change, or open a Command Prompt window to use system tools such as DiskPart from the command line.

Using File History to protect files and folders

File History is designed as a "set it and forget it" feature. After you enable this backup application, it first copies all personal data files in your personal profile to a secondary drive, usually an external device or a network location. File History then scans the file system at regular intervals (hourly, by default), looking for newly created files and changes to existing files, and adds those files to the backup store.

You can browse the backed-up files by date and time or search the entire history, and then restore one or more of those backed-up files to their original location or to a different folder.

But first, you have to go through a simple setup process.

Setting up File History

Although the File History feature is installed by default, it's not enabled until you designate a drive to serve as the backup destination. This drive is typically an external storage device, such as a USB-attached hard drive, or a network location. On desktop PCs with multiple internal hard disks, you can choose a second internal hard disk as the File History location. Removable drives, such as USB flash drives, are not eligible. The File History setup wizard will show you only eligible drives when you set up File History for the first time.

> ### CAUTION
>
> Be sure you specify a File History volume that is on a separate physical drive from the one that contains the files you're backing up. Windows will warn you, sternly, if you try to designate a separate volume on the same physical drive as your system drive. The problem? One sadly common cause of data loss is the failure of the drive itself. If the backups and original files are stored on the same drive, a hardware failure wipes everything out. Having backups on a separate physical drive allows them to remain independent.

To turn on File History for the first time, open Settings > Update & Security > Backup. Click Add A Drive to scan for available File History drives. The File History wizard responds by showing you all drives that are eligible for use as a File History destination. Figure 15-16 shows a system that has two external USB hard drives attached. Selecting one of the available locations turns on the File History service and begins the backup process, with the backup frequency set to one hour.

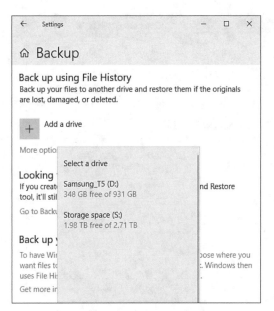

Figure 15-16   Before you can enable File History, you must specify a location (preferably an external USB drive) to hold the backed-up files.

File History is yet another example of a feature caught in the transition from the classic Windows Control Panel to the new Settings app. The overlap between old interface and new is more pronounced here than elsewhere. From the old Control Panel (in File History, click Advanced Settings) or the new Settings app (on the Backup page, click More Options), you can change the backup interval and time period for saving backups. With one notable exception, the options are identical in effect but different in appearance.

To add a network share for which you have read/write permission, you need to use the old-style Control Panel. From Settings > Update & Security > Backup, click More Options > See Advanced Settings to open File History in Control Panel. Then click Select Drive; if you previously added a network location for use with File History, select it here. To add a shared network folder for the first time, click Add Network Location, and use the browse button or enter the full path of a shared folder to which you have read/write access. If necessary, enter and save alternative network credentials. Select the newly added drive, as we've done in Figure 15-17, and click OK. With that task out of the way, you can return to the more modern Settings page.

When you first enable and run File History, it creates a full copy of all files in the locations you designated for backup. That list contains either the default locations or your customized list. (We describe how to create a custom backup list in the next section.)

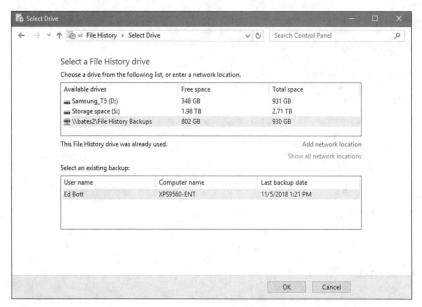

Figure 15-17   To use a network drive with File History, you must first add it to the list of available drives using the old Control Panel settings.

There's nothing complicated or proprietary about File History volumes. The following rules apply to external drives and shared network folders:

- Windows creates a FileHistory folder on the destination drive, with a separate private subfolder for each user. Thus, on a device that includes multiple user accounts, each user's files can be backed up separately.

- Within each user's private subfolder are one or more additional subfolders, one for each device backed up. This folder arrangement allows you to use a single external drive to record File History backups on different devices.

- Each backup set includes two folders. The Configuration folder contains XML files and, if necessary, index files to allow speedier searches. The Data folder contains backed-up files, which are stored in a hierarchy that matches their original location.

- Backed-up files are not compressed. File names are the same as the original, with a date and time stamp appended (in parentheses) to distinguish different versions. As a result, you can browse a File History drive in File Explorer and use search tools to locate a file or folder without using the File History app.

CAUTION

Files stored on a File History drive are not encrypted by default. Anyone who has physical possession of the drive can freely read any files stored there. If you're concerned about confidential information contained in an external File History drive, we recommend you encrypt the drive. (See "Encrypting with BitLocker and BitLocker To Go" in Chapter 18, "Windows security and privacy," for detailed instructions.) As an alternative, consider saving File History to a shared network folder for which you have appropriate permissions.

By default, File History checks your designated drives and folders once an hour, saving copies of any new or changed files as part of the operation. You can adjust this setting in either direction, choosing from nine intervals that range from every 10 minutes (if you really hate the idea of ever losing a saved file) to once daily.

File History backups are saved by default forever. (You receive a warning when your File History drive is full.) However, you can alter the Keep Saved Versions setting to 1, 3, 6, or 9 months or 1 or 2 years. The "set it and forget it" Until Space Is Needed setting allows File History to automatically jettison old backups to make way for new ones when the drive is full.

Click More Options on the Backup page in Settings to adjust either option.

TROUBLESHOOTING

Some files are missing from file history backups

Because of the unique way File History organizes and names backed-up files, you might find that some files aren't backed up properly. This can happen, for example, if you append a version date and time to the name of a file, particularly if the file is deeply nested within multiple subfolders. Those extra characters, added to an already long path, can cause the file name in the File History folder to exceed the maximum path limit of 260 characters. You can spot these errors easily in the File History event logs. To get to those logs quickly from the Backup page in Settings, click More Options > See Advanced Settings. In the classic Control Panel, click Advanced Settings and then click Open File History Event Logs To View Recent Events Or Errors. Resolve any issues by moving the original files or subfolders to a location with a path name that's sufficiently shorter.

Choosing locations to back up

By default, File History backs up all folders in the current user profile (including those created by third-party apps) as well as the contents of local folders that have been added to custom libraries.

➤ For an overview of what's in a default user profile and instructions on how to work with libraries, see Chapter 9, "Storage and file management."

CHAPTER 15

To manage the list of folders backed up by File History, open Settings > Update & Security > Backup > More Options. Scroll down to view the folder list on the Backup Options page.

To remove any folder from this list, select its name and then click or tap Remove. To add a folder from any local drive, click or tap Add A Folder and then select the location using the Select Folder dialog box.

NOTE

Although the OneDrive folder is included by default in the list of folders to be backed up by File History, only files that are synced to the local drive are backed up to File History.

At the end of the list is an Exclude These Folders option. It's useful when you want to avoid filling your File History drive with large files that don't require backing up. If you routinely put interesting but ephemeral video files into a subfolder in your Downloads folder, for example, you might choose to exclude that Videos subfolder completely from File History, while leaving the rest of the Downloads folder to be backed up.

When a File History drive fills up, you can either change the settings to remove old backed-up files and make room for new ones or swap in a new drive. If you choose the latter option, click or tap the Stop Using Drive button on the Backup Options page, remove the old drive, and set up the new one.

Restoring files and folders

File History backups give you multiple ways to recover files that are lost, damaged, or accidentally deleted. You can restore the entire contents of a folder or drive as part of the recovery from a hard drive crash, for example. You can even resuscitate an earlier version of a document so that you can recover content you changed or deleted in a later draft.

The simplest way to recover an earlier version of an existing file or folder is to start from File Explorer. If you know which version you want, right-click the file in File Explorer and choose Restore Previous Versions. That opens the file's properties dialog box with the Previous Versions tab selected, displaying a list of available backed-up versions sorted by date, as shown in Figure 15-18.

The arrow to the right of the Open button at the bottom of the Previous Versions list gives you a choice of how to open the selected item. Clicking Open works especially well for Office documents; you get a read-only copy of the document in its original application. That way, you won't accidentally overwrite the current version of the document with the older one you just opened.

Click Open In File History to use the File History application instead. (We'll say more about the File History application in a moment.)

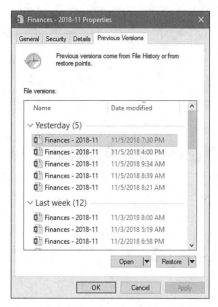

Figure 15-18   When you know exactly which file you want to restore, it's often quickest to get it from the Previous Versions tab in File Explorer.

The second button beneath the File Versions list also provides a pair of choices: Click Restore to overwrite the current version, or click Restore To and save a copy to a different location. If you attempt to restore a previous version of a file to the original location and the original file still exists, you'll see the Replace Or Skip Files dialog box, which gives you an opportunity to change your mind or save the new file as a copy in the same location. If you want to restore a copy without deleting the original, click Compare Info For Both Files and then select the check box for both the original file and the restored previous version, as shown in Figure 15-19. The restored copy will have a number appended to the name to distinguish it from the original.

Not sure which version you want? Select a version and click Open In File History to preview that version. Or select a document and then, on the File tab in File Explorer, click History. That option opens a preview of the most recent saved version in the File History app. Use the back button below the main window to go back in time until you find the right version. Right-click the big green button for Restore and Restore To options.

The File History app offers a distinctly different take on browsing backed-up files. Although it resembles File Explorer in some respects, it adds a unique dimension—the ability to choose a set of saved files from a specific date and time, and then scan, scroll through, or search that entire set of files.

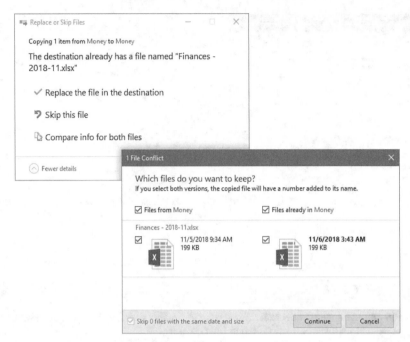

Figure 15-19 To restore a previous version of a file without replacing the original, click the Compare Info For Both Files option and then select both versions in the File Conflict dialog box.

You're most likely to use the File History app in one of the following two ways:

- To restore some or all files from a backup (after reinstalling Windows, for example), go to Settings > Update & Security > Backup. Click More Options and then, at the bottom of the Backup Options page, click Restore Files From A Current Backup. If you haven't set up File History yet, choose the external drive or network location where the backup is located.

- To restore one or more files or folders, open File Explorer, select the file or folder you're interested in recovering, and then click History, in the Open group of the ribbon's Home tab.

Figure 15-20 shows the File History app, which has an address bar, navigation controls, and a search box along the top, very much like File Explorer. What's different are the time stamp (above the file browsing window) and the three controls below the window that allow time control without the need for flux capacitors or other imaginary time-machine components.

Figure 15-20   In its Home view, the File History app shows all files and folders set for regular backup. Scroll left for older backups, right for more recent ones.

The legend at the top of the window tells you the date and time of the currently displayed backup. Use the Previous Version and Next Version controls at the bottom of the window to move between backups. (You can also use the keyboard shortcuts Ctrl+Left/Right Arrow.)

Within the File History app window, you can open folders to see their contents. An address bar at the top, along with the invaluable up arrow beside it, allows you to navigate as you might in File Explorer. As with File Explorer, you can use the search box in the upper-right to narrow the results by file type, keyword, or file contents. Because file names rarely provide enough detail to determine whether a specific file is the one you're looking for, File History has a preview function. Double-click a file to show its contents in the File History window. Figure 15-21 shows one such preview of an Excel workbook, with the full path and file name in the address bar and a scrollbar along the right for moving through the document in the preview window. You can choose to preview individual tabs in the workbook, just as you can scroll through slides in a PowerPoint presentation or pages in a Word document.

To restore a file or folder you deleted or overwrote, move backward through the backups until you reach the desired date. Double-click to open a folder; use Ctrl+click to select multiple items. When you've made your selections, click the big green button to restore the selected items to their original location. If you'd prefer to restore the items to a separate location, right-click the green button and click Restore To.

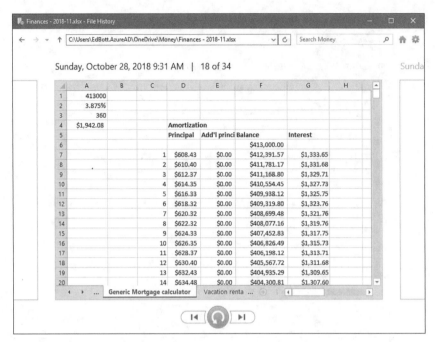

Figure 15-21   File History is capable of previewing most popular file types, including images, PDF files, and Microsoft Office documents like this Excel workbook.

The option to restore entire folders is especially useful when you're switching to a new PC. After you complete one last backup on your old PC, plug the File History drive into your new PC, and then use the big green Restore button to copy your backed-up files to corresponding locations on the new PC.

As with File Explorer, you can change the view of files in the File History browsing window. By using the two shortcuts in the lower-right corner, you can quickly switch between Details and Large Icons view. (The latter is particularly useful when looking through folders full of digital photos.)

Inside OUT

Transfer your File Explorer smarts to File History

There's no need to open a menu or click a tiny icon to change the view in File History. Any of the eight predefined views, from Content through Extra Large Icons, can be invoked with its keyboard shortcut, Ctrl+Shift+*number*. Any number between 1 and 8 works, with Ctrl+Shift+2 switching to Large Icons view and Ctrl+Shift+6 to Details view. These same shortcuts work in File Explorer as well.

Using the Reset option to recover from serious problems

One of the signature features of Windows 8 turned out to be quietly revolutionary: an easy way for anyone to reset Windows to its original configuration using a Refresh or Reset command, with no technical skills required.

Windows 10 significantly refines that capability under a single Reset command. The most important change eliminates the need to have a disk-hogging OEM recovery image in a dedicated partition at the end of the hard drive. In Windows 10, that recovery image and its associated partition are no longer the primary recovery option. Instead, Windows 10 accomplishes recovery operations by rebuilding the operating system to a clean state using existing system files.

This push-button reset option has the same effect as a clean install, without the hassles of finding drivers and without wiping out potentially valuable data. The Reset This PC option is at the top of the list on the Recovery page in Settings, as shown earlier in Figure 15-15. It's also the featured choice on the Troubleshoot menu when you restart in the Windows Recovery Environment, as shown in Figure 15-22. Beginning with Windows 10 version 1703, Windows Defender Security Center includes a Fresh Start option on the Device Performance And Health page that offers the same reset option in a friendlier environment.

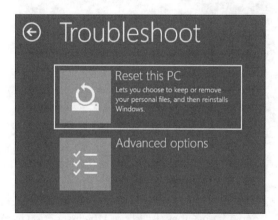

Figure 15-22   You can reset your Windows 10 PC by starting the Windows Recovery Environment and choosing the top option shown here.

When you reset a PC, Windows 10 and its drivers are restored to the most recent rollup state. After the reset is complete, the PC includes all updates except those installed in the past 28 days, a design that allows recovery to succeed when a freshly installed update is part of the problem.

For PCs sold with Windows 10 already installed, any customized settings and desktop programs installed by the manufacturer might be restored with the Windows 10 reset. These customizations are saved in a separate container, which is created as part of the OEM setup process.

All of the default preinstalled Windows apps (Photos, Weather, Mail, and Calendar, for example) are restored, along with any Windows apps that were added to the system by the OEM or as part of an enterprise deployment. App updates are downloaded and reinstalled via the Store automatically after recovery.

Windows desktop programs are not restored and must be manually reinstalled. Likewise, any previously purchased Store apps are discarded and must be reinstalled from the Store.

Resetting a PC isn't something you do accidentally. The process involves multiple confirmations, with many opportunities to bail out if you get cold feet or realize that you need to do just *one* more backup before you irrevocably wipe the disk. The first step offers you the option to keep your personal files or remove everything, as shown in Figure 15-23.

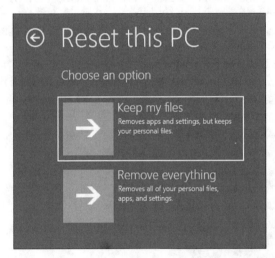

Figure 15-23   The Reset This PC option let you choose whether to keep your personal files or remove everything and start with a completely clean slate.

If you're performing the reset operation in preparation for selling or donating your computer, you'll probably want to use the second option. Otherwise, choose the first option to retain your personal files.

If you're removing everything on a system with more than one drive, you can choose to remove files from only the drive where Windows is installed or from all drives. The reset process also includes an option to scrub data from the drive so that it cannot easily be recovered using disk utilities. The Fully Clean The Drive option can add hours to the process. Note that this option, while thorough, is not certified to meet any government or industry standards for data removal.

If you made it this far through the process, you have only one more confirmation to get through. That dialog box, shown in Figure 15-24, shows the choices you made, with one last Cancel option. To plunge irreversibly ahead, click Reset.

Figure 15-24   This is your last chance to back out when resetting a PC.

The reset option is a tremendous time-saver, but it's not all-powerful. Your attempts to reset Windows can be thwarted by a handful of scenarios:

- If operating system files have been heavily corrupted or infected by malware, the reset process will probably not work.

- If the problem is caused by a cumulative update that is more than 28 days old, the reset might not be able to avoid that problem.

- If a user chooses the wrong language during the out-of-box-experience (OOBE) phase on a single-language Windows version (typically sold in developing countries and regions), a complete reinstallation might be required.

If the reset option doesn't work, the best option is reinstalling with the assistance of a recovery drive, as we describe in Chapter 2.

Using the Windows 7 Backup program

Windows 10 includes the Windows Backup program, which was originally released as part of Windows 7. Its feature set is basically the same as its predecessor, and it's included primarily for compatibility with backups created using that older operating system. (In fact, the name of the executable file, Sdclt.exe, is an inadvertent giveaway of just how old this program is. It's short for SafeDocs Client, the original name of this feature when it debuted as part of a very early Windows Vista beta release.)

If you have a working backup routine based on the Windows 7 Backup program, we don't want to stand in your way. The version included with Windows 10 does all the familiar tasks you depend on, and we suggest you carry on. After all, the best backup program is the one you use.

For Windows 10, there are better backup utilities, but we continue to recommend the Windows Backup program for the one task it does exceptionally well: Use it to make a system image backup that can re-create a complete PC configuration, using a single drive or multiple drives. Restoring that system image creates a perfect copy of the system configuration as it existed on the day that system image was captured, without the need to reinstall and reconfigure applications.

To restore an image backup, boot into the Windows Recovery Environment, choose an image file to restore, and complete the process by restoring from your latest file backup, which is likely to be more recent than the image. (Depending on the age of the backup image, you might also need to install the latest feature update for Windows, followed by the latest cumulative quality update.) The image files that Windows Backup creates are largely hardware independent, which means that—with some limitations—you can restore your backup image to a new computer of a different brand and type.

Inside OUT

Use a system image to save your custom configuration

The single greatest use for a system image backup is to clean up an OEM configuration, leaving Windows intact, removing unwanted software, and installing your favorite apps. Being able to return to a baseline configuration quickly is a trick that IT pros learned long ago as a way of deploying Windows in large organizations. By mastering the system image backup feature, you can accomplish the same result even in an environment with a few PCs instead of a thousand.

Creating a system image backup

To create a system image, go to Settings > Update & Security > Backup and click Go To Backup And Restore (Windows 7). You can skip a few clicks by typing **sdclt** in the search box or the Run box. That opens the tool shown in Figure 15-25.

When you first open Windows Backup, a message alerts you that the program has not been set up. You can ignore that message and the options in the center of that window, and instead click the Create A System Image link at the left side of the window. That opens the efficient Create A System Image wizard. The first step asks you to define a destination for your system image.

The ideal destination for a system image backup is a local hard disk, internal or external. If the Windows Backup program detects a drive that qualifies, it suggests that destination in the list of hard disks at the top of the dialog box. The second option lets you choose a DVD writer as the target for the backup operation; while this option might have made sense a decade ago, we do not recommend it today.

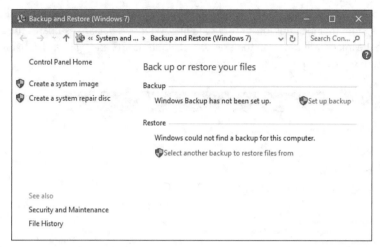

Figure 15-25   The vintage Windows 7 Backup tool isn't necessary for file backup tasks, but it's ideal for capturing a complete image of a Windows installation for disaster recovery.

TROUBLESHOOTING

Windows Backup says your drive is not a valid backup location

If you try to choose a removable drive that is not a hard drive, such as a USB flash drive or SD card, Windows Backup will return this error message: "The drive is not a valid backup location." In its conventional backup role, Windows Backup can save data files on just about any storage medium. System image backups, however, must be saved on a fixed or removable hard disk (not portable media) formatted using NTFS or in a network location.

When you create a system image backup, the resulting image file stores the complete contents of all selected drives during its first backup. If the backup target is a local (internal or external) hard drive, subsequent backup operations store only new and changed data. Therefore, the subsequent, incremental backup operation typically runs much faster, depending on how much data has been changed or added since the previous image backup operation.

If you choose a shared network folder as the backup destination, you can save only one image backup. Any subsequent image backup wipes out the previous image backup.

If you have multiple hard drives, Windows displays a dialog box in which you choose the volumes you want to include in the backup. By default, all volumes that contain Windows system files (including the EFI System Partition and the Windows Recovery Environment) are selected. If other volumes are available, you can optionally choose to include them in the image backup as well.

The disk space requirements for an image-based backup can be substantial, especially on a well-used system that includes lots of user data files. Windows Backup estimates the amount of disk space the image will use, as in the example in Figure 15-36, and will warn you if the destination you choose doesn't have sufficient free disk space.

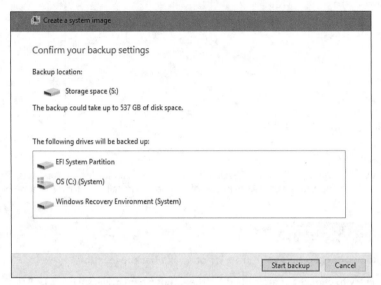

Figure 15-26   The Windows boot volume (indicated by the logo on the drive icon) and other system volumes must be included in a system image. Other volumes, such as a dedicated data drive, are optional.

After you confirm your settings, click Start Backup to begin the process of building and saving your image.

System images are stored in virtual hard disk (VHD) format. Although the data is not compressed, it is compact because the image file does not include the hard drive's unused space and some other unnecessary files, such as hibernation files, page files, and restore points. Incremental system image backups on a local drive are not written to a separate folder. Instead, new and updated files (actually, the changed blocks in those files) are written to the same VHD file. The older blocks are stored as shadow copies in the VHD file, allowing you to restore any previous version.

The final step of the image backup process offers to help you create a system repair disc on a writable CD or DVD. This option might be useful for an older PC, but it's redundant if you already created a recovery drive as described earlier in this chapter.

Inside OUT

Save multiple image backups on a network

If you specify a shared network folder as the destination for an image backup, beware of the consequences if you try to reuse that location for a subsequent backup of the same computer. If the backup operation fails for any reason, the older backup will be overwritten, but the newer backup will not be usable. In other words, you'll have no backup.

You can avoid this risk by creating a new subfolder in the shared network folder to hold each new image backup. The disadvantage, of course, is that each image file will occupy as much space as the original disk, unlike an incremental image backup on an external hard drive, which stores only the changed data.

Restoring a system image backup

The system image capabilities in Windows Backup are intended for creating an emergency recovery kit for a single PC. In that role, they function exceptionally well. If your hard drive fails catastrophically, or if you want to wipe your existing Windows installation and start with a clean custom image you created a few weeks or months ago, you've come to the right place.

Your options (and potential gotchas) become more complex if you want to use these basic tools to work with a complex set of physical disks and partitions. That's especially true if the disk layout to which you want to restore an image has changed from the time you created the original image—if you replaced the original system disk with one that has a larger capacity, for example.

In this section, we assume you created an image backup of your system disk and want to restore it to a system that is essentially the same (in terms of hardware and disk layout) as the one you started with. In that case, you can restart your computer using a recovery drive or bootable Windows 10 installation media and then choose the Repair Your Computer option.

Choose Advanced Options and then select System Image Recovery, as shown in Figure 15-27.

If you're restoring the image backup to the same system on which it was originally created, and the external drive containing the backup file is available, you should see a dialog box proposing that option. Verify that the date and time and other details of the image match the one you want to restore, and then click Next to continue.

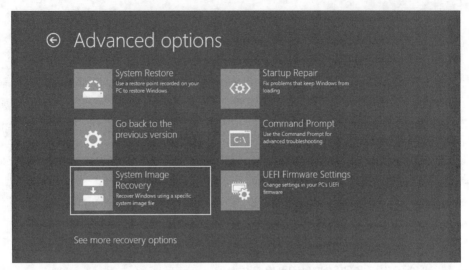

Figure 15-27   By restarting using the Windows Recovery Environment, you can wipe the current device clean and replace its contents with a saved system image backup.

If the image file you're planning to restore from is on a network share or if you want to use a different image, choose Select A System Image and then click Next. You'll see a dialog box that lists additional image files available on local drives. Select the correct file, and then click Next to select a specific image backup. If the image file you're looking for is in a shared network folder, click the Advanced button and then click Search For A System Image On The Network. Enter the network location that contains your saved image, along with credentials (a user name and password) that have authorized access to that location.

Restoring an image backup completely replaces the current contents of each volume in the image file. The restore program offers to format the disk or disks to which it is restoring files before it begins the restore process; if you have multiple drives or volumes and you're nervous about wiping out valuable data files, it offers an option to exclude certain disks from formatting.

The important point to recognize about restoring a system image is that it replaces the current contents of system volumes with the exact contents that existed at the time of the image backup you select. That means your Windows system files and registry will be returned to healthy (provided the system was in good shape when you performed your most recent backup and that no hardware-related issues have cropped up since then). Whatever programs were installed when you backed up your system will be restored entirely. All other files on the restored disk, including your documents, will also be returned to their prior states, and any changes made after your most recent backup will be lost.

CAUTION

If you keep your documents on the same volume as your system files, restoring a system image is likely to entail the loss of recent work—unless, of course, you have an up-to-date file backup, or you have the good fortune to have made an image backup almost immediately before your current troubles began. The same is true if you save documents on a volume separate from your system files but have included that data volume in your image backup. If you have documents that have not been backed up, you can avoid losing recent work by first copying them to a disk that will not be affected by the restore process—a USB flash drive, for example, or some other form of removable media. You can use the Command Prompt option in the Windows Recovery Environment to copy these documents. (For details about using the Command Prompt option, see "Working at the Command Prompt" in Chapter 19.) If you do have a recent file backup, first restore the image backup and then restore your backed-up datafiles.

The main hardware limitation for restoring a system image backup is that the target computer must have at least as many hard drives as the source system, and each drive must be at least as big as its corresponding drive in the source system. This means, for example, that you can't restore a system image from a system that has a 500-GB hard drive to a system with a 256-GB SSD, even if the original system used far less than 256 GB of drive space. Keep in mind also that on a system with multiple physical disks, you might have to adjust BIOS or firmware settings to ensure that Windows restores the image of your system volume to the correct drive.

If your new computer meets the space requirements, restoring a system image should work. This is true even when the source and target computers use different disk controllers. Similarly, other differences—such as different graphics cards, audio cards, processors, and so on—shouldn't prevent you from restoring a system image to a different computer, because hardware drivers are isolated from the rest of the image information and are rebuilt as part of the restore process. (You might need to reactivate Windows because of hardware changes.)

TROUBLESHOOTING

Your backup folders are "empty"

If you use File Explorer to browse to the folder containing your system image backup, when you rest the mouse pointer over a folder name, the pop-up tip might identify it as an "Empty folder." Alarmed, you right-click the folder and choose Properties, only to find that the folder apparently contains 0 bytes, 0 files, and 0 folders. Don't worry. This is the normal condition when your backups are stored on an NTFS volume because, by default, only the System user account has permission to view the files. (That's a reasonable security and reliability precaution, which prevents you or another user from inadvertently deleting a key backup file.) If you're confident in your ability to work safely with backup files in their native format, the solution is simple: Double-click the folder name. Follow the prompts, including a User Account Control (UAC) consent dialog box, to permanently add your user account to the folder's permissions list, giving you Full Control access to the folder.

CHAPTER 15

Configuring and using System Restore

The System Restore feature is a relatively minor part of the recovery toolkit in Windows 10, but it can be useful for quickly undoing recent changes that introduced instability. When System Restore is enabled, the Volume Shadow Copy service takes occasional snapshots of designated local storage volumes. These snapshots occur before Windows Update installs new updates and when supported software installers run. You can also create snapshots manually—a sensible precaution before you make system-level changes.

System Restore snapshots take note of differences in the details of your system configuration—registry settings, driver files, third-party applications, and so on—allowing you to undo changes and roll back a system configuration to a time when it was known to work correctly.

NOTE

In Windows 7, the volume snapshots created by System Restore also included a record of changes to data files on designated drives, allowing you to restore previous versions of those data files. In Windows 10, this capability has been moved into the File History feature, which we described in detail earlier in this chapter.

Note that System Restore monitors all files it considers system-related, which includes executable files and installers. If you download the latest version of a favorite utility and store it in your Downloads folder, it will be removed if you roll back to a System Restore checkpoint from before it was downloaded.

Inside OUT

What's in a restore point?

Restore points in Windows 10 include a full copy of the registry at the time of the snapshot as well as information about changes made to specific files on that volume since the previous snapshot was created. Historically, files are monitored if they include any of 250+ file-name extensions specifically designated for monitoring. This list (which cannot be modified) contains many file types that are clearly programs and system files, with extensions such as .exe, .dll, and .vbs. But it also includes other files you might not think of as system files, including .inf and .ini. You can see the entire list at *https://bit.ly/monitored-extensions*. The information there is most useful for programmers and system administrators, but you might want to browse the extension list if you're curious why System Restore deleted a file.

To check the status of the System Restore feature, type **System Protection** in the search box and then click the Create A Restore Point link; or use the undocumented shortcut **systempropertiesprotection**. Either option takes you to the System Protection tab of the System Properties dialog box in Control Panel. There, under Protection Settings, you'll find a list of internal and external NTFS-formatted drives. (See Figure 15-28.) A value of On indicates that restore points are being created automatically for the associated drive.

Figure 15-28   By default, System Restore monitors changes to the system drive. Select another drive and click Configure to enable System Protection for that drive.

Using the System Properties dialog box, you can enable or disable automatic monitoring for any local drive. On previous versions of Windows, system protection is fully enabled for the system drive by default and is disabled for all other local drives. In our experience, Windows 10 typically disables system protection; we're not aware of any documentation that explains how or why Windows 10 chooses to enable or disable this feature, but the obvious reason is to save disk space. After a successful upgrade, we recommend that you check these settings and, if you find this feature important, re-enable system protection for the system drive at least.

You can manually create a restore point at any time for all drives that have system protection enabled. Click the Create button at the bottom of the System Protection tab to open the Create A Restore Point dialog box. Enter a meaningful description and then click Create to enter the descriptive text.

To turn system protection on or off, or to adjust the amount of space it uses, select a drive from the Available Drives list and then click Configure. That opens the dialog box shown in Figure 15-29.

CHAPTER 15

Figure 15-29   Use the Max Usage slider to adjust the amount of disk space used by System Restore snapshots.

The information under the Disk Space Usage heading shows both the current usage and the maximum amount of space that will be used for snapshots before System Protection begins deleting old restore points to make room for new ones. Move the Max Usage slider to change the amount of disk space reserved for restore points. We recommend using no more than 5 percent of the disk, up to a maximum of 10 GB, on volumes that are larger than 64 GB.

If you're concerned about disk space usage and you're confident you won't need to use any of your currently saved restore points, you can click the Delete button in the lower-right corner under the Disk Space Usage heading to remove all existing restore points without changing other System Protection settings.

Rolling back to a previous restore point

The most common reason to roll back to a previously saved restore point is to undo the destabilizing effect of a freshly installed program or driver that conflicts with other software or drivers on your system. First, if possible, uninstall the offending program or driver, and then apply the restore point captured before the installation. That should remove any problematic system files and registry settings that were left behind by the uninstaller.

To see a list of recent restore points, type **rstrui** at a command prompt, or click System Restore on the System Protection tab of the System Properties dialog box. (If you're running under a standard user account, you'll need to enter an administrator's credentials in a UAC dialog box to continue.) That opens the System Restore wizard, shown in Figure 15-30, with the most recent restore point selected.

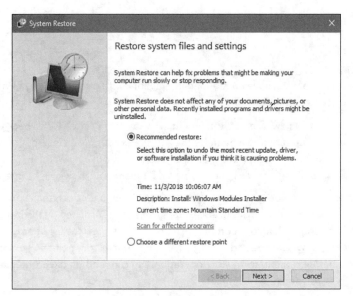

Figure 15-30   The System Restore wizard recommends the most recent restore point. Select the option at the bottom of this dialog box to see older restore points.

To choose a restore point other than the most recent one, click Choose A Different Restore Point and then click Next.

What impact will your choice of restore points have? To see a full list of programs and drivers that will be deleted or restored, select the restore point you're planning to use, and then click Scan For Affected Programs. That displays a dialog box that lists every change you made since that restore point was created. (Note that this list does not warn you about any executable files that might be deleted from your Desktop, Downloads, or other folders.)

After selecting a restore point, click Next to display a series of confirmation dialog boxes. After you successfully convince the system that, yes, you really want to do this, the System Restore wizard creates a new restore point, labeled Undo: Restore Operation, which makes it possible to restore the current configuration if this troubleshooting operation doesn't solve the underlying problem. Then, after a restart, it replaces current system files and registry settings with those in the restore point you selected.

When System Restore reinstates a previously saved configuration using a restore point, your data files—documents, pictures, music files, and the like—are not tampered with in any way. (The only exception is if you or a program created or saved a file using one of the file-name extensions from the list of monitored extensions, as described in the previous section.)

Inside Out

Watch out for System Restore gotchas

Using System Restore can have unintended interactions with other features of Windows 10. Here are a few to watch out for:

- If you create a new user account and then use System Restore to roll back your system configuration to a point before the new account was created, the new user will no longer be able to sign in, and you will receive no warning. (The good news is that the new user's unencrypted documents will, however, be intact.)

- System Restore does not uninstall programs, although it does remove executable files, dynamic-link libraries (DLLs), and registry entries created by the installer. To avoid having orphaned program shortcuts and files, view the list of programs and drivers that will be affected when you return to the restore point and uninstall them before running the restore operation. You can reinstall the program after the restore operation is complete.

- Any changes made to your system configuration using the Windows Recovery Environment are not monitored by System Protection. This can produce unintended consequences if you make major changes to system files and then roll back your system configuration with System Restore.

Although you can restore your system to a previously saved restore point from the Windows Recovery Environment, neither you nor Windows can create a new restore point from that location. As a result, you cannot undo a restore operation that you perform by starting from the Windows Recovery Environment. You should use System Restore in this mode only as a last resort if you are unable to start Windows normally to perform a restore operation.

PART IV

For IT professionals and Windows experts

When is a PC not a PC? When it's a *virtual machine.*

A virtual machine (sometimes called a *VM*) is, effectively, a computer within a computer. It runs in an isolated session on the *host computer*, under the control of a system-level software layer called a *hypervisor*. The operating system running within the virtual machine is called the *guest operating system.* A VM can run the same software as a physical PC and can interact over a virtual network with other PCs and with web-based services. Crucially, a VM doesn't require any hardware beyond what's already part of the host PC.

Business editions of Windows 10—Pro, Enterprise, and Education—include a built-in hypervisor and associated management tools that are collectively part of a feature set called Hyper-V. This option is especially useful for developers, IT pros, and researchers in the following situations:

- If you need to run a program that was written for an earlier version of Windows and does not work properly in Windows 10, you can run it in a virtual machine using that older version of Windows.

- Developers who need to test their programs in different Windows versions or under different resource configurations can set up a virtual machine for each target platform or configuration.

- Security researchers and curious users who want to test software of unknown provenance or explore potentially dangerous websites can reduce the risks by working within the confines of a virtual machine (assuming it's properly isolated from the host and the host network). If a virus or other malware is found, the host machine remains unscathed, and the virtual machine can be rolled back to a safe state.

- IT pros and enthusiasts who want to test a new prerelease version of Windows or experiment with an alternative non-Microsoft operating system such as Linux can do so in a virtual machine. This way, they can try the software without having to dedicate a physical machine or risking their main system.

- Authors of books like this one can use virtual machines not only to test various setups but also to capture images of screens that would be impossible to grab using ordinary screen-capture tools (for example, images showing sign-in screens or even Windows setup before Windows itself is fully functional).

There are, of course, some jobs for which virtual machines are inappropriate. Any task that requires direct access to physical hardware, such as the use of a GPU to encode and decode video files, should be reserved for physical hardware. Likewise, any workload that depends on low latency and precise timing is likely to perform unacceptably in a VM.

Virtual machines are also highly portable. You can move a VM to a new host by simply copying a few files.

To use Hyper-V, your system must meet certain minimum requirements, and you might need to enable the Hyper-V feature, as described in the next section. After that is done, you use Hyper-V Manager to create virtual machines. With enough system resources, you can then run one or more virtual machines, each operating independently of the others. Because they function as independent computers, each virtual machine can run a different version of Windows—32-bit or 64-bit, old or new, server or desktop—or even other operating systems that work on PC-compatible hardware.

NOTE

The hypervisor included in Windows 10 is also used to enable virtualization-based security features, such as Hypervisor-Enforced Code Integrity (HVCI). For more on this group of features, see "Windows security and privacy" in Chapter 18.

Getting started with Hyper-V on Windows 10

Hyper-V (or, more accurately, the Hyper-V role) has long been a power feature in server editions of Microsoft Windows, allowing IT managers to use a single physical machine to host various server roles, each in its own virtual machine. Since the release of Windows 8 in 2012, Microsoft has included so-called Client Hyper-V in Pro and Enterprise editions of Windows, to the great delight of IT professionals, developers, security researchers, and tech enthusiasts.

NOTE

Although this chapter offers a thorough introduction to Windows-based virtualization, there's plenty of technical detail that didn't fit in these pages. For a more comprehensive reference, see the official documentation, "Hyper-V on Windows 10," at *https://docs. microsoft.com/en-us/virtualization/hyper-v-on-windows/.*

The feature sets of Client Hyper-V and its counterpart in Windows Server 2016 overlap but are not a perfect match. In Windows 10, Client Hyper-V gains some additional features, such as production checkpoints, better support of older operating systems, and the ability for users to change memory and other settings without first shutting down a virtual machine. Feature updates since the original release of Windows 10 have added support for Secure Boot and Trusted Platform Modules in VMs; nested virtualization, allowing virtual environments to host additional virtual machines; a Quick Create tool for setting up a VM; better memory allocation; and a Default Switch option that makes virtual network connections easier to manage on laptop PCs.

The Hyper-V platform includes the Hyper-V hypervisor and a group of services that do the work of managing virtual hardware, connecting to virtual networks, and running virtual machines. In particular, the Virtual Machine Management Service (Vmms.exe) and the Hyper-V Host Computer Service (Vmmcompute.exe) both run under the credentials of the currently signed-in user; other parts of the Hyper-V infrastructure run under local system and service accounts, allowing VMs to run even when no user is signed in.

Separate from the hypervisor and related Hyper-V services, Client Hyper-V includes a set of management tools. Two of them are worth calling out here:

- **Hyper-V Manager (Virtmgmt.msc)** is a Microsoft Management Console snap-in that provides management access to the virtualization platform. Using Hyper-V Manager, you can create a new virtual machine; adjust the configuration of an existing VM; configure virtual networking and storage hardware; import, export, and share VMs; and adjust the settings of the Hyper-V platform itself.

- **Virtual Machine Connection (Vmconnect.exe)** is a Windows desktop program that allows you to interact with a running virtual machine using the keyboard and mouse on the host PC. The application can run in a window, in which its contents act as a virtual monitor for the VM, or in full-screen mode, where the virtual machine's display takes over the host PC's display.

We cover both of these essential tools in more detail later in this chapter.

Inside OUT

Determine whether your computer supports Hyper-V

On a PC that's already running Windows 10, checking for Hyper-V support is as easy as opening the System Information app (Msinfo32.exe). Scroll to the bottom of the System Summary tab to see four entries that begin with "Hyper-V," as shown here:

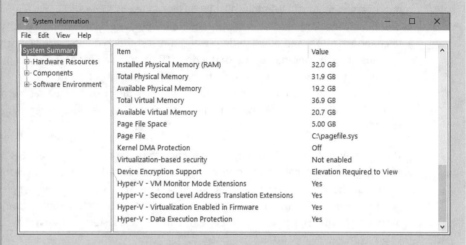

If you see the value *Yes* for every item on that list, you can turn on Hyper-V. (If this section shows *A hypervisor has been detected*, then Hyper-V has already been set up and you're good to go.)

To check Hyper-V compatibility on a PC running an older version of Windows, use the CoreInfo utility from Windows Sysinternals, which is available from *https://bit.ly/sysinternals-coreinfo*. At an elevated command prompt, enter **coreinfo –v** and look at the values for VMX and EPT.

For an Intel processor, an asterisk in the VMX line means the processor supports hardware-assisted virtualization. An asterisk in the EPT line indicates support for Second Level Address Translation (SLAT), a requirement for running Hyper-V; a hyphen in that space indicates that the processor does *not* support SLAT. For an AMD processor, the line to look for is NP. Note that you'll get valid results only if a hypervisor is *not* already running. (But if it's already running, you didn't need to run this diagnostic test anyway, did you?)

Setting up Hyper-V

Before you get started with Hyper-V, be sure your computer meets the system requirements. Because each virtual machine uses system resources on a par with a standalone computer, the requirements are somewhat steep:

- **A CPU with Hyper-V features enabled.** Your computer must have a 64-bit processor that supports virtualization in the firmware and has Hardware-Enforced Data Execution Prevention enabled. Most 64-bit processors sold by Intel and AMD in the past few years have this capability. In addition, support for Second-Level Address Translation (SLAT) is required.

- **A 64-bit version of Windows 10 Pro, Enterprise, or Education.** Hyper-V is unavailable on 32-bit versions and is also not part of Windows 10 Home.

- **At least 4 GB of RAM.** With 4 GB of total RAM, you can probably run one or two low-resource virtual machines simultaneously. In our experience, you need at least 8 GB of total RAM for satisfactory performance with one or more virtual machines running Windows.

- **Copious disk space.** Each virtual machine is stored in files on your hard drive. The size can vary considerably depending on how you configure your virtual machines (for example, the operating system and the size of the VM's virtual hard disks), how many checkpoints you save, and so on—but expect to use at least 20 GB of disk storage for each virtual machine.

With those prerequisites in place, you're ready to turn on the Hyper-V features, which are installed but are off by default. To do so, open Windows Features, shown in Figure 16-1. (In the search box, type **features** and then click Turn Windows Features On Or Off.)

Figure 16-1 To select all the Hyper-V-related entries, select the top-level Hyper-V check box.

CHAPTER 16

Click the plus sign by the top-level Hyper-V entry to show all the subentries. If your computer does not fully support Hyper-V, the Hyper-V Hypervisor entry is not available.

Inside OUT

Using Hyper-V on a computer that lacks hardware support

Hyper-V Management Tools, the first subentry under Hyper-V, can be installed on any computer running any edition of Windows 10. Therefore, even if the Hyper-V Hypervisor entry is dimmed (which means your computer isn't capable of hosting virtual machines), you can use Hyper-V Management Tools to manage virtual machines that are hosted on a different physical computer (in most cases, a computer running Window Server). To run virtual machines on your own computer, you must enable the Hyper-V Hypervisor.

Select Hyper-V (which also selects all the available subentries) to enable it, and then click OK. After a few moments, Windows asks you to restart your computer.

Alternatively, you can enable Hyper-V by using Windows PowerShell. Use this cmdlet:

```
Enable-WindowsOptionalFeature –Online –FeatureName Microsoft-Hyper-V –All
```

Using Hyper-V Manager

Hyper-V Manager is the program you use to create, configure, manage, and run virtual machines. When you start Hyper-V Manager, the initial view, shown here, might leave you scratching your head. You're faced with a barren console window that has only one available action:

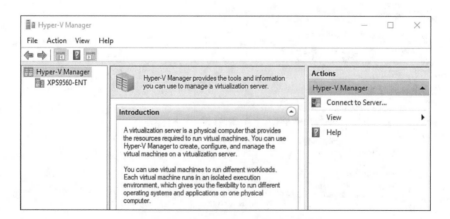

The trick is to select a "server" (in this case, your local computer) in the left pane, the console tree. (On computers that do not have Hyper-V Platform enabled, the only option is to choose

Connect To Server from the Actions pane, which allows you to connect to a different virtualization server.) That action reveals far more information and options, as shown in Figure 16-2.

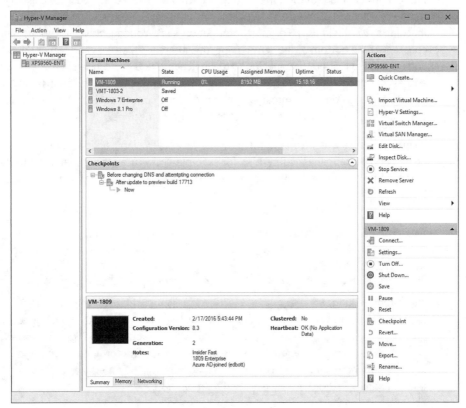

Figure 16-2   The bottom of the Hyper-V Manager window shows details about the currently selected virtual machine, with available actions for that VM on the right.

TROUBLESHOOTING

The name of your computer doesn't appear in the console tree

If your computer's name doesn't appear under Hyper-V Manager in the console tree, it's probably because either your account lacks the necessary privileges or your computer is not running the Hyper-V Hypervisor and associated services. The first problem can occur if you're signed in using a standard account. To fix it, right-click Hyper-V Manager in Start, choose Run As Administrator, and supply credentials for an administrator account. To ensure that your computer is running the Hyper-V Hypervisor, be sure you're running a 64-bit version of Windows 10, and be sure your computer supports Hyper-V, as described in the previous section. If your computer meets the requirements, check to be sure that Hyper-V Platform is selected in Windows Features.

When you select a Hyper-V host in the console tree (in this case, your PC running Windows 10 Pro or Enterprise), the center pane lists the virtual machines available on that host and shows a bit of information about the current state of each one. Below that, you'll see a list of checkpoints for the selected virtual machine. (A *checkpoint* captures the configuration and data of a virtual machine at a point in time. For more information, see "Working with checkpoints" later in this chapter.) At the bottom of the center pane, the Summary, Memory, and Networking tabs show additional details about the selected virtual machine. Here you can see at a glance what IP address has been assigned to the virtual machine, how much memory is in use, and so on. The thumbnail image on the Summary tab also provides a convenient launching method for the virtual machine; double-click it to connect to that virtual machine.

As in other console applications, the right pane shows available actions for the items selected in the left and center panes. Figure 16-2, for example, shows the actions that apply to the Hyper-V host running on the local computer named XPS9560-ENT and to the virtual machine named VM-1809.

Inside OUT

Add notes to help explain a virtual machine's configuration

In the settings for every virtual machine is a Name field that includes a free-form box where you can record notes about that VM. We recommend that you get in the habit of using these notes to record details that will help you or a colleague understand the details of a configuration (including the default account for signing on) without having to poke around in the VM's settings. Those notes can be especially useful when you're reopening a VM that's been unused for months or even years.

What's in a virtual machine?

Creating and configuring a virtual machine isn't particularly different from building a physical PC, except that instead of snapping memory modules into motherboards and connecting disk drives to SATA ports, you assemble virtual components using Hyper-V management tools. In fact, every virtual machine created using Hyper-V is built from the same small group of virtual components. With one noteworthy exception, the CPU, your virtual machine is unable to directly access hardware that's part of the host PC.

You can see all of those components by opening Device Manager within a virtual machine. Figure 16-3, for example, shows Device Manager expanded to show a virtual disk, a virtual DVD-ROM drive, a virtual keyboard, a virtual storage controller, and an assortment of virtual system devices on a virtual motherboard.

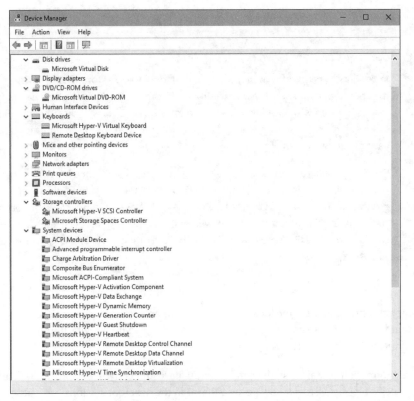

Figure 16-3   Virtual machines are made up of virtual components, as you can see when you open Device Manager from within a Windows 10 VM as we've done here.

In most cases, it's considerably easier to upgrade a virtual PC than it is to perform the corresponding task on a physical PC. To add more virtual memory or a second virtual storage device, for example, all you need to do is shut down the VM and adjust a few settings in that VM.

We'll get to the tools for creating and reconfiguring VMs later in this chapter. In the remainder of this section, we explain how Hyper-V stores the different pieces that make up a VM.

The most basic building block is the virtual machine configuration file, which is stored in a binary format using the .vmcx file extension. By default, these configuration files are stored in %ProgramData%\Microsoft\Windows\Hyper-V; you can specify an alternate location when you create a new VM, and you can move configuration files to a different folder or drive using Hyper-V Manager. (%ProgramData% is an environment variable that is set to C:\ProgramData on a standard Windows installation.)

CHAPTER 16

Inside OUT

Use PowerShell to edit a .vmcx file

In previous versions of Hyper-V, configuration details were stored in XML-formatted data files that could be viewed and edited using any text editor. The new binary file format introduced with Windows 10 and Windows Server 2016 isn't directly editable, and as a result it's impossible to use Hyper-V Manager to work with a configuration file that hasn't been registered with the current Hyper-V host.

For serious tinkerers, however, there's always the Hyper-V module for Windows PowerShell, which is installed along with Hyper-V Manager. As Ben Armstrong, a program manager on Microsoft's Hyper-V team, explains, it's possible to import a configuration file, modify it using PowerShell cmdlets, and then save the result as a new configuration file. For details, see his blog post, "Editing a .VMCX file," at *https://bit.ly/edit-vmcx-powershell*.

Other files stored in the same location include .vmgs and .vmrs files, which contain information about the current state of a running VM, and the smart paging file, which supplements dynamic memory when you restart a VM.

The information contained in the configuration file instructs Hyper-V how to allocate resources to specific types of virtual hardware, as outlined in the next four sections.

Machine generation

In Windows 10, Hyper-V supports two types of machines. This choice is new to the Hyper-V client in Windows 10 and offers some trade-offs between compatibility and features.

- Generation 1 supports a wide range of guest operating systems, including most versions of Windows (32-bit and 64-bit) and Linux. The virtual hardware in a generation 1 virtual machine is typical of that found in BIOS-based PCs for many years.

- Generation 2 supports only 64-bit Windows versions: among desktop operating systems, Windows 8, Windows 8.1, and Windows 10 are supported; support for Windows Server as a guest operating system is restricted to Windows Server 2012 and later versions. Generation 2 also supports newer versions of many Linux distributions.

NOTE

For a complete discussion of the differences between the two VM generations, including a list of supported operating systems, visit *https://bit.ly/Gen1Gen2*.

In addition, generation 2 removes support for attaching physical DVD drives and other older hardware to a virtual machine. But a generation 2 virtual machine has modern UEFI-based firmware, which enables Secure Boot and booting from a network adapter, SCSI hard drive, or virtual DVD. In addition, generation 2 virtual machines enable new Hyper-V features, such as the ability to adjust memory or add a network adapter while the virtual machine is running. A new feature that first appeared in Windows 10 version 1703 adds a Zoom Level command to the View menu in a Virtual Machine Connection window for generation 2 machines; with this command, you can set the display scaling to 100%, 125%, 150%, or 200%.

As we explain later in this chapter, you must make the choice of generation at the time you create a VM, and you can't change it after that initial selection.

Memory

Like its physical counterpart, a virtual machine needs memory. When a VM is running, the memory assigned to that VM is reserved by Hyper-V and can't be used by the host PC. If you assign a fixed amount of memory to a VM configuration, running that VM can put significant memory pressure on the host PC. If your host PC has 16 GB of RAM, for example, and you set the RAM value to 8 GB for a VM, your host PC is effectively limited to 8 GB for Windows and all other activities when that VM is running, even if the VM is using only a fraction of the memory assigned to it.

To ease this pressure, Hyper-V in Windows 10 includes a feature called *dynamic memory,* which allows you to make more efficient use of the memory in the host PC.

When you enable the Dynamic Memory option for a VM, you assign two additional values for memory: Minimum RAM and Maximum RAM. That configuration allows the VM to grab physical memory when it needs it (especially when starting up) but releases that memory when it's no longer in use so that it's available for the host PC.

Figure 16-4 shows memory usage in a VM that is configured with 4096 MB (4 GB) of RAM, with Dynamic Memory enabled, Minimum RAM set to 2048, and Maximum RAM set to 8192.

In that Task Manager window, you can see the RAM configuration, 4.0 GB, in the upper-right corner. That's the amount of RAM that was allocated at startup, exactly as it would look on a physical PC with 4 GB of RAM. In this VM, however, you can see from the Memory Usage scale that only 2.0 GB of physical RAM from the host PC is in use. The Maximum Memory value at the bottom right shows that this VM is ready and able to increase its RAM to 8.0 GB if necessary (and if that physical RAM is available on the host PC).

Dynamic Memory is an excellent way to conserve memory when running Hyper-V on a system with limited physical RAM. If you have ample system resources and want to occasionally run VMs with a fixed amount of RAM, leave that option disabled.

We discuss the different ways to manage memory usage in VM configurations later in this chapter.

CHAPTER 16

Figure 16-4   Unlike a physical PC, virtual machines can be configured with dynamic memory. This VM is allowed to use a minimum of 2.0 GB and a maximum of 8.0 GB of RAM.

Storage controllers and virtual disks

Every Hyper-V virtual machine includes a virtual storage controller. On a Generation 1 VM, this virtual component mimics a legacy IDE controller. On a Generation 2 VM, it acts like a SCSI controller.

Part of the basic configuration of a VM is, of course, a virtual hard disk that attaches to that virtual controller. Hyper-V in Windows 10 supports two virtual disk file formats: the legacy VHD format and the newer VHDX format.

The legacy VHD format is limited to a total size of 2 TB. VHDX files, on the other hand, can be as large as 64 TB, provide better data resiliency, and support advanced 4K sector technology; you can also expand a VHDX file on the fly without having to shut down the VM in which it's being used.

An important attribute of a virtual disk that distinguishes it from a physical disk is the disk type, which can be one of the following three choices:

- **Fixed size.** This type of virtual disk uses exactly as much disk space on the Hyper-V host as its configured size. The size of the VHD file doesn't change based on the amount of data stored within it.

- **Dynamically expanding.** Choose this disk type when you want to conserve physical disk space on the Hyper-V host and the workloads you plan to use on the VM are not disk-intensive. The virtual disk file starts out small and grows as you add data to it within the VM. (You can't, of course, overturn the laws of physics; as your virtual hard disk expands, it will use a corresponding amount of physical disk space.)

- **Differencing.** This advanced disk type starts with a parent disk that remains intact; any changes you make in this virtual disk affect only the file containing the child disk and can be reverted easily.

On a generation 2 virtual machine, you also have the option to share a virtual disk file that already exists. If you have a spare physical disk partition available, you can create a virtual disk and attach that physical drive to it directly. This option offers excellent performance but is impractical on most desktop configurations.

Generation 1 VMs also allow the use of virtual DVDs, which are most useful when you want to mount an ISO file to install a new operating system in the VM. If you're feeling especially nostalgic, you can even create a virtual floppy disk.

We discuss the mechanics of creating and managing virtual disks later in this chapter.

Networking

Support for basic networking in Hyper-V requires two components: a *virtual network adapter*, configured separately for each VM, and a *virtual switch*, which is managed by the Hyper-V platform. The default virtual network adapter is called a *Hyper-V specific network adapter* and is available for both generation 1 and generation 2 machines. In generation 1 machines only, you can install a *legacy network adapter* capable of booting directly to a network and running unsupported operating systems.

By default, a new virtual machine is set up as a standalone computer with no network connection. It can't connect to the internet or to other computers on your network. That disconnected configuration might be useful for some testing scenarios, but for most situations, you'll probably want to give your virtual machines access to a network connection.

To do that, you must first configure the virtual network adapter to connect to a virtual switch; that action connects the virtual network adapter in your virtual machine to the physical network adapter in your physical computer, thereby allowing the VM to connect to the outside world. For each virtual switch you configure, Hyper-V creates a corresponding virtual network adapter on the host PC that handles communication to other hosts and to the internet. Here, for example, is what the virtual adapter for the default switch looks like in Network And Sharing Center.

CHAPTER 16

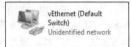

In current versions of Hyper-V on Windows 10, every VM has access to a preconfigured default network switch that communicates with the host PC and other PCs using Network Address Translation (NAT). To use this switch, when you get to the point in creating a new virtual machine where you configure networking, simply select Default Switch from the drop-down list. (See "Configure networking," later in this chapter.)

You can create additional custom switches to accommodate other network configurations, and then choose the type of virtual switch you need for each VM, at startup time or while the VM is running.

To create a virtual switch or make changes to an existing one, open Hyper-V Manager and then, in the Actions pane (or on the Action menu), click or tap Virtual Switch Manager. Then select the type of switch you want to create:

- **External.** This is the correct choice for a VM that you want to use as if it were another PC on your local network. This configuration binds the virtual switch to your computer's physical network adapter so that you can access your physical network. Assuming your physical network adapter is connected to the internet, your virtual machines using this type of switch also have internet access.

- **Internal.** An internal virtual switch allows connections among virtual machines on the host PC using the same virtual switch; those VMs can also connect to the host PC and to the internet using the virtual network adapter (vEthernet) on the host PC.

- **Private.** Use a private virtual switch to set up a network that comprises only the virtual machines running on your physical computer and using the same virtual switch. This network is isolated from all physical computers, including the Hyper-V host on which it's installed.

When you click or tap Create Virtual Switch, you're asked for more details, as shown in Figure 16-5. Click OK to complete the switch creation.

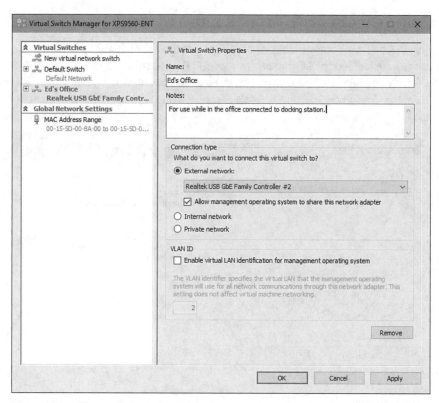

Figure 16-5 If your computer has more than one physical network adapter, specify the one you want to use for a new switch under External Network.

Creating and managing virtual machines

Beginning with Windows 10 version 1709, Hyper-V supports two ways of creating a new virtual machine from within Hyper-V Manager. The Quick Create option was introduced in version 1703, and in version 1709 it adds support for a gallery of predefined virtual machine images. This option allows you to create a VM with just a few clicks; if you're comfortable with the settings it makes on your behalf, this can be a useful tool.

The alternative is the traditional New Virtual Machine Wizard, which walks you step by step through configuring each virtual component. The process can feel tedious, but it also results in much greater control over the VM's configuration.

Our discussion begins with the newer, streamlined option.

CHAPTER 16

Using Quick Create to configure a new VM

The Quick Create command appears at the top of the Actions pane for a Hyper-V server (which in this case is a desktop PC running Windows 10 Pro), as shown earlier in Figure 16-2. Clicking Quick Create opens a Create Virtual Machine dialog box like the one shown in Figure 16-6. From this dialog box, you can choose a predefined image or specify a local source of installation media, as we've done here.

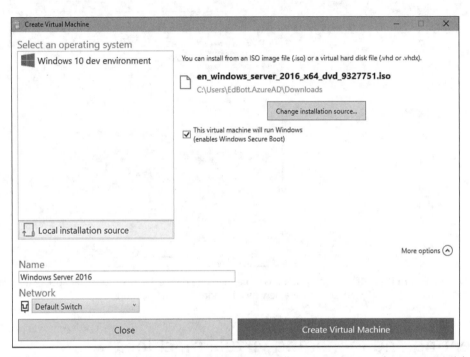

Figure 16-6   With just a single dialog box, Quick Create allows you to answer the most essential questions posed by the New Virtual Machine Wizard.

As of late 2018, two options are available in the gallery for a default installation of Hyper-V on Windows 10. The Windows 10 Dev Environment package includes an evaluation version of Windows 10 Enterprise and requires a download of more than 12 GB; the Ubuntu 18.04.1 LTS option allows you to quickly set up a VM running this popular Linux distribution and requires a download of approximately 1.5 GB.

It's certainly possible that Microsoft will add more packages to this default gallery; until that happens, those most likely to use this feature are organizations that want to make custom images available for internal development and test groups. For details on how to add your own virtual machine images to the Quick Create gallery, see this post from Microsoft's Virtualization Blog: *https://bit.ly/hyperv-gallery-new-vm*.

Inside OUT

Get ready-to-run virtual machines

As part of its support for web developers, Microsoft offers fully configured virtual machines you can download and run. Each one has a different guest operating system with certain software installed. These virtual machines are for testing and evaluation and expire after 90 days, but instructions provided with the virtual machine files explain how to use the files after expiration. You can find these virtual machine files at *https://bit.ly/ free-vms-webdev*.

If nothing in the Quick Create gallery meets your requirements, take advantage of the last option to create a VM using local installation media. From the Quick Create dialog box, select Local Installation Source, click the Change Installation Source button, and navigate to the ISO or VHD/VHDX file you want to use for installation or as a template.

We recommend that you click More Options to display controls where you can enter a descriptive file name and select a virtual network adapter. You can specify three settings from this dialog box.

- **Operating System.** Click Change Installation Source to specify the location of your OS installation disk, which must be in the form of an ISO image or a virtual hard disk file.

- **Name.** The text you enter here will be used to identify the VM in the Virtual Machines list in Hyper-V Manager.

  The check box under Change Installation Source enables Secure Boot, a feature of UEFI-based computers. For more information, see "Advanced security options" later in this chapter.

- **Network.** Here you select a virtual network switch for the VM. Unless you've created a custom network switch, choose Default Switch here.

With those details complete, click Create Virtual Machine. Hyper-V creates your new VM using default settings and displays a final dialog box with two buttons. The first allows you to connect to the VM immediately; the second opens the Settings dialog box for the new VM, where you can adjust the amount of memory, tinker with hard drives, and make any other necessary changes.

CHAPTER 16

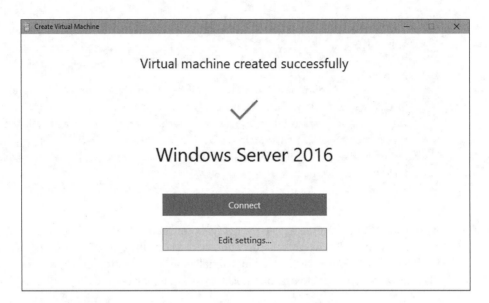

We discuss exactly how (and why) to change those settings later in this chapter.

Inside OUT

Don't use Quick Create for an older operating system

Quick Create always creates a generation 2 virtual machine—a setting that cannot be changed. As described in the previous section, "What's in a virtual machine?" a generation 2 machine is the appropriate choice when the guest operating system you plan to use is a recent 64-bit version of Windows or a recent Linux distribution. If you're setting up a VM to run an older operating system, such as Windows 7, you're better off using the New Virtual Machine Wizard and selecting generation 1, which has virtual hardware that's better supported by earlier operating systems.

Using the New Virtual Machine Wizard

If you want step-by-step control over the process of creating a new VM, avoid Quick Create. Instead, open Hyper-V Manager and, in the Actions pane, click or tap New > Virtual Machine. That action launches the New Virtual Machine Wizard. Navigating through the wizard leads you through the process of setting up a virtual machine. Use the Next and Previous buttons or the links along the left side to step through each group of settings. At any point in the wizard, you can click Finish to create a virtual machine that uses default values for any wizard pages you skip.

The first page of the wizard is a text-only Before You Begin page, which you can banish for good by selecting Do Not Show This Page Again. The remainder of this section describes your options at each succeeding step of the wizard.

NOTE

For fast results, you can open the New Virtual Machine Wizard and immediately click Finish. As it turns out, however, that up-front efficiency is just an illusion, as is the corresponding Quick Create option. When using the wizard in this fashion, you'll need to spend time and effort later manually changing the generic default name for the VM and the virtual hard disk, adjusting the size of available memory, and attaching installation media. In addition, the default settings create a generation 1 VM, which can't be changed to a generation 2 configuration.

Specify name and location

After you step through the Before You Begin page, the wizard asks you to provide a name for your virtual machine. Replace the generic New Virtual Machine entry with a name that'll help you differentiate this virtual machine from others you might create. (The wizard will use this entry again later, as the suggested name for the virtual hard disk you create.) If you don't like the proposed storage location for the virtual machine files, select the check box and specify another, as shown in Figure 16-7.

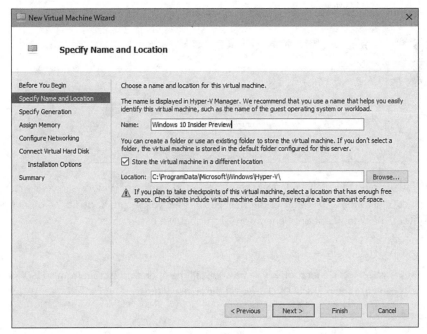

Figure 16-7   Use a descriptive name to help identify the VM in Hyper-V Manager. We recommend storing configuration files in the default location unless you have a separate, dedicated data drive.

The default location is %ProgramData%\Microsoft\Windows\Hyper-V\. If your computer has a small system drive—a common configuration in some desktop systems that use a solid-state drive for system files and a large hard disk for data files—you might want to store the files elsewhere. Keep in mind that a virtual machine can occupy 10–40 GB or more, and each checkpoint can consume equivalent amounts of space.

It's possible to change the location where the virtual machine configuration files are stored after you create the VM, but it's not easy. The virtual hard disk can be moved by right-clicking the machine name and choosing the Move option, for example, and the paging file location can be changed by adjusting the VM configuration, but these options aren't available for the core configuration files. To completely move all the pieces of a virtual machine at a later time, you can import a virtual machine, copy it, and store it in a different location. You're much better off choosing a suitable location *before* you create the virtual machine.

Specify generation

On the Specify Generation page, shown here, select either Generation 1 or Generation 2 for the style of virtual machine you need. (For a discussion of the differences, see "Machine generation," earlier in this chapter.)

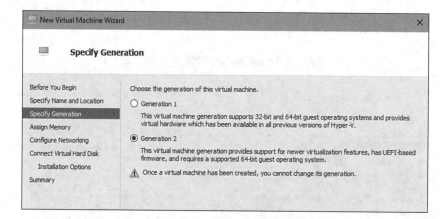

If you're going to install a relatively new, supported version of Windows in your virtual machine, select Generation 2 to enable additional features such as Secure Boot. For an older operating system, the default option, Generation 1, is probably a better choice.

NOTE

If you select Generation 2, you must install the operating system from an ISO file; you can't use the physical DVD drive on the Hyper-V host.

Assign memory

On the Assign Memory page, shown in Figure 16-8, you specify the amount of RAM to assign to the VM during startup. This amount remains assigned to the VM when it's running unless you select the Use Dynamic Memory For This Virtual Machine option. (For an explanation of how dynamic memory works, see "Memory," earlier in this chapter.)

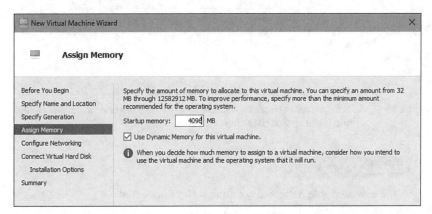

Figure 16-8   By selecting the Use Dynamic Memory For This Virtual Machine check box, you can use memory more efficiently, which can improve performance when physical memory is scarce.

Note that the wizard does not allow you to specify values for Minimum RAM and Maximum RAM. Instead, if you use the New Virtual Machine Wizard and enable dynamic memory, Hyper-V assigns 512 MB and 1048576 MB, respectively. You can exercise far more granular control over memory by adjusting the settings for a VM after you create it, as we explain a bit later in this chapter.

Configure networking

On the Configure Networking page, shown in Figure 16-9, you specify the virtual network switch where you want to connect your virtual machine's network adapter. The default option is Not Connected, which results in a virtual machine that's isolated from all other computers (physical and virtual) and from the internet. To connect to the host PC and to the internet, select Default Switch (a new feature, introduced in Windows 10 version 1709, which uses NAT to connect to your computer's network) or select a virtual network switch you created previously.

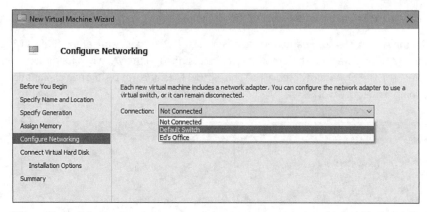

Figure 16-9   Select a virtual network switch to connect to the outside world. The Default Switch option is the appropriate choice for most VMs.

TROUBLESHOOTING

The only available networking option is Not Connected

In Windows 10 version 1703 and earlier, Hyper-V did not include a default network switch. In those older versions, you had to create a virtual network switch before con-necting a VM to a network, as described earlier in "Networking." If you're running a cur-rently supported Windows 10 version and the Default Switch option is missing, the most likely explanation is that you or another administrator removed it. You can re-create this switch by shutting down any running VMs and then removing and reinstalling the Hyper-V Platform feature, as described earlier in "Setting up Hyper-V."

Connect virtual hard disk

Use the Connect Virtual Hard Disk page, shown in Figure 16-10, to set up the virtual machine's first virtual hard disk. By default, the New Virtual Machine Wizard creates a dynamically expanding virtual hard disk, using the VHDX format and a default name based on the name you entered in the first step. If you want to create a fixed-size virtual hard disk or use the older VHD format, choose the Attach A Virtual Hard Disk Later option and customize your VM after you complete the wizard.

Just like a physical computer, a virtual machine can have multiple hard drives; the wizard allows you to create or attach the system drive only. By default, this drive is created in a subfolder of the virtual machine location you specified earlier, where it's accessible to any user who signs in on the host PC. You can override that default and store the virtual hard disk on any physical disk that's accessible to the Hyper-V host.

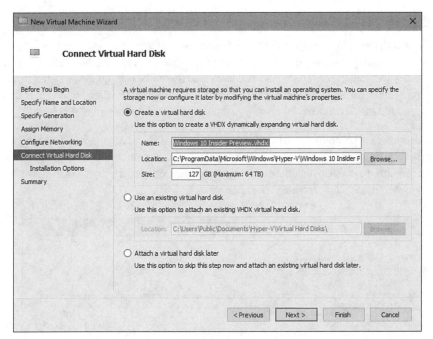

Figure 16-10   With the first option, you create a virtual hard disk. Choose one of the other options to use an existing virtual hard disk.

In addition to specifying the name and location of your virtual hard disk file, you must specify the disk's capacity, in gigabytes. Be sure you create a virtual hard disk that's big enough to store the operating system, programs, and data you plan to use on the virtual machine. Although you don't want to go overboard, don't worry too much about specifying a size that's too big. As we noted earlier, a dynamically expanding VHDX file starts small and can grow as needed; just make sure the location you choose on the physical disk has enough space to accommodate the virtual drive file as it grows.

> ### NOTE
>
> **Changing the name or location of a virtual hard disk is a tedious process that requires multiple steps. Likewise, resizing a virtual hard disk after it has been created involves tinkering with partitions in the virtual machine. To avoid those hassles, we recommend putting some thought into getting this setting right from the beginning.**

If you have an existing virtual hard disk you want to use instead of creating a new one, select the second option on this wizard page.

Installation options

The Installation Options page, shown in Figure 16-11, allows you to specify how and when you want to install an operating system in your new virtual machine. Because this is a generation 2 virtual machine, the only options available are to use an ISO image file or install from a network server running enterprise deployment tools. (Generation 1 VMs offer options to install from the physical CD/DVD drive on the Hyper-V host or from a bootable virtual floppy disk.)

Like a physical computer, a virtual machine is useless without an operating system, so installing one should be your first order of business unless you're using a virtual hard disk that already has an operating system installed. Select the appropriate option, specify the location of your operating system installation media, and click Next.

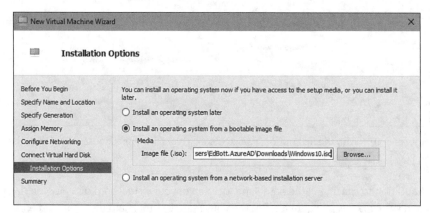

Figure 16-11   These options are available for a generation 2 VM. Options for installing from a physical CD/DVD drive or a virtual floppy disk are available only for generation 1 VMs.

This brings you to a Summary page, where you can review your settings before clicking Finish to complete the wizard.

At this point, even though you specified installation options, you still don't have a working virtual machine. Now back in Hyper-V Manager, you have two choices: You can select the newly created VM and then fine-tune its settings (as described in the following section). Or you can double-click the new virtual machine to open it in a Virtual Machine Connection window. Then click or tap the Start button on the toolbar or choose Start on the Action menu. This "powers on" your virtual machine and launches the operating-system setup from the location you specified in the wizard.

> ## TROUBLESHOOTING
>
> **Your VM displays a network message instead of booting to a virtual DVD.**
>
> If you start your newly configured VM for the first time and see a message telling you that the VM is attempting a "PXE network boot using IPv4," you need to adjust the boot order for the VM to give the virtual DVD drive a higher priority than the network adapter.
>
> Open the Settings dialog box and click Firmware (if this is a generation 1 VM, click BIOS). In the Boot Order list, select the Network Adapter entry and click Move Down until that entry is at the bottom of the list. Save the revised settings and restart the virtual machine. Click in the Virtual Machine Connection window and then tap a key when you see the "Press any key to start from DVD" prompt.

Changing settings for a virtual machine

As we noted earlier in this chapter, you can freely modify most of the virtual hardware associated with a virtual machine—for example, adding virtual memory, expanding a virtual hard disk, or connecting a virtual DVD drive. The one exception is the machine generation, which cannot be changed after its initial configuration. You can also perform management tasks, such as adjusting how the VM behaves when you shut down or restart the host PC.

To dive into these settings, open Hyper-V Manager, select the virtual machine you want to reconfigure, and then, near the bottom of the Actions pane, click or tap Settings. (If that menu is not visible, right-click the VM name to see a shortcut menu containing the same options.) The Settings dialog box, shown in Figure 16-12, contains two groups of option: one for the virtual hardware and the other for management settings. Note that some hardware options available here differ slightly, depending on the machine generation.

The Processor settings shown in Figure 16-12 are primarily designed for Hyper-V on servers containing multiple processors. Virtually all PCs designed for use with Windows 10 contain a single processor with multiple cores, and the settings in that dialog box do not apply. If you try to assign more than one virtual processor to a virtual machine, Hyper-V ignores the setting.

Some settings can be changed even while a machine is running (which is important for virtual machines running critical tasks), especially on generation 2 virtual machines. Other configuration changes, however, require that the VM be turned off (not just saved).

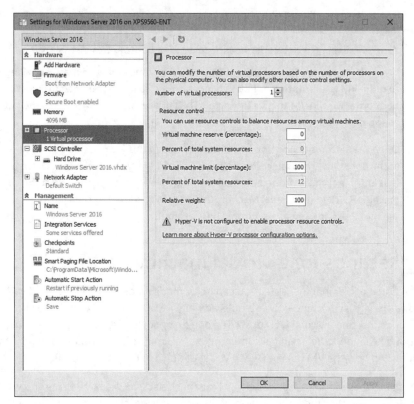

Figure 16-12   Use this Settings dialog box to adjust a wide array of options that are not available when using Quick Create or the New Virtual Machine Wizard.

Inside OUT

Mount or unmount a virtual DVD quickly

Any disk image in ISO format can appear as a virtual DVD drive, and there's no need to go through the Settings dialog box to mount or unmount a virtual drive. Instead, to attach an ISO file as a drive within a running virtual machine, click Media from the VMConnect console, and then click DVD Drive > Insert Disk. Choose an ISO file, and click OK. To unmount a virtual drive, use the Eject <*ISO filename*> option from the DVD Drive menu.

The following sections highlight some of the most important options you can set using the Settings dialog box.

Fine-tuning virtual memory usage

As with a physical PC, adding memory is the single most important thing you can do to improve performance. The balancing act with a virtual machine is finding the right configuration that doesn't hobble performance on the host PC.

Options on the Memory tab are identical for both generations of virtual machines. When dynamic memory is enabled, you can specify minimum and maximum amounts of memory to be available to that VM. If you're obsessed with memory tuning, you can also change buffer sizes for dynamic memory and adjust the priority for memory usage when multiple virtual machines compete for a limited supply of physical RAM.

Figure 16-13, for example, shows the memory configuration for a VM running Windows Server 2016. Note that we've increased the Minimum RAM setting from its default value of 512 MB to 4096 MB and lowered the default Maximum RAM value of 1,048,576 MB to 8192 MB.

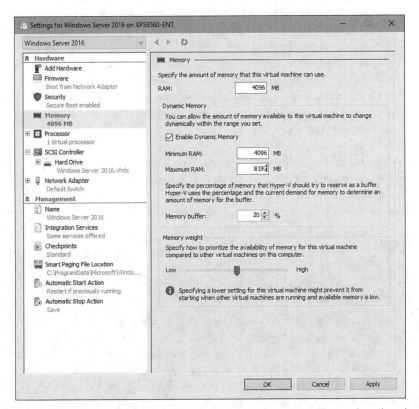

Figure 16-13   Using these dynamic memory settings, the VM will never have less than 4 GB of RAM available to it. When needed, it can use as much as 8 GB of memory but no more.

CHAPTER 16

There's no right or wrong way to adjust these settings, which depend on how you plan to use the VM. For example, if you're testing a Windows Insider Preview build of Windows 10 and you plan to switch to that VM as soon as you start up your host PC, you can safely allocate an amount of RAM equal to the total physical RAM on your system. By contrast, if your goal is to have two VMs running in the background at all times while you do your daily productivity tasks on the host PC, you'll want to restrict the amount of RAM for those VMs, even if that means they occasionally encounter some memory pressure.

Using dynamic memory ensures that each machine gets as much memory as it needs, but it doesn't reserve a fixed amount of memory (which would preclude other virtual machines or the host operating system from using that memory).

TROUBLESHOOTING

Installing a guest operating system fails with a memory-related error

In some configurations, the installation of the guest operating system might fail even though the dynamic memory settings appear to allocate sufficient resources. The problem occurs when the system assigns a minimal amount of memory to the VM at startup, and that amount causes the installer to believe the system doesn't meet minimum requirements. The solution is to increase the value for RAM so that it is at least equal to the minimum required for installing the operating system. After installation is complete, Windows will reduce the amount of assigned memory, if appropriate, according to the Minimum RAM value for that VM.

If you plan to run only one virtual machine, or if you know how much memory your virtual machine will need to perform its given tasks, you can turn off dynamic memory and specify a fixed amount of memory. This setup works more like a physical computer, in that whatever memory you specify is equal to the total amount of installed RAM in the virtual machine.

Inside OUT

Find out how much RAM a VM is using.

As we noted earlier in this chapter, you can use Task Manager's Performance tab to check on memory usage when you're working directly with a virtual machine. But you don't need to go to those lengths to check on memory usage when a VM is running in the background. Instead, open Hyper-V Manager, select the VM whose resource usage you want to check, and then click the Memory tab in the status pane below the Virtual Machines list. In the example shown here, Assigned Memory is larger than Memory Demand, reflecting the 20 percent default buffer used for dynamic memory.

VMT-1803-2

Startup Memory:	4096 MB	**Assigned Memory:**	2296 MB
Dynamic Memory:	Enabled	**Memory Demand:**	1928 MB
Minimum Memory:	2048 MB	**Memory Status:**	OK
Maximum Memory:	8192 MB		

Summary   Memory   Networking

Adding, removing, and adjusting virtual disks

For most garden-variety VMs, the default configuration is sufficient: a single virtual disk used as the system drive and a virtual DVD available for installing software. For some tasks, however, you might want to add a second virtual hard disk, or you might need to change the size or format of an existing disk. This section covers your available options.

Adding a new virtual disk

To add a new virtual disk to an existing VM, follow these steps:

1. Open Settings and click the entry for the VM's disk controller: SCSI Controller on a generation 2 machine, or one of the two IDE Controllers on a generation 1 machine.

   ### NOTE

   The system disk on a generation 1 machine must be attached to an IDE controller. Each IDE controller on a generation 1 machine can connect up to two devices. If you attempt to connect a new secondary drive to a controller that already has two devices attached, your attempt will fail with an error message. If both of the default IDE controllers are full, use the SCSI Controller instead.

2. From the list on the right, choose Hard Drive and click Add. Hyper-V automatically selects an unused location on the controller and displays the settings for that location, as shown in Figure 16-14.

CHAPTER 16

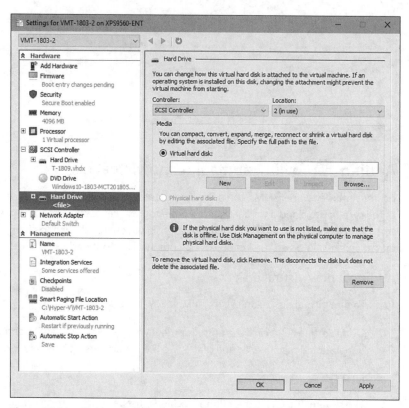

Figure 16-14 Clicking the New button on this page launches a wizard that walks you through configuring a virtual hard disk.

3. Click New to open the New Virtual Hard Disk Wizard and complete its steps:

- **Choose A Disk Format (VHD/VHDX).** This option is available only for a generation 1 machine. For generation 2 machines, the default format is VHDX and this step is unavailable.

- **Choose A Disk Type.** Dynamically Expanding is the default and is usually the correct choice for a VM running a modern operating system; you can also choose Fixed or Differencing. (For an explanation of how each type is used, see "Storage controllers and virtual disks," earlier in this chapter.)

- **Specify A Name And Location.** Change the default name ("New Virtual Hard Disk") to something descriptive, and adjust the location if necessary.

- **Configure Disk.** Accept or change the default size of 127 GB, or copy the contents of an existing physical or virtual disk to the newly created disk.

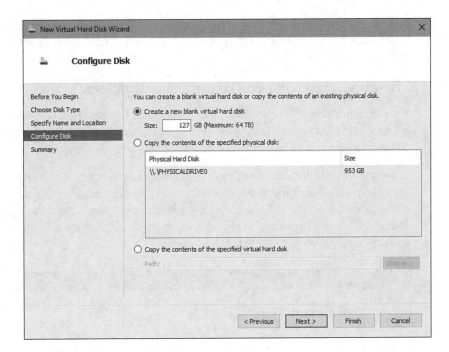

4.   Complete the wizard to add your hard disk.

Note that this sequence is the equivalent of attaching a new drive to a physical PC. If the virtual machine is running Windows, you'll need to use the Disk Management console to add the drive, format it if necessary, and assign a drive letter.

> ➤ **For details on how to set up a new hard drive, see Chapter 9, "Storage and file management."**

Removing or replacing a virtual disk

Removing a virtual disk from a VM configuration is a straightforward process. You might choose to do so if you created a secondary disk for test purposes and no longer need it. From the Settings dialog box for the VM, click the drive in the Hardware pane on the left, and then click the Remove button on the right.

Although it's possible to remove the system drive from a VM, it's hard to imagine why you would want to do that. You're more likely to replace one virtual disk with another, a task you can complete by selecting the virtual disk, clicking the Browse button in the pane on the right, and then choosing the replacement drive. As an alternative, you can also click New to replace the existing disk with a blank disk for a clean start.

CHAPTER 16

In either case, note that removing or replacing the disk does not remove the underlying VHD/VHDX file. If you want to reclaim that storage space on the host PC, you'll need to do so manually, from File Explorer.

Inspecting, expanding, and converting virtual disks

If you're curious about the size, format, and other details of a virtual hard disk, select its entry in the left pane of the Settings dialog box and then, on the right, click Inspect. That opens a small dialog box packed with all the essential details, including the current file size and the maximum disk size.

To expand a virtual disk or convert it to a different format or disk type, you need to first remove any checkpoints from the virtual machine (a process we explain later in this chapter). After doing so, shut down the VM, select the hard disk from the Settings dialog box, and click Edit. That opens yet another wizard, as shown in Figure 16-15, with Compact, Convert, and Expand options that are relatively easy to follow.

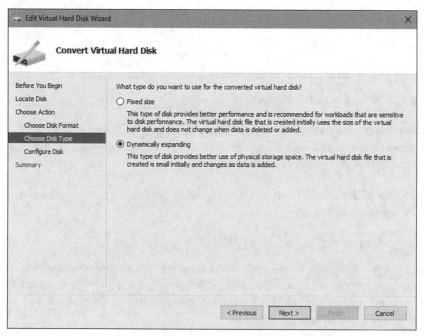

Figure 16-15   Use the Edit Virtual Hard Disk Wizard to convert a dynamically expanding disk to fixed size, or vice versa. You can also convert between VHD and VHDX formats here.

CAUTION

Changing the format, disk type, or size of a virtual hard disk runs a small but meaningful chance of data loss. As a precaution, we recommend backing up the VHD/VHDX file before performing the conversion of resizing.

If you find you've run out of virtual disk space (or are in imminent danger of doing so), use the Expand option to increase the size of the drive. Note that the additional space you create is not

automatically added to any disk volumes in your virtual machine. You'll need to open the VM
and use Disk Management to expand the volume to use the newly added space.

Advanced security options

On generation 2 VMs only, the Security tab offers the same security features you get with Windows 10 running on a UEFI-based physical PC. Figure 16-16 shows these options for a virtual
machine running a preview release of Windows. Note that Secure Boot is enabled using the
Microsoft Windows template. For a virtual machine running a distribution of Linux that supports Secure Boot, choose the Microsoft UEFI Certificate Authority template instead. (The third
option, Open Source Shielded VM, is available only on hosts running Windows Server 2016.)

This tab also contains an option to enable a virtual Trusted Platform Module (TPM), which allows
the disks in a virtual machine to be encrypted with BitLocker Disk Encryption. On older releases of
Windows 10, enabling this feature required some special preparation; these steps are not required
as of the Windows 10 Anniversary Update, version 1607. For more details, see the TechNet article
"Generation 2 virtual machine security settings for Hyper-V," at *https://bit.ly/gen2-vm-security*.

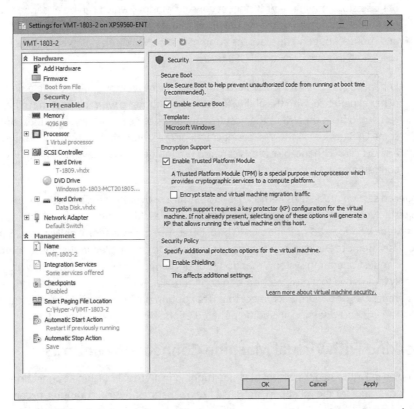

Figure 16-16   On a generation 2 virtual machine, you can turn on Secure Boot and, optionally, create
a virtual Trusted Platform Module to use BitLocker Disk Encryption on virtual disks.

CHAPTER 16

Automatic start and stop actions

You use the final two options under the Management heading to specify what happens to a virtual machine when you shut down or start the Windows 10 Hyper-V host. For most purposes, the correct setting for Automatic Stop Action is Save; for Automatic Start Action, you can configure a VM to start automatically (with or without a delay) or start the VM only if it was running when the system shut down previously.

Running a virtual machine

As the final step in creating a virtual machine, as described earlier in this chapter, you double-click the name of a virtual machine in Hyper-V Manager to open the machine in a Virtual Machine Connection window. (Clicking Connect in the dialog box that appears after you set up a new machine using Quick Create does the same thing.) You then click the Start button on the toolbar to power on the machine. You can run the virtual machine session in a Virtual Machine Connection (VMConnect) window using one of two session types:

- Basic sessions run in the VMConnect console window, which can be expanded to any resolution supported by the virtual display adapter. This type of session accepts keyboard and mouse input and displays the contents of the VM display; however, there's no access to audio hardware or external USB devices.

- Enhanced sessions, which debuted with Hyper-V in Windows 8.1, provide a significantly richer experience, with the ability to share the Clipboard with the host machine, redirect audio from the VM to the host PC's speakers or headphones, share local drives and some USB devices in the VM, connect to a printer through the host PC, and sign in with a smart card. Enhanced sessions can also use multitouch displays and multiple-monitor configurations.

Enhanced session mode uses Remote Desktop Protocol over the virtual machine bus (VMBus); as a result, you can only use an enhanced session with a VM running a supported guest operating system: Windows 8.1 or Windows 10 (Pro, Enterprise, or Education); or Windows Server 2012 R2 or later. Remote Desktop connections do not have to be enabled in the guest operating system. For guest operating systems that don't support enhanced sessions, such as Windows 7 Pro, the only alternative to a basic session is to configure a network connection in the VM and use the Remote Desktop client to connect to it. That option provides several of the features available in an enhanced session, including a shared Clipboard and audio support.

Working with Virtual Machine Connection windows

As shown in Figure 16-17, a virtual machine running in a Virtual Machine Connection window looks (and, for the most part, acts) just like a separate physical computer, except that it's contained in a window on your desktop. In this example, we're even able to capture a screen-shot of the sign-in screen, which isn't possible on a physical PC.

Figure 16-17   To work safely with a preview release of Windows 10, you can run it in a Virtual Machine Connection window.

Use the toolbar at the top of the window (or the corresponding commands on the Action menu) to operate the virtual machine.

From left to right, the buttons have the following functions:

- **Ctrl+Alt+Del.** Because the Ctrl+Alt+Del key combination is reserved by Windows 10 on your physical computer, when you press it while you're using a virtual machine, the key combination goes to your host computer. To mimic the effect of Ctrl+Alt+Del within a virtual machine, press Ctrl+Alt+End, or click or tap this toolbar button.

- **Start.** This button turns on a virtual machine that is off.

- **Turn Off.** This button turns the virtual machine off, but it does so by effectively unplug-ging the machine. This, of course, is a quick but not graceful way to shut down a com-puter (even a virtual one), and you'll lose any unsaved data.

- **Shut Down.** Clicking this button is equivalent to using the Shut Down command on the Start menu, and the machine goes through the usual shutdown process. Note that some unusual configurations (usually older, unsupported operating systems) do not allow the use of the Shut Down command in Hyper-V. For a virtual machine without this support, use commands within the virtual machine to shut down properly.

- **Save.** This button saves the virtual machine state and then turns it off, releasing all resources to the host PC. The process is much like hibernation on a physical computer. When you next start the virtual machine, you return immediately to where you left off.

- **Pause/Resume.** Pausing a virtual machine stops it temporarily but does not fully release its resources, as the Turn Off, Shut Down, and Save options do.

- **Reset.** Resetting a virtual machine discards any changes and reboots using the last saved version.

- **Checkpoint.** This button creates a checkpoint, which is a snapshot of the virtual machine's state and its data. For more information, see "Working with checkpoints" later in this chapter.

- **Revert.** This button restores the virtual machine to its condition at the previous check-point and restarts the virtual machine.

- **Basic/Enhanced Session.** On guest operating systems that support it, this button toggles the virtual machine between basic session mode and enhanced session mode. For more information, see the next section, "Using enhanced session mode."

- **Share.** Use this option, introduced in version 1709, to export the entire virtual machine configuration and data files (but not checkpoints) to a compressed file in VMCZ format. You can then copy that file to another PC running Hyper-V and double-click to import the VM.

Within the Virtual Machine Connection window, you use the virtual machine just as you would a physical computer, with only a few exceptions:

- When you run an older, unsupported guest operating system, using a mouse is not as fluid as it is when your guest operating system is Windows 7 or later. In those configura-tions, the mouse can become trapped when you click inside the virtual machine window. To release it, press Ctrl+Alt+Left Arrow.

- Not all of your physical computer's hardware is available in all virtual machines. For example, access to the physical DVD drive on the Hyper-V host is not available in generation 2 virtual machines. (You can, however, mount an ISO image as a DVD drive.) For generation 1 machines, only one virtual machine can use a physical DVD drive at any given time. (To release the DVD drive from one virtual machine so that you can use it in another, use commands on the Media menu.)

  USB devices, audio devices, and some other local resources work only in enhanced session mode. (For more information, see "Using enhanced session mode.")

When you close the Virtual Machine Connection window, note that your virtual machine continues to run. By closing the window, all you're doing, in effect, is turning off the monitor. To shut down or turn off the virtual machine, you should use the appropriate buttons on the Virtual Machine Connection window. If that window is closed, reopen it by using Hyper-V Manager.

Using enhanced session mode

As we noted earlier, Hyper-V support in earlier versions of Windows included severe limitations on access to physical hardware from a VM. You could overcome some of these limitations (specifically, audio playback and file copying) by using Remote Desktop Connection to connect to a virtual machine, but that option requires a working network connection to the virtual machine.

The solution in Windows 10 is *enhanced session mode*, which solves many of these shortcomings. With enhanced session mode, you can redirect the following resources from your physical computer to a virtual machine in a Virtual Machine Connection window:

- Audio devices

- Printers

- Plug and Play devices

- Clipboard (which you use to copy and paste files and other information between the virtual machine and your physical computer)

> ## Inside OUT
>
> *Determine at a glance whether you're in enhanced session mode*
>
> Need a quick way to tell whether your machine is running in enhanced session mode? Look at the speaker icon in the notification area of your virtual machine's taskbar. If it has a red X, that's because no audio device is available, which means you're in basic session mode.

Alas, enhanced session mode comes with its own limitations. As noted earlier, it works only with Windows 8.1 (or Windows Server 2012 R2) and later versions as the guest operating system. And in enhanced session mode you can't change the resolution of the virtual machine's monitor using commands within the virtual machine. (For a workaround, see the following tip.) However, a new capability built in to Windows 10 version 1703 and later allows you to change resolution simply by dragging the borders of the Virtual Machine Connection window; when you do so, the guest operating system automatically adjusts to the new resolution.

If your virtual machine is running an operating system that supports enhanced session mode, you can switch between basic and enhanced session mode by clicking or tapping the next-to-last button on the Virtual Machine Connection toolbar.

You can enable and disable enhanced session mode on a per-server or per-user basis. To view or change either setting, in Hyper-V Manager select the host name from the tree on the left and then, under the host name in the Actions pane, click or tap Hyper-V Settings. In the Hyper-V Settings dialog box that appears, you'll find enhanced-session-mode settings under Server and User.

Inside OUT

Change screen resolution for an enhanced mode session

Within an enhanced session mode window, using the normal Windows settings for changing screen resolution leads to this message: "The display settings can't be changed from a remote session." (Enhanced session mode, in effect, uses Remote Desktop Connection to connect to the virtual machine; hence, the message about a "remote session.") As described earlier, Hyper-V in Windows 10 version 1703 and later lets you change the resolution simply by dragging the edges of the Virtual Machine Connection window. However, this makes it difficult to precisely set a standard resolution—which might, for example, be a requirement for compatibility testing.

If you need to change the screen resolution to a specific size, switch to basic session mode and then close the Virtual Machine Connection window. In Hyper-V Manager, click Connect to open a new Virtual Machine Connection window, and you'll be greeted by a dialog box in which you can specify the screen resolution.

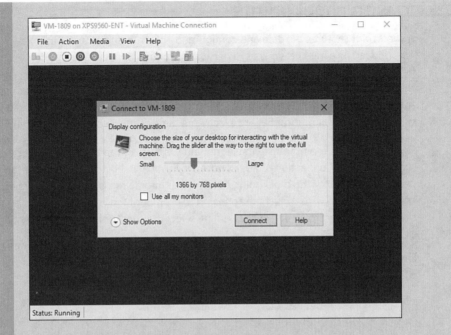

In this same dialog box, clicking Show Options adds a Local Resources tab to the dialog box. On that tab, you specify which local resources—that is, printers, drives, and other devices from the host computer—you want to use within the virtual machine. For more information about these settings, see "Connecting to another computer with Remote Desktop" in Chapter 13, "Windows networking."

One of the most effective uses of an enhanced session is to effectively work with a virtual machine as if it were a complete replacement for the host PC. To do so, move the resolution slider to Full Screen. If your host PC has multiple monitors, select the Use All My Monitors check box. Click Connect, and the virtual machine expands to fill the entire display (or displays). The only indication that you're working with a virtual machine is the toolbar at the top of the screen. That bar includes the name of the VM and the host PC in the center and standard Minimize, Restore, and Close buttons on the right. If the status bar gets in the way of something on the screen, you can slide it left or right. To hide it completely, click the Pin icon at the far left. When the status bar is hidden, you can show it by moving the mouse pointer to the top of the screen and allowing it to remain there briefly.

Working with checkpoints

A *checkpoint* captures the data and configuration of a running virtual machine—a snapshot in time. Indeed, in earlier versions of Hyper-V, checkpoints were called *snapshots*. A checkpoint can be restored so that you can quickly and easily return your virtual machine to an earlier time—this capability is particularly valuable for providing a consistent test environment for evaluating software. After the testing is complete, revert to the previous checkpoint to start another round of testing under conditions that are exactly the same as they were before the previous test.

To capture a checkpoint from within a running VM, click or tap the Checkpoint button on the Virtual Machine Connection toolbar, or use the keyboard shortcut Ctrl+N. You can provide a descriptive name for the checkpoint, but no other interaction is required. The checkpoints you collect for a given virtual machine appear in the center of the Hyper-V window, as shown in Figure 16-18. To revert to an earlier checkpoint, select the checkpoint and, in the Actions pane, click or tap Apply.

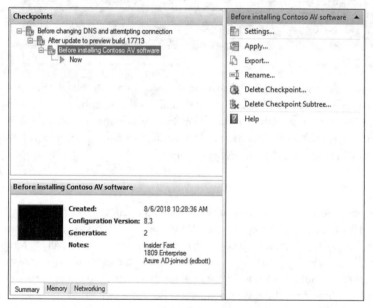

Figure 16-18   When you select a checkpoint in the center pane, a list of applicable actions for that checkpoint appears in the bottom of the Actions pane.

Microsoft engineers discovered that droves of Hyper-V users use checkpoints as a form of backup. (Although it doesn't provide the full capabilities of a more traditional backup program—such as the ability to restore individual folders and files—it's convenient and easy.) However, the checkpoint feature as implemented in earlier Hyper-V versions is far from ideal for backup. Because those checkpoints (now called *standard checkpoints*) include information on the virtual machine state, running applications, and network connections, restoring one often takes you to an unstable condition (for example, the same network connections might not be available).

In response, Client Hyper-V in Windows 10 adds a new type of checkpoint called a *production checkpoint*. A production checkpoint uses the Volume Snapshot Service (VSS) backup technology to save the data and configuration of a running virtual machine but not its state. This provides a much better backup solution, and it's now the default checkpoint in Hyper-V. You can still use standard checkpoints if you prefer; to make the switch, open Settings for a virtual machine and, under Management, click Checkpoints:

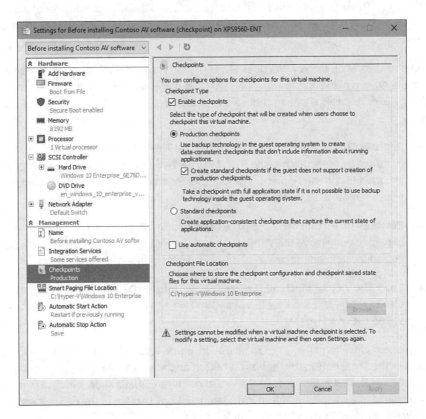

Effective with version 1709, Hyper-V adds a Use Automatic Checkpoints check box. This option automatically creates a checkpoint when you start a VM, giving you the option to roll back without having to remember to create checkpoints. The next time you shut down and restart the virtual machine, you'll have the option to revert to the previous checkpoint. This option is automatically on for new Windows 10 VMs. If you're concerned that this option is too resource-intensive, disable it.

Importing, exporting, and moving VMs

If you have a virtual machine running on one Windows 10 PC and you want to move or copy that VM to a different Windows 10 PC, you have two options.

The first is to use the Export function. Start by shutting down the VM you want to move or copy. Then, in Hyper-V Manager, select the VM and click Export in the Actions menu. In the resulting dialog box, specify a location that has sufficient free disk space to hold all the files associated with the VM (a folder on a removable hard disk, for example, or a network share) and then click Export. This operation (which can take a long time depending on the size of the virtual disks associated with the VM) saves your files in three separate subfolders in the location you specified.

To import the VM on the new PC, open Hyper-V Manager and click Import Virtual Machine from the Actions menu. In the Import Virtual Machine Wizard, browse to the location that contains the exported files and then choose one of the three options on the Choose Import Type page:

- **Register The Virtual Machine In-Place (Use The Existing Unique ID).** Use this option if you are permanently moving the VM to the new Hyper-V host and you want to use the exported files in their current location. This option makes sense if you copied the files from a removable hard drive to a data folder on the new PC, for example.

- **Restore The Virtual Machine (Use The Existing Unique ID).** Use this option if you want to permanently move the VM to the new Hyper-V host and copy the exported files to the default location on the new PC. The exported files remain in place.

- **Copy The Virtual Machine (Create A New Unique ID).** This option is appropriate if you plan to continue using the old VM and you want to create an independent copy of the VM on the new Hyper-V host.

A slightly simpler alternative is the Share option, introduced in version 1709. From a running VM, click the Share button (the rightmost button on the Virtual Machine Connection toolbar) or press Ctrl+H. That action exports the virtual machine configuration and data files (but not checkpoints) to a compressed file in VMCZ format. Copy that file to the new Hyper-V host and double-click to import the VM to default locations.

Finally, if you've run out of disk space on the host PC and need to move all or part of a VM to a new, more capacious drive, shut down the VM and click Move. The resulting wizard allows you to move virtual disk storage or an entire virtual machine to a new location or locations of your choosing. The VM remains registered in Hyper-V Manager; only the location of associated data files changes.

Alternatives to Hyper-V

Client Hyper-V is the easiest way to work with virtual machines in Windows 10, but it's not the only way. Two relatively new options provide alternatives that might make sense if you're a candidate for virtualization.

Windows 10 supports the use of Hyper-V Containers, which are self-contained virtual environments that can manage workloads without requiring the overhead (and licensing cost) of a full operating system.

Container support is new and still developing. For an overview, see the information at *https://bit.ly/Windows10-containers*.

Microsoft Azure is a cloud-based service capable of running virtual machines that don't require local resources. Azure VMs are charged on a pay-as-you-go basis, making them ideal for test environments and important servers where downtime is not an acceptable option. If you have a Visual Studio subscription, your account includes a monthly allowance for Azure usage, with ready-made Windows 10 and Linux virtual machines available. For more details, see *https://azure.microsoft.com/en-us/services/virtual-machines/*.

Managing business PCs

Throughout this book, our emphasis has been on how individuals can get the most out of Microsoft Windows: learn how to use its many features, save time with shortcuts and work-arounds, and customize it to suit specific needs. Most of this information applies equally to a wide variety of devices—including tablets, laptops, and desktop PCs—in a wide variety of environments. Whether you use Windows as a standalone system, in a home network, in a small business network, or as a tiny cog in a ginormous enterprise-scale operation, you can make use of this knowledge.

In this chapter, however, we depart from that focus on the individual to provide an overview of topics, products, and techniques that are useful primarily on business networks. Most require a business edition of Windows: Windows 10 Pro or Windows 10 Enterprise. (Windows 10 Education editions can also use most of these features, as can Windows 10 Pro Workstation.) In addition, many of these features rely on Active Directory services, which are available only on centrally managed networks running Windows Server. Azure Active Directory provides a cloud-based subset of those management tools without the requirement to operate a local server.

Of course, we don't have the space in this book—or any other single book—to fully docu-ment the wealth of business tools Microsoft makes available for Windows 10. Instead, our goal here is to provide a survey of some widely used tools, along with pointers to more in-depth information.

Using a domain-based network

Elsewhere in this book, we describe setup, configuration, and usage of peer-to-peer (or *workgroup*) networks. This is the type of network most commonly found in homes and small businesses, and it does not require a server; each computer on the network is an equally empowered peer, and access to the device and its data is managed locally.

Windows 10 Pro, Enterprise, and Education editions can also be configured in an Active Direc-tory domain. The traditional Active Directory domain-based network requires at least one computer running a version of Windows Server. This is sometimes called *on-premises Active Directory* to differentiate it from a newer, cloud-based alternative called Azure Active Directory (Azure AD).

Both variants of Active Directory provide identity and access services, allowing users to sign on to any cloud or on-premises web application using a wide variety of devices, and to sign on to domain-joined devices. All computers and user accounts on the network can be centrally managed through the server or through a web-based Azure AD dashboard. An on-premises domain controller offers full, policy-based management capabilities. Azure AD provides a more limited set of management tools, although like most Microsoft Azure–based services, it continues to increase in functionality. When you have more than a handful of computers in a network, connecting them to a Windows domain makes them much easier to manage.

If you use a business-focused Microsoft cloud service such as Office 365 (Business and Enterprise subscriptions) or Microsoft Dynamics CRM (among others), your subscription already includes Azure AD.

A detailed description of domains and Active Directory is (well) beyond the scope of this book. Here are some resources to get you started:

- Microsoft Azure: *https://azure.microsoft.com*

- Azure Active Directory: *https://azure.microsoft.com/services/active-directory*

- Windows Server: *https://www.microsoft.com/cloud-platform/windows-server*

Managing computers with Group Policy

Active Directory administrators use Group Policy to configure computers throughout sites, domains, or organizational units. In addition to setting standard desktop configurations and restricting what settings users are allowed to change, administrators can use Group Policy to centrally manage software installation, configuration, updates, and removal; specify scripts to run at startup, shutdown, sign in, and sign out; and redirect users' profile folders (such as Documents) to folders on a network server. Administrators can customize all these settings for different computers, users, or groups.

In a domain environment, Group Policy enables an administrator to apply policy settings and restrictions to users and computers (and groups of each) in one fell swoop. With a workgroup, you must make similar Group Policy settings on each computer where you want such restrictions imposed. Nonetheless, Group Policy can be a useful tool for managing computers on a small network or even for managing a single computer.

Each feature update to Windows 10 typically includes a liberal assortment of new Group Policy settings. A full list of new policy settings grouped by feature update is available at *https://bit.ly/new-group-policy-settings*. That page also includes download links for the complete set of Administrative Template (.admx) files for the most recent Windows 10 feature update. (As of December 2018, when we prepared this revision, the list of new policy settings for versions 1803 and 1809 were not yet available.)

For each .admx file, Microsoft also provides a downloadable spreadsheet that lists the policy settings for computer and user configurations included with that version. Because this spreadsheet is cumulative, it includes all policy settings that apply to all versions of Windows 10. The list also provides other details about each setting, such as the scope of the setting (machine or user), the registry value it controls, and whether a setting change requires a sign-off or reboot to take effect. For version 1803, this spreadsheet is at *https://www.microsoft.com/en-us/download/details.aspx?id=56946*.

The list is huge—thousands of entries—but you can use Excel to sort, filter, or search the list to find policy settings of interest. If you're evaluating when and how to deploy a new feature update for Windows 10, use the New In Windows 10 column in this spreadsheet to display only the settings that are new in any version of Windows 10. Figure 17-1 shows this spreadsheet, configured as a list, with an Excel filter set to show only policies that are new in version 1803.

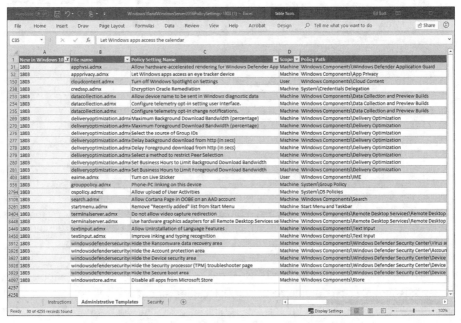

Figure 17-1   With each new version of Windows 10, Microsoft updates a spreadsheet documenting the new policies. Filter that list to show only policies that are new in a specific version, as we've done here for version 1803.

Using Local Group Policy Editor

In this book's examples, we use Local Group Policy Editor (Gpedit.msc) to show how to adjust policy settings. That way, you can follow along even if you don't have access to the Group Policy Management console on a domain controller or don't need the power of Active Directory. Setting Group Policy in an Active Directory domain uses fundamentally similar methods and policies.

To begin exploring Group Policy, in the Start search box type **group policy** and then tap or click Edit Group Policy. As shown in Figure 17-2, Local Group Policy Editor appears in the familiar Microsoft Management Console format.

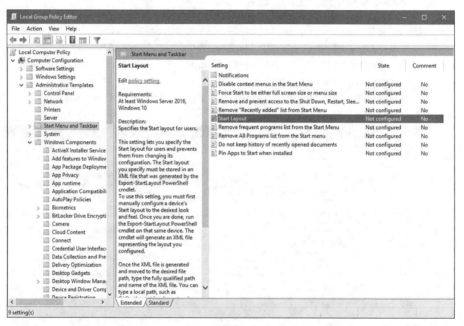

Figure 17-2   Selecting a folder or a subfolder in the left pane shows all policy settings associated with that group in the right pane. When you select a setting, a description of the setting appears.

The Computer Configuration branch of Group Policy includes various computer-related settings, and the User Configuration branch includes various user-related settings. The line between computer settings and user settings is often blurred, however. Your best bet for discovering the policies you need is to scan them all. You'll find a treasure trove of useful settings, including many that can't be made any other way short of manually editing the registry. In the Administrative Templates folders, you'll find several hundred computer settings and even more user settings, which makes this sound like a daunting task—but you'll find that you can quickly skim the folder names in Local Group Policy Editor, ignoring most of them, and then scan the policies in each folder of interest.

To learn more about each policy, simply select it in Local Group Policy Editor, as shown in Figure 17-2. If you select the Extended tab at the bottom of the window, a description of the selected policy appears in the center pane.

> ## Inside OUT
>
> ### Customize Start and taskbar behavior and appearance
>
> The policy setting shown in Figure 17-2 controls one aspect of Start. Many more policies—most of them located in User Configuration > Administrative Templates > Start Menu And Taskbar—manage all manner of Start details, such as the appearance of suggestions and most-used apps in the app list on Start. For more information about these policy settings, go to *https://bit.ly/start-policy*.

NOTE

Some settings appear in both User Configuration and Computer Configuration. In a case of conflicting settings, the Computer Configuration setting always takes precedence.

Changing policy settings

Each policy setting in the Administrative Templates folders has one of three settings: Not Configured, Enabled, or Disabled. By default, all policy settings in the local Group Policy objects are initially set to Not Configured.

To change a policy setting, in Local Group Policy Editor, double-click the name of the policy setting you want to change or click the Policy Setting link that appears in the center pane of the Extended tab. A dialog box then appears, as shown in Figure 17-3.

Beside each setting's option buttons is a large area where you can add your own remarks about a policy, which can come in handy later when you are trying to remember why you changed a specific policy. The Help pane below this Comment area includes detailed information about the policy setting (the same information that appears in the center pane of the Extended tab). The pane to the left of the Help pane offers options relevant to the current policy. Previous Setting and Next Setting buttons make it convenient to go through an entire folder without opening and closing individual dialog boxes.

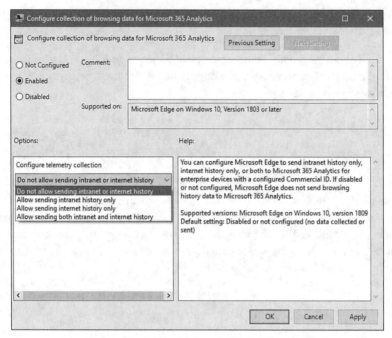

Figure 17-3   When a policy setting has configurable options, like those shown here under Configure Telemetry Collection, they're available only when the policy is set to Enabled.

Management tools for enterprise deployments

In larger organizations, managing PCs individually is impractical. For large-scale Windows deployments, administrators typically use centralized management software for a variety of tasks: to deploy Windows, to administer updates for Windows and other software, to manage hardware inventory and track software licenses, and to apply policies throughout an organization. These tasks traditionally apply to PCs that are owned and managed by the organization, but increasingly they're being applied to personal devices that are used to access company services and store company data. This option typically uses mobile device management (MDM) software, which can configure security policies on devices from a wide variety of manufacturers, including PCs running Windows 10. This option is often referred to as Bring Your Own Device (BYOD).

Enterprise administrators have a wide selection of third-party MDM and system management tools they can use for a network with a large number of Windows 10 PCs. This section lists three Microsoft tools you're likely to encounter in such an environment.

Microsoft Intune

Intune is a component of Microsoft Enterprise Mobility + Security. It integrates with Azure Active Directory for identity and access control and can enforce security settings for information on Office 365 Business and Enterprise subscriptions. You'll find full documentation for Microsoft Intune at *https://docs.microsoft.com/intune/*.

System Center Configuration Manager (SCCM)

As you might guess from the name, System Center describes a family of management tools for managing devices and users, both on-premises and in the cloud. Configuration Manager is a console-based application that enables an enormous range of capabilities, including allowing administrators to distribute applications, manage devices, and enforce network security. It integrates with other management tools, including Microsoft Intune, to give administrators excellent visibility into the status of their network.

Full documentation for System Center is located at *https://docs.microsoft.com/sccm/*.

Windows Server Update Services (WSUS)

In the Windows-as-a-Service era, Microsoft expects most of its customers running Windows 10 PCs in homes and small businesses to connect directly to Windows Update servers. In large organizations, administrators typically want more control over the update process. WSUS provides that control by allowing administrators to manage their own update servers, approving updates to Windows and hardware devices only after they're confident that they'll install without issues.

The official documentation for WSUS is at *https://bit.ly/WSUS-intro*.

Managing apps

You might want to control the apps that are installed on employees' computers. Of course, you want to be sure that the apps they install and run are safe; the last thing you need is malware spreading throughout your organization. Perhaps you want to limit availability of productivity-killing apps. Or maybe you need a way to manage licenses throughout your company.

Managing app distribution in an organization

The Microsoft Store for Business and Education (previously known as the Windows Store for Business) provides a way for organizations to make volume purchases of Windows apps. App licenses can be allocated to certain users in your organization, and licenses can be reclaimed and reused. Organizations can create a private store for their employees that includes a curated collection of apps from the Microsoft Store. In addition, you can add and distribute your own private line-of-business apps.

As with the Microsoft Store available to the public, the Microsoft Store for Business and Education manages updates for apps, ensuring that all your users automatically receive the most recent updates.

The requirements for using the Microsoft Store for Business and Education are not too rigorous: To begin the setup process, you must have an Azure AD account for your organization. To install apps from the Store, employees must be running Windows 10 version 1511 or later and must have an Azure AD account.

For complete details about Microsoft Store for Business and Education, including how to set up your store and "stock" it with apps, visit *https://bit.ly/windows-store-for-business*.

Securing apps with AppLocker

AppLocker is a feature of Windows Enterprise and Education editions that lets an administrator control which apps and files users can run. AppLocker rules apply to all types of executable files, including scripts, app installers, and dynamic-link libraries (DLLs) as well as program files; it's a comprehensive tool for dictating what is allowed to run. AppLocker rules can be applied to security groups or individual users.

AppLocker is most effective when it's deployed throughout a large organization using Group Policy on Active Directory.

> ➤ For complete information about AppLocker, start at *https://bit.ly/applocker-overview*.

Managing the browsing experience

In Windows 10, Microsoft Edge has replaced Internet Explorer as the default browser. Microsoft Edge offers improvements in security and speed over Internet Explorer, which is no longer being actively developed and is available only for legacy purposes. Large businesses are most likely to use websites or line-of-business web applications, on the internet or on a private intranet, that were designed specifically for Internet Explorer (using ActiveX controls, for example, or legacy document modes) and won't run on Microsoft Edge or any third-party browser.

Upgrading these applications or finding alternatives to business-critical websites can be expensive and impractical. To allow these sites to run properly while still using Microsoft Edge as the default browser, you can use a feature called Enterprise Mode. With that configuration enabled, Microsoft Edge checks an Enterprise Mode Site List before opening any page; if it finds the URL for the requested page, it automatically hands off the site to Internet Explorer.

> ➤ For complete details about Microsoft Edge and its relationship to the legacy product Internet Explorer, see Chapter 8, "Microsoft Edge and Internet Explorer."

To use Enterprise Mode, you must first create a list of sites you want to open in Internet Explorer. The easiest way to create the list (an XML file) is with Enterprise Mode Site List Manager, a free tool from Microsoft that you can download from *https://bit.ly/emslm-v2*. Figure 17-4 shows this tool in action.

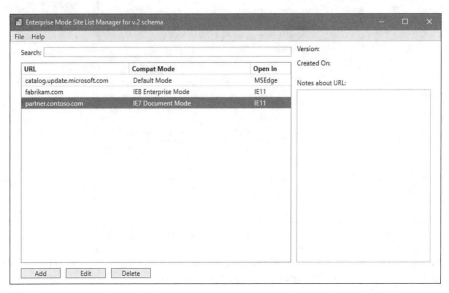

Figure 17-4   Use the Enterprise Mode Site List Manager to enter the URLs and compatibility settings for sites that require Internet Explorer 11; then click the File menu and save the result as an XML file.

With the list saved as XML and placed on a network location accessible to your users, you must then turn on a Group Policy setting that causes Microsoft Edge to use the Enterprise Mode site list. Most organizations will use Group Policy deployed through Active Directory to apply this policy, but you can accomplish the same goal using the Local Group Policy editor. Navigate to Administrative Templates > Windows Components > Microsoft Edge and open the Configure The Enterprise Mode Site List setting, as we've done in Figure 17-5.

Inside OUT

Manage other browsing features

While you have your Group Policy editor open to Administrative Templates > Windows Components > Microsoft Edge, this is an excellent time to look at other policy settings that control the way Microsoft Edge works. You can, for example, disable the use of extensions, specify home pages, prevent the use of InPrivate browsing, and so on.

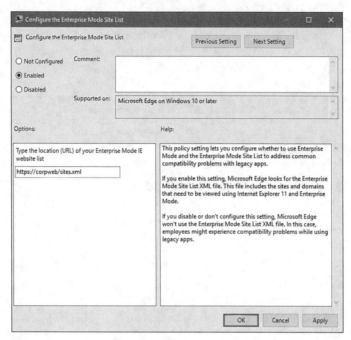

Figure 17-5 To configure this policy, select Enabled and then enter the URL of the site list you created with Enterprise Mode Site List Manager.

With an Enterprise Mode site list in place and enabled by Group Policy, when a user visits a site
on the list using Microsoft Edge, a message like the one shown next appears in the Microsoft
Edge window. Clicking Open With Internet Explorer starts Internet Explorer and opens the page
in a new window.

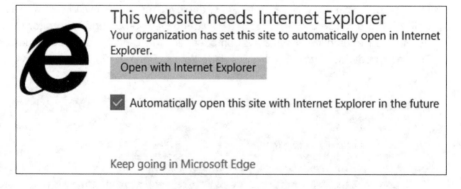

Enterprise Mode has other capabilities that make it useful in some situations, such as an option
to open intranet sites in Internet Explorer, the ability to automatically open a site in Microsoft Edge from Internet Explorer, compatibility with sites that depend on rendering engines
as ancient as Internet Explorer 5, and more. For more details, visit *https://docs.microsoft.com/
en-us/microsoft-edge/deploy/emie-to-improve-compatibility*.

Managing special-purpose computers

Throughout this book, we focus almost exclusively on desktop and notebook PCs that are con-figured for use by a single primary user, with secondary accounts set up as needed for others in a family or business who occasionally need to use that device. In businesses, however, other scenarios are sometimes appropriate. In the following sections, we look at two specialized Windows configurations: shared PCs and kiosk devices.

Using shared PC mode

A school or business might find it useful to have a shared PC—one that can be used by any student or employee as needed, or one that you want to make available for temporary use by customers and visitors. A feature introduced in Windows 10 version 1607 called *shared PC mode* makes this easier than in previous versions.

Shared PC mode requires that the computer be joined to an Active Directory or Azure Active Directory domain. After that step is complete, an administrator applies a series of customizations using mobile device management software, such as Microsoft Intune, or a provisioning package created with the Windows Configuration Designer (WCD), which is free in the Microsoft Store, *https://www.microsoft.com/store/productId/9NBLGGH4TX22*. Figure 17-6 shows the first step of creating a provisioning package using WCD.

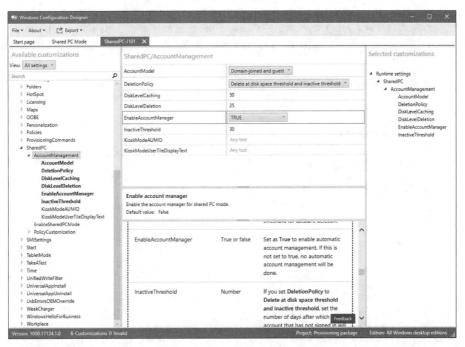

Figure 17-6   Smaller organizations that don't have access to mobile device management software can use the Windows Configuration Designer to create a Shared PC provisioning package.

Using either method, you can configure the shared PC to allow access by anyone with an account in the organization's directory, guests, or both. You can also configure what happens to an account when a user signs off: Automatically delete the account, or save the cached data for faster sign-in next time.

You'll find step-by-step instructions for setting up and using shared PC mode at *https://bit.ly/ shared-pc-mode*.

Setting up a kiosk device

Another common scenario in business is to set up a kiosk device—a computer that is set up to do only one thing. An office might use this computer as a check-in device for guests; a retail business could put a kiosk PC on the retail floor and allow customers to use the device's touch-screen to view a product catalog or check prices. You could configure a device using these tools to run a single app, such as a banking program or an inventory app, while eliminating the risk that a worker will inadvertently allow the machine to be compromised by using a web browser or an email program.

In the initial release of this feature, a kiosk device was capable of running a single app only. As of version 1809, Windows 10 supports several additional kiosk configurations, including multi-app kiosks, which display a simplified Start menu that makes it possible for kiosk users to choose from a list of allowed apps. You can also configure a kiosk device to run Microsoft Edge in a variety of configurations—as a public browser with user data protected, for example, or as a digital sign or interactive display showing the contents of a single site. If you choose Microsoft Edge as the single app to run, the Set Up A Kiosk page in Settings offers these two options:

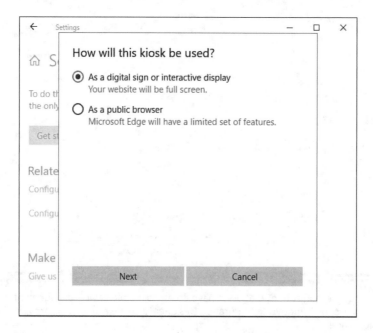

➤ For more details about setting up a kiosk device in any supported configuration, including a reference guide for the required XML settings, see "Configure kiosks and digital signs on Windows desktop editions," at *https://bit.ly/kiosk-configure*. For details about configuring a PC to use Microsoft Edge in kiosk mode, see *https://bit.ly/ms-edge-kiosk-mode*.

Click Next to specify the default URL where the browser will return after a defined period of inactivity, which will also reset the current browser session.

You can configure a kiosk-mode device in multi-app mode or any browsing configuration using an XML file and mobile device management software such as Microsoft Intune, or you can create a provisioning package using Windows Configuration Designer, as we discussed earlier in this section.

In a small business without a dedicated IT staff or centralized management tools, you can configure a single-app kiosk to run a UWP app, using a feature called *assigned access*. Go to Settings > Accounts > Family & Other Users. (On a PC joined to Azure AD or a domain, this option is Other Users.) Click Assigned Access under the Set Up A Kiosk heading, and then click Get Started to specify the user account and app that will run in kiosk mode. Figure 17-7 shows the resulting options, where we created a new local account called Kiosk-1 and specified the Weather app as the only one allowed to run.

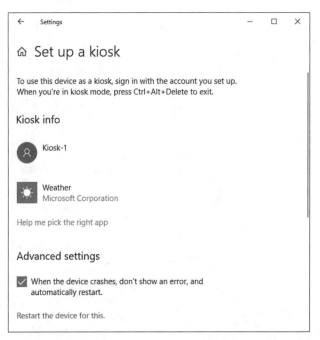

Figure 17-7 In single-app kiosk mode, a local account, which cannot be an administrator, is allowed to run one and only one app—in this case, the Microsoft Weather app.

NOTE

To learn more about local accounts, see "Creating and managing user accounts" in Chapter 11, "Managing user accounts, passwords, and credentials."

If you chose Microsoft Edge as the default app, the options available here allow you to change the browsing mode, specify a new default page, and adjust the timeout period.

We recommend that you choose the option to create a new account for kiosk use; when you do so, Windows automatically configures that account to sign in automatically at startup. If you choose an existing account, users will need to sign in using that account's password.

With your device thus configured, turn it on, and it launches directly to the app you selected, running in a full screen and lacking all the usual Windows accoutrements, including the Start button and taskbar. To escape, press Ctrl+Alt+Delete, whereupon you can sign in using another account.

To undo or adjust this setup, return to Settings > Accounts > Family & Other Users. Click Assigned Access, click to select the user account configured for kiosk mode, and click Remove Kiosk. Click the app name to reveal a Change Kiosk App button that allows you to choose a different app.

Windows security and privacy

We don't mean to be scaremongers, but they *are* out to get you. Computer attacks continue to increase in number and severity each year. And while the big data breaches—the loss of millions of credit card numbers from a major retailer or the loss of millions of personnel records from the U.S. government—command the most media attention, don't think that the bad guys wouldn't like to get into your computer, too. Whether it's to steal your valuable personal data or hold it for ransom, appropriate your computing resources and bandwidth, or use your PC as a pathway into a bigger target with whom you do business, there are plenty of actors with bad intent.

In this chapter, we examine the types of threats you're likely to face at home and at your office. More importantly, we describe some of the more significant security improvements made in Microsoft Windows 10—many of which are in layers you can't see, such as hardware-based protection that operates before Windows loads.

Beginning with Version 1703, Windows 10 includes a new modern app that functions as a dashboard for common security functions. This chapter introduces the new Windows Security app (previously called Windows Defender Security Center), which offers access to other visible security features, including Windows Defender Firewall, Windows Defender Antivirus, and Windows SmartScreen. This chapter also covers other, related security features, including User Account Control and BitLocker Drive Encryption.

Understanding security threats

A decade ago, the threat landscape for Windows users was dominated by viruses and worms. Ah, for the good old days! The modern threat landscape is much more complex and, unfortunately, more insidious. Today, an attacker is likely to be part of an organized crime ring or even acting on behalf of a state-sponsored organization, and attacks are typically designed to go unnoticed for as long as possible.

A rogue program, installed without your knowledge and running without your awareness, can perform malicious tasks and transfer data without your consent. This category of software is often referred to as *malware*.

The goal of the bad guys is to get you to run their software. They might, for example, convince you to install a *Trojan*—a program that appears legitimate but actually performs malicious actions when it's installed. This category of malware doesn't spread on its own but instead uses social engineering (often using popular social networking sites such as Facebook and Twitter) to convince its victims to cooperate in the installation process. As part of its payload, a Trojan can include a downloader that installs additional malicious and unwanted programs. Some Trojans install a "back door" that allows an outside attacker to remotely control the infected computer.

What's in it for the bad guys? Money, mostly, gathered in various ways, depending on how the attackers got through your defenses. Here are just a few examples:

- A *password stealer* runs in the background, gathers user names and passwords, and forwards them to an outside attacker. The stolen credentials can then be used to make purchases, clean out bank accounts, or commit identity theft.

- Bad guys prey on fear with rogue security software (also known as *scareware*), which mimics the actions and appearance of legitimate antivirus software. If you install one of these programs, it inevitably reports the presence of a (nonexistent) virus and offers to remove the alleged malware—for a fee, of course. A related category includes tech-support scams, in which a Windows user receives a phone call from a scammer masquerading as a Microsoft support professional.

- The fastest rising star in the malware hall of shame continues to be *ransomware*, a form of digital blackmail in which a program encrypts all your data files and offers to unlock them only upon payment of a ransom.

- *Phishing attacks*, which use social engineering to convince visitors to give away their sign-in credentials, are a separate but potentially devastating avenue to identity theft that can strike in any browser using any operating system.

You can review lists of current malware threats, along with links to details about each one, at the Windows Defender Security Intelligence site, *https://bit.ly/malware-encyclopedia*. For a more comprehensive view of the changing threat landscape, Microsoft Secure issues a twice-yearly report, using data from hundreds of millions of Windows users and other sources. You'll find the latest Microsoft Security Intelligence Report at *https://microsoft.com/security/sir*.

SECURING YOUR COMPUTER: A DEFENSE-IN-DEPTH STRATEGY

A multidimensional threat landscape requires a multilayered approach to protecting your PC and your network. The big-picture goal is to secure your device, secure your data, secure your identity, and block malware. On a home or small business network, those layers of security include the following:

- **Use a hardware router to protect your broadband connection.** This is an essential part of physical security, even if your network consists of a single PC.

- **Enable a software firewall, and keep it turned on.** You can use Windows Defender Firewall, which is included with Windows 10, or a third-party firewall such as those included with security suites. To learn more, see "Blocking intruders with Windows Defender Firewall" later in this chapter.

- **Strengthen the sign-in process.** Biometric sign-in using a fingerprint reader or facial recognition with Windows Hello offers much more than convenience. Because biometric sign-in is linked to a specific device, it provides effective two-factor authentication. If you sign in using a Microsoft Account or Azure AD, turn on two-factor authentication to prevent your credentials from being used if they're stolen. For more information, see "Managing the sign-in process" in Chapter 11, "Managing user accounts, passwords, and credentials."

- **Set up standard user accounts, and keep User Account Control enabled.** Standard accounts help to prevent (or at least minimize) the damage that an untrained user can do by installing untrusted programs. User Account Control (UAC) helps in this regard by restricting access to administrative tasks and virtualizing registry and file-system changes. For details, see "Introducing access control in Windows" in Chapter 11 and "Preventing unsafe actions with User Account Control" later in this chapter.

- **Keep Windows and vulnerable programs up to date.** Windows Update handles this chore for Windows, Office, and other Microsoft programs, as well as for the Adobe Flash software included with Microsoft Edge and Internet Explorer. You're on your own for third-party programs. We provide an overview of security updates in Chapter 5, "Managing updates."

- **Use an antimalware program, and keep it up to date.** Windows Defender Antivirus, which is included with Windows 10, provides antimalware protection, but many third-party solutions are also available. For details, see "Using Windows Defender Antivirus" later in this chapter.

- **Protect yourself from threats in email messages.** At a minimum, your email solution should block or quarantine executable files and other potentially dangerous attachments. In addition, effective antispam features can block scripts and prevent phishing attempts.

- **Use parental controls to keep kids safe.** If you have children who use your computer, family safety features in Windows can help you keep them away from security threats and keep them from wandering into unsafe territory online by restricting their computer activities in other ways. In Windows 10 version 1703 and later, these features have moved to the new Windows Security app. For details, see "Controlling your family's computer access" in Chapter 11.

Security And Maintenance, included in the classic Control Panel, monitors many of these areas to be sure you're protected, and it displays an alert if something needs attention.

CHAPTER 18

> The new Windows Security app offers a similar overview in a slightly different format. For details, see "Monitoring your computer's security" later in this chapter.
>
> The most important protective layer—and the one that's most easily overlooked—is user education and self-control. Everyone who uses a computer must have the discipline to read and evaluate security warnings when they're presented and to allow the installation only of software that is known to be safe. (Although a user with a standard account can't install or run a program that wipes out the entire computer, he can still inflict enough damage on his own user profile to cause considerable inconvenience.) Countless successful malware attacks worldwide have proven that many users do not have adequate awareness of safe computing basics.

New security features in Windows 10

Because the bad guys are always upping their game, a hallmark of each new version of Windows is a number of new and improved security features. Windows 10 is no exception. In this section we enumerate changes available in Windows 10 Home and Windows 10 Pro; several additional features are included with Windows 10 Enterprise on a managed network.

Securing devices

Security features in Windows 10 begin with support for modern hardware designs. Although Windows 10 continues to support legacy hardware, some security features require two elements that have become standard on most newer computers:

- **Unified Extensible Firmware Interface (UEFI).** UEFI is a firmware interface that replaces the BIOS, which has been a part of every PC since the beginning of personal computing. Among other improvements, UEFI enables Secure Boot and Device Encryption, features that are described in the following pages. PCs designed for Windows 8 and later must use UEFI.

- **Trusted Platform Module (TPM).** A TPM is a hardware chip that facilitates encryption and prevents altering or exporting encryption keys and certificates. The presence of a TPM makes it easy to turn on BitLocker Drive Encryption (described later in this chapter). Other security features in Windows 10, such as Measured Boot and Device Guard, require the presence of a TPM.

With UEFI and TPM in place, Windows 10 is able to secure the boot process. (Many recent malware attacks take control of the system early in the boot process before Windows is fully running and before antimalware programs spring into action. This type of malware is called a *rootkit*.) The Windows 10 boot process steps through the following features:

- **Secure Boot.** Secure Boot, a basic feature of UEFI, prevents the use of any alternative operating system loader. Only an operating system loader that's digitally signed using a certificate stored by UEFI is allowed to run. (A conventional BIOS allows interruption of the boot process to use any operating system loader, including one that's been corrupted or compromised.)

- **Early Launch Antimalware (ELAM).** Antimalware software that has been certified and signed by Microsoft—including compatible third-party programs as well as Windows Defender Antivirus—loads its drivers before any other third-party drivers or programs. This sequence of events allows the antimalware software to detect and block attempts to load malicious code.

- **Measured Boot.** With this feature, measurements of the UEFI firmware and each Windows component are taken as they load. The measurements are then digitally signed and stored in the TPM, where they can't be changed. During subsequent boots, the new measurements are compared against the stored measurements.

Securing data

The increased mobility of PCs also increases the risk of theft. Losing a computer is bad enough, but handing over all the data you've stored on the computer is potentially a much greater loss. Windows 10 includes new features to ensure the thief can't get your data.

- **Device encryption.** On devices that support InstantGo, data on the operating system volume is encrypted by default. (Formerly called Connected Standby, InstantGo is a Microsoft hardware specification that enables advanced power-management capabilities. Among other requirements, InstantGo devices must boot from a solid-state drive.) The encryption initially uses a clear key, but when a local administrator first signs in with a Microsoft account, the volume is automatically encrypted. A recovery key is available when you sign in using that Microsoft account at *https://onedrive.com/recoverykey*; you'll need the key if you reinstall the operating system or move the drive to a new PC.

- **BitLocker Drive Encryption.** BitLocker Drive Encryption offers similar (but stronger) whole-volume encryption, and on corporate networks, it allows centralized management. In Windows 10, BitLocker encrypts drives more quickly than in previous Windows versions; additional speed comes from the new ability to encrypt only the part of a volume in use. For more information, see "Encrypting with BitLocker and BitLocker To Go" later in this chapter.

Securing identities

It seems like every week we hear about another data breach where millions of user names and passwords and other personal data have been stolen. There's a thriving market for this type of information because it enables the thieves to sign in anywhere using your credentials.

CHAPTER 18

Furthermore, because many people use the same password for different accounts, criminals can often use the stolen information to gain unauthorized access to a theft victim's other accounts. Windows 10 offers a handful of features that make passwords less problematic.

With Windows 10, enterprise-grade two-factor authentication is built in. After enrolling a device with an authentication service, the device itself becomes one factor; the second factor is a PIN or a biometric, such as a fingerprint or facial recognition.

After Windows Hello signs you in, it enables sign-in to networks and web services. Windows Hello supports Microsoft accounts, Active Directory and Azure Active Directory (Azure AD) accounts, and any identity provider that supports the Fast ID Online (FIDO) v2.0 standard. Your biometric data remains securely stored in your computer's TPM; it's not sent over the network.

With this combination of authentication methods, an attacker who has a trove of user names and passwords is stymied. To unlock your encrypted information (and, by extension, gain the ability to sign in to your web services), he needs the enrolled device. And a thief who steals your computer needs your PIN or biometric data. Active Directory, Azure Active Directory, and Microsoft accounts support this new form of credentials; other services are sure to follow.

➤ For more information about Windows Hello, see "Managing the sign-in process" in Chapter 11.

Blocking malware

Since the days of Windows 7, several features that block malicious software have been beefed up:

- **Address Space Layout Randomization (ASLR).** ASLR is a feature that randomizes the location of program code and other data in memory, making it difficult for malware to carry out attacks that write directly to system memory because the malware can't find the memory location it needs. In Windows 10, memory locations are scrambled even more. And because the randomization is unique to each device, a successful attack on one device typically won't work on another.

- **Data Execution Prevention (DEP).** DEP is a hardware feature that marks blocks of memory so that they can store data but not execute program instructions. Windows 10 can't be installed on a system that doesn't support DEP.

- **Windows Defender Antivirus.** In Windows 7, Windows Defender is a lightweight anti-spyware program, and antimalware features require the installation of Windows Security Essentials, a free add-on for Windows 7. But starting with Windows 8 and continuing in Windows 10, those features are built into the operating system itself. Windows Defender Antivirus, which is included with all Windows 10 editions, supports ELAM, described earlier in this chapter, which means that it can defend against rootkits that attempt to co-opt the boot process. Version 1709 adds controlled folder access, a feature that makes it easier to protect data from ransomware and other malicious software. For more information, see "Using Windows Defender Antivirus" later in this chapter.

- **SmartScreen.** The goal of SmartScreen is similar to that of Windows Defender Antivirus: Stop malicious code from running, thus avoiding the headache of cleaning up damage after a successful attack. But SmartScreen takes a completely different approach: Instead of looking for signatures of known bad programs, it checks a hash of each executable downloaded from an online source against Microsoft's application-reputation database. Files that have established a positive reputation are deemed safe and are allowed to run, whereas files with a negative reputation (or those that are unknown and potentially dangerous) are blocked.

  When SmartScreen was introduced in Windows 7, it was a feature of Internet Explorer. Beginning with Windows 8, SmartScreen became an integral part of Windows (and continues to be a feature of Internet Explorer and, in Windows 10, Microsoft Edge). Therefore, it prevents all unknown programs that originated from an online source—including those downloaded with a non-Microsoft browser—from running. SmartScreen works not just as you download a program in a browser but any time you attempt to run such a program.

- **Exploit protection.** These advanced settings, previously available only as part of a separate download called the Enhanced Mitigation Experience Toolkit, allow administrators to adjust DEP, ASLR, and other features that affect code execution. These settings can be configured on a systemwide basis or on a per-application basis. To see the full range of settings, go to Settings > Update & Security > Windows Security. Then click App & Browser Control, which opens the Windows Security app. In Windows Security, scroll to the bottom of the page and click Exploit Protection Settings. For full documentation, see *https://bit.ly/win10-exploit-protection*.

Configuring privacy options

You don't need to be a conspiracy theorist to be concerned about privacy. Some companies abuse your trust by taking your information—often without your knowledge or consent—and sharing it with others who hope to profit from that information. Even a trustworthy third party can slip up and allow your private information to be stolen from its servers in a security breach. In the European Union, the General Data Protection Regulation (GDPR) requires organizations (including Microsoft) to follow strict privacy controls when collecting, processing, and storing personal data within the EU, and some privacy advocates have argued that those protections should be extended worldwide.

Because Windows 10 is tightly integrated with cloud services, some of your information is stored, with your permission, on Microsoft-owned servers. Likewise, Microsoft requests permission when you first set up a user account to use some of your information to provide personalized suggestions; for example, opting in to the Cortana service allows the use of location data from your device and appointments from your calendar to give you reminders about when you need to leave for a meeting. In addition, Windows 10 shares what Microsoft calls *diagnostic data* (also sometimes called *telemetry* data) for the purpose of improving the reliability of the operating system.

Diagnostic data, which is collected by the Connected User Experiences And Telemetry service, includes information about the device and how it's configured, including hardware attributes such as CPU, installed memory, and storage. This data also includes details about quality-related events and metrics, such as uptime and sleep details and the number of crashes or hangs. Additional basic information includes a list of installed apps and drivers. For systems where the diagnostic data is set to a level higher than Basic, the information collected includes events that analyze the interaction between the user and the operating system and apps.

Microsoft insists that its diagnostic-data system is designed to prevent any privacy issues. "We collect a limited amount of information to help us provide a secure and reliable experience," the company says. "This includes data like an anonymous device ID and device type. ... This doesn't include any of your content or files, and we take several steps to avoid collecting any information that directly identifies you, such as your name, email address or account ID."

NOTE

For a full discussion of how Windows 10 diagnostic data works, with an emphasis on how to manage settings for collecting diagnostic data in an organization, see *https://bit.ly/configure-telemetry*.

Some of your personal information is used to provide more relevant advertising in apps. If you opt to turn off that personalization, you'll still see ads, but those ads will not be based on your browsing history or other information about you. Regardless of your privacy settings, Microsoft does not use your email, chat, files, or other personal content to target ads.

A single privacy statement covers most of Microsoft's consumer products and services, including Windows 10 and related services. For information about the privacy policy and to make choices about how Microsoft uses your data, visit *https://privacy.microsoft.com*. (A direct link to the Windows section of the Microsoft privacy statement is also available at Settings > Privacy > Privacy Statement.)

More important still, Windows includes a raft of options for controlling your privacy. You'll find them under the Privacy heading in Settings, where you can specify which apps are allowed to use each of your computer's many devices, whether to disclose your location, whether to let Cortana better know your voice and word pronunciations, and so on. (Other privacy options for Cortana can be found in Settings > Cortana > Permissions & History.)

For each privacy option, you'll find a link to the Microsoft privacy statement and links to additional information as well as the controls for making settings. The privacy statement is detailed yet clearly written, and it's an important aid for deciding which options to enable. You should examine each of these options carefully and decide for yourself where the proper balance is between your personal privacy and convenience.

To minimize the collection of diagnostic data, for example, go to Settings > Privacy > Diagnostics & Feedback. Under the Diagnostic Data heading, shown in Figure 18-1, choose the Basic setting. (Note that the Diagnostic Data option is set to Full and cannot be changed on PCs that are configured as part of the Windows Insider Program; a message in bright red text at the top of the page explains why the controls are unavailable.)

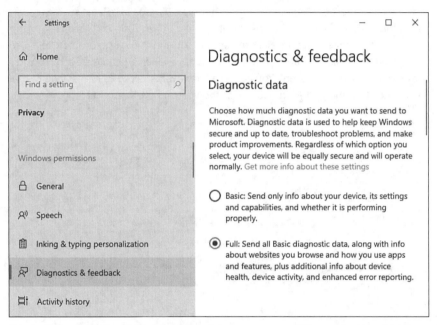

Figure 18-1   If you'd prefer to share the minimum amount of diagnostic data with Microsoft's telemetry servers, choose the Basic option here.

In earlier versions of Windows 10, a third option, Enhanced, was available on this page. That option is still available in Group Policy settings, but we cannot think of any good reason to prefer it in place of the Basic and Full settings.

A fourth level, Security, is available via Group Policy and device management software. Note that this setting applies only to devices running Windows 10 Enterprise edition; if you select it on a device running Windows 10 Pro, Windows ignores the policy and uses the Basic setting. The Security option disables Windows Update and should thus be used only when an alternative update mechanism such as Windows Server Update Services is available.

To view and configure these settings, open the Local Group Policy Editor, Gpedit.exe, and navigate to Computer Configuration > Administrative Templates > Windows Components >

Data Collection and Preview Builds. Double-click Allow Telemetry and set its value to Enabled to see all four levels under Options.

In early 2018, Microsoft added two advanced tools that allow you to inspect and manage diagnostic data on your computer. These tools are available on all Windows 10 editions beginning with version 1803.

The first is Diagnostic Data Viewer, an app that displays the collected data so you can see for yourself exactly what is going to Microsoft. To use Diagnostic Data Viewer, go to Settings > Privacy > Diagnostics & Feedback and turn the View Diagnostic Data switch to On. (In version 1803, this switch is labeled Diagnostic Data Viewer.) Then click the Open Diagnostic Data Viewer button. (If you haven't yet installed the app, you'll land in the Microsoft Store, where you can download and install the app.) In Diagnostic Data Viewer, type in the Search box to look for text within a diagnostic event. You can also filter events; click the funnel icon to the right of the search box to display filtering options, as shown in Figure 18-2.

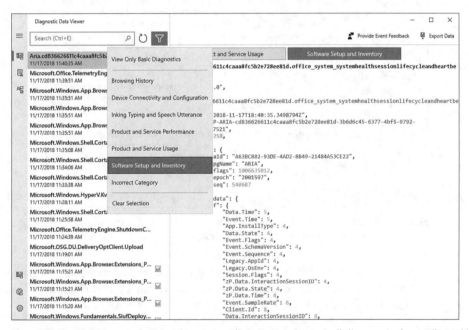

Figure 18-2 The Diagnostic Data Viewer app allows you to inspect all diagnostic data collected by Windows 10.

The second tool added as of version 1803 allows you to request that Microsoft erase diagnostic data that has been collected from the current device. To do so, open Settings > Privacy > Diagnostics & Feedback, and then click Delete under the Delete Diagnostic Data heading. After you make this request, Windows displays the Last Delete Request date to the right of the Delete button.

Monitoring your computer's security

Over the first few years of Windows 10, security settings have steadily migrated from the old-style Control Panel to a more modern presentation. The latest incarnation is the Windows Security app, which you might know by its original name, Windows Defender Security Center. You can open Windows Security directly from its place on the Start menu's app list, or use the slightly unconventional navigation options in Settings > Update & Security > Windows Security. That Settings page includes a big Open Windows Security button and seven headings, each of which opens or switches to the Windows Security app with the respective page selected. Figure 18-3 shows the Windows Security home page, displaying the status of seven groups of security-related settings.

Figure 18-3   The Windows Security dashboard offers a consolidated view of security status. Clicking any item provides access to settings for that group of features.

As expected, Windows Security provides status information even when it's not open. A badge over the app's icon in the notification area of the taskbar shows the current security status with a green check mark, a yellow exclamation point, or a red X and, if necessary, options for resolving problems. Additional notifications of activity (results of recent virus scans, for example) appear in Notification Center. Click the gear icon in the lower-left corner of the Windows Security app window to configure these options, as shown in Figure 18-4.

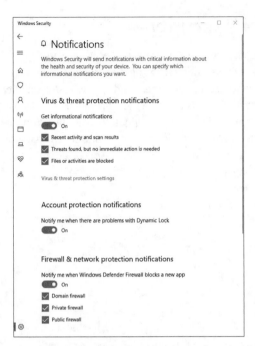

Figure 18-4   If you don't want to be bothered with noncritical notifications from Windows Defender Antivirus, such as successful scans that detect no threats, clear the Recent Activity And Scan Results check box.

Preventing unsafe actions with User Account Control

Widely scorned when it was introduced more than a decade ago as part of Windows Vista, User Account Control (UAC) intercedes whenever a user or program attempts to perform a system administrative task and asks for the consent of a computer administrator before commencing what could be risky business. Since that rocky start, UAC has been tuned to become an effective security aid—without the annoyance factor that plagued the original implementation.

UAC works in conjunction with a feature called Mandatory Integrity Control, which assigns a measure of trust called an *integrity level* to every system object, including processes and registry keys. Processes that run at the System integrity level cannot be directly accessed by any user account. A process with a High integrity level is one that is capable of modifying system data and requires an administrator access token. Most normal processes run with a Medium integrity level and require a standard user access token. (Store apps run with the AppContainer integrity level, and web browsers other than Microsoft Edge run at Low or Untrusted integrity levels. A standard user account can run either type of app, but the lower integrity level effectively creates a "sandbox" that prevents those apps from modifying objects with higher integrity levels.)

In Windows 10, user accounts you set up after the first one are standard user accounts by default; although they can carry out all the usual daily computing tasks, they're prevented from running any process with a High integrity level. These restrictions apply not just to the user; more importantly, they also apply to any programs launched by the user.

At sign-in, Windows creates a token that's used to identify the privilege levels of your account. Standard users get a standard token, but administrators get two: a standard token and an administrator token. (This dual-token configuration is called Admin Approval Mode.) The standard token is used to open Explorer.exe (the Windows shell), from which all subsequent programs are launched. Child processes inherit the token of the process that launches them, so by default, all applications run as a standard user—even when you're signed in with an administrator account. Any activity that runs a process with a High integrity level requires an administrator token; if your account provides that token, the program runs. This process is called *elevation*. Note that an elevated process can, in turn, run additional processes as an administrator.

> ➤ For information about user accounts, see Chapter 11. For a detailed technical discussion of UAC, see "How User Account Control Works," at *https://bit.ly/how-UAC-works*.

Most modern Windows desktop programs and all Store apps are written so that they don't require administrator privileges for performing everyday tasks. Programs that truly need administrative access (such as utility programs that change computer settings) request elevation—and that's where UAC comes in.

What triggers UAC prompts

The types of actions that require elevation to administrator status (and therefore display a UAC elevation prompt) include those that make changes to system-wide settings or to files in %SystemRoot% or %ProgramFiles%. (On a default Windows installation, these environment variables represent C:\Windows and C:\Program Files, respectively.) Among the actions that require elevation are the following:

- Installing and uninstalling most desktop applications (except those converted into app packages and delivered through the Microsoft Store, or those that install completely into the user profile)

- Installing device drivers that are not included in Windows or provided through Windows Update

- Installing ActiveX controls

- Changing settings for Windows Defender Firewall

- Changing UAC settings

- Configuring Windows Update

- Adding or removing user accounts

- Changing a user's account type

- Running Task Scheduler

- Editing the registry

- Restoring backed-up system files

- Viewing or changing another user's folders and files

Within the classic Windows desktop interface (including the remnants of Control Panel that have yet to migrate to Settings), you can identify in advance many actions that require elevation. A shield icon next to a button or link indicates that a UAC prompt will appear if you're using a standard account.

If you sign in with an administrator account (and if you don't change the default UAC settings), you'll see fewer consent prompts than if you use a standard account. That's because the default setting uses Admin Approval Mode, which prompts only when a program tries to install software or make other changes to the computer, but not when you make changes to Windows settings—even those that would trigger a prompt for a standard user with default UAC settings. Windows uses this automatic elevation, without the expected UAC prompt, for certain programs that are part of Windows. Programs that are elevated automatically are from a predefined list; they must be digitally signed by the Windows publisher, and they must be stored in certain secure folders.

CHAPTER 18

LIMITATIONS OF USER ACCOUNT CONTROL

User Account Control isn't a security silver bullet. It's one layer of a defense-in-depth strategy.

Some Windows users assume that UAC consent dialog boxes represent a security boundary. They don't. They simply represent a place for an administrator to make a trust decision. If a bad guy uses social engineering to convince you that you need his program, you've already made a trust decision. You'll click at least a half-dozen times to download, save, and launch the bad guy's program. A UAC consent request is perfectly normal in this sequence, so why wouldn't you click one more time?

If this scenario bothers you, the obvious solution is to adjust UAC to its highest level. Among other changes, this setting disables the autoelevation behavior. (For details on how to do this, see "Modifying UAC settings" later in this chapter.) If a program tries to use this subterfuge to sneak system changes past you, you'll see an unexpected consent dialog box from the system. But as soon as you provide those elevated credentials, the code can do anything it wants.

A better alternative is to sign in using a standard account, which provides a real security boundary. A standard user who does not have the administrator password can make changes only in her own user profile, protecting the system from unintended tampering.

Even running as a standard user doesn't provide complete protection. Malware can be installed in your user profile without triggering any system alarms. It can log your keystrokes, steal your passwords, encrypt your personal data files and hold them for ransom, and send out email using your identity. Even if you reset UAC to its highest level, you could fall victim to malware that lies in wait for you to elevate your privileges and then does its own dirty work alongside you.

As we said, enabling UAC is only one part of a multilayered security strategy. It works best when supplemented by a healthy skepticism, good training, and up-to-date antimalware software.

Dealing with UAC prompts

When you attempt to run a process that requires elevation, UAC evaluates the request and then displays an appropriate prompt. If you signed in to the current session with an administrator account, the most common prompt you're likely to see is the consent prompt, which is shown in Figure 18-5. Check the name of the program and the publisher, and click Yes if you're confident that it's safe to proceed. (Note that the default action is No; if you absentmindedly press Enter, Windows will cancel the elevation request.)

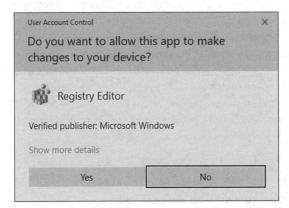

Figure 18-5   For a program that's digitally signed, clicking Show More Details displays a link to the associated certificate.

If, on the other hand, you signed in to the current session with a standard account, any attempt to run a program that requires elevation displays the credentials prompt, which is shown in Figure 18-6. The user must provide the credentials of an administrator (that is, user name and password, smart card, or biometric authentication, depending on how sign-in options are configured on the computer); after entering those credentials, the application opens using the administrator's access token.

Figure 18-6   To perform an administrative task, a standard user must enter the full credentials for an administrator account.

By default, the UAC dialog box sits atop the secure desktop, which runs in a separate session that requires a trusted process running with System privileges. (If the UAC prompt were to run in the same session as other processes, a malicious program could disguise the UAC dialog box, perhaps with a message encouraging you to let the program proceed. Or a malicious program could grab your keystrokes, thereby learning your administrator sign-in password.) When the secure desktop is displayed, you can't switch tasks or click any open window on the desktop. (In fact, in Windows 10 you can't even see the taskbar or any other open windows. When UAC invokes the secure desktop, it displays only a dimmed copy of the current desktop background behind the UAC dialog box.)

TROUBLESHOOTING

There's a delay before the secure desktop appears

On some systems, you have to wait a few seconds before the screen darkens and the UAC prompt appears on the secure desktop. There's no easy way to solve the slowdown, but you can easily work around it. In the User Account Control Settings (described in the next section, "Modifying UAC settings"), you can take the protection level down a notch. The setting below the default provides the same level of UAC protection (albeit with a slight risk that malware could hijack the desktop), except that it does not dim the desktop.

NOTE

If an application other than the foreground application requests elevation, instead of interrupting your work (the foreground task) with a prompt, UAC signals its request with a flashing taskbar button. Click the taskbar button to see the prompt.

It becomes natural to click through dialog boxes without reading them or giving them a second thought. But it's important to recognize that security risks to your computer are real and that actions that trigger a UAC prompt are potentially dangerous. Clearly, if you know what you're doing, and you click a button to open Registry Editor or run a desktop program you just downloaded from a trusted location, you can blow past that security dialog box with no more than a quick glance to be sure it was raised by the expected application. But if a UAC prompt appears when you're not expecting it—stop, read it carefully, and think before you click.

Modifying UAC settings

To review your User Account Control options and make changes to the way it works, type **uac** in the search box on the taskbar or in Settings, and then click Change User Account Control Settings. A window similar to the one shown in Figure 18-7 appears.

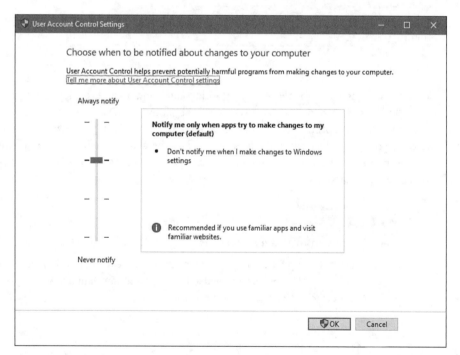

Figure 18-7   We don't recommend changing the default UAC settings unless you fully understand the consequences.

Your choices in this window vary slightly depending on whether you started the current session using an administrator account or a standard user account. For standard user accounts, the top setting is the default; for administrator accounts, the second setting from the top is the default. Table 18-1 summarizes the available options.

Table 18-1   User Account Control settings

Slider position	Prompts when a program tries to install software or make changes to the computer	Prompts when you make changes to Windows settings	Displays prompts on a secure desktop
Standard user account			
Top (default)	✔	✔	✔
Second	✔	✔	
Third	✔		
Bottom (off)			
Administrator account			
Top	✔	✔	✔
Second (default)	✔		✔
Third	✔		
Bottom (off)			

To make changes, move the slider to the position you want. Be sure to take note of the advisory message at the bottom of the box as you move the slider. Click OK when you're done—and then respond to the UAC prompt that appears. Note that when you're signed in with a standard user account, you can't select one of the bottom two options, even if you have the password for an administrator account. To select one of those options, you must sign in as an administrator and then make the change.

TROUBLESHOOTING

User Account Control settings don't stick

If you find that nothing happens when you make a change to User Account Control settings, be sure you're the only one signed in to your computer. Simultaneous sign-ins that use Fast User Switching can cause this problem.

Inside OUT

Use Local Security Policy to customize UAC behavior

On PCs running Windows 10 Pro, Enterprise, or Education, an administrator can use the Local Security Policy console to modify the behavior of UAC. Start Local Security Policy (Secpol.msc), and open Security Settings > Local Policies > Security Options. In the details pane, scroll down to the policies whose names begin with "User Account Control." For each policy, double-click it and then click the Explain tab for information before you decide on a setting. With these policies, you can make several refinements in the way UAC works—including some that are not possible in the User Account Control Settings window. (Administrators on Windows-based enterprise networks can also configure these options using Group Policy management tools.) For details about each of these policies, see "User Account Control Group Policy and registry key settings" at *https://bit.ly/10uac-gpo*.

Regardless of your UAC setting, the shield icons still appear throughout Control Panel, but you won't see UAC prompts if you've lowered the UAC protection level. Clicking a button or link identified with a shield immediately begins the action. Administrators run with full administrator privileges; standard users, of course, still have only standard privileges.

CAUTION

Don't forget that UAC is more than annoying prompts. Universal Windows apps will not run when UAC is disabled. Only when UAC is enabled does an administrator run with a standard token. Only when UAC is enabled do web browsers run at Low integrity level to thwart web-based attacks. Only when UAC is enabled does Windows warn you when a rogue application attempts to perform a task with system-wide impact. And, of course, disabling UAC also disables file and registry virtualization, which can cause compatibility problems with applications that use fixes provided by the UAC feature. For all these reasons, we urge you not to select the bottom option in User Account Control Settings, which turns off UAC completely.

Blocking malware

The best way to fight unwanted and malicious software is to keep it from being installed on any PC that's part of your network. You can install third-party software for this task, or you can use Windows Defender Antivirus, which is included with every edition of Windows 10.

Windows Defender Antivirus runs as a system service (two services, to be precise: Windows Defender Antivirus Service and Windows Defender Network Inspection Service); it uses a scanning engine to compare files against a database of virus and spyware definitions. It also uses heuristic analysis of the behavior of programs to flag suspicious activity from a file that isn't included in the list of known threats. It scans each file you access in any way, including downloads from the internet and email attachments you receive. (This feature is called *real-time protection*—not to be confused with scheduled *scans*, which periodically inspect all files stored on your computer to root out malware.)

Using Windows Defender Antivirus

In general, you don't need to "use" Windows Defender Antivirus at all. As a system service, it works quietly in the background. The only time you'll know it's there is if it finds an infected file; one or more notifications will pop up to alert you to the fact.

Nonetheless, there are a few settings you can tweak and a few tasks you can perform manually. As of Windows 10 version 1809, all these options have moved to the Windows Security app (known as Windows Defender Security Center in version 1803 and earlier). Display the Virus & Threat Protection page to see details about the most recent scan (manual or automatic). Under normal circumstances, this number should be zero; if Windows Defender Antivirus detected a threat, it displays the details and offers options for dealing with the threat, as shown in Figure 18-8.

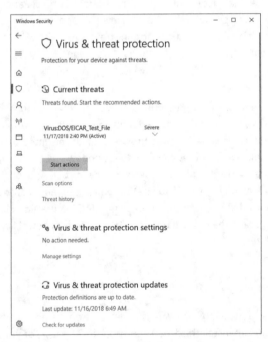

Figure 18-8   This page in Windows Security provides an overview of the most recent scan with the option to address any threats.

Click Manage Settings, under the Virus & Threat Protection Settings heading, to open a page containing a group of switches for adjusting the behavior of Windows Defender Antivirus. (In version 1803, don't look for Manage Settings; instead, click the Virus & Threat Protection Settings heading.)

Slide the Real-Time Protection switch to Off to temporarily disable protection (an option you should use only for short periods and only if you're certain you're not allowing malware to sneak onto your PC as a result of actions that would otherwise be blocked). The Cloud-Delivered Protection and Automatic Sample Submission options work together to help block threats that have not yet been identified in a signature. Most people should keep these options turned on.

Finally, in the Exclusions section, you can specify files, folders, file types (by extension), or processes you want Windows Defender Antivirus to ignore. This option is especially useful for developers working with files that might otherwise trigger alarms.

Manually scanning for malware

The combination of real-time protection and periodic scheduled scanning is normally sufficient for identifying and resolving problems with malware and spyware. However, if you suspect you've been infected, you can initiate a scan on demand. To immediately scan for problems, open the Virus & Threat Protection tab in Windows Security (shown earlier in Figure 18-8) and click Quick Scan (Scan Now in version 1803). This option kicks off a scan that checks only the places on your computer that malware and spyware are most likely to infect, and it's the recommended setting for frequent regular scans.

For a more intensive (or more focused) inspection, click Scan Options (Run A New Advanced Scan in version 1803), which leads to a page containing three options in addition to Quick Scan. Choose Full Scan if you suspect infection (or you just want reassurance that your system is clean) and want to inspect all running programs and the complete contents of all local volumes. Click Custom Scan if you want to restrict the scan to any combination of drives, folders, and files. The Windows Defender Offline option is useful for removing persistent infections that are able to successfully block Windows Defender Antivirus in normal operation. It requires a restart and can take a significant amount of time.

CHAPTER 18

Inside OUT

Run a scan from a script or a scheduled task

Windows Defender Antivirus includes a command-line utility you can use to automate scans with a script or a scheduled task. You'll find MpCmdRun.exe in %ProgramFiles%\Windows Defender. For details about using the utility, open an elevated Command Prompt window and run the program with no parameters.

Dealing with detected threats

If Windows Defender Antivirus detects the presence of malware or spyware as part of its real-time protection, it displays a banner and a notification in Action Center and, in most cases, resolves the problem without requiring you to lift a finger.

To learn more about its findings, open Windows Security and, on the Virus & Threat Protection tab click Threat History. Select Quarantined Threats to see recently removed items, or click See Full History for a more complete listing. Windows Security shows the name, alert level, and detection date of the quarantined item or items. Click See Details for additional information about detected threats.

Blocking ransomware with controlled folder access

One of the pernicious threats in recent times is *ransomware*. Typically, this type of malware works in the background to encrypt all your documents and other files. Upon completion, the program displays a digital ransom note: *If you ever want to see your files again, send us money.* Supposedly, after you pay up (usually via untraceable digital currency), the hijacker sends you a decryption key and instructions for recovering your files.

A feature introduced in version 1709 prevents malicious and suspicious apps from making changes to any files stored in designated folders—typically, all your document folders. To enable this feature, on the Virus & Threat Protection page in Windows Security, click or tap Manage Ransomware Protection. Turn on Controlled Folder Access to enable this feature and its two configurable settings. The Protected Folders link allows you to view and modify the list of folders monitored by this feature. A second link, Allow An App Through Controlled Folder Access, leads to a page where you can whitelist an app that you know to be safe. You'll need to do this only if Controlled Folder Access blocks an app you trust; most legitimate apps are on a known-good list and need no further clearance to go about their work.

On this same page, you'll find details about file recovery options for OneDrive and OneDrive for Business accounts.

Stopping unknown or malicious programs with SmartScreen

SmartScreen, which began as a feature in Internet Explorer in Windows 7, is used to identify programs that other users have run safely. It does so by comparing a hash of a downloaded program with Microsoft's application-reputation database. (It also checks web content used by Microsoft Store apps.)

This reputation check occurs when you download a program using Microsoft Edge or Internet Explorer. SmartScreen also kicks in when you attempt to run a program you downloaded from the internet—regardless of what browser you use.

Programs with a positive reputation run without fuss. Programs that are known to be bad or that have not yet developed a reputation are blocked. A message similar to the one shown in Figure 18-9 appears.

Figure 18-9   When you attempt to run a downloaded program that doesn't have an acceptable reputation in the SmartScreen database, a message like this appears.

If you're certain that a program is safe, you can override the block by clicking the Run Anyway button. With default settings in place, you then need the approval of someone with an administrator account before the program runs. Don't say you weren't warned.

To configure Windows Defender SmartScreen settings, including those for Microsoft Edge and for app content in Microsoft Store apps, open Windows Security and click the App & Browser Control tab.

Blocking intruders with Windows Defender Firewall

Typically, the first line of defense in securing your computer is to protect it from attacks by outsiders. Once your computer is connected to the internet, it becomes just another node on a huge global network. A firewall provides a barrier between your computer and the network to which it's connected by preventing the entry of unwanted traffic while allowing transparent passage to authorized connections.

CHAPTER 18

Using a firewall is simple, essential, and often overlooked. You'll want to be sure that all network connections are protected by a firewall. You might be comforted by the knowledge that your portable computer is protected by a corporate firewall when you're at work and that you use a firewalled broadband connection at home. But what about the public hotspots you use when you travel?

And it makes sense to run a software-based firewall on your computer even when you're behind a residential router or corporate firewall. Other people on your network might not be as vigilant as you are about defending against viruses, so if someone brings in a portable computer infected with a worm and connects it to the network, you're toast—unless your network connection has its own firewall protection.

Windows includes a two-way, stateful-inspection, packet-filtering firewall called, cleverly enough, Windows Defender Firewall. Windows Defender Firewall is enabled by default for all connections, and it begins protecting your computer as it boots. The following actions take place by default:

- The firewall blocks all inbound traffic, with the exception of traffic sent in response to a request by your computer and unsolicited traffic that has been explicitly allowed by creating a rule.

- All outgoing traffic is allowed unless it matches a configured rule.

You notice nothing if a packet is dropped, but you can (at your option) create a log of all such events.

Using Windows Defender Firewall with different network types

Windows Defender Firewall maintains a separate profile (that is, a complete collection of settings, including rules for various programs, services, and ports) for each of three network types:

- **Domain.** Used when your computer is joined to an Active Directory domain. In this environment, firewall settings are typically (but not necessarily) controlled by a network administrator.

- **Private.** Used when your computer is connected to a home or work network in a workgroup configuration.

- **Guest or public.** Used when your computer is connected to a network in a public location, such as an airport or a library. It's common—indeed, recommended—to have fewer allowed programs and more restrictions when you use a public network.

If you're simultaneously connected to more than one network (for example, if you have a Wi-Fi connection to your home network while you're connected to your work domain through a virtual private network, or VPN, connection), Windows uses the appropriate profile for each connection with a feature called multiple active firewall profiles (MAFP).

You make settings in Windows Defender Firewall independently for each network profile. The settings in a profile apply to all networks of the particular type to which you connect. (For example, if you allow a program through the firewall while connected to a public network, that program rule is then enabled whenever you connect to any other public network. It's not enabled when you're connected to a domain or private network unless you allow the program in those profiles.)

➤ **For more information about network types, see "Setting network locations" in Chapter 13, "Windows networking."**

Managing Windows Defender Firewall

Earlier in this chapter, we described the Windows Security app, which includes Firewall & Network Protection as one of the categories it monitors. The icon on that app's home page displays the current status of Windows Defender Firewall, with a green check mark indicating that Windows Defender Firewall is on and protecting the current network connection.

Clicking the Firewall & Network Protection icon offers access to additional status information as well as links to advanced configuration options. Figure 18-10, for example, shows the firewall status for a Windows 10 PC with multiple network connections: one to a private network and the other to a public network.

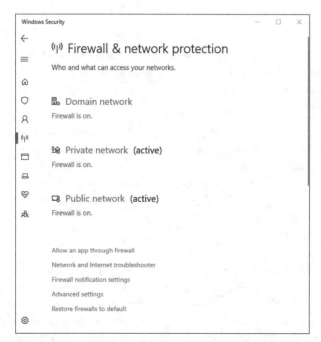

Figure 18-10   Click any network entry to see additional firewall status information for that network as well as an on/off switch. The links at the bottom lead to more advanced controls.

CHAPTER 18

Click any of the three network entries to see a status page for that connection, with a simple on/off switch for the firewall for that network type, as shown here:

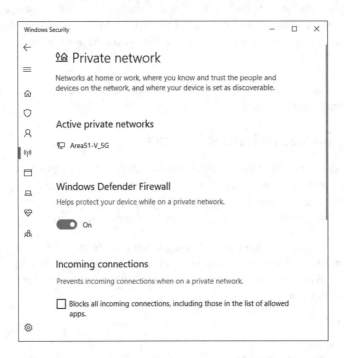

In general, the only reason to turn off Windows Defender Firewall is for brief (and extremely cautious) troubleshooting purposes, or if you have installed a third-party firewall that you plan to use instead of Windows Defender Firewall. Most compatible third-party programs perform this task as part of their installation.

The Blocks All Incoming Connections check box provides additional protection from would-be intruders. When it's selected, Windows Defender Firewall rejects all unsolicited incoming traffic—even traffic from allowed programs that would ordinarily be permitted by a rule. Invoke this mode when extra security against outside attack is needed. For example, you might block all connections when you're using a suspicious public wireless hotspot or when you know that your computer is actively under attack by others.

NOTE

Selecting Blocks All Incoming Connections does not disconnect your computer from the internet. Even in this mode, you can still use your browser to connect to the internet. Similarly, other outbound connections—whether they're legitimate services or some sort of spyware—continue unabated. If you really want to sever your ties to the outside world, open Settings > Network & Internet and disable each network connection. Alternatively, use brute force: physically disconnect wired network connections and turn off wireless adapters or access points.

As you'll discover throughout Windows Defender Firewall, domain network settings are available only on computers that are joined to a domain. You can make settings for all network types—even those to which you're not currently connected. Settings for the domain profile, however, are often locked down by the network administrator by using Group Policy.

The traditional alternative for monitoring the status of Windows Defender Firewall is the Control Panel application of the same name. That dashboard is still available, but its primary tasks—allowing a program through the firewall or blocking all incoming connections—are now accessible directly from links at the bottom of the Firewall & Network Protection page in Windows Security. Click Allow An App Through Firewall, for example, to display a list of allowed apps and features like the one shown in Figure 18-11.

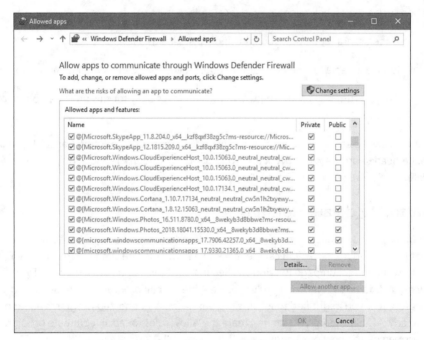

Figure 18-11   Click Change Settings, and then select or clear a check box to control connections over each network type by a specific app or feature.

The Allowed Apps And Features list includes programs and services that are installed on your computer; you can add others, as described in the following section. In addition, program rules are created (but not enabled) when a program tries to set up an incoming connection. To allow connections for a program or service that has already been defined, simply select its check box for each network type on which you want to allow the program. (You need to click Change Settings and approve a UAC consent request before you can make changes.)

In each of these cases, you enable a rule in Windows Defender Firewall that opens a pathway in the firewall and allows a certain type of traffic to pass through it. Each rule of this type increases your security risk to some degree, so you should clear the check box for all programs you don't need. If you're confident you won't ever need a particular program, you can select it and then click Remove. (Many items on this list represent apps or services included with Windows and don't allow deletion, but as long as their check boxes are not selected, these apps present no danger.)

The first time you run a program that tries to set up an incoming connection, Windows Defender Firewall asks for your permission by displaying a dialog box. You can add the program to the allowed programs list by clicking Allow Access.

When such a dialog box appears, read it carefully:

- Is the program one that you knowingly installed and ran?

- Is it reasonable for the program to require acceptance of incoming connections?

- Are you currently using a network type where it's okay for this program to accept incoming connections?

If the answer to any of these questions is no—or if you're unsure—click Cancel. If you later find that a needed program isn't working properly, you can open the allowed apps list in Windows Defender Firewall and enable the rule.

Restoring default settings

If you've played around a bit with Windows Defender Firewall and perhaps allowed connections that you should not have, you can get back to a known secure state by opening the Firewall & Network Protection page in Windows Security and clicking Restore Firewalls To Default. Be aware that doing so removes all rules you've added for all programs. Although this gives you a secure setup, you might find that some of your network-connected programs no longer work properly. As that occurs, you can re-create the Allow rules for each legitimate program, as described on the previous pages.

Advanced tools for managing Windows Defender Firewall

If you have any experience at all configuring firewalls, you'll quickly realize that the Windows Defender Firewall settings in Windows Security cover only the most basic tasks. Don't take that as an indication that Windows Defender Firewall is underpowered. To the contrary, you can configure all manner of firewall rules, allowing or blocking traffic based on program, port, protocol, IP address, and so on. In addition, you can enable, disable, and monitor rules; configure logging; and much more. With advanced tools, you can also configure Windows Defender Firewall on remote workstations. Because the interface to these advanced features is rather daunting, Windows 10 provides the simplified firewall management tools described earlier in this chapter.

These basic tools are adequate not only for less experienced users but also for performing the routine firewall tasks needed by information technology (IT) professionals and others.

Nonetheless, our tour of security essentials would not be complete without a visit to Windows Defender Firewall With Advanced Security, a snap-in and predefined console for Microsoft Management Console (MMC) that offers granular control over rules, exceptions, and profiles. From the Firewall & Network Security page in Windows Security, click Advanced Settings to open Windows Defender Firewall With Advanced Security, as shown in Figure 18-12.

Figure 18-12   In the left pane, click Inbound Rules or Outbound Rules to view, configure, create, and delete firewall rules. The Domain Profile appears even on a computer that's not part of a Windows domain.

➤ For detailed documentation, see "Windows Defender Firewall with Advanced Security" at *https://bit.ly/win10-firewall-advanced*.

Inside OUT

Open Windows Defender Firewall with Advanced Security directly

You don't need to open Windows Security to get to Windows Defender Firewall With Advanced Security. In the search box, type **wf.msc** and press Ctrl+Shift+Enter to run it as an administrator.

CHAPTER 18

Encrypting information

Windows provides the following encryption tools for preventing the loss of confidential data:

- BitLocker Drive Encryption provides another layer of protection by encrypting entire hard-disk volumes. By linking this encryption to a key stored in a Trusted Platform Module (TPM), BitLocker reduces the risk of data being lost when a computer is stolen or when a hard disk is stolen and placed in another computer. A thief's standard approach in these situations is to boot into an alternate operating system and then try to retrieve data from the stolen computer or drive. With BitLocker, that type of offline attack is effectively neutered.

- BitLocker To Go extends BitLocker encryption to removable media, such as USB flash drives.

- Encrypting File System (EFS) is an older technology that encrypts the contents of files so that even if someone is able to obtain the files, that person won't be able to read them. The files are readable only when you sign in to the computer using your user account.

NOTE

The BitLocker Drive Encryption and Encrypting File System features are not available in Windows 10 Home. Encrypting a removable drive with BitLocker To Go requires Windows 10 Pro, Enterprise, or Education; the resulting encrypted drive can be opened and used on a device running Windows 10 Home (or, for that matter, any edition of Windows 7 or later).

Encrypting with BitLocker and BitLocker To Go

BitLocker Drive Encryption can be used to encrypt entire NTFS volumes, which provides excellent protection against data theft. BitLocker can secure a drive against attacks that involve circumventing the operating system or removing the drive and placing it in another computer. BitLocker provides the greatest protection on a computer that has TPM version 1.2 or later; on these systems, the TPM stores the key and ensures that a computer has not been tampered with while offline. If your computer does not have a TPM, you can still use BitLocker on your operating system volume, but an administrator must first turn on the Group Policy option "Allow BitLocker without a compatible TPM." In that configuration, you must supply the encryption key on a USB flash drive or enter the operating system volume password each time you start the computer or resume from hibernation. Non-TPM systems do not get the system integrity check at startup.

With BitLocker To Go, a feature introduced in Windows 7, you can encrypt the entire contents of a USB flash drive or other removable device. If it's lost or stolen, the thief will be unable to access the data without the password.

To apply BitLocker Drive Encryption or BitLocker To Go, right-click the drive in File Explorer and then click Turn On BitLocker. BitLocker asks how you want to unlock the encrypted drive—with a password, a smart card, or both. After you have made your selections and confirmed your intentions, the software gives you the opportunity to save and print your recovery key, as shown in Figure 18-13. (Note that this PC is connected to an Azure AD account; if it were connected to a Microsoft account, the first option would offer to save the encryption key to that account.)

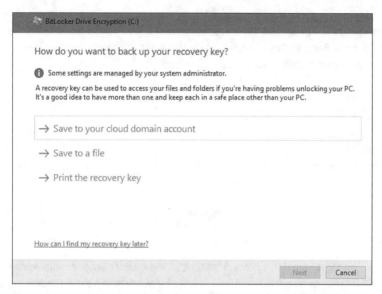

Figure 18-13   The option of saving the recovery key to an Azure AD or Microsoft account is new with Windows 10.

Your recovery key is a system-generated, 48-character, numeric backup password. If you lose the password you assign to the encrypted disk, you can recover your data with the recovery key. BitLocker offers to save that key in a plain text file or cloud storage; you should accept the offer and store the file in a secure location.

Inside OUT

Store your recovery keys on OneDrive or in Azure AD

If you're signed in with a Microsoft account, the Save To Your Microsoft Account option saves the recovery key on OneDrive, making it possible to recover quickly from an encryption problem, provided that you have another Internet-connected device from which to recover the key. You'll find the recovery keys for every device associated with your Microsoft account at *https://onedrive.com/recoverykey*.

When you're signed in with an Azure AD account, the Save To Your Cloud Domain Account option saves the recovery key in your organization's Azure AD portal. A Global Administrator can sign in at *https://portal.azure.com* and retrieve the recovery key from the Devices tab.

With all preliminaries out of the way, BitLocker begins encrypting your media. This process takes a few minutes, even if the disk is freshly formatted. However, if you're in a hurry, you can opt to encrypt only the used space on the drive. This choice can save you a considerable amount of time if your disk contains only a small number of files.

To read a BitLocker-encrypted removable disk, you need to unlock it by using whatever method you stipulated. If you're prompted for a password you have lost or forgotten, click More Options and then click Enter Recovery Key. In case you have several recovery-key text files, BitLocker To Go gives you the key's identification code:

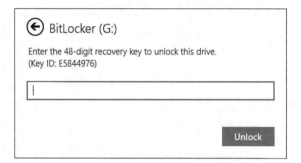

Find the entry on OneDrive (*https://onedrive.com/recoverykey*) or the text file whose name matches the identification code, and then enter the recovery key in the BitLocker dialog box. You'll be granted temporary access to the files, which is good until you remove the disk or restart the computer. At this point, you might want to change the password; type BitLocker in the search box and click Manage BitLocker. Select the encrypted removable drive and then click Change Password.

To remove BitLocker encryption from a disk, use the Manage BitLocker option, select the encrypted drive, and click Turn Off BitLocker. The software will decrypt the disk; allow some time for this process.

> ➤ **For more information about BitLocker, see *https://bit.ly/BitLocker-win10*.**

Using the Encrypting File System

EFS provides a secure way to store sensitive data in files, folders, or entire drives on PCs running Windows 10 Pro, Enterprise, or Education. Windows creates a randomly generated file encryption key (FEK) and then transparently encrypts the data, using this FEK, as the data is being written to disk. Windows then encrypts the FEK using your public key. (Windows creates a personal encryption certificate with a public/private key pair for you the first time you use EFS.) The FEK, and therefore the data it encrypts, can be decrypted only with your certificate and its associated private key, which are available only when you sign in with your user account. (Designated data-recovery agents can also decrypt your data.) Other users who attempt to use your encrypted files receive an "access denied" message. Even administrators and others who have permission to take ownership of files are unable to open your encrypted files.

You can encrypt individual files, folders, or entire drives. (You cannot, however, use EFS to encrypt the boot volume—the one with the Windows operating system files. For that, you must use BitLocker.) We recommend you encrypt folders or drives instead of individual files. When you encrypt a folder or drive, the files it contains are encrypted, and new files you create in or copy to that folder or drive are encrypted automatically.

To encrypt a folder, follow these steps:

1. In File Explorer, right-click the folder, choose Properties, click the General tab, and then click Advanced, which displays the dialog box shown next. (If the properties dialog box doesn't have an Advanced button, the folder is not on an NTFS-formatted volume and you can't use EFS.)

2. Select Encrypt Contents To Secure Data. (Note that you can't encrypt compressed files. If the files are already compressed, Windows clears the compressed attribute.)

3. Click OK twice. If the folder contains any files or subfolders, Windows then displays a confirmation message:

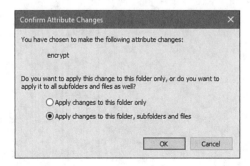

NOTE

If you select Apply Changes To This Folder Only, Windows doesn't encrypt any of the files currently in the folder. Any new files you create in the folder, however, including files you copy or move to the folder, will be encrypted.

After a file or folder has been encrypted, File Explorer displays its name in green. This minor cosmetic detail is the only change you're likely to notice. Windows decrypts your files on the fly as you use them and reencrypts them when you save.

CAUTION

Before you encrypt anything important, you should back up your file-recovery certificate and your personal encryption certificate (with their associated private keys), as well as the data-recovery-agent certificate, to a USB flash drive or to your OneDrive. Store the flash drive in a secure location. To do this, open User Accounts in Control Panel, and then click Manage Your File Encryption Certificates.

If you ever lose the certificate stored on your hard drive (because of a disk failure, for example), you can restore the backup copy and regain access to your files. If you lose all copies of your certificate (and no data-recovery-agent certificates exist), you won't be able to use your encrypted files. To the best of our knowledge, there's no practical way for anyone to access these encrypted files without the certificate. (If there were, it wouldn't be very good encryption.)

To encrypt one or more files, follow the same procedure as for folders. You'll see a different confirmation message to remind you that the file's folder is not encrypted and to give you an opportunity to encrypt it. You generally don't want to encrypt individual files because the information you intend to protect can too easily become decrypted without your knowledge. For example, with some applications, when you open a document for editing, the application creates a copy of the original document. When you save the document after editing, the application saves the copy—which is not encrypted—and deletes the original encrypted document. Static files that you use for reference only—but never for editing—can safely be encrypted without encrypting the parent folder. Even in that situation, however, you'll probably find it simpler to encrypt the whole folder.

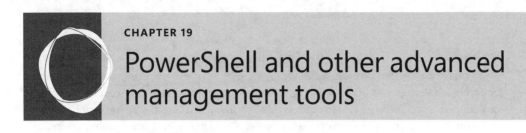

The simplest way to accomplish most tasks in Windows 10 is with the help of the graphical user interface—the dialog boxes and Settings pages where you can define preferences and change settings.

But just because that's usually the easiest way doesn't mean it's the only way. Most such tasks have an alternative that you can exercise via the command line or by making changes to the Windows registry. If you're a system administrator or help desk technician, using command-line tools can save time, especially when you incorporate them into scripts. And for some tasks, using a command-line tool is the only way to get a specific job done.

In this chapter, we offer detailed instructions on how to use the Windows Command Processor (Cmd.exe), a classic tool that hasn't lost any of its power with age. We also introduce Windows PowerShell, a .NET-based command-line shell and scripting language tailored to work with every facet of Windows. This chapter provides an essential overview of the PowerShell language, with pointers to additional learning resources.

We also cover the powerful Registry Editor utility (Regedit.exe), starting with an explanation of how the Windows registry works, and we finish with a quick overview of the many advanced management tools based on the Microsoft Management Console.

But we start with a question you'll need to answer the first time you sit down in front of a PC running Windows 10.

Command Prompt or PowerShell?

Most of the features we discuss in this chapter have been around for many years, and there are few if any substantive changes in their behavior in Windows 10. A modification that debuted in Windows 10 version 1703 is worth noting here, however. Windows PowerShell is now the default command-line shell, replacing the venerable Windows Command Processor, Cmd.exe.

CHAPTER 19

This change is apparent in the default configuration of the Quick Link menu, which appears when you right-click Start or press Windows key+X: where it previously contained menu items for Command Prompt and Command Prompt (Admin), those slots are now occupied by entries for Windows PowerShell and Windows PowerShell (Admin), respectively. Similar changes are visible on the File menu in File Explorer and when you hold down Shift as you right-click in any empty space when viewing the contents of a folder in File Explorer. (A Command Prompt shortcut that opens the Windows Command Processor is still available on the All Programs menu, in the Windows System folder.)

Which command shell should you use? That's entirely a matter of personal preference. PowerShell is, of course, newer and more powerful. It also has a steeper learning curve. Thanks to aliases (which we describe in more detail in "Interacting with PowerShell" later in this chapter), you can continue using many familiar command-line tools in the new environment.

If you find a task that you don't know how to accomplish in the new shell, it's easy enough to switch to the Windows Command Processor environment on the fly: After opening a PowerShell window (with or without administrative rights), type **cmd** and press Enter. When you're finished working with the Cmd.exe environment, type **exit** and press Enter to return to the PowerShell prompt. To open a separate Command Prompt window, use the command **start cmd**.

But if you have a library of scripts and shortcuts that were explicitly designed for the classic Command Prompt, or if you'd prefer not to climb the PowerShell learning curve at all, it's easy enough to undo the new configuration and reestablish Command Prompt as the default shell. Open Settings > Personalization > Taskbar, and look for the switch labeled Replace Command Prompt With Windows PowerShell In The Menu When I Right-Click The Start Button Or Press Windows Key+X. Slide that switch to the Off position, and you're back to the status quo ante.

One other related capability that we didn't mention in earlier editions of this book is worth noting here. In any File Explorer window, you can open a Command Prompt window or a PowerShell window by entering a command in the File Explorer address bar; type **cmd** or **powershell** and then press Enter to open the respective shell. The folder from which you enter the command becomes the current directory in the shell window. (*Directory* is the MS-DOS-era term for *folder*, and you'll encounter it frequently in command names, help files, and so on.) Note that a session launched in this fashion does not have administrative rights.

Inside OUT

Run the Bash shell natively in Windows

In March 2016, Microsoft announced it would be offering developers the ability to work with the Ubuntu user space and Bash shell, running natively (not in a virtualized environment) in Windows 10. The technology, which relies on a new Windows Subsystem for Linux (WSL), enables developers to use command-line utilities such as grep, awk, and sed, and run Bash scripts that rely on these utilities. You can also launch Windows binaries directly from a WSL command prompt.

As of version 1709, the Bash shell/WSL environment is officially released and no longer requires installing developer (beta) releases. During the preview period for the Creators Update, Microsoft replaced the underlying WSL version with Ubuntu 16.04 (Xenial); this version is installed by default on all new Bash on Ubuntu on Windows instances and is available in the Microsoft Store.

For more information on how to get started, including articles and blog posts, see the Microsoft Docs page at *https://docs.microsoft.com/en-us/windows/wsl/about*.

Working in a Command Prompt session

To open a Command Prompt window, run Cmd.exe. You can do this by double-clicking any shortcut for Cmd.exe, but because you like to type, you might find it easiest to tap the Windows key to position the insertion point in the search box, type **cmd**, and then press Enter. To open a second or subsequent Command Prompt window when one is already open, you can type **start** in the window that's already running.

Running with elevated privileges

Your activities in a Command Prompt session are subject to the same User Account Control (UAC) restrictions as anything else you do in Windows. If you use Command Prompt to launch a program (for example, Registry Editor) that requires an administrative token, you'll be asked to confirm a UAC prompt before moving on. If you plan to run several such tasks from Command Prompt, you might prefer to run Cmd.exe itself with elevated privileges. To do this, use any of the following techniques:

- Type **cmd** in the search box and press Ctrl+Shift+Enter.

- Right-click any shortcut for Command Prompt and then click Run As Administrator, or press Ctrl+Shift as you click the shortcut or press Enter.

- Use the appropriate command on the Quick Link menu: click Command Prompt (Admin), or click Windows PowerShell (Admin) and then enter **cmd**.

Windows displays the word *Administrator* in the title bar of any Command Prompt window running with elevated privileges.

Starting Command Prompt at a particular folder

If you run Cmd.exe from its location in %SystemRoot%\System32, the session begins with that folder as the current directory. If you run Cmd from the Start menu, Windows uses the location specified in the Start In field for the Start > Windows System > Command Prompt shortcut: %HOMEDRIVE%%HOMEPATH%. To run a Command Prompt session at a different folder, hold down the Shift key while you right-click the folder in File Explorer. On the shortcut menu, click Open PowerShell Window Here, and then enter **cmd**.

Starting Command Prompt and running a command

By using the **/C** and **/K** command-line arguments, you can start a Command Prompt session and immediately run a command or program, which we refer to as *commandstring* in this section. The difference between the two is that **cmd /C *commandstring*** terminates the Command Prompt session as soon as *commandstring* has finished, whereas **cmd /K *commandstring*** keeps the Command Prompt session open after *commandstring* has finished. Note the following:

- You must include either /C or /K if you want to specify a command string as an argument to Cmd. If you type **cmd *commandstring***, the command processor simply ignores *commandstring*.

- While *commandstring* is executing, you can't interact with the command processor. To run a command or program and keep the Command Prompt window interface, use the Start command. For example, to run Mybatch.bat and continue issuing commands while the batch program is running, type

```
cmd /k start mybatch.bat
```

- If you include other command-line arguments along with **/C** or **/K**, **/C** or **/K** must be the last argument before *commandstring*.

Using AutoRun to execute commands when Command Prompt starts

By default, Command Prompt executes on startup whatever it finds in the following two registry values:

- The AutoRun value in HKLM\Software\Microsoft\Command Processor

- The AutoRun value in HKCU\Software\Microsoft\Command Processor

The AutoRun value in HKLM affects all user accounts on the current machine. The AutoRun value in HKCU affects only the current user account. If both values are present, both are executed—HKLM before HKCU. Both AutoRun values are of data type REG_SZ, which means they can contain a single string. To execute a sequence of separate Command Prompt statements, therefore, you must use command symbols or store the sequence as a batch program and then use AutoRun to call the batch program.

You can also use Group Policy objects to specify startup tasks for Command Prompt.

Editing the command line

When working at a command prompt, you often enter the same command multiple times or enter several similar commands. To assist you with repetitive or corrective tasks, Windows includes a feature that recalls previous commands and allows you to edit them on the current command line. Table 19-1 lists these editing keys and what they do.

Table 19-1   Command-line editing keys

Key	Function
Up Arrow or F3	Recalls the previous command in the command history
Down Arrow	Recalls the next command in the command history
Page Up	Recalls the earliest command used in the session
Page Down	Recalls the most recently used command
Left Arrow	Moves left one character
Right Arrow	Moves right one character
Ctrl+Left Arrow	Moves left one word
Ctrl+Right Arrow	Moves right one word
Home	Moves to the beginning of the line
End	Moves to the end of the line
Esc	Clears the current command
F7	Displays the command history in a scrollable pop-up box
F8	Displays commands that start with the characters currently on the command line
Alt+F7	Clears the command history

Using command symbols

Old-fashioned programs that take all their input from a command line and then run unaided can be useful in a multitasking environment. You can turn them loose to perform complicated processing in the background while you continue to work with other programs in the foreground.

To work better with other programs, many command-line programs follow a set of conventions that control their interaction:

- By default, programs take all their input as lines of text typed at the keyboard. But input in the same format also can be redirected from a file or any device capable of sending lines of text.

- By default, programs send all their output to the screen as lines of text. But output in the same format also can be redirected to a file or another line-oriented device, such as a printer.

- Programs set a number (called a *return value*) when they terminate to indicate the results of the program.

When programs are written according to these rules, you can use the symbols listed in Table 19-2 to control a program's input and output or chain programs together.

Table 19-2 Command symbols

Symbol	Function
<	Redirects input
>	Redirects output
> >	Appends redirected output to existing data
|	Pipes output
&	Separates multiple commands in a command line
&&	Runs the command after && only if the command before && is successful
||	Runs the command after || only if the command before || fails
^	Treats the next symbol as a character
(and)	Groups commands

The redirection symbols

Command Prompt sessions in Windows allow you to override the default source for input (the keyboard) or the default destination for output (the screen).

Redirecting output   To redirect output to a file, type the command followed by a greater-than sign (>) and the name of the file.

Using two greater-than signs (> >) redirects output and appends it to an existing file.

Redirecting input   To redirect input from a file, type the command followed by a less-than sign (**<**) and the name of the file.

Redirecting input and output   You can redirect both input and output in a command line. For example, to use Batch.lst as input to the Sort command and send its output to a file named Sorted.lst, type the following:

```
Sort < batch.lst > sorted.lst
```

Standard output and standard error   Programs can be written to send their output either to the standard output device or to the standard error device. Sometimes programs are written to send different types of output to each device. You can't always tell which is which because, by default, both devices are the screen.

The Type command illustrates the difference. When used with wildcards, the **Type** command sends the name of each matching file to the standard error device and sends the contents of the file to the standard output device. Because they both go to the screen, you see a nice display with each file name followed by its contents.

However, if you try to redirect output to a file by typing something like this:

```
type *.bat > std.out
```

the file names still appear on your screen because standard error is still directed to the screen. Only the file contents are redirected to Std.out.

With Windows, you can qualify the redirection symbol by preceding it with a number. Use **1>** (or simply >) for standard output and **2>** for standard error. For example:

```
type *.bat 2> err.out
```

This time the file contents go to the screen and the names are redirected to Err.out.

The pipe symbol

The pipe symbol (**|**) is used to send, or pipe, the output of one program to a second program as the second program's input. Piping is commonly used with the More command, which displays multiple screenfuls of output one screenful at a time. For example:

```
help dir | more
```

This command line uses the output of Help as the input for More. The More command filters out the first screenful of Help output, sends it to the screen as its own output, and then waits for a keystroke before sending more filtered output.

Inside OUT

Pipe command-line output to the clipboard

Using the Clip utility, introduced with Windows Vista, you can pipe the output of a command to the Windows Clipboard, from whence you can paste it into any program that accepts Clipboard text. Typing **dir | clip**, for example, puts a listing of the current directory's files on the Clipboard. You can also redirect the contents of a file to the Clipboard by using the < symbol. Typing **clip < myfile.txt**, for example, transfers the contents of myfile.txt to the Clipboard.

Inside OUT

Customize Command Prompt windows

You can customize the appearance of a Command Prompt window in several ways. You can change its size, select a font, and even use eye-pleasing colors. And you can save these settings independently for each shortcut that launches a Command Prompt session so that you can make appropriate settings for different tasks. To customize the current Command Prompt window, click the Control menu icon at the left side of the title bar, and then click Properties on the Control menu. (If Command Prompt is running in full-screen mode, press Alt+Enter to switch to window display.) To customize future sessions, click the Control menu icon in a Command Prompt window, and then click Defaults on the Control menu.

An introduction to Windows PowerShell

Microsoft describes Windows PowerShell as a "task-based command-line shell and scripting language designed especially for system administrators." That means you can use PowerShell for the same kinds of tasks you're accustomed to performing with Cmd.exe, and you can use its scripting power to automate routine work. If you're a Windows user who occasionally likes to take advantage of the power of text-based command-line tools such as Ipconfig or Netsh, you'll find that PowerShell lets you interact with the operating system in all the old familiar ways—and a good many new ones as well. If you're accustomed to using batch programs, VBScript, or JScript to automate administrative tasks, you can retain your current scripting investment but take advantage of the additional capabilities afforded by PowerShell's object orientation and .NET Framework foundation as your scripting needs grow.

Among the advantages PowerShell offers over previous shells and scripting platforms are the following:

- **Integration with the Microsoft .NET Framework.** Like more traditional develop-ment languages, such as C#, PowerShell commands and scripts have access to the vast resources of the .NET Framework.

- **Object orientation and an object-based pipeline.** All PowerShell commands that gen-erate output return .NET Framework objects rather than plain text, eliminating the need for text parsing when the output of one command provides input to a second.

- **A consistent, discoverable command model.** All of PowerShell's commands (or "cmdlets," as they are called) use a verb-noun syntax, with a hyphen separating the two components. All cmdlets that read information from the system begin with Get; all those that write information begin with Set. These and other similar consistencies make the lan-guage easy to learn and understand. Each cmdlet has a help topic that can be retrieved by typing **get-help** *cmdletname* (where *cmdletname* is the name of a cmdlet). You can use a **–Whatif** parameter to test the effect of a cmdlet before you execute it.

- **Universal scripting capability.** A PowerShell script is a text file, with the extension .ps1, containing PowerShell commands. Any commands that can be used interactively can be incorporated into a script. Scripting structures, such as looping, branching, and variables, can also be used interactively—that is, outside the context of a script.

- **A focus on administrators.** PowerShell includes features of particular interest to sys-tem administrators, such as the ability to work with remote computers; access to system resources such as files, folders, registry keys, events, and logs; and the ability to start and stop services.

- **Extensibility.** Developers can extend the PowerShell language by importing modules—packages of PowerShell commands and other items. Office 365 administrators, for example, can download Office 365 PowerShell modules and connect to an Office 365 tenant to manage the entire family of Office 365 apps and services. For details, see *https://bit.ly/office365-powershell*.

The following pages introduce PowerShell. Our discussion focuses primarily on the use of PowerShell as an interactive command shell because PowerShell scripting is itself a book-length subject. For sources of additional information, see "Finding additional PowerShell resources" later in this chapter.

Starting PowerShell

To launch Windows PowerShell, right-click Start (or press Windows key+X) and choose Windows PowerShell or Windows PowerShell (Admin) from the Quick Link menu. Alternatively, type **powershell** into the search box; the Windows PowerShell application should appear at or near the top of the results list. Nearby you'll also find the 64-bit and 32-bit versions of the

Windows PowerShell Integrated Scripting Environment (ISE). The ISE is a multitabbed graphical environment of particular use for developing and debugging scripts.

As Figure 19-1 shows, PowerShell's default appearance offers a minimal command-line interface similar to that of Cmd.exe. The *Windows PowerShell* label in the title bar and above the copyright notice, along with the letters *PS* at the beginning of the command prompt, are the only distinguishing details.

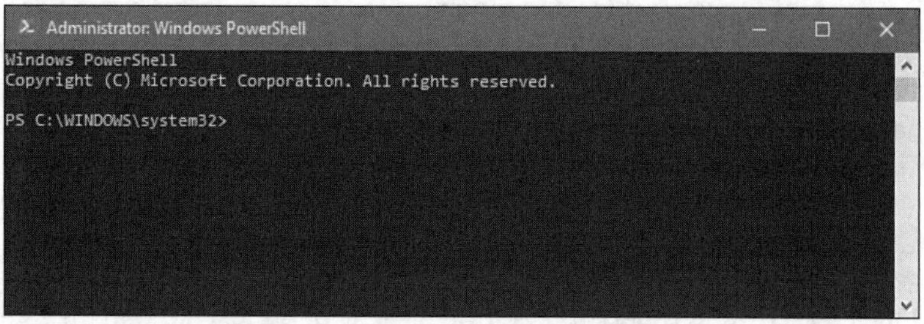

Figure 19-1 An uncustomized (default) PowerShell window looks a lot like a Command Prompt window.

Interacting with PowerShell

If you're an old hand at the command prompt but new to PowerShell, the first thing you might want to try is using some of Cmd.exe's familiar internal commands. You'll discover that most such items—for example, *dir*, *cd*, *md*, *rd*, *pushd*, and *popd*—still work in PowerShell. Redirection symbols, such as > to send output to a file and >> to append output to a file, work as well, and you can pipe lengthy output to More, just as you're accustomed to doing in Cmd.exe. PowerShell uses aliases to map Cmd.exe commands to its own cmdlets. Thus, *dir* is an alias for the PowerShell cmdlet *Get-Childitem*; *cd* is an alias for PowerShell's *Set-Location*. You can create your own aliases to simplify the typing of PowerShell commands that you use often; for details, see "Using and creating aliases" later in this chapter.

Like any other command prompt, PowerShell can be used to launch executables. Typing **regedit**, for example, launches Registry Editor; typing **taskschd** launches Task Scheduler. (Note that with PowerShell you also can work directly with the registry without the use of Registry Editor; for details, see "Editing the Windows registry" later in this chapter.)

Using cmdlets

The core of PowerShell's native vocabulary is a set of cmdlets, each consisting of a verb, followed by a hyphen, followed by a noun—for example, *Start-Service*. A cmdlet can be followed by one or more parameters; each parameter is preceded by a space and consists of a hyphen connected to the parameter's name followed by a space and the parameter's value. So, for example,

```
Get-Process -Name iexplore
```

returns information about any currently running processes named iexplore.

With parameters that accept multiple values, you can use a comma to separate the values. For example,

```
Get-Process -Name iexplore, winword, excel
```

generates information about Microsoft Word and Excel as well as Internet Explorer.

Many cmdlets use positional parameters. For example, the **–Name** parameter for *Get-Process* is positional. PowerShell expects it to come first, so you can omit **–Name** and simply specify the names of the processes in which you're interested.

If you omit both the first positional parameter and its value, PowerShell typically assumes a value of *. So, for example,

```
Get-Process
```

returns information about all running processes, as shown in Figure 19-2.

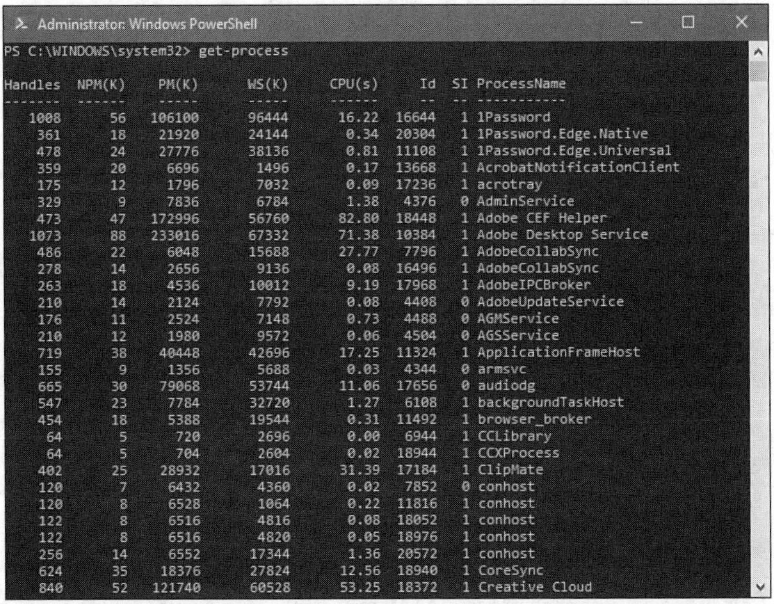

```
PS C:\WINDOWS\system32> get-process

Handles  NPM(K)    PM(K)      WS(K)   CPU(s)     Id  SI ProcessName
-------  ------    -----      -----   ------     --  -- -----------
   1008      56   106100      96444    16.22  16644   1 1Password
    361      18    21920      24144     0.34  20304   1 1Password.Edge.Native
    478      24    27776      38136     0.81  11108   1 1Password.Edge.Universal
    359      20     6696       1496     0.17  13668   1 AcrobatNotificationClient
    175      12     1796       7032     0.09  17236   1 acrotray
    329       9     7836       6784     1.38   4376   0 AdminService
    473      47   172996      56760    82.80  18448   1 Adobe CEF Helper
   1073      88   233016      67332    71.38  10384   1 Adobe Desktop Service
    486      22     6048      15688    27.77   7796   1 AdobeCollabSync
    278      14     2656       9136     0.08  16496   1 AdobeCollabSync
    263      18     4536      10012     9.19  17968   1 AdobeIPCBroker
    210      14     2124       7792     0.08   4408   0 AdobeUpdateService
    176      11     2524       7148     0.73   4488   0 AGMService
    210      12     1980       9572     0.06   4504   0 AGSService
    719      38    40448      42696    17.25  11324   1 ApplicationFrameHost
    155       9     1356       5688     0.03   4344   0 armsvc
    665      30    79068      53744    11.06  17656   0 audiodg
    547      23     7784      32720     1.27   6108   1 backgroundTaskHost
    454      18     5388      19544     0.31  11492   1 browser_broker
     64       5      720       2696     0.00   6944   1 CCLibrary
     64       5      704       2604     0.02  18944   1 CCXProcess
    402      25    28932      17016    31.39  17184   1 ClipMate
    120       7     6432       4360     0.02   7852   0 conhost
    120       8     6528       1064     0.22  11816   1 conhost
    122       8     6516       4816     0.08  18052   1 conhost
    122       8     6516       4820     0.05  18976   1 conhost
    256      14     6552      17344     1.36  20572   1 conhost
    624      35    18376      27824    12.56  18940   1 CoreSync
    840      52   121740      60528    53.25  18372   1 Creative Cloud
```

Figure 19-2 Typing **Get-Process** without parameters produces information about all running processes.

In some cases, if you omit values for an initial positional parameter, PowerShell prompts you to supply the parameter. For example, in response to

```
Get-Eventlog
```

CHAPTER 19

PowerShell will do you the courtesy of prompting for the name of an event log. (Event logs are large; it wouldn't be reasonable to ask for all of them at once.)

For information about any particular cmdlet, type **get-help** followed by the cmdlet name.

Using the pipeline

You can use the pipe operator (**|**) to supply the output of one cmdlet as input to another. You can connect as many cmdlets as you please using the PowerShell pipeline, as long as each cmdlet to the right of a pipe operator understands the output of the cmdlet to its left. Because PowerShell cmdlets return full-fidelity .NET objects rather than text, a cmdlet to the right of a pipe operator can operate directly on properties or methods of the preceding cmdlet's output.

The following paragraphs provide examples of the use of piping to format, filter, and sort the output from various Get- cmdlets.

Formatting output as a list   The default output from many Get- cmdlets is a table that presents only some of the resultant object's properties (about as many as the width of your display is likely to accommodate). For example, the cmdlet

```
Get-Service
```

generates a three-column display that includes only the Status, Name, and DisplayName properties.

If you pipe the same output to *Format-List*,

```
Get-Service | Format-List
```

PowerShell, no longer constrained by display width, can display more of the object's properties (as shown in Figure 19-3), including in this case such useful items as the dependencies of each service and whether the service can be paused or stopped.

In some cases, you'll find the *Format-List* cmdlet, with no parameters, is equivalent to *Format-List –Property* *. But this is by no means always the case. For example,

```
Get-Process | Format-List
```

returns four properties for each process: ID, Handles, CPU, and Name. Asking for all properties produces a wealth of additional information.

To generate a list of particular properties, add the **–Property** parameter to *Format-List* and supply a comma-separated list of the properties you want to see. To see what properties are available for the object returned by a cmdlet, pipe that cmdlet to *Get-Member*:

```
Get-Process | Get-Member -Itemtype property
```

(Omitting the **–Itemtype** parameter returns methods as well as properties.)

Figure 19-3 By piping a cmdlet to *Format-List*, you can see more of a resultant object's properties.

Formatting output as a table Perhaps you want tabular output but with different properties from those that your cmdlet gives you by default. *Format-Table* does the trick. For example,

```
Get-Service | Format-Table -Property name, dependentservices, servicesdependedon
```

generates a table consisting of these three enumerated properties. Note that PowerShell's console output is constrained by your console width, no matter how many properties you ask to see. For results that are too wide to display, redirect output to a file (using the **>** operator) or try the *Out-Gridview* cmdlet, described next.

Generating an interactive graphical table Piping the output to *Out-Gridview* generates a graphical tabular display you can filter, sort, and copy easily into other programs, such as Excel, that accommodate tabular data. For example,

```
Get-Process | Select-Object * | Out-Gridview
```

produces output comparable to that shown in Figure 19-4. Note that in this example, *Get-Process* is piped first to *Select-Object* * because *Out-Gridview*, unlike *Format-Table*, does not include a **–Property** parameter. *Select-Object* * passes all properties of the object returned by *Get-Process* along the pipeline to *Out-Gridview*.

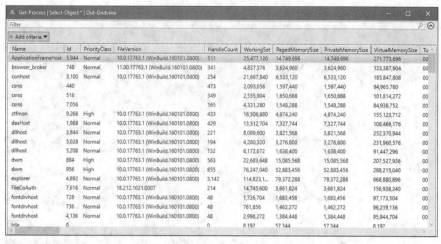

Figure 19-4 The *Out-Gridview* cmdlet produces a graphical tabular display you can sort, filter, and copy into a spreadsheet.

You can manipulate the *Out-Gridview* display with techniques comparable to those used by many other programs:

- To sort the display, click a column heading; click a second time to reverse the sort.

- To change the position of a column, drag its heading. You can also rearrange columns by right-clicking any column head, choosing Select Columns, and then using the Move Down and Move Up buttons in the Select Columns dialog box.

- To remove columns from the display, right-click any column heading, click Select Columns, and then use the << button in the Select Columns dialog box.

- To perform a quick filter, enter text in the line labeled Filter. For example, to limit the display in Figure 19-4 to processes with properties containing the word *Microsoft*, type **Microsoft** on the Filter line.

- To filter on one or more specific columns, click the Add Criteria button. In the drop-down list that appears, select check boxes for the columns on which you want to filter and then click Add.

Filtering output   To filter output from a cmdlet, pipe it to the *Where-Object* cmdlet. With *Where-Object*, you encapsulate filtering criteria in a script block, between curly braces. The following example filters output from *Get-Service* so that only services whose status is Stopped are displayed:

```
Get-Service | Where-Object {$_.Status -eq "Stopped"}
```

Sorting output   You can use the *Sort-Object* cmdlet to sort the output from a cmdlet on one or more of the resultant object's properties in a variety of useful ways. If you omit the **–Property** parameter, *Sort-Object* sorts on the default property. For example,

```
Get-Childitem | Sort-Object
```

sorts the contents of the current directory by Name, the default property in this case. To sort on multiple properties, follow **–Property** with a comma-separated list. *Sort-Object* sorts on the first named property first, sorting items with identical values for the first property by the second property, and so on. Sorts are ascending by default; to sort in descending order, add the parameter *–Descending*.

By piping *Sort-Object* to *Select-Object*, you can do such things as return the largest or smallest *n* items in a resultant object. For example,

```
Get-Process | Sort-Object -Property WS | Select-Object -Last 10
```

returns the processes with the 10 largest values of the working set (WS) property. Using **–First 10** instead of **–Last 10** gives you the items with the smallest values.

Piping output to the printer   To redirect output to the default printer, pipe it to *Out-Printer*. To use a nondefault printer, specify its name, in quotation marks, after *Out-Printer*. For example,

```
Get-Content C:\Users\Craig\Documents\Music\Sonata.sib | Out-Printer
"Microsoft Print To PDF"
```

sends the content of C:\Users\Craig\Documents\Music\Sonata.sib to the device named Microsoft Print To PDF.

Using PowerShell features to simplify keyboard entry

PowerShell is a wordy language and doesn't take kindly to misspellings. Fortunately, it includes many features to streamline and simplify the task of formulating acceptable commands.

Using and creating aliases   An alias is an alternative formulation for a cmdlet. As mentioned earlier, PowerShell uses aliases to *translate* Cmd.exe commands to its own native tongue—for example, *cd* to *Set-Location*. But it includes a great many more simply for your typing convenience; *gsv*, for example, is an alias for *Get-Service*. And you can create aliases of your own.

To see what aliases are currently available (including any you created yourself during the current session), type **get-alias**. To see whether an alias is available for a particular cmdlet, pipe *Get-Alias* to *Where-Object*, like this:

```
Get-Alias | Where-Object { $_.definition -eq "Set-Variable" }
```

This particular command string inquires whether an alias is available for the *Set-Variable* cmdlet. If you type this, you'll discover that PowerShell offers two: *sv* and *set*.

To create a new alias, type **set-alias *name value***, where *name* is the alias and *value* is a cmdlet, function, executable program, or script. If *name* already exists as an alias, *Set-Alias* redefines it. If *value* is not valid, PowerShell won't bother you with an error message—until you try to use the alias.

Aliases you create are valid for the current session only. To make them available permanently, include them in your profile. See "Using your profile to customize PowerShell" later in this chapter.

Abbreviating parameter names   Aliases are dandy for cmdlets, but they're no help for parameter names. Fortunately, with PowerShell you can abbreviate such names. The commands *Get-Process –name iexplore* and *Get-Process –n iexplore* are equivalent. As soon as you've typed enough of a parameter name to let PowerShell recognize it unambiguously, you can give your fingers a rest. And, of course, you can combine aliases with parameter abbreviations to further lighten your load.

Using Tab expansion   As a further convenience, with PowerShell you can complete the names of files, cmdlets, or parameters by pressing Tab. Type part of a name, press Tab, and PowerShell presents the first potential completion. Continue pressing Tab to cycle through all the possibilities. Note, however, that Tab expansion works only with the noun portion of a cmdlet; type the verb and the hyphen, and then you can use Tab expansion for the noun.

Using wildcards and regular expressions   Like all its Windows-shell predecessors, PowerShell supports the * and ? wildcards—the former standing in for any combination of zero or more characters, the latter for any single character. PowerShell also provides a vast panoply of "regular expressions" for matching character strings. For details about regular expressions in PowerShell, type **get-help about_regular_expressions**.

Recalling commands from the command history   PowerShell maintains a history of your recent commands, which makes it easy to reuse (or edit and reuse) a command you already entered. To see the history, type **get-history**. Each item in the history is identified by an ID number. Type **invoke-history ID** to bring an item to the command line. On the command line, you can edit an item before executing it. With the exception of Alt+F7, the editing keys available in Cmd.exe (which are listed in Table 19-1) work the same way in PowerShell.

The number of history items retained in a PowerShell session is defined by the automatic variable $MaximumHistoryCount. By default, that variable is set to 64. If you find you need more, you can assign a larger number to the variable. For example, to double the default for the current session, type **$MaximumHistoryCount = 128**. To change the history size for all sessions, add a variable assignment to your profile. For more information, see "Using your profile to customize PowerShell" later in this chapter.

Using PowerShell providers for access to file-system and registry data

PowerShell includes a set of built-in providers that give you access to various kinds of data stores. Providers are .NET Framework–based programs, and their data is exposed in the form of drives, comparable to familiar file-system drives. Thus, you can access a key in the HKLM registry hive with a path structure similar to that of a file-system folder; for example, the path HKLM:\Hardware\ACPI specifies the ACPI key of the Hardware key of the HKLM hive. Or, to use a quite different example, you can use the command *Get-Childitem env:* to get a list of current environment variables and their values.

Table 19-3 lists PowerShell's built-in providers. For more information about providers, type **get-help about_providers**.

Table 19-3   Built-in providers

Provider	Drive	Data store
Alias	Alias:	Currently defined aliases
Certificate	Cert:	X509 certificates for digital signatures
Environment	Env:	Windows environment variables
FileSystem	(varies)	File-system drives, directories, and files
Function	Function:	PowerShell functions
Registry	HKLM:, HKCU:	HKLM and HKCU registry hives
Variable	Variable:	PowerShell variables
WSMan	WSMan:	WS-Management configuration information

The following paragraphs provide some basic information about working with the file system and registry.

Working with the file system   For very simple file-system operations, you might find that familiar Cmd.exe commands are adequate and easier to use than PowerShell cmdlets. The built-in aliases listed in Table 19-4 let you stick with time-honored methods. PowerShell supports the familiar single period (**.**) and double period (**..**) symbols for the current and parent directories, and it includes a built-in variable, $Home, that represents your home directory (by default, equivalent to the %UserProfile% environment variable).

Table 19-4   File-system aliases

Alias	PowerShell cmdlet
cd, chdir	Set-Location
copy	Copy-Item
del	Remove-Item
dir	Get-Childitem
move	Move-Item

md, mkdir	New-Item
rd, rmdir	Remove-Item
type	Get-Content

The PowerShell cmdlets, however, include valuable optional parameters:

- **–Confirm and –Whatif.** The –Confirm parameter, used with *Copy-Item*, *Move-Item*, *Remove-Item*, or *Clear-Content*, causes PowerShell to display a confirmation prompt before executing the command. (*Clear-Content* can be used to erase the contents of a file.) If you use the **–Whatif** parameter, PowerShell shows you the result of a command without executing it.

- **–Credential.** Use the **–Credential** parameter to supply security credentials for a command that requires them. Follow **–Credential** with the name of a user, within double quotation marks. PowerShell will prompt for a password.

- **–Exclude.** You can use the **–Exclude** parameter to make exceptions. For example, *Copy-Item directory1*.* directory2 –Exclude *.log* copies everything, excluding all .log files, from Directory1 to Directory2.

- **–Recurse.** The **–Recurse** parameter causes a command to operate on subfolders of a specified path. For example, *Remove-Item x:\garbagefolder*.* –Recurse* deletes everything from X:\Garbagefolder, including files contained within that folder's subfolders.

- **–Include.** By using the **–Include** parameter in conjunction with **–Recurse**, you can restrict the scope of a command. For example, *Get-Childitem c:\users\craig\documents* –Recurse –Include *.xlsx* restricts a recursive listing of C:\Users\Craig\Documents to files with the extension .xlsx.

- **–Force.** The **–Force** parameter causes a command to operate on items that are not ordinarily accessible, such as hidden and system files.

For detailed information about using these parameters with *Set-Location*, *Get-Childitem*, *Move-Item*, *Copy-Item*, *Get-Content*, *New-Item*, *Remove-Item*, or *Get-Acl*, type **get-help cmdletname**.

Working with the registry The built-in registry provider provides drives for two registry hives: HKLM and HKCU. To change the working location to either of these, type **set-location hklm:** or **set-location hkcu:**, respectively. Use standard path notation to navigate to particular subkeys but enclose paths that include spaces in quotation marks—for example, *set-location "hkcu:\control panel\accessibility"*.

To display information about all subkeys of a key, use *Get-Childitem*. For example,

```
Get-Childitem -Path hkcu:\software\microsoft
```

returns information about all the subkeys of HKCU:\Software\Microsoft.

To add a key to the registry, use *New-Item*. For example,

```
New-Item -Path hkcu:\software\mynewkey
```

adds the key mynewkey to HKCU:\Software. To remove this key, type **remove-item –path hkcu:\software\mynewkey**.

To copy a key, use *Copy-Item* and specify the source and destination paths; like this, for example,

```
Copy-Item -Path hkcu:\software\mykey hkcu:\software\copyofmykey
```

To move a key, use *Move-Item*. The command

```
Move-Item -Path hkcu:\software\mykey -Destination hkcu:\software\myrelocatedkey
```

copies all properties and subkeys associated with HKCU:\Software\Mykey to HKCU:\Software\Myrelocatedkey and deletes HKCU:\Software\Mykey.

To display the security descriptor associated with a key, use *Get-Acl*. To see all the properties of the security descriptor, pipe this to *Format-List –Property **. For example,

```
Get-Acl -Path hkcu:\software\microsoft | Format-List -Property *
```

generates a display comparable to this:

CHAPTER 19

For more information about working with the registry, type **get-help registry**.

Discovering PowerShell

PowerShell provides plenty of resources to help you learn as you go. You can display help information about any cmdlet by typing **get-help cmdletname**. For example, to read help about *Get-Help*, type **get-help get-help**. If you omit the first *get,* PowerShell helpfully pipes the help text to More. So, for example, if you type **help get-help**, PowerShell pauses the output after each screenful.

Among the useful parameters for *Get-Help* are the following:

- **–Examples.** To display only the name, synopsis, and examples associated with a particular help text, add the **–Examples** parameter.

- **–Parameter.** To get help for a particular parameter associated with a cmdlet, include **–Parameter**. Specify the parameter name in quotation marks.

- **–Detailed.** To get the description, syntax, and parameter details for a cmdlet, as well as a set of examples, use the **–Detailed** parameter. (Without this parameter, the examples are omitted; with **–Examples**, the syntax information is omitted.)

- **–Full.** For the works, including information about input and output object types and additional notes, specify **–Full**.

- **–Online.** For the latest information that Microsoft has, including additions or corrections to the native output of *Get-Help*, specify **–Online**. The relevant information from Microsoft Docs will appear in your browser.

The information made available via the **–Online** parameter is more current and more accurate than what's provided in the Windows help file for PowerShell. For the most recent updates, visit the PowerShell Scripting page in Microsoft Docs, *https://bit.ly/scripting-with-powershell*.

Finding the right cmdlet to use

The *Get-Command* cmdlet can help you figure out which cmdlet is the right one to use for a given task. Type **get-command** with no arguments to get the names and definitions of all available cmdlets, functions, and aliases. *Get-Command* can also give you information about non-PowerShell executables. If you type **get-command ***, for example, you'll get a huge list including all files in all folders included in your current %Path% environment variable.

Either global list (with or without the non-PowerShell executables) is likely to be less than useful when you just want to know which cmdlets are available for use with a particular object. To get such a focused list, add the **–Noun** parameter. For example, type **get-command –noun eventlog** to get a list of the cmdlets that use that noun; you'll be rewarded with the names and definitions of *Clear-Eventlog, Get-Eventlog, Limit-Eventlog, New-Eventlog, Remove-Eventlog, Show-Eventlog,* and *Write-Eventlog*. You can get a list focused similarly on a particular verb by using the **–Verb** parameter.

Scripting with PowerShell

A PowerShell script is a text file with the extension .ps1. You can create a script in any plain text editor (Notepad will do fine), or you can use the Integrated Scripting Environment (ISE).

Anything you do interactively with PowerShell you can also do in a script. The reverse is true as well; you can take lines from a script, including those that involve looping or branching structures, and execute them individually outside the context of a script. For example, if you type

```
For ($i=1; $i -le 5; $i++) { "Hello, World" }
```

at the PowerShell command prompt, PowerShell performs the familiar greeting five times.

Using PowerShell's history feature, you can transfer commands you have used interactively into a script. That way you can test to see what works and how it works before committing text to a .ps1 file.

For example, the command

```
Get-History | Foreach-Object { $_.commandline } >> c:\scripts\mynewscript.ps1
```

appends the CommandLine property from each item in your current history to the file C:\ Scripts\Mynewscript.ps1. (If the path doesn't exist, the command returns an error.) Once you have transferred your history to Mynewscript.ps1 in this manner, you can edit it in Notepad by typing **notepad c:\scripts\mynewscript.ps1**.

Running PowerShell scripts

Although files with the extension .ps1 are executable PowerShell scripts, running one is not quite as straightforward as double-clicking a .bat file. In the first place, if you double-click a .ps1 file in File Explorer, you'll get an Open File—Security Warning dialog box, from which the only forward step leads to Notepad. In effect, the default action for a PowerShell script in File Explorer is Edit.

Second, the first time you try to run a script by typing its name at the PowerShell command prompt, you might see a distressing message displayed in red letters and with possibly unwelcome detail. This means that PowerShell has declined to run your script "because the execution of scripts is disabled on this system." You need to change PowerShell's execution policy, as described next.

Third, even after you've cleared the execution-policy hurdle, you might still be rebuffed if you try to run a script stored in the current directory. That's because PowerShell requires a full path specification, even when the item you're running is stored in the current directory. For example, to run Displayprocessor.ps1, which resides in the current directory, you must type **.\displayprocessor**.

Getting and setting the execution policy

PowerShell's power can be used for evil ends. The majority of Windows users will never run PowerShell, but many will have .ps1 files lying about on their system or will download them inadvertently. To protect you from malice, PowerShell disables script execution until you explicitly enable it. Enabling execution requires a change to the execution policy.

Note that your profile script (if you have one) is subject to the same execution policy as any other script. (See "Using your profile to customize PowerShell" later in this chapter.) Therefore, it's pointless to set an execution policy by means of a profile script; that script itself will not run until you've enabled script execution elsewhere.

The following execution policies, listed here from least permissive to most, are available:

- **Restricted.** The default policy. No scripts are allowed to run.

- **AllSigned.** Any script signed by a trusted publisher is allowed to run. PowerShell presents a confirmation prompt before running a script signed by a publisher that you have not designated as "trusted."

- **RemoteSigned.** Scripts from local sources can run. Scripts downloaded from the internet (including scripts that originated as email or instant-messaging attachments) can run if signed by a trusted publisher.

- **Unrestricted.** All scripts can run, but PowerShell presents a confirmation prompt before running a script from a remote source.

- **Bypass.** All scripts are allowed to run.

Execution policies can be set separately for the following scopes:

- **Process.** Affects the current PowerShell session only. The execution policy is stored in memory and expires at the end of the session.

- **CurrentUser.** The execution policy is stored in a subkey of HKCU and applies to the current user only. The setting is retained between PowerShell sessions.

- **LocalMachine.** The execution policy is stored in a subkey of HKLM and applies to all users at this computer. The setting is retained between PowerShell sessions.

If policies are set at two or more of these scopes, the Process policy takes precedence over the CurrentUser policy, which takes precedence over the LocalMachine policy. Execution policy can also be set via Group Policy, however, and settings made in that manner trump any of the foregoing scopes. (Group Policy settings can be made in either the Computer Configuration or User Configuration node; a Computer Configuration setting trumps any other.)

To see the execution policies in effect at all scopes, type **get-executionpolicy –list**.

To set an execution policy, use *Set-ExecutionPolicy*. To set a policy at the LocalMachine scope, you need to be running PowerShell with administrative privileges.

The default scope for *Set-ExecutionPolicy* is LocalMachine, so if you're planning to apply a policy to all users at your computer, you can omit the **–Scope** parameter. For example, if you're comfortable disabling all of PowerShell's script-execution security measures, including warning prompts, you can type **set-executionpolicy bypass**. For a slightly more protective environment, type **set-executionpolicy unrestricted**.

To set a policy at the CurrentUser or Process scope, add **–Scope** followed by **CurrentUser** or Process. Note that you can also set an execution policy at the Process scope by adding an **–Executionpolicy** argument to a command that launches PowerShell. For example, from a command prompt in Cmd.exe, in PowerShell, or on the Start menu, you can type **powershell –executionpolicy unrestricted** to launch PowerShell with the Unrestricted execution policy at the Process scope.

To remove an execution policy from a particular scope, set that scope's policy to Undefined. For example, if you set a Process policy to, say, Bypass, and you would like PowerShell to revert to the policy at the next level of precedence (CurrentUser, if a policy is set there, or LocalMachine, if not), type **set-executionpolicy undefined –scope process**.

Using your profile to customize PowerShell

Your profile is a script that PowerShell executes at the beginning of each session. You can use it to tailor your PowerShell environment to your preferences. Your profile must have the following path and file name:

`$Home\Documents\WindowsPowerShell\Microsoft.PowerShell_profile.ps1`

where $Home is a system-generated *PowerShell* variable corresponding to the environment variable %UserProfile%. You can see where this is on your system by typing **$profile**, and you can edit an existing profile by typing **notepad $profile**. If you have not yet created a profile, you can type the following:

`if (!(test-path $profile)){New-Item -Type file -Path $profile -Force}`

PowerShell will create the file for you in the appropriate folder. Then you can type **notepad $profile** to edit the blank file.

You can use your profile to customize PowerShell in a variety of ways. Possibilities to consider include changing the default prompt and creating new aliases.

PowerShell's prompt is derived from a built-in function called Prompt. You can overwrite that function with your own. For example, the function

`Function prompt {"PS [$env:computername] $(Get-Date) > "}`

replaces the built-in PowerShell prompt with the letters PS, followed by your computer name, followed by the current date and time. For more information about PowerShell prompts, type **get-help about_prompts**.

To add new aliases to the ones PowerShell already offers, include *Set-Alias* statements in your profile. (See "Using and creating aliases" earlier in this chapter.)

Using the PowerShell ISE

A feature introduced with PowerShell 2.0 allows you to issue commands and work with scripts in a graphical environment. This ISE includes a command pane, a script pane, and an output pane. The output pane displays the results of any commands you issue in the command pane or any scripts you run in the script pane.

Windows PowerShell ISE is a desktop app that you can launch from Start. Alternatively, at a PowerShell prompt or in a Command Prompt window, type **powershell_ise**.

The ISE supports multiple tabs, so you can open several scripts at once. Click File > New to open a new blank tab (for example, to write a new script) or File > Open to open an existing script in a new tab. To run the current script, click Debug > Run/Continue, press F5, or click the green arrow in the middle of the toolbar. You can use other commands on the Debug menu to set and remove breakpoints and step through execution.

The ISE offers all the usual amenities of a graphical environment. You can resize and rearrange the panes, for example. You can use the View menu's Zoom commands (or adjust the slider in the lower-right corner of the window) to make the text display larger or smaller. And you can easily select and copy text from one pane to another or from the ISE to another application.

The ISE uses its own profile, separate from the one you use to customize PowerShell itself. The path and file name are as follows:

$Home\Documents\WindowsPowerShell\ProfileISE.ps1

and you create the file by typing:

```
if(!(Test-Path $profile)){New-Item -Type file -Path $profile -Force}
```

Finding additional PowerShell resources

This chapter's discussion of PowerShell has barely nicked the surface. For further exploration, we recommend the following:

- *Windows PowerShell Step by Step*, Third Edition, by Ed Wilson (Microsoft Press, 2015)

- *Windows PowerShell Cookbook*, Third Edition, by Lee Holmes (O'Reilly Media, 2013)

- "PowerShell Documentation" at *https://docs.microsoft.com/en-us/powershell/*

- The "Hey, Scripting Guy!" blog at *https://bit.ly/scripting-guy*

- "Getting Started with Windows PowerShell" at *https://bit.ly/powershell-get-started*

Editing the Windows registry

The Windows registry is the central storage location that contains configuration details for hardware, system settings, services, user customizations, applications, and every detail—large and small—that makes Windows work.

NOTE

The registry is the work of many hands, over many years, and capitalization and word spacing are not consistent. With readability as our goal, we made our own capitalization decisions for this book, and our treatment of names frequently differs from what you see in Registry Editor. No matter. Capitalization is irrelevant. Spelling and spacing must be correct, however.

Although it's convenient to think of the registry as a monolithic database, its contents are actually stored in multiple locations as separate *hive* files, alongside logs and other support files. Some of those hive files are read into memory when the operating system starts; hive files that contain user-specific settings are stored in the user profile and are loaded when a new user signs in.

The Boot Configuration Data (BCD) store has its own file on the boot drive. The core hives for Windows—the Security Account Manager (SAM), Security, Software, and System—are securely stored in %SystemRoot%\System32\Config. Two hives that contain settings for local and network services are located in %SystemRoot%\ServiceProfiles\LocalService and %SystemRoot%\ServiceProfiles\NetworkService, respectively. User-specific hives are stored as part of the user profile folder.

The Hardware hive is unique in that it has no associated disk file. This hive, which contains details about your hardware configuration, is completely volatile; that is, Windows 10 creates it anew each time you turn your system on.

NOTE

You can see where the hives of your system physically live by examining the values associated with HKLM\System\CurrentControlSet\Control\HiveList. Windows assigns drive letters after assembling the registry, so these paths do not specify drive letters.

You can't work with hive files directly. Windows 10 is designed in such a way that direct registry edits by end users are generally unnecessary. When you change your configuration by using the Settings app or Control Panel, for example, Windows writes the necessary updates to the

CHAPTER 19

registry for you. Likewise, when you install a new piece of hardware or a new program, the setup program makes the required registry changes; you don't need to know the details.

On the other hand, because the designers of Windows couldn't provide a user interface for every conceivable customization you might want to make, sometimes working directly with the registry is the only way to make a change. Even when it's not the only way, it might be the fastest way. Removing or modifying registry entries is occasionally a crucial part of troubleshooting and repair as well. Windows includes a registry editor you should know how to use—safely. This section tells you how.

CAUTION

Most Microsoft support articles contain a dire warning about the risks associated with editing the registry. We echo those warnings here. An incorrect registry modification can render your system unbootable and, in some cases, might require a complete reinstall of the operating system. Use Registry Editor at your own risk.

Understanding the Registry Editor hierarchy

Registry Editor (Regedit.exe) offers a unified view of the registry's contents as well as tools for modifying its contents. You'll find this important utility on the All Apps list, under the Windows Administrative Tools category. It also shows up when you use the search box. Alternatively, you can type **regedit** at a command prompt or in the Run dialog box. Registry Editor has been virtually unchanged since the last century. However, beginning in version 1703, you might have noticed some small but long-needed improvements: an address bar, new keyboard shortcuts for traversing the registry, and the addition of a View-menu command with which you can select the font for displaying the registry.

Figure 19-5 shows a (mostly) collapsed view of the Windows 10 registry, as seen through Registry Editor.

The Computer node appears at the top of the Registry Editor tree listing. Beneath it, as shown here, are five root keys: HKEY_CLASSES_ROOT, HKEY_CURRENT_USER, HKEY_LOCAL_MACHINE, HKEY_USERS, and HKEY_CURRENT_CONFIG. For simplicity's sake and typographical convenience, this book, like many others, abbreviates the root key names as HKCR, HKCU, HKLM, HKU, and HKCC, respectively.

Root keys, sometimes called *predefined keys,* contain subkeys. Registry Editor displays this structure in a hierarchical tree in the left pane. In Figure 19-5, for example, HKLM is open, showing its top-level subkeys.

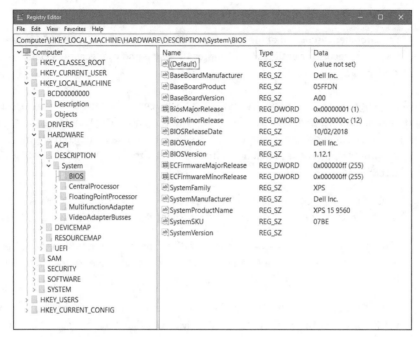

Figure 19-5 The registry consists of five root keys, each of which contains many subkeys.

Subkeys, which we call *keys* for short, can contain subkeys of their own, which in turn can be expanded as necessary to display additional subkeys. The address bar near the top of the Registry Editor window shows the full path of the currently selected key: Computer\HKLM\HARDWARE\DESCRIPTION\System\BIOS, in the previous figure.

NOTE

One of the Registry Editor changes introduced in version 1703 is the address bar. In it, you can type a registry path and press Enter to jump directly to that key, much as you can for jumping to a folder in File Explorer. For the root keys, you can type the full name or the commonly used abbreviations described earlier.

To go to the address bar and select its current content, press Alt+D or Ctrl+L, the same keyboard shortcuts that work in File Explorer as well as most web browsers. Previous versions of Registry Editor displayed the path in a status bar at the bottom of the screen, but you couldn't edit it or select it for copying.

The contents of HKEY_LOCAL_MACHINE define the workings of Windows itself, and its subkeys map neatly to several hives we mentioned at the start of this section. HKEY_USERS contains an entry for every existing user account (including system accounts), each of which uses the security identifier, or SID, for that account.

NOTE

For a detailed discussion of the relationship between user accounts and SIDs, see "What are security identifiers?" in Chapter 11, "Managing user accounts, passwords, and credentials."

The remaining three predefined keys don't exist, technically. Like the file system in Windows—which uses junctions, symlinks, and other trickery to display a virtual namespace—the registry uses a bit of misdirection (implemented with the REG_LINK data type) to create these convenient representations of keys that are actually stored within HKEY_LOCAL_MACHINE and HKEY_USERS:

- HKEY_CLASSES_ROOT is merged from keys within HKLM\Software\Classes and HKEY_USERS*sid*_Classes (where *sid* is the security identifier of the currently signed-in user).

- HKEY_CURRENT_USER is a view into the settings for the currently signed-in user account, as stored in HKEY_USERS*sid* (where *sid* is the security identifier of the currently signed-in user).

- HKEY_CURRENT_CONFIG displays the contents of the Hardware Profiles\Current subkey in HKLM\SYSTEM\CurrentControlSet\Hardware Profiles.

Any changes you make to keys and values in these virtual keys have the same effect as if you had edited the actual locations. The HKCR and HKCU keys are generally more convenient to use.

Registry values and data types

Every key contains at least one value. In Registry Editor, that obligatory value is known as the default value. Many keys have additional values. The names, data types, and data associated with values appear in the right pane.

The default value for many keys is not defined. You can think of an empty default value as a placeholder—a slot that could hold data but currently does not.

All values other than the default always include the following three components: name, data type, and data. Figure 19-6, for example, shows customized settings for the current user's lock screen. (Note the full path to this key in the address bar at the top of the Registry Editor window.)

The SlideshowEnabled value (near the bottom of the list) is of data type REG_DWORD. The data associated with this value (on the system used for this figure) is 0x00000000. The prefix 0x denotes a hexadecimal value. Registry Editor displays the decimal equivalent of hexadecimal values in parentheses after the value.

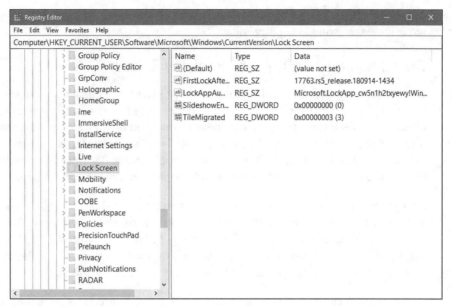

Figure 19-6 Selecting a key on the left displays all its values on the right.

The registry uses the following data types:

- **REG_SZ.** The SZ indicates a zero-terminated string. This variable-length string can contain Unicode as well as ANSI characters. When you enter or edit a REG_SZ value, Registry Editor terminates the value with a 00 byte for you.

- **REG_BINARY.** The REG_BINARY type contains binary data—0s and 1s.

- **REG_DWORD.** This data type is a "double word"—that is, a 32-bit numeric value. Although it can hold any integer from 0 to 2^{32}, the registry often uses it for simple Boolean values (0 or 1) because the registry lacks a Boolean data type.

- **REG_QWORD.** This data type is a "quadruple word"—a 64-bit numeric value.

- **REG_MULTI_SZ.** This data type contains a group of zero-terminated strings assigned to a single value.

- **REG_EXPAND_SZ.** This data type is a zero-terminated string containing an unexpanded reference to an environment variable, such as %SystemRoot%. (For information about environment variables, see "Interacting with PowerShell" earlier in this chapter.) If you need to create a key containing a variable name, use this data type, not REG_SZ.

Internally, the registry also uses REG_LINK, REG_FULL_RESOURCE_DESCRIPTOR, REG_RESOURCE_LIST, REG_RESOURCE_REQUIREMENTS_LIST, and REG_NONE data types. Although you might occasionally see references in technical documentation to these data types, they're not visible or accessible in Registry Editor.

Browsing and editing with Registry Editor

Because of the registry's size, looking for a particular key, value, or data item can be daunting. In Registry Editor, the Find command (on the Edit menu and also available by pressing Ctrl+F) works in the forward direction only and does not wrap around when it gets to the end of the registry. If you're not sure where the item you need is located, select the highest level in the left pane before issuing the command. If you have an approximate idea where the item you want is located, you can save time by starting at a node closer to (but still above) the target.

After you locate an item of interest, you can put it on the Favorites list to simplify a return visit. Open the Favorites menu, click Add To Favorites, and supply a friendly name (or accept the default). If you're about to close Registry Editor and know you'll be returning to the same key the next time you open the editor, you can skip the Favorites step because Registry Editor always remembers your last position and returns to that position in the next session.

Registry Editor includes a number of time-saving keyboard shortcuts for navigating the registry:

- To move to the next subkey that starts with a particular letter, simply type that letter when the focus is in the left pane; in the right pane, use the same trick to jump to the next value that begins with that letter.

- To open a key (revealing its subkeys), press Right Arrow or Alt+Right Arrow.

- To collapse the subkeys of the current key, press Left Arrow or Alt+Left Arrow. With all subkeys collapsed, either action moves up one level in the subkey hierarchy. To move up a level without closing the subkeys as you move up, press Alt+Up Arrow.

- To move to the top of the hierarchy, press Home.

- To quickly move between the left and right panes, use the Tab key.

- In the right pane, press F2 to rename a value, and press Enter to open that value and edit its data.

Some of these shortcuts, added in version 1703, match the behavior of File Explorer shortcuts, allowing you to apply your knowledge of that program to Registry Editor.

Once you are comfortable using these keyboard shortcuts, you'll find it's usually easier to zip through the subkey hierarchy with a combination of arrow keys and letter keys than it is to open outline controls with the mouse.

Changing data

You can change the data associated with a value by selecting a value in the right pane and pressing Enter or by double-clicking the value. Registry Editor pops up an edit window appropriate for the value's data type:

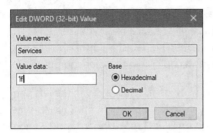

Adding or deleting keys and values

To add a key, select the new key's parent in the left pane, open the Edit menu, point to New, and click Key. The new key arrives as a generically named outline entry, exactly the way a new folder does in File Explorer. Type a new name.

To add a value, select the parent key, open the Edit menu, and point to New. On the submenu that appears, click the type of value you want to add. A value of the type you select appears in the right pane with a generic name. Type over the generic name, press Enter twice, enter your data, and press Enter once more.

To delete a key or value, select it and then press Delete. Note that deleting a key also deletes every value and subkey associated with it.

Using the Reg command

One expert-level option is to use the Reg command in a Command Prompt window or in a batch file or script. Type **reg /?** to see the full list of eligible arguments for the reg command (query, add, export, import, and so on). Each of those variants has its own syntax help. Try **reg add /?** to see the correct syntax for adding a value.

Backing up and restoring parts of the registry

Before you make any changes to the registry, consider using System Restore to set a restore point, which includes a snapshot of the registry as it currently exists. Taking this precaution allows you to roll back any ill-advised changes.

➤ For information about using System Restore, see "Rolling back to a previous restore point" in Chapter 15, "Troubleshooting, backup, and recovery."

CHAPTER 19

In addition, or as an alternative, you can use the Export command in Registry Editor to back up the portion of the registry where you plan to work. Registry Editor can save all or portions of your registry in any of four different formats, but only one is relevant in the modern era.

The Registration Files option creates a .reg file, which is a text file that can be read and edited in Notepad or a similar program. A .reg file can be merged into the registry of a system running any version of Windows. When you merge a .reg file, its keys and values replace the correspond-ing keys and values in the registry. By using .reg files, you can edit your registry "offline" and add your changes to the registry without even opening Registry Editor. You can also use .reg files as an easy way to share registry settings and copy them to other computers.

To export a portion of the registry before you work on it, select a key in the left pane, and then click File > Export. (Easier still, right-click a key and click Export.) In the Save As Type list in the Export Registry File dialog box, select Registration Files (*.reg). Under Export Range, choose Selected Branch and then click Save. The resulting file includes the selected key and all its sub-keys and values.

CAUTION

Exporting a registry hive file using the Registry Hive Files format saves the entire hive; importing the saved file replaces the entire contents of the selected key with the con-tents of the file—regardless of its original source. That is, it wipes out everything in the selected key and then adds the keys and values from the file. The potential for chaos is obvious, and the benefits are not worth the risk, in our estimation.

If you saved your backup as a .reg file, you use the same process to import it. (As an alternative, you can double-click the .reg file in File Explorer without opening Registry Editor.) The complete path to each key and value is stored as part of the file, and it always restores to the same loca-tion. This approach for recovering from registry editing mishaps is fine if you did not add new values or subkeys to the section of the registry you're working with; it returns existing data to its former state but doesn't alter the data you added.

TROUBLESHOOTING

You used a registry cleaner and your system is no longer working properly

The registry is often inscrutable and can appear messy. Misguided attempts at cleanup can cause unexpected problems that are nearly impossible to troubleshoot, which explains why Microsoft is so insistent with its warnings that improper changes to the registry can prevent your computer from operating properly or even booting. We've never found a so-called registry cleaner that justifies the risk it inevitably entails. If you find yourself with a misbehaving system after using a registry cleaner, use the Reset option to recover your system and start over. And this time, don't bother to install that unnecessary utility.

Automating registry changes with .reg files

The .reg files created by the Export command in Registry Editor are plain text, suitable for reading and editing in Notepad or any similar editor. Therefore, they provide an alternative method for editing your registry. You can export a section of the registry, change it offline, and then merge it back into the registry. Or you can add new keys, values, and data to the registry by creating a .reg file from scratch and merging it. A .reg file is particularly useful if you need to make the same changes to the registry of several computers. You can make and test your changes on one machine, save the relevant part of the registry as a .reg file, and then import the saved file to the registry on other machines that require it.

Figure 19-7 shows a .reg file. In this case, the file was exported from the HKCU\Software\ Microsoft\Windows\CurrentVersion\Explorer\Advanced key, shown in Figure 19-8.

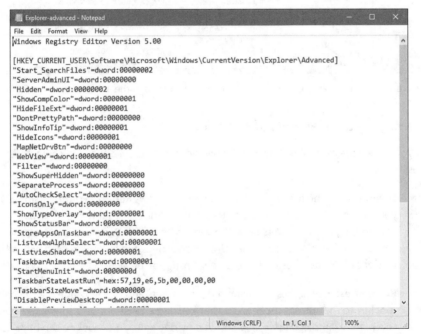

CHAPTER 19

Figure 19-7   A .reg file is a plain-text file suitable for offline editing. This .reg file was exported from the key shown in Figure 19-8.

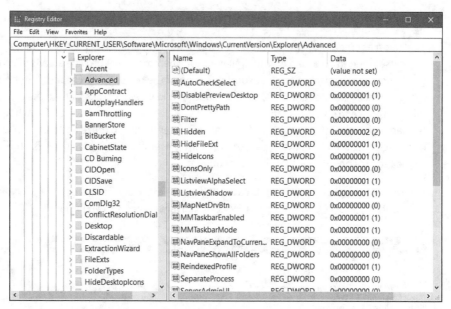

Figure 19-8   This key's name, values, and data are recorded in the .reg file shown in Figure 19-7.

Identifying the elements of a .reg file

As you review the examples shown in the two figures, note the following characteristics of .reg files:

- **Header line.** The file begins with the line "Windows Registry Editor Version 5.00." When you merge a .reg file into the registry, Registry Editor uses this line to verify that the file contains registry data. Version 5 (the version used with Windows 7 and later versions, including Windows 10) generates Unicode text files, which can be used with all supported versions of Windows as well as the now-unsupported Windows XP and Windows 2000.

- **Key names.** Key names are delimited by brackets and must include the full path from the root key to the current subkey. The root key name must not be abbreviated. (Don't use HKCU, for example.) Figure 19-7 shows only one key name, but you can have as many as you want.

- **The default value.** Undefined default values do not appear in .reg files. Defined default values are identified by the special character **@**. Thus, a key whose default REG_SZ value was defined as MyApp would appear in a .reg file this way:

  `"@"="MyApp"`

- **Value names.** Value names must be enclosed in quotation marks, whether or not they include space characters. Follow the value name with an equal sign.

- **Data types.** REG_SZ values don't get a data type identifier or a colon. The data directly follows the equal sign. Other data types are identified as shown in Table 19-5.

Table 19-5 Data types identified in .reg files

Data type	Identifier
REG_BINARY	hex
REG_DWORD	dword
REG_QWORD	hex(b)
REG_MULTI_SZ	hex(7)
REG_EXPAND_SZ	hex(2)

A colon separates the identifier from the data. Thus, for example, a REG_DWORD value named "Keyname" with value data of 00000000 looks like this:

```
"Keyname"=dword:00000000
```

- **REG_SZ values.** Ordinary string values must be enclosed in quotation marks. A backslash character within a string must be written as two backslashes. Thus, for example, the path C:\Program Files\Microsoft Office\ is written like this:

```
"C:\\Program Files\\Microsoft Office\\"
```

- **REG_DWORD values.** DWORD values are written as eight hexadecimal digits, without spaces or commas. Do not use the 0x prefix.

- **All other data types.** Other data types—including REG_EXPAND_SZ, REG_MULTI_SZ, and REG_QWORD—appear as comma-delimited lists of hexadecimal bytes (two hex digits, a comma, two more hex digits, and so on). The following is an example of a REG_MULTI_SZ value:

```
"Addins"=hex(7):64,00,3a,00,5c,00,6c,00,6f,00,74,00,00,75,00,73,00,5c,00,\
31,00,32,00,33,00,5c,00,61,00,64,00,64,00,64,00,69,00,6e,00,73,00,5c,00,\
64,00,71,00,61,00,75,00,69,00,2e,00,31,00,32,00,61,00,00,00,00,00,00,00
```

- **Line-continuation characters.** You can use the backslash as a line-continuation character. The REG_MULTI_SZ value just shown, for example, is all one stream of bytes. We added backslashes and broke the lines for readability, and you can do the same in your .reg files.

- **Line spacing.** You can add blank lines for readability. Registry Editor ignores them.

- **Comments.** To add a comment line to a .reg file, begin the line with a semicolon.

Using a .reg file to delete registry data

.Reg files are most commonly used to modify existing registry data or add new data. But you can also use them to delete existing values and keys.

To delete an existing value, specify a hyphen character (minus sign) as the value's data. For example, to use a .reg file to remove the value ShellState from the key HKCU\Software\ Microsoft\Windows\CurrentVersion\Explorer, add the following lines to the .reg file:

```
[HKEY_CURRENT_USER\Software\Microsoft\Windows\CurrentVersion\Explorer]
"ShellState"=-
```

To delete an existing key with all its values and data, insert a hyphen in front of the key name (inside the left bracket). For example, to use a .reg file to remove the key HKCR\.xyz\shell and all its values, add the following to the .reg file:

```
[-HKEY_CLASSES_ROOT\.xyz\shell]
```

Merging a .reg file into the registry

To merge a .reg file into the registry from within Registry Editor, open the File menu and click Import. Registry Editor adds the imported data under the appropriate key names, overwriting existing values where necessary.

The default action for a .reg file is Merge—meaning merge with the registry. Therefore, you can merge a file into the registry by simply double-clicking it in File Explorer and answering the confirmation prompt.

Registry virtualization

One of the longstanding fundamental principles of security in Windows is that it prevents applications running under a standard user's token from writing to system folders in the file system and to machine-wide keys in the registry, while at the same time enabling users with a standard account to run applications without running into "access denied" roadblocks.

Some older applications that require administrator-level access are still in use in Windows 10, but standard users can run them without hassle. That's because User Account Control uses registry virtualization to redirect attempts to write to subkeys of HKLM\Software. (Settings in HKLM apply to all users of the computer; therefore, only administrators have write permission.) When an application attempts to write to this hive, Windows writes instead to a per-user location, HKCR\VirtualStore\Machine\Software. Like file virtualization, this is done transparently; the application (and all but the most curious users) never know this is going on behind the scenes.

NOTE

When an application requests information from HKLM\Software, Windows looks first in the virtualized key if it exists. Therefore, if a value exists in both the VirtualStore hive and in HKLM, the application sees only the one in VirtualStore.

Note that because the virtualized data is stored in a per-user section of the registry, settings made by one user do not affect other users.

NOTE

Registry virtualization is an interim solution to application compatibility problems. It was introduced with Windows Vista; at that time, more than 10 years ago, Microsoft announced its intention to remove the feature from a future version of the operating system. It is still a feature in Windows 10 but is increasingly less important as software developers adapt their apps to modern security requirements. For more information about registry virtualization, see *https://bit.ly/registry-virtualization*.

Automating tasks

Windows 10 provides several ways to automate tasks. The built-in Task Scheduler tool allows you to create tasks using a point-and-click interface; batch commands and scripts, especially those using Windows PowerShell, represent the most common automation alternative.

Task Scheduler

Task Scheduler is a Microsoft Management Console (MMC) snap-in that supports an extensive set of triggering and scheduling options. Scheduled tasks can run programs or scripts at specified times, launch actions when a computer has been idle for a specified period of time, run tasks when particular users sign in or out, and so on. Task Scheduler is also tightly integrated with the Event Viewer snap-in, making it possible to use events (an application crash or a disk-full error, for example) as triggers for tasks.

Windows and third-party apps make extensive use of Task Scheduler to set up maintenance activities that run on various schedules. You can also create custom tasks. For full documentation on this tool, see *https://docs.microsoft.com/windows/desktop/TaskSchd*.

Automating command sequences with batch programs

A batch program (also commonly called a *batch file*) is a text file with a .bat filename extension that contains a sequence of commands to be executed. You execute the commands by entering the file name at a command prompt. Any action you can take by typing a command at a command prompt can be encapsulated in a batch program.

When you type the name of your batch program at the command prompt (or when you specify it as a task to be executed by Task Scheduler and the appropriate trigger occurs), the command interpreter opens the file and starts reading the statements. It reads the first line, executes the command, and then goes on to the next line. On the surface, this seems to operate just as though you were typing each line yourself at the command prompt. In fact, however, the batch program can be more complicated because the language includes replaceable parameters, conditional and branching statements, the ability to call subroutines, and so on. Batch programs can also respond to values returned by programs and to the values of environment variables.

Automating tasks with Windows Script Host

Microsoft Windows Script Host (WSH) provides a way to perform more sophisticated tasks than the simple jobs that batch programs are able to handle. You can control virtually any component of Windows and of many Windows-based programs with WSH scripts.

To run a script, you can type a script name at a command prompt or double-click the script's icon in File Explorer. WSH has two nearly equivalent programs—Wscript.exe and Cscript.exe—that, with the help of a language interpreter dynamic-link library such as Vbscript.dll, execute scripts written in VBScript or another scripting language. (Cscript.exe is a command-line program; Wscript.exe is its graphical counterpart.)

With WSH, the files can be written in several languages, including VBScript (a scripting language similar to Microsoft Visual Basic) and JScript (a form of JavaScript). All the objects are available to any language, and in most situations, you can choose the language with which you are most comfortable. WSH doesn't care what language you use, provided the appropriate interpreter dynamic-link library is available. VBScript and JScript interters come with Windows 10; interpreters for Perl, KiXtart (KixKIXE), Python, RexxHex, and other languages are available elsewhere.

Using Microsoft Management Console

Microsoft Management Console (MMC) is an application that hosts tools for administering computers, networks, and other system components. By itself, MMC performs no administrative services. Rather, it acts as the host for one or more modules, called *snap-ins*, which do the useful work. MMC provides user-interface consistency so that you or the users you support see more or less the same style of application each time you need to carry out some kind of computer management task. A combination of one or more snap-ins can be saved in a file called a Microsoft Common Console Document or, more commonly, an MMC console.

Creating snap-ins requires expertise in programming. You don't have to be a programmer, however, to make your own custom MMC consoles. All you need to do is run MMC, start with a blank console, and add one or more of the snap-ins available on your system. Alternatively, you can customize some of the MMC consoles supplied by Microsoft or other vendors simply by adding or removing snap-ins. You might, for example, want to combine the Services console with the Event Viewer console, the latter filtered to show only events generated by services. You might also want to include a link to a website that offers details about services and service-related errors. Or perhaps you would like to simplify some of the existing consoles by removing snap-ins you seldom use.

MMC consoles use, by default, the file name extension .msc, and .msc files are associated by default with MMC. Thus, you can run any MMC console by double-clicking its file name in a File Explorer window or by entering the file name at a command prompt. Windows 10 includes several predefined consoles; the most commonly used ones, described in Table 19-6, can be easily found by typing their name in the search box.

Inside OUT

Avoiding User Account Control problems with MMC consoles

Consoles can be used to manage all sorts of computer hardware and Windows features: With a console, you can modify hard-drive partitions, start and stop services, and install device drivers, for example. In other words, MMC consoles perform the types of tasks that User Account Control (UAC) is designed to restrict. In the hands of someone malicious (or simply careless), consoles have the power to wreak havoc on your computer.

Therefore, when using an MMC console, you're likely to encounter a User Account Control request for permission to continue. If UAC is enabled on your computer, the type of request you get and the restrictions that are imposed depend on your account type and the console you're using. Some consoles, such as Device Manager (Devmgmt.msc), display a message box informing you that the console will run with limitations. (In effect, it works in a read-only mode that allows you to view device information but not make changes.) Others block all use by standard user accounts. To ensure that you don't run into an "access denied" roadblock when performing administrative tasks while signed in with a standard account, always right-click and then click Run As Administrator.

Table 19-6   Useful predefined consoles

Console name (file name)	Description
Computer Management (Compmgmt.msc)	Includes the functionality of the Task Scheduler, Event Viewer, Shared Folders, Local Users And Groups, Performance Monitor, Device Manager, Disk Management, Services, and WMI Control snap-ins, providing control over a wide range of computer tasks.
Certificate Manager (Certmgr.msc)	Uses the Certificates snap-in to view and manage security certificates for the current user. A similar console, Certlm.msc, manages certificates on the local machine.

Console name (file name)	Description
Device Manager (Devmgmt.msc)	Uses the Device Manager snap-in to enable administration of all attached hardware devices and their drivers. See Chapter 14, for more information on configuring hardware.
Disk Management (Diskmgmt.msc)	Uses the Disk Management snap-in for configuring disk volumes and partitions. For details, see "Managing hard disks and other storage devices," in Chapter 14.
Event Viewer (Eventvwr.msc)	Uses the Event Viewer snap-in to display all types of logged information. See "Event Viewer" in Chapter 15.
Hyper-V Manager (Virtmgmt.msc)	Uses the Hyper-V Manager snap-in to provide an environment for creating, modifying, and running virtual machines. See Chapter 16, "Hyper-V," for details.
Local Users and Groups (Lusrmgr.msc)	Uses the Local Users and Groups snap-in to manage local user accounts and security groups. For more information, see "User accounts and security groups" in Chapter 11.
Performance Monitor (Perfmon.msc)	Uses the Performance Monitor snap-in to provide a set of monitoring tools. See Chapter 12, "Performance and power management," for details.
Print Management (Printmanagement.msc)	Uses the Print Management snap-in for managing printers and print jobs.
Services (Services.msc)	Uses the Services snap-in to manage services in Windows. For details, see "Managing services" in Chapter 12.
Task Scheduler (Taskschd.msc)	Uses the Task Scheduler snap-in for managing tasks that run automatically.
Trusted Platform Module (TPM) Management (Tpm.msc)	Displays information about and enables configuration of a computer's TPM chip.
Windows Firewall With Advanced Security (Wf.msc)	Uses the Windows Firewall With Advanced Security snap-in to configure rules and make other firewall settings. For details, see "Advanced tools for managing Windows Defender Firewall" in Chapter 18, "Windows security and privacy."

CHAPTER 19

Maximizing productivity on a portable PC

The modern portable PC is packed with feats of hardware engineering wizardry, miniaturizing powerful components to previously unheard-of sizes. On the software side, similar efforts have been successful in coaxing ever more battery life out of those designs. The upshot is you can now take a portable PC running Windows 10 on the road and do work that is nearly identical to what you can accomplish back at the office.

There are, however, some key differences that make up our discussion in this chapter. When you're traveling, for example, your portable PC is unlikely to have the advantage of a fast, always-on broadband connection. Likewise, you're limited to the amount of data storage inside that laptop, without easy access to USB- and network-attached storage devices.

Security is also an ongoing concern when you travel, especially when you find yourself connecting to public Wi-Fi networks with no guarantee that your packets and passwords aren't being intercepted.

We cover all these topics in this chapter. We know there's some inevitable overlap with similar discussions earlier in this book, but our focus here remains on the unique challenges of computing on the go. We begin with the biggest challenge of all: battery life.

Managing battery life

Sometimes you want the full power of your PC, especially if you're trying to accomplish a resource-intensive task on a tight schedule and you know that you'll be back within range of AC power well before your battery is in danger of running out of juice. Under other circumstances, when the workload is light, and you know it will be many hours before you'll be able to recharge your device, you want to make that battery last as long as possible.

Being able to accomplish either goal requires mastering one essential skill first: the ability to quickly assess how much power capacity remains in the current session.

For a quick estimate of remaining battery life, click the battery icon in the notification area. That opens a flyout menu that shows the remaining battery life, expressed as a percentage. When the laptop is plugged into a charger, this menu also estimates the amount of time before the battery is fully charged, as shown in Figure 20-1.

Figure 20-1   Click the battery icon in the taskbar to display this flyout menu, which shows remaining battery life and offers a slider to control how Windows uses the battery.

When the portable PC is plugged in, this flyout also displays an estimate of the time remaining before the device is fully charged. When running on battery power, Windows displays an estimate of the time remaining. (If you don't see either detail, just wait; Windows needs a few minutes of charging or discharging time to make an accurate estimate.)

For a more complete display of information about the current battery status, click the Battery Settings link at the bottom of that flyout menu (or take the long way around by going to Settings > System > Battery). On that page, you'll find a similar display of remaining battery life and, if available, estimated charging time. But that Settings page also includes some additional controls, as shown in Figure 20-2.

Unless you look carefully, you might miss the most important troubleshooting tool on the Battery page in Settings. After running your portable PC on battery power for at least a few hours (and preferably at least a day), click See Which Apps Are Affecting Your Battery Life. That opens a page that contains details similar to those shown in Figure 20-3.

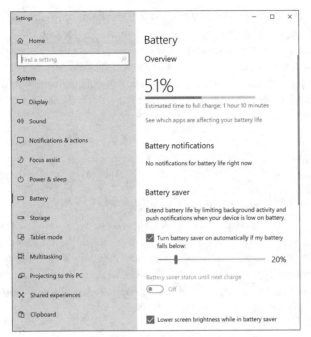

Figure 20-2   This Settings page shows the same information available on the Battery flyout menu, but it also includes a link to a diagnostic tool for tracking down power-hungry apps.

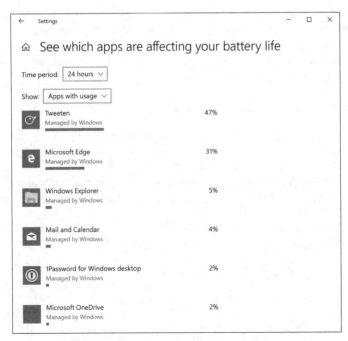

Figure 20-3   After running your Windows 10 laptop PC on battery power over the course of a full day, you can see which apps are most responsible for draining the battery.

Use the three options on the Time Period menu to change the scale of activity to 6 Hours, 24 Hours, or 1 Week; the values returned show activity on a per-app basis for all times during the selected period when your device was running on battery power. That's pretty powerful diagnostic information. Used properly, it can help you diagnose which apps are most responsible for draining your PC's battery. Armed with that information, you can either choose not to use those apps when power saving is high on the agenda, or you can look for configuration changes in the apps at the top of the list to help reduce their hunger for power.

Inside OUT

Don't forget to check the batteries on your peripheral devices

If you carry essential add-on devices when you travel, be sure to check their battery level before you leave, unless you want to experience the frustration of having your noise-canceling Bluetooth headphones stop working one-hour into a trans-Atlantic flight. Recent additions to the Bluetooth device status pages in Settings make it possible to check battery life at a glance for modern Bluetooth devices. For details, see "Setting up Bluetooth devices," in Chapter 14, "Hardware and devices."

Battery Saver and other power management options

To quickly change the way in which Windows uses the battery during the current session, open the Battery flyout menu and use the slider to choose one of the options ranging from Best Performance (on the right) to Best Battery Life (on the left). Moving the slider all the way to the left turns on the Battery Saver feature; you can also turn on Battery Saver using its Quick Actions button at the bottom of Action Center.

While Battery Saver is on, Windows automatically adjusts the following settings:

- The Mail, People, and Calendar apps no longer sync automatically.

- Most apps that normally run in the background are blocked from doing so. OneDrive, for example, sends a notification that it has temporarily stopped syncing local changes to the cloud. You can override this action by clicking the Sync Anyway button in Action Center.

- Display brightness (one of the biggest factors in battery usage) is reduced by 30 percent. Hardware manufacturers can change this default setting.

- All noncritical telemetry uploads are blocked.

- All noncritical downloads from Windows Update are blocked.

While Battery Saver is enabled, Windows displays an overlay of a leaf on the battery icon in the taskbar, in Settings, and in the Battery flyout menu.

By default, Windows 10 automatically turns on Battery Saver when remaining battery life falls below 20 percent. Use the slider on the Battery page in Settings to change that threshold or clear the Turn Battery Saver On Automatically check box to continue running at your chosen power mode until you reach the Low or Critical battery level. At those two settings, you can ask Windows to show a notification or perform an action. For example, you might ask to see a notification when remaining battery level drops to 10 percent and have Windows automatically hibernate when it reaches 5 percent.

You'll find these settings for the current power plan in the old Control Panel, in the Power Options category, under the Advanced Settings tab for the current power plan. (For more detailed instructions on how to work with power plans, see "Power management on desktop systems," in Chapter 12, "Performance and power management.") Expand the Battery heading to expose options for setting Low and Critical levels and defining notifications and actions for each level.

Monitoring long-term battery life and capacity

Over time, if you're paying attention, you develop an instinctive sense for how long your battery will last and when you should begin looking in earnest for a power outlet. Windows 10 also allows you to generate a battery report that gives you a more precise measurement of your battery's history. The report also allows you to observe the decline in battery capacity that inevitably occurs over time. To generate a battery report, open a Command Prompt window and run the command **powercfg /batteryreport**. That action generates a file in the current folder called Battery-report.html; double-click that file to view the report in a browser window.

Figure 20-4 shows the Battery Life Estimates section of one such report. The values under the Active heading show actual battery life for each session, with an average at the bottom of the list.

Battery life estimates
Battery life estimates based on observed drains

PERIOD	AT FULL CHARGE		AT DESIGN CAPACITY	
	ACTIVE	CONNECTED STANDBY	ACTIVE	CONNECTED STANDBY
2018-10-11 - 2018-10-18	7:35:24	368:28:09 4 % / 16 h	7:07:50	346:10:06 5 % / 16 h
2018-10-18 - 2018-10-25				
2018-10-25 - 2018-11-01	6:50:19	870:50:48 2 % / 16 h	6:28:19	824:08:42 2 % / 16 h
2018-11-01 - 2018-11-08	6:18:52	284:29:19 6 % / 16 h	5:58:33	269:13:56 6 % / 16 h
2018-11-08	4:14:03	245:03:21 7 % / 16 h	4:00:26	231:54:50 7 % / 16 h
2018-11-09	-	-	-	-
2018-11-10	-	-	-	-
2018-11-11	-	-	-	-
2018-11-12				
2018-11-13	8:39:30	1054:09:36 2 % / 16 h	8:06:06	986:24:18 2 % / 16 h
2018-11-14	7:33:30	297:25:30 5 % / 16 h	6:58:48	274:39:31 6 % / 16 h
2018-11-15	7:29:15	110:45:11 14 % / 16 h	6:54:51	102:16:32 16 % / 16 h
2018-11-16	5:09:04	133:01:26 12 % / 16 h	4:45:13	122:45:40 13 % / 16 h
2018-11-17	11:50:24	2375:45:35 1 % / 16 h	10:56:58	2197:03:54 1 % / 16 h
2018-11-18	7:58:04	313:52:22 5 % / 16 h	7:22:07	290:15:52 6 % / 16 h
2018-11-19	7:47:39	276:51:05 6 % / 16 h	7:12:29	256:01:40 6 % / 16 h

Current estimate of battery life based on all observed drains since OS install

| Since OS install | 8:46:20 | 354:01:07
5 % / 16 h | 8:06:45 | 327:23:27
5 % / 16 h |

Figure 20-4 Run a battery report to generate an HTML-formatted report that shows, among other things, actual battery life for a portable PC.

Mobile connectivity

At home or in the office, with an always-on broadband connection, you probably don't think of data as a scarce resource. But on the road, where you typically connect to the internet through mobile data services or Wi-Fi networks managed by other people, that's an essential factor to keep in mind.

We cover the basic techniques for connecting to public and private Wi-Fi networks in Chapter 13, "Windows networking," along with similar details for "tethering" a mobile phone as a Wi-Fi hotspot, and won't repeat those instructions here. Instead, we focus on cellular connectivity options that allow connection over high-speed LTE mobile networks. These features are beginning to appear in some new Windows 10 devices, including the Surface Pro and Surface Go lines from Microsoft.

On a device that's equipped with an LTE modem, you'll see a Cellular page under the Network & Internet category in Settings. You'll need to insert a SIM card from your mobile provider or, on devices that have a built-in eSIM card, configure that connectivity according to the data provider's instructions. Figure 20-5 shows a properly configured LTE modem on a Windows 10 PC.

Figure 20-5 On a Windows 10 PC equipped with an LTE cellular modem, you have a wide selection of options for tightly controlling mobile data usage.

If continuous connectivity is more important than managing your mobile data budget, you can select Let Windows Manage This Connection and set the Use Cellular Data Instead Of Wi-Fi option to When Wi-Fi Is Poor. If, on the other hand, your mobile data comes at a steep price, you might choose to connect to the LTE connection manually.

➤ As is the case when you set up your mobile phone as a hotspot and connect to it via Wi-Fi, you can monitor data usage on a per-connection basis. For details, see "Mobile hotspots and other metered connections," in Chapter 13.

WHAT'S IN YOUR TRAVEL BAG?

Unless you're just stepping out for a couple hours at the local coffee shop, traveling with a Windows 10 PC requires some additional hardware, including cables and adapters.

We recommend keeping a small, lightweight travel bag packed with those necessaries. The benefit of having everything in a single bag is it means you're less likely to forget a crucial item. The most important accoutrement is your laptop charger; if you have a spare charger, you can keep it in the bag full time. We also recommend keeping a USB Ethernet adapter and an Ethernet cable, for those occasions when a wired network is available. A USB flash drive (encrypted with BitLocker To Go, of course) can be enormously useful for casual data transfers. If your portable PC includes a USB Type-C connector, consider bringing a mini-hub with video, network, and additional USB Type-A ports. You never know when those will come in handy.

On the optional-but-nice-to-have list, consider a small set of headphones (with microphone) for occasions when you need to play audio or make a Skype call without disturbing fellow travelers. A compact portable power strip is useful when you find yourself in an old hotel room with minimal AC power options. And if you expect to spend more than a few minutes a day working on your notebook, an external Bluetooth mouse can really increase your productivity.

Storage

How do you make sure you have the data files you need when you hit the road? If you use OneDrive (or an equivalent cloud service), the challenge is one of organizing your work files into folders in the cloud and then letting OneDrive's sync feature do the heavy lifting.

The other option is downright old-fashioned but still effective. If your portable PC has an expansion slot for an SD or MicroSD card, you can use that removable storage to physically transfer data between PCs. Because it's a separate physical device from the primary storage, you can also use it for File History backups.

➤ For details on backing up and restoring files with File History, see "Using File History to protect files and folders," in Chapter 15, "Troubleshooting, backup, and recovery."

Figure 20-6 shows a portable PC with a 128-GB system drive and a removable MicroSD card that holds 256 GB, or twice as much data.

Two facts are worth noting when using this type of removable storage. First, it's typically far slower than the solid-state drives used on a modern laptop PC. For performance reasons, you should avoid using this type of removable storage for data files where the ability to read and write quickly is important, such as Hyper-V virtual machines. Second, bear in mind that it's especially important to encrypt a removable storage device so that if it's lost or stolen, your personal data is safe from prying eyes.

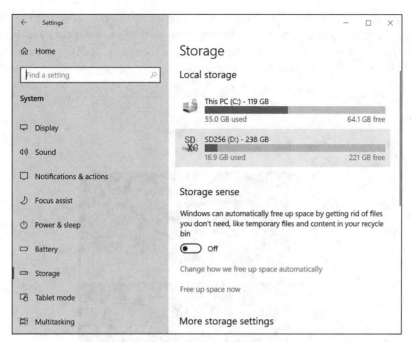

Figure 20-6 Adding removable storage to a portable PC can dramatically expand its storage capacity.

Windows 10 and your mobile phone

The Windows 10 Mobile platform is, alas, no more. We recognize that some of our readers still proudly use Windows 10 phones, and we salute their loyalty, but that doesn't change the fact Microsoft has exited the phone business and has no plans to get back in.

For those who have moved on to mobile phones running the Android OS, there are some consolations. Microsoft has been actively engaged in developing apps for Android, including several that enable direct connections between an Android Phone and a PC running Windows 10. (These features are still in their early stages of development and are not yet available on devices running Apple's iOS.)

Making this connection requires installing matching apps on each device. On the PC side, you'll need a Microsoft Store app called Your Phone, which is available at *https://www.microsoft. com/store/productId/9NMPJ99VJBWV*. From the Google Play Store, download Microsoft's Your Phone Companion app and install it on the Android device. (The app is available at *https://play. google.com/store/apps/details?id=com.microsoft.appmanager*.)

After following the instructions to connect the two devices using a Microsoft account, you can do two phone-related tasks from your PC. The Your Phone app shows the 25 most recent photos and screenshots from your phone, as in the example in Figure 20-7. Snap a picture on the phone, and you no longer need to jump through hoops to get it onto your PC. Drag a photo from Your Phone into File Explorer or an app or share it. Or double-click to edit the picture in Microsoft Photos or the default photo editor.

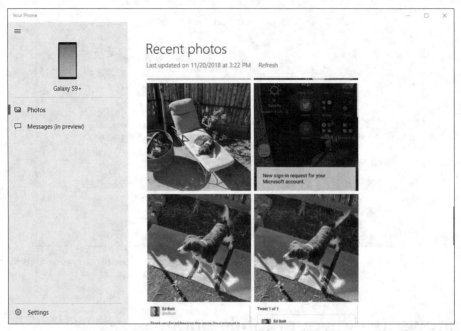

Figure 20-7   Use the Your Phone app to copy or share the 25 most recent photos or screenshots from your Android phone directly from a PC running Windows 10.

The Your Phone app also syncs SMS messages from your phone, allowing you to carry on limited conversations from your desktop PC or laptop. As of late 2018, the Your Phone app doesn't support MMS-formatted messages, which means you'll need to pick up your phone to see photos sent as attachments to text messages or to participate in conversations with multiple people.

Windows 10 editions and licensing options

When Windows 10 was first released to the public in 2015, its lineup of editions was refreshingly simple. Since then, the list has expanded significantly. Each edition encompasses a specific set of features, sometimes coupled with licensing options and geographic restrictions.

Despite that seemingly confusing assortment, however, we suspect most of our readers will have no problem sorting through their choices. When you purchase a new PC through traditional retail channels, you're likely to have a choice of two and only two editions: Home and Pro. (A new option, Windows 10 Pro for Workstations, is available only on extremely powerful hardware not normally found alongside conventional PCs.) Likewise, IT pros responsible for deployment of Windows PCs in large organizations typically upgrade PCs running Windows 10 Pro to some flavor of Windows 10 Enterprise; their choices are most often dictated by licensing agreements rather than individual features.

NOTE

As if the waters weren't already muddy enough, Microsoft introduced a new edition of Windows in May 2017 and then, several months later, revised its strategy and effectively eliminated that edition. Microsoft announced Windows 10 S with some fanfare as part of the introduction of the Surface Laptop; this new edition was intended to be a subset of Windows 10 Pro, primarily for the education market (but probably attractive in some enterprise settings as well). As part of that launch event, some of Microsoft's hardware partners announced lower-cost PCs also running Windows 10 S.

In 2018, Microsoft revised its strategy for this edition, relegating "S Mode" to the status of a feature available with multiple editions of Windows 10. On a Windows 10 PC running in S mode, configuration settings restrict installation of apps to those that are delivered through the Microsoft Store. Windows 10 in S mode also sets Microsoft Edge as the default browser and uses Bing as the default search engine. Neither setting can be changed. S mode can be disabled by going to Settings > Update & Security > Activation and choosing Switch To Windows 10 Home or Switch To Windows 10 Pro. That leads to the Microsoft Store and a Switch Out Of S Mode page. Note that this switch, once made, is irreversible.

Yes, the Windows 10 family also includes devices running Windows 10 Mobile, although Microsoft has stopped development of that variant and no longer manufactures or sells Windows smartphones. Windows 10 also runs on the Xbox One gaming console and the HoloLens virtual reality headset, and sometime in the not-so-distant future, you might encounter the Windows 10 IoT (Internet of Things) edition, which is for use in specialized hardware such as automated teller machines and "smart" devices that lack a display. But our focus in this appendix is on the editions of Windows 10 designed for use on traditional PCs and PC-like devices such as tablets.

Windows 10 editions at a glance

Although the assortment of Windows editions might be confusing, their progression is, for the most part, consistent. Each edition contains all of the features of the previous edition, along with a set of unique features that you can evaluate to decide whether the cost of upgrading is justified.

In this section, we describe the core features included with Windows 10 Home and then describe the additional features included as part of each successive upgrade. You can use this information to decide whether to upgrade from Home to Pro when you're shopping for a new PC, for example. You can also use this information to help decide which PCs on a corporate network should be upgraded to Enterprise edition using your organization's volume license agreement or one of the newer subscription-based options.

We start with a brief discussion of hardware configurations. Table A-1 lists technical limits related to CPU and memory support that might affect your purchase or upgrade decision.

Table A-1   Supported hardware configurations in Windows 10

Hardware component	Supported configurations
Number of CPUs/cores	Windows 10 Home: One physical processor. Windows 10 Pro, Enterprise, or Education: One or two physical processors. Windows 10 Pro for Workstations: Up to four physical processors. All editions support multicore processors, up to a maximum of 32 (x86) or 64 (x64) cores per physical processor.
Addressable memory (RAM)	32-bit (x86) editions: 4 GB maximum (because of 32-bit memory architecture, usable memory is typically 3.5 GB or less). 64-bit (x64) editions: 128 GB for Windows 10 Home; 2 TB for Windows 10 Pro, Enterprise, or Education; 6 TB for Windows 10 Pro for Workstations

For our discussion of specific editions, we start with those available preinstalled on new PCs and in retail channels. We follow that with editions available for deployment within large enterprises, organizations, and educational institutions.

Retail and OEM editions

Consumers and businesses that acquire Windows on a new device or as a retail upgrade typi-cally have their choice of two editions: Windows 10 Home and Windows 10 Pro. Since the initial release of Windows 10, Microsoft has introduced one new retail/original equipment manufac-turer (OEM) edition: Windows 10 Pro for Workstations.

NOTE

In some markets, you might find Single Language, KN, and N variations of the two retail and OEM editions. Using a Single Language version means you can't install an additional language pack or change the base language unless you update to the full, language-neutral version. N versions are available in the European Union, and KN versions are offered in South Korea; both editions have had several media playback features removed as a result of legal proceedings between Microsoft and regulators in those jurisdictions. For most Windows installations in developed countries and regions, the standard Home and Pro editions are the preferred choices.

All these editions are available preinstalled on new PCs from original equipment manufactur-ers and are also available as retail products in shrink-wrapped boxes or as downloads from the Microsoft Store and third-party online stores.

Home

Windows 10 Home includes all the core features that we describe in detail in this book. That includes the complete Windows 10 user experience, with its customizable Start menu and task-bar, as well as the modern Settings app that offers access to system settings formerly included in Control Panel. It also includes the technical architecture of Windows 10: the NTFS file system, TCP/IP networking, power management, the Windows Search index, and Cortana.

With the exception of some high-end configurations that include multiple processors and mas-sive amounts of system memory, there's no difference in hardware support between Windows 10 Home and higher editions. Any device that has a compatible Windows driver will work on Windows 10 Home, including multiple displays, touchscreens, and pens that support the Win-dows Ink platform.

Every edition of Windows receives security and feature updates through Windows Update, although the Home edition lacks some configuration options available in more advanced edi-tions. Likewise, the security infrastructure of Windows 10 Home supports Trusted Platform Modules, Secure Boot, and Windows Hello biometric authentication. Some advanced security features, such as BitLocker Drive Encryption, require Pro or Enterprise editions.

And, of course, every edition of Windows 10 includes the same assortment of apps, including Microsoft Edge and Internet Explorer 11.

Pro

Windows 10 Pro includes the same core features as Windows 10 Home, with the addition of features that are primarily of interest to business users and corporate network administrators. All the features in the following list are also available in Enterprise and Education editions.

- **Client Hyper-V.** With proper hardware support, allows users to create a virtual machine (VM), install Windows or another operating system on the VM, and use it as if it was a separate physical device.

- **Language packs.** Changes the Windows 10 interface to add language packs and switch between languages for displaying menus, dialog boxes, and other elements.

- **Encrypting File System.** Enables strong encryption of files and folders on an NTFS-formatted volume.

- **BitLocker Drive Encryption.** Allows an entire drive to be encrypted, protecting its contents from unauthorized access if the computer is lost or stolen.

- **BitLocker To Go.** Encrypts data on removable media such as USB flash drives and external drives. (Devices running Windows 10 Home can read storage devices encrypted using this feature but cannot manage BitLocker To Go encryption.)

- **Domain join/Group Policy management.** Allows the device to join a Windows domain and be managed by using Active Directory and Group Policy.

- **Windows Information Protection.** Provides advanced control over data files, including encryption and remote wipe.

- **Enterprise Mode Internet Explorer (EMIE).** Using network configuration files, administrators can define compatibility settings for sites accessed using Internet Explorer, including those on corporate intranets, enabling the continued use of older web apps that aren't compatible with Microsoft Edge.

- **Remote Desktop (server).** Allows remote access to the full Windows experience on the current PC; the connection is made over the network using Remote Desktop Protocol from a client program running on any Windows PC, Mac, or supported mobile device. (Devices running Windows 10 Home can connect to a PC that allows incoming Remote Desktop sessions, but can't share its own resources in this fashion.)

- **Azure Active Directory support.** Allows a Windows 10 device to join Azure Active Directory, with a single sign-in to cloud-hosted apps.

- **Business Store for Windows 10.** Allows an organization to provision apps and packaged Windows desktop programs in a restricted area of the Microsoft Store for installation by employees.

- **Windows Update for Business.** Allows central management of security updates and new features delivered through Windows Update, with the option to configure limited delays for quality updates and longer delays (up to one year) for feature updates.

Pro for Workstations

In 2017, Microsoft announced Windows 10 Pro for Workstations, a new edition that is intended for use on "server-grade hardware" that is much more powerful than the average desktop PC, typically with multiple CPUs and massive amounts of memory. By design, these workstations perform compute-intensive tasks such as computer-aided design and video rendering, which need hardware resources far beyond what even a high-end desktop PC can deliver.

The feature set for this edition is similar to that of Windows 10 Pro. Where it differs is in its hardware support.

Windows 10 Pro for Workstations includes support for devices with persistent memory (also known as non-volatile memory, or NVDIMM-N), the fastest data storage possible on workstations. It supports SMB Direct file transfers, over network adapters that use Remote Direct Memory Access (RDMA) for faster throughput and very low latency. As an alternative to the traditional NTFS file system, it supports the newer ReFS (Resilient File System), which is optimized for large data volumes spread over multiple physical disks.

Editions for organizations

Windows 10 Enterprise is available as an upgrade for PCs that already have an underlying license for Windows 10 Pro. Windows 10 Education provides equivalent features for large networks in academic environments (K-12 and university) and allows upgrades from Windows 10 Home or Pro editions. In the past, Enterprise updates required a Volume License agreement. Those agreements are still the primary means for acquiring an Enterprise license, but, as we discuss in this section, Microsoft has introduced new subscription options that make Enterprise upgrades available for small businesses and individuals.

Enterprise

The following list enumerates features that are available only in Windows 10 Enterprise editions. On corporate networks, you have the option to enable some additional features by upgrading to the Enterprise edition as part of a volume license agreement with Software Assurance.

- **Start menu customization.** Provides standard Start menu layouts defined by administrators and prevents users from altering the standard user experience.

- **AppLocker.** Enables administrators of enterprise networks to create an authorized list of programs that users can install and run.

- **Credential Guard.** Supports multifactor authentication using smart cards and biometric information.

- **Device Guard.** Allows organizations to lock down a Windows 10 device so that only approved apps and desktop programs can be installed or run, preventing the installation of most forms of malware and any unauthorized software.

- **Windows To Go Creator.** Allows the installation of Windows 10 Enterprise or Education on certified, high-performance USB drives that can boot and run in secure, self-contained mode, isolated from access by the host PC.

- **Windows 10 Defender Advanced Threat Protection.** Available only with Windows 10 Enterprise E5 subscriptions, provides detection of online threats and attacks.

- **BranchCache.** Increases network responsiveness of applications in environments running on Windows Server 2008 R2 and later.

- **DirectAccess.** Provides secure connections (without a virtual private network, or VPN) between a client PC running Windows 10 and a remote server running Windows Server 2008 R2 or newer.

- **Location-aware printing.** Helps domain-joined computers find the correct printer when a user moves between office and home networks.

Enterprise E3 and E5

In the past two years, Microsoft has expanded the availability of Windows 10 Enterprise upgrades through subscription offerings called Windows 10 Enterprise E3 and E5, available only through Microsoft partners who are part of the Cloud Service Providers program. The feature set for these editions is identical to Enterprise edition sold through volume license agreements. The most important distinction is that these subscription editions are tied to an Azure Active Directory account and can be installed on up to five PCs for each user.

Microsoft 365

The Microsoft 365 offerings (formerly Secure Productive Enterprise E3 and E5) include Windows 10 Enterprise as part of a package that also includes Office 365 and a variety of management, analytics, security, and compliance tools collectively branded Enterprise Mobility + Security. The Windows 10 portion of this package contains the same feature set as other Enterprise edition offerings.

Enterprise LTSB/LTSC

The Long Term Servicing Channel (LTSC) was previously known by the equally awkward moniker Long Term Servicing Branch (LTSB). Microsoft releases new versions of Windows 10 to the Long

Term Servicing Channel every two to three years. The two most recent releases in this channel are Windows 10 Enterprise LTSB 2016 and Windows 10 Enterprise LTSC 2019, which was released in October 2018.

Despite the name change, the product is the same at its core. Each LTSB/LTSC release contains the same features as other editions from the same release cycle, with two noteworthy exceptions:

- LTSB/LTSC releases do not receive feature updates through Windows Update.

- These releases do not contain many in-box applications that are included with other editions, including Microsoft Edge, Microsoft Store, Cortana (limited search capabilities remain available), Mail, Calendar, OneNote, Weather, Microsoft News, Photos, Camera, Groove Music, and Alarms & Clock.

Deploying this edition allows administrators to limit deployment of new features in Windows 10, installing reliability and security updates only; this feature is designed for use on specialized equipment in mission-critical environments and is available only in the Enterprise edition.

Editions for educational institutions

At schools and other institutions of learning, administrators can enable advanced features by upgrading to Windows 10 Pro Education and Windows 10 Education. These specialized editions provide education-specific default settings but are otherwise essentially equivalent to the Pro and Enterprise editions.

Administrators in education environments can provision new devices with the Set up School PCs app or Windows Configuration Designer. They can also deliver "digital assessments" with the Take a Test app. These features work with all desktop Windows 10 editions except Windows 10 Home.

Institutions that have deployed Windows 10 Pro and Enterprise in managed environments can configure the product to have similar feature settings to Windows 10 Pro Education and Windows 10 Education using Group Policy settings.

For specific details about these Windows 10 editions and configuration options, see *https:// bit.ly/win10-education*.

Pro Education

Windows 10 Pro Education is effectively a variant of Windows 10 Pro that provides education-specific default settings similar to those in Windows 10 Education. It is available on new devices purchased with discounted K-12 academic licenses through OEM partners. (These discounted licenses are sometimes referred to as National Academic or Shape the Future.) This edition is also available through Volume Licensing channels.

Education

According to Microsoft's official documentation, "Windows 10 Education is effectively a variant of Windows 10 Enterprise that provides education-specific default settings. These default settings disable tips, tricks and suggestions & Microsoft Store suggestions." It is available only through Volume Licensing channels.

If you have a hankering for new Windows features, all you have to do is wait. Microsoft releases new feature updates for Windows twice a year, targeting release dates in March and September. These full upgrades are delivered at no charge through Windows Update to properly licensed devices running Windows 10.

This accelerated release schedule is a key part of the "Windows as a Service" model for Windows 10, where upgrades arrive far more frequently than before.

Still not fast enough for you? Then feel free to sign up for the Windows Insider Program, which is free of charge and open to anyone who wants to receive preview releases of Windows as they work their way through the development process. This open approach makes it significantly easier than in previous Windows versions to track the development process and see what's coming next.

By running preview builds, you can try out new features as they develop. More importantly, the program gives you the opportunity to report bugs and provide feedback and suggestions that can influence the direction of those features.

The Insider program is, of course, ideal for Windows enthusiasts, but it's also of value to IT professionals who want to avoid unpleasant surprises when new versions are rolled out to the public. In this appendix, we explain how to manage your participation in the Windows Insider Program.

How the Windows Insider Program works

Microsoft introduced the Windows Insider Program in 2014 when it announced Windows 10, delivering the first preview release days later. The program has continued nonstop since then, expanding in 2017 to include business users as well as personal accounts.

You don't need to pay a fee or pass a test to join the Windows Insider Program. All you have to do is complete two steps. First, go to *https://insider.windows.com*, read the terms and conditions, and sign up using a Microsoft account or an Azure Active Directory address. After completing that prerequisite, you can take the second step by configuring any device running Windows 10 to install Insider Preview builds.

Inside OUT

What's different about the Windows Insider Program for Business?

To join a device to the Windows Insider Program for Business, use an Azure Active Directory (Azure AD) account to register; the Azure AD account option is available only if the device is connected to your corporate network using that account. When you install a preview build on an Azure AD–joined device using that Azure AD account, an additional My Company page appears in the Feedback Hub, where you can see and upvote feedback submitted by other members of your organization.

If you are a Global Administrator of an Azure AD enterprise domain, you can also register that domain with the Windows Insider Program. Doing so allows you to manage Insider builds on corporate devices by applying policies. It also ensures that feedback from your users is not shared with outsiders.

For details on how to configure the Windows Insider Program for Business on an enterprise domain, see *https://insider.windows.com/en-us/for-business-organization-admin/*.

Unless you're an experienced software tester, you should approach these preview builds with caution. By definition, they are unfinished, with known and unknown issues that can potentially expose you to system crashes and data loss. The best test platforms are secondary PCs or virtual machines that are properly backed up.

Another significant issue associated with setting up access to Insider Preview builds is the need to install feature updates far more frequently than the normal twice-yearly schedule. Even the most conservative settings for the Windows Insider Program involve installing a full feature update roughly every month or so. More aggressive Insider settings can increase the disruption factor dramatically, with builds typically released weekly during normal development cycles and the pace of updates increasing to several times per week as developers reach the end of the cycle and prepare for the public release.

Joining a device to the Windows Insider Program is not a decision to be made lightly. If you decide you want to stop receiving preview builds and go back to the current release channel, you can safely do so during the brief interval after a new Windows version is released to the Semi-Annual Channel. At that time, you can safely disconnect a device from receiving Insider builds without having to reinstall Windows. At all other times, however, you'll almost certainly have to back up your data and perform a clean reinstall of Windows.

If you're cognizant of the risks and willing to accept the trade-offs, keep reading to learn how to set up a Windows 10 PC to receive Insider builds.

Inside OUT

Stop unauthorized users from switching to Insider builds

If you manage PCs in an office or home, you probably don't want to have preview builds installed on them without your permission. To prevent users from creating headaches for you and your support staff, take the following steps:

On any PC running Windows 10 Pro, Enterprise, or Education, you can apply a Group Policy setting to block changes to Insider settings on that PC. On versions of Windows 10 up to and including 1703, go to Computer Configuration > Administrative Templates > Windows Components > Data Collection And Preview Builds, and then set the policy Toggle User Control Over Insider Builds to Disabled.

Beginning with Windows 10 version 1709, the corresponding settings are in Computer Configuration > Administrative Templates > Windows Components > Windows Update > Windows Update for Business.

On devices running Windows 10 Home (which doesn't support Group Policy settings), your best option is to configure standard user accounts, which require permission from an administrator (you) to access Windows Insider Program settings.

APPENDIX B

Joining the Windows Insider Program

After registering at *https://insider.windows.com,* you're ready to configure a Windows 10 device to receive Insider Preview builds. Go to Settings > Update & Security > Windows Insider Program and click Get Started.

The first step is to link your PC to the registered Insider account. In most cases, the Microsoft account you use to sign in to Windows 10 is the best choice here. Then walk through the wizard's steps to configure your Insider settings, as shown in Figure B-1.

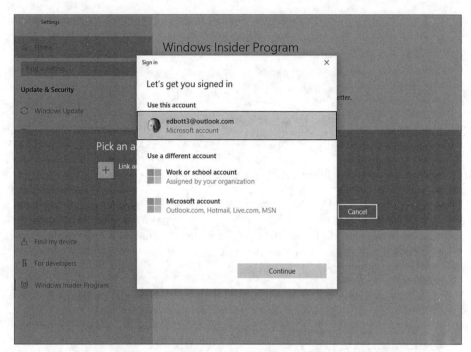

Figure B-1   If you're willing to accept the risks of installing preview builds in exchange for the opportunity to influence the direction of Windows, click Get Started and link an account that you've registered with the Windows Insider Program.

After that step is complete, you need to choose one of three Insider Preview channels:

- **Just Fixes, Apps, And Drivers.** This channel offers access to apps and drivers before the general public, but you won't receive new Windows builds.

- **Active Development Of Windows.** For most of our readers, this option is the appropriate choice. Enrolling in this channel provides access to new builds in the development cycle for the next release of Windows. When development is complete and that version is released to the Semi-Annual Channel (Targeted), you can stop receiving Insider Preview builds, or you can continue to the next feature update.

- **Skip Ahead To The Next Windows Release.** At the end of the development cycle for a given feature update, Microsoft stops introducing new features and focuses solely on stabilizing the build for release. Meanwhile, another team of engineers begins developing for the next feature update. At that point, anyone who chooses this option will be among the first to begin receiving those new builds. Note that Microsoft limits the number of Insiders in this channel, so don't be surprised if you're unable to choose this option.

Finally, you need to choose the pace at which you want to receive preview builds. Each level represents a release group that is in between Microsoft's internal testing groups and the current public release:

- **Fast.** Preview builds go to this group of Insiders first. The benefit of being first to see a new feature is balanced by the risk of being the first to experience a new bug. You can report those bugs using the Feedback Hub.

- **Slow.** Devices configured for this level receive preview builds after they've had a chance to be thoroughly tested by the Fast ring. These builds are likely to be more stable because they incorporate fixes based on feedback from testers in the Fast ring.

- **Release Preview.** This is the most conservative ring of all, available for selection only when Microsoft begins releasing new builds near the end of the development cycle for a feature update. Insiders who choose this level can also receive updated Microsoft apps and driver updates.

Before you can complete the configuration process, you must click through two bold and very stern warnings, which list the risks we discussed earlier. After a restart, you're ready to begin receiving new builds. The current Insider Preview release that matches your preferences will download and install automatically, just like any feature update.

After configuring a device to receive Insider Preview builds, you should see some new options in the Windows Insider Program section in Settings > Update & Security. There, you can change your Insider Level and the pace at which you receive new builds. To use a different account with a specific device, register that account with the Windows Insider Program. Then click the account card at the bottom of that Settings page and use the Change or Unlink buttons.

APPENDIX B

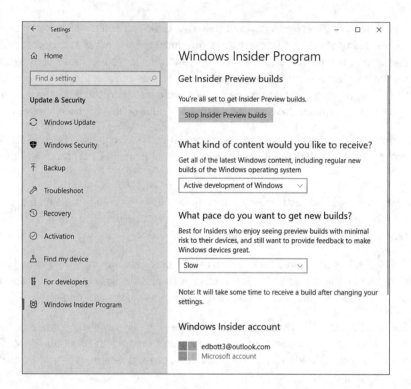

Insider Preview builds arrive via Windows Update, as normal. After installing an Insider Preview build, you can see a few changes. For starters, a watermark with the words "Evaluation copy" and the Insider Preview build number appears in the lower-right corner of the screen, above the clock in the notification area. (This watermark disappears briefly near the end of a development cycle, as Microsoft prepares the final preview builds for the official release.)

In addition, on a PC configured to receive Insider Preview builds, some privacy settings can't be adjusted. The Diagnostic And Usage Data settings, for example, are set to the default levels, where they provide the maximum feedback to Microsoft. As you can see in Figure B-2, the corresponding Settings pages disclose that the Windows Insider Program has taken control of those options.

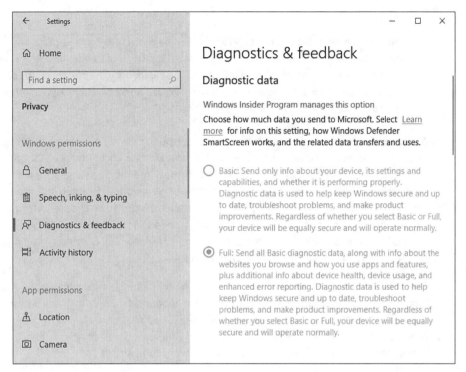

Figure B-2 When a device is configured to receive Insider Preview builds, you cannot change the settings shown here.

Those options return to normal when you change the configuration of a device so that it no longer receives Insider Preview builds and is back on the Semi-Annual Channel.

Inside OUT

Making sense of Windows code names

Each new Windows 10 feature update has its own code name, which you can use to track that version as it works its way through the development process, a process called "flighting." The initial release of Windows 10, in July 2015, was code-named Threshold, and the second release, version 1511, was identified as Threshold 2. The Anniversary Update, version 1607, was code-named Redstone, and subsequent feature updates were code-named Redstone 2, Redstone 3, Redstone 4, and Redstone 5.

Those code names are mostly useful to those who have enrolled in the Windows Insider Program and are actively testing upcoming versions. The first public preview release from the Redstone 5 flight arrived for those in the Skip Ahead group well before version 1803 (the formal name of what had previously been Redstone 4) became publicly available. The designation "rs5" in the file name for a download of a preview build is a giveaway to informed observers that the new build belongs to the Redstone 5 development cycle.

NOTE

At the time we wrote this book, Microsoft had begun actively testing the version of Windows that will be released in the first half of 2019. Instead of a codename, this release was identified as 19H1 in its Insider flight details. To identify the current status of Insider Preview releases for Windows 10 PC, Server, and IoT, go to the Flight Hub at *https://docs.microsoft.com/windows-insider/flight-hub/.*

When running an Insider Preview build, you can suspend delivery of new builds for up to seven days. Go to Settings > Update & Security > Windows Update, click Advanced Options, and then slide the Pause Updates switch to the On position. You might choose to make this change if you're in the midst of a big project and don't want your work to be interrupted by a large download that could take an hour or more to install. You might also choose to stop updates temporarily if you're traveling. As a member of the Windows Insider Program, however, that delay is limited to a week. (For a device in the public Semi-Annual Channel, you can use the same option to pause updates for up to 35 days.)

To see the full range of options available to you as an Insider, go back to Settings > Update & Security > Windows Insider Program and click the Stop Insider Preview Builds button at the top of the page. That opens a large dialog box like the one shown next. Options let you change to a slower update pace, take a break for up to 7 days (the same pause option we just discussed), roll back to the last Windows release, or exit the program completely.

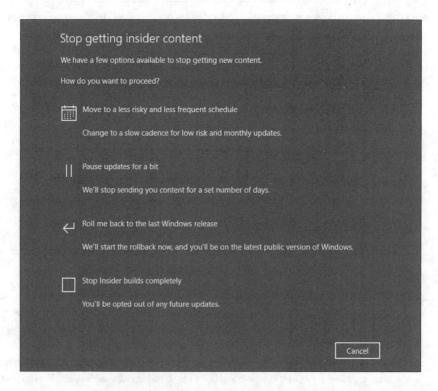

The Roll Me Back To The Last Windows Release option doesn't actually stop you from receiving preview builds. Instead, it takes you to the Recovery page in Settings, where the option to roll back is available only if you installed a single preview build less than 10 days ago. If you've installed multiple Insider Preview builds during the current development cycle, the options here allow you to roll back to the previous Insider build or reset your PC to the current public release, keeping your personal files but losing any installed apps and settings.

To switch to a different registered Insider account (for example, if you want to use a personal account rather than a work account), click the account name to reveal Change and Unlink buttons.

Keeping track of what's in each preview build

Every new Insider Preview release is accompanied by copious documentation. To catch up on just the highlights, visit *https://insider.windows.com/en-us/previews-highlights*. That page lists each build in the active development cycle, in reverse chronological order, with a few bullet points listing the features that are new or significantly improved in that build. Beneath each build's entry is a link to the corresponding set of release notes on the Windows Insider Blog, which discusses those features in more detail and includes detailed lists of general fixes as well as known issues. To browse through all release notes, go to *https://blogs.windows.com/windowsexperience/tag/windows-insider-program*.

APPENDIX B

Inside OUT

Read the release notes when installing a preview build

Every preview release of Windows 10 is accompanied by copious notes documenting features that are new or changed in the current release, as well as issues that have been fixed from previous builds and—crucially—known issues that might affect your PC's performance or stability.

It is, of course, human nature to ignore these notes and plunge headlong into a new preview release. As tempting as the prospects of new features might be, we strongly urge you to at least skim each set of release notes, especially the Known Issues section, before using a new preview release. Doing so can save you frustration and needless troubleshooting when you run into a feature that's not working correctly. In rare cases, it can also prevent the annoyance of a failed install when a known issue affects specific hardware or software installed on your device.

Links to those same release notes are also available in the Feedback Hub app, on the Announcements tab; click the megaphone icon in the navigation pane to see the full list, as shown here.

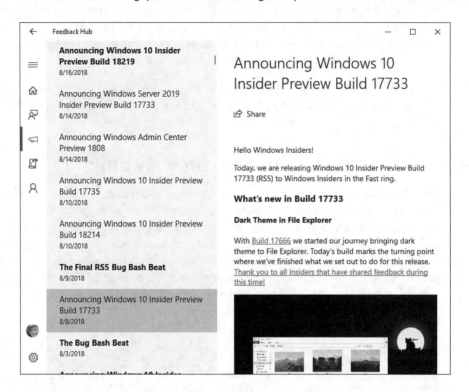

That's not the only purpose of the Feedback Hub app, of course, as we consider in the next section.

Submitting and tracking feedback

The Windows Insider Program is, by design, a feedback loop. The primary means for offering bug reports and suggestions to Microsoft is via the aptly named Feedback Hub app.

That loop is a crucial step in ensuring that serious bugs are caught and fixed before they reach the general public. A prime example of just how important that task is occurred when Microsoft released the October 2018 Update, version 1809. Only days later, the rollout of that feature update was paused for more than a month after early adopters reported two serious bugs with the new update.

Ironically, Windows Insiders had done the job they were supposed to do, with multiple Insiders reporting both bugs during the course of testing preview builds. Microsoft's engineers had missed those reports in the flood of data from the Feedback Hub. To help ensure that those reports are taken more seriously, the Windows team added a new Severity field to the feedback form.

The Feedback tab, shown in Figure B-3, allows you to view and search all items submitted by the Insider community, adding your own comments and upvoting items to make a suggestion more visible to the Microsoft employees designing and coding upcoming Windows releases.

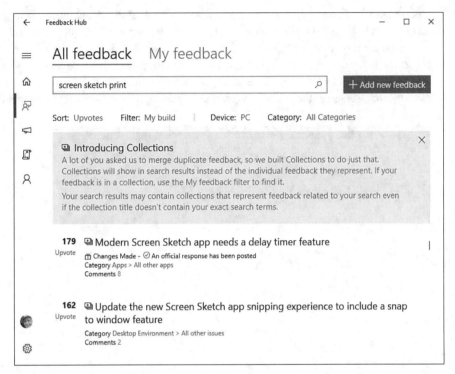

Figure B-3   Before creating a new feedback item, use the search box to find previous reports.

Before you click the Add New Feedback button, we recommend using the search box to find previous reports on the same issue. If you find one that already covers the issue you were planning to report, consider clicking the Upvote button (to the left of a summary item and below the heading when you open the full feedback item). If you have additional details that are relevant, open the item and add a comment. (You can also comment on comments.)

A few suggestions for getting the most out of the Feedback Hub app:

- Use the Sort options to change the display of search results. Choose Trending to see items that are getting the most current activity; click Upvotes to show feedback items that have already proven popular and might benefit most from your support.

- Choosing My Build from the Filter list can help you avoid seeing outdated feedback and confirm that an issue you're experiencing is also being reported by others using the same build. Clearing that option can help you report a longstanding issue that was reported in previous builds and is still occurring in a current build.

- Take advantage of some relatively recent Filter options to identify issues that have been addressed by the Windows development team. Select the Changes Made and Official Response categories to see items that contain these details.

If you can't find an existing feedback item, click Add New Feedback and fill in the three-part form shown in Figure B-4. Provide clear details in the subject line so that others can find your issue, and choose the correct category in step 2. Pay special attention to the Additional Details section, which includes a new section for ranking the severity of the issue on a scale of 1 (Minor Issue) to 5 (Broken Or Unusable Experience) and allows you to attach screenshots, log files, or even record a series of steps to help an engineer understand exactly what you're seeing.

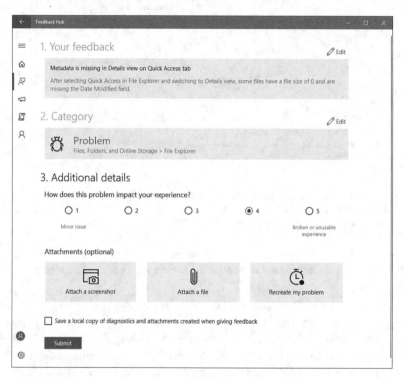

Figure B-4   The Recreate My Problem and Record My Suggestion options allows you to show a sequence of events that an engineer can reproduce, making a bug report or suggestion far more effective.

Help and support resources

We hope this book is helpful. We also know that even if we had unlimited pages and multiple volumes to fill, there's no way we could answer every question or cover every nook and cranny of a product as rich and diverse as Microsoft Windows 10. And, of course, in the "Windows as a Service" model, Windows 10 continues to evolve with new and reworked features. We've updated this edition to include all existing features as of version 1809, but Microsoft began delivering new features in preview builds to members of the Windows Insider Program within days of delivering that update.

So, we've put together this appendix to serve as a compendium of places where you can go to find help, troubleshooting tips, how-to guides, drivers, utilities, and advice.

Our list starts with official resources, collated and curated by Microsoft, but we also include community-based resources where you're likely to find reliable answers.

Online help

Over the years, what longtime Windows users call "the Help file" has evolved, with the internet serving as the greatest agent of change. As recently as Windows 7, a Help And Support link on the Start menu led to Compiled HTML Help (.chm) files, readable with a built-in Windows utility (Hh.exe) that acts like a special-purpose browser.

That utility is still included with Windows 10, and you can still find a few .chm files (mostly for third-party products) if you search hard enough, but for Windows 10 itself most help is available online, where it's easily updated without the hassle of having to deliver those revised files to a billion or so PCs.

So, for most basic questions, your first stop should be the web—specifically, Microsoft's search engine, Bing, which delivers results directly from Microsoft Help when you ask a question about Windows. Figure C-1 shows one such question, with the answer in a box above all other search results and the source clearly labeled as "Help from Microsoft."

Figure C-1 Microsoft's Bing search engine delivers results directly from its collection of online Help from Microsoft if you ask the right questions.

If a specific search doesn't return the official answer you're looking for, try rephrasing the question. If that's still not delivering the necessary answers, browse through Windows Help online (*https://support.microsoft.com/products/windows?os=windows-10*), which contains tutorials and instructions for common tasks, organized by category, with a search box to help deliver more refined results, as shown in Figure C-2. (Note that Microsoft continues to tinker with the layout of this page, but the basic organization remains the same.)

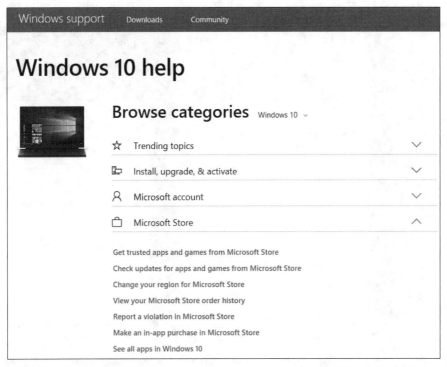

Figure C-2   Windows Help online is organized by category. Use the arrow to the right of each heading, as in the "Microsoft Store" example shown here, to see a list of topics containing explanations and instructions.

Inside OUT

Ask Cortana for help

Cortana doesn't have the entire Windows 10 help library memorized, but you can get help with some tasks. Ask the right question, and you might get a search result that has a large question mark icon to its left. That's your indication you've found a Help topic, which looks like this when you click the search result.

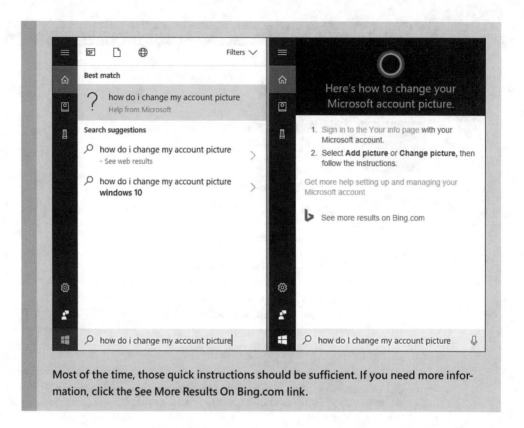

Most of the time, those quick instructions should be sufficient. If you need more information, click the See More Results On Bing.com link.

Sometimes, of course, you're not looking for a detailed explanation or step-by-step instructions but simply trying to find a Windows setting without having to dig through menus or dialog boxes. For that type of chore, you have your choice of no fewer than three separate places to start a search:

- **The search box on the taskbar.** Entering a search term (in this case, the word *display*) in the search box on the taskbar returns a short but usually well-focused set of results. The results are the same regardless of whether you have enabled Cortana, as shown next.

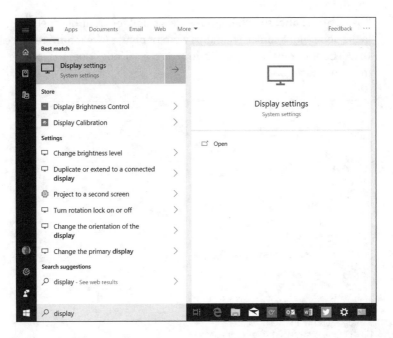

- **The Settings search box.** Click Start > Settings (or use the keyboard shortcut Windows key+I) and enter a word or phrase in the search box in the center, just below the Windows Settings heading. (If you're browsing a subsection of Settings, use the search box above the navigation pane.) Note that the top of the Show All Results list contains matching entries from the modern Settings app, followed by results from the desktop Control Panel, with the latter identifiable by their colorful icons, as shown here:

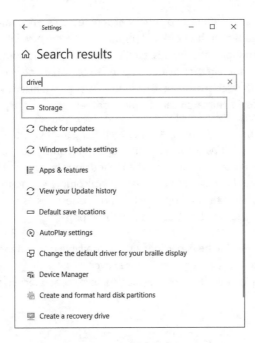

- **The Control Panel search box.** The classic desktop Control Panel has its own search box in the upper-right corner. Entering a word or phrase here returns results exclusively from the All Control Panel Items list. As you can see, its index does not include options from the modern Settings app:

For traditionalists, one bit of local help is available on a Windows 10 device, courtesy of a Microsoft Store app called Tips. (In Windows 10 releases before version 1703, this app was called Get Started). The app, shown in Figure C-3, is installed with Windows 10 and updated through the Microsoft Store. It received a complete visual makeover in Windows 10 version 1709.

The content in the Tips app is basic, offers an overview of core features, and is aimed primarily at nontechnical users. Most readers of this book will probably find little new information there, but it's an excellent resource to suggest to friends, family members, and coworkers who could benefit from it. Click Recommended in the navigation pane to see what's new in the latest feature update, or click Collections to choose from a list of topic areas, organized as index cards. Click any topic to see short tips, in animated card format, for that topic.

You can open Tips directly from Start. An alternative entry point comes via pop-up tips that appear occasionally after you install Windows 10, suggesting that you try out new features. Those tips are designed to be unobtrusive and won't appear if you already used the feature the tip is intended to introduce. But if you want to eliminate them completely, go to Settings > System > Notifications & Actions. Slide the Get Tips, Tricks, And Suggestions As You Use Windows switch to the Off position and you won't be bothered by those pop-ups.

> ➤ An additional source of detailed help in Windows 10 is available through the Troubleshooting section under Settings > Update & Security. We cover these guided tools as well as online Fix It resources in Chapter 15, "Troubleshooting, backup, and recovery."

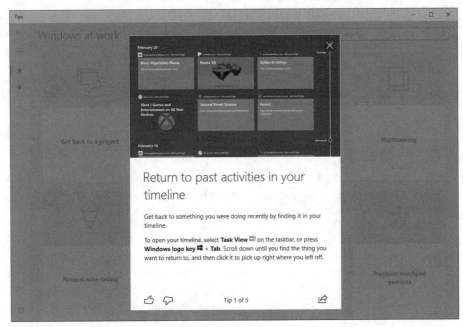

Figure C-3   The Tips app is installed with Windows 10 and is intended primarily for beginners and nontechnical users.

Online reference material from Microsoft

Microsoft's commitment to ongoing support of Windows 10 includes an enormous library of training aids and reference material. This section lists the most important of these resources.

Microsoft Docs

The well-organized index at *https://docs.microsoft.com* is your starting point for Microsoft Docs, which contains all of Microsoft's technical documentation along with reference materials and tutorials for software developers, hardware designers, and IT professionals. The information is thorough, well organized, and expanding at an impressive rate. The IT Pro section is likely to be of most interest to readers of this book.

Microsoft Knowledge Base

Knowledge Base (KB) articles are official support documents that provide details about known issues, workarounds, security updates, new features, and anything else that the Microsoft Support organization deems worthy of formal publication.

Every Knowledge Base article has a unique ID number you can use as a search term to locate a specific document. Security updates, for example, are documented with KB numbers so that IT pros can read details about what a specific update does.

To search for specific information in the Knowledge Base, start with this search term:

```
site:support.microsoft.com/en-us/help "windows 10"
```

If your Windows 10 language is something other than US English, replace **en-us** with the prefix for your regional settings.

Save that search in your browser's Favorites bar or bookmarks and use it as the starting point for any future searches, appending your search terms in the search box. The results list will contain only documents that have been formally published in the Knowledge Base.

Microsoft IT Pro Center

Microsoft IT Pro Center (*https://www.microsoft.com/itpro*) is Microsoft's hub for technical information written primarily for IT pros. The site, formerly part of the TechNet brand, includes news, technical articles, and downloads for all Microsoft products.

To focus exclusively on information about Windows 10, visit the Windows 10 information hub within the Microsoft IT Pro Center: *https://www.microsoft.com/itpro/windows-10*.

The library for Windows is continually expanding as new technical articles are added. The content, written for IT pros and experts, is thorough and sometimes extremely technical, in sharp contrast to the consumer-friendly general help pages. It's worth bookmarking that page and visiting occasionally to see what's new.

Microsoft Virtual Academy

This online learning resource (*http://microsoftvirtualacademy.com*) is an excellent source of free training on a wide range of topics, including Windows 10. Available content includes prerecorded courses, live events (and archives of previous events), and books, with walk-throughs and demos bringing complex topics to life. New content is added regularly.

Getting technical support

If you can't find an answer in the Knowledge Base, or if a problem seems to be unique to your system configuration, you can turn to Microsoft's support forums for help.

Microsoft Community

Nontechnical users running consumer versions of Windows should start with the Microsoft Community forums at *https://answers.microsoft.com*. These threaded message boards are organized into categories—choose Windows, and then Windows 10 to find the most relevant answers.

It's tempting to start by clicking Ask A Question, but a much better strategy is to use the search box to see whether anyone else has reported a similar issue. After entering the Windows 10 topic area, click the search icon in the upper-right corner and enter your search term in the box. Choose Current Scope from the drop-down list to ensure that you see only answers relevant to Windows 10.

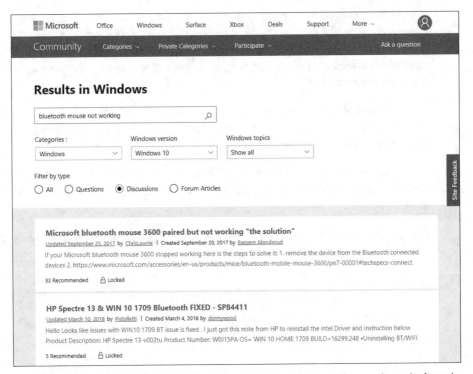

Figure C-4   Use the filter options beneath the search box to narrow the search results from the Microsoft Community forums.

If your search doesn't turn up the answer you're looking for, click Ask A Question to begin composing a question of your own. (You can use this same form to start a discussion if you want to raise an issue that doesn't require an answer.) When posting to the Community forums, try to be as specific as possible, providing relevant details about your system configuration and hardware as well as any troubleshooting steps you've already tried and their results.

Note that support in these forums is provided by community members as well as Microsoft support personnel. You're also likely to run into an occasional Microsoft MVP (Most Valuable Professional). There's no guarantee you'll get a satisfactory answer, but we can testify from personal experience that this route has been successful for many people.

To keep track of a discussion, sign in with your Microsoft account and use the notification options at the bottom of any message. You'll receive an email at the address associated with your Microsoft account whenever anyone replies to the message; this is true regardless of whether you started the discussion yourself or found an existing discussion that you want to follow.

TechNet forums

If you're an IT pro and have a question or want to start a discussion with other like-minded and experienced individuals, go to the TechNet forums, *https://social.technet.microsoft.com/forums*. Topics available here include a much broader range of Microsoft products and technologies than those covered in the Community forums, with a special emphasis on deploying and using Windows in the enterprise.

The basic rules of these more advanced message boards are similar to those we recommend for the Microsoft Community forums: search first and ask a new question only if you can't find an existing discussion that addresses your issue.

Search options for the TechNet forums allow you to select multiple forums, shown on the left in Figure C-5, and then find specific topics within that selection by using a search box above the message list.

Use the filtering and sorting options (above the message list) to narrow your search further or make specific answers easier to locate.

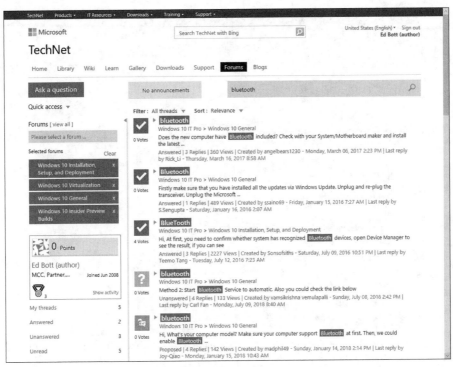

Figure C-5 Choose one or more TechNet forums from the list on the left, and then use the search box at the top of the message list to narrow your results.

Free and paid support from Microsoft

Getting answers from fellow Windows users has the advantage of being free and easily accessible, but sometimes you need formal support from Microsoft engineers.

Microsoft provides free support for security issues. If you suspect your computer has been infected with malware, for example, you can request and receive support at no charge. Other support options might be covered under a product warranty that's provided if you purchase Windows directly from Microsoft, or you can open a support ticket (called an "incident") for a fee.

Visit the Microsoft Answer Desk online at *http://support.microsoft.com/contactus* to see your support options. Listings on that page direct you to the appropriate technical support resources for different business categories.

As an alternative, use the Get Help app, which is installed by default with Windows 10. This app prompts you through an AI-powered chat session with a virtual agent. If that doesn't provide the answer you're looking for, you can click Talk To A Person to get non-virtual support. Figure C-6 shows the options available when we asked for help with a Windows activation issue.

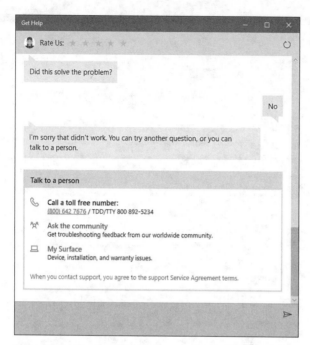

Figure C-6   Use the Get Help app to chat online or talk with a support representative. Note that some options might require payment.

The Windows roadmap

If your organization uses Windows, you should make a special effort to stay on top of what's coming in future updates to Windows 10. That task is not as easy as it should be.

Around the time Microsoft began development of Windows 10, it offered an online roadmap listing business features under development. That page is no longer available. As an alternative, we recommend following the various Microsoft blogs that we describe later in this chapter.

There are still some clues you can find about future plans for Windows 10. Microsoft Edge, for example, has its own roadmap, at *https://bit.ly/ms-edge-platform-status*. If you or your company build or deploy web-based applications, this is an important site to know about.

And, of course, it's just as important to know in advance which parts of the Windows operating system are heading off into the sunset, so that you have time to switch to suitable replacements. For each new feature update, Microsoft publishes a list of features that are removed or planned for replacement. You'll find this list for the October 2018 Update at *https://bit.ly/windows-10-deprecated-1809*; for the April 2018 Update at *https://bit.ly/windows-10-deprecated-1803*; for the Fall Creators Update, version 1709, at *https://bit.ly/windows-10-deprecated-1709*.

The corresponding list for the earlier Creators Update, version 1703, is at *https://bit.ly/windows-10-deprecated-1703*.

In addition to reading those engineering and support documents, you can check in regularly at Microsoft's network of official blogs covering the Windows ecosystem. The following represent valuable information sources we recommend adding to your reading list:

- Microsoft runs its own mini network of Windows blogs that includes the Windows Experience blog, Windows For Your Business, the Microsoft Edge Dev Blog, and the Microsoft Devices Blog. Separate blogs are available in other languages, including Chinese, Spanish (Latin America), Russian, Polish, and Japanese. A comprehensive directory is located at *https://blogs.windows.com/windows-blog-directory/*.

- A relatively recent addition to the Microsoft lineup of business software is Microsoft 365, which combines Office 365, Windows 10, and Enterprise Mobility + Security for business and enterprise customers. The Microsoft 365 team runs a blog at *https://www.microsoft.com/en-us/microsoft-365/blog/*.

- You'll find a large assortment of technical blogs at the Microsoft Tech Community, including business areas like financial services and healthcare as well as product-focused blogs. An index is available at *https://techcommunity.microsoft.com/t5/custom/page/page-id/Blogs*.

- Skype has its own network of blogs as well, with product announcements, updates, tips and tricks, and more. Start at *https://blogs.skype.com/*.

- Developers can go to *https://blogs.msdn.microsoft.com/* for content on Azure, Visual Studio, PowerShell, the Universal Windows Platform, and of course Windows 10. The MSDN network includes official blogs from product teams as well as personal, sometimes highly technical blogs by individual Microsoft employees.

And, of course, there are dozens of unofficial online news sources of varying credibility that will happily keep you up to date on Windows 10 rumors and news. (Sometimes what appears to be news is really just a rumor.)

Do you need a bit of help keeping track of news topics? Feel free to enlist Cortana's assistance. Open Cortana's Notebook, click Manage Skills, select News, and add Windows 10 as a topic to track.

Index

Symbols

* (asterisk), in searches, 371, 377
–Confirm parameter, 716
–Credential parameter, 716
–Detailed parameter, 718
–Examples parameter, 718
–Exclude parameter, 716
–Force parameter, 716
–Full parameter, 718
$GetCurrent folder, 39
–Include parameter, 716
@mentions, inserting in email messages, 212-213
.nfo files, 425
–Online parameter, 718
–Parameter parameter, 718
| (pipe) symbol, 705-706
? (question mark), in searches, 378
–Recurse parameter, 716
.reg files, 731-734
~ (tilde), in searches, 378
.vmcx files, editing, 616
$Windows.~BT folder, 38
$Windows.~WS folder, 39
32-bit versions of Windows 10, 33
64-bit versions of Windows 10, 33
802.11ac, 464
802.11ax, 464
802.11g, 463
802.11n, 464

A

accent colors, choosing, 122-124
accented characters on Touch Keyboard, 105
access control entry (ACE), 413
access control lists (ACLs), 413
accessibility settings, choosing, 142-144

accessing
    computers, 408-410
        managing, 410-414
        permissions/rights, 414
        restricting assigned access, 410
    networks, 574
        checking status, 447-449
        configuring sharing, 483-484
        connecting printers, 495
        hidden connections, 464-465
        Hotspot 2.0, 468
        location settings, 459-460
        mobile hotspots, 457-459
        Nearby Sharing, 468-471
        Remote Desktop, 471-477
        Remote Desktop Connection, 477-480
        sharing files, 481-489
        sharing printers, 489-491
        TCP/IP configuration, 451-456
        tools, 449-450
        troubleshooting, 495-503
        wireless connections, 461-464
        wireless security, 465-467
    PowerShell, 715-717
    ransomware, blocking, 686
    Safe Mode, 573
    user accounts, 415-418
accounts
    Administrator, 417
    Azure Active Directory (Azure AD), 384, 670, 695, 754
        configuring, 389-391
        registering for Windows Insider Program for Business, 760
    biometric sign-ins, configuring, 402
    creating, 384-386
    deleting, 393-395
    Dynamic Lock, configuring, 404

email
    adding/deleting, 209
    Focused Inbox, 211-212
    linking, 209
    notification options, 210-211
    security, 667
    syncing, 209-210
Guest, 417
local
    configuring, 388-389
    modifying passwords, 398
    selecting, 388-389
    signing in during installation, 44
Microsoft, 670
    configuring, 386-388
    selecting, 386-388
    signing in during installation, 44
modifying, 392-393
passwords, configuring, 398-399
permissions/rights, 414
picture passwords, configuring, 401-402
PINS, configuring, 400-401
selecting, 386
settings
    changing picture in, 73
    syncing, 70-71
sharing, 405
    adding users, 406-407
    configuring access, 408-410
    managing access, 410-414
    restricting assigned access, 410
sign-in methods, managing, 395-397
sign-out methods, configuring, 403-404
standard, security, 667
switching, 403-404
user, 415-418
    Azure Active Directory accounts, selecting, 389-391
    creating, 384-386

Plug into learning at

microsoftpressstore.com

The Microsoft Press Store by Pearson offers:

- Free U.S. shipping

- Buy an eBook, get three formats – Includes PDF, EPUB, and MOBI to use with your computer, tablet, and mobile devices

- Print & eBook Best Value Packs

- eBook Deal of the Week – Save up to 50% on featured title

- Newsletter – Be the first to hear about new releases, announcements, special offers, and more

- Register your book – Find companion files, errata, and product updates, plus receive a special coupon* to save on your next purchase

Discounts are applied to the list price of a product. Some products are not eligible to receive additional discounts, so your discount code may not be applied to all items in your cart. Discount codes cannot be applied to products that are already discounted, such as eBook Deal of the Week, eBooks that are part of a book + eBook pack, and products with special discounts applied as part of a promotional offering. Only one coupon can be used per order.